SOFTWARE PROJECT MANAGEMENT

Subramanian Chandramouli

Senior Manager, Cognizant Technology Solutions

Saikat Dutt

Director, Cognizant Technology Solutions

Pearson

Associate Editor—Acquisitions: Neha Goomer
Editor—Production: Nikhil Rakshit

ISBN: 978-93-325-4214-3

First Impression

Published by Pearson India Education Services Pvt. Ltd, CIN: U72200TN2005PTC057128

Head Office: 1st Floor, Berger Tower, Plot No. C-001A/2, Sector 16B, Noida – 201 301,Uttar Pradesh, India.

Registered Office: Featherlite, 'The Address' 5th Floor, Survey No 203/10B, 200 Ft MMRD Road,Zamin Pallavaram, Chennai - 600044
Website: in.pearson.com; Email:companysecretary.india@pearson.com

Digitally printed in India by Trinity Academy for Corporate Training Ltd, New Delhi in the year of 2025.

To God, who has blessed me beyond belief.
My parents, M. Subramanian and S. Lalitha, for their constant inspiration.
To my wife, R. Ramya, for her endless support.
To my ambitious and loving daughter, C. Sri Siva Ranjani.
To my fun-loving and loving son, C. Shri Krishna.
Thank you all, for allowing me to stretch to my potential.

—Subramanian Chandramouli

This book is dedicated to the people without whom the dream could not have come true. My parents, Tarun Kumar Dutt and Srilekha Dutt; constant inspiration and support from my wife, Adity; and unconditional love of my sons, Deepro and Devarko.

—Saikat Dutt

CONTENTS

SECTION IV: SOFTWARE PROJECT EXECUTION, MONITORING AND CONTROL

FOREWORD

One of the main reasons for software failure is inadequate planning. A disciplined approach towards software project management can help in avoiding such issues. While there are many learning tools and published materials available on software project management, the authors of this book have uniquely provided a comprehensive and complete coverage of the subject. The flow of this book follows the generic flow of software projects, like initiation, planning, execution, monitor, and control and closure. The critical topics, like estimation techniques, metrics along with project management methodologies are also explained in detail which helps in understanding these concepts in entirety. It is my belief that this book will help college students and practitioners to expand their understanding on software project management and its associated concepts that covers the entire syllabus.

The science of software project management is always a high-profile area for IT professionals and, thus, understanding the importance and basic concepts of software project management is essential for the aspiring software professionals. This book is a serious compilation of the software project management concepts, techniques, and disciplines. It is written for those professionals who expects to excel in project management. For the casual readers, this book, for its simplicity, would serve as an impressive knowledge resource. For the project management professionals, this book would provide immense benefits because of its subjective depth and informative details. Overall, it will help students as well as professionals to easily understand the various concepts with confidence.

I admire the pictorial representations for conceptual clarification and the easy step-by-step approach, adopted in this book, for explaining a number of difficult concepts. The authors have explained most of the crucial project management concepts to produce an outstanding book that provides readers with an excellent understanding of software project management. This book is extremely well-conceptualized and well-written. It is, undoubtedly, a highly valuable book for the aspiring software professionals. The expertise of the authors, shines through the pages of this well-written book, is a road map for success and a must read for all IT students and software project management professionals.

I hope that readers will find this book useful and it will provide them the knowledge and resources they need in their lifelong career development as software management professionals. I strongly recommend this book for enhanced performance and results.

Dr. Indranil Bose

Professor and MIS Group Coordinator
Faculty Coordinator, IIMC Case Research Centre
Indian Institute of Management, Calcutta

PREFACE

Repeated requests from software professionals, who are the readers of our previous books, for a comprehensive book covering all gamut of software project management, encouraged us to write this book. The trend in number of software project failures due to inadequate project management is still disturbing. Even though, some improvements made over the past few years, but it needs further improvements. So, we thought to write this book, specifically, for college students and junior managers, for their easy understanding of the concepts of software project management and projects execution successfully.

Due care has been taken to present the concepts in a simple and easy manner in this book. The pictorial representations, for explaining a number of complex-natured concepts and several examples included in this book, will facilitate in-depth understanding of the topics. Though, this book is primarily designed for using as a textbook for courses on software project management, but it can also serve as a good point of reference for software practitioners.

We have tried to provide an ideal blend of practical as well as theoretical concepts of software project management in this book. It explains the agile concepts and also handling of international projects for the benefit of modern software project managers which will enable them to excel in executing projects in respective domains.

Why This Book?

There are many concepts in software project management which require critical reading and in-depth understanding. It was our endeavour to present the concepts in easily understandable manner and to explain in lucid language. All the complex topics are decomposed into sub-topics to help readers understand the concepts easily. Based on real project experience and pictorial representations, plenty of explanations and examples are given to facilitate easy assimilation of the concepts.

Whom is This Book for?

Readers of this book will gain a thorough understanding of the principles of software project management. Technical managers and management practitioners will get an insight of how to weave software project management into the overall software engineering process. Students, developers, and technical managers with a basic background in computer science will find the material in this book easily readable.

How This Book is Organized?

Each chapter of this book starts with an introductory paragraph which gives an overview of the chapter and an idea of the topics covered in the chapter. Sample questions at the end of the chapters would help students prepare for relevant examinations. For quick review of the topics, a recap summary is given at the end of each chapter.

No matter whether a project is big or small, but for successful delivery, project management is an integral part. Software project delivery is not just about writing codes, but it is also about ensuring that proper project management processes along with standard testing of the implemented codes are in place. Effective project management is only possible with effective planning, monitoring, controlling and proper implementation of metrics management. Testing includes unit testing, system testing, integration testing and activities like writing test cases, test plan, and executing those test cases. This book covers all these essentials topics.

Notes for Instructors

This book can be used in an introductory course in software project management or as a supplementary text in undergraduate level software project management courses. An introductory graduate level or an undergraduate level course in software project management can be covered by using this book.

Subramanian Chandramouli
Saikat Dutt

ACKNOWLEDGEMENTS

The journey through our professional career has been very enriching so far. Along the way, several individuals have been instrumental in providing us with guidance, opportunities and insights we needed to excel in our fields. We are grateful to Pearson Education for coming forward to publish this book. Sojan Jose, Anita Yadav, Neha Goomer and Nikhil Rakshit of Pearson Education were always kind and extremely helpful throughout this work. Their review with abundant patience and professional touch has added a lot of value to this book. We would like to convey our gratitude to Chandra Sekaran, Executive Vice Chairman at Cognizant Technology Solutions; Pradeep Shilige, Senior Vice President at Cognizant Technology Solutions; and Utkarsha Gosavi, Director at Cognizant Technology Solutions, for their constant encouragement and support. With their vast experience and knowledge, they not only helped us in enriching professionally, but also guided us in taking this project to a successful completion.

Subramanian Chandramouli

Saikat Dutt

I need to thank a wonderful and cheerful man, Chandrasekhar, CIO at Standard Chartered Bank, who encouraged me a lot when he launched my first book 'Virtual Project Management Office'. I need to thank a good human being, a good family friend of mine, Natarajan, who encouraged me to work on this subject and helped me to understand complex topics through easy mind-mapping in logical way. He gave me the first writing assignment in 1999, for a technical subject. Balu Mohan Rao, Senior Vice President at Scope International; Govindaswamy Abbupillai, Senior Vice President at Mahindra Satyam; Sriram K., Senior Vice President at Mahindra Satyam; and Narayana Murthy K., Vice President at Mahindra Satyam. I would like to express my gratitude to all those who provided support, talked things over and offered comments. Especially, I want to thank my father, M. Subramanian; mother, S. Lalitha; wife, R. Ramya; and two kids, Shrikrishna and Shrisivaranjani, who were unfailingly supportive and encouraging during the long months I spent glued into my computer while writing this book. Last and not least, I beg forgiveness of all those who have been with me over the course of the years and whose names I have failed to mention. I am, especially, indebted to G. Rajesh Kumar, Government Arts College (autonomous), Nandhanam, Chennai, for meticulously reading through a number of drafts of this book and for his helpful suggestions, advice and constructive comments.

Subramanian Chandramouli

This book wouldn't have been possible without constant inspiration and support from my lovely wife, Adity. My parents have always been enthusiastic about this project. They tirelessly helped me providing continuous guidance at every necessary step. The unconditional love and affection that my sons, Deepro and Devarko, ushered on me, constantly motivated me to work hard on this crucial project.

This book is the culmination of all the learnings that I received from many well-reputed professionals Mr. the industry. I was fortunate to work with them and gained valuable knowledge under their aegis. It helped me rightly molding my professional career. Mr. Kollol Hazra, Managing Director, CSG Systems International, India; Dr. Rathi Dasgupta, former Managing Director, Intec India; Prof Indranil Bose, Indian Institute of Management, Kolkata (IIMC) provided guidance and encouragements in different aspects of my life as well as professional career. I would also like to thank some people blessed with highly-intellectual minds. They have helped me in gaining valuable knowledge which has become an integral part of this book. To name them, Saikat Biswas, Head–Customer Engineering and Delivery at Sixth Sense Media; and Indrajit Sanyal, Director and Head–System Integration and Package Solution at Ericsson, comes to my mind first.

My heartfelt thanks goes to all those wonderful people who contributed in many ways in conceptualizing this book and wished success of this project.

Saikat Dutt

About the Authors

Subramanian Chandramouli, PMP, PMI-ACP, is a recognized industry thought leader in project and program management. He has authored two books, PMP Certification Excel with Ease and PMI Agile Certified Practitioner Excel with Ease, were published by Pearson Education. He is an alumnus of IIM Kozhikode. He is a prolific writer of business management articles dealing with delivery management, competitiveness, IT, organizational culture and leadership. His vast experience includes corporate and project governance, customer relationship management and organization strategy.

Subramanian Chandramouli was an active member in PMI OPM3 and PMCDF project works. He is a certified Green Belt in six sigma methodology and also ITIL (F) Certified. He is actively associated with academia and various research professional bodies in India.

A continuous learner and conference enthusiast, Subramanian Chandramouli has authored a paper on Strategy-based Service Model which won the 1st runner up award at the International IT Service Management Conference, 2013 (ITSM-2013). He has also authored a paper titled 'SCRUM TEA Model—Best Practices of Agile Program Management'. It received the second runner award by QAI at the International Program and portfolio Conference, 2013.

Saikat Dutt, PMP, PMI-ACP, CSM, is the author of the book 'PMI Agile Certified Practitioner—Excel with Ease' published by Pearson Education. He is a Project Management Professional (PMP) and PMI Agile Certified Professional certified by Project Management Institute (PMI), USA, and also a Certified Scrum Master (CSM). Saikat has more than 17 years of IT industry experience. He has expertise in managing large-scale, multi-location and mission critical projects. Saikat holds a B.E. degree from Jadavpur University, Kolkata. He is working as a Director in Cognizant Technology Solutions. He is an active speaker on project management methodologies and Agile Best Practices in several forums. He is also actively involved with IIM Calcutta to develop case studies taught in global business schools.

Section I

Basics of Software Project Management

1

Introduction to Software

1.1 Introduction to Software

The success of mankind in performing a process with more accuracy and efficiency commenced with the advent of computers. The digitized computing machines, developed in 1940s, merely carried out arithmetic operations marking the first steps towards the development of today's highly-evolved computers. The progress made in the field of computing today was never predicted. We cannot talk about computers without mentioning the components used in creating this wonder device. In a similar fashion, man has developed many such small and useful gadgets which are cumulatively aiding in making our everyday life easier and comfortable.

Every device that man has invented has remarkably simplified his life. Inventions like pulley, wheel, and finally the computer—all these have taken away the stress and strain from our lives.

The first generation computers performed very simple calculations and yielded results, which were of little consequence, at the cost of high energy consumptions and being bulky in size. But today, computers are power-packed machines whose power of calculation, analysis, comparison of the details and decision making is second to none. The role of humans is reduced to that of mere approvers of the decisions of computers. There is no domain which does not use the powers of this incredible device. Extended functionalities of the computer have eliminated the efforts that humans had to invest so far, which can now be channelled to better and more important use. The primary components of computer were a memory space to store the variables, a procedure to perform the operations, and a display to show the results to the user. The instructions to the computer were provided by a wired component that was very messy. Then the idea of storing the programmed instructions in the device itself came up, leading to no further need to input every single instruction manually. This concept brought forward the requirement of a programming language to construct a procedure for every task. A programming language has certain formats to guide the user in easier and faster design of a program. Programs of individual functions grouped together form the software. Software is a collection of similar tasks which provides the single interface to the user to obtain the results for a variety of requests. It is, thus, the controlling units of a hardware component. Both the components complete the computer structure, one without the other is useless. A memory device, a power unit, capacitors, resistors, processor, monitor, and various cables to connect—are the hardware components used in a computer.

The software defines functions of data transfer, path of control messages and the input and output traffic between hardware.

This book contemplates on the concepts of software and its various stages of development, and discusses why it is so necessary in the success of computers. Software development involves many arduous tasks which have evolved to the present stage. Different methods have been proposed to develop software and deploy it in the environment needed. The development of software does not end, but continues till the next version is developed. The development team continues its relationship with the software by periodically updating it, meeting the ever-increasing demands and needs of the clients and the end users. Software engineering deals with the designing and delivery of software to the clients' complete satisfaction. The birth of software, the phases, and the levels of applicability, the roles it play in the functioning of computers are discussed in the following topics.

1.1.1 What is Software?

Software is defined as the tool with a designated order of instructions that directs a computer to perform specific operations and provide the desired results after obtaining the requirements of the users. The methodology of how to perform the operations in an optimal path to get accurate results in a quick manner states the function of computer software.

Software is comprised of procedures, rules, software related documents and the associated basic data to run the software..

Software = Computer Programs (Instructions) + Procedures + Rules
+ Associated Documents + Data

Procedures and rules include step-by-step guide of how to install (deploy) a software, and how to use an installed software. Documents include requirement documents, design documents and testing-related documents. In order to run the software, basic data needs to be fed in.

Computer software resides in the memory space of a computer, commanding it in every situation. The process of the software begins with the booting of the computer till it is shut down.

Point to Remember

Software = Computer Programs (Instructions) + Procedures + Rules
+ Associated Documents + Data

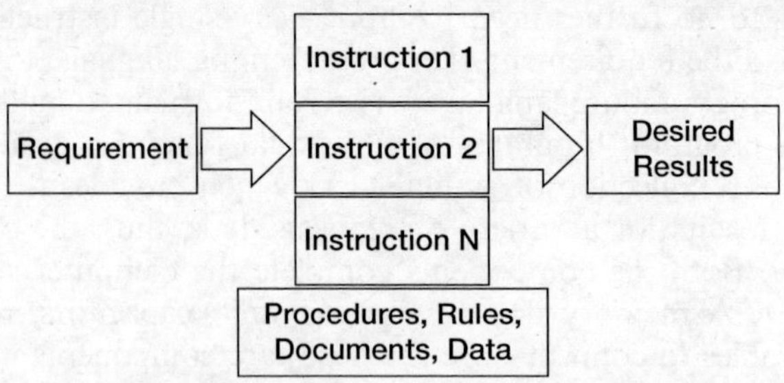

Figure 1.1 Components of Software

Examples of software:

1. Microsoft Word
2. Microsoft Excel
3. Microsoft PowerPoint
4. Linux
5. MySQL
6. Adobe Photoshop

1.1.2 Evolving Role of Software

Software has evolved from a single instruction provided to the machine to the present stage of decision-making software (Figure 1.2). Initially, the devices were operated by inputting single real time instructions; later a programming language framed a structure for programs to be combined into software. The software then was divided into categories based on their implementation areas.

Individual programs perform an operation; collectively, they form software and perform a function for the user (Figure 1.3). Software are of two types. This classification is based on the areas they command, namely, Application Software and System Software.

System Software comprises the programs which are concerned with the operations of the hardware components (Figure 1.3). The technical functioning of the computer is dependent on the operating system, built-in with a number of adequate system software that controls the transfer of messages handling the internal processes, which are mostly abstracted from the external users of the computer.

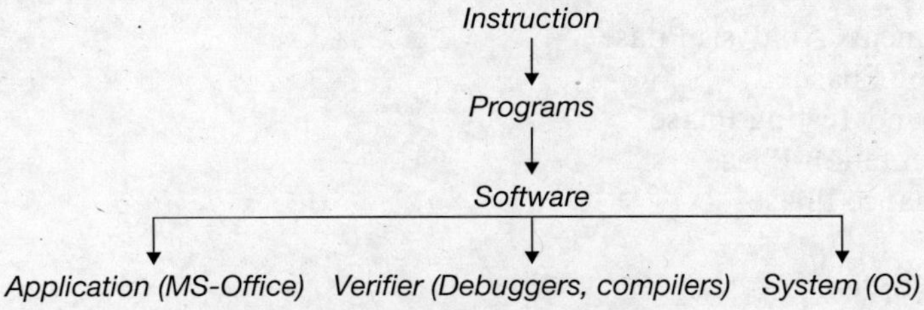

Figure 1.2 Evolution of Software

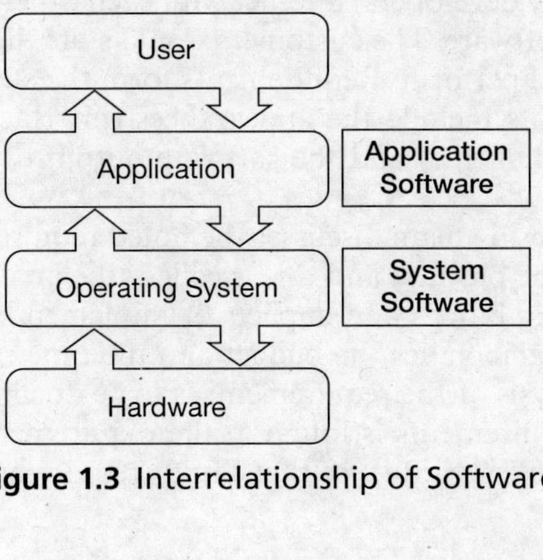

Figure 1.3 Interrelationship of Software

Examples:

1. Operating System like DOS, Windows and Linux.
2. Device Drivers (Hardware Controllers) like video-driver software.

Application Software consists of programs designed to carry out operations for a specific application meant purely for the tasks of the user. It obtains the inputs and processes them with the instructions already defined (Figure 1.3). They have no access to the hardware or the pre-recorded system software of the device. Intended for interfacing and interacting with the user, they are adorned with the unifying taste of the users.

Examples: MS-Office suite, Microsoft Calculator, Notepad, etc.

There are other types of software which are dedicated to the verification of the programs in terms of coding, formats, flow of control and order of execution. These verifying software do not involve in any other parts of the operations. They are used to detect and report the syntax errors in the designed program. Without the report of verifiers and stated rectifications the program is not allowed to execute.

Examples: Compilers and Debuggers.

1.1.3 Phases in Software Development

The phases in software development define the steps at every stage of organizing the development of software. Each step is called a phase. Each phase will have at least one deliverable (output).

The general software development phases are as follows:

1. Requirements Analysis Phase
2. Designing Phase
3. Coding and Testing Phase
4. Implementation Phase
5. Maintenance Phase

Requirements Analysis

Requirements analysis is the first phase of software development in which the customer and the business analysts (usually developers) interact with each other and document the necessities of the outcome of the software. The customers would state their requirements—how and what the end product should perform. Requirements form the stepping stone of any project or product. The requirements include the appearances (interface requirements), the functionalities (functional requirements) and the software output expectations (non-functional requirements).

The Requirements gathering team discusses the noted requirements with the experts, for their implementation into the product and this is called 'the analysis part of the phase'. An expert team analyses the possibilities and impacts of implementing the stated requirements. Analysis of the requirements includes the budget and the time required for completing the product. The complete analysis of the requirements is to be documented for future reference.

If a problem in the requirements is found at the requirements analysis stage, it would then be very easy to fix the issue. But, if that faulty requirement percolates through the stages of design and coding, then it would cost 10–100 times more to fix the same. Capturing the requirements fully and correctly at the early stages of a project is essential to keep the project profitable.

Types of Requirements include:

- Functional Requirements
- Non-functional Requirements
- Interface Requirements

The steps in Requirement Engineering phase include:

- Feasibility Study
- Eliciting Requirements
- Requirement Analysis
- Specifying and Validating Requirements
- Requirements Management

Requirement Analysis Models (Approach) includes:

- Structured Analysis Model
- Object-oriented Analysis Model

We will discuss 'Requirement Engineering Principles' in Chapter 2, and 'Requirement Analysis Modelling' in Chapter 3.

Designing

During the design phase, the software requirement is converted into design models. Each design outcome is verified and validated before moving to the next phase.

Design of the software depends on the level of complexity of the product, the graphical interfaces required and simplicity needed in usage of the end users. The design should not leave out any of the agreed requirements of the user. The Design Phase acts as a bridge between the Requirement Analysis phase and Coding Phase. Design phase converts the business requirements into technical requirements. The design has no functionality, but is relevant only to the structure of the product. Design of the software product should be:

1. Precise and Specific
2. Conform to budget and requirements
3. A direct solution to the problem

Modularity, Cohesion, Coupling and layering are the factors to be considered while designing a software. UML is a modelling language used in modeling software and non-software systems. We will discuss UML and the above factors in detail in the later chapters.

Software Design includes Data Design, Architectural Design, User Interface Design, Procedural Design, and Deployment Level Design.

We will discuss 'Software Design Concepts' in Chapter 4. It covers design models, architectural engineering, etc. Chapter 5 is about object-oriented concepts, it covers class, objects, inheritance, polymorphism, design patterns, etc. Chapter 6 is about object-oriented analysis, it covers use case modelling, UML Notations, etc. Chapter 7 discusses user interface design.

Coding and Testing

Coding is defined as the phase where the document format is transformed into lines of codes in programming languages. Coding is done, in a typical waterfall model, after the requirement analysis (requirement clarification) and design phase. Writing standardized codes for software not only helps maintain it properly once it is built, but also helps enhancing the code easily at a later point of time. It also helps in identifying and fix the bugs quickly and easily. So, writing correct code alone is not enough, focus should be given on writing a standard code. Lines of code are the instructions which execute a program in the environment where it is supposed to be. The designs in high-level language are converted into machine-level language for implementation in the real-world environment. We will be discussing the various coding conventions and coding standards in detail in the subsequent chapters.

After the coding phase is completed, the lines of code have to be tested for ensuring its right functionality in the platform. Testing is carried out by a separate team of experts (software testers) specialized in generating sample cases and subjecting the product to various tests. Only after the product has been proved to be reliable over the tests, it enters into the implementation phase. We will be discussing the process of testing and its procedures in detail in the subsequent chapters.

Chapters which are related to coding and testing aspects are:

Chapter 8—Software Coding
Chapter 9—Introduction to Software Measurement and Metrics
Chapter 10—LOC Function Point and Object-oriented Metrics
Chapter 19—Software Testing Plan and Test Case preparation
Chapter 20—Software Test Automation

Implementation

This phase involves the introduction of the developed software into the market and to the end users. This phase is also called 'deployment phase'. The tested software product is then implemented in the customer's domain. The software developed, is installed in the platform for its prescribed function. The success of the implemented product lies with the likability and higher preferences it obtains from the users. There are similar products satisfying the same functionalities of competing companies in the market vying for attention. Hence, the implemented product should be simple to use and accurate for the use of financial and trading organizations.

Maintenance

Software Maintenance is the core aspect of software engineering. After the system development, the system gets deployed into the production environment. The process of modifying the production system after the delivery in order to correct the faults, improving performance and adapting to the changing environment is called software maintenance. The duty of the team of developers does not end after the product is implemented, but continues for a considerable length of time. Training has to be provided to the clients and users for handling the product. Without proper training and knowledge on how the product works, there are chances of errors and failures. Not every user is skilled in the technical aspects of the software other than the developers themselves. Over and above this, the software should be maintained and upgraded with ever increasing demands and requirements of the clients and end users. All the changes in the maintenance stage are clearly documented for further references. When a new product of similar characteristics is in need to be developed, these documents are referred for analysing the components which could be reused. The reusable component shortens the time and effort of the development team by facilitating them to skip the design and coding process for that particular portion of the code. We will discuss maintenance and its corresponding process in Chapter 9—Introduction to Software Measurement and Metrics.

1.1.4 Software Characteristics

A software has the following characteristics (Figure 1.4).

1. **It should be complete:** The software product being developed should meet all the requirements of the customers. No matter how complex the product is, the requirements agreed upon should be present in the product. The final product should not miss out any of the required functions.
2. **It should be exclusive and reliable:** Unique software delivers ensured performance to a particular problem. A software should concentrate on the given problem or requirements. The solution obtained after using the software should be distinct. The software needs to be stable for a considerable time and usage, providing unfailing service.
3. **It should be precise:** Unwanted steps and operations should be eliminated and shorter operations with the right solution preferred. Unwanted steps lead to the wastage of resources, manpower and thus the cost. These extra operations would have no extra effect on the final solution of the software. Selective and adequate processes should be enough and thus the structure needs to be clear-cut.
4. **It should be efficient:** A well-organized software produces optimal result at every moment of usage. The structure of the software needs to obey a strict and pre-defined order to be efficient. It should also be flexible in nature so that it can be extended at a later point of time.

1.1.5 Changing Nature of Software

At the beginning, binary instructions were fed into computers. Today, software has evolved to a matured level. We have sophisticated tools to develop software and no longer require to type in binary instructions. Now, we have object-based software development.

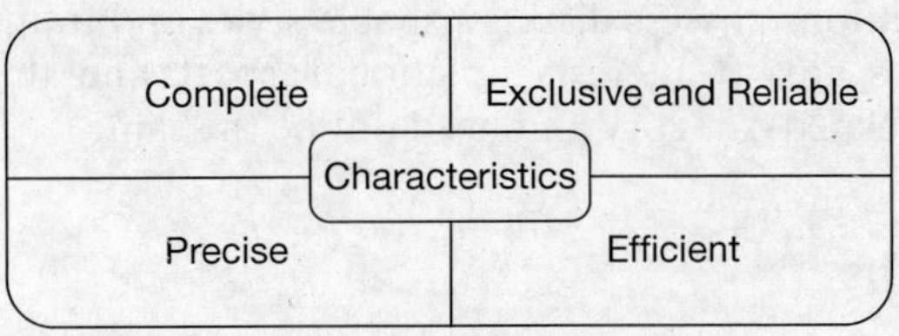

Figure 1.4 Characteristics of Software

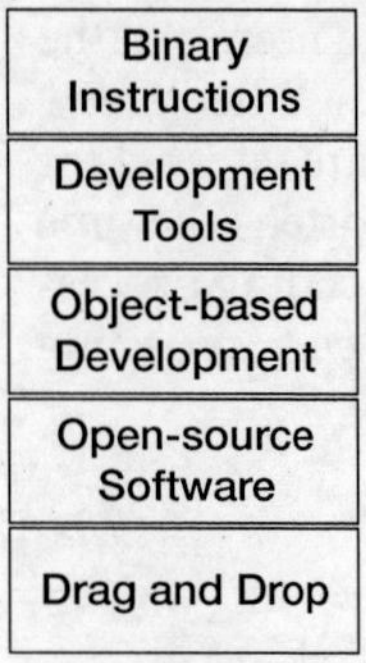

The urge of ever-increasing features and demands of the business users lead to the changes necessary in software development. Source codes were once visible only to the development team. But now, it is available even to the customers. Open-source software is a big hit in the market and anybody can change the code while using and customizing it as per needs. Tools are now developed to facilitate the users to design a software product themselves by dragging and dropping the components (contents) at their intended positions. Software development tools have simplified the design and implementation phases drastically. The process of developing software has become simpler.

In-built Software

Various mechanisms of automobiles, planes, and robots employed for various operations in the fields of military and research involves dedicated software with complex operations and decision-making skills. These devices need embedded software as they involve serious analysis and the ability to take appropriate actions at the right time. The in-built software are deeply sensitive and efficient software prescribing the intelligence functions of the devices. The intelligence includes decision-making skillsets since no human can be practically involved to command robots, which is, for example, reporting on the atmospheric conditions of the planet Mars. Mostly, engineering and scientific researches engage this type of software, reducing participation of men in inhuman conditions.

System-based Software

The system-based software also has some prescribed functions, but they are limited to simpler devices. Home computers or computers of any kind necessitate an operating system and additional driver software for the functioning of the entire system. The system-based software are related to the programs which defines the functionality of the hardware components of a particular computer. The operation of a computer as a whole is facilitated by the system software containing the basic instructions and modes of operations at different instances of the end user. Without this software, the hardware is a mere machine. Compliers, linkers and debuggers are also some of the important system software for testing the programs.

Application-based Software

These kinds of software are purely subject to the delivery of a service at user request. They obtain an input condition or a query from the end user, analyses it and displays the results on the monitor. They are not as much complex as the forementioned type. The structure and the language used for the applications vary by a large measure, like for a web-based application the HTML and XML languages are used. For a database application, an ORACLE program is used. Different applications possess distinguishable styles and frameworks. Every field has its very own requirements, area of interests, functional aspects and, thus, different application software belong to the related category and need not be the same.

1.1.6 Software Myths

Software development entails many myths. These myths have created an incomplete and false image of the software development processes. Some of the myths are as follows:

Software is Better Than Implementing Devices

Devices are prone to the wear and tear associated with usage. Software is theoretically known to change indefinitely with alterations in the codes and reusability factors. Software does not come with an expiry date, but practically, there is a limit to the usage. Even though the changes are easier to be updated in the software than devices, they need to be verified.

Reusability Ensures Better Solution

The conceptual model of reusing a component is an incredible strategy to improve the performance in designing and implementing software. But, there is a major factor of adaptability of the existing component into the newer component. Certain modifications may be needed in the component to be reused. Hence, only testing identifies the errors and creates a report. Further remedial actions are taken for a component to be the best fit into the product.

Additional Features Adds Efficiency

As already mentioned, the product being developed needs to be a direct and dedicated solution to the present problem. A more straightforward software is preferred over a software with additional and unwanted features. One has to understand that the product cannot run accurately at the very first time itself, and testing alone cannot identify all the problems.

More Designers—More Delay

This is absolutely not true since the developers team comprises of engineers with vast knowledge of the strategies of rapid development. Expertise and experience of supplementary engineers surely help the product to be deployed at a faster rate.

1.1.7 What is Software Engineering?

Software engineering comprises of strict disciplines which needs to be followed to develop a programmable solution to solve the problems of the customers.

Strategies are defined to obtain a runnable, efficient and maintainable software solution which takes care of the costs, quality, resources and other expenditures. These strategies have been proposed by various engineers after implementing and analysing the merits and demerits of each strategy.

1.1.8 Why Study Software Engineering?

Software engineering encompasses every concept and standard of the disciplines involved in the creation of designs, coding and thus developing maintainable software complying with the available resources and budget constraints. Without a minimal knowledge of software engineering and its disciplines, the developer would find it difficult to cope and control a vast expanse of designing, converting the design into a code, and finally implementing and upgrading the product in keeping with the changing market and conditions. Every developer cannot just jump into the ocean of creativity and in-depth programming skills without a sound concept of software engineering terminologies.

1. It is the basis of any software development.
2. It helps to produce reliable, reusable and quality software.
3. Software engineering understands the customer needs and develops software.

4. It helps developers understand the disciplines of software life cycle.
5. It helps developing software in an efficient way.
6. Software engineering teaches us the best practices of software development.
7. Software engineering helps writing software which can be easily integrated with other software.

1.1.9 Generic View of Software Engineering

The sequential steps which describe the stages of a product being developed are the generic view of software engineering (Figure 1.5).

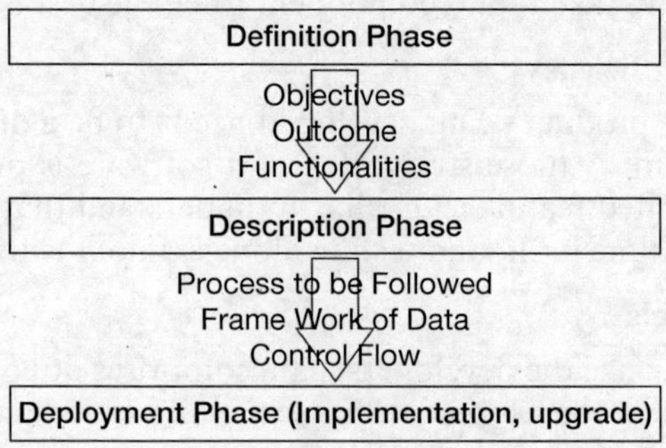

Figure 1.5 Generic View of Software Engineering

Every action, required for the development, is categorized into three generic stages (phases) as:

1. **Definition Phase:** The desired outcomes, functionalities and objectives are obtained from the customers and are documented. These objectives are the driving force for a product to be developed. The team of developers and customers agree upon the final and feasible list of goals to be implemented into the product.
2. **Description Phase:** The next generic phase takes the necessary steps for further development; the desired outcomes are framed with optimal preceding and succeeding processes. The framework of data and control flow in a product, how the processes are ordered, how the functionalities are defined are described in this phase.
3. **Deployment Phase:** After the processes are described, they have to be transformed into corresponding coding and implemented in the real-world environments. Implementation of the software product also includes the training provided to the customers and the end users, the maintenance and upgradations at regular intervals.

1.1.10 Role of Management in Software Engineering

Management of software products depends on the following factors (Figure 1.6).

Participants

Members with varied skill sets, from the team member to the team leader and manager, are responsible for every process of software development. The customers are the initial

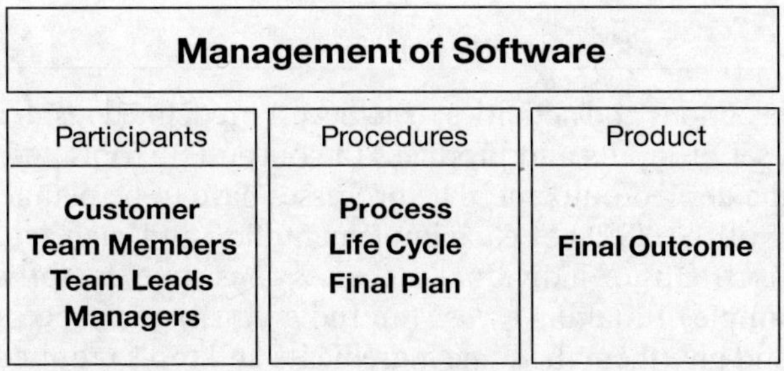

Figure 1.6 Participants, Procedures and Product

participants of the project. They put forward their problems and request a solution. Team of skilled personnel discuss different solutions obeying the technical and administrative constraints. This participating team of developers is assigned by the top level management based on the acquired and proficiency level of each member. Staffing requires analysis of how proficient a member is in a particular field.

Managers play a crucial role in software development. A manager is not only responsible for the final outcome of a project, but also responsible for the execution of the project from the beginning to the end. A manager prepares a plan and tries to execute the project as per laid out plan to create the deliverables. He is also responsible for managing scope, time, cost and quality of the overall project.

Procedure

Procedure describes the way in which a product is developed. The order and types of procedures are devised by the team members and the final plan to be implemented is approved by the team manager. Managers also determine the life cycle which has to be followed among the various models. The best option would help conserving resources and money invested by the management. A slight deviation from the proposed procedure would affect the efficiency of an entire process.

Product

Selection of the best plans and procedures, assigning the right and efficient staff to the project ensures the success of the project and, thereby, ensuring the final outcome of the project called 'the product' (Figure 1.7). A product is the outcome of a project.

There are many models related to product development, evolved from the earliest era of software development. Product models help creating quality product through proper process.

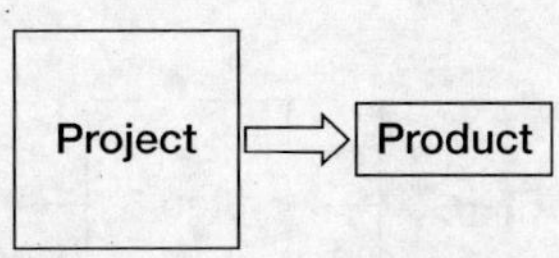

Figure 1.7 Project vs Product

1.2 Software Process

Any set of inter-related actions and activities to achieve a predefined result is called 'a process'. A process has its own set of inputs and produces the output(s). Tools and techniques acts on the process to create the desired outcome. The processes have to be planned with utmost care and the understanding of the effects of each implementation and each activity on the product by all the stakeholders. Groups of individual processes constitute the software as a whole.

Let us take an example of making a *dosa* (an Indian dish) as a process. If we call five different people (chefs) and give them the same ingredients and tools required to make *dosa*, will the output be the same? The size and taste of the *dosa* is bound to vary. Why is it so? This is not only because of the difference in skills possessed by the chefs, but also due to difference in techniques they have learnt over a period of time. Thus, we need to understand and learn the techniques of a process to produce a better output.

In the next few sections, an overview of the different processes of software development is discussed.

1.2.1 The Linear Sequential Model

Linear action means sequence of actions which describes the order in which the execution of activities are planned and followed.

The process of development (Figure 1.8) is divided into a sequence of actions (steps) from requirements analysis, designing, coding and testing, implementation and finally maintenance. Each activity is carried out in a linear order (in sequential fashion) and no other order of execution is followed other than the flow mentioned. The result of the first activity is forwarded to the next stage and thus to the final stage. Without the completion of the previous step and forwarding the result, the next activity cannot be executed. It follows a strict sequence and strongly believes that no step could be overlapped.

This model is a straightforward approach. Other names of the Linear Sequential Model are Predictive Life Cycle Model, Waterfall Model and Classical Life Cycle Model. Prototyping Model and Rapid Application Development Models can be the best examples of this model.

Examples for Linear Sequential Model include developing a portal which follows the steps of Requirement Analysis, Design, Coding, Testing and Implementation.

The advantages of Linear Sequential Model are as follows:

1. It is very easy to understand.
2. It is easy for implementation.
3. It is widely used and known to all involved; hence, all stakeholders understand this.
4. It identifies deliverables and milestones upfront.

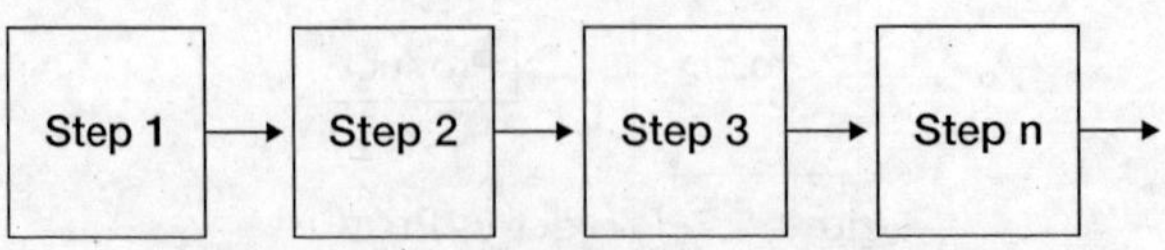

Figure 1.8 Linear Sequential Model

The disadvantages of the Liner Sequential Model are as follows:

1. This model assumes that requirements can be frozen before starting the Design Phase which is not true in most of the situations.
2. Requirements are elaborated over a period of time.
3. Strictly following this model takes longer time to finish the project as each step takes its own time.
4. Specialists are required to run each step which is difficult in long-term projects.

1.2.2 Layered Technology

Similar to the linear sequential model, the layered technology (Figure 1.9) introduced the concept of using the software technologies and terminologies even better than the previous strategies. A layered approach ensures a much stronger product. The layered model of software engineering divides the activities in four broad categories:

1. **Quality Process:** For a successful engineering process, there should be a strong base of quality processes.
2. **Process:** The software engineering processes ensure that all the technology layers work together and enables timely development of the software system.
3. **Methods:** The methods in software engineering provide technical capabilities to the system. The requirement analysis, design, modelling, development, testing, etc., are the tasks related to the methods.
4. **Tools:** The tools provide the support to the Process and Methods by making the tasks automated or semi-automated.

Let us consider an example. Roads are constructed in three layers (Figure 1.10). The bottom layer is a combination of clay and large stones, followed by another layer of smaller stones and tar. The next layer combines tar and even smaller stones for providing a neat finish. The quality of the roads depends on the tar used; the number of times ran over by a roller machine and the time given to those combinations to settle down. The layered technology resembles many construction techniques which ensures a well-built structure.

Layers are responsible for defining the activities in an order of execution. The layers begin with the requisition of input conditions and storing them at a location, and the next layers are dedicated to describing the most advantageous processes and methodologies to produce the preferred outcome. The final layer concentrates on submission of the designed product with the best quality beyond every difficulty.

Developing a quality product includes serious approaches, such as selection and engagement of valued resources and staff.

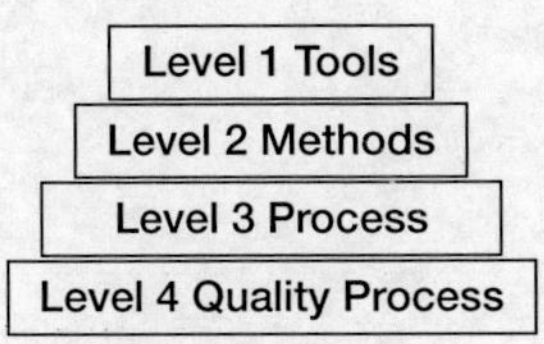

Figure 1.9 Layered Technology

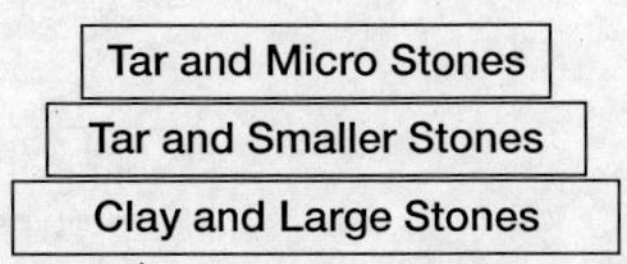

Figure 1.10 Example of Layered Technology

1.2.3 Prototyping Model

The product once developed by using Layered approach cannot be reversed easily. But, in real-life situations, the requirements are subject to numerous changes till they are implemented into the product.

Hence, the prototyping model (Figure 1.11) was proposed with a completely different strategy. Every product to be developed initially receives requirements from the customers. With the given requirements, a sample or test model called 'the prototype' is developed and displayed to the customer. The customers would respond with their opinion and rectifications needed to the current prototype. The prototype is altered till the customer is satisfied with the style, design and execution of the processes. Otherwise, the development team continues to consider different options for creating the prototype. The final list of requirements reported will lead the development team to the next phase of design.

There are two types of prototypes (Figure 1.12) developed in this model, namely, evolutionary and throw-away prototypes.

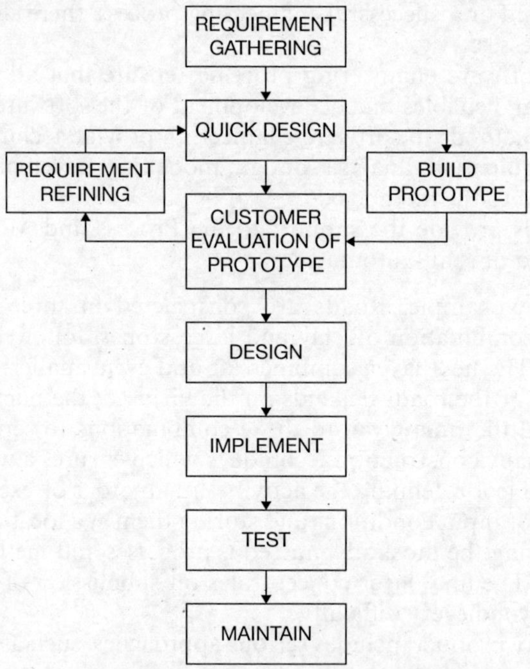

Figure 1.11 Prototyping Model

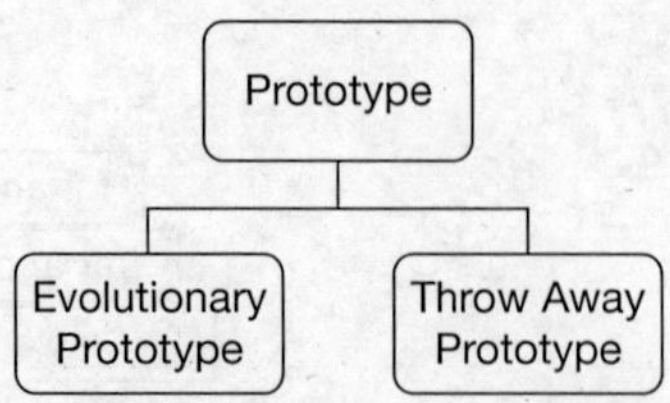

Figure 1.12 Prototyping Model

The former type will be reused and the changes are implemented in that particular prototype. The new changes and corrections are updated in the existing prototype until the final list of requirements is obtained without wasting the used resources. The other type, as the name suggests, destroys the wrong prototypes. Thrown away prototypes are proved to be wrong and thus the new prototypes are developed in the next stages. The resources used in the previous prototypes are either freed or rejected.

Point to Remember

The two types of prototypes are: (1) evolutionary prototype; and (2) Throw-away prototype.

1.2.4 RAD Model

RAD model stands for Rapid Application Development Model. This model is the methodology proposed for quicker design and deployment of a product (Figure 1.13). This model includes the technologies and concepts of prototyping and iterative designs. RAD model requires a very short time span of 60–90 days for completing the software and delivering it to the customer. Unlike the traditional approaches, many innovative and simpler strategies of less time consuming activities are executed by the team of developers. RAD model proves to be the most preferable solution to quick needs and implementation of web-based applications. An organization needs to promote itself through World Wide Web by deploying a web application. This application has to be a simple to use and produce the desired results. Already present with numerous applications in web-based concepts, the customer may have to just refer available applications and select from the same. Reuse of existing prototypes in the referred application facilitates the faster deployment of new application.

RAD model includes the following five phases for development.

1. Business modelling
2. Data modelling
3. Process modelling
4. Application generation
5. Testing and turnover

Business Modelling

Business modelling is the stage in which the types of information that are prime factors of the application are defined. The category of information involved in the processes, the procedures which use the information for various computations, initiators of the information and transfer of data between the processes are defined in the business modelling phase. With the details of the information being processed, the area of functionality of the application can be determined.

Data Modelling

The obtained information from the previous phase is filtered into useful and meaningful sets of data. They are refined into entities of high importance. The characteristics of the entities

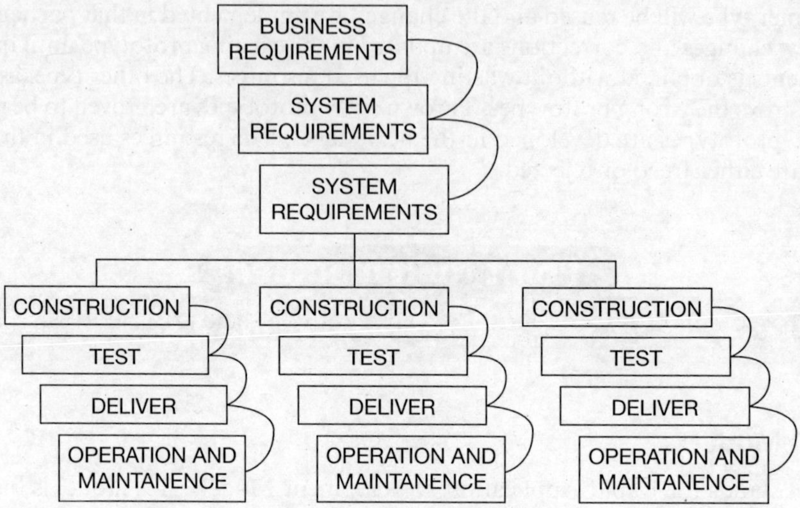

Figure1.13 RAD Model

and their relationships are also defined in this data modelling phase. Attributes and entities enable a better understanding of the chief factors around which an entire processes are framed.

Process Modelling

Process modelling defines the activities needed to process the entities. Every instruction is framed in this phase. The instructions are concerned with the processing of the data from the initial to the final stages of the application. Processes are defined for the storage and retrieval of the objects, their attributes and their associated metrics. Without proper design of these processes, the desired outcome cannot be achieved.

Application Generation

Application generation is a phase which uses automated tools to generate the working model of the designed application. The automated tools are used for faster analysis of similar components for reuse thus saving time in making new designs. Software tools have provided a huge range of amenities for faster deployment of an application with the same accuracy.

Testing and Turnover

The final phase is to test the correctness and consistency of the developed application. With such a short time and implementation of many reusable components, the accuracy of the application has to be tested with greater care. Reusing a component involves increased risk factors since the interfacing modules need to relate the different modules of varying applications.

Points to Remember

The business modelling is the stage in which the types of information that are prime factors of the application are defined. Application generation is a phase which uses automated tools to generate the working model of the designed application.

1.2.5 Process Framework

Framework activities are processes of basic functionalities and they are common to almost all software products. These actions can be applied to every product without any further modifications. For example, a user login form always proceeds the further session for every user. The login form consists of only two requirements: Username and Password. A new application with the same requirement (user login form) need not create a new design, but can reuse it with the whole module. The login form also requires a database for storing user-names and corresponding passwords.

Process Framework

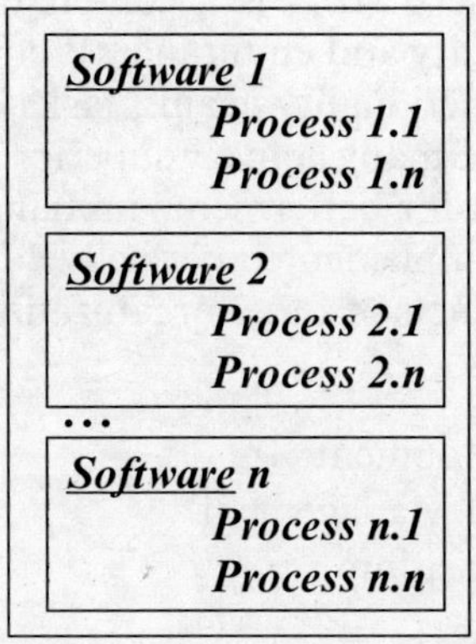

Analysis of the Process Framework Activities

Gathering the Necessities: The customary **process framework** activities begins with the analysis and observations made on the requirements. This process called 'the Requirement Gathering phase', involves intended customers and the team of developers. Concluding the requirement gathering process produces a list of gathered and approved requirements.

Scheduling and Staff Allocation: Based on the gathered information, the plans about the model selected for development, processes framed and analysis on the feasible risks are made. In addition, the schedule for the development is also agreed on. Members are assigned tasks depending on the knowledge possessed by them and the knowledge required for the tasks.

Design and Deployment: The team members start to design and develop the coding for their assigned task. The design process may be eliminated by reusing a module. Efficient modelling and processes eases the risks at the later stages of a product.

Supplementary Framework Activities: The product being developed has to be checked whether it proceeds in the right path at regular intervals. Slight deviations from the intended path would result in start the whole process over again. Risk analysis is also another major course of action to prevent disastrous outcomes at the end. Detection and mitigation of risks at the earlier stages would shorten the final process.

Points to Remember

Framework activities are processes of basic functionalities and they are common to almost all software products. These actions can be applied to every products without any further modifications.

1.2.6 Capability Maturity Model Integration (CMMI)

Capability Maturity Model Integration (CMMI) is an approach for improving the process level operations (Figure 1.14). The CMMI is a compilation of many best approaches to enhance a product's efficiency, quality and endurance. It collects the strategies for improving the processes at many levels of functionality, teams, tasks, sub-tasks and the whole project. As the name denotes, integration of many actively superior methodologies are combined and incorporated into a single product for betterments in many ways. Individual products have their own processes designed and implemented perfectly. Identifying such best processes and integrating them into the new products of other organizations is the ultimate goal of CMMI. The levels of CMMI are as follows.

1. Product and Service Development
2. Service Establishment and Management
3. Product and Service Acquisition

The products are the functional units to be designed and the services are functionalities of such products. Integrating numerous individual services into a product is the prime accomplishment of CMMI. The services are analysed for resemblance, the level of matching and how well they suit themselves into the new product.

CMMI Levels

The CMMI model was evolved from the Software CMM for integrating many different and well-organized models into new models. There are five evolutionary levels of the model which are:

1. Initial
2. Repeatable
3. Defined
4. Managed
5. Optimizing

The **initial** level is a poorly controlled phase with no proper designation of the schedule and the resources needed for development. The primary necessities are analysed, selected and advanced to the next level of the model. In the succeeding level, certain processes are chosen to produce the desired outcomes after organizing the schedule and resources needed. Yet those processes are in need of additional consistency in the **repeatable** level. The control processes are ordered and in position.

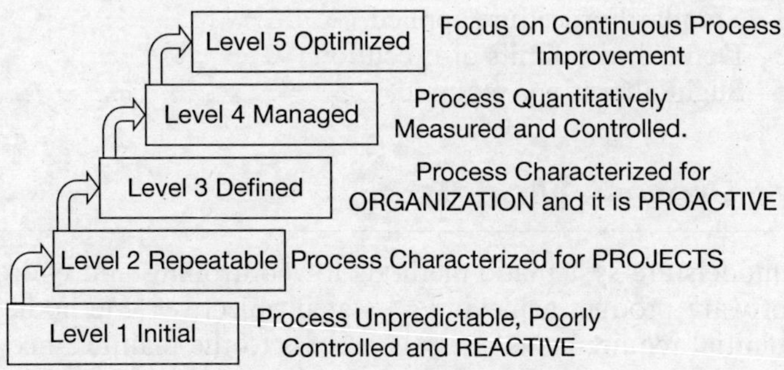

Figure 1.14 CMMI Levels

The third level **defined** requires stringent measures to be followed. The processes are regulated, well-understood and, thus, properly ordered. The consistency of all the processes is achieved in this stage. **Managing level** is the fourth level in which adequate steps are taken to determine the actions to update and upgrade the processes in the product. The level defines measures for widening the functionality of every process. This level forwards its outcome to the **optimizing** level. This level concentrates on smoothening of approaches for better, faster and risk-free execution of the processes.

All these levels are proposed to achieve a process incremental model helping the development team to nominate an efficient product with minimal effort.

PCMM (People Capability Maturity Model) is another model of Capability Maturity Model released in 1995 (book form in 2001) and it deals with the improvement of human resources (assets) of organizations. People Management Process: Areas addressed in PCMM contains common futures and key practices.

1.2.7 Process Pattern

In a software development life cycle, there is a standard order of activities for completing a task. The order cannot be altered, as the pattern has been proven as the most optimal solution. There will not be another alternative with an equal strength of an existing pattern. Patterns compile a set of activities or tasks or actions, following a prescribed sequence of execution. These patterns are considered in software life cycles, customer communication, coding, reviews and test patterns.

1.2.8 Process Assessments

Every process has its own strength, weakness and associated risks. These factors have to be assessed to determine the level of applicability. A process with high risks and weaknesses cannot be applied in a product. The strength of all possible affirmative solutions has to be reviewed to decide on the applicable solution and on the first alternative. Evaluation of the strengths, weaknesses and risks of every process against a process model is called Process Assessment. Process assessment describes the results of evaluation as:

- **Incomplete**—Still needs revision and modifications
- **Performed**—Completes definition and satisfies the customer
- **Managed**—Controlled and maintained

- **Established**—Standard procedure applied
- **Predictable**—Defined with limits of execution
- **Optimizing**—Slight alterations required

1.3 Software Process Models

Software process models are systematic methods for controlling and coordinating the development of a software product achieving all stated objectives. Methodical processes are followed from the initial requirements analysis process to the maintenance phase. The systematic processes provide guidelines and prevent the development team from deviating from the intended path leading to a failure. Software process models help the developer team to recognize the following:

1. Set of tasks, sub-tasks and interfaces
2. Resources needed for every process
3. Adequate time span

Traditional Software Process Models

Traditional approaches of software process do not include the developments and simplified procedures attained today. We already discussed the linear sequential model in previous pages. Some of the traditional approaches are explained here.

1.3.1 Waterfall Model

Waterfall Model (Figure 1.15) is the first and foremost methodology of Software Development Life Cycle (SDLC). The original methodology comprises of the activities—Requirements Specification (phase 1), Design (phase 2), Construction (phase 3), Integration (phase 4), Testing (phase 5), Debugging (phase 6), Installation (phase 7) and Maintenance (phase 8). These activities are proceeded downwards, one after the other (like a waterfall). This conceptual model is based on the construction strategies as no other ideas were suitable for a development process. The process model of construction activity is to design a blueprint, collect all the raw materials for construction, organize the workers and determine the time needed for the project to be completed.

The waterfall model was devised by Royce in 1970, and many organizations implemented this process model in earlier days. The necessities and conditions are obtained from the customer in the first step. This specification and analysis is obviously the first process which leads the developer team. The developer team will start to design a framework for achieving the objectives. Design of a software product is like a blueprint of a construction site. Following the efficient design, the coding begins. This resembles a construction with walls. Testing is the phase which ensures correctness of the product being developed. Without testing, any product cannot be allowed to be implemented in the real-world environments. The maintenance process cannot be predicted and assumed. The software needs additional features after deployment based on the demand of users and customers.

All the processes of the waterfall model ensue in sequential order. These processes are documented, the confirmed information are printed and stored for future references. This model is also called the document driven approach.

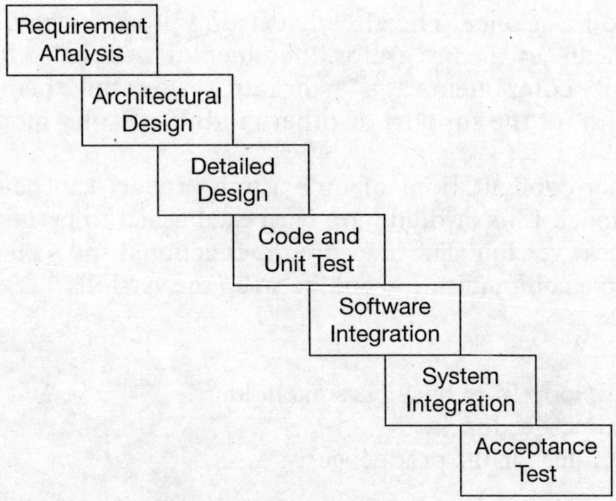

Figure 1.15 Waterfall Model

Advantages of the Waterfall Model:

1. Easy to understand.
2. Easy for implementation.
3. Widely used and known; hence, all stakeholders understand this.
4. Identifies deliverables and milestones upfront.

Disadvantages of the Waterfall Model:

1. Does not match well with reality.
2. It is unrealistic to freeze the requirement upfront.
3. Software is delivered only at the final phase.
4. Difficult and expensive to make changes (CRs always).

1.3.2 Incremental Process Model

The incremental model is one of the evolutionary models which overcame the drawback of the linear execution style of the waterfall model (Figure 1.16). Incremental model has the capability of progressing independently and simultaneously. Separate teams can work individually to produce a product assigned once the requirements are gathered. The whole product is achieved by integrating all of the individual components developed.

The major advantage of the incremental model is that the consecutive steps do not have to wait till the preceding function completes its activity. This assisted the team of developers to complete the design process much faster. The large and complex problems can be divided into a number of smaller and unique tasks, providing a better chance to solve them. The incremental model is suitable for applications which need additions and alterations in its contents after certain time periods. For example, the shopping mall application needs to introduce new offers and concessions on the price list of all items for festive seasons. They cannot be stable at all times and the waterfall model is not the right method to develop the product. The constraints of time and expenses justified the need of the incremental model at once. The already existing product can be combined with a new requirement by means of the integrator. Incremental model also facilitated the isolation of errors and faulty components at a faster rate, the modules being independent and capable of running without the support of other modules. Faulty modules remain intact until rectified.

Versions and higher configurations of an existing product can be developed with the incremental process model. Links would have been established to permit the linkage of additional features in a next version. The links are the functional spots of the integrator component which builds up a communication link between the versions.

Advantages:

1. Quick feedback loop from business stakeholders.
2. Focus on customer feedback.
3. Customer gets a feel of the product early.

Disadvantages:

1. Scheduling of development is difficult with the incremental model.
2. Even though the final product is given in pieces, tracking and monitoring is difficult.
3. Testing needs to be exhaustive in each part.

Evolutionary Process Models

The Evolutionary process models smoothens the process of software development in a number of ways. Its strategies are of prototypes, overlapping and autonomous. The demerits of linear sequential models are eliminated and it is among one of the best process models in software development. Some of the evolutionary process models are as follows.

- Spiral Model
- Components-based Development Model
- Formal Methods Model

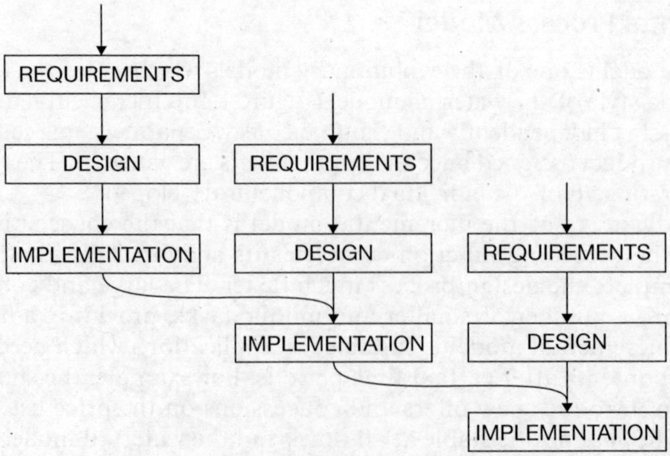

Figure1.16 Incremental Model

1.3.3 Spiral Model

The spiral model was proposed by Boehm, as an evolutionary model, introduced the concept of risk analysis in the earlier stages of development process. Other name of Spiral Model is Risk Spiral Model. This model combines the software development life cycle with Risk Management principles to control the risks at an early stage of the project.

The previously mentioned methodologies did care about the detection of risks but only near end of the project, which increased the burden of rework. If a risk is found to be too disastrous, then the product has to be designed anew. Taking the importance of a risk management process and testing process into account, the spiral model defined new strategies.

A spiral model encompasses the iterative steps in a spiral representation as shown in Figure 1.17. Each circle in the model denotes a succeeding level of the previous state. These are divided task regions which represents the selective process. The task regions may vary from the complexity level of different products.

The planning part includes the tasks of designing an efficient framework as a solution to the objectives. Planning also happens in steps. Life Cycle Plan is prepared first. Development Plan is prepared in the next level; Integration Plan is prepared at the last level.

In the Risk Analysis Phase the prototype is developed. The risk analysis would report the identification and effects of the present risks in the prototype. Assessments of risks at every rotation of the spiral evolution reduce the problems and time required for solving them at the final stage. The risk analysis strategies have to be stringent enough such that even small errors are not left out. Prototyping, incremental and premature risks detection proves this method to be an efficient method over the other process models. Elimination of risks occurs in next iteration. The feedback from the customers is noted for updating the next prototype. The final prototype is developed after incorporating the stated suggestions and subjecting it to the risk analysis process.

Construction and release also happens in iterative fashion based on the base prototype developed. At every level it is also strengthened and final level is the final code to be delivered to the customer.

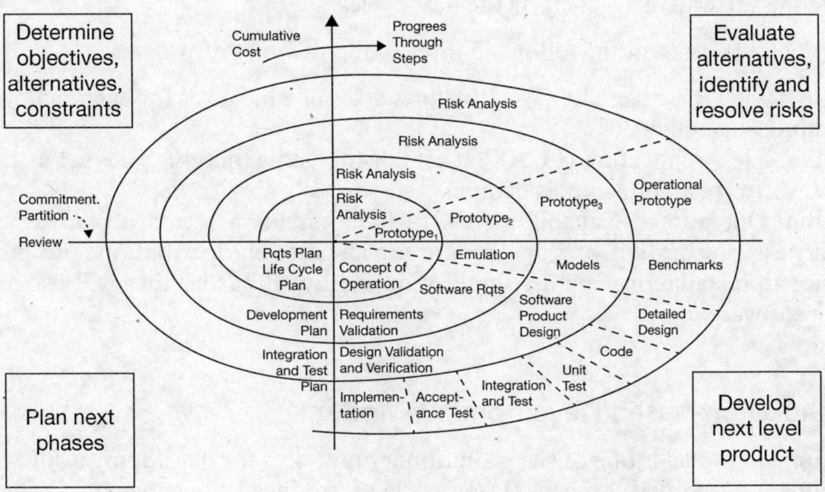

Figure 1.17 Spiral Model

The number of iterations is determined by the team manager depending on the rectifications made and completion of the product. The cost and schedule cannot be assumed right at the initial phase as the prototypes are altered at every rotation. The team manager adjusts cost and time metrics after every circle. The spiral model is selected for software of higher level organizations.

Points to Remember

A spiral model encompasses the iterative steps in a spiral representation. Each circle in the model, denotes a succeeding level of the previous state. There are divided task regions which represent the selective process.

WIN-WIN Spiral Model

The results are based on the negotiations made by the customers. WIN-WIN result is decided for the best negotiations. The customers have their own requirements and needs concerning the system or product. The customer wins by getting the system or product that satisfies the majority of the customer's needs. The developer has some criteria and budgets given by their organization and the developer wins by working towards realistic and achievable budgets and deadlines. Boehm's WIN-WIN spiral model defines a set of negotiation activities at the beginning of each pass around the spiral.

Before defining the set of requirements of the system the win condition for the system are set by the customer. After identifying stakeholders of the system we need to set win-win conditions

The WIN-WIN spiral model introduces three process milestones, called anchor points. These points help to establish the completion of one cycle around the spiral and provide decisions before the software project starts the next cycle.

The anchor points represent the following three different views of progress:

1. Life Cycle Objectives (LCO)—It defines a set of objectives for each major software engineering activity.
2. Life Cycle Architecture (LCA)—It establishes goals that must be met as the system and software architecture is defined.
3. Initial Operational Capability (IOC)—It represents a set of objectives associated with the preparation of the software for installation/distribution, site preparation prior to installation, and assistance required by all parties that will use or support the software.

1.3.4 Component-based Development Model

This development model is one of the evolutionary practices for developing a software product. Component-based development (Figure 1.18) introduced the concept of reusability to the fullest extent. After analysis of the requirements, instead of entering into the design

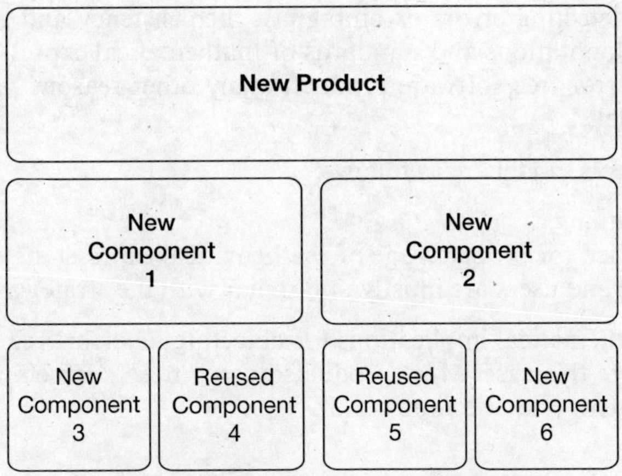

Figure 1.18 Component-based Model

phase, components or modules of existing similar products are checked for their match. Software reuse is the main motto of this evolutionary model. This model serves best where faster and cheaper deployment of the desired product is required.

Requirements Comparison

The requirements for a new product are compared with the recorded list of requirements from the existing products. The percentage of match between the new and existing requirements is evaluated. The extent of match should be considerably high enough to be a perfect match.

Modification and Implementation

After suitable matches or near matching components are identified, these sections are replaced by the existing matches. But the question is whether a 100% match can be obtained or not. The answer is a NO in most cases. Any component cannot be directly implemented into a new product. The near matching product needs some modifications to meet the stated requirements. Interfacing needs to be perfect in order to make the reusable component adapt to a new environment. Modifications and redesigning of interfaces are comparatively easier than designing a whole new component.

Risk Analysis

Integration of existing modules has a greater level of risks than the newly developed components. The outcome of the product may be similar but the preceding and succeeding activities may disturb the new component. Hence a more sincere risk analysis methodology is required for eradication of the risks.

The cost, manpower and time can be reduced to a great extent by this evolutionary process model. Prototyping and spiral model and thus component based software engineering, enhances the speed of developing a product.

1.3.5 The Formal Methods Model

There are some methodologies of strong technical and mathematical background for eliminating most of the errors missed out by other paradigms. Applying mathematical constants improves the rate of detecting errors of ambiguity, inconsistency and irregularity. The errors are quantified with notations and standards of mathematical expressions. Although this approach ensures an error free software product, many other reasons prevent the usage of Formal Methods Model.

The disadvantages of this model are as follows:

- It is time consuming.
- Training is needed for proper usage of mathematical expressions.
- Customers and end users are mostly unfamiliar with the strategy.

Knowledge of the mathematical implications for detecting an error-free software product is an absolute prerequisite this case. Most products do not need such efficient methodologies after considering the extra cost and time factor.

1.3.6 Software Engineering Process

Engineering a process requires a dedicated and disciplined order of activities with a clear-cut view of how to reach the destination. A software product of high significance needs a pertinent roadmap leading to the objectives. Deriving such an efficient path towards the destination can be achieved only if the order is adhered to completely. The engineering process has gained the expertize in many of today's applications and products. The engineering process unlike other problem solving strategies and design approaches, orders the activities with respect to profound technical information of the product statement.

Software engineering process differs from the ordinary process models in the following ways. Normal problem-solving strategies define and solve the problem continued by verification of the proposed solution. Whereas in engineering processes, the software requirements are analysed and specified, designing and implementation of a suitable product and finally verifying the designed product with respect to the specified requirements. Efficiency is promoted as the prime factors are narrowed down and the knowledge of the processes is fed to every employee and participant. This knowledge is acquired by experience from previous successful projects and exposure to the technical background.

Primary Steps of Software Engineering Process

As mentioned, the initial step is to '**Analyse**' and '**Specify**'. The requirements are analysed in general aspects, such as, identifying the main objectives of the entire product, analysing the associated objectives of next importance and other indirect activities that support the objectives, problem identification and determination of the functional and non-functional requirements. These functional and non-functional requirements are the resources which have a direct or indirect impact on the outcome of the product. These analyses produce a list of specifications on the requirements and the identified problem.

Designing and Implementation of a well-organized technical plan would reduce the number of designs to meet the goals of product. Once the design has been proved to be an efficient solution, it can be developed as a prototype subject to examination of the customer for any changes. The prototype eliminates the chances of later delays if properly verified. A prototype is extended with full functionalities and implemented in the final product.

Verifying the deployed product involves the cross-checking of how well the whole product works in the real-time environment. Usually, the product is developed to be enhanced by adding additional features to it as and when the demands arise. The data design and the flow design are separately verified to ensure maximum efficiency. Functional design verifies the relationships among the existing processes and checks if there are any conflicts in the transfer of data between the available functions.

1.3.7 Business Process Engineering

Software is employed in almost every field, mostly in business applications. Software products implemented in business areas are never constant as the customers and end users need features of global influence which is ever-evolving. Distributed environments of a same business process cannot be the same. Operational responsiveness is the ability of a software product to communicate with customers having different queries. The serviceable business processes are intended to respond and provide solutions regarding the business outsources and purpose. The detailed information on the services available to the customers is promised to every requester with 100 percent satisfaction.

Operational responsiveness advocates the principles, intentions, and functional aspects of a particular organization. The organization develops a software product with its business processes employed. The software developed, concentrates on the devoted business processes unlike other software solutions.

1.3.8 Fourth Generation Techniques

The Fourth Generation Techniques (4GT) combines distinguished directory of software tools with assisting amenities for a software developer. Non-procedural languages for database maintenance and data manipulation operations, high-end graphics interfacing, spreadsheet operations, drag and drop creations of web-based applications are some of the separate high level 4G technologies. Imagine a whole system implementing all of these separate techniques into a single procedure. Fourth Generation techniques are designed to generate the source code themselves only with the minimal specification from the designer. The developer does nothing much other than inputting complete requirements and other conditions. Positioning the preconditions, post conditions and the conditions at the correct location would be enough; the rest of coding is taken care of automatically by the procedure itself. After the mentioning of such conditions a non-operational prototype is developed as a sample output. Another foremost point is that the customer is able to understand every functionality and error-prone zones in the prototype. This procedure aids the faster development and deployment of a software product with greater interactive sessions and participation of a customer. As all the processes eliminate the abstraction like other terminologies, entire process becomes completely visible from the coding to framed structure. The major drawback is that a customer himself may lack in the optimal way of describing the requirements and unwanted processes may be wasting the efficiency of the Fourth Generation Techniques. This technique includes the following process:

- Requirements Specification
- Prototype Design
- Implementation
- Constructing the Original Framework

1.4 Software Product

1.4.1 Characteristics of a Good Software Product

A good software product should possess the following characteristics:

Completeness: The developed software product should cover all the stated and agreed requirements without missing out any.

Consistency: Operations of the product should be stable and capable of handling the problems in implementation.

Durability: The customers may vary in technical and geographical aspects. The product should respond to a diversity of environments.

Efficiency: The product should not waste the resources, like the memory spaces allocated for the processes and also minimize the execution and waiting time of operations.

Security: The stored contents and the input statements of the software should be confidential and conserved if they possess a high significance.

Interoperability: Communication between other processes and environments should be possible to make a product universally acceptable.

1.4.2 Engineering Aspects of Software Products

A software product has different views of understanding. Speaking of technical and engineering aspects, a software product will provide customers an abstract image of the product. Engineering aspects contemplates the description of a product in terms of its practical implications and impacts over the platform. The technical aspects include the following.

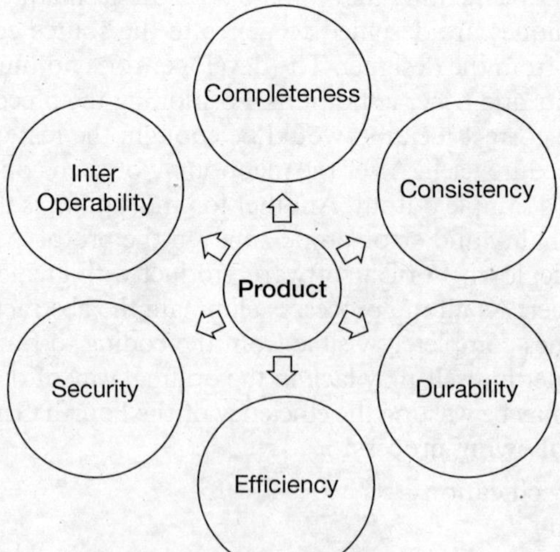

Figure 1.19 Product Characteristics

Purpose

The aim of a software product needs a strong justification and, thus, emphasizing the purpose of being developed. The areas the product description is supposed to cover are the necessary conditions for the product to work and the dependability on other processes.

Process

Definition of the operations needs engineering skills for the right placement and interrelationships. The experience of the developers in previous projects aids them for better design approaches. Unlike normal methodologies, engineering a process needs strong background of the construction ideologies.

1.4.3 Role of Management in Software Products

Management plays an important role in driving the processes of development in the right path benefitting the customer and organization. The ultimate goal is to limit the budget and achieve a reasonable profit satisfying the quality standards. Managing the development process includes the following steps.

Defining the Vision

The goal of the organization is different from that of objectives of the product. The vision is the force which motivates the developer team. This defines the standards and principles of the organization apart from the desired outcomes of the product. The vision keeps the team on track to maintain the standards in any condition.

Defining the Plan

The plans are the set of actions acting on inputs and producing set of outputs. Plan is the blueprint which has to be followed for achieving the outcomes. The plan encompasses many individual processes, structured in an ordered sequence. This structure defined is an optimal solution for perfect execution of operations. Without a proper plan, the solution cannot be obtained as promised. There are also additional plans designed as a backup in case of failures. The alternative plans are also numbered as the first alternative and so. Secondary options are initiated only if the optimal plan fails to succeed.

Defining the Designation

Every participating member in a development process is assigned with a role and jobs to perform. The leader of the team has supplementary duties to ensure that every activity is performed as scheduled and as planned. Every member follows the vision and principles of the organization besides their prescribed role. The members are categorized according to their authority level and decision making capability. But, all members have the liberty to express their views and ideas over the tasks.

Testing the Pathway

Testing is an important process in managing the defined plans. Testing includes the verification of the correctness and consistency of the product, checking on whether the resources are properly used, and budget and time constraints are obeyed. This testing process ensures that the development team can proceed in the path as defined. The pathway reports the deviation from the defined path if the results are different from the sample outputs.

Supportive Activities

There are many associated processes besides the normal procedures. Licensing product as the registered outputs of a particular organization and marketing the products among the competing organizations are some of the additional activities which support delivery of the software product. End user training has to be provided after delivery for efficient utilization. Not every user can readily use the software product as many may lack even the basic knowledge of the understanding the functionality.

We will be discussing the project management concepts in the following chapters:

Chapter 13—Project Management Introduction
Chapter 14—Risk Analysis and Management
Chapter 15—Communication and Team Management
Chapter 16—Project Time and Cost Management
Chapter 17—Project Stakeholder Management

1.4.4 Role of Metrics and Measurements

The terms of representing the quality and quantity of a particular process are metrics and measures. They are used in determining the level of any means in the form of numbers or units. Understanding these terms needs the definition of data points. These are units which denote the condition of a process, the variables involved and the errors in a particular spot.

When a single data point has been collected, a measure has been established. A **measurement** is the representation of data points after a review of a whole module or processes collectively. Measurements are of two types, they are either direct or indirect. Direct measurements denote the values after quantifying the errors in lines of code, resources misuse and memory misuses. Indirect measurements estimate the errors in functionality, complexity, reliability and maintainability.

Metrics are quantitative details obtained by monitoring and controlling the budget and time span of the product. Any deviations from the scheduled path would be reported by the metric values observed at regular intervals.

We will be discussing software measurement and metrics in Chapter 9, 'Introduction to Software Measurement and Metrics' and in Chapter 10, 'LOC Function Point and Object-oriented Metrics'.

1.4.5 Product Engineering Overview

Global implementation of software products has forced the introduction of many innovative techniques for delivering a high quality product within a short duration and expenses. This urge had driven the methodologies towards simpler and faster completion motives. Agile methodology, Pair Programming, Extreme Programming and Reusability are some of the concepts that enable today's goals. Product engineering methodology groups all these strategies and the resultant method has overcome all the drawbacks of traditional methodologies. This engineering model is purely dedicated to the development of products, differentiating it from software or process engineering concepts.

SUMMARY

In this chapter, we discussed the definition of software which is: A software is defined as a tool with designated order of instructions, performing tasks to provide desired results after obtaining the requirements of the users. Software has evolved from a single instruction provided to the machine to the present stage of decision-making software.

- The general software development phases are described as follows:
  1. Requirements Analysis Phase
  2. Designing Phase
  3. Coding and Testing Phase
  4. Implementation Phase
  5. Maintenance Phase
- General Software Characteristics:
  1. It should be complete.
  2. It should be exclusive and reliable.
  3. It should be precise.
  4. It should be efficient.
- Software Myths
  1. Software is better than implementing devices.
  2. Reusability ensures better solution.
  3. Additional features adds efficiency.
  4. More designers, more delay.
- Software engineering comprises of strict disciplines which needs to be followed to develop a programmable solution to solve the problems of the customers.
- Why Study Software Engineering?
  1. It is the basic of any software development.
  2. Software engineering understands the customer needs and develops software.
  3. It helps the developers to understand the disciplines of software life cycle.
  4. It helps to develop software in an efficient way.
  5. Software engineering teaches us the best practices of software development.
  6. Software engineering helps write software which can be integrated easily with other software.
- Generic View of Software Engineering
  1. Definition Phase
  2. Description Phase
  3. Deployment Phase
- Management of the software products depends on the following factors:
  Participants (people), Procedure and Product. Product is the outcome of the Project.
- Linear Sequential Model was the initial step of developing a software product, otherwise, known as the Life Cycle Model. Each activity is carried out in a linear order and no other order of execution is followed other than the flow mentioned.
- A layered approach ensures a much stronger product. Basic level is being ensured strongly before going to the next level.
- Prototype Model—With the given requirements, a sample or test model called the prototype is developed and displayed to the customer. There are two types of prototypes namely, evolutionary and throw away prototypes.

- The RAD model stands for Rapid Application Development Model. It is the methodology proposed for quicker design and deployment of a product.
- Framework activities are processes of basic functionalities and they are common to almost all software products. These actions can be applied to every product without any further modifications.
- Capability Maturity Model Integration is an approach for improving the process level operations. There are five levels of the model which are evolutionary.
  1. Initial
  2. Repeatable
  3. Defined
  4. Managed
  5. Optimizing
- The Waterfall Model was devised by Royce in 1970, and many organizations implemented this process model in earlier days. Incremental Model has the capability of independent and simultaneous progression. A Spiral Model encompasses the iterative steps in a spiral representation. Each circle in the model denotes a succeeding level of the previous state. In component-based models, after analysis of the requirements, instead of entering into the design phase, components or modules of existing similar products are checked for their match.
- The Fourth Generation Techniques (4GT) combines distinguished directory of software tools with assisting amenities for a software developer.
- Characteristics of good software products
  1. Completeness
  2. Consistency
  3. Durability
  4. Efficiency
  5. Security
  6. Interoperability

Discussion Points

1. Provide three examples of software projects that can follow the Waterfall Model. Give specific examples.
2. Is it possible to combine various process models? If so, provide a few examples.
3. List down the merits and demerits of Waterfall Model.
4. Is it very important to understand the customer's problem before developing a software solution? Justify.
5. Apply Spiral Model or Waterfall Model for development of a Railway (Train) Reservation System.
6. Suppose, you have to build a product to determine the inverse of 2.656885 to four decimal places. Once the product has been implemented and tested, it will be thrown away. Which life-cycle model will be used for this assignment? Give reasons for the answer.
7. Consider an automated ticket-issuing system used by the passengers while reserving seats in a government bus. Design an architecture based on the model.

EXERCISES

PART A (Objective-type Questions)

1. All of the following are components of software, except
   A. Instructions
   B. Rules
   C. Data
   D. Compact Disk
2. Which part of software packages explains about how to install (deploy) a software?
   A. Computer Programs
   B. Procedures
   C. Rules
   D. Documents
3. Which of the following is not an example of Operating System?
   A. DOS
   B. Windows
   C. Linux
   D. PowerPoint
4. Name the software comprising of programs concerned about the operations of the hardware components of a computer.
   A. System Software
   B. Application Software
   C. User Interface Software
   D. Hardware Interface Software
5. Which of the following is not part of general Software Development Phase?
   A. Requirement Analysis Phase
   B. Customer Acceptance Phase
   C. Coding and Testing Phase
   D. Implementation Phase
6. In which phase of software development customers and the business analysts interact with each other?
   A. Requirement Analysis Phase
   B. Design Phase
   C. Coding Phase
   D. Implementation Phase
7. All of the following are the types of requirements, except
   A. Functional Requirements
   B. Non-functional Requirements
   C. Interface Requirements
   D. Feasibility Requirements
8. Which of the following is not a step of Requirement Engineering phase of a project?
   A. Feasibility Study
   B. Eliciting Requirements
   C. Requirement Analysis
   D. Design
9. Which of the following phase acts as a bridge between the Requirement Analysis Phase and Coding Phase?
   A. Feasibility Study Phase
   B. Design Phase
   C. Testing Phase
   D. Eliciting Requirement Phase
10. All of the following are the types of Software Design, except
    A. Architectural Design
    B. User Interface Design
    C. Deployment Level Design
    D. Database Design
11. Implementation Phase can also be called Deployment Phase.
    A. True
    B. False
12. The software product being developed should meet all the requirements of the customer, no matter how complex the product is. This characteristic of software is referred as
    A. It should be complete.
    B. It should be reliable.
    C. It should be precise.
    D. It should be efficient.
13. Unique software delivers ensured performance to a particular problem (or) a software should concentrate on the given

problem or requirements. This characteristic of software is referred to as
A. It should be complete
B. It should be reliable
C. It should be precise
D. It should be efficient

14. Unwanted steps and operations should be eliminated and shorter operations with the right solution preferred. This characteristic of software is referred as
A. It should be complete
B. It should be reliable
C. It should be precise
D. It should be efficient

15. The software being well-organized produces an optimal result at every moment of usage. This characteristic of software is referred as
A. It should be complete
B. It should be reliable
C. It should be precise
D. It should be efficient

16. A software development process in which sequence of actions describes the order comprising the execution of activities are planned and followed is called
A. V-Model
B. Linear Sequential Model
C. Simple model
D. Design model

17. Which of the following is one of the disadvantages of Linear Sequential Model?
A. This is a very complex model.
B. This model is not understood by most software professionals.
C. This model assumes that requirements can be frozen before starting the Design Phase which is not true in most of the situations.
D. This model needs more resources than other models.

18. Which of the following is the lowest layer (categories) of the Layered Technology?
A. Quality Process
B. Methods
C. Tools
D. People

19. Which software development model is used as the most preferable model for web-based application development?
A. CAD
B. RAD
C. TAD
D. Layered Model

20. Which of the following is not one of the phases of RAD model?
A. Business modelling
B. Data modelling
C. Testing and turnover
D. Program writing

21. A model of Capability Maturity Model released in 1995 which deals with the improvement of human resources (assets) of the organization is called
A. PCMM
B. ICMM
C. CMMI
D. CMM level 5

22. Which of the following is not a product characteristic?
A. Completeness
B. Consistency
C. Profitable
D. Efficiency

23. Operations of the product should be stable and capable of handling the problems in implementation. This is referred to as
A. Completeness
B. Consistency
C. Efficiency
D. Interoperability

24. The product should not waste the resources, execution and waiting time of operations and the memory spaces allocated for the processes. This is referred as
A. Completeness
B. Consistency
C. Efficiency
D. Interoperability

25. Communication between other processes and environments should be possible to make a product universally acceptable. This is referred as
A. Completeness
B. Consistency
C. Efficiency
D. Interoperability

26. Third Level of CMMI model is known as
A. Repeatable
B. Defined
C. Managed
D. Optimizing

27. The level of CMMI in which adequate steps are taken to determine the actions to update and upgrade the processes in the product. The level defines measures for widening the functionality of every process.
A. Repeatable
B. Defined
C. Managed
D. Optimizing

28. This level of CMMI concentrates on smoothening of approaches for better, faster and risk-free execution of the processes is
A. Repeatable
B. Defined
C. Managed
D. Optimizing

29. Which software development model was devised by Royce in 1970?
A. Waterfall Model
B. Incremental Model
C. Iterative Model
D. RAD Model

30. Which of the following is one of the characteristics of software?
A. It should be exclusive and reliable.
B. It should be profitable.
C. It should have some cost.
D. It is developed by some people.

31. Which of the following is one of the disadvantages of linear sequential model?
A. This is a very complex model.
B. This model is not understood by most software professionals.
C. This model assumes that requirements can be frozen before starting the design phase which is not true in most of the situations.
D. This model needs more resources than other models.

PART B (Answer in one or two lines)

1. Define the term 'software'.
2. What are all the components of a software?
3. Give three examples of software.
4. List down the generic software development phases.
5. Define system software.
6. Define application software.
7. What are all the types of requirements?
8. Name two requirement analysis models.
9. Write notes on software maintenance.
10. Write any three characteristics of software.
11. What is software engineering?
12. Write any three reasons for studying software engineering.
13. What is a process? Write notes on it.
14. Write notes on Linear Sequential Model.
15. List down few advantages of the linear sequential model.
16. Mention the disadvantages of the linear sequential model.
17. Write notes on layered technology.
18. What are all the categories used in layered model of software engineering?
19. Write a note on prototyping model.
20. What are all the types of prototypes?
21. What is evolutionary prototype model?
22. What is throw-away prototype?
23. Write a short note on RAD model.
24. Write a short note on CMMI.
25. What are all the levels of CMMI model?
26. What is process pattern?

27. What is Waterfall Model?
28. What are the advantages of Waterfall Model?
29. What are the disadvantages of the Waterfall Model?
30. What is Incremental Model?
31. What are the advantages of Incremental Model?
32. What are all the disadvantages of Incremental Model?
33. What is Evolutionary Process Model?
34. Give some examples of the Evolutionary Process Model.
35. Write a note on the Spiral Model.
36. What is Win-Win Spiral Model?
37. Write a note on component-based development model.
38. What are the characteristics of a good software product?

2

Introduction to Software Project Management

2.1 Introduction

Project management has been practiced successfully for years (even 2000 years before) in civil engineering projects across the globe. Only in the early 1950s, which is marked as the beginning of modern project management, organizations started recognizing the importance of project management and started applying the project management concepts systematically. So project management as a separate discipline evolved and derived from the best practices of engineering and management disciplines. Henry Gantt and Henry Fayol are the pioneers in the field of project management. Henry Gantt used Gantt chart as a project management tool used for project planning and controlling. Henry Fayol introduced five management functions (initiation, planning, execution, monitoring, controlling and closing) which laid the foundation of project and program management disciplines.

Software project management became famous in the early 1990s due to the emergence of various information technology products and software to speed up business cycle and, in turn, the global economy.

Organizations aspire to not only complete projects successfully, but also execute them professionally to stay on top of competition, this objective assuming ever more significance in times of economic recession. The only way to achieve effective execution of the projects and realizing the desired outcome of a project is by performing strict project management. Even if all the technical aspects are correctly set up and the architecture of the product is robust, a project may fail because of the weak project management process. Completing the project within the triple constraint of time, cost, scope and maintaining the desired quality is the primary objective of the project management framework.

In this chapter, we will learn the definition of process, project and project management; and also discuss the advantages of project management, role of a project manager, activities covered by software project management, project management life cycle, management and the problems with software projects.

CASE STUDY

Introduction to Project Management

Pratap, Senior Vice President of ABC Company which is an IT service provider, asked the quality assurance department to arrange for an internal special PMR (Project Management Review) meeting for a project named 'GKP Insurance Automation Project'. This project is a strategic initiative at the customer's end and needs to go live exactly on the scheduled date. Each day of delay, for the project to go live, will cost around USD 20,000 losses to GKP Insurance. The product (outcome of GKP Insurance Automation Project) is targeted at end-users (sales agents) who have sales volumes of over a 1000 artefacts a year. Typical customers would be large scale, large volume and multi-geographic agents. Go-live dates of the product are being fixed during the release roadmap creation for a particular year, irrespective of estimated effort and requirement readiness for the given scope. This customer is also ready to give out few more projects, worth US$ 4 million to ABC Company, if they execute this project successfully. At present all those projects are in the pipeline. ABC company maintains a matrix structure wherein they have horizontals such as competency (technical competency units), and verticals such as business units. There were about 3000 bugs reported by the customer on one of the requirement analysis document delivered for sign-off. Customer GKP escalated this issue to the higher officials of ABC Company.

The PMR meeting was attended by all the internal stakeholders of the project of ABC Company which includes the program manager, competency leaders, project manager, on-site coordinator, and sponsor of the project, few important team members and technical leads of the project. The project manager of this project is Mahesh who is from Java Competency. He was promoted last year, because of his excellent performance in Java architecting.

Pratap asked the following questions to the stakeholders in the meeting:

1. Who is responsible for this issue among all the stakeholders?
2. Why did this issue occur?
3. Was a review planned for all the deliverables? If so, what was the outcome?
4. What is needed to be done to avoid the similar issues in the future?

At the end of the review meeting, Pratap identified that the project schedule was not updated properly, tasks were improperly tracked. For this reasons, the internal review of the deliverables did not happen. He asked the program manager to guide the project manager to overcome the situation. He also discussed about the importance of a proper plan and project schedule in the project. Pratap asked the project manager to prepare a detailed plan on how he will tackle the situation by putting down a detailed set of activities. The plan was reviewed on weekly basis by Pratap until the end of the project. Below is the email from the customer at the end of the project which shows the importance of a project manager and project planning.

> I just wanted to take some time and say THANK YOU for providing Mahesh as our Project Manager. He did an excellent job by managing the GKP Insurance Automation Project. He put a project plan in place very effectively and worked with my team to launch it. This has been a very challenging project and many changes have taken place in it. All of these changes were out of his control and we appreciate his willingness to be flexible in working with timelines and meeting our target dates on time. Even with this project not fully completed, we would not have gotten this far without his documented project work plan and his scheduling of meetings with all the teams to keep us on track for the items we could control. I would not hesitate to have him manage my projects in the future, if we ever have a need.

2.2 Definition of Process

Set of interrelated actions and activities to achieve a predefined result is called as process. Process has its own set of inputs and produces the output(s). Tools and techniques act on the process to create the desired outcome. A typical process has three components, namely, input, tools and techniques, and output. Input comprises of the things that are necessary to run the process. Input is transformed to output in a process by using the specified tools and techniques.

Example 1

Let us take an example of making *Dosa* (an Indian dish). Making Indian *Dosa* can be considered as a process.

Inputs:	batter (soaked rice and *dal*), oil
Tools and Techniques:	gas stove, a *tawa*, a spatula
Output:	*dosa*

Let us look into the activities involved in making *dosa*.

1. Heat a tawa and grease it with little bit of oil.
2. Pour about 3/4 cup batter (soaked rice and *dal*) at the centre of the *tawa.*
3. Gently spread the batter to make a circular shape.
4. Drizzl 1 tsp of oil around the edges of the *dosa.*
5. Using a spatula/spoon to gently lift the *dosa* and flipping it over after 30 seconds.
6. Cook the other side also for another 40 seconds.
7. Remove from the *tawa*.
8. Get the *dosa* served.

These activities constitute a process—a set of interrelated activities performed to achieve a prespecified service, that is, making a *dosa*. If we call five different people (chefs), give them the same ingredients and tools required to make *dosa*, and also the process that we have defined above, printed in a sheet of paper, will the output be the exactly same? The size and taste of the *dosa* made by different chefs is bound to vary. Why is it so? This is not only because of the difference in skills possessed by the chefs, but also due to the techniques they have learnt over a period of time. Thus, we need to understand and learn the techniques of a process in order to produce a better output.

Example 2

Browsing (i.e., surfing the Internet) can be considered as a process.

Inputs:	URL address
Tools and Techniques:	Computer, browser
Output:	Web page display

Let us look at the activities involved in browsing:

1. Switch on the system.
2. Enter the specified password for the system.
3. Click on the browser.
4. Type the address in the URL space.
5. Get the specified webpage.

Every process has its own strength, weakness and associated risks. These factors have to be discovered to determine the level of applicability. Evaluation of the strengths, weaknesses and risks of every process against a process model is called 'process assessment'.

Process assessment describes the results of evaluation. Following are the possible results of process evaluation.

- **Incomplete:** Still needs revision and modifications.
- **Performed:** Complete definition and satisfies the customer.
- **Managed:** Controlled and maintained.
- **Established:** Standard procedure applied.
- **Predictable:** Defined with limits of execution.
- **Optimizing:** Slight alterations required.

2.2.1 Methods Versus Methodology

Methods can be defined as an ordered sequence of actions. Methodology is the study of scientific methods. It can also be defined as a set of methods chosen for achieving a purpose or set of purpose. For example, strategies for gathering project requirements is called 'requirement collection method'.

2.3 People, Process and Product

Management of software products depends on the following factors (Figure 2.1).

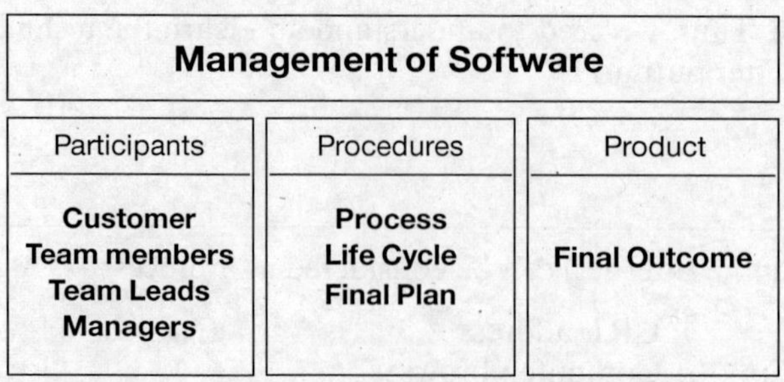

Figure 2.1 Participants, Procedures and Product

2.3.1 Participants/People

Members of various skill sets, from the team member to the team leader and manager, are responsible for acting on every process of software development. The customers are the initial and important participants of a product. They put forward their problem and request a solution which, in turn, acts as requirements of a project. A team of skilled personnel will discuss the different possible solutions obeying the technical and administrative constraints in order to fulfil the customers requirements. This participating team of developers are assigned by the top-level management based on the acquired and proficiency level of each member. Staffing requires the analysis of how proficient a member is in a particular field. Managers play a crucial role in the development of software. He is not only responsible for the final outcome of a project, but also responsible for the execution of the project from the beginning to the end. A manager prepares a plan and tries to execute the project as per the plan in order to create the deliverables. The manger is also responsible for managing time, cost, scope and quality of the overall product outcome.

2.3.2 Procedure/Process

Procedure describes the way in which a product is developed. The order and types of procedures are devised by the team members. The final plan to be implemented is approved by the team manager. Managers also determine the life cycle which has to be followed among the various models. The best option would help to conserve the resources and money invested by the management. A slight deviation from the proposed procedure would affect the efficiency of the entire process.

2.3.3 Product

Selection of the best plans and procedures, assigning the right and efficient staff to the project, ensures the success of the project, thereby, ensuring the final outcome of a project is called 'the product'. Product is the outcome of a project. There are many models of developing a product, evolved from the very early era of software development. Different models proposed, increased the efficiency of team of developers by altering and speeding up the actions of normal methods.

Following are the special characteristics of a software product.

Invisibility: It is very difficult to represent software using the existing geometric models. When bridge is being unstructed, it is easily seen that the progress of the project is visible, but the same is not possible with a software product. Software project management helps overcome this situation through various measurement techniques of software.

Complexity: Complexity is always associated with any software. In fact, the complexity associated with a software product is more than any other visible products. This may be due to unknown factors associated with the complexity. Since there is no visibility of the internal parts of a software product, the complexity increases further.

Conformity: Software project conforms to the requirements specification document and checking the conformity is highly difficult as interpretation of the requirements may vary from one person to another. Conformity can be checked at every step in a physical product construction, but doing the same is difficult with a software product.

Flexibility: Software products are always built with flexibility to enhance it at a later point of time which is very rare in physical products. This flexibility aspect also increases the complexity of the software product.

2.4 Definition of Project

Project Management Institute (PMI) defines a project as a temporary endeavour undertaken to create a unique product, service or result. Project is also progressively elaborated. Outcome of a project is product or service or defined result.

All of us have been involved in various projects in our personal life, business and industry. Following are the examples of projects:

Personal Life Projects

- Obtaining an MCA/MBA degree
- Getting married

Business-related Projects

- Finding suitable business
- Finding ROI of a business
- Forming a business

Industry-related Projects

- Construction of a building
- Laying a road
- Designing and launching a space rocket
- Constructing a bridge
- Election campaigning

Projects may vary depending on its size (say number of people, number of lines of code, number of screens, etc.) and duration (say number of total project days or timeline). Project may also vary in complexity (simple, medium, and complex projects).

Here are some examples of Information Technology-based projects.

- Creating a website that support administration of talent resources inside a company (workforce management software).
- Creating a system to track all financial activities within a company (finance management software).
- Creating a time management system (timesheet management system).
- Creating a billing management system for a company (billing management system).
- Developing a cloud-based business intelligence solutions for the insurance industry (insurance management system).
- Automating loan process in a bank using java technology (loan management system).

Gartner Top 10 Technology Trends for 2014

Gartner Symposium/ITxpo is the world's most important gathering of high level CIOs of bigger organizations. This event delivers independent and objective contents with the authority of the world's leading IT research and advisory organization, and provides access to the latest solutions from key technology providers. IT executives rely on Gartner Symposium/ITxpo to gain insight into how their organizations can use IT to address business challenges and improve operational efficiency. (*Source:* www.gartner.com/newsroom/id/2603623)

The top ten strategic technology trends for 2014 include:

1. **Mobile Device Diversity and Management:** The unexpected consequence of 'bring your own device' (BYOD) programs is a doubling or even tripling of the size of the mobile workforce. Enterprise policies on employee-owned hardware usage need to be thoroughly reviewed and, where necessary, updated and extended. Gartner's advice is to 'balance flexibility with confidentiality and privacy requirements'.
2. **Mobile Apps and Applications:** Gartner predicts that through 2014, improved JavaScript performance will begin to push HTML5 and the browser as a mainstream enterprise application development environment. Gartner recommends that developers focus on creating expanded user interface models including richer voice and video that can connect people in new and different ways. Apps will continue to grow while applications will begin to shrink.
3. **The Internet of Everything:** The Internet is expanding beyond PCs and mobile devices into enterprise assets such as field equipment, and consumer items such as cars and televisions. The combination of data streams and services created by digitizing everything creates four basic usage models: Manage, Monetize, Operate and Extend.
4. **Hybrid Cloud and IT as Service Broker:** Bringing together personal clouds and external private cloud services is an imperative. Enterprises should design private cloud services with a hybrid future in mind and make sure future integration/interoperability is possible.
5. **Cloud/Client Architecture:** Cloud/client computing models are shifting. In the cloud/client architecture, the client is a rich application running on an Internet-connected device, and the server is a set of application services hosted in an increasingly elastically scalable cloud computing platform. The cloud is the control point and system or record and applications can span multiple client devices. The increasingly complex demands of mobile users will drive apps to demand increasing amounts of server-side computing and storage capacity.
6. **The Era of Personal Cloud:** The personal cloud era will mark a power shift, away from devices and toward services. In this new world, the specifics of devices will become less important for the organization to worry about, although the devices will still be necessary. Access to the cloud and the content stored or shared from the cloud will be managed and secured, rather than solely focusing on the device itself.
7. **Software Defined Anything:** Software-defined anything (SDx) is a collective term that encapsulates the growing market momentum for improved standards for infrastructure programmability and data centre interoperability; driven by automation inherent to cloud computing, DevOps, and fast infrastructure provisioning.
8. **Web-scale IT:** Web-scale IT is a pattern of global-class computing that delivers the capabilities of large cloud service providers within an enterprise IT setting by rethinking positions across several dimensions. This goes beyond re-designing facilities to be more energy efficient to also include in-house design of key hardware

components such as servers, storage and networks. Web-oriented architectures allow developers to build very flexible and resilient systems that recover from failure more quickly.

9. **Smart Machines:** Through 2020, the smart machine era will blossom with a proliferation of contextually aware, intelligent personal assistants, smart advisors (such as IBM Watson), advanced global industrial systems and public availability of early examples of autonomous vehicles. The smart machine era will be the most disruptive in the history of IT.
10. **3-D Printing:** Worldwide shipments of 3-D printers are expected to grow 75 percent in 2014 followed by a near doubling of unit shipments in 2015. The consumer market hype has made organizations aware of the fact that 3-D printing is a real, viable and cost-effective means to reduce costs through improved designs, streamlined prototyping and short-run manufacturing.

Attributes of a Project: Three keywords defining the term 'project' are Temporary, Unique and Progressive Elaboration. They are called 'the attributes of a project'.

The Temporary Nature of a Project: Temporary does not imply short in duration or use-and-throw. A project can run for 1 day or 1 year or 100 years. But temporary does mean that a project should have a definite planned start date and definite planned end date.

The Unique Nature of a Project: A project involves set of work that has not been attempted before and creating an outcome that has not been created before and is, therefore, unique. However, unique does not mean that a project is completely made up of unique work creating unique components. We may use reusable components of past projects or existing systems to simplify our efforts.

Progressive elaboration: Progressive elaboration indicates developing software or documents in steps with continuous improvements. Goals and objectives that are set in the beginning are slowly elaborated and made clearer, and more detailed as the project progresses.

- Sometimes, product characteristics are progressively elaborated. Progressive elaboration is the characteristic of a project that integrates the concepts of the unique and the temporary attributes.
- Start with nothing and slowly move forward to create valuable results.
- Progressive elaboration allows a project management team to manage at a greater level of detail as the project moves along. Basically, it is the process of identifying the characteristics of a project.

A project requires various types of resources which include people, software, hardware, tools or other assets. People with different knowledge, skill set and experience are also required in order to execute projects.

A project usually has a customer and sponsor. A customer helps to execute a project successfully and acts as single point of contact as per the contract. A sponsor funds the project without which we cannot start a project.

A project always involves uncertainties. Project risk is an uncertain factor.

2.4.1 Project Constraints

Constraints are the factors which limits the options of a project and, in turn, forces the project manager to act within the constraints. Constraints in a project are mostly related to cost, time, scope and quality added as a fourth constraint at later point of time. They are called 'triple constraints of a project'. Triple constraints can be drawn in the form of a triangle where each side represents one of the three constraints. This is also called 'the project triangle'.

Scope constraint represent the constraints (limited options) related to work of the project, what must be done to create the product. Customer wanting the executing organization to do unit testing, system testing, performance testing—are examples of scope (work)-related constraints. Time constraints are related to the amount of time available to finish a project. Customer wanting to finish a project before 31st of December 2014, is a time constraint. Cost constraint represents the constraints related to the available budget of a project. Sponsor wanting a project to be executed within a specified budget, is a cost constraint.

Time: Time required to execute a project is calculated by summing up all the individual efforts required to do the tasks within the project. Tasks are prioritized along with various dependencies in a project schedule. Dependencies also affect the overall schedule of the project and so task dependencies are considered as constraints. Number of resources available to do a task is also a constraint which affects the overall schedule of the project.

Cost: Cost of a project depends on number of resources used in the project, experience level of the resources used in the project, salary level of the resources deployed into the project, various equipment types used to do the work, etc.

Scope: Scope is the work to be done to create the product and is related to what the project is supposed to accomplish, and the accomplishment happens by executing various related works. Scope of a project is directly related to the number of functionalities to be included in the system and the complexity of those functionalities. If the number of functionalities in a system increases, obviously the work (scope) to finish the project also increases. If the complexity of the functionality increases, then the work (scope) to accomplish that functionality also increases. Scope of a project depends on the requirements of the project.

These three constraints usually competes with each other. If the customer increases the scope (work) of the project, then it impacts the timeline of the project and also increases the cost of the project. If the customer wants the project to be completed early, it will lead to decreased scope and increased cost. Changing the cost constraints will also affect the scope and timeline. A project manager needs to keep a close eye on all the three parameters together.

Discussion Points

1. Discuss, how 'obtaining an MCA or MBA degree' can be considered as a project.
2. Discuss, how 'election campaigning' can be considered as a project.

2.4.2 Environmental Factors That Mandate Projects in Organizations

A project is being executed in an organization due to market demand, business needs, customer requests, technological advances and legal requirements. The following table describes the reasons that mandate projects in an organization along with examples.

Environmental Factors That Mandate Projects

Market demand	A bank initiates a project to offer customers an option to transfer money to other accounts over the Internet, following an increase in intrabank and interbank transactions and also increased usage of the Internet.
Business needs	A company initiates a new project to design a portal for business-to-business transactions as the current manual process of transaction takes lot of time and the cost involved is high, lot of errors in the manual transactions.
Customer requests	A bank initiates a project to develop a loan automation system to automate verification and sanction, as the existing manual system generated customer dissatisfaction. Customer feedback required a new system to reduce processing time and errors.
Technological advances	Whenever a new technology comes to market, every company manufactures a proof of concept (POC) product in the new technology to showcase its ability in the new technology. For example, when Java was introduced in late 1990s, many companies initiated POC projects in Java technology to showcase their ability in the new technology and generate new business.
Legal requirements	New health care laws might require modifications or new programming in the existing health care system.

2.4.3 Stakeholders

Stakeholders, as we know, are those members or entities who are actively involved in project execution or whose interests may be positively or negatively affected by project outcomes.

Examples of stakeholders: Customer, project manager, team members, executing organization, sponsor of the project and end users.

Customer: Organizations/individuals purchasing the project. Customer is one who signs the contract with the vendor (executing organization). Project Manager is responsible for all the project deliverables. He is responsible for managing an entire project. A project manager need not be a technical expert. Team members are the set of people who are working at the ground level to complete the project successfully.

The executing organization is, otherwise, called vendor. It employs its resources to accomplish the project. Vendors sign the contract with the customer and take ownership for executing the project. Sponsor provides financial assistance for the project. (*Note:* Customer need not give the money at the beginning of the project, but we need money to start the project and this is provided by the sponsor). Most of the projects fail, because we do not consider the end users as project stakeholders. End users are those who actually uses the product once it is implemented. We need to identify end users at the appropriate time and involve them in the project to make it successful.

The general characteristics of stakeholders are as follows.

- Stakeholders are affected by the project.
- Project is affected by the stakeholders.
- Stakeholder expectations is 'untold' in most of the time.

- Stakeholders often have conflicting objectives.
- Differences among stakeholders are resolved in favour of the customer.

Types of Stakeholders

Internal to the project team: These stakeholders will be under the direct managerial control of the project manager. Team members are the best example of this type of stakeholders.

External to the project team, but within the same organization: These stakeholders will not be under the direct managerial control of the project manager, but they belong to the same organization as the project manager. Project Management Office (PMO) is the best example of this type of stakeholders. Project manager might need the assistance of the PMO to choose the correct template for project reporting.

External to both the project team and the organization: These stakeholders will not be under the direct managerial control of the project manager and also not belong to the same organization as the project manager. Customer(s) and end user(s) are the best examples of this type of stakeholders. This relationship is usually based on a legally binding contract.

Identification of stakeholders: It is a process of identifying the people, groups, entities or organizations that could impact or be impacted by the decisions taken in the project, activities executed in the project, or outcome of the project as a whole. It is important to analyse and document relevant information regarding stakeholders' interests, involvement, interdependencies, influence, and their potential impact on project success. Identification of stakeholders is critical for project success. The key benefit of the process of identifying stakeholders is, it allows the project manager to identify the appropriate stack of work for each stakeholder or group of stakeholders. After identifying the stakeholders, the project manager can involve them into the project at appropriate time. Project manager needs to analyse stakeholders' level of interest, their individual expectations, as well as their importance and influence over the project. This initial assessment of interest, influence and impact should be reviewed and updated regularly as it will change over a period of time. This also enables the project manager to focus on the relationships with stakeholders which is necessary to ensure the success of the project.

Discussion Point

Discuss why stakeholders often have conflicting objectives?

Note: Customers always want experienced resources to be deployed in their projects. Sponsors does not allow this as it affects the cost of the project.

2.4.4 Project Management

Although many may believe project management to be just little more than paperwork, it is in reality, a complex activity—both an art and a science. Project management is the application of knowledge, skills, tools and techniques to the project activities to meet the project requirements. Project management, thus converts the abstract into the concrete, or an organization's vision to reality. While defining project management, the following three keywords are important.

1. Knowledge
2. Skills
3. Tools and Techniques

One may gain knowledge by going through books, browsing the Internet, reading magazines, and hearing from others, etc. We need to continuously apply knowledge in order to develop our skills. Similarly, the project manager should know the tools and techniques in order to function in a project management environment.

Skills Required for Project Managers

Driving projects successfully from from the beginning to the closure is the ultimate responsibility of a project manager. He needs to ensure that all the objectives of the project are met. It is also the responsibility of the project manager to lead the team, motivating them to execute the project work successfully. To handle a project successfully, a project manager is required to equipped with the following skills.

1. **Clear Communication:** Communication is the important skills of a project manager. One of PMI's (Project Management Institute) survey states that more than 90% of project managers' time goes doing communication. A project manager needs to communicate in all directions with the stakeholders of the project.
2. **Forecasting Skill:** Being the manager of the project, he needs not only to track and report the project status, but also forecast the project successfully. Spotting problems/risks proactively and reducing the impact of those problems helps accurately forecasting the project.

Analytical Thinking: This helps in forecasting projects. A project manager, apart from collecting data, also analyses those to take appropriate actions. Nowadays, a number of handy project management tools are available for data and information analysis. One such tool is Earned Value Technique.

Team Management Skill: Project management itself is a team effort. Robust planning is possible only with the help of the team. Team management skills include motivation skills, negotiation skills, problem-solving skills and coaching skills.

Interpersonal Skills: The following interpersonal skills are very important for a project manager.

- Leadership
- Team Building
- Conflict Management
- Communication
- Motivation
- Influencing
- Decision Making
- Negotiations
- Political and Cultural Awareness

A project manager not only applies his own knowledge, skills, tools and techniques to the project, he also needs to utilize the team members' knowledge, skills and techniques into the project. In order to do this, a project manager needs to have the required soft skills to manage a project. Project management involves controlling scopes, time, costs, risks, and quality throughout the life cycle of a project. It is useful to organizations that attempt to build unique product/service/results. Project management helps in delivering on-time, on-budget of product/service/results as per the agreed specification.

High-level Project Management Activities (Project Management Responsibilities)

1. Feasibility study of the project
2. Initiating the project
    - Setting expectations with all stakeholders
3. Planning the project
    - Plan the work of the project
    - Plan the schedule, cost, quality, communication of the project
    - Plan the human resources of the project
    - Plan the risk management aspects of the project
    - Plan the stakeholder management of the project
4. Execution of the project
    - Execute the integrated plan
    - Acquire human resources
    - Develop human resources
    - Perform quality assurance
    - Manage communication
5. Control of the project
    - Control the work of the project
    - Control the schedule, cost, quality, communication the project
    - Control the human resources of the project
    - Control the risks of the project
    - Control the stakeholder management of the project
6. Prepare project reports
7. Archive the entire project documents
8. Close the project

Feasibility Study of the Project

The worthiness of a proposed software system should be determined before putting efforts on building the system.

Feasibility study itself can be considered as a sub-project of a longer project. It helps in deciding whether the proposed system is worthwhile. It has the following characteristics:

- Whether the system contributes to organizational objectives.
- Whether the system can be developed using the currently available technology and within specified time and budget.
- Whether the system can easily be integrated with other surrounding systems as required by the overall architecture.

Project Initiation

If feasibility study indicates that a project is viable, then the project initiation and planning takes place.

- Initiation phase helps to set the expectations among all stakeholders.
- It ensures proper infrastructure to start the project.

- It is called 'concept phase'
- Will initiate if it is a new project
- Authorized to continue an existing project
- Determine the project objectives
- Assign a project manager
- Identify the stakeholders

Setting expectations among stakeholders of the project is the element critical to project success and this ensures to get the buy-in from all stakeholders and also helps to get their view and hurdles if any to execute the respective work. Initiation phase is also an opportunity for the stakeholders to connect and know each other.

Identifying Project Infrastructure

Identifying project infrastructure is critical for project planning and, in turn, to project's success. The following steps are useful in identifying ideal infrastructure for a project.

1. Going through the requirement documents of the project for infrastructure requirements.
2. Identifying the current project needs and future strategic planning (extension).
3. Identifying and referring infrastructure standards and guidelines.
4. Going through the project organization structure which will guide the software and infrastructure requirements of the project.

Project Planning

If a feasibility study indicates that the project is viable, then the project initiation and planning takes place. For a bigger project, the planning happens in steps as more information about the project is known with the progress of time. A high-level plan is drawn at the beginning. It will be elaborated to a detailed plan in steps. This is called 'progressive elaboration'.

Planning process are the process for formulating and revising the project goals and objectives. It helps in detailed understanding of the overall project. Most of the project's time is spent over the planning processes. A project manager, with the help of project team, develops the project management plan. Planning helps to cross-check customer's understanding, and also helps to execute the project in order, and helps in identifying and organize the tasks properly. Without planning, it is very difficult to measure the deviation and it becomes highly difficult to finish the project on-time.

A project planning process needs to cover all the knowledge areas of the project in detail, like:

- Plan the work of the project
- Plan the schedule the project
- Plan the cost of the project
- Plan the human resources of the project
- Plan the quality of the project
- Plan the communications of the project
- Plan the risks of the project
- Plan the stakeholder management of the project

Project Execution

A project plan identifies the activities to be carried out in order to create a product. Execution of a project plan is called 'project execution'.

- Most of the project's cost would be spent on this process.
- All the work packages/plans that were designed and developed during planning will be executed.
- Implement approved 'change requests' and team building.

The following activities are performed during the execution phase of a project:

- Executing the integrated plan
- Acquiring human resources
- Developing human resources
- Performing quality assurance
- Managing communication

Controlling and Project Monitoring

Controlling ensures the actual project execution happens as per the plan.

Monitoring and controlling phases of a project regularly monitor project performance against performance measurement baseline. It also recommends 'change requests' as part of contolling. It also verifies the scope of the project against set of requirements. It helps monitoring and controlling entire project work.

First, we need to monitor and observe the deviation. If there is any deviation between project execution and plan, a change is proposed. Change leads to either change in plan or change in the execution or change in both the aspects of a project.

For executing a project, the time, resource and the cost needs to be estimated and budgeted first. Once a project starts, the actual time, resource and cost estimates closely monitored against the plan and necessary corrective actions would be initiated in case of any deviation. This is the main principle of project planning and monitoring.

Closing:

- Main goal is formally and orderly end the project activities
- Involves contract closure as well as archiving any project records, documents, etc.
- Procurement audits and payments are made.

We need to organize the tasks due to the following reasons:

- Proper organization helps us understand the pitfalls/gaps in the overall tasks.
- Proper organization of tasks helps us do better monitoring and controlling of the task.
- Proper organization of tasks helps to report the correct status to the management.
- Proper organization of tasks increases the customer confidence level.

Controlling of projects happens at all the knowledge areas of the project, namely:

- Control the work of the project
- Control the schedule the project
- Control the Cost of the project
- Control the Human Resources of the project
- Control the Quality of the project
- Control the communications of the project
- Control the Risks of the project
- Control the stakeholder management of the project

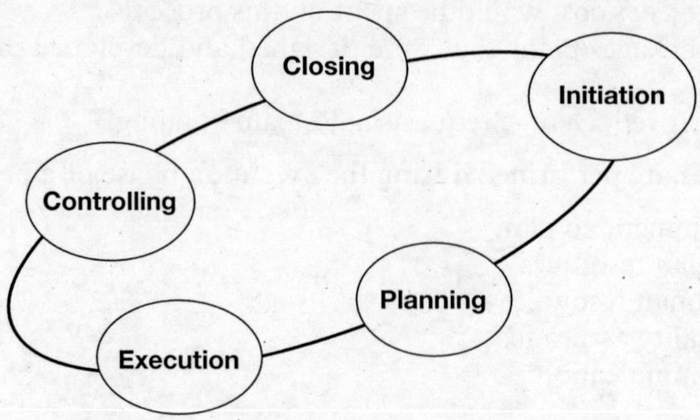

Figure 2.2 Project Management Life Cycle

Project Management Life Cycle

The following five project management functions creates a project management life cycle.

1. Initiation
2. Planning
3. Execution
4. Monitoring and control
5. Closure

Note: Feasibility study happens well before a project is initiated. It is not part of the project management life cycle, but usually happens before a project starts.

2.4.5 Knowledge Areas of Project Management

As we know that the spectrum of project management is very wide and it can be divided into the following 10 groups called 'knowledge areas'.

1. Project scope management
2. Project time management
3. Project quality management
4. Project communication management
5. Project risk management
6. Project cost management
7. Project human resource management
8. Project integration management
9. Project procurement management
10. Project stakeholder management

2.4.6 Project Organization Structure

Organization structure is the hierarchical relationships of various entities within an organization that collaborate with each other for project execution purpose. Different organizations, by virtue of their objectives and core philosophies, carry different organizational structures.

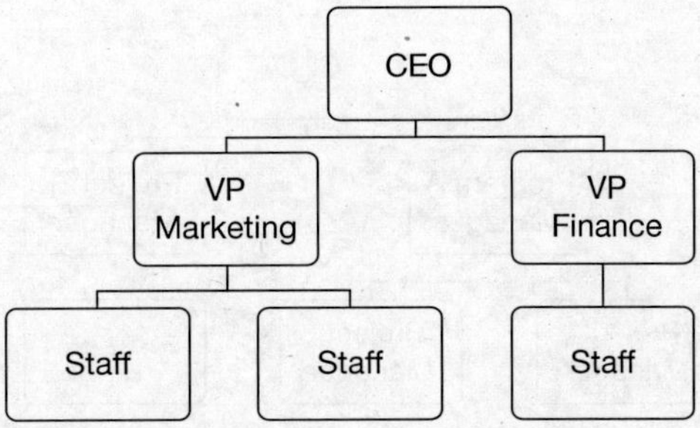

Figure 2.3 Example of a Functional Structure

The structure of an organization determines the operational model used in the organization. Organizational structure determines the responsibilities for different functions and entities.

There are different organizational structures depending on their objectives and ambience. The structure of an organization determines the operation models of the organization. Organizational structure determines the responsibilities for different functions and entities.

The organizational structure sets the level of authority, roles and responsibilities, and the reporting structure within a project.

2.4.7 Functional Structures

Figure 2.3 represents a functional structure of an organization. Here, the entire structure of the organization is based on the function each part executes, such as production department, marketing department, HR department, finance department, at the higher level. Functional department executes its own project work for its department.

The project manager has the least power and all management activities are done by functional managers, like finance manager, marketing manager, etc.

Key characteristics:

- Clear reporting hierarchy and communication channels.
- Skills are specific to the staff in a department.
- Projects/project team are specific to the department.
- Communication between departments flows through functional managers down to the project team.
- Project manager may be known as a project coordinator or team leader.

Advantages	**Disadvantages**
1. Easy management of functional specialists. 2. Cleary defined career path for employees. 3. Team members reports to only a single reporting manager. 4. Grouping of associates based on skill sets.	1. No career path in the project management. 2. Project Manager has little or no authority.

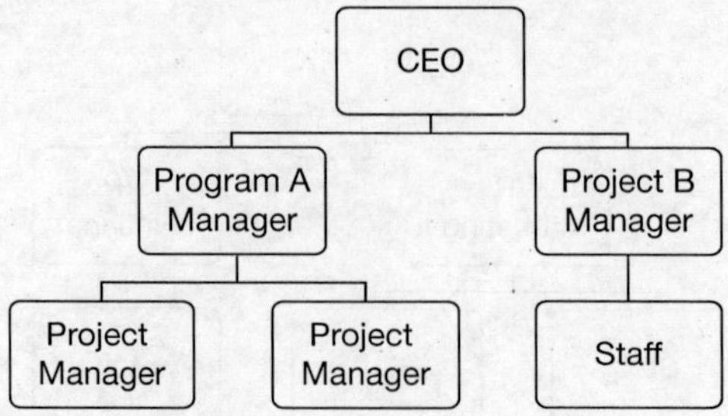

Figure 2.4 Example of a Projectized Structure

2.4.8 Projectized Structure

Figure 2.4 represents a Projectized Organization Chart of an organization. Entire structure of the organization is based on the projects it does. The project manager has total control over all projects. Project manager has full authority to assign priorities, apply resources, and direct the work of persons assigned to the project.

In the projectized structure, team members are often co-located (working in the same area). Most of the organization's resources are involved in the project work, meaning, whatever the work they do is for the projects. They have organizational units called 'departments' and they report directly to the project manager.

Key characteristics:

- The PM has complete or close to complete power over the project team.
- PM works full time on the project with his team.
- Has full time administrative staff to help expedite the project
- Loyalties are formed towards the project, and not to the functional manager.

Advantages	**Disadvantages**
1. More effective communication. 2. Loyalty to the project. 3. More control over the project.	1. No home when the project is completed. 2. Resources may not be utilized properly. 3. Resources may not get a chance to groom in a single business area (functional).

2.4.9 Matrix Structure

Figure 2.5 represents a matrix organization structure. A matrix structure is the combination of both function and project-based structure. Actually, this structure combines the best of both the structures. A complex project mostly fits into matrix type of organization structure. In a matrix organization, personnel performance measurements is not a responsibility of the project manager and it is the responsibility of the functional manger. The role of a project manager is more that of a coordinator or expediter than that of a true project manager.

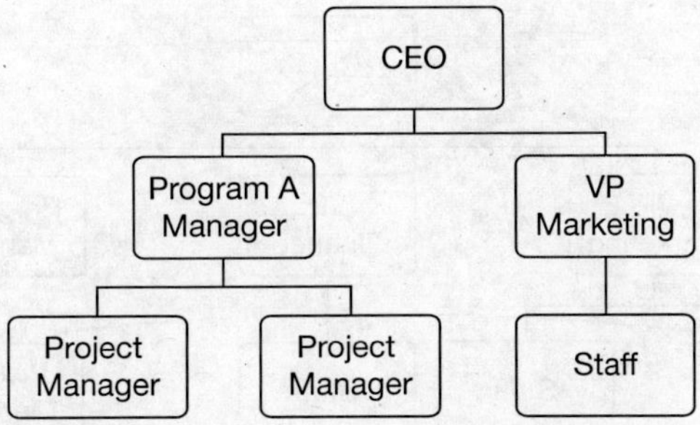

Figure 2.5 Example of a Matrix Structure

Project expeditor basically acts as a staff assistant to an executive who is ultimately responsible for the project.

In a matrix organization, the team members reports to and remain responsible to both the functional manager and project manager. Effective management of this dual relationship is definitely a challenge and should be the responsibility of the project manager. Team building is most difficult in matrix type of structure due to dual reporting structure.

- A project team is formed by taking staffs from the functional organization.
- Some of the staffs report to both project manager and functional manager.
- The functional manager is responsible for administrative portion of duties and the assignment of his staff to specific project.
- Project manager is responsible for executing projects.

Advantages	**Disadvantages**
1. Highly visible project objectives 2. Improved project manager control over resources 3. Better coordination	1. More than one boss 2. Need extensive policies and procedures 3. Higher potential for conflict

2.4.10 Strong Matrix

Figure 2.6 represents a strong matrix structure of an organization. In a strong matrix organization, the project manager has greater authority or power than the functional manager. They have most of the characteristics of the projectized structure. They have full-time project managers and full-time administrative staff for the project.

2.4.11 Weak Matrix

Figure 2.7 represents a weak matrix structure of an organization. In a weak matrix organization, a project manager does not have as much power as the functional manager. In a weak matrix, the project manager's role might be more of a project expediter or project

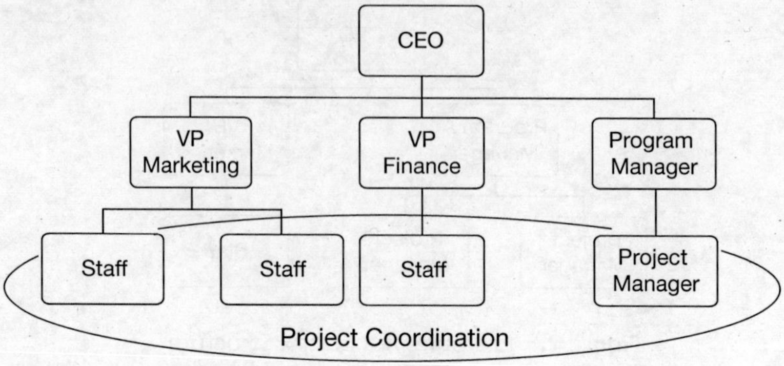

Figure 2.6 Example of a Strong Matrix Structure

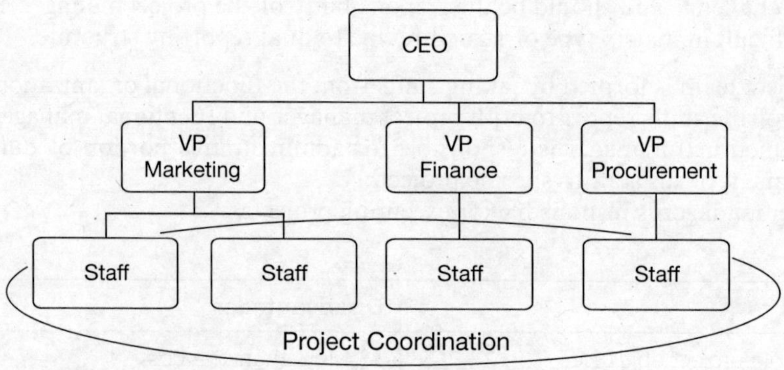

Figure 2.7 Example of a Weak Matrix Structure

coordinator. There is no official designation or role as project manager in this type of structure. The project expediter acts primarily as a staff assistant and communications coordinator. The expediter cannot personally make or enforce decisions. The project coordinator has some power to make decisions, some authority, and reports to a higher-level manager.

2.4.12 Balanced Matrix

Figure 2.8 represents a balanced matrix structure. It recognizes the need of the project manager, but does not provide him full authority over the project and project funding.

In a balanced-matrix organization, the power of the functional manager and the project manager are almost same and in balance.

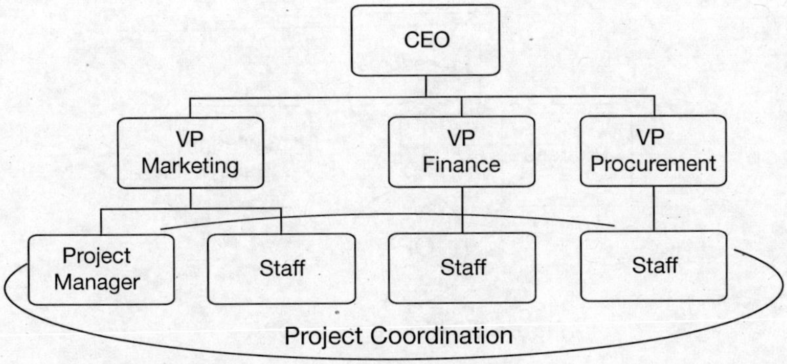

Figure 2.8 Example of a Balanced Matrix Structure

Comparison of Matrix Structures					
PM's / Type of Matrix	Title	Focus	Authority	Time	Reports into
Weak Matrix	Project Coordinator/ Project Leader	Split between project and functional	Minimal	Part time on project	Functional Manager
Balanced Matrix	Project Manager	Project work	Balanced	Full time on project	Functional Manager, but shares power for project.
Strong Matrix	Project Manager	Project work	Complete	Full time on project	Manager of projects

A tight matrix is a concept where all team members involved are brought together in one location to solve a particular problem. It is not related to organizational structure.

Exercise 2.1: Select the structure based on the characteristics		
Project manager is having high authority	Projectized	Functional
No home for team members	Projectized	Functional
Project manager as project co-ordinator	Weak matrix	Strong matrix
Mostly like functional organization	Weak matrix	Strong matrix

2.4.13 Organization Process Assets

Organization process includes process related to assets from the organizations involved in the project that can be used to influence the project success (Figure 2.9). Updating OPA is generally, the responsibility of the project team members.

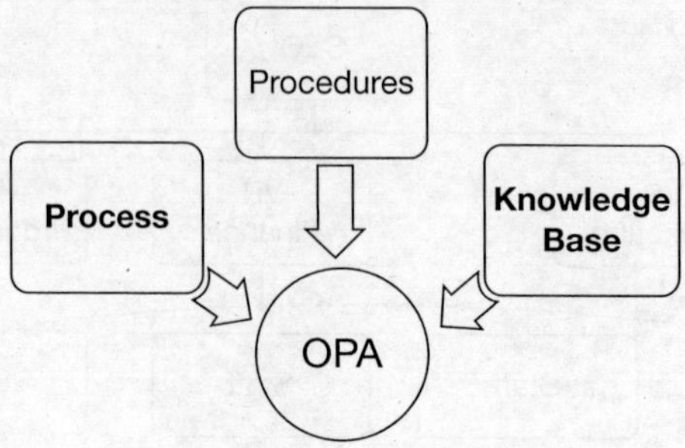

Figure 2.9 Contents of OPA

OPA is grouped into two categories, namely:

1. Processes and procedures
2. Corporate knowledge base

Example of process assets include formal and informal plans, procedures, process, guidelines, lessons learnt and historical information.

Usually, OPA will be in the form of an Intranet site, so that people can refer the procedure or process quickly. This Intranet will also have the filled in templates and documents from other projects for reference. Most of the organization calls this 'QMS Site' (Quality Management System).

Does your organization have a QMS site? What are all the contents of it?

Discussion Points

1. In which organization structure, you, as a project manager, would want to work and why?
2. Did you work in different types of structures like this before? If so, what are all the difficulties you faced?
3. If you are a functional manager, how will you give comfort level to a project manager?

2.4.14 Pitfalls of Project Management

1. Project and project management are designed to solve problem(s). If we are not able to understand the problem, the project will fail.
2. Project and project management are designed to solve problem(s). If we choose a wrong problem, then the project will fail.
3. Project management fully depends on planning. 100% correct planning is possible only at the end of a project.
4. Customers are changing their requirements frequently. That is always a problem for the project manager.
5. Tracking projects become difficult when the number of resources exceed the manageable level.
6. Project visibility is usually unclear at the beginning of a project when we tend to freeze the plan.

7. All the data are not provided by the customer to the project manager.
8. Customer wants everything in the system (greed), not restricting the functionalities, which may lead to project failures.
9. Project executing organization does not have proper mix of resources which may lead to project failure.
10. Human resources continuously getting changed in the project is a problem for the project manager.
11. Not performing right kind of estimation (cost, schedule, etc.) is a problem.
12. Identifying and managing all the risks in the project is difficult in nature.
13. Technology change is always a problem for the project manager.
14. Lack of quality standards and measures.
15. Poor definition of roles and responsibilities in the project.

Program: It is a group of projects managed in a coordinated way to obtain benefits and control that would not have been obtained had the projects been managed separately.

- According to the PMBOK®, *a program is a group of projects managed in a coordinated way to obtain* benefits *and control that would not have been obtained had the projects been managed separately.*
- Program management focuses on project interdependencies and helps determining the optimal approach for effectively managing them.
- An example of a program would be a new communications satellite system program comprising projects for designing the satellite, constructing and integrating the individual systems, and launching the satellite.

Portfolio: By portfolio, we refer to a collection of projects or programs that have been grouped together to facilitate effective management to meet strategic business objectives.

Portfolio management refers to the selection process based on the needs, profitability and affordability of the proposed projects.

The projects or programs that belong to a portfolio may not necessarily be interdependent or directly related.

Portfolio management also refers to the centralized management of one or more portfolios.

Project Management Office (PMO)

- The primary function of a Project Management Office (PMO) is to support project managers in a variety of ways.
- The PMO manages methodologies, standards, overall risks/opportunities, and interdependencies among projects at the enterprise level.
- The PMO also manages the project team and organizes the common services of projects.
- The Project Management Office (PMO) is the department or group that defines and maintains the standards of process, generally related to project management, within the organization.
- PMO reports to CEO/CIO/COO/VP-Projects.
- PMO is responsible for periodic review, providing assistance to the PM and resolving issues.
- Project Manager directly reports to the PMO, if that exists.
- PMO delegates authority to individual PMs if it has a formal grant of authority from the Executive Management.

Discussion Points

1. What are all the quality characteristics that you will look into while buying a kilogram of bread from the market?
2. If there is a trade-off between quality and grade, how would you convince a customer? (Customers usually demand higher quality and higher grade at the same time.)

SUMMARY

- **Process:** Set of inter-related activities performed to create pre-specified products, services, or results.
- **Project:** The PMI defines a project as a temporary endeavor undertaken to create a unique product, service, or result.
- **Progressive elaboration:** It is the characteristic of a project that integrates the concepts of the unique and the temporary: Start with nothing and slowly move forward to create valuable results.
- **Program:** It is a group of projects managed in a coordinated way to obtain benefits and control that would not have been obtained if the projects were managed separately.
- **Portfolio:** By portfolio, we refer to a collection of projects or programs that have been grouped together to facilitate effective management to meet strategic business objectives.

3

Information Technology: The Context of Software Project Management

3.1 Introduction

Projects labelled as Information Technology (IT) Projects are usually different in nature than the other industry-specific projects as IT caters to the needs of various industries and business domains in the name of IT Projects. IT Projects usually involve collaboration with various business people and end users to understand its business process before designing the requirements acceptable for the end users. Choosing the best available and suitable technology fitting the need is a challenge. Managing IT Projects in the banking domain requires a different skill set than managing IT projects in insurance or manufacturing domains.

3.2 Characteristics of Information Technology Team Members

IT projects requires stakeholders with an optimum combination of business and technical skills along with knowledge of the IT industry and project management skills. Finding suitable people who have the knowledge and skills in all these areas is difficult and, hence, IT projects run with collaborative skills. Because of this, nowadays, top companies have started recruiting people from various fields, like business, biology, medicine, arts and other areas and then training them to their specific needs. IT companies started giving generic titles such as 'Consultant', 'Associate', 'General Manager', 'Director', etc., can easily be applicable to all these diversified people.

Technology, in the IT industry, also changes over the years and requires constant update of knowledge. Few years before (in 1990s) FoxPro and dBase were very famous. Now, in 2000, we are talking about JAVA, PHP, Android. In a few years, newer technology may emerge and IT project members will need to adapt to the situation through learning those softwares to excel and execute projects successfully.

Government policies also changes over a period of time, which caters to the changes in the IT industry and, in turn, the IT stakeholders need to gain quick knowledge of those policies. Obama's health care insurance reforms and changes in policies cater to the change in all health care insurance related IT projects.

Project management is a set of specialized skills required to manage projects. But, in the IT industry, people at the ground level are only given training on technology and, due to this, it become difficult for people to switch from technological layer to project management layer.

There has been a lot of changes in the process of developing software in the past 10 years. Agile is a topic of growing importance. Nowadays, many customers want their project to be executed using the Agile methodology. Agile is a software development methodology based on iterative and incremental development. IT team members need to align the project life cycle model to Agile Life Cycle Model. Agile methodology requires lot of generalists rather than specialists and hence team members are expected to know and master all the aspects of projects like technological aspects, business aspects, customer management aspects, etc.

3.3 Introduction to System View of Project Management

Projects cannot run in an isolated mode. It needs to integrate with various elements of the organization in order to create better values for the stakeholders. A project manager needs to understand the organizational context to run the project better. In order to solve complex problems in projects, the project manager needs to consider a holistic view of the project and how it operates within the organizational boundaries and systems.

3.4 Definition of System

A system is made up of various elements called 'components' (Figure 3.1) which are connected together as a whole. Properties of each component form the properties of the system as a whole.

A system can be described as a working model build for a specific purpose and made up of various interrelated sub-systems which, in turn, depend on various activities and interactions. The arrangement and activities of sub-systems affect the performance of the overall system.

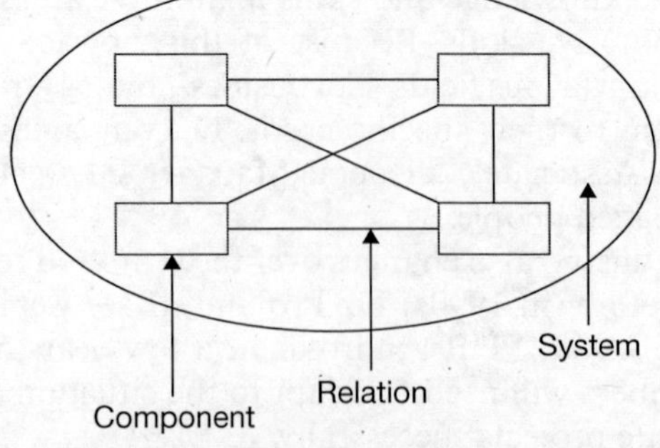

Figure 3.1 Structure of a System

3.5 Different Types of Systems

The three types of systems are as follows:

1. **Human System:** Human body as a whole consisting of various sub-systems.
2. **Mathematical System:** Mathematical equation made up of other equations.
3. **Physical system:** House, building, etc., which are also made up of sub-systems.

3.5.1 Open System vs Closed System

The boundaries of a system may be chosen at a defined level suitable for the purpose of system formation.

Systems that have clear external boundaries are called 'closed systems'. Closed system is the system which has no relationship with their environment (Figure 3.2). Systems that have link with their environment are called 'open systems'. Open system exchanges energy, information or other things with their environment. Open systems are more common in nature.

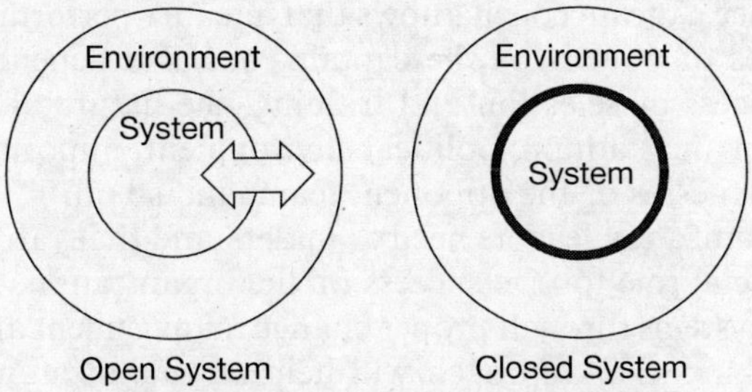

Figure 3.2 Open vs Closed System

3.6 Systems Thinking

Barry Richmond coined the term 'Systems Thinking' in 1987. It is the art and science of making reliable inferences about behaviour by developing an increasingly deep understanding of underlying structure. The essence is seeing the inter-relationships of the structural parts rather than linear cause-and-effect chains of the structural parts.

System Thinking concept (Figure 3.3) can be applied in many different fields and is described as a meta-discipline. In software context, software is considered as a large complex

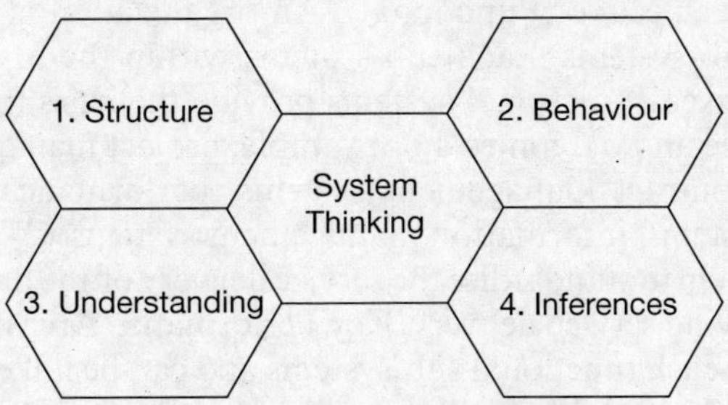

Figure 3.3 System Thinking

system which consists of multiple sub-systems. In this context, system thinking is a holistic approach that focuses on the way a software system's various parts (sub-systems) interrelate with each other and behaves over time and within the context of larger systems. Bigger system's behaviour is controlled by its dynamic structure of sub-systems.

Systems thinking can be considered a management discipline that examines the system with the linkages and interactions between its components.

3.6.1 Importance of Systems Thinking

1. It can help us to design smart and enduring system.
2. It gives more accurate and long-term solutions to problems.
3. It helps us to get an overall view of the system.

3.6.2 Systems Thinking to Improve Organization Effectiveness

The ability of leaders to lead and manage within an organization is compared to team sports like cricket. Often the abilities of captains, players, and teams are given as examples to what makes a great performance. A team coach knows that a team's performance not only depends on individual capabilities of players or the captain, but also depends on a range of supporting systems like process of selection and training, the nature of the pitch, supporters, geographic dimensions of the stadium, political environment, importance of that particular game, strengths and weaknesses of the opponent team, and so on.

In a similar way, organization leaders need to understand that various sub-systems of the organization plays a crucial role for the success of the organization. A conscious approach on managing those sub-systems through proper change management and leadership concepts using the Systems Thinking (ST) approach will help an organization achieve high performance. Systems Thinking (ST) approaches help in understanding and describing how various organizational systems perform and identifying ways to improve them.

There are three approaches to organizational systems, namely:

1. Functional Systems Approach
2. Structural Systems Approach
3. Interpretative Systems Approach

1. Functional Systems Approach

A functional systems approach (Figure 3.4) provides a solid framework for investigating the complex interrelationships between individuals and their social, material, and psychological worlds (John-Steiner, et al., 1998). This approach is used for simple systems. This gives importance to unitary perspective (Functional). An organization is considered to be made of a lot of functional sub-systems. Each sub-systems within the organization are designed to achieve specific objectives. Functional systems provide the basis for developing standards of repeatable best practice and outcomes. For example, project management systems, invoice management systems, contract management systems, performance management systems, training management systems, information management systems.

Functional systems help to standardise the service delivery of the organization and, thereby, provide means for improving service delivery. Key Performance Areas (KRAs) and Indicators (KPIs) can be defined for each functional sub-systems and can be linked with each other at the organizational level. It can be used to improve performance of individual sub-systems and, in turn, the overall organization performance.

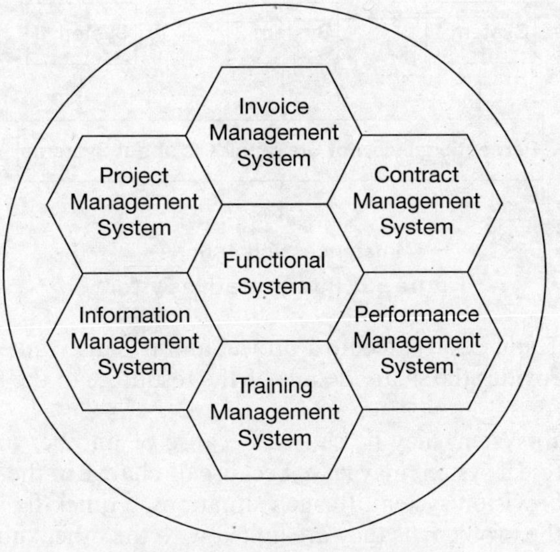

Figure 3.4 Functional System

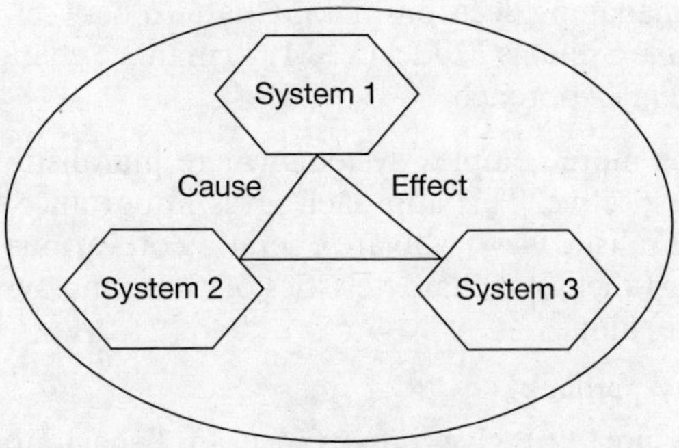

Figure 3.5 Structural System

Methodologies to improve functional systems include:

1. Lean Six Sigma approach for reduction of waste elements
2. CMMI (Capability Maturity Model Integration)
3. OPM3 Models (Organization Project Management Maturity Model)
4. Customer Satisfaction Survey

2. Structural Systems Approach

An organization is considered to be made of lot of structural sub-systems. Every subsystem within the organization is linked with each other through 'links' and 'loops' to form the overall organization structure which also results in predictable cause and effects. This approach is used for complicated systems (Figure 3.5). This gives importance to unitary perspective (structural). A system can be linked with 'N' number of other sub-systems for different purposes. For example, HR management system is linked with project management system as

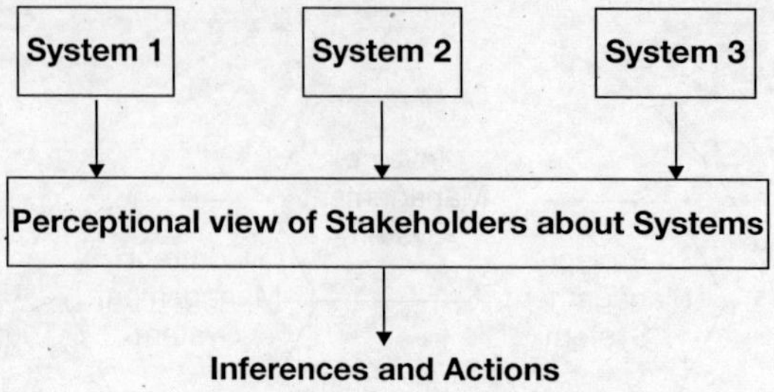

Figure 3.6 Interpretative System

it provides the needed resources to execute a project and it is also linked with financial management system as it provides the salary details of the resources to the financial management system.

Problem in one sub-system may be caused because of another linked sub-system. For example, people in a project system may leave because of change in the reimbursement policy system or in the salary revision system. In such situations, a quick-fix in one system will not help completely solve the problem as they are linked with the other sub-systems.

The methodologies to improve structural systems include:

1. Identifying and managing decision-making pattern between various sub-systems.
2. Formulating Viable Systems Model (VSM) to manage changing environment.
3. Interpretive Systems Approach.

This approach is used for more complex systems where pluralistic view gives best results, rather than a unitary perspective. This approach gives importance to the interpretation of different stakeholders (pluralistic view) who are operating on various subsystems, rather than physical characteristics or functional characteristics of those sub-systems or view of a single entity (unitary perspective) alone.

3. Interpretative Systems Approach

Interpretive systems (Figure 3.6) give importance to behavioural outcome aspects of sub-systems and organizational environment in which those sub-systems operates.

This gives importance to the views of stakeholders which may be subjective in nature, but caters to the need of the stakeholder involvement in the success of the organization.

Methodologies to improve interpretive systems include:

1. Forming Strategic Options Development and Analysis (SODA) for solving planning and policy-related issues.
2. Modelling Human Activity Systems (HAS). It can be applied to a wide range of organizational performance-related issues.

3.7 Problems with Systems Thinking

Complete and accurate prediction is not possible with systems thinking. This can be explained in terms of Chaos theory. According to which, the behaviour of dynamical systems are highly sensitive to initial conditions. A small difference in initial conditions will yield widely-diverging outcomes at a later point of time—a response known as the butterfly effect.

3.8 Systems Philosophy

This philosophy talks about how a project relates to the whole organization. The project manager needs to follow a systems philosophy to understand and execute the project better.

3.9 Systems Analysis

It is the process of studying a procedure or business in order to identify its goals and purposes and create systems and procedures that will achieve them in an efficient way. It evaluates a system's problems, opportunities, constraints, and needs. The analyst examines alternative approaches to solutions for improving the current situation by identifying action points.

3.10 Systems Management

Systems management takes the input from analysts and manages the change towards the betterment of the system. System changes addresses issues related to business, technology and the whole organization.

3.11 Systems Approach

System Approach of project management emerged in early 1950s. Three important elements are system philosophy, system analysis and system management. All these elements work towards the success of the project and do what is best for the organization.

3.12 Three Sphere Model of System Management

Organization is a system which is made up of Business, Technical and Organizational elements.

3.12.1 Understanding Business

Understanding customer's requirement alone is not sufficient for the successful execution of projects. IT project manager needs to understand the business objectives to be achieved by implementing IT projects. One of the main reasons for IT project success is to understand the business objectives clearly. Business Objectives are the results the IT project is intended to attain. Business objectives should be identified early in the project and is part of Project Charter. The business objectives will set the triple constraints of the projects namely scope constraints, time constraints, and cost constraints. If business objectives are unclear, it could lead to project failures.

SMART (Specific, Measurable, Achievable, Realistic, Time-bound) business objectives leads to the success of a project.

Specific: Define business objectives precisely and accurately without scope for misinterpretation.

Measurable: Measurable performance specifications needs to be defined for the set business objectives.

Achievable: Set challenging and achievable objectives that encourage people.

Realistic: Objectives should be realistic in nature.

Time-bound: Include the date by which you will achieve the objectives.

Examples for SMART Goal

By implementing new contract management system (IT Project), customer business is going to sign new contracts with 20 new vendors in the next three months. Customer will contact 15 of potential vendors each month through this system. By 15h January 2015, customers will be working with these new suppliers.

IT Projects managers must be able to identify measurable business objectives. After identifying business objectives, Project manager needs to identify appropriate stakeholders of the projects who can be involved in the project and who can help to achieve the identified business objectives. After identifying the stakeholders, the needs of the stakeholders are also to be tracked and prioritized in the overall project plan. Balancing the needs of the stakeholders are crucial aspects of project success. Interpersonal skills of the project managers help to handle this situation which includes communication management, conflict management, issue management and negotiation skills.

The following questions help understanding business objectives of the IT projects:

1. What would be the impact of this IT Project in business community?
2. What would be the cost of maintaining IT Project outcome after implementation?
3. Who will get affected after implementation of the said project?
4. How much efforts saved by the users because of this IT Project implementation?
5. What are the current business problems faced by business users?

3.12.2 Understanding Technology

IT project managers need to know the capabilities and deficiencies of the current technology and tools and be ready to adopt new emerging technologies. Extendibility to new technology is very important consideration while creating a software. IT project managers are not expected to be technical experts, but they should be able to understand the impacts of these technologies on business community and long-term business objectives.

1. What operating system the IT product will support?
2. What database software to be used?
3. What scripting language to be used?
4. What browsing software and versions to be used?
5. What is the current network support?
6. What are all the hardware used in the production environment?
7. What are all the non-functional Requirements (NFR) of a system?

3.12.3 Understanding Organizations

Organizational elements can be viewed as having four different frames: structural, human resources, political and symbolic.

Structural Frame: It focuses on structural aspects of the organization, like organization structure, reporting relationships, roles and responsibilities of various positions and their interaction levels. Organization chart represents the structural frame of the organization. Information technology department can be centralized or decentralized depending on the situation.

Human Resource Frame: Human Resources are important elements for any organization. They actually execute all organizational activities and, hence, an organization needs to be aligned with the human resource needs. If human resource needs are taken care of, then automatically organization needs will be taken care of. Information technology aspects in human resource frame takes care of various learning and development aspects of the human resources to execute IT projects.

Political Frame: This can be considered as a combination of structural and human resource frame. Due to this, various interest groups are formed within the organization. Organizations are considered as a combination of individuals and interest groups. Managing politics within this group through better conflict management techniques helps the organization. This political frame also gets created due to its structural frame. Politics, here, is directly related to authority and responsibility levels within the organization. In a projectized organization, a project manager has more power; in a functional structure, a functional manager has more power.

Symbolic Frame: This represents the cultural aspects of the organization. Since an organization is part of the culture within which it operates, by understanding the societal culture we can easily understand the organizational culture. There are different symbols, colours, words which represents the culture through which we can understand an organization.

Organization Structure: There are different organizational structures depending on their objectives and ambience. The structure of an organization determines the operation model of the organization. Organizational structure determines the responsibilities for different functions and entities. The organizational structure sets the level of authority, roles and responsibilities and the reporting structure within the project.

The following types of organization structures have been discussed in Chapter 2.

1. Functional Structure
2. Projectized Structure
3. Matrix Structure

3.13 Need for Organizational Commitment to IT Projects

Organization's commitment to IT is crucial for its success. If the organization has negative attitude towards IT, then it is very difficult to execute IT projects.

Information technology helps a business and organization to grow faster and better and an organization needs to understand and invest money on IT. If the organization considers investment in IT as burden, then sailing through the competition will be difficult.

Information technology helps analysing various business elements quickly and making quick business decisions. IT also helps in the innovation part of business and working smarter, leading to huge savings for organization in long term. Organizations need to invest in IT with long-term and short-term focus, leading to sustainability.

Organizations that understand the importance of IT, appoint positions such as Chief Technology Officer (CTO) and Chief Information Office (CIO) in order to run the information technology part of the business who take leadership roles in promoting IT within the organization.

Information technology not only helps in conducting Research and Development, but also helps a lot to understand the customers through its CRM and Analytics Software. Understanding customers better helps the organization to serve them better which, in turn, increases the business of the organization. Hence, IT should be considered as integral part of the organization.

3.14 Need for Organizational Standard

1. Organization standards help to execute projects consistently.
2. Organization standards help and connect various projects.
3. Organization standards are also helpful in comparing projects within the organization. Standards ensure consistency.
4. Standards also pave the path for continuous improvement of a process.
5. Standards help to get external certifications.
6. Standards help in easy auditing.
7. Standards ensure consistency in the status reports shared with the top management by various projects.
8. Standards also help to take quick decisions based on project related information.
9. Implementation of standards demonstrates an organization's commitment to IT project execution.

3.15 The Importance of Top Management Commitment

Top management commitment is very important for any project's success. It is also applicable for IT projects. If a project is not in the top priority list of top management, then it may not get the proper support in the next levels too. Top management commitment indirectly fetches the buy in from other departments to execute the projects successfully. Getting adequate resources to execute projects will be difficult without top management commitment. It is very difficult to run IT projects without top management commitment towards it.

3.16 Stakeholder Management

Every project involves multiple individuals or groups who directly or indirectly get impacted by the project. So, keeping all of them informed about the project status, regularly communicating with them, dealing with their conflicting interests—require considerable effort and planning.

3.16.1 Stakeholders and Their Characteristics

Stakeholders are those team members or entities who are actively involved in project execution or whose interests may be positively or negatively affected by project outcomes. The following list presents their characteristics.

- Stakeholder interests may be either positively or negatively impacted by the project.
- Alternatively, stakeholders may influence project execution and project results.
- It is important for project planners to identify all stakeholders and their requirements. Sometimes, individual stakeholder requirements may be implicit and not explicitly stated. For instance, in one of the requirements gathering workshop, a customer said that he wanted a 'world-class system'. When he was probed further, it came to be known that he wanted a system with background in golden colour and transaction response time of 5 seconds.
- Stakeholders may have conflicting interests and objectives—managing stakeholders may not be so easy.
- Involving stakeholders in the initiation phase of the project improves the probability of success of the project.
- In general, differences among stakeholders must be resolved in favour of the customer or end user.

3.16.2 Identify Stakeholder Process

There is no hard-and-fast rule that can be used in stakeholder identification. Rules for judging stakeholder involvement is always situation specific: rules that work in one situation may not work in another. The best way to identify stakeholders is by asking the right questions. The questions given in the following list are guidelines—a preliminary road map—and by no means exhaustive.

1. Who are the team members, entities, or organizations likely to be affected or to benefit from the intended project outcome?
2. Who would be assigned responsibility for the tasks entailed by the project?
3. Who is likely to move for or against the intended objective of the project?
4. Who can make improvements to the tasks entailed by the project? (Who can do it the better way?)
5. Who can contribute to the financial and technical resources required by the project?

Answers to these questions, which would vary across organizations, would likely yield a list of stakeholders. Procurement documents are the main inputs of this process along with the project charter.

Procurement documentation helps identifying stakeholders referred in the contract and procurement documents.

The three main steps in identifying right stakeholders are as follows (Figure 3.7):

Step 1: Identify all potential stakeholders and relevant information.

Step 2: Identify the potential impact or support each stakeholder could generate and use a power/interest grid to classify them.

Step 3: Assess how the stakeholders are likely to react or respond in various situations to help plan influencing them to enhance support or mitigate negative impacts.

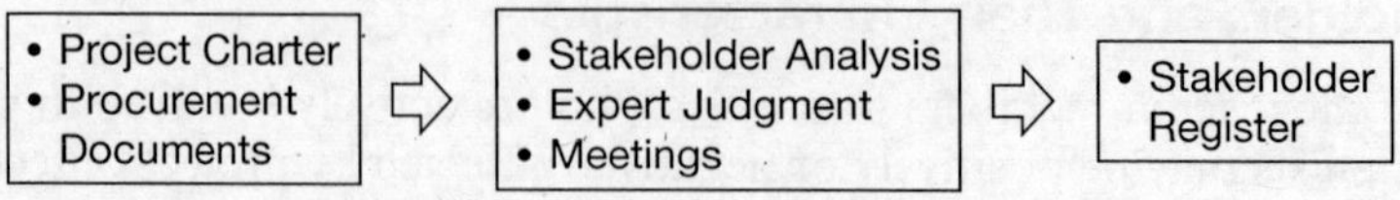

Figure 3.7 Identify Stakeholders

Step 1

Project managers use group dynamic techniques, whereby key project team members are asked to identify all possible stakeholders of the project. The Crawford Slip is another popular technique used for this purpose. This technique can be used to rapidly collate ideas from a large group of people.

Crawford is actually one of the original forms of brain-writing. The sponsor who pays money for the project is a key stakeholder. Individuals who sign on the project deliverables (usually customers) are stakeholders. The organization that executes this project is also a stakeholder as it stands to benefit through project execution. The organization that buys the outcome of the project is also a stakeholder since its members are benefitted. The organization that provides resources for executing the project is a stakeholder. Project managers, team members and functional managers are stakeholders. You can identify new stakeholders by asking the existing stakeholders.

Step 2

Stakeholder Register: A stakeholder register carries the following elements:

1. Identification elements of stakeholder
2. Influencing stage of the stakeholder
3. Classification of stakeholder

Figure 3.8 depicts the contents of a stakeholder register. It usually contains name, designation, influence stage and classification. Depending on their skill levels, stakeholders will be involved in the appropriate life cycle of the project and this is called 'influence stage'. For example, stakeholders having high proficiency level in designing will get involved only in the designing stage of the project.

In Figure 3.8, R. Ramya and K. Balachandran seem to have high proficiency in design and so are being involved only in the design stage of the project. There are people who are continuously involved throughout the project life cycle. In this figure, Pavan Kumar, the application manager, is involved continuously throughout the life cycle of the project because of the nature of the work he handles. Stakeholder classification like 'supporter', 'neutral', and 'resistor' depends on the nature of the stakeholders. If they are negatively impacted by the outcome of the project, they are classified as 'supporters'. They are classified as 'neutral' if they are neither 'supporters' nor 'resistors'.

Step 3

Stakeholder management is a difficult task requiring the formulation of a comprehensive stakeholder management strategy. Stakeholder analysis involves the following steps:

- Identify all potential project stakeholders' relevant information, such as their roles, departments, interests, knowledge, expectations, and influence levels.
- Analyse the potential impact or support each stakeholder could generate, and classify them so as to define an approach strategy. In large stakeholder communities, it is important to prioritise the stakeholders to ensure the efficient use of effort to communicate and manage their expectations.

Name	Designation stage	Influence	Classification
Pavan Kumar	Application Manager	All	Supporter
Siva Ranjani	Technical Consultant	Design, Coding	Neutral
R. Ramya	Architect	Design	Resistor
Shri Krishna	Business Manager	All	Neutral

Figure 3.8 A Stakeholder Register Template

	POWER (LEVEL OF AUTHORITY)	INTEREST (LEVEL OF CONCERN)	INFLUENCE (LEVEL OF INVOLVEMENT)	IMPACT (EFFECT OF INVOLVEMENT)
POWER		MODEL1	MODEL2	MODEL3
INTEREST	MODEL1			
INFLUENCE	MODEL2			
IMPACT	MODEL3			

Figure 3.9 Stakeholder Classification Model

- Assess how key stakeholders are likely to react or respond in various situations in order to plan how to influence them to enhance their support and mitigate potential negative impacts.

A stakeholder analysis matrix is a tool used to represent a project's stakeholder management strategy. The following are the contents of a stakeholder analysis matrix:

1. Stakeholder's name
2. Stakeholder's impact level
3. Stakeholder's interest level
4. Strategies for gaining support from this stakeholders'

A typical stakeholder analysis matrix may be obtained by adding a column to the stakeholder register template (Figure 3.9) titled 'Strategies for Gaining Support'. This strategy is based on the classification of the customer defined in Step 2 along with the influencing stage of the customer defined in Step 3.

Stakeholder Classification Model

Figure 3.9 shows three stakeholder classification models based on the power and the interest, influence and impact grids.

Model 1: Classifies the stakeholders based on Power and Interest

Model 2: Classifies the stakeholders based on Power and Influence

Model 3: Classifies the stakeholders based on Power and Impact

Power indicates the level of authority of a person; Interest indicates the level of concern a person has for the project; Influence indicates the level of involvement shown on the project; Impact is the effect due to the level of involvement.

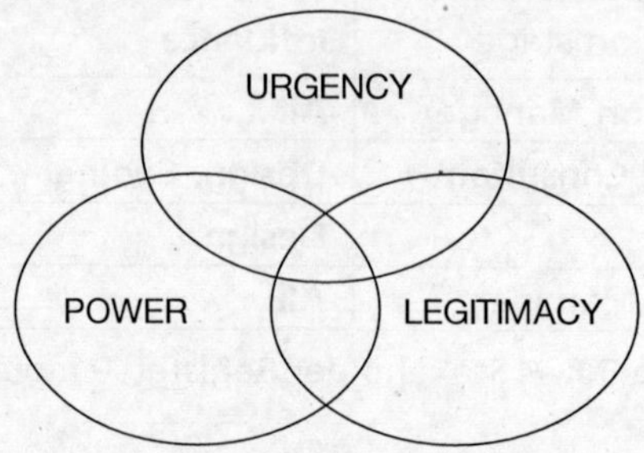

Figure 3.10 Salience Model of Stakeholder Classification

Another popular stakeholder classification model is the Salience Model (Figure 3.10). It is based on power, urgency, and legitimacy grids. Power indicates the level of authority of a person, urgency indicates the need for immediate action and legitimacy indicates whether the involvement is appropriate or not. A grid (Venn diagram) is drawn based on the above three factors to find out the types of stakeholders.

Planning Stakeholder management is critical and vital to the success of projects and the project manager.

3.16.3 Plan Stakeholder Management Process

Planning Stakeholder management is critical and vital to the success of projects. The project manager cannot execute a project alone. The contribution of the people (stakeholders) in executing the process laid down by the project manager is important, as it is difficult to execute the project without such contribution. Communication with stakeholders is vital to project management. The project manager needs to establish clear lines of communication with all stakeholders and keep them involved in and aware of the projects progress from time to time. Engaging the right kind of people (people with the right skills) in the right way in a project at the right time makes a big difference to the success of the project. Stakeholder management plan has to be shared and shaped by key stakeholders to ensure that it meets the needs of those interested in the successful outcome of a particular project.

Tools and Techniques of the Plan Stakeholder Management Process

Expert Judgment: Here, the experience gained from similar kind of projects in managing the stakeholders/process of stakeholder management is put into use. The Dos and Don'ts are implemented based on the expertise gained from previous projects.

Meetings: In order to develop a stakeholder management plan which is realistic and accepted by the entire team, it is better to conduct team meetings while drawing the stakeholder management plan. This meeting should be attended by stakeholders such as project sponsors and others who are responsible for the project and its success. The project manager can also conduct this meeting with selected team members who have good knowledge of the stakeholders.

Stakeholder Analysis: Stakeholders are classified on the basis of their interests, influence and involvement in the project. Such a classification helps a project manager to focus on the complementary functions and relationships among stakeholders necessary to ensure project success.

Output of the Plan Stakeholder Management Process

Stakeholder Management Plan: It specifies the process of managing stakeholders. The purpose of the stakeholder management plan is to provide a framework for the following aspects of the stakeholders:

1. Identify each stakeholder and the corresponding group (classification), both internal and external to the project.
2. Define roles and responsibilities of each group clearly so that the project can utilize them properly.
3. Define communication methods clearly and specify how the stakeholder groups will interact.
4. Define escalation mechanism clearly, if not defined already.
5. Provide a means to set clear expectations among all stakeholders.

The amount of time allocated to stakeholder management depends on the complexity and schedule of the project and its corresponding goals.

3.16.4 Manage Stakeholder Engagement Process

Project managers need to engage stakeholders throughout the life cycle of a project in order to utilise them better for the success of the project. Most of the time, bringing in the right people will solve most of the problems. While we engage stakeholders, we may come across a few issues that need to be managed with our communication skills, management skills and interpersonal skills. Issues can be managed with proper planning by creating an issue log that helps to compile, analyse and manage the issues.

Project communication with stakeholders is an important part of any project. A project manager needs to establish lines of communication with all stakeholders and also develop a mechanism to keep them involved and aware of the project's progress and status. Stakeholder management plan defines an approach to communications and a mechanism to provide project data to stakeholders. The stakeholder management plan can be formal or informal, highly detailed or broadly framed, based on the needs of the project. In addition to the data gathered in the stakeholder register, the stakeholder management plan often provides:

- Desired and current engagement levels of the key stakeholders.
- Impact level of the stakeholders.
- Identified interrelationships and potential overlap between stakeholders.
- Stakeholder's communication requirements for the current project phase.
- Information to be distributed to stakeholders, including language, format, content, and level of detail.
- Reason for the distribution of that information and the expected impact on stakeholder's engagement.
- Time frame and frequency for the distribution of required information to stakeholders.
- Method for updating and refining the stakeholder management plan as the project progresses and develops.

It may be necessary to develop different strategies for the different groups identified during the Identify Stakeholder Process. Some possible methods of communication are:

- Progress reports
- Meetings and briefings
- User groups (email groups)
- Access to documentation (Requirements)

Tools and Techniques of Manage Stakeholder Engagement Process

Meetings: To resolve an issue in a way that is realistic and accepted by the stakeholders. It is better to conduct team meetings while addressing issues. This meeting should also be attended by other stakeholders, such as project sponsors and others who are responsible to contrive a solution to the problem at hand. The project manager can also conduct this meeting with selected team members who have good knowledge of the matter of contention.

Reporting Systems: Reporting systems are standard tools that help to capture, store and distribute the information needed to manage and control stakeholders, thereby, helping to resolve open issues. These also help managers to report performance and progress of a project and resolve issues.

3.16.5 Control Stakeholder Engagement Process

Project managers need to engage stakeholders throughout the life cycle of the project to utilize them better for the project to succeed. Controlling stakeholder engagement is critical for the success of the project.

Inputs of the Control Stakeholder Engagement Process

Project Management Plan: Project Management Plan is the main input of this process which talks about the course (the how part) of controlling the engagement of stakeholders. Various subsidiary plans (including Stakeholder Management Plan), which are part of the main project management plan, help in charting a suitable mechanism for stakeholder engagement.

Issue Log: It is a LIVE updated document which contains a list of on-going and closed issues of the project. The various issues related to the engagement of stakeholders are managed using this document. The 'issue log' can also be used to organize the current issues of the project based on various parameters (its priority, status, etc.) so as to control it in a systematic way.

Work Performance Data: Work performance data is the input for the control stakeholder engagement process. It includes data associated with the degree of compliance and data related to managing and controlling the stakeholders, such as number of issues, number of open issues and number of challenges faced by the project team.

Tools and Techniques to the Control Stakeholder Engagement Process

Expert Judgment: The experience of experts is vital to control stakeholder engagement. Skill levels based on similar kind of previous activities are also considered as expert judgment. We may utilize the competence of experts to analyse existing historical information and use it to define better stakeholder control and solve the current issues of stakeholders. We may also use expert judgment to evaluate the various options available and choose the best one. Usually, personnel of senior management, SMEs and external consultants are used for this purpose.

Meetings: To resolve an issue in a way that is realistic and accepted by the stakeholder, it is better to conduct team meetings while addressing issues. This meeting should also be attended by other stakeholders such as project sponsors and others who are responsible for contriving a solution to the problem at hand. The project manager can also conduct this meeting with selected team members who have good knowledge of the matter of contention.

Report Systems: Report systems are standard tools that help to capture, store and distribute the information needed to manage and control stakeholders, thus, helping resolve open issues. These also help managers to report performance and progress of a project in resolving issues.

SUMMARY

- Stakeholders are those team members or entities who are actively involved in project execution or whose interests may be positively or negatively affected by project outcomes.
- Once the stakeholders are identified, their details are maintained in a stakeholder register. This document usually contains name, designation, influence stage and classification.
- A contract is a formal and legally binding agreement between two or more parties, individuals, businesses, organizations, or government agencies, by which the contracted parties exchange goods or services of value to each other.
- A system is made up of various elements called 'components' which are connected together as a whole. Properties of each component form the properties of the system as a whole.
- Three different types of systems:
  1. **Human System:** Human body as a whole consisting of various sub-systems.
  2. **Mathematical System:** Mathematical equation made up of other equations.
  3. **Physical System:** House, building, etc., which are also made up of sub-systems.
- Closed System is the system which has no relationship with their environment. Systems that have link with their environment are called Open Systems. An open system exchanges energy, information or other things with their environment. Open systems are more common in nature.
- Importance of Systems Thinking:
  1. It can help us design smart and enduring systems.
  2. It gives more accurate and long-term solutions to problems.
  3. It helps us get an overall view of the system
- Three approaches to organizational systems:
  1. Functional Systems Approach
  2. Structural Systems Approach
  3. Interpretive Systems Approach
- **Systems Philosophy:** This philosophy talks about how a project relates to the whole organization. A project manager needs to follow a systems philosophy to understand and execute the project in an efficient.
- **System Analysis:** It is the process of studying a procedure or business of the system in order to identify its goals and purposes and in turn identify procedures that will achieve them in an efficient way. It evaluates a system's problems, opportunities, constraints, and needs. The analyst examines alternative approaches to solutions for improving the current situation by identifying action points.

EXERCISES

PART A (Objective-type Questions)

1. The main output of the identify stakeholders process is
A. Risks Register
B. Stakeholder Plan
C. Stakeholder Register
D. Stakeholder Management Strategy

2. If stakeholder is having additional information needs, which of the following documents will be updated?
A. Stakeholder Register
B. Risk Register
C. Stakeholder Management Strategy
D. Issue Log

3. All of the following are the content of a stakeholder register, except
A. Assessment Information
B. Identification Information
C. Stakeholder Classification
D. Urgency of the need of information

4. Following are the contents of stakeholder management strategy, except
A. Key stakeholders who can significantly impact the project.
B. Level of participation in the project desired for each identified stakeholder.
C. Stakeholder groups and their management.
D. Urgency of the need of information of stakeholders.

5. Who is responsible for stakeholder expectation management?
A. Project Leader
B. Customer
C. Project Manager
D. Project Sponsor

6. Which of the following is the most common way to represent stakeholder management strategy?
A. Stakeholder Register
B. Risk Register
C. Stakeholder Analysis Matrix
D. Stakeholder Impact Matrix

7. Your manager asked you to find an approach to increase the support and minimize negative impacts of stakeholders throughout the entire project life cycle. What did he ask you to create?
A. Risks Register
B. Stakeholder Plan
C. Stakeholder Register
D. Stakeholder Management Strategy

PART B (Write the answers in one or two lines)

1. What do you mean by stakeholder of a project?
2. List the three-step process to identify stakeholders.
3. List the contents of a stakeholder analysis matrix.
4. What do you mean by power and urgency of stakeholders?
5. How is communication management related to project stakeholder management?
6. Define System.
7. List the three different types of systems.
8. What is the difference between closed-system and open-system?
9. Define system thinking.
10. Mention three benefits of systems thinking.
11. List the three approaches to organizational systems.
12. Write a short note on functional system approach.
13. Write a short note on structural system approach.
14. Define systems philosophy.
15. What is system analysis?

Section II

Software Project Initiation

4

Software Project Evaluation

4.1 Introduction

Continuous competition in the marketplace forces organizations to evaluate each and every projects before investing in them. Along with monetary benefits, several other factors need to be considered to decide whether a project is worth undertaking. Assessing current and future market demand, financial viability and return on investment, alignment with the organizational strategy, technical feasibility with the currently available technology, etc., are some of the focus areas that help in decision making about taking up a new project. In this chapter, we will discuss, how an organization can systematically evaluate software projects for implementation considerations.

4.2 Project Analysis

The first and the most critical step in making projects successful is the analysis phase. This step takes into account various parameters that are crucial to ensure that the right project is started at the right time. Before starting a project, it is important to know from where funds would be available, how the investors would get back their money from the project, how the demand of the product will be and what kind of risks may arise during the life cycle of the project. In the subsequent sections, we will discuss these various parameters and how they are analysed in this phase.

4.2.1 Market and Demand Analysis

Market and demand analysis is critical as the facility, capacity and location planning can only be taken up based on market demand and project viability. An incorrect market analysis may lead to flawed facility and capacity planning which, in most cases, is irreversible. Evaluation of an investment proposal should always be backed by a strong market and demand analysis, thus leading to correct forecasting.

There are several qualitative and quantitative demand forecasting models which try to eliminate the subjectivity in the forecast and make it more reliable and repetitive. Based on the time horizon for which it is undertaken, the demand forecasting is grouped into three broad categories:

- Short-term demand forecasting that is used for short-term planning decisions.
- Medium-term demand forecasting that is used for technology or site selection.
- Long-term demand forecasting that is used for site selection and long-term objective setting of the organization.

There are few attributes which need to be kept in mind for producing a good demand forecasting. Those are as follows:

Accurate: It is important to keep track of the accuracy of forecasting by comparing the past forecasts with the current actual demand. It will help you fine-tune the assumptions made during creation of the forecast. As forecast is an attempt to predict the future, it may not always be completely accurate, but it should be regularly revisited to avoid big surprises.

Plausible: The assumptions made at the time of creating the forecasts should be reasonable and hold well when probed closely.

Economic: Though forecasting is an important activity, it should not be too expensive to create a forecast. While fine-tuning a forecast, it is important to make sure that the improvement gained is more than the cost of fine-tuning the forecast.

Quick: The creation of the demand forecast should not take unreasonably long time. Also, it should be easy to take quick and effective decisions based on forecasting.

Available on-time: The methodology followed for forecasting should be easy enough so that the forecast can be updated if there is any change in the assumptions or market.

Durable: The forecast should have stable relationship with the parameters. So, if the parameters change, it is easy to make necessary changes in the forecast.

Given here are some of the widely used qualitative and quantitative demand forecasting techniques. We will discuss these briefly to get an idea of how these are used for arriving at an accurate forecast.

Qualitative Techniques: These techniques do not employ any calculation or use any past data, but are based mainly on the experience levels of the persons doing the demand forecast. These are quick ways to create forecasts and if the group of people participating in this type of forecast are chosen carefully, then the result may be quite satisfactory.

Collective Opinion Survey: The opinion of the sales personnel and the managers involved in various levels of sales are collected through a survey to make basic analysis and demand forecasting. As the sales personnel know the customers best, they will be able to provide valuable inputs regarding required product features, competitive pricing, competitors, and market policies, etc., which are important factors for determining the demand forecast.

The drawback of this kind of forecasting is that this is person dependent and may vary based on the experience levels of the sales personnel. Also, if they are new into this domain and have exposure to only a small portion of the market, then their forecast will not be accurate.

Survey of Customers Intention: This method tries to get the opinion from the customers regarding things, like what they want from a product, the future demand and the pricing.

This is normally a questionnaire-based survey involving few big customers who can represent a particular segment of the industry.

This is an effective technique if there are few big institutions which drive the market for a product, but the challenge is that the customer may not have a good idea about the future demand, especially, in case, many similar products are available in the market.

Delphi Method of Demand Forecasting: Delphi method is a collective opinion method which aims at arriving at a consensus of the participating members. The participants are normally the experts in market research and demand forecasting. The co-ordinator sends out the questionnaire to a set of experts who will fill up the expected demand and send back to the co-ordinator. Then the co-ordinator collates the data, edits those to check the incomplete answers and summarises the predictions. Based on the summary, a new set of questionnaire is prepared and sent to the participants. The co-ordinator repeats the process of collating, editing and summarizing the responses until a consensus is reached among the experts who might have diverse background.

The strong point of this methodology is that this removes the bias from the forecasting process by restricting the direct interaction between the experts. Based on how diverse the experts are in the group, several insights about the market demand, policies and features may come out.

Nominal Group Technique: This is a kind of Delphi technique where a group of seven to ten experts interact with each other to reach a consensus. During their group discussion, the experts write down the assumptions and the demand forecasts for each item. The facilitator then makes sure that the assumptions and forecast for each item by each of the participants is discussed and a consensus is reached to arrive at the final forecast.

Quantitative Techniques: These techniques try to remove the subjective nature of the demand forecasting by making it based on data and analysis. The dependency on the experience levels of the experts have been tried to be removed by doing this.

Simple Average Method: This is the simplest form of the quantitative demand forecasting technique where the average of the actual demand for a certain period in the past is considered as the current demand. For example, the actual market demand for last 12 months is recorded and the average is taken to find out the demand for this month.

Simple Average = Sum of demand of all periods/Number of periods

The problem with this technique is that all the past periods are given the same importance, whereas the recent data should get more importance. This problem is addressed in the moving average method.

Moving Average Method: A constant number of periods is chosen for this calculation and once this number is reached, the older data is discarded and the new periods are added. This makes sure that the less relevant older data is kept out of calculation for demand forecasting.

Moving Average = Sum of demand of chosen period/Number of chosen period

For the moving average, to give an accurate result, the number of chosen period should be kept constant over time.

Weighted Moving Average: Though moving average takes care of removing the old and less relevant data from the calculation, it is further refined in the weighted moving average method where the recent period data is multiplied by a higher weightage value so that those figures get more importance in the forecasting calculation.

$$\text{Weighted Moving Average} = m_1 \times V_1 + m_2 \times V_2 + m_3 \times V_3 + \cdots + m_n \times V_n$$

Where $m_1, m_2, \ldots, m_n$ are the weightages assigned to each period data and $V_1, V_2, \ldots, V_n$ are the actual demand data from previous periods.

The weightages are critical for this technique and should be assigned by the market analyst to remove the bias from the data, like seasonal demand surge.

Exponential Smoothing Methods: This technique takes help of the computer programs to assign the weightage for the weighted moving average and the weightage increases exponentially starting from the oldest period as it moves towards the current period. As the weightages change exponentially rather than linearly, it helps in smoothing the effect of older data to give priority to the more recent data. The expression looks like:

$$\text{Forecast of the next period demand} = W \times \text{Actual demand of most recent period} + (1 - W) \times \text{Demand forecast for the most recent period}$$

Adaptive Exponential Smoothing: This technique is used in case the demand is not stable or there is no known pattern for the demand. Here, the value of W is not fixed, but it is allowed to fluctuate over time in line with the pattern of demand fluctuation.

Projection by Curve Fitting: This is a graphical way of projecting the demand. The actual demand data for an organization collected over a period of time is plotted in the graph and a linear or a curved line fitting the data is created as the trend for demand in that organization. For any new time period, it is simple and easy to find out the demand forecast from the graph, once it is created in the first step. Figure 4.1 shows how this technique is used.

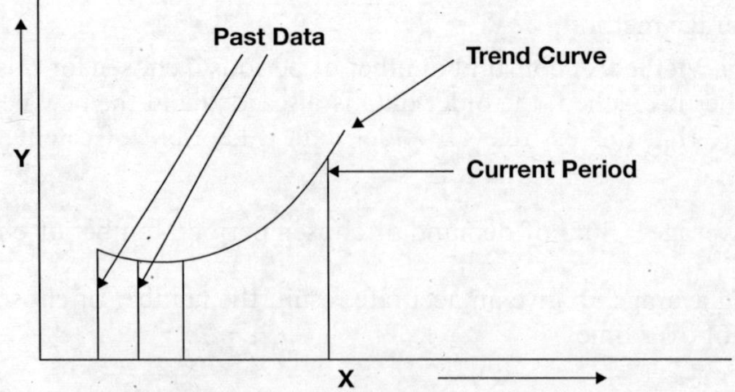

Figure 4.1 Demand Forecasting by Curve Fitting

4.2.2 Strategic Assessment

The first step of strategic assessment is to define the strategic plan. This is an organization level plan where the organization decides what they plan to achieve in short term as well as long term and how it will allocate the resources to achieve these goals. The three basic questions that the organization should answer at this stage are:

- What do we do?
- For whom do we do it?
- How do we succeed?

Projects and Strategic Planning: Projects are often utilized as a means of achieving an organization's strategic plan, whether the project team is employed by the organization or is a contracted service provider.

Exercise 4.1: Why does any organization do projects?

Organizations do projects for the following strategic considerations:

1. A market demand
2. An organization need
3. A customer request
4. A technological advance
5. A legal requirement

Market Demand
Example: A bank initiates a project to offer customers the ability to transfer money to other accounts over the Internet as these kinds of intra and interbank transactions have increased.

Business Need
Example: A company initiates a new project to design a portal for business-to-business transaction as the current manual process of transaction is very slow.

Customer Request
Example: Loan automation system to automate the loan process as the current manual system creates customer dissatisfaction. Many customers wanted something to be done to reduce the time and the errors due to manual system.

Technological Advance
Whenever a new technology comes to the market, every company does Proof of Concept (POC) Project in the new technology introduced to showcase their ability in the new technology. For example, when JAVA was introduced to the market in late 90s, every company started doing POC Projects in JAVA technology to showcase their ability in the new technology to get new projects form the customer.

Legal Requirement
New income tax laws might require modifications or new programming to the existing income tax system.

A project or a group of projects (often termed 'programme') should be aligned with the overall strategy of the organization. This stage is called 'strategic assessment'. The questions should be answered at the strategic assessment stage are as follows:

- How does this project contribute to the organization's overall goal? For example, the new system may help the organization in expanding to the new geographies.
- How does the proposed system fit into the existing information system? For example, will it replace any part of it with more efficient system or will it interface with the existing systems to provide the desired outcome?
- Is this project viable (commercially or technically)? For example, the currently available software in the market may not be able to provide the type of functionalities that this project is expecting to provide, which may delay the overall project delivery and finally the financial viability may be an issue.
- Is the timing right? For example, due to a new government regulation the proposed new software will have a huge market demand.
- Are proper resources available? Manpower, capital, hardware, and software everything should be considered as resource.
- How does this proposed project affect the organization structure? For example, the proposed system may plan to automate the order processing unit, making the workforce in that department redundant.
- How it will affect the brand value of the organization? Based on the success or failure of the project, will the image or brand value of the organization get positively or negatively affected?
- How does it affect the workforce of an organization? Is there any way the skill base or the manning levels of the employees gets affected by this project?

The project should be evaluated against the organization's objectives, and the context for assessing individual project for its success or failure needs to be set at this stage. Let us take the example of a software development project taken up by an organization which already has a well-defined organization-wide information system. It is obvious that the newly developed software system should become part of the overall information system and should be evaluated in the context of this existing system.

4.2.3 Technical Assessment

Along with the strategic alignment of the projects, it is important to evaluate the technical aspects as well. The functionalities planned for the software are evaluated against the capability of available software and hardware. Any constraint imposed by the existing information system plan, of the organization, should also be considered at this stage, to determine if the project will be technically successful.

4.3 Economic Assessment and Cost–Benefit Analysis

After Strategic and technical assessment, the most common analysis employed for project evaluation is economic assessment. Cost–benefit analysis is the process for conducting economic assessment. As suggested by the name, cost–benefit analysis is done by comparing the expected cost of development and operations, with the benefits that it will reap. While considering benefits, along with monetary benefits, several other possible benefits are also considered which may be intangible in nature. Cost–benefit analysis is often employed to decide which project is the best among the available options and also to prioritize among the projects, so that the resources can be allocated most efficiently.

The cost–benefit analysis considerations are as follows:

- Expected cost of developing a system.
- Expected cost of operating a system (i.e., set-up and running costs).
- Benefits obtained.

Two standard steps for this analysis are as follows:

- Identify and estimate the costs and benefits of engaging into a project.
- Convert all the costs and benefits in a common unit for easy comparison.

Net Benefit = Total Benefit – Total Cost

Let us understand the costs as mentioned above.

Development Cost: This includes the salary and other employment cost of the staff, any infrastructure requirement, and software licences, etc.

Set-up Cost: This includes the costs involved in implementing the system, such as any hardware, training, documentation, etc.

Operation Cost: After the system is installed, the costs involved in running the system, like staffing for monitoring the performance of the system, hardware and software maintenance, etc., are bucketed under this head.

It is also important to understand the types of benefits which can be derived as the outcome of a project.

Benefits are quite difficult to quantify in monetary terms even if they are identified.

Direct Benefits: These benefits are those realized directly from using the implemented system. For example, reduction in workforce due to automation software is a direct benefit and can be assessed easily.

Assessable Indirect Benefits: These are the secondary benefits obtained from the use of the new system, because it is more user-friendly or performance intensive. For example, after an upgrade, the database processing efficiency had increased which led to completion of more work order than earlier leading to more business.

Intangible Benefits: These are generally the long-term indirect benefits and are difficult to quantify. For example, the new look and feel of a website had created more interest among the users and that can generate more business in the longer term.

The overall calculation of total cost and total benefit is not sufficient for taking any business decision. Rather the cost–benefit analysis should forecast the cash flow over a period of time, right from the beginning of the project, which gives the organization the visibility of fund flow and investment requirements.

4.3.1 Cash Flow Forecasting

Cash flow forecasting provides the estimation of cash flow over time. At the beginning of the project, the cost is greater than the benefit which gives a negative cash flow, meaning—a need

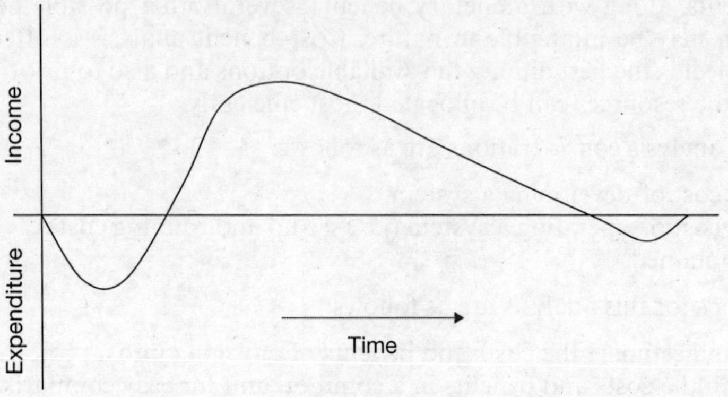

Figure 4.2 Cash Flow Forecasting

for investment. Once the software is in use, the organization starts realizing the benefits. Figure 4.2 shows how the cash flow graph looks like for a project over the time period.

As you can see, the expenditure and income both needs to be considered in the forecasting. It is not easy to forecast all the incomes or expenditures right at the beginning of the project. So, the forecast needs to be revisited at regular intervals during project execution.

4.3.2 Cost–Benefit Evaluation Techniques

There are various cost–benefit evaluation techniques that consider the timing of the costs, and benefits and the relative size of benefit with respect to the cost. Figure 4.3 gives an overview of the economic models available for cost–benefit analysis.

Payback Period	**Present Value (PV)**
The amount of time to recover initial cost	A series of future cash flows expressed in today's value (monetary) **PV = FV / (1 + r)ⁿ**; FV = Future value R = rate of interest; n = # of time periods
Future Value (FV)	**Net Present Value (NPV)**
FV = PV * (1 + r)ⁿ; PV: Present Value; r = rate of interest; n = # of time periods	Accurate value for the project in today's dollars
Internal Rate of Return (IRR)	**Return on Investment (ROI)**
Investments return on **profitability.** Similar to bank interests it is also called Discounted Cash Flow Rate of Return (DCFROR)	Is a **return ratio** that compares the net benefits of a project vs its total cost
Life Cycle Cost	
Development Cost + Maintenance Cost + Operation Cost + Disposal Cost	

Figure 4.3 Economic Models

Payback Period: Payback period is the unit of time (amount of time) required to recover (get back) the initial amount invested. This is the time required for the cumulative income from the project to become equal to cumulative expenditure on the project.

The advantages of this model are that this is based on simple calculation and provides a clear idea of when the break-even (the point at which the cumulative income equals cumulative expenditure) will be reached.

Owing to its simplicity, there are many disadvantages—It does not consider the future inflow which means it does not give any value to the cash flow after payback period; it ignores the time value of money and makes no adjustment for risk or interest factors.

Here is an example of how payback period is calculated. Suppose, an organization invests \$40,000 to start a business (it includes all the resource costs, infrastructure costs, etc.) and the flow of money (income) to the company due the business is as follows:

Cash Inflow Statement

Year	Inflow ($)
2011	5,000
2012	15,000
2013	20,000
2014	25,000
2015	15,000
2016	10,000

The amount invested at the beginning (\$40,000) is given back by the business in three years \$(5000 + 15000 + 20000) and so the payback period of the business is three years. If there are multiple projects from which we have to prioritize one based on the payback period, then the project with lowest payback period is the better choice as we are able to recover the investment faster.

Payback period is also otherwise called Break-Even Point as shown in Figure 4.4. We need to draw a graph plotting Time at X-axis vs Revenue (\$) the at Y-axis. Draw a line for revenue and another for cost. Break-even point is the point at which the cost line meets the revenue line.

Net Present Value (NPV): It is the accurate value of all the future inflow or outflow in the business in today's value (present value). The cash flow summary adjusted to reflect the time value of money is called Discounted Cash Flow (DCF). This analysis takes into account the

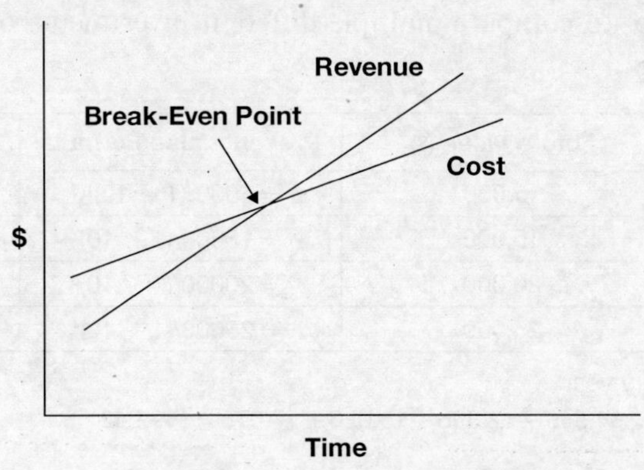

Figure 4.4 Payback Period

series of cash flows happening in future and converts them to today's value. The aggregate of these cash flow streams is called 'net present value'.

So, there are two important parameters considered for this calculation—the amount of time between the present time and the actual cash flow, and the interest rate (i.e., discount rate). As the amount of time interval between now and cash flow time increases, the present value of that cash flow decreases. Similarly, as the interest rate (discount rate) increases, the present value of the future cash flow decreases.

$$\text{Discount Factor} = 1/(1 + r\,\%)^t;\ r = \text{interest rate};\ t = \text{time interval}$$

We need to convert the future value into the present value and then the sum of all the present value gives NPV (Net Present Value). The process of moving future amounts back into the present value is called Discounting. Figure 4.5 shows how the NPV is calculated for a project based on the future cash flow figures.

Choose the project with the highest NPV.

Return on Investment (ROI): ROI is used for measuring the performance of an investment by comparing it with the net benefit and, is also, a useful means to compare different investment options. ROI is being calculated using the formula of Benefit to Cost.

$$\text{ROI} = \text{Benefit/Cost} \times 100\%$$

The benefit is the Average Annual Profit and the cost is Total Investment.

$$\text{Average Annual Profit} = \text{Net Profit/Total Number of Years}$$

For example, if the net profit in a project over five years is \$50,000 after investing \$100,000, then the ROI calculation using the above formula is as follows:

$$\text{Average Annual Profit} = 50{,}000/5 = 10000$$

$$\text{ROI} = (10{,}000/100{,}000) \times 100\% = 10\%$$

The disadvantage with the above calculation is that it does not take into account the time value of money which is not a realistic calculation. If we take the Discount Rate into consideration, the formula looks like:

$$\text{Discounted ROI} = \text{NPV of Benefits/NPV of Costs}$$

Discounted ROI considers the future value of the money (benefits and costs).

ROI is a useful tool to compare multiple different investments or to track the performance of the projects.

S. No.	Year	Future Value (\$)	Present Value Formula	Present Value (\$)
1	2014	5,000	$= 5000/(1 + .10)^1$	4545
2	2015	15,000	$= 15000/(1 + .10)^2$	12396
3	2016	20,000	$= 20000/(1 + .10)^3$	15026
4	2017	25,000	$= 25000/(1 + .10)^4$	17075

Interest Rate = 10% flat every year

From the above table, NPV = \$4,545 + 12,396 + 15,026 + 17,075 = \$49,042

Figure 4.5 Present Value vs Future Value

Internal Rate of Return (IRR): ROI is, otherwise, called as IRR. It provides return in terms of Percentage. IRR is a measure of how quickly the investment in a project will increase in value. IRR is the interest rate at which NPV of cash flow stream is equal to zero.

MARR stands for Minimum Attractive Return of Rate. It is the minimum rate of return on investment, in a project, a manager or company is willing to accept before starting a project.

4.4 Risk Evaluation

Along with the financial analysis, another important factor considered during project evaluation is the risks associated in taking up a project. Risk evaluation is meant for analysing whether the project will be able to meet its objectives and, thus, decide whether to proceed with the project or not. It also helps in shortlisting the projects to proceed with, from a list of projects, based on the risks associated with each of them. Organizations prefer to proceed with the less risky project even if the return is more on the high-risk ones.

4.4.1 Risk Identification and Ranking

Risks have two main characteristics—likelihood of occurrence, and impact. While identifying and ranking the risks, it is important to take into account both these aspects. By likelihood we mean, the chance or probability that a risk will occur; and by impact we mean the loss or benefit arising from the risk in case it occurs. For example, the probability of a hardware crash before the production 'go-live' may only be 5%, but the impact will be loss of business worth millions of dollars. In this case, the organization will decide to invest on a backup hardware in case the risk occurs.

There are two easy ways employed for risk identification and ranking. Those are as follows:

Relative Valuation Method: In this method, we place a value between 1 and 10 on the likelihood of occurrence of the risk, and again a value between 1 and 10 for the impact or severity. The product of these two values gives the relative risk score for a particular risk. We need to understand here that this is a relative scoring technique as we are assigning the numbers comparing a risk with other risks in our radar. Let us check the following example showing how we can calculate the total risk score of a project before we decide whether to take it up for implementation or not.

Risk Category	Likelihood	Impact	Risk Score
Other vendor releases the same product before us	3	9	27
The cost of hardware increases before go-live	8	3	21
Not enough skill set in the market to develop this product	9	8	72
Cash flow will be discontinued by the sponsors	2	9	18
Total risk score of project	–	–	138

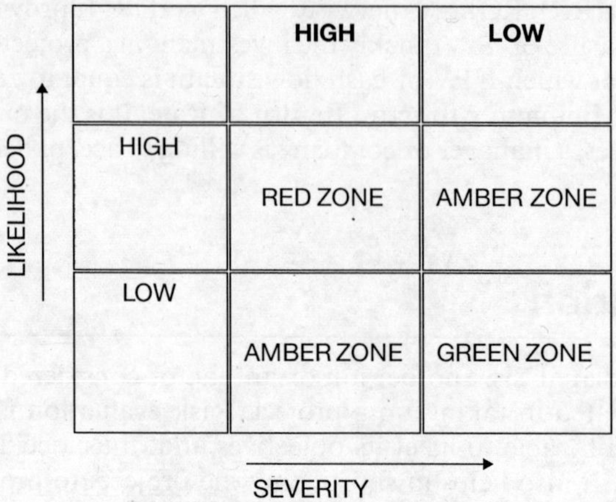

Figure 4.6 Four Square Method

Similarly, the risk score for different other projects, which are also under consideration, can be found out for the same set of parameters and then the organization will take a decision on which project to go ahead with.

Four Square Method: This method assesses the Severity and Likelihood of the risks and plots the valuations within four squares as shown in Figure 4.6. As it can be observed, the most impacting and most likely risks will appear in the RED zone which needs to be evaluated with maximum details.

For example, while starting a software project on a newly released platform, the team has identified the following risks:

1. The platform being at its nascent stage, there will be several defects inside it which may hamper the architecture of the proposed software project. This is a very high impact risk, as the project viability depends on this. But, if this new platform was released by a reputed software organization, like Oracle or IBM, etc., then there is less chance of this happening.
2. The cost of the new platform is very high, which means the project needs to be performed at a very low margin and higher management support may not be there. This is very likely to happen, and without higher management support the project will come to a halt. Thus, this is a high impact and high likelihood risk.
3. This being a new technology, the skill set of the resources will not be high and, thus, there will be a risk of missing the deadline. This is also a likely higher risk as the platform is a new one and there won't be trained resources readily available. But, the impact can be greatly reduced as the vendors who create new software, arrange for training the resources too. Thus, the impact is less for this risk.
4. The existing employees of the organization may not be ready to work on a new platform. This is less likely to happen and the impact is also low as there is an option of getting new people from the market and getting them trained in this platform.

So, if we plot these four-risks within the four squares, then it will look like Figure 4.7.

Case Study: ROI, NPV and IRR

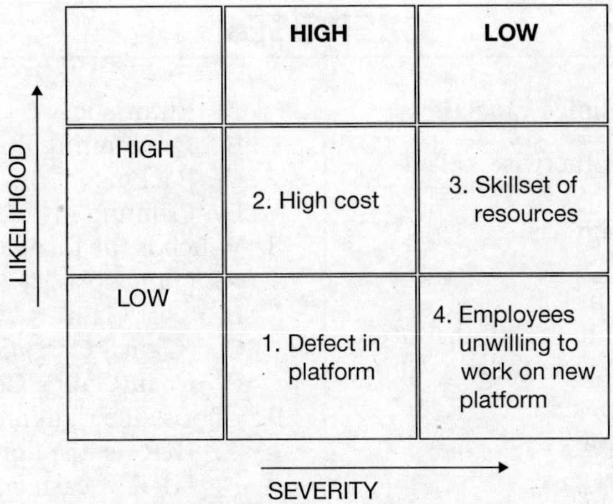

Figure 4.7 Four Square Method Example

SUMMARY

This chapter discusses the various investment evaluation techniques, like ROI, NPV and IRR.

- **Market and Demand Analysis:** Market and demand analysis is critical as the facility, capacity and location planning can only be taken up based on the market demand and project viability. An incorrect market analysis may lead to flawed facility and capacity planning, which in most cases, is irreversible. Evaluation of an investment proposal should always be backed by a strong market and demand analysis leading to correct forecasting.
- **Cash Flow Forecasting:** Cash flow forecasting provides the estimation of cash flow over time. At the beginning of the project, the cost is greater than the benefit which gives a negative cash flow, meaning—a need for investment.
- **Risk Evaluation:** Risk evaluation is meant for analysing whether the project will be able to meet its objectives and to decide whether to proceed with the project or not. It also helps in shortlisting the projects to proceed with, from a list of projects, based on the risks associated with each of them.
- **Payback Period:** Payback period is the unit of time (amount of time) required to recover (get back) the initial amount invested. This is the time required for the cumulative income from the project to become equal to cumulative expenditure on the project.
- **Net Present Value (NPV):** It is the accurate value of all the future inflow or outflow in the business in today's value (Present Value). The cash flow summary adjusted to reflect the time value of money is called Discounted Cash Flow (DCF). This analysis takes into account the series of cash flows happening in future and converts them to today's value.

  The aggregate of these cash flow streams is called 'Net Present Value'.

EXERCISES

Part A (Multiple-choice Questions)

1. Payback period is, otherwise, called
   A. Break
   B. Break-Even Point
   C. Profit Point
   D. Profit-Even Point
2. It is the accurate value of all the future inflow due to business in today's value.
   A. Future value
   B. Gross Present Value
   C. Present Value
   D. Net Present Value
3. Company usually accepts the rates which are greater than
   A. MIRR
   B. IRR
   C. MARR
   D. Cost
4. Which of the following is true?
   A. Money earned or spent today is worth more than money spent or earned in future.
   B. Money earned today is worth more than money earned in future, but money spent today is worth less than money spent in future.
   C. Money spent today is worth more than money spent in future, but money earned today is worth less than money earned in future.
   D. Money earned or spent in future is worth more than money spent or earned today.
5. MARR stands for
   A. Money Assured Rate of Return
   B. Maximum Assured Rate of Return
   C. Minimum Attractive Rate of Return
   D. Maximum Attractive Rate of Return
6. The rate at which organization discounts future money is known as
   A. Opportunity Cost
   B. Sunk Cost
   C. Overhead Cost
   D. Profit Cost
7. The process of moving future amounts back into the present value is known as
   A. Futuristic
   B. Discounting
   C. Backing
   D. Profiting
8. Which is the formula for ROI?
   A. Gain/Cost
   B. Cost/Gain
   C. (Gain – Cost)/Cost
   D. Cost/(Gain – Cost)
9. Choose the right answer.
   A. IRR is the interest rate in which NPV of cash flow is equal to 0.
   B. ROI of agile projects are usually lesser than the traditional way of executing projects.
   C. We usually choose projects with smallest NPV.
   D. The cost of termination in agile projects are much higher than the cost of termination in traditional projects.
10. If a project can bring in \$8 million in revenue for a total investment of \$4 million and, if profit margin is 20 per cent. ROI is
    A. 20%
    B. 40%
    C. 10%
    D. 5%

Part B (Answer in one or two lines)

1. What are the different types of demand forecasting techniques?
2. Write a note on qualitative demand forecasting techniques.
3. Describe different quantitative demand forecasting techniques.
4. What is strategic assessment?
5. Describe NPV with an example.
6. Describe IRR with an example.
7. What are the different risk evaluation techniques?
8. What is meant by cash flow analysis? Describe it giving an example.

5

Contract Management

5.1 Introduction

Contract management or contract administration deals with the management of contracts with the customers, vendors, suppliers and employees. An organization can wear different hats while dealing with different sets of people—sometimes as a vendor, sometimes as a customer or sometimes as a supplier. Contract management departments are the highly specialized teams. They often have representatives from finance and legal departments. Before going into the details of contract management, let's discuss the procurement processes and when we should get intó contracts.

5.2 Contract

A contract is a formal legally binding agreement between two or more parties, individuals, businesses, organizations, or government agencies, by which the contracted parties exchange goods or services of value with each other. Contracts also specify restrictions on certain actions of the contracted parties during the tenure of the contract.

Contract can also be used as a risk management tool as it is used for transferring risk of delivery from the parent organization to the contracted supplier. 'Centralized Contracting' refers to a separate contracting office that handles contracts for all projects of the organization. In 'De-centralized Contracting', a contract administrator is assigned for each project of the organization.

Force Majeure is a powerful and unexpected event such as hurricane or other disasters. It is a common clause in contracts which essentially frees both parties from liability or obligation when an extraordinary event or circumstance happens beyond the control of the parties.

Points to Remember

Privity is a contractual information between customer and vendor (just between you and me), and it occurs most commonly in the contract of sale of goods or services. 'Horizontal Privity' arises when the benefits from a contract are to be given to a third party and 'Vertical Privity' involves a contract between two parties, with an independent contract between one of the parties and another individual or company.

The salient features of a contract are as follows:

- A contract may be written, using formal or informal terms, or it may be entirely verbal, although the former type is generally preferred. The terms of a contract for, that is, who, what, where, when, how, and which of the agreement—define the binding promises of each party to the contract.
- A contract clearly states the acceptance criteria of the contracted product or service. A contract is generally deemed fulfilled only if all its terms are fulfilled.
- Remedies for resolving differences that may arise during the period of a contract are also documented in it. The terms of a contract clearly define the actions—or inactions—of the contracted parties that constitute a breach of the contract, as well as force majeure conditions.
- A contract may be used as a risk management tool, because it transfers risk from the buyer to the seller. Organizations typically handle contracts either through a centralized contracting office, which handles all project contracts entered into by the organization, or through decentralized contract administrators, one of whom is assigned for each project executed by the organization.
- The terms of a contract should meet applicable legal requirements governing contracts to establish the validity of a contract.
- In a contract, a seller may be referred to as a contractor, sub-contractor, vendor, service provider, or supplier.
- In a contract, a buyer may be referred as a client, a customer, a prime contractor, a contractor, an acquiring organization, a governmental agency, a service requestor, or a purchaser.
- Depending upon the area of application, a contract is sometimes called an agreement, an understanding, a subcontract, or a purchase order.
- The roles of a buyer and a seller are pre-determined when teaming agreement document is present. A teaming agreement is an arrangement between different business entities to come together as a team in order to perform the activities of a particular project.
- If a buyer expects a seller to begin a high-priority, business-critical project immediately, then the seller needs 'letter of intent' or 'letter of contract' from the buyer to start work immediately.

5.2.1 Different Contract Types

Depending on the payment terms, contracts can of various types. These are:

Fixed-price Contract (Lump-sum Contract): This type of contract involves a fixed total price for the whole project and usually scope of the project is well-defined for this. The buyer knows what he is buying and the seller knows what he is selling and there is no confusion regarding the scope of the contract between the parties engaged. Fixed Prices contract with Economic Price Adjustment (FP EPA) is a fixed price contract which takes into consideration price changes due to inflation and market conditions, especially when the project duration is long.

Cost-reimbursable Contracts: This category of contract involves reimbursement to the seller the actual costs incurred by the seller, plus a fee typically representing seller's profit. Few subcategories of this type of contract are:

- **Cost-Plus-Fee (CPF) or Cost-Plus-Percentage of Cost (CPPC):** Seller is reimbursed for the allowable costs for performing the contract work and he receives a fee (this is the profit for the seller) calculated as an agreed-upon percentage of the costs.

- **Cost-Plus-Fixed-Fee (CPFF):** Seller is reimbursed for allowable costs for performing the contract work and also receives a fixed fee (this is the profit for the seller) calculated as a percentage of the estimated project costs. The fixed fee does not vary with actual costs unless the project scope changes.
- **Cost-Plus-Incentive-Fee (CPIF):** Seller is reimbursed for allowable costs for performing the contract work and receives a pre-determined fee, an incentive bonus, based on achieving certain performance objective levels set in the contract and, this is like performance bonus. In some cases, if the final costs are less than the expected costs, then both the buyer and seller benefit from the cost savings based upon a pre-negotiated sharing formula defined in the contract. Sometimes, instead of incentives, there may be penalties if the cost or time exceeds the stipulated units defined in the contract.

Time and Material (T&M) Contracts: T&M contracts are a hybrid type of contractual arrangement that contains aspects of both cost-reimbursable and fixed-price type arrangements. Here, the seller receives money per unit of time (say $X per hour) irrespective of the volume work accomplished.

Now, we are familiar with different types of contracts. Given here are the relative advantages and disadvantages of each type of contracts. Note, every type of contracts have their own benefits or constraints. Based on the project situations, contracts will be judiciously used.

Fixed-price

Advantages	Disadvantages
• Less work to manage • Seller has incentive to control costs • More company experience with this type of contract • Buyer knows total price	• Seller may charge extra on change orders • Seller may 'shortcut' Scope of Work • More work for buyer to write Scope of Work • More expensive than cost reimbursable—seller adds price for risk taking

Cost-plus-fixed-fee

Advantages	Disadvantages
• Lower cost than fixed price • Less work to write Scope of Work • Cheaper than fixed price, because seller does not add risk factor.	• Requires auditing • More work to manage • Seller has moderate incentive • Total price is unknown

Time and Materials

Advantages	Disadvantages
• Quick—simple form of contract • Brief contract • Good choice for hiring staff augmentation labour	• Profit is in every hour billed • Seller has no incentive to control costs • Appropriate for small projects

The main difference between these contract types: who is bearing more risk during the contract tenure, whether it is the buyer or the seller.

Salient Attributes of Different Types of Contracts

Contract Type	Contract Scope Definition	Risk	Payment
Fixed-price	Well-defined	Seller assumes risk	Fixed total
Cost reimbursable	Not well-defined	Buyer assumes risk	Per actual cost plus fee
Time and materials	Not well	Buyer assumes risk	Per unit of time seller spends on work activities

Figure 5.1 represents the risk spectrum for each types of contracts.

Exercise: Find and Match the Contract Type Based on the Situations Given Below.

The buyer will pay salaries for all the employees, rent for the office and the actual cost of Broadband and other communicative devices plus an additional $35,000 per month.	Cost Plus Incentive Fees
The customer will pay the vendor a total of $35,000 for one year for support services.	Time and Material
The customer will pay $25 per hour per resource but will not pay more than $20,000 per month.	Fixed Price
The customer will pay salaries of the employees, Internet and other communication services, rent and other facilities. An additional $4,000 per month for each month the vendor provides an average of 25 issues resolved per person per week with waiting time of the end users under four hours per issue.	Cost-plus-fixed-fee

Exercise: Answers

The buyer will pay salaries for all the employees, rent for the office and the actual cost of Broad band and other communicative devices plus an additional $35,000 per month.	Cost-plus-fixed-fee
The customer will pay the vendor a total of $35,000 for one year for support services.	Fixed-price
The customer will pay $25 Per hour per resource but will not pay more than $20,000 per month.	Time and Material
The customer will pay salaries of the employees, Internet and other communication services, rent and other facilities. An additional $4,000 per month for each month the vendor provides an average of 25 issues resolved per person per week with waiting time of the end users under four hours per issue.	Cost-plus-incentive-fees

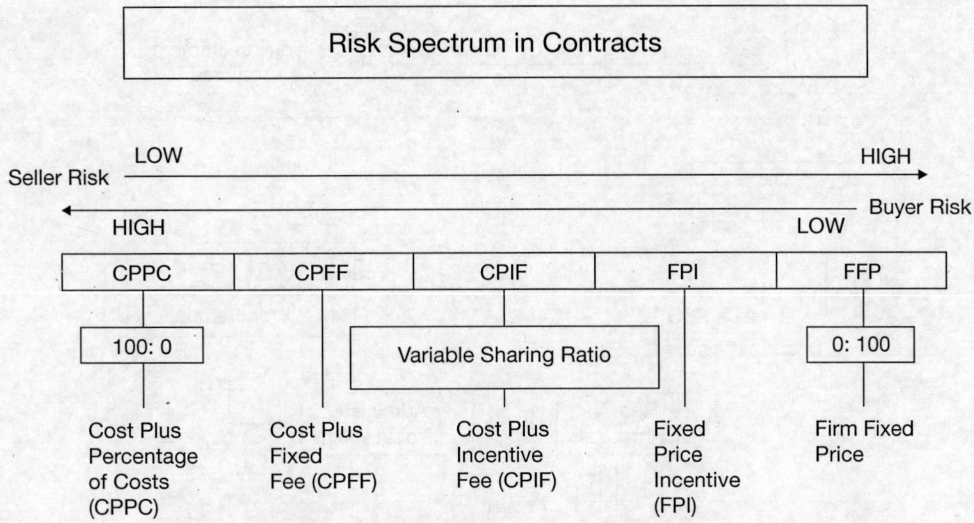

Figure 5.1 Risk Spectrums in Contracts

5.3 Contract Management and Procurement Process

Every organization gets involved in the procurement activities where the supplier is an important stakeholder. We all understand that an organization may not be able to create all the things itself that it needs for running a project and thus should buy or outsource few items. It is important to manage the procurement process effectively while executing a contract with the supplier. Thus, 'Contract Management' is a key focus area in each organization. One important activity that is taken up before even considering the contracts is the analysis of whether to create a work item internally within the organization or to get it created through a third party or vendor. This is called 'Make or Buy' analysis.

5.3.1 Make or Buy Analysis

Make or Buy analysis is used to determine whether a particular product can be produced cost effectively by the performing organization or must be procured from outside the organization. The flowchart in Figure 5.2 explains this process.

The goal of Make or Buy analysis is to determine whether to acquire outside support and, if so, then:

1. What to acquire?
2. When to acquire?
3. How to acquire?
4. How much to acquire?

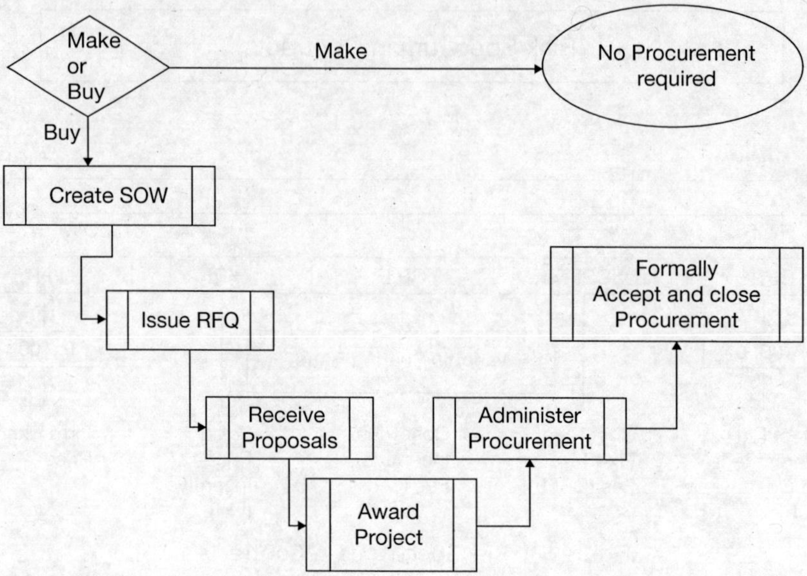

Figure 5.2 Contract Management Flow

The analysis includes the consideration of:

- The indirect and direct costs of in-house manufacturing.
- Any extra capacity or resources that may be available within the performing organization during the course of project execution.
- Possible use of proprietary or business critical activity of the performing organization that may represent its core business or core competency.

Make or Buy decisions are governed by a simple rule: The option that entails lesser cost while ensuring compliance to project scope requirements should be chosen. Although cost is the main criterion to decide the procurement, there are other factors which should be considered like competency level, skill sets, capacity level, and intellectual properties involved in the product.

For example, if the organization feels that it has the desired competency level, it can make the product, rather than outsource it. If the performing organization feels that a third party organization has better competency suitable for the product, then it may outsource the product instead of manufacturing the product in-house. The same is applicable for skill sets required for developing the product.

If the organization does not have the capacity to produce the required product, then it has no option than to go for outsourcing. Tailoring shops outsource to smaller shops during heavy demand periods like Diwali, etc. Demand level is also to be considered when taking a Make or Buy decision. If the organization does not have the required capacity then it needs to consider the cost of adding the required capacity before opting to outsource its business.

The organization also needs to consider the Intellectual Property (IP) rights associated with the product. While outsourcing, the organization needs to ensure that the product IP rights of the organization are not violated. If the product is very innovative, then it is better not to go for outsourcing.

Here is an example of the Make or Buy analysis.

Example: You are considering whether to buy or make a software product.

- If you buy, the cost is $60,000, and the cost of procurement and integrating in your company is $2,000.
- If you wish to develop the product yourself, it would require 7 software engineers to work for 3 months. Salary of each software engineer is $3,000 per month. The overhead costs apportioned to the project will be $1,000.

Choose the best option based on the given situation.

Answer: If you buy, cost is: $60,000 + $2,000, i.e., $62,000.
If you develop, cost is: $3,000 × 7 × 3 + $1,000 = $64,000.

So, it is better to buy where the cost is less and save $2,000.

However, the real-life procurement decisions are seldom simple.

5.3.2 Contract Planning

The contract or procurement management plan (a component of the project management plan) describes how a project team will acquire goods and services from outside the performing organization. The procurement management plan describes how the procurement processes will be managed and carried out, from developing procurement documentation through contract closure. In the process, the purchasing decisions in the project and the goals get documented. The approach and the process of procurement are detailed here with the objective of identifying potential sellers. The following are the contents of a typical procurement management plan.

- Types of contracts used and description about it.
- Process for managing multiple providers.
- How procurement will be coordinated effectively.
- Standardized documents to be used for procurement process.
- Identifying pre-qualified selected sellers, if any.
- Constraints and assumptions of procurement process.
- Evaluation criteria for procurement.
- Procurement metrics to be used to the procedure to collect it.

The typical checklist used for creating an effective procurement management plan looks quite similar to the list as given here. It ensures that all the important points are covered in the plan.

- What type of contract is to be used?
- Is there any risk or issue in the proposed contract?
- Is there any need for performing independent estimate as one of the contract evaluation criteria?
- Whether the performing organization has a prescribed procurement, contracting, or purchasing department.
- Is there any need for standardized procurement documents?
- How to manage multiple suppliers?
- How to coordinate procurement with other project aspects, such as scheduling and performance reporting?
- Is there any constraints and assumptions that could affect planned procurements?
- How to handle the Make or Buy decisions and link them to Resourcing and Scheduling activities?

Procurement Management Plan also tries to provide a guideline of how to shortlist a vendor or supplier from multiple bidders. This is called 'source selection criteria'. It is included as a part of the procurement documents so that the sellers are also aware of the same. Some possible source selection criteria are as follows:

- **Understanding of need:** How well does the seller's proposal address the procurement statement of work?
- **Overall or lifecycle cost:** Will the selected seller produce the lowest total cost of ownership (purchase cost plus operating cost)?
- **Technical capability:** Does the seller have, or can the seller be reasonably expected to acquire, the technical skills and knowledge needed?
- **Risk:** How much risk is embedded in the statement of work, how much risk will be assigned to the selected seller and how does the seller mitigate risk?
- **Management approach:** Does the seller have, or can the seller be reasonably expected to develop, management processes and procedures to ensure a successful project?
- **Technical approach:** Do the seller's proposed technical methodologies, techniques, solutions, and services meet the requirements stated in the procurement documents or are they likely to provide more or less than the expected results?
- **Warranty:** What does the seller propose to warrant for the final product, and for what time period?
- **Financial capacity**: Does the seller have, or can the seller reasonably be expected to obtain, the necessary financial resources?
- **Production capacity and interest:** Does the seller have the capacity and interest to meet potential future requirements?
- **Business size and type**: Does the seller's enterprise meet a specific category of business such as small business (disadvantaged, specific programs, etc.) as defined by the organization or established by governmental agency and set forth as a condition of the agreement award?
- **Past performance of sellers:** What has been the past experience with the selected sellers?
- **References:** Can the seller provide references from previous customers verifying the former's work experience and compliance with contractual requirements?
- **Intellectual Property right:** Does the seller assert intellectual property rights in the work processes or services they will use or in the products they will produce for the project?
- **Proprietary right:** Does the seller assert proprietary rights in the work processes or services they will use or in the products they will produce for the project?

Figure 5.3 reflects the flow of contract management process.

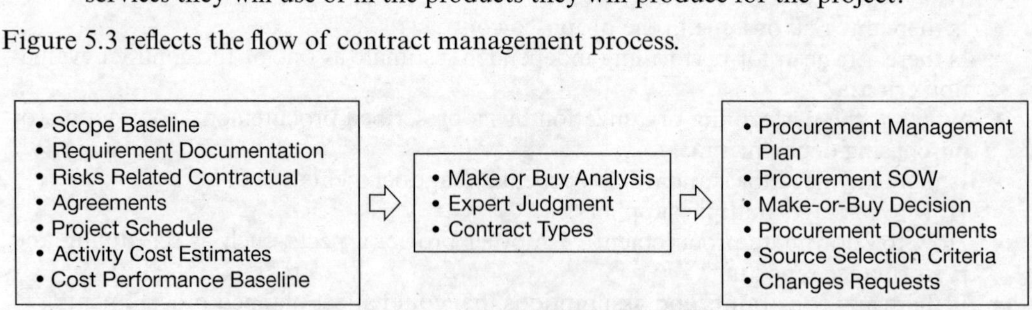

Figure 5.3 Contract Planning Flow

5.3.3 Contract Documentation

Contract or procurement of documents are used to seek proposals from prospective sellers when the buy decision is taken. Terms such as bid, tender, or quotation are generally used when the sellers selection decision is based on price and terms. Request for proposal is generally used when considerations such as technical skills or technical approach are given significant weightage.

Contract Statement of Work (SOW)
A contract Statement of Work (SOW) is the outcome of Plan Procurement process and after which the buyer issues a Request for Quotation (RFQ) to receive proposals.

SOW is the document wherein the seller describes the work to be completed and/or the product to be delivered. The description is in sufficient detail to enable prospective sellers to determine whether they are capable of effectively handling the contracted work or not. At the end of the Contract Planning phase the Contract SOW is issued, following which the buyer issues a Request for Quotations (RFQ). Interested sellers would return the RFQ with their proposals. The SOW document may not be complete in terms of full project scope at the beginning. It is further refined into the project scope statement in the project initiation and planning stages.

Request for Quotation
Requests for quotation (RFQ) is generally used when the decision to select sellers is expected to be based largely on quotation submitted. This is used for projects, usually of low dollar value and when the vendor's other related information like their competency level, and unique capabilities are known in advance.

Request for Proposal
Requestsfor proposal (RFP) is generally used when the decision to select sellers is expected to be based largely on prospective sellers' technical skills or unique capabilities. When an organization submits the proposal, it should include its unique capabilities like organization strength, competency level, number of projects executed similar to the proposed project, and other appropriate data like customer feedback. It takes more time to write a RFP compared to a RFQ.

Request for Information
Request for information (RFI) is generally used when the decision to select sellers is expected to be based largely on the information provided.

Procurement Agreement
A procurement agreement includes terms and conditions, and may incorporate other items that the buyer specifies regarding what the seller is to perform or provide, it is the project management team's responsibility to make sure that all agreements meet the needs of the project, while adhering to the organizational procurement policies.

The components in an agreement document may include the following:

- Statement of work or deliverables
- Schedule baseline
- Performance reporting
- Period of performance

- Roles and responsibilities.
- Seller's place of performance.
- Pricing rationale and payment terms. Frequency or milestones for the payments, late payment fees, reasons for non-payment. As a response to inaccurate invoices, the buyer cannot stop all payments. They can, however, stop payments on disputed amounts.
- Place of delivery.
- Inspection and acceptance criteria.
- Product support.
- Limitation of liability.
- Fees and retainer—Whether an amount of money, usually 5 percent or 10 percent, will be withheld from each payment. This money is paid when all the final work is completed and helps ensure completion.
- Penalties/Incentives—Will the seller receive any benefit for aligning with the buyer's objectives of time, cost, quality, risk and performance?
- Insurance and performance bonds.
- Subordinate subcontractor approvals.
- Change request handling.
- Termination clause and dispute resolution mechanisms.
- Force Majeure—A situation that can be considered an act of God, such as fire or freak electrical storm, which is an allowable excuse for either party not meeting contract requirements. If a force majeure occurs, it is considered to be no one's fault. It is usually resolved providing the seller with an extension of time on the project.
- Waiver clauses.
- Warranties—Promises of quality for the goods or services that are delivered under the contract, usually restricted to a certain time period.
- Intellectual property—Ownership of the intellectual property (patents, trademarks, copyrights, processes, source code, books) used in connection with or developed as part of the contract. This may also include warranties of the right to use certain intellectual property in performance of the contract.
- Material Breach—if there is a breach that is so large that it may not be possible to complete the work under the contract.

The buyer and the seller both will administer the procurement contract for similar purposes. Each of them ensures that both parties meet their contractual obligations and that their own legal rights are protected. The legal nature of the contractual relationship makes it imperative that the project management team knows of the legal implications of actions taken when controlling any procurement.

5.3.4 Contract Execution

It is the process of collecting seller responses, selecting seller based on the criteria defined, and awarding contract. In this process, the client team will receive bids, quotes or proposals and will apply previously defined selection criteria to select one or more sellers who are qualified to perform the work.

As discussed, RFP and RFQ are the two means used for getting the proposal and price quotes from the seller. There are several steps that are taken to analyse the responses or proposal to identify the best suited one.

Bidders' Conference—Meetings with prospective sellers are held prior to the preparation of a proposal to clarify doubts, if any. This conference also clarifies doubts on the procurement process.

- Bidder conference ensures that all prospective sellers have a clear, common understanding of the procurement.
- Responses to seller's clarifications by the buyers may be incorporated into the procurement documents as amendments.

Proposal Evaluation Techniques—There are different techniques available to rate and score proposals. In addition to performance criteria defined in the procurement document, expert judgment is also being used to evaluate the proposals. The criteria for selecting the seller should be defined well in advance, and these criteria may already be an organizational process asset. The criteria may include price, past performance of seller, seller's technical capabilities, years the company has been in business, creativity of solution, etc. The criteria will be weighted based on importance.

Independent Estimates—Most of the time, the procuring organization prepares its own independent estimates of the costs to validate the pricing in the proposals. Without independent estimates, it is very difficult to cross check the pricing given in the proposals.

Advertising—Placing advertisements in general-circulation publications, newspapers, or in specialty publications, such as journals is a common way to call for proposals. Indian Railways use newspaper as a mode of getting proposals from vendors. There are some clients who advertise only within a closed circle asking them to take part in bidding process. For example there are bigger organizations that have their own Offsite Development Centres (ODCs) and they advertise only among these ODCs for bidding.

Figure 5.4 shows a contract execution flow.

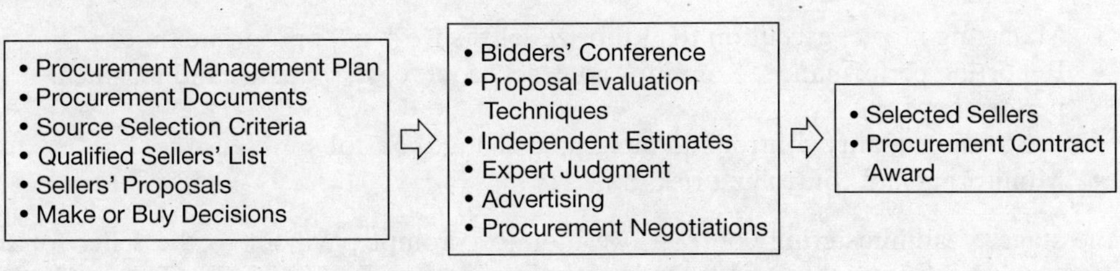

Figure 5.4 Contract Execution Flow

5.3.5 Contract Negotiation

The aim of contract negotiation is to create a mutually acceptable result in terms of scope, price and other criteria. This kind of mutual agreement should be reached prior to signing the contract.

The classic definition of contract reveals the five rights of contract or procurement, which are the actual preferences or interests of professionals during a contract negotiation. The five rights are:

1. The right quality as agreed.
2. In the right quantity as agreed.

3. At the right time as agreed.
4. From the right place as agreed.
5. At the right cost as agreed.

The aim of contract negotiation in its barest form is to get mutual agreement for these five rights.

Selected Sellers: At the end of the contract execution and contract negotiation, the sellers who have been judged to be in a competitive range based upon the outcome of the proposal or bid evaluation are selected. With these selected sellers, a draft contract is negotiated which will be the actual contract when an award is made.

Procurement Contract Award: A contract is awarded to each selected seller and one project may be awarded to multiple vendors also. The contract can be in the form of a complex document or a simple purchase order and is a mutually binding legal agreement that obligates the seller to provide the specified products, services, or results, and obligates the buyer to pay the seller as per the terms defined in the contract.

5.3.6 Administer Contract

After the contract is agreed upon it should be monitored and managed closely. Administer Contract is the process of managing procurement relationships, monitoring and managing the contract performance and making changes and corrections as needed in the contract terms. The project team must be aware of the legal implications of actions they can take or face during administration of the contract.

The project management processes related to procurement are as follows:

- Managing project execution to authorize seller's work at appropriate time.
- Reporting performance to monitor contract scope, cost, schedule and technical performance.
- Performing quality control and integrated change control.
- Monitoring and controlling risks.

At the stage of administering contract, we monitor prompt payment to the seller for the contracted work. Contract can be amended anytime in accordance with the Change Control terms of the contract. Such amendments may not always be equally beneficial to both the buyer and the seller.

Contract Change Control System: It defines the step by step process through which the contract may be modified. It includes:

- Paperwork, if any.
- Tracking systems for changes.
- Dispute-resolution procedures during execution.
- Approval procedures of CRs.
- Performance reporting about contract.
- Payment system as per contract.

Inspections and Audits: Inspections and audits are required by the buyer and supported by the seller as specified in the contract can be executed to identify any weaknesses in the seller's work processes or deliverables. Audits of the contractor facilities are mandated by several quality management standards as well. An important objective of inspections and audits is to report on seller performance. Performance reporting refers to the communication from the project management team to the performing organization's management on the performance of contractors as per contract terms. To this end, audits generate information on the effectiveness of the seller in delivering on contractual obligations, deviations if any from the terms of the contract, and the performance levels of the seller with respect to the service level agreements spelled out in the terms of the contract.

Performance Reporting: It involves information about how effectively the seller is achieving the contractual objectives? Is there any deviation from the contract? What is the performance level of Service Level Agreement if any, set for contract?

Payment System: Payments outstanding to the seller are handled by an accounts payable system of the performing organization. It must follow appropriate reviews and approvals made by the project management team. The payments system, which is jointly implemented by the project management team and accounts payable department, tracks payment per the terms of the contract and reports on deviations, if any. The project management team, in its own interest, should implement processes to ensure that payments outstanding to the compliant sellers are made on time. Obviously, sellers would appreciate on-time payments, which is likely to have a direct bearing on quality and the schedules of the deliverables.

Claims Administration: Contested changes are those changes to the contract requested by the buyer or the seller with regard to which the buyer and the seller have not been able to agree. These contested changes are called 'claims, disputes, or appeals'. Claims are processed, monitored, and managed throughout a contract's life cycle, usually in accordance with the terms of the contract. Outright disputes are best resolved through negotiated settlements; legal processes, such as arbitration and litigation are, generally, the least preferred among the dispute resolution options available.

Records Management System: A records management system refers to a specific set of processes mostly related to contract control functions and automation tools. These are consolidated and combined into a whole as part of a project management information system. It is used by project managers to manage contract and procurement documentation and records.

Figure 5.5 shows a step-wise workflow that takes place during the contract administration process.

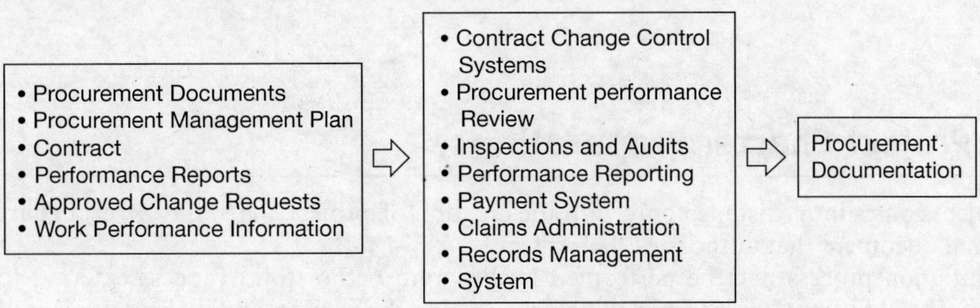

Figure 5.5 Contract Administer Flow

5.3.7 Contract Closure

Settlement and completion of the contract, including resolution of any open items is involved in the contract closure stage. It includes product verification and administrative closeout.

Procurement documentation (input for closure) includes, but is not limited to:

- Signed contract.
- Supporting schedules for the contract.
- Requested and approved contract changes and its documents.
- Seller-developed technical documentation for the projects.
- Seller performance reports for the contract.
- Financial documents of the contract.
- Contract-related inspection results, if any.

Procurement Audits: Structured and well established reviews of the procurement process, from procurement planning through administer procurements. It helps to identify successes and failures (lessons learned). Procurement audit is usually planned and conducted at regular intervals.

Negotiated Settlements: Resolving disputes through negotiation is a primary goal, but when everything fails, then litigation in the court (least preferred) is the only solution.

Closed Contracts: The buyer provides the seller (through its authorized contract administrator) a formal written notice that the contract has been completed. Requirements for formal contract closure are usually defined in the terms of the contract, and usually is a part of contract management plan.

Updates of the Organizational Process Assets are generated by a complete set of indexed contract documentation, including the closed contract', by adding the 'deliverable acceptance' and by adding the 'lessons learned and best practices documentation.'

During the initiation phase of the project, it is decided what portion of the project will be done in-house and what will be outsourced to an external vendor. For the part that will be done in-house it is very important to get it started with proper understanding of the scope and right stakeholders are engaged. Project charter preparation is the phase during which the project is formally started in an organization.

5.4 Project Charter Preparation

A project comes into existence only with the creation of project charter. A project charter is a formal document that authorizes the project.

Initiation process may be performed by Program or Portfolio Process external to the project. Feasibility study is conducted before selecting the project, and it also sets clear objectives for the project.

Some salient features of project charter are:

1. It formally authorizes the project or the Current Iterative Cycle.
2. It documents the initial requirements of the current iterative cycle that satisfy the Stakeholder's needs and expectation.
3. In multiphase project this process is used to validate or refine the decisions made during previous iterations.

The contents of a project charter are as follows:

1. Requirements that satisfy the customer, sponsor, and other stakeholders' needs, wants and expectations.
2. Business needs, high-level project description or product requirements.
3. Project purpose or justification for the project.
4. Assigned Project Manager (Iterative Cycle Manager) and her authority level.
5. Stakeholder's influences.
6. Functional organizations and their participation.
7. Organizational, environmental and external assumptions/constraints.
8. Business case justifying the project, including ROI and summary budget.

Project Charter Sign-off: A project charter is not complete until we receive sign-off from the project sponsor. The charter states the goals of the project and deliverables, if any, and the time, resources, and costs needed to meet those defined goals. Project charter keep changing throughout the course of the project.

The important inputs to the project charter are SOW and business case. Figure 5.6 shows the process for developing a project charter.

SOW: This is the document given to the vendor by the customer. This explains how the customer expects the vendor to execute the project. It basically contains the narrative description of the products or services to be delivered as an outcome of the project. SOW is provided by the customer along with a request for proposal (RFP) document. Next time, before you start the project, please ensure that you have the SOW document of the project. It helps the vendor (executing organization) to serve the customer best.

The SOW References

1. **Business Needs:** Why the customer is doing the project? Is it based on market demand/ legal requirement/technological advance, etc.?
2. **Product Scope Description:** This is the main content of SOW which describes the characteristics of the product. The product requirements will, generally, have limited details during the initiation process.
3. **Strategic Plan:** It describes an organization's strategic goals.

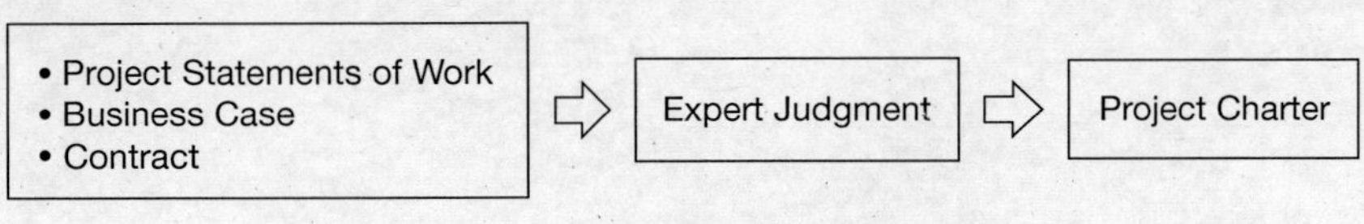

Figure 5.6 Project Charter Creation Flow

Business Case

It provides the necessary information from a business point of view to determine whether the project is worth the required investment. Business needs and the cost benefit analysis are the contents of the business case document. Customer provides the business case document.

Constraints and Assumptions: Project assumptions are defined as those factors that do not exist at the time of planning, but are considered to be true, real, or certain in the opinion of the project manager. Because of the inherent uncertainty regarding project execution, assumptions require to be made for planning of resources, vendors, start and end dates, contract signing, and the like. Of course, these assumptions need to be valid and demand judgment and experience from the project planners.

Constraints are the factors that limit the options of a project manager for project execution. These factors are considered as the primary risk factors for a project. A project may have more than one constraint at the same time. Such as scope-related constraints, quality-related constraints, team size-related constraints, schedule-related constraints, team experience-related constraints. For example, you may get only limited budget sanctioned for your project. It is a constraint on the project which is cost-related. Constraints may also be related with each other, and this increases the complexity, and limits options.

SUMMARY

- A contract is a formal legally binding agreement between two or more parties, individuals, businesses, organizations, or government agencies, by which the contracted parties exchange goods or services of value with each other.
- The make or buy analysis is used to determine whether a particular product can be produced cost effectively by the performing organization or must be procured from outside the performing organization.
- A project charter is a formal document that authorizes a project.
  - It formally authorizes a project or the current iterative cycle.
  - It documents the initial requirements of a CIC that satisfy the stakeholder's needs and expectations.
  - In multi-phase projects, this process is used to validate or refine the decisions made during previous iterations.

EXERCISES

PART A (Objective-type Questions)

1. Which of the following documents represent mutually binding agreements that obligates the seller to provide specified products or services?
   A. Procurement document
   B. Statement of work
   C. Contract
   D. Proposal
2. Depending on the application area of contracted work, a seller may be referred to use all of the following terms, except
   A. Contractor
   B. Vendor
   C. Service provider
   D. Purchaser
3. Which of the following types of contracts are typically preferred by customers?
   A. Firm-fixed price
   B. Time and material contract
   C. Cost reimbursable contract
   D. Cost-plus-percentage contract
4. Which of the following types of contract is used whenever a seller's performance period spans over many years?
   A. Firm-fixed-price
   B. Fixed-price-plus (with) incentive
   C. Fixed-price with EPA
   D. Cost reimbursable contract
5. All of the following factors are selection criteria used in selecting sellers, except
   A. Management approach
   B. Technical capability
   C. Technical approach
   D. Known company
6. When are bidder conferences held?
   A. Prior to submission of bids.
   B. After submission of proposals.
   C. After contracts have been entered into.
   D. After submission of proposals, but before contracts have been entered into.
7. A CPPC contract has an estimated cost of \$140,000, with an agreed profit of 20% of the costs. The actual cost of the project is \$120,000. What is the total amount to be reimbursed to the seller on the basis of the above figures?
   A. \$144,000
   B. \$140,000
   C. \$168,000
   D. \$120,000
8. A buyer expects a single price for a new project. What type of contract does the customer have in his mind?
   A. RFP   C. Proposal
   B. RFI   D. IFB
9. If a buyer pays a seller \$55 per hour plus material cost per actuals, then type of contract has been negotiated between the buyer and the seller?
   A. T&M
   B. Fixed bid
   C. Cost-plus-incentive
   D. Cost-plus-cost
10. If a buyer wants a seller to begin on a high-priority, business-critical project immediately. In such a situation, what would the seller need from the buyer to start the work immediately?
    A. RFP
    B. RFQ
    C. Letter of contract
    D. Letter of negotiation

PART B (Answer in one or two lines)

1. What is a contract?
2. Describe fixed-price and cost-reimbursable contracts.
3. Describe CPF, CPFF and CPIF types of contracts.
4. What is a T&M contract?
5. Discuss the relative advantages and disadvantages of different contract types.
6. Describe the make or buy analysis process.

6

User Management

6.1 Introduction

Every project involves multiple individuals or groups called 'stakeholders' who directly or indirectly get impacted by the project. So, keeping all these parties informed about the project progress, regularly communicating with them, dealing with conflicting interest requires considerable effort and planning.

Users represent important stakeholder groups who use or gain the benefits of the project outcome. A representative set of user groups at senior level is to be involved in the project with significant authority to take important decisions on behalf of the end users. They must be empowered to make important decisions about the project outcome.

6.2 Top Reasons for Project Failures

If we look into the prime reasons for project failures of many sources; lack of user involvement plays a top spot directly and indirectly with the following other reasons which are also related to users involvement.

1. Failure to set and manage expectations (user-related).
2. Failure to adequately identify, document and track requirements (requirement related to end users).
3. Cultural and ethical misalignment (usability related).
4. Misalignment between the project team and the business or end users' needs (user related).
5. Poor project team integration between clients, users and supply chain (user related).
6. Ineffective engagement with stakeholders (user related).

6.3 Usability

'Usability refers to the extent to which a product can be used by specified users to achieve specified goals with effectiveness, efficiency and satisfaction in a specified context of use.'

—ISO 9241-11

'Human-centered design is characterized by: the active involvement of users and a clear understanding of user and task requirements; an appropriate allocation of function between users and technology; the iteration of design solutions; multi-disciplinary design.'

—ISO 13407

Approximately 63% of software projects exceeds their estimates, with the top four reasons, all related to product usability. Evidence shows that product usability is the market differentiator of the future. 'If you do not do usability testing on your product, then the customer will do it for you, which will cost you more'.

Usability is the degree of UID consideration which takes care of making the system effective, efficient and satisfying for the users by taking into account the human psychology and physiology of the users. Usability is linked to the human psychology and physiology of the users of the system.

6.3.1 Measuring Usability

Effectiveness: A user's ability to successfully use a website to find information and/or accomplish tasks.

Efficiency: A user's ability to quickly accomplish tasks with ease and without frustration.

Satisfaction: How satisfied the user is with site.

Error frequency and severity: How often users make errors while using the system, how serious the errors are, and how users recover from the errors.

Memorability: A user's ability to remember enough to use the site effectively after his or her first visit.

(*Source*: www.usability.gov)

6.3.2 Five E-models of Usability

Effective: How completely and accurately the project tasks are completed or goals are achieved by end users—Indicators of effectiveness include learn ability, error prevention, and quality of navigation. The third key aspect of effectiveness is navigation. Users need to have a feeling of comfort about what they need to do in order to complete their task.

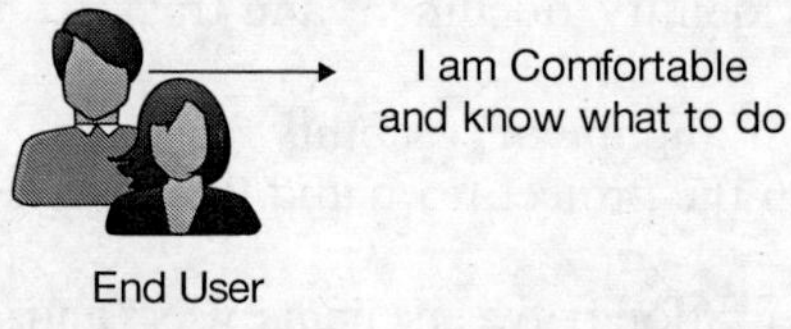

Efficiency: How quickly this work can be completed by the end users; efficiency is a simple measure of productivity—how fast a user can perform a set of tasks without making any errors.

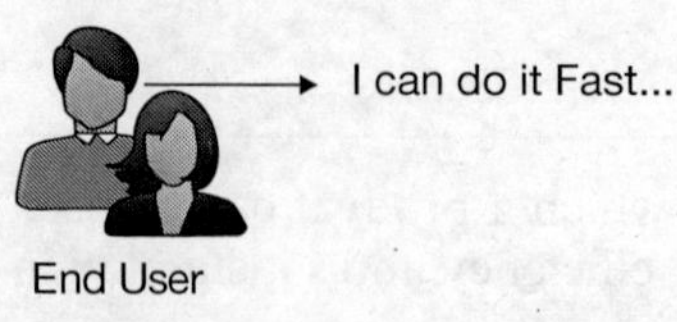

Engaging: How pleasant and satisfying it is to use.

Error Tolerant: How well the product prevents errors and can help the user recover from mistakes that do occur.
Easy to Learn: How well the product supports both the initial orientation and continued learning throughout the complete lifetime of use. The learn ability of a UI refers to the time it takes the user to learn how to use it.

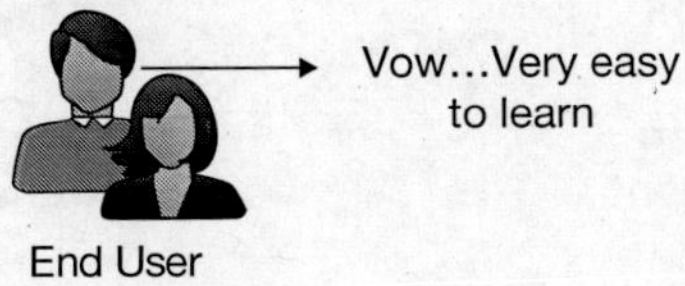

6.4 Role of Users in Projects

Systematic application of user-centered design techniques helps to build usability into the product or system. Project managers needs to move from customer centric project management approach to user centric project management approach, to avoid last minute failures. Involving users in the project management life cycle is of paramount importance for the project success. A user's role may vary from project to project and it depends on the features available to project users in the final product being developed.

6.4.1 Goals of User-centric Project Management

1. It improves project success rate. User involvement in project management contributes to 16% of project success.
2. Standardize the Collect Requirement Process. Clear statement of requirements contributes to 13% of project success.
3. Prioritizing usability in the project.
4. Best results are obtained from introducing usability engineering early into the development cycle, resulting in better initial designs and reduced development churn.

When users are involved in the project then it automatically fetches top management commitment, which contributes to 14% of project success. User involvement also fetches competent staff for the project (as it indirectly has top management commitment) which contributes to 7.2% of project success.

Considering the importance of user involvement, Project Management Institute (PMI) introduced (Figure 6.1) various processes which are related to user management in its project management standard, according to Project Management Body of Knowledge (PMBOK®). In the latest edition of PMBOK®, a new knowledge area called 'Stakeholder management' has been introduced.

User Role in Project Management

Users' need to be involved continuously in the project management life cycle. It consists of initiation, planning, execution, monitoring controlling and closing stage of the project.

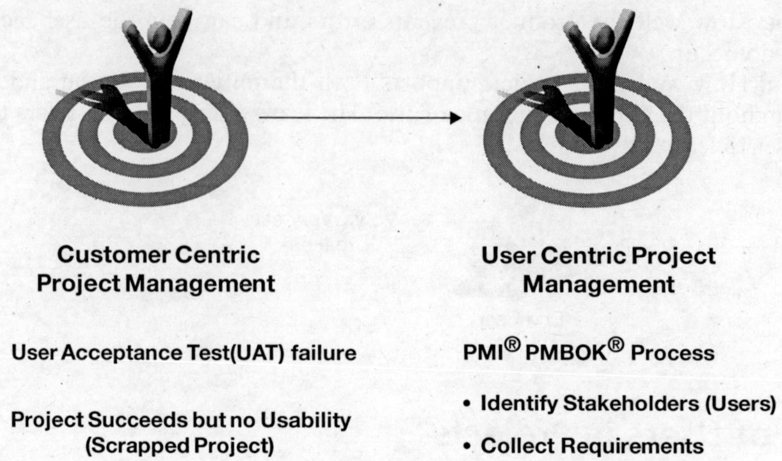

Figure 6.1 Importance of User Centric Project Management

Role of User in the Initiation Stage of the Project

1. Agree and commit the resources (users) required for the successful execution of the project.
2. Ensure the agreements are in line between end users and the project team.

User Role in the Planning Stage of the Project

1. Provide user requirements in terms of quality, functionality and ease of use.
2. Representing the interest of all users of the project deliverables.
3. Ensuring the end users' needs are accurately specified in the requirement documents.
4. Clarifying the project teams doubts related to requirements, quality and usability.
5. Defines acceptance criteria and quality criteria of the project with end user perspective.
6. Ensure user requirements are captured specified in the project plan accurately and completely.
7. Identify risks from end user perspective.
8. Posting unresolved user issues to project governance board for consideration.

User Role in the Execution and Control Stage of the Project

1. Verify processes and procedures and reviews to assess user requirements.
2. Act as a communication bridge between the end user community and the project team.
3. Monitor and report on the user aspects of the project continuously ensuring user needs.
4. Ensure scope validation of the project with strong user involvement.
5. Resolving conflicting user requirements.
6. Monitor and control risks identified from end user perspective.

User Role in Closure Stage of the Project

1. Ensuring the end solution meets the quality, functionality and ease of use.
2. Ensuring the end solution meets the user expectations realizing the business benefits.
3. Sign-off project deliverables against the agreed quality acceptance criteria.

6.4.2 Role of Users in Various stages of Software Development

Users' needs to be involved continuously in the project life cycle, which consists of requirement collection, design, coding, testing, implementation, etc. User goals, user needs, user connect (communication) and user testing are very important in the life cycle of the projects (Figure 6.2).

User Centric Requirement Gathering Activities

1. Identify the people who can determine the requirements.
2. They must have knowledge of the business need.
3. Hold requirements gathering workshops and interviews or other techniques.
4. Document the requirements.
5. Circulate requirements for review and feedback.
6. Make updates and seek sign-off.

Requirements of the project are nothing but user needs of the project; and reaching a consensus in gathering requirement is very important for the project success.

Consensus in Gathering User Requirements

A group reaches consensus when all members agree upon a single alternative, and each group member can honestly say: 'I believe that you understand my point of view and that I understand yours. Whether or not I prefer this decision, I support it and it is the best solution for us at this time.'

Reaching consensus is achievable with the following elements:

1. Communicate requirements effectively: Listen actively, pay attention to others, ask questions for clarification; do not assume intent.
2. Encourage participation by all: Make sure all user views are heard.

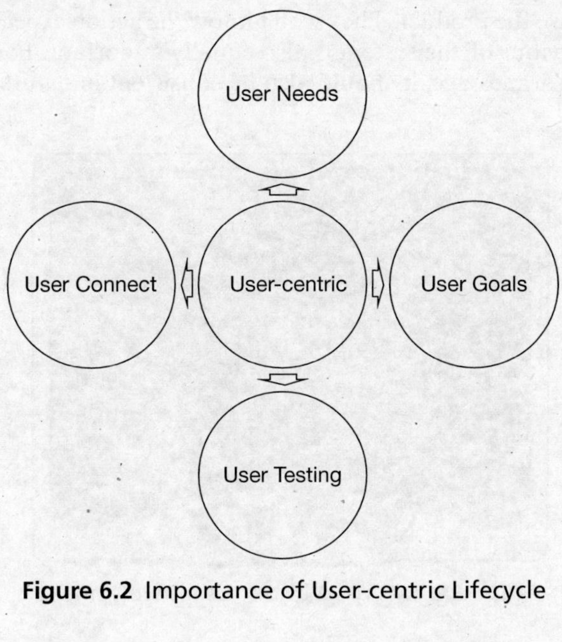

Figure 6.2 Importance of User-centric Lifecycle

3. Share information, interests, ideas and feelings.
4. Approach the problem with an open mind, not a preconceived solution.
5. Use the problem solving process—step by step.
6. Do not VOTE; do not bargain or trade support.

User-centric Design Activities

One important part of the design process is the User Interface Design (UID). It plays a crucial role in the success of software projects. UI is not only the reflection of the functionalities of the system, but also the reflection of culture of the end users. For example, white colour is the symbol of purity in Western cultures, whereas the same colour is the symbol of bad luck in India, Japan and China. Pink colour is appreciated in Japan, but not in India. If the portal/website is intended for particular demographics, then we need to choose the colours appreciated by that particular region.

Lets give an example that depicts the importance of UID.

Customer requirement is very simple here: They want to design a gas stove with four burners and four on/off switches for each burner. Now see the first cut design without user involvement. Can you identify the problem in this design (Figure 6.3)? The first (in the row) on/off switch is for which burner? Confusion arises right? Note: The following design works completely but users will find it difficult to use.

So what is the solution to solve the above problem? There can be multiple solutions but the following solution is cost effective (Figure 6.4). There seems to be no confusion with the below model on usability. This clearly shows the importance of user involvement in the design stage of the product.

Consistency in design across the product is also very important to avoid confusion with the user groups.

Without consistent representation, a user may struggle to understand what they are looking at for and how to use the product. They won't know the action expected (behaviour) from them. Consistent behaviour of the system is also equally important. For example: When the system pops out an error message, it should also be consistent in nature and understandable by everybody.

Figure 6.3 Design Without User Involvement

Figure 6.4 Design with User Involvement

Usability Testing

For any application the comfort of the end user is a very important requirement. The more the ease with which the users can learn and use the application the better it is. In usability testing the tester looks out for various aspects of usability like efficiency, intuitiveness, aesthetics and ergonomics. Usability testing has to be preferably done early in the lifecycle so that UI and workflow changes do not cause substantial rework later. Testers first get familiarized with the domain and application functionality. They identify the different roles, corresponding workflows and tasks performed by the end users. Each tester performs the identified tasks to evaluate the application for usability by identifying violations of usability standards, inconsistencies and overall look and feel. Then finally recommendations are made to rectify issues.

6.5 UID in Detail

One important part of the design process is the UID. UI plays a crucial role in the success of software projects. First impression is the best impression and hence first look into the UI should impress the end users. It is not only the reflection of the functionalities of the system but also the reflection of the culture of the end users. For example, white colour is the symbol of purity in Western cultures whereas the same colour is the symbol of bad luck in India, Japan and in China. Pink colour is appreciated in Japan, but not in India. If the portal/web site is intended for particular demographics then we need to choose the colours appreciated by that region. In addition to that, each colour has its own meaning (Figure 6.5) and it also needs to be considered while choosing the colour. Given here are the names of a few colours and their common meanings.

- **Black**: mystery, secrecy
- **Blue**: coolness, peace
- **Brown**: strength, stability
- **Gray**: maturity, reliability
- **Green**: life, naturalness, health
- **Orange**: warmth, courage
- **Red**: danger, energy, power, aggression
- **White**: purity, freshness, peace
- **Yellow**: happiness, brightness, joy

Figure 6.5 Colours and Their Characteristics

Usability measurement plays a crucial role in the success of any product and it is applicable for software systems and the portals also. In this chapter, let us see few important usability concepts and procedures of applying the same.

6.5.1 Concepts of User Interface

As shown in Figure 6.6, the three basic components of UI are:

- End users
- User interface
- System (machine)

A UI helps people (users) interact with a machine (system). UI includes its own software and hardware components which helps users interact with the machine (system).

UI input allows users to manipulate the system. UI output helps the users to understand the system behaviour. In general, UI helps for human machine interaction.

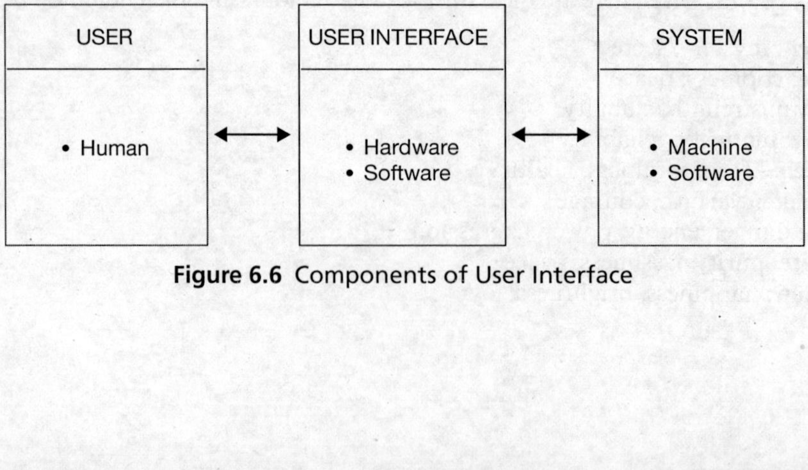

Figure 6.6 Components of User Interface

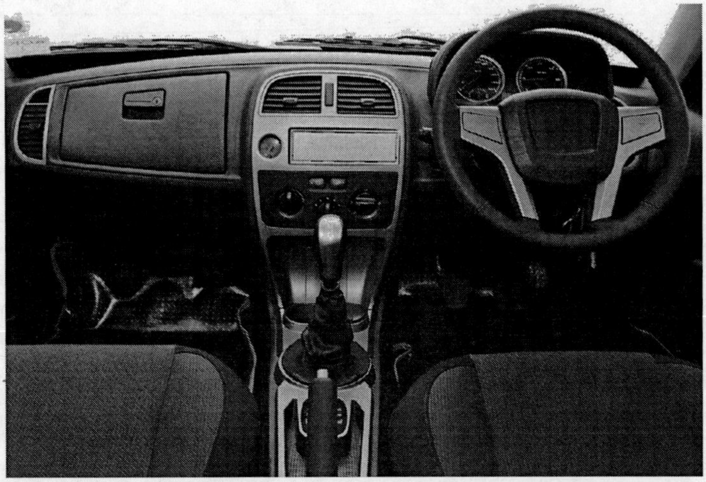

Figure 6.7 User Interface Example

For example, while driving a car, the driver (user) uses the accelerator, break, clutch, and gearing system to interact with the engine of the car (machine). They all act as user interface inputs. Speedometer, fuel level meters helps the driver to understand the engine. They act as user interface output (Figure 6.7).

The goal of the UI is to effectively control the machine (system) at the user's end and passing the feedback from the machine (system) back to the user in an efficient manner which helps the user to make decisions. It means the user needs to provide minimal input to achieve the desired output and stopping the machine to provide undesired output.

The design of the UI is directly linked to the disciplines of ergonomics and psychology.

The following is the definition of Ergonomic by International Ergonomics Association (IEA). (*Source*: www.iea.cc)

Ergonomics (or human factors) is the scientific discipline concerned with the understanding of the interactions among humans and other elements of a system which helps to optimize human well-being and overall system performance.

UI is also called HCI (human–computer interface) and NMI (man–machine interface).

6.5.2 Elements of the User Interface

User Interface has four elements (Figure 6.8), namely:

1. Users
2. Tasks
3. Contents
4. Environment

Users interact with the system through the UI. Tasks are the activities performed by the users to interact with the system. Contents are the output of the system that is displayed to the users through the UI. The environment in which these tasks are executed are also part of the UI.

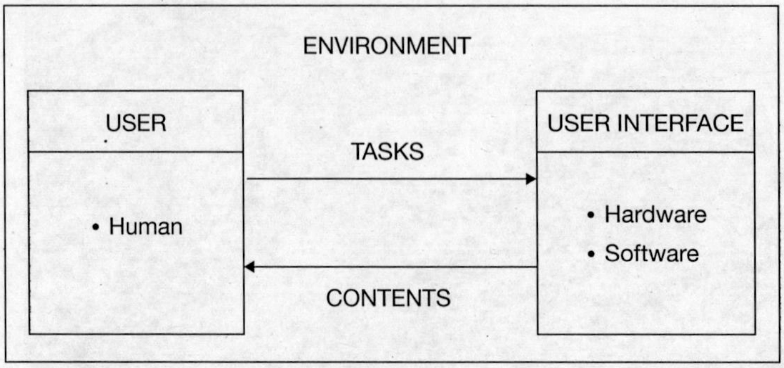

Figure 6.8 User Interface Elements

Based on the four elements, the analysis is also classified into four types:

1. User Analysis
2. Tasks Analysis
3. Contents Analysis
4. Environment Analysis

6.5.2.1 User Analysis

In User Analysis (Figure 6.9), we are trying to understand the end users as well as understand how the end users use the system which will help them to design the UI in better way. Information about the end users can be obtained directly from them in the form of interview and also by way of input from others who interact with the end users like sales, marketing and support people. We can prepare a basic set of questions that can be used to gather the information from all the above set of people.

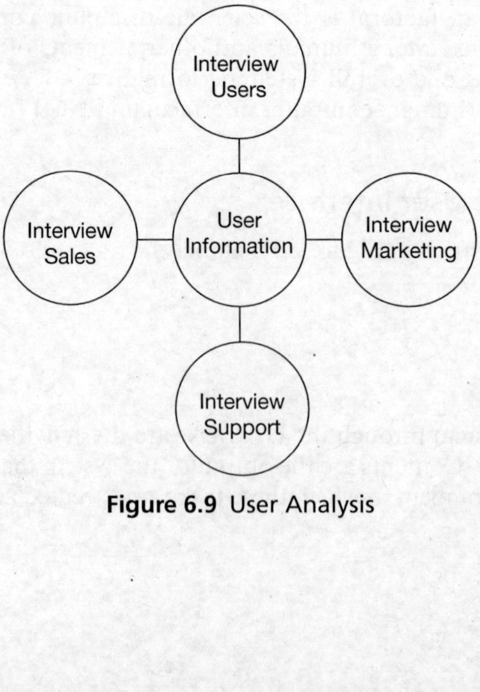

Figure 6.9 User Analysis

- User interviews conducted directly with the end users to understand the basic information about them, their likings, mental models, etc.
- Sales input (interviews) conducted with the sales people who interact with end users on a regular basis to understand more about the latter.
- Marketing input (interviews) conducted based on a market analysis to understand the likings of the segmentations.
- Support input (interview) happens to understand the likings of the users and what will work and what will not work out.

User Analysis Questions

Following questions are samples of User Analysis questions which help to understand the end users.

1. What level of formal education does the user have?
2. Age of the user.
3. Home country of the user.
4. Gender of the end user.
5. Primary spoken language of the user.
6. Office hours of the user.
7. Is the system integral part of the user's work?
8. Can the user learn the system by looking into user manuals?
9. Is the user trained to use the system?
10. Does the user know the technology behind the system or want to know the technology?
11. Is the user is a Subject Matter Expert of the system?
12. Consequences if the user makes a mistake in the system?

6.5.2.2 *Task Analysis*

In 'Task Analysis' (Figure 6.10) we are trying to understand the tasks done by the end users under a specific circumstance. We try to understand the sub tasks done by the end users, its sequence levels, hierarchical levels, problems faced by the end users while executing the tasks As an output of task analysis, user case diagram is drawn which helps to understand how the end users perform the tasks along with the workflow of the interaction. It helps to understand the overall flow of the users as well as the tasks performed by the users.

Task Analysis Questions

Following questions are sample 'Task Analysis' questions which help to understand the tasks performed by the end users.

1. List of tasks performed by the particular end user.
2. What are all the sub tasks of the tasks described above?
3. What are all the sequencing levels of the sub tasks defined above?
4. What are all the hierarchical levels of the sub tasks?
5. How work flow moves from one user to the other?
6. Who is the next user acting on the task(s) performed by this user?
7. What is the duration of the tasks performed?

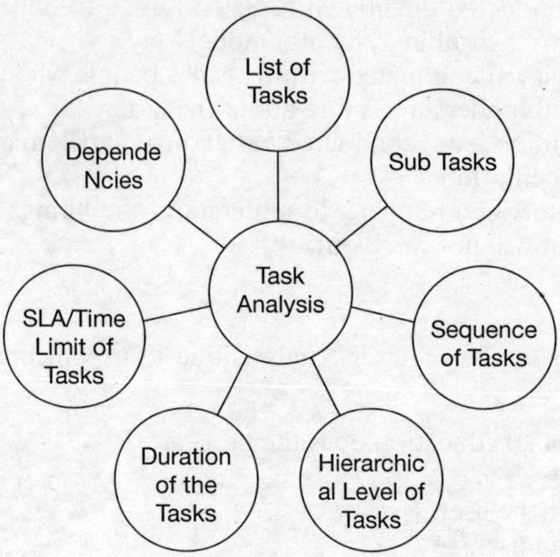

Figure 6.10 Task Analysis

8. Is the task performed manual or automated?
9. Is there any email communication to other users about the tasks?
10. Is there any Service Level Agreement set for the tasks with the customer?
11. Is there any time limit for the tasks to be performed?
12. Tasks depend on the external parties (inside and outside the organization)?

6.5.2.3 Content Analysis

Content Analysis (Figure 6.11) is an important element of the overall UI as it directly satisfies the end users. It helps the end users to understand the machine language. Content may be in

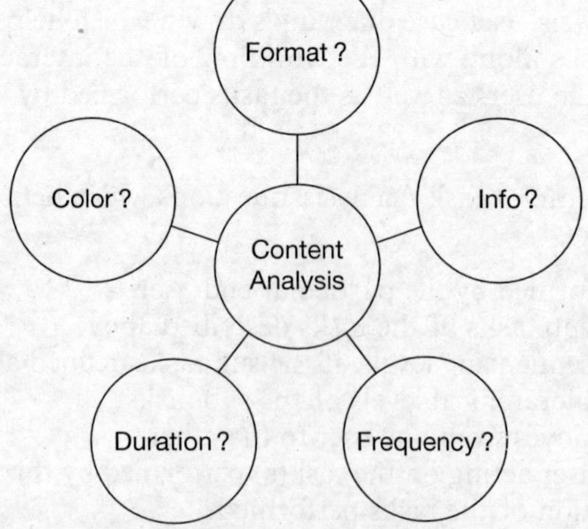

Figure 6.11 Content Analysis

the form of single word, graphical representation or in the form of sound files. For example, reverse guider fitted into the car gives a deep beep sound if there is any object nearby the car prompting the driver to apply the break. In few cars the reverse guider system also has a visual display in the front that can be used by the driver. Content analysis helps to understand the content requirement of the users. Display content may be acquired from already stored database of the system as well as data transmitted from external system to the application. For example: Radio system being used in a car. The format of the content is the main component of the study along with the data/information to be displayed.

Content Analysis Questions

Following questions are sample 'Content Analysis' questions which help to understand the contents.

1. What information is required by the end user?
2. What is the form of content? (graphics tables, text)
3. What is the frequency of updation of the content? (is it LIVE update?)
4. How long the content needs to be displayed? (is it permanent display?)
5. Can the user customize the place holder of the information (content)?
6. How can colour be used to enhance the understanding? (RED/GREEN, etc.)
7. Can the user navigate through the information?

6.5.2.4 Work Environment Analysis

Work Environment Analysis (Figure 6.12) plays a crucial role to understand whether the designed product is fitting into the environment. For example, the intensity level of the head-

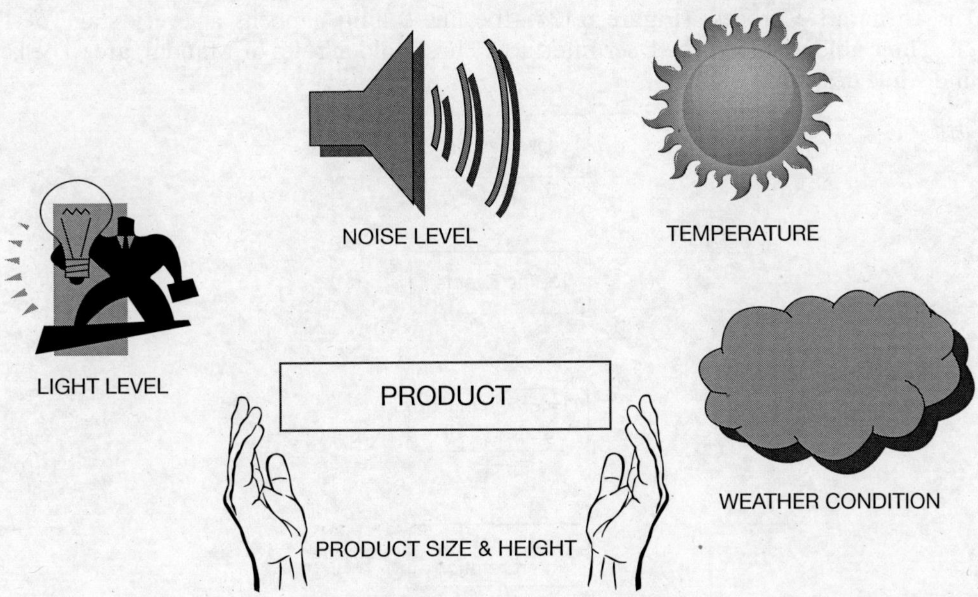

Figure 6.12 Environment Analysis

light in a car will always be higher than the intensity of the light used inside the car. Both are bulbs, but the light intensity levels vary and it depends on the environment in which it operates. Same logic is applicable to software products also. For example, surrounding noise level plays a crucial role while designing an audio/video system.

Environmental Factors to be Analysed

1. Surrounding temperature
2. Surrounding noise level
3. Surrounding light level
4. Time restrictions if any
5. Weather condition
6. Space (place size) limitation
7. Product size, height
8. Input device to be used
9. Size of the input device
10. Output device to be used
11. Size of the output device
12. Alternatives Input and Output device

Point to Remember

Based on the four elements the analysis is also classified into four types: User Analysis, Tasks Analysis, Contents Analysis, Environment Analysis.

6.5.3 Designing the User Interface

UID is an iterative process (Figure 6.13)—the fine-tuning happens at every stage of the design. Three golden rule of the User Interface (Three golden rules of Mandal) are to be kept in mind while designing the UI.

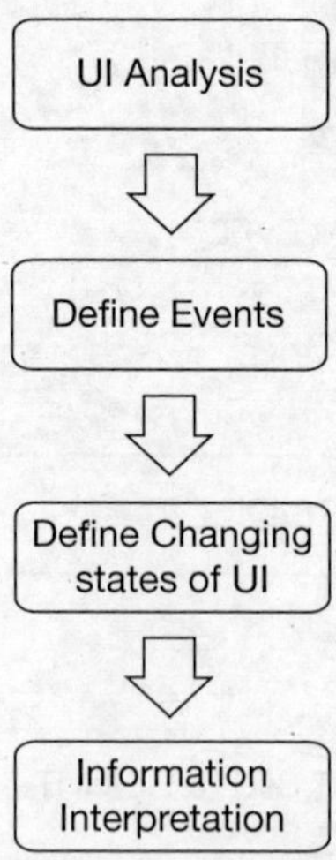

Figure 6.13 User Interface Design

Three golden rules of Mandal are:

- Place users in control
- Reduce users' memory load
- Make the interface consistent

UIDs Steps:

1. Do User Interface Analysis (User Analysis, Tasks Analysis, Content Analysis, Environment Analysis)
2. Define the events changing the UI state
3. Depict the UI state
4. How the user interprets the stats of the system from the information provided

UID starts with the analysis of the UI which we already discussed above. The questionnaires prepared will help the designer to understand the users, tasks, contents and the environment better.

Events consists of series of actions (tasks) performed by the end users. Events are performed on the Interface Objects through clicks, reading, writing, etc. So we need to define the Interface Objects and the corresponding actions of the users. Interface objects are classified into Source Objects, Target Object, and Application Object. Source Objects are placed over the target object. Application Objects represents the applications and are specific to the application for example 'List' data displayed on the screen. After identifying the objects, the designer needs to identify the actions performed by the objects (Figure 6.14). Interface designer creates the layout of the screen (Screen Layout) after identifying all the objects and its actions.

Screen layout design generally involves the following steps:

1. Graphical design of the overall screen.
2. Placement of icons and place holders.
3. Proper titling to the screen and place holders.
4. Definition of menu items and its actions.
5. Placement of objects on the place holders and its actions.
6. User help facilities (Help menu).
7. Appropriate error message.

Designing Dialogue

Sequence in which the information is displayed (output) and obtained (input) from the end users is called dialogue. In other words, dialogue is the sequence in which the information is exchanged between the end users and the system.

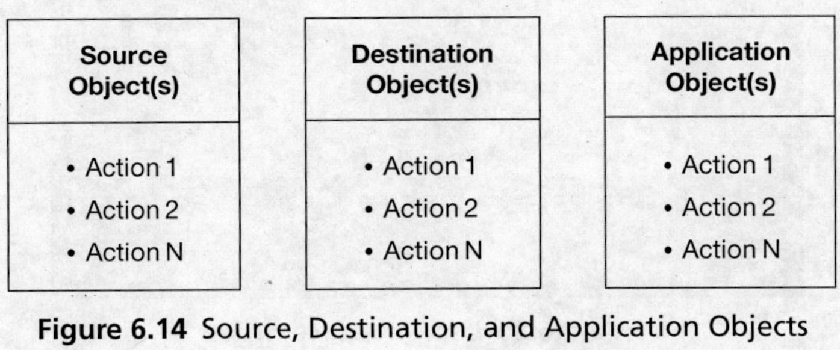

Figure 6.14 Source, Destination, and Application Objects

Three major steps in designing the dialogue are:

1. Designing the sequence of information (dialogue)
2. Building a prototype for the dialogue
3. Assessing usability of the dialogue using prototype

Guidelines for designing the dialogues are:

1. Simple and easy
2. Maintain consistency
3. Maintain the sequence
4. Focus on control

6.5.3.1 Common UID Issues

1. Improper error messages to the users (Figure 6.15).
2. No proper menu labelling.
3. Improper help facilities to the users.
4. Response time of the system.

UI should convert the system errors which are technical in nature into a user specific error message which is understandable by the users in their business language. Basically we need to covert the technical message into a simple business message, so that it is easy for business users to interpret and act accordingly.

Following are the characteristics of the error messages:

1. It is easily understandable and non-judgmental.
2. The message should not blame the end users under any circumstance.
3. The message should also use visual cue so that the end users understand it easily.
4. The message should indicate the reason for the error (For example: Input File format is not correct, etc.).
5. The message should indicate advice to overcome the current situation (For example: Input File format is not correct. Please correct the format and try this option again).
6. Even successful transaction is to be shown to the customer in the form of message. (For example: Application successfully submitted. Please check the email for the next step).

Figure 6.15 User Interface Issues

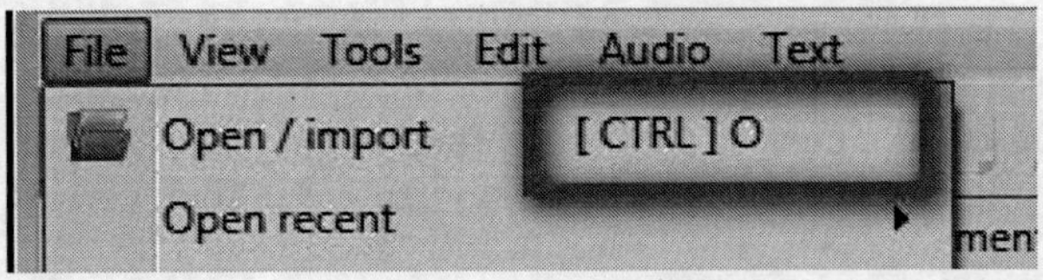

Figure 6.16 Menu

Menu labelling is to be designed in such a way that it is easy and consistent across all the screens. It should have the internationalization facility if required. It should also display consistently across all environments.

Menu labelling should address the following (Figure 6.16):

1. Are all menu labels self-explanatory?
2. Short cut options available for menu actions? (Example: CTRL O, etc.)
3. Can menus be customized by the users?
4. Are sub menus consistent with the main menu?

Help manuals should describe all the scenarios of the system and it should be written in easy language so that any novice can understand and use the system. Response time of the system is very important and it needs to be taken care of even while designing the UI.

6.5.4 User Interface Evaluation

While evaluating the UI we need to act as a pseudo user experiencing the system, thereby come out with the difficulties we are facing which in turn can lead to the improvement action plan.

Factors to be considered while evaluating/reviewing the UI:

1. Time spent by the users to perform tasks.
2. Response time of the system (each screen and actions).
3. Amount of learning the users should undergo.
4. Memory load on the users.
5. How easy the help and error messages are?
6. Complexity of the UI look and feel (how easily the users are able to understand what he needs to perform).
7. Check UI rules being followed in the design.

6.5.5 Golden Rules of UID

Three golden rules of Mandal are:

- Place users in control.
- Reduce users' memory load.
- Make the interface consistent.

Source: theomandel.com/resources/golden-rules-of-user-interface-design/

Each rule has its own sub-rules.

The first main rule is placing the users in control, which includes providing customizable screen based on the user profile, proper help, providing proper navigation of the system, providing different options to the customers for interacting with the system, interactive display system etc. By providing control to the users, they feel as if they own the system and start liking the system.

The second main rule is reduce users' memory load—which includes providing visual cues, promoting visual clarity, provide interface short cuts, etc. By reducing the users' memory load, it becomes easy for the customer to use the system.

The third main rule is making the interface consistent. This is not only to ensure keeping the look and feel of the users consistent across the pages but also includes continuity from one screen to the other in terms of experience, expectations, predictability.

Points to Remember

Three famous golden rules of Mandal are:

- Place users in control.
- Reduce users' memory load.
- Make the interface consistent.

6.5.6 User Interface Models

6.5.6.1 User Profile Model

In this model the entire UID is based on the user profile of the system like his age, gender, general experience, education level, culture, personality, frequency of usage (novice user, intermittent user, frequent users), knowledge (syntactic and semantic).

Steps for user profile model:

1. Establish the profile of the users and capture all the profile information above.
2. Capture the knowledge of the users (syntactic knowledge, semantic knowledge).
3. Identify the frequency of usage (novice, intermittent, frequent user).
4. Design the UI based on the user profile defined.

6.5.6.2 Design Model

In this model the UI is derived (designed) based on the requirement of the system. Entire design is constrained by the information depicted in the requirements. Requirements include the interface, data, and architectural requirements.

6.5.6.3 Implementation Model

This model looks into the requirement and sees the best possible way of implementing the requirements. So it takes care of the look and feel of the interface as well as the requirements of the system. This model is also in alignment with user's mental model, thereby users feel comfortable using it. It links the user profile model with user's mental model.

6.5.6.4 *User's Mental Model*

This takes care of the user's perception of using the system. User's mental model is considered before designing the UI. Accuracy here depends on the user's profile because user profile and user mental model are related to each other.

6.6 Role of Users in System Implementation

Systems implementation consists of two phases, namely:

1. Construction of the new system.
2. Delivery of that system into production environment.

User involvement in system implementation is critical to its success. In order to get the acceptable of the system (2nd phase of system implementation) it is better to involve the users in the beginning stage itself (1st phase of system implementation). User participation in the requirement gathering, design, testing and then delivery of that system (operation of information systems) has several positive results. Implementing user knowledge and utilizing their expertize leads to better long lasting solutions and users also will react positively to the entire change process of system implementation. Construction of the new system (Phase 1) is done by team of information system specialists who usually have different levels of knowledge, skill sets, experience, interests, priorities than the people who will be using the system (Users of phase 2). This is generally referred as the user-designer communications gap. Success of the overall system implementation largely depends on narrowing down this user-designer communication gap and so professional project managers will concentrate on this aspect during system implementation.

Users always will have the following common doubts in their mind regarding the system:

1. Will the implemented system change the way I (user) work currently?
2. Do I need to learn different skill sets to use the implemented system?
3. How quickly can I learn the system?
4. Will the new system implement all the functionalities I currently do?
5. Will the system deliver the information I need, to do my work?
6. How easily can I retrieve the data required to do my work?
7. What will happen if some problem occurs in the system?
8. What levels of data security is implemented in the system?

Requirements that are to be implemented into the system are to be prioritized appropriately based on the needs of the user and market signals. End users are to be educated on how best to communicate their needs to the developer. Implementation team needs to be educated on the importance of user involvement in the system life cycle. Without end users' involvement in the system implementation stage, the end product may not meet the user needs. End users should have knowledge on their company's strategy and business process. They also transfer that knowledge to the vendors who will build the system. They receive questions and doubts from the end users community and the system implementation team. End users representative should have the knowledge to generate answers to both the parties with the help of other parties and his own knowledge and competencies.

We can classify the roles of users in the overall system implementation into four types namely:

- Organizational role
- Competency role
- Education and training role
- System coach role

Organizational role involves in deciding and finalizing the time of roll out (system implementation), deciding on tasks to be carried out before the implementation date, forming a controlling committee who are the owners of the tasks; Commissioning a communication model involving various stakeholders so that the communication is smooth; Forming a governance model ensuring the system implementation is on time; Clarifying doubts; resolving conflicts; Forming right information model along with communication, ensuring smooth flow of information to various stakeholders getting their buy-in and involvement for the system implementation.

Competency role is connected with competence and skills possessed by the key users. This role needs to utilize end users competency, knowledge, skills in order to ensure smooth implementation of the system. This role needs to know organization strategies, plans, process to carry out system implementation in multiple stages. This role needs to ensure that the key users actively participate in explaining as-is system to IT implementation team along with to-be system expectations also. In order to explain to-be system, they also need to have knowledge of Information Technology. The key users also get involved in checking the final system and give sign-off approval.

Educational and training role supports the IT implementation team for carrying out training to all the end users of the system once it is implemented (after going live). Competency role members can take this role easily but it requires different skill sets. They need to prepare complete training material about the system in a way that all the end users understand it clearly. This role needs to have training skills, presentation skills in addition to knowledge about the system and also possess the ability to present individual merits of the implemented system. This role also conveys the functionalities of the system to senior management who are not directly involved in the implementation process.

System coach role is taken by one of the key users of the system who is well-versed with the new implemented system. They are actually users with thorough system knowledge who also understands the company environment and the line of business. They act as change agents. They transfer their knowledge to the rest of organization's employees.

6.7 Stakeholders and Their Characteristics

Involving appropriate stakeholders at appropriate time in the project increases the success probability of the project and hence in addition to involving users we also should know how to involve other stakeholders of the project. Stakeholders are those team members or entities who are actively involved in project execution or whose interests may be positively or negatively affected by project outcomes.

6.7.1 Stakeholders and Their Characteristics

The following list presents Stakeholders salient characteristics:

- Stakeholder interests may be either positively or negatively impacted by the project.
- Alternatively, stakeholders may influence project execution and project results.

- It is important for project planners to identify all stakeholders and their requirements. Sometimes individual stakeholder requirements may be implicit and not explicitly stated. For instance, in one of the requirements gathering workshop, a customer said that he wanted a 'world class system' When he was probed further, it came to be known that he wanted a system with background in golden colour and transaction response time of 5 seconds.
- Stakeholders may have conflicting interests and objectives—Managing stakeholders may not so easy.
- Involving stakeholders in the initiation phase group improves the probability of a positive outcome for the project.
- In general, differences among stakeholders must be resolved in favour of the customer or end user.

Point to Remember

Stakeholders can be positively or even negatively influenced by the project.

6.7.2 Identifying the Stakeholders

There exists no hard-and-fast rule to be applied in stakeholder identification. Rules for judging stakeholder involvement is always situation specific: Rules that work in one situation may not work in another. The best way to identify stakeholders is by asking the right questions. The questions given in the following list are guidelines—a preliminary road map—and by no means exhaustive:

1. Who are the team members, entities, or organizations likely to be affected or to benefit from the intended project outcome?
2. Who would be assigned responsibility for the tasks entailed by the project?
3. Who is likely to move for or against the intended objective of the project?
4. Who can make improvements to the tasks entailed by the project? (Who can do it the better way?)
5. Who can contribute to the financial and technical resources required by the project?

Answers to these questions, which would vary across organizations, are likely yield a list of stakeholders. Procurement documents are the main inputs of this process along with the project charter.

Procurement documentation helps to identify stakeholders referred to in the contract and procurement documents.

The three main steps in identifying the correct stakeholders are as follows (see Figure 6.17):

Step 1: Identify all potential stakeholders and relevant information

Step 2: Identify the potential impact or support each stakeholder could generate and use a power/interest grid to classify them

Step 3: Assess how the stakeholders are likely to react or respond in various situations to help plan influencing them to enhance support or mitigate negative impacts.

Step 1: Project managers use group dynamic techniques, whereby key project team members are asked to identify all possible stakeholders of the project. The Crawford slip is another popular technique used for this purpose. This technique can be used to rapidly collate ideas from a large group of people.

Figure 6.17 Identify Stakeholders

Crawford is actually one of the original forms of brain-writing. The sponsor who pays money for the project is a key stakeholder. Individuals who sign on the project deliverables (usually customers) are stakeholders. The organization that executes this project is also a stakeholder as it stands to benefit through project execution. The organization that buys the outcome of the project is also a stakeholder since its members are benefitted. The organization that provides resources for executing the project is a stakeholder. Project managers, team members, and functional managers are stakeholders. You can identify new stakeholders by asking the existing stakeholders.

Step 2:

Stakeholder Register

The stakeholder register carries the following elements:

1. Identification elements of stakeholder
2. Influencing stage of the stakeholder
3. Classification of stakeholder

Figure 6.18 shows the contents of stakeholder register. It usually contains name, designation, influence stage, classification. Depending on their skill levels stakeholders will be involved in the appropriate life cycle of the project and this is called influence stage. For example, stakeholders having high proficiency level in designing will get involved only in the designing stage of the project.

In Figure 6.18, R. Ramya and K. Balachandran seems to have high proficiency in design and so are being involved only in the design stage of the project. There are people who continuously involve throughout the life cycle of the project. In this figure, Pavan Kumar, the application manager, involves continuously throughout the life cycle of the project because of the nature of the work he handles. Stakeholder classification like 'supporter', 'neutral', and 'resistor' depends on the nature of the stakeholders. If they are negatively impacted by the outcome of the project, they are classified as 'supporters'. They are classified as 'neutral' if they are neither 'supporters' nor 'resistors'.

Name	Designation	Influcnce stage	Classification
Pavan Kumar	Application Manager	All	Supporter
Siva Ranjani	Technical consultant	Design, Coding	Neutral
R.Ramya	Architect	Design	Resistor
Shri Krishna	Business Manager	All	Neutral

Figure 6.18 A Stakeholder Register Template

Step 3

Stakeholder management is a difficult task requiring the formulation of a comprehensive stakeholder management strategy. Stakeholder analysis involves the following steps:

- Identify all potential project stakeholders and relevant information, such as their roles, departments, interests, knowledge, expectations, and influence levels.
- Analyze the potential impact or support each stakeholder could generate, and classify them so as to define an approach strategy. In large stakeholder communities, it is important to prioritize the stakeholders to ensure the efficient use of effort to communicate and manage their expectations.
- Assess how key stakeholders are likely to react or respond in various situations, in order to plan how to influence them to enhance their support and mitigate potential negative impacts.

A stakeholder analysis matrix is a tool used to represent a project's stakeholder management strategy.

The following would be the contents of a stakeholder analysis matrix:

1. Stakeholder name
2. Stakeholder impact level
3. Stakeholder interest level
4. Strategies for gaining support from this stakeholder

A typical stakeholder analysis matrix may be obtained by adding a column to the stakeholder register template (Figure 6.18) titled 'Strategies for Gaining Support'. This strategy is based on the classification of the customer defined in Step 2 along with the influencing stage of the customer defined in Step 3.

Stakeholder Classification Model

Figure 6.19 shows three stakeholder classification models based on the power and the interest, influence and impact grids.

Model 1: Classifies the stakeholders based on Power and Interest

Model 2: Classifies the stakeholders based on Power and Influence

Model 3: Classifies the stakeholders based on Power and Impact

Power indicates the level of authority of a person; Interest indicates the level of concern a person has on the project; Influence indicates the level of involvement shown on the project; Impact is the effect due to the level of involvement.

	POWER (LEVEL OF AUTHORITY)	INTEREST (LEVEL OF CONCERN)	INFLUENCE (LEVEL OF INVOLVEMENT)	IMPACT (EFFECT OF INVOLVEMENT)
POWER		MODEL1	MODEL2	MODEL3
INTEREST	MODEL1			
INFLUENCE	MODEL2			
IMPACT	MODEL3			

Figure 6.19 Stakeholder Classification Model

Another popular stakeholder classification model is the Salience Model (Figure 6.20), which is based on the power, urgency and legitimacy grids. Power indicates the level of authority of a person; Urgency indicates the need for immediate action and Legitimacy indicates whether the involvement is appropriate or not. A grid (Venn diagram) is drawn based on the above three factors to find out the type of stakeholders.

6.7.3 Managing the Stakeholder Engagement

Project Managers need to engage stakeholders throughout the lifecycle of a project in order to utilize them better for the success of the project. Most of the time, bringing in the right people will solve most of the problems. While we engage stakeholders, we may come across a few issues that need to be managed with our communication skills, management skills and interpersonal skills. Issues can be managed with proper planning by creating an issue log that helps to compile, analyze and manage the issues.

Project communication with stakeholders is an important part of any project. A project manager needs to establish lines of communication with all stakeholders and also develop a mechanism to keep them involved and aware of the project's progress and status. Stakeholder management plan defines an approach to communications and a mechanism to provide project data to stakeholders. The stakeholder management plan can be formal or informal, highly detailed or broadly framed, based on the needs of the project. In addition to the data gathered in the stakeholder register, the plan often provides:

- Desired and current engagement levels of key stakeholders.
- Scope and impact of change to stakeholders.
- Identified interrelationships and potential overlap between stakeholders.
- Stakeholder communication requirements for the current project phase.
- Information to be distributed to stakeholders, including language, format, content, and level of detail.
- Reason for the distribution of that information and the expected impact to stakeholder engagement.
- Time frame and frequency for the distribution of required information to stakeholders.
- Method for updating and refining the stakeholder management plan as the project progresses and develops.

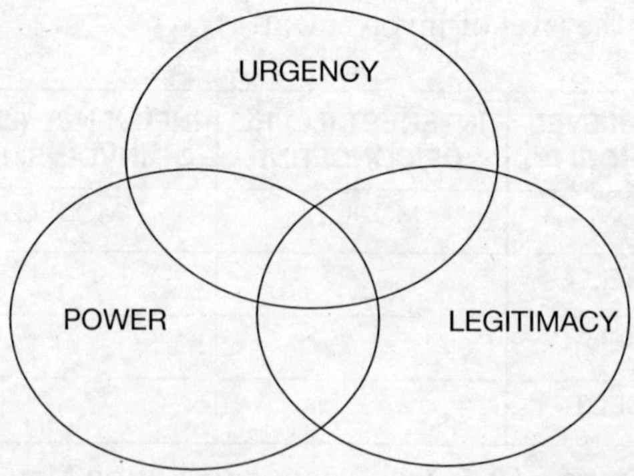

Figure 6.20 Salience Model of Stakeholder Classification

It may be necessary to develop different strategies for the different groups identified during the collect requirement process. Some possible methods of communication are:

- Progress reports
- Meetings and briefings
- User groups (email groups)
- Access to documentation (requirements)

Meetings

To resolve an issue in a way that is realistic and accepted by the stakeholder, it is better to conduct team meetings while addressing issues. This meeting should also be attended by other stakeholders such as project sponsors and others who are responsible to contrive a solution to the problem at hand. The project manager can also conduct this meeting with selected team members who have good knowledge of the matter of contention.

Reporting Systems

Reporting systems are standard tools that help to capture, store and distribute the information needed to manage and control stakeholders, thereby helping to resolve open issues. These also help managers to report the performance and progress of a project in resolving issues.

SUMMARY

Usability: '[Usability refers to] the extent to which a product can be used by specified users to achieve specified goals with effectiveness, efficiency and satisfaction in a specified context of use.'—ISO 9241-11.

'Human-centered design is characterized by' the active involvement of users and a clear understanding of user and task requirements; an appropriate allocation of function between users and technology; the iteration of design solutions; multi-disciplinary design.'—ISO 13407

Goals of User-centric Project Management

1. It improves Project Success Rate. User involvement in project management contributes to 16% of project success.
2. Standardize the Collect Requirement Process. Clear statement of requirements contributes to 13% of project success.
3. Prioritizing usability in project.
4. Best results are obtained from introducing usability engineering early into the development cycle—resulting in better initial designs and reduced development churn.

Consensus in gathering User Requirements

A group reaches consensus when all members agree upon a single alternative, and each group member can honestly say 'I believe that you understand my point of view and that I understand yours'. 'Whether or not I prefer this decision, I support it and it is the best solution for us at this time.'

User Centric Design Activities

One important part of the design process is the UID. It plays a crucial role in the success of software projects. UI is not only the reflection of the functionalities of the system but also the reflection of the culture of the end users. For example, white colour is the symbol of purity in Western cultures, whereas the same colour is the symbol of bad luck in India, Japan and in China.

Pink colour is appreciated in Japan, but not in India. If the portal/website is intended for particular demographics then we need to choose the colours appreciated by that particular region.

User Interface

User Interface (UI) is not only the reflection of the functionalities of the system but also the reflection of the culture of the end users.

Usability measurement plays a crucial role in the success of any product and it is applicable for the software systems and the portals also. In this chapter let us see few important usability concepts and procedures of applying the same.

A User Interface has three basic components, namely

- End Users
- User Interface
- System (Machine)

User Interface has four elements, namely

1. Users
2. Tasks
3. Contents
4. Environment

Based on the four elements, the analysis is also classified into following four types

1. User Analysis
2. Tasks Analysis
3. Contents Analysis
4. Environment Analysis

In user analysis, we are try to understand the end users as well as how the end users use the system which will help them to design the UI in a better way. Information about end user's can be obtained directly from them in the form of interview and also by way of input from others who interact with the end users, like sales, marketing and support people.

In task analysis, we are try to understand the tasks done by the end users under a specific circumstance. We try to understand the sub-tasks done by the end users, its sequence levels, hierarchical levels, problems faced by them while executing the tasks. As an output of task analysis, user case diagram is drawn which helps to understand how the end users perform the tasks along with the workflow of the interaction.

Content analysis is an important element of the overall UI as it directly satisfies the end users. It helps the end users to understand the machine language. Content may be in the form of single word, graphical representation or in the form of sound files.

Work Environment analysis plays a crucial role as the designed product is fitting into the environment. For example, the intensity level of the headlight in a car will always be higher than the intensity of the light used inside the car.

The three golden rules of Mandal are:

- Place users in control
- Reduce users' memory load
- Make the interface consistent

Designing Dialogue: Sequence in which the information is displayed (output) and obtained (input) from the end users is called 'dialogue'. In other words, dialogue is the sequence in which information is exchanged between the end users and the system.

Common UID issues:

1. Improper error messages to the users
2. No proper menu labelling
3. Improper help facilities to the users
4. Response time of the system

We can classify the roles of users in the overall system implementation into four types, namely

- Organizational role
- Competency role
- Education and training role
- System coach role

There are no hard-and-fast rules applicable for identification of stakeholders.

Rules for judging stakeholders' involvement is always situation-specific, Rules that work in one situation may not work in another. The best way to identify stakeholders is by asking them right questions. The questions given in the following list are guidelines. It is a preliminary road map and by no means exhaustive.

The stakeholder register carries the following elements:

1. Identification elements of stakeholder
2. Influencing stage of the stakeholder
3. Classification of stakeholder

Stakeholder Classification Models:

Model 1: Classifies the stakeholders based on Power and Interest

Model 2: Classifies the stakeholders based on Power and Influence

Model 3: Classifies the stakeholders based on Power and Impact

EXERCISES

PART A (Objective-type Questions)

1. User Interface is not only the reflection of the functionalities of the system, but also a reflection of the culture of the end users.
A. True B. False

2. Blue colour indicates
A. Mystery, secrecy
B. Strength, stability
C. Purity, freshness, peace
D. Coolness, peace.

3. Which of the following is not an element of User Interface?
A. Users C. Environment
B. Contents D. Business Logic

4. Sequence in which the information is displayed (output) and obtained (input) from the end users is called
A. Dialogue C. Environment
B. Output D. Interface

5. Which of the following is not part of common User Interface Design Issues?
A. Improper error messages to the users
B. Improper help facilities to the users
C. Response time of the system
D. Improper calculations

6. This model takes care of the user's perception of using the system.
   A. Design Model
   B. User's Mental Model
   C. Implementation Model
   D. Usability Model
7. The degree of UID consideration, which takes care of making the system effective, efficient and satisfying for the users by taking into account the human psychology and physiology of the users is called
   A. Usability
   B. User Satisfaction
   C. User Ability
   D. User Comfort Level
8. The main output of the identify stakeholders process is
   A. Risks register
   B. Stakeholder plan
   C. Stakeholder register
   D. Stakeholder management strategy
9. If stakeholder is having additional information needs, then which of the following documents would be updated?
   A. Stakeholder register
   B. Risk register
   C. Stakeholder management strategy
   D. Issue log
10. All of the following are content of stakeholder register except
    A. Assessment Information
    B. Identification Information
    C. Stakeholder Classification
    D. Urgency of the need of information
11. Following are the contents of stakeholder management strategy, except
    A. Key stakeholders who can significantly impact the project.
    B. Level of participation in the project desired for each identified stakeholder.
    C. Stakeholder groups and their management.
    D. Urgency of the need of information of stakeholders.
12. Who is responsible for stakeholder expectation management?
    A. Project leader
    B. Customer
    C. Project manager
    D. Project sponsor
13. Which of the following is the common way to represent stakeholder management strategy?
    A. Stakeholder register
    B. Risk register
    C. Stakeholder analysis matrix
    D. Stakeholder impact matrix
14. Your manager asked you to find an approach to increase the support and minimize negative impacts of stakeholders throughout the entire project life cycle. What did he ask you to create?
    A. Risks register
    B. Stakeholder plan
    C. Stakeholder register
    D. Stakeholder management strategy

PART B (2 Marks Questions)

1. List any three colours with its characteristics.
2. Name three basic components of User Interface.
3. List down the three golden rules of Mandal.
   Place users in control.
4. What is design model?
5. What is user's mental model?
6. What is implementation model?
7. Define usability.
8. What is Task Effectiveness?
9. What do you mean the term 'stakeholder of a project'?
10. List down three step process to identify stakeholders.
11. List down the contents of stakeholder analysis matrix.
12. What do you mean by power and urgency of stakeholders?
13. How is communication management related to project stakeholder management?

7

Requirement Management

7.1 Introduction

The software project life cycle starts with capturing the requirements of the project. A product is developed or a project is executed to capture requirements which takes them to the next level. Managing the requirements and its various stages, like gathering, documenting and disseminating requirements are the keys to the success of any project. Though it sounds easy, but gathering the requirements effectively and managing them efficiently is a complex task and need to be handled in a systematic manner. The requirement management principles help to perform this job in a better way.

According to industry average, more than 90% of the software projects fail due to faulty or incomplete requirement capturing. This certainly gives the idea of how important these steps are for the success of any software project. In this chapter, we will discuss the different aspects of requirement management with steps and guidelines.

7.2 Understanding Requirements—Needs

Before getting into the details of requirement management, we should understand what requirement is.

Definition of requirement in IEEE Std. 610.12-1990 is given as, 'a condition or capability needed by a user to solve a problem or achieve an objective'; and 'a condition or capability that must be met or processed by a system or system-component to satisfy a contract, standard, specification, or other formally imposed documents.'

This means requirements are originated from the user needs which are captured and tracked to satisfy the contracts, specifications and standards.

The definition of requirement management is:

> 'Project Management Institute (PMI) defines requirement management as the discipline or process of planning, monitoring, analyzing, communicating and controlling requirements. It is a continuous process throughout the project. It involves communication between project team members and stakeholders and adjustments to requirement changes throughout the course of the project.'
>
> —*Project Management Institute*

The whole range of activities related to requirements from inception and understanding it for tracking and maintaining the requirements is termed as requirement management.

7.3 Importance of Requirements

The requirements form the stepping stone of any project. If a software project starts without properly understanding the user needs or without exploring the multiple dimensions of the requirements, there will be misalignment at the end between the final result delivered and user's expectations from the project resulting in lot of reworks.

Usually, primary focus is only given to the construction stage of the software development which leads to lot of problems at the end.

Software project has the objective of completing the project within certain time and budget. The primary cause of schedule and budget overrun is the rework due to incomplete requirement understanding.

Figure 7.1 shows the relative cost of repairing a defect at each stage of software project life cycle. It is evident that, earlier an error is detected easier and cheaper is to fix it.

For example, if a problem in the requirement is found at the requirement's review stage, then it will cost less (say $X) to fix the issue, but as that faulty requirement percolates through later stages, it would costs more to fix the same, three times of the same cost to fix it during the design stage, 5–10 times of the same cost to fix it during the construction stage, 10 times of the same cost to fix it during the system testing stage of the project, 10–100 times of the same cost to fix it during post-release phase. So, identifying and fixing the errors at early stage cost less to the organization.

This signifies that, capturing the requirements fully and correctly at the early stage of the project is essential to keep the budget profitable. The only way to ensure this is to follow a disciplined requirement management process.

Point to Remember

The cost of fixing an error in the system increases exponentially with the stages of the project.

Cost to Correct an Error		Stage Detected				
		Requirement	**Design**	**Construction**	**System Test**	**Post-release**
Stages Introduced	Requirements	1X	3X	5-10X	10X	10-100X
	Design	–	1X	10X	15X	25-100X
	Construction	–	–	1X	10X	10-25X

Figure 7.1 Cost of Fixing Errors at Different Stages

7.4 Types of Requirements

Requirements are categorized into three main types. These are discussed here.

7.4.1 Functional/User Requirements

The set of requirements which defines what the system will do or accomplish are called functional requirements. These are the requirements which determine how the software will behave to meet certain user needs.

The requirements may be for performing some calculations, data manipulations, processing, logical decision making etc. which form the basis of the business rules. Functional requirements are often captured as 'Use Cases'. Functional requirements are the main driver for the application architecture of the system. An example of functional requirement is—a retail shop billing software must have the functionalities of capturing commodity prices, calculate the discounts, generate the bill, print the invoice etc.

7.4.2 Non-functional/System Requirements

Functional requirements are supported by non-functional requirements. The quality attributes, design and architecture constraints which the system must have possessed are called the non-functional requirements.

Some of the quality attributes of the system from end users' view are—performance, availability, usability and security.

Some of the system quality attribute from developers view are—reusability, testability, maintainability and portability.

The non-functional (system) requirements are critical in most of the software projects than the functional requirements. Non-functioanl requirements caters to the architectural needs of the overall system, whereas functional requirements caters to the design needs of the overall system.

The non-functional requirements may be related to the product or organization or the external requirements of the system.

Examples for product related non-functional requriements are—performance, availability, maintainability, portability, reliability, security, scalabability, testability and usability.

Examples for organization related non-functional requirements are—standard requriements, and implementation requriements.

Examples for external non-functional requirements are—legal requirements, ethical requirements.

Example of non-functional requirements are:

The system should be available 24×7 (Availability)

The system should save or fetch 1000 records in 1 second, etc. (performance)

Measuring Non-functional Requirements (NFRs): We need to first define measurable criteria for each non-functional requriements and, then realize the metrics by measuring it. For example, availability can be defined in terms of percentage first and, then define the duration within which we are going to measure it. In order to measure the availability, we can say that availability of the system in the past one week is 100% as the sytem was running continuously without any down time (another related metrics). A Service Level Agreement (SLA) is reached with the customer for setting an agreed level of availability depending on the stability of the system. If the system is more stable without any down time, we can fix the agreed limit of availability as 100%. If the system is not stable, then there will be frequent system shutdowns and target availability needs to be reducedaccordingly (say 90% or 95%).

Aproaches to NFRs: Non-functional requirement can be approached in two ways—firstly, product-oriented approach; secondly, process-oriented approach. As the name suggests, the product oriented appraoch concentrates the product and its associated non-functional requirement aspects. Similarly, process oriented approach concentrates on process and its associated non-functional requirement aspects. The second approach to NFRs are qualitative vs quantiative appraoch. Qualitative approach concentrates on non-numeric related NFRs while quantitative approach concentrates on the numeric aspects of the NFRs.

7.4.3 Interface Specification

Most of the software systems do not work alone. In order to work, it needs to interact with other systems. They interact with many other systems to receive and send data, get help in processing logic, store information in other systems for different reasons. The interaction requirement of one system with another is defined in the interface specification.

This helps in building different systems in such a fashion that they can seamlessly interact with each other to produce the desired outcome. In the previous example, the retail shop billing system may interact with another system—an inventory system to make sure that the warehouse keeps track on the stock of the material at hand and the protocol of how these two systems interact with each other are captured in the interface specification document.

Points to Remember

Functional requirements define what a system must do to fulfill the user needs; non-functional requirements put forth the constraints on design and architecture while the interface specification define how the system will interact with other external systems.

7.5 Steps of Requirement Management

Requirement management discipline deals with end-to-end handling of requirements. The way the requirements are captured, analysed, stored and tracked comes under this discipline. The important aspects, like handling the changes to the existing requirements and introduction of new requirements during the requirement phase as well as throughout the life cycle of the project are part of the requirement management principles.

Discussion Points

If there is no requirement management process defined for a project, what will be the problems faced by the team?

1. ______________________________
2. ______________________________
3. ______________________________
4. ______________________________

The first step of managing requirements is to prepare the plan on how the requirements will be managed throughout the life cycle of a project. A **Requirement Management Plan** describes how to manage the following:

- Requirement identification
- Requirement change
- Requirement status tracking
- Requirement traceability

7.5.1 Requirement Identification

The requirement identification is the first step in requirement management. This creates the baseline set of requirements on which the implementation team starts working.

Though, the requirements life cycle may vary based on the application domain, there are few generic steps that are common across all types of software projects. Requirement lif-eycle includes requirement development and requirements management (Figure 7.2). The basic aims of requirements life cycle process are to provide a mechanism to understand the user needs, analysing the need, assessing the feasibility, specifying and validating the requirements and proposed solutions, managing the requirements over the whole life cycle of the project which are described below:

- Feasibility study
- Eliciting requirements
- Requirement analysis
- Specify and validate requirements

Figure 7.2 shows, how each step of requirement life cycle are related to each other.

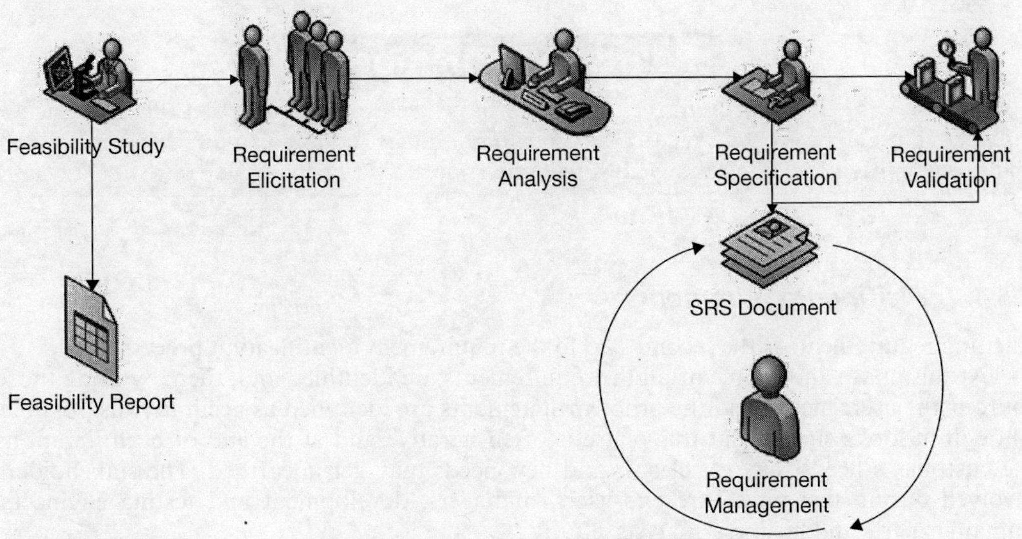

Figure 7.2 Requirements Life cycle

7.5.1.1 Feasibility Study

Feasibility study is the first step for the requirement identification process. The worthiness of the proposed software system should be determined before spending efforts on building the system.

A feasibility study helps in deciding whether the proposed system is worthwhile and has the following characteristics.

- Whether the system contributes to organizational objectives.
- Whether the system can be developed using the current available technology and within specified time and budget.
- Whether the system can easily be integrated with other surrounding systems as required by the overall architecture.

Thus, the feasibility can be classified into three broad categories:

Operational Feasibility: This checks the usability of the proposed software. If the operational scope is high, then the proposed system will be used more, ensuring the acceptance from the sponsors of the project.

Technical Feasibility: This checks whether the level of technology required for development of the system is available with the software firm including the hardware resource requirement, software development platforms and other software tools.

Economic Feasibility: This checks whether there is enough scope for returns by investing in this software system. All the costs involved in developing the system including the software licenses, hardware procurement, manpower cost, etc. needs to be considered while doing this analysis. The cost benefit ratio is derived as the result of this exercise and the stakeholders take a decision on the justification of going ahead with the proposed project.

Points to Remember

Before investing in any project, the sponsors will be keen to know whether the investment is worth and the project can succeed technically as well as economically. Thus, a feasibility study step provides the insight to all stakeholders at the very beginning.

7.5.1.2 Eliciting Requirements

Eliciting requirements is the second step fo the requirement identification process.

At this phase, the source of all the requirements are identified and, then, by using those sources, the users' needs and the problem statements are identified as accurately as possible. Though, it looks simple, but this phase is often iterative and at the end of each iterations the customer's needs may get clearer and new needs may get unearthed. The stakeholders involved during this phase are end-users, managers, development and testing engineers, domain experts and business analysts, etc.

7.5.1.2.1 Identifying Stakeholders Before the requirements are gathered for a system, it is important to know the people who can contribute and help in gathering the requirements. Missing key stakeholders during the requirement elicitation phase can lead to missing those important requirements which may cause rework at the later stage. Stakeholder identification is, thus, the first step in starting the requirement elicitation.

People or entities (organizations) actively involved in the projects, otherwise, affected by outcome of the defined project are called as stakeholders.

Discussion Points

Can you think who are the important stakeholders for a medical insurance claim processing software development project?

1. ______
2. ______
3. ______
4. ______

7.5.1.2.2 Characteristics of Stakeholders Stakeholders interests may either positively or negatively impacted by the performance of the project. Stakeholders may influence a project and its results.

It is important for the project manager to identify all the stakeholders and their requirements (sometimes requirements may be implicit and not explicitly stated—the project manager should also try to understand such requirements). Stakeholders may have conflicting interests and objectives. So, managing stakeholders may not be so easy. Involving stakeholders in the project phases improves probability of success of the project.

Stakeholder involvement is always situation-specific. What works in one situation may not be appropriate in another. By asking few simple questions, we can identify appropriate and required stakeholders. Though, it is not intended to provide an exhaustive list of questions here, but this will surely give us a fare idea of the type of questions appropriate for this purpose. These are:

1. Who are the people likely to be affected/benefited?
2. Who is responsible for what we intend to do?
3. Who is likely to move for or against what is intended?
4. Who can make what is intended better way?
5. Who can contribute to financial and technical resources?

Points to Remember

Properly identifying stakeholders and managing the stakeholders' expectations hold the key to success in any project. Maintaining a prioritized list of stakeholders according to their stakes in the project helps in avoiding the bottlenecks created by them at the later stage of a project.

Problems in Eliciting Requirements

- Users not sure
- Communication gap
- Conflicting requirements
- Volatile requirements

Figure 7.3 Problems in Eliciting Requirements

7.5.1.2.3 Problems in Eliciting Requirements Figure 7.3 depicts the problems in eliciting requirements. Different problems arises while eliciting requirements are as follows:

- **Users not sure about the requirement:** This situation arises often when the system to be developed is a new system and there is no corresponding manual system or any old software system that can be analysed to get the requirement. In this situation, the users will be looking for either similar systems developed elsewhere or mock-up screens, workflows, prototypes, etc. during the requirement gathering stage which will aid their imagination in coming up with the requirements for the new system.
- **Communication gap:** Even if the end users and stakeholders are clear about the need from the new system to be developed, they may find it difficult to express the same in concrete manner due to their less exposure to the computing systems. They may state the requirements in an ambiguous or non-testable fashion. Sometimes, the obvious basic requirements may be omitted and they concentrate on explaining the peripheral requirements. The system engineer needs to drive the stakeholders in right direction throughout the requirements stage, so that the focus is maintained on important requirements only.
- **Conflicting requirements:** This problem increases with the number of stakeholders involved in the project. There may be conflicting need and priorities in each stakeholder's mind, based on the business areas they are covering. For example, a stakeholder from the marketing team will try to put requirements that will expedite the creation of new products, while the end users of the system will look for efficient screens that help easy data capture. During the analysis phase, the requirement analyst and the client should collaboratively discuss and resolve any conflicting requirement coming out from multiple stakeholders.
- **Volatile requirements:** Requirements may get changed during the elicitation stage due to entry of new stakeholders who has different perspective of the system. Though, this is helpful in clarifying the requirements better, but it sometimes creates friction between the requirement engineer and the stakeholders due to continuous change in the scope.

Discussion Points

Suppose, you are the end-user of a mainframe-based banking software which is going to be replaced by a new JAVA-based software. Have the requirement engineers from this new company had approached you to understand the requirements for the new system? How will you make sure that they have noted down all your requirements, correctly?

1. ____________________
2. ____________________
3. ____________________
4. ____________________

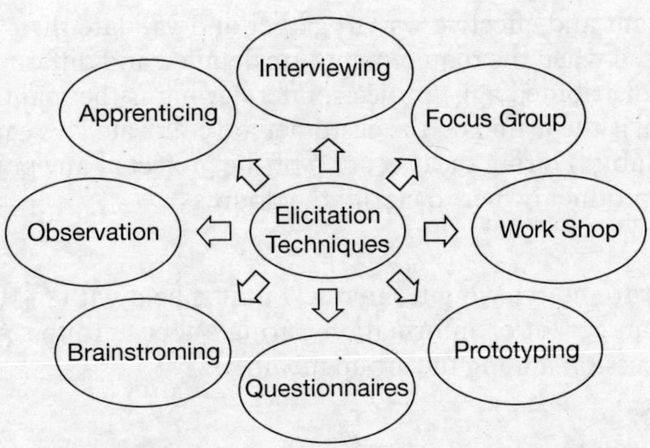

Figure 7.4 Requirement Elicitation Techniques

7.5.1.2.4 Requirement Elicitation Techniques Based on the project scope, domain, customer preparedness, etc., one or combination of multiple techniques needs to be used for gathering the requirements in an organized manner. Several techniques (Figure 7.4) can be applied for eliciting requirements are as follows:

- Interviewing
- Focus groups
- Facilitated workshops
- Prototyping
- Questionnaires
- Brainstorming
- Direct observation
- Apprenticing

Interviewing
Begin the interviews with stakeholders who are believed to have the most complete understanding of the requirements. Face-to-face interaction with users through individual interviewing is the primary source of requirements (Figure 7.5).

Figure 7.5 Interview Technique

This is an important and effective way to gather and validate their requirements. Interview techniques are used when the requirements are detailed and differing opinions are likely or are sought. In the distributed agile projects, interviewing is the main technique to gather the requirements. Even if the team and the customer are collocated we can use interview technique to clarify the doubts. During the execution of the project at any point of time interview may happen with the product owner to clarify the doubts.

Focus Groups

Focus group is similar to interviewing technique, but it is held with 6–10 people at a time in the same group. We can get lot of information during a focus group session because of the enhanced level of discussion among the group members.

Types of Focus Groups

Two-way Focus Group. Here two focus groups are used. One focus group will continuously watch other focus group so that the interaction happens as per predefined rule and proper discipline is being followed.

Dual Moderator Focus Group—Model 1. Like two different focus groups in the given model, here two moderators also does the job. While, one looks into the disciplne, the other looks into the content flow. This helps in ensuring smooth progress of the session as well as the entire topics of discussion is covered.

Dual Moderator Focus Group—Model 2. In this model also, two moderators are there, but they take completely opposite stands. It means if one says something is impossible, another says why it is not possible. This is more helpful in finding the pros and cons of both the opposite views and will be helpful to take a final decision.

Respondent Moderator Focus Group. Respondents are asked to act as the moderator temporarily and because of this, they take ownership of the session and hence we can collect the requirements successfully and the outcome will be helpful (Figure 7.6).

Figure 7.6 Focus Group Technique

Client Participant Focus Group. Client representatives participate in the discussion and will ensure ownership from the client over the decision taken. Most of the projects fail at the last stage of the project life cycle particularly in user acceptance testing (UAT) phase. The reason being the client may not take the ownership there as the end users have more ownership. But client participant focus group helps to overcome these kind of problems.

Mini Focus Group. Groups are restricted to four or five members rather than 8–12 and is helpful to avoid confusion. It will be easy for us to manage and gather the requirements quickly.

Teleconference Focus Group. In this type of group, telephone network is used to facilitate the discussion sessions.

Online Focus Group. In online focus group, computers connected via the Internet are used to facilitate the discussion sessions.

Facilitated Workshops

Workshops (Figure 7.7) can be used for rapidly pulling together a good set of requirements. Workshops are very quick and the best way to gather requirements than all the other techniques. A workshop is expensive, because it involves many people, but it saves a large amount of time for us. Requirements are discussed at the high level. Workshops are being useful in situations when the requirements are focused on one area of business in which the participants have knowledge and consensus is being sought. In workshops, different alternatives are given to the customers to choose the correct option.

Prototyping

The word 'prototype' is derived from the Greek word 'prototypon'. Prototypes and models are the best ways of presenting ideas to users. They give users a glimpse of what they might get. More requirements are likely to emerge when users see what they will get and through

Figure 7.7 Facilitated Workshop Technique

your suggestion. This technique aims at the users to express their requirements. Prototype is used to get feedback from the user. Business logic may not be coded in prototyping. Experimental systems are developed using prototyping. It is actually the initial version of the system.

Points to Remember

During the requirement phase, the prototype is generally a document-based prototype where the user interface design, use cases, overall look and feel and navigation, etc. are discussed with the end users. The scope of working prototype normally comes at the construction phase.

Types of Prototype

As discussed in Chapter 1, there are two major classifications of prototypes, namely, evolutionary prototype and throw-away prototype.

The former type will be reused and the changes are implemented in that particular prototype. The new changes and corrections are updated in the existing prototype until the final list of requirements is obtained, without wasting the used resources. The other type, as the name suggests, destroys the wrong prototypes. Thrown away prototypes are proved to be wrong and thus the new prototypes are developed in the next stages. The resources used in the previous prototypes are either freed or rejected. Figure 7.8 represents different types of prototypes.

Proof-of-Principle Prototype (*Bread Board*). Only intended design is tested here and visual appearance is not in scope of this prototype. Few working codes are part of it just for understanding purpose.

Form Study Prototype. Only visual appearance instead of functionalities is considered here.

Visual Prototype. It simulates the appearance, colour, fonts and surface textures of the intended product, but no representation of the final function(s) of the final product.

Functional Prototype. It is also called working prototype, because it simulates the actual functionality of the intended work.

Questionnaires

Questionnaires can be used to collect input from multiple stakeholders quickly which can be consolidated to create a list of requirements. As the stakeholders targeted for the questionnaire, they need not be physically present with the requirement elicitation team. This process can be run with a large number of participants in quite inexpensive fashion.

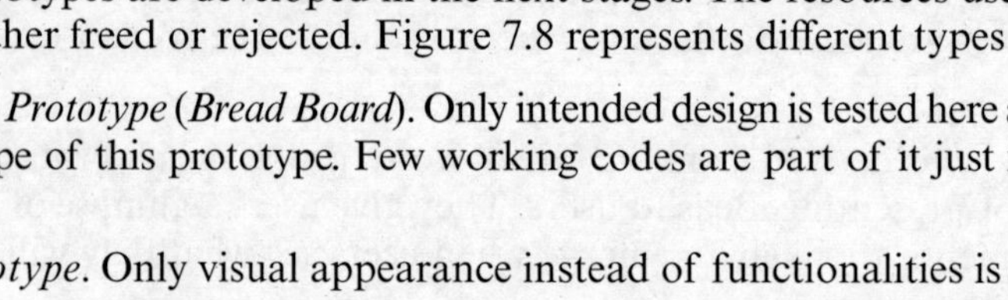

Figure 7.8 Types of Prototypes

But the questionnaires have their own limitations, like designing an exhaustive questionnaire becomes difficult, especially if the complexity of the system is high. As the stakeholders are not in direct contact with the elicitation team, there may be ambiguity in questions which lead to erroneous responses. Moreover, the response rate may be low and may need lot of follow-up for getting sufficient input through this technique.

Brainstorming

This is a powerful technique with which a large number of requirements or ideas can be generated in short period of time.

- In these groups, members meet face-to-face and rely on both the verbal and non-verbal interactions to communicate with each other.
- The main purpose of the brainstorming technique is to get as many ideas as possible togather different views of the requirement and, thereby, helping to capture better requirements.

In a typical brainstorming session about six people are involved and they sit around a table. The group leader states the problem in a clear and understandable manner so that it is understood by all the participants involved. Members are allowed to suggest as many alternatives as they can in a given length of time. No criticism is allowed. Alternative ideas generated are also are recorded and is used for analysis and discussions at later stages. Brainstorming, however, is merely a process to generate ideas, it may not be effective for decision making purpose.

Discussion Points

Do you think the brainstorming sessions can help in a situation where the end users does not have clear idea of the features they want from the software to be developed?

1. ______
2. ______
3. ______
4. ______

Direct Observation and Apprenticing

In many cases, a new system is developed to replace an existing system in which either a lot of manual intervention is involved or it is not efficient and suitable for conducting the job. In such scenarios, it is very useful to gather knowledge of the requirement by observing what is actually done by the user of the system. This is far more powerful than going through the documents of the capability of the existing system as it provides opportunity to capture the real motivation behind going for the new system.

A better technique will be the apprenticing model where the requirement engineer is performing the tasks that the user of the system is carrying out. Though, this requires the understanding of the business process carried out by the user, but has huge benefit of getting an in-depth vision into what tasks the users are performing with the current system and the areas they need improvement or automation in the new system.

7.5.1.3 Requirement Analysis

Requirement analysis is the third step of the requirement identification process. The aim of the elicitation phase is just to gather the requirements, whereas in the analysis phase the requirements are understood in detail. This is the phase which bridges the gap between the requirement engineering and design. Thus, the requirement analyst refines the data, functional and behavioral constraints of the software which acts as the input to the design. Various modeling techniques are used during the analysis phase which supports in problem evaluation and solution synthesis during this stage.

The focus areas for the analyst during this stage are:

A. Externally observable data objects
B. Flow and content of information
C. Software functionality elaboration
D. Behaviour of the software on external input
E. Interface requirements
F. Design constraints

After analysing each of these areas, the analyst starts working on the solution part, that is, the system architecture, database requirements, etc. He discusses with the customer to make sure that the system design is based on the customer's need. For example, the data flow analysis may reveal that a real time interface is not required in the system which will reduce the complexity and cost of the proposed solution. The analyst creates models of the system in order to capture the data requirement and flow, functional processing, operational behaviour and information content. These models become the stepping stone for the software design phase.

The following modeling techniques are widely used in requirement analysis and are discussed in the next chapter.

- Use case
- System models (Context, Behavioral, Data, Object, Structure methods)
- Data modeling
  - Data flow diagram
  - Data dictionary
  - Entity relationship model
  - Control flow model
  - Decision tables
- Information modeling
- Object-oriented analysis
- Scenario-based modeling
- Flow-oriented modeling
- Class diagram

7.5.1.4 Specifying Requirements

After successful completion of requirement elicitation and analysis, the next step is to put all the knowledge gathered in those steps in a clear, concise and unambiguous manner so that the design and development teams can use it going forward. This is called 'the requirement specification phase.'

While specifying the requirements, it is also important that the same is validated with the customers and users to demonstrate that what the customer really wants is captured at this stage. Software Requirement Specification (SRS) is the outcome of this requirement specification and validation stage.

Specifying Requirements in Software Requirement Specification (SRS) Document

Once created, SRS document becomes the main source for any requirement clarification and dissemination to all stakeholders. There are several purposes that the SRS document can be used for:

- It may form the basis for the contractual agreement between the customer and the suppliers. The suppliers in an unambiguous fashion describe what will be developed as part of the project and, thus, any change in this agreed understanding will be re-negotiated between the customer and the suppliers.
- This is the foundation document for the test engineers to develop their strategy on how to test the proposed system fully.
- The design and development team start their work based on this document. As all the stakeholders think through what they need from the system and get it documented in the SRS, the chance of redesign or re-construction work gets minimized, if the SRS is developed well.
- It is also helpful in the resourcing.

Discussion Points

List down the qualities of a SRS document which will help it to become the primary reference document for all the requirements?

1. ____________________
2. ____________________
3. ____________________
4. ____________________

- Budgeting, scheduling and pricing for the project are based on the volume and complexity of the requirements captured in this document. The modern estimation techniques take direct input from the use cases and models developed in the SRS.
- A good SRS ensures that future maintainability of the project and enables the customer to switch into a different supplier during the maintenance phase of the project. The new supplier's team will use the SRS document as the primary artifact to understand the capabilities wanted by the stakeholders from the system and can validate that against the developed capabilities.

SRS Template IEEE Standard

The aim of the SRS document is to provide the understanding of what the stakeholders want from the system and how the system should behave to cater to those needs. As discussed above, this document forms the foundation for the downstream processes like design, construction and testing. Thus, it is very important and proper care is taken while creating this document. IEEE Standard '*IEEE Recommended Practice for Software Requirements Specifications*' (IEEE Std-830-1993) provides a template for creating the SRS document as shown below in Figure 7.9.

IEEE Standard SRS Template

1. Introduction
- 1.1. Purpose
- 1.2. Scope
- 1.3. Definitions, acronyms & abbreviations
- 1.4. References
- 1.5. Overview

2. Overall Description
- 2.1. Product perspective
  - 2.1.1. System interfaces
  - 2.1.2. User interfaces
  - 2.1.3. Hardware interfaces
  - 2.1.4. Software interfaces
  - 2.1.5. Communications interfaces
  - 2.1.6. Memory constraints
  - 2.1.7. Operations
  - 2.1.7. Site adaptation requirements
- 2.2. Product functions
- 2.3. User characteristics
- 2.4. Constraints
- 2.5. Assumptions and dependencies
- 2.6. Apportioning of requirements

3. Specific Requirements
- 3.1 External interface requirements
  - 3.1.1 User interfaces
  - 3.1.2 Hardware interfaces
  - 3.1.3 Software interfaces
  - 3.1.4 Communication interfaces
- 3.2 Specific requirements
  - 3.2.1 Sequence diagrams
  - 3.2.2 Classes for classification of specific requirements
- 3.3 Performance requirements
- 3.4 Design constraints
- 3.5 Software system attributes
  - 3.5.1 Reliability
  - 3.5.2 Availability
  - 3.5.3 Security
  - 3.5.4 Maintainability
- 3.6 Other requirements

4. Supporting Information
- 4.1 Table of contents and index
- 4.2 Appendixes

Figure 7.9 IEEE Standards SRS Template

- Correctness
- Completeness
- Consistency
- Verifiability
- Clarity
- Priority
- Modifiability

Figure 7.10 Checklist for Writing Good SRS

Based on the application domain, complexity and involvement of other third party systems, the sections may get added or removed from the above template.

Checklist for Writing a Good SRS

The consumers of the SRS document are all the stakeholders of the project—the customer, end users, project engineers, interface developers, managers etc. Thus, ensuring the correctness and completeness of this document is crucial for the success of each stage of the project. The below checkpoints (Figure 7.10) provide a guideline on how to create a SRS document that serves its purpose.

1. **Correctness**
   (a) Will the requirement meet the customer's need?
   (b) Does the requirement capture how the system should transform, produce and provide the exact outcome expected from the system?
   (c) The correctness of requirements typically refers to the accuracy of the requirements and whether everything agreed is delivered.
2. **Completeness**
   (a) Are all the requirements captured which will form a system that fully provides solution to the customer's problem?
   (b) Are each requirement detailed enough and supported by necessary diagrams, figures, data and use cases so that all the stakeholders get their necessary input from the requirement?
   (c) Are all functional, non-functional and interface requirements captured for the system?
3. **Consistency**
   (a) Are there requirements which are in conflict with each other? This may happen in case multiple stakeholders have different view of the proposed system and provide requirements which create conflicts while grouped together.
   (b) Are the terminology, diagrams, tables and figures are consistent and provide a consistent view of the proposed system?
4. **Verifiability**
   (a) Are the requirements verifiable—which means will the test engineers be able to check whether the requirement fulfills the customer need at entirety before the product is shipped to customer.
   (b) Are the requirements validated and verified by all the stakeholders before those are base-lined for consumption of downstream processes?
5. **Clarity**
   (a) Is the requirement statement explicit enough and can be interpreted in one way only? Along with unambiguous language it is important to take the help of pictorial representations like diagrams, figures and use cases to eliminate ambiguity in requirements.
   (b) Will the design and construction engineer be able to determine the single way of implementation from the requirement document? In case there are multiple interpretations of a requirement possible then there is possibility that it is implemented in a way not desired by the customer and thus causes rework.
6. **Priority**
   (a) Is the relative priority of the requirement vis-a-vis the others captured? Prioritization of the requirements is important as that drives the plan for implementing those. In case when the project is under time or budget constraint, the priority of the requirements become important as it will provide clear guideline of which requirements should be tackled first, and which requirements are less important.
7. **Modifiability**
   (a) How much dependency the requirement has on other requirements? This will depict how easily the requirements can be modified. A requirement which has dependency on several other requirements should be structured in a fashion so that the impact of any modification to this requirement across other requirements can be easily traceable. There are several requirement management tools like Doors, RequisitePro, etc., available which help in this regard.

Point to Remember

Note the seven points to be taken care of in a good SRS document—correctness, completeness, consistency, verifiability, clarity, priority and modifiability.

7.5.1.5 Validating Requirements

Validating requirements is an important step as invalid requirements may cost high to rectify at later stages of the project. The main aim of requirement validation is to make sure the customer needs are captured completely, clearly and consistently.

The validation step should provide enough confidence to all the stakeholders that the proposed system will provide all the features required and will be completed within the time and budget allocated for the project. The different roles involved in the validation process are:

1. Customer
2. End user
3. Domain expert
4. Architect
5. Construction and test engineer
6. Third party systems interacting with the proposed system

There are different approaches taken for validating the requirements as follows.

Walkthroughs, Reviews and Inspections

There is some subtle difference between the validation processes – walkthroughs, reviews and inspection.

Walkthroughs: This is an informal process where the author of the document presents the document to a group of people and the observations or issues found by the group of people are reported and corrected after the walkthrough session. Normally, minutes of the meeting are not maintained for the walkthrough sessions.

Reviews: This may be either formal or informal process where the group of stakeholders will critically go through the SRS document and check that:

(a) The standards and guidelines available in the organization are followed in the document.
(b) The completeness, consistency and other points mentioned in the *Checklist for writing a good SRS* are followed.
(c) All the requirements could be traced back to their origin. This will make sure only the valid requirements are captured and implemented and not just any wish-list from the user groups.

Normally, the minutes of the review sessions are captured and all the findings are tracked till satisfactory closure.

Inspection: This is a more structured way of review where the non-conformances found in the SRS document based on the point discussed above are listed as defects which are tracked till the defects are closed satisfactorily.

Modeling and Prototyping

Creating models and prototypes are other approaches for validating the requirements.

Models: Use case modeling using Unified Modeling Language (UML) is the most frequently used technique for capturing and validating the business case, interactions and flows in the proposed system.

Prototypes: As discussed in section *Requirement Elicitation* the prototyping method is very effective way to validate the technical feasibility and the user need because a smaller version of the actual system is developed and showcased to the stakeholders. So, prototypes can be considered as the **executable** models used for requirement validation.

7.5.2 Requirement Change

Requirements are bound to change during the course of time. There can be several reasons behind the requirements change:

1. The customer and the users of the system get more insight into the system as they see few working prototypes of the system. This leads to change in existing requirements and emergence of new requirements. This is very common phenomena as no human being can foresee a future system fully just by thinking about it. Take a simple example of designing the interior of your house. While providing the specification, you have to imagine how the different furniture will be oriented, the colors of the walls, electrical fittings and all. But when you see the first model design created by the designer, you get more concrete idea on how things will look like and you made modifications to the design more confidently. The changes may occur till the different pieces of the interior are built and fixed. In the similar fashion, as more insight comes out of the system as we progress on the project, there may be changes or clarifications to the existing requirements.
2. The market and the business needs are ever changing. To cope up with the changing market needs the specification of the product to be developed may have to be changed.
3. The priority of the requirements may change due to change in market scenario, business priority change and change in view point of the different stakeholders of the system. Figure 7.11 shows the for requirements change management flow.

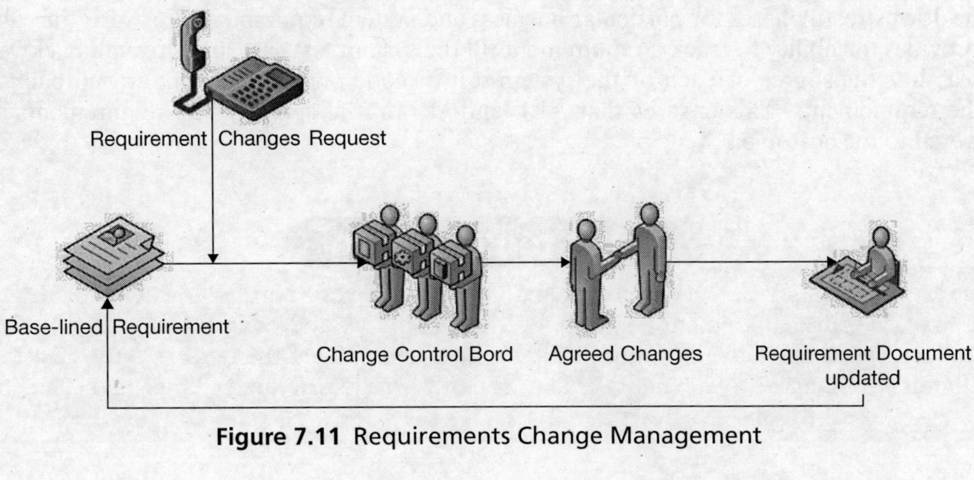

Figure 7.11 Requirements Change Management

A strong change management process is essential in tracking the requirement changes. This will ensure that all the changes are incorporated during the project and minimize the chance of missing out on the new requirements or changes that have been found after the requirements phase of a project.

Change Control Process

Once the initial requirements are agreed upon with different stakeholders, it is important that any change in those requirements is controlled well. Changes in requirements are almost always related to change in project effort, timeline and cost. By introducing a *Change Control Board* all the stakeholders try to make sure that everyone gets good transparency on the changes agreed upon. A change control board normally is a group of people comprising of members from each stakeholder groups who are directly linked to the project outcome. This group sets forth the steps to be followed whenever a change or new requirement crops up after the initial set of requirements are signed off by everyone.

7.5.3 Requirement Status Tracking

After the requirement gathering phase, the set of requirements get base-lined which can be modified after the change control board approves a requirement for implementation. It is important to track the status of the all these requirements throughout the life cycle of the requirement, i.e., till the requirements are available to the customer. This is to make sure that at any point of time the stakeholders should be able to find out the progress on this requirement. A sample of the change status tracker is in Figure 7.12.

7.5.4 Requirement Traceability

The most commonly used artifact to track the requirements in each stage of the project life cycle, such as design, construction, unit testing and system testing is by maintaining the tracing information in a traceability matrix as shown in Figure 7.13.

Note that each column of this table can be used to capture and maintain the traceability in the downstream phases for particular business and system requirement. Forward traceability provides the ability to track a requirement till the system test case and through backward traceability, the source of each of the system test or code or design can be traced back up to the requirements. This ensures that ALL and ONLY the agreed upon requirements are delivered to the customer.

Points to Remember

Due to the complexities involved in handling the changes, there is a general tendency for 'try to avoid' requirement changes. But, for a lengthy and complex project, requirement change is inevitable and, thus, rather than pushing back the customer to resist the requirement change, it is more advisable to plan for a well-structured change management process.

Change Request Details														Change Request Implementation Details					
					Impact														
CR Id	Request-ed By	Request-ed Date	Priority	Change Descrip-tion	Sl. No.	CI Id	Name	Existing Version	Esti-mated Effort (in PH)	CR Ap-proved By	CR Ap-proved Date	CR Sta-tus	Reason (if Rejected / Deferred / Cancelled)	Planned Start Date	Planned End Date	Actual Start Date	Actual End Date	Actual Effort (in PH)	CR Imple-menta-tion Status
					1														
					2														
					3														
					4														
					5														

Figure 7.12 Change Request Tracker

Re-quire-ment Clarifi-cation	Business Require-ments	System Require-ments		NFR Require-ments	Related Re-quire-ments	User Interface Proto-type	System Testing		Perfor-mance Testing		Design				Coding		Unit Testing		Integration Testing	
Clarifi-cation ID	Business Require-ment ID	System Require-ment ID	System Use Case ID	NFR Require-ments ID	Related Re-quire-ment ID	Screen/ Wire-frame ID	Docu-ment Name (SCI ID)	Test Case ID	Docu-ment Name (SCI ID)	Test Case ID	Com-ponent/ Class Diagram ID	Se-quence Diagram	Use Interface Specifi-cation-Screen ID/Name	Data-base Tables	Program / Source Code File Name(s)	Method/ Stored Proce-dures	Docu-ment Name (SCI ID)	Test Case ID	Docu-ment Name (SCI ID)	Test Case ID

Figure 7.13 Requirement Traceability Matrix

7.6 Case Study on Requirement Review

A SRS review checklist is a critical item for the requirement phase of a project. Here is a sample checklist that covers the aspects discussed in the SRS creation and validation sections.

Software Requirements Specification Review Checklist				
		Yes	**No**	**Not Applicable**
Completeness				
	Is there a table of contents?			
	Are all figures, tables, and diagrams labeled?			
	Are all figures, tables, and diagrams cross-referenced?			
	Are all terms defined?			
	Are all terms indexed?			
	Are all units of measure defined?			
	Are areas where information is incomplete, because development hasn't started been specified?			
	Is the missing information defined in the requirement?			
	Should any requirement be specified in more detail?			
	Should any requirement be specified in less detail?			
	Are all of the requirements defined?			
	Is the entire requirement related to functionality included?			
	Are there any requirements which make you feel uneasy?			
	Are all of the requirements related to performance included?			
	Are all of the requirements related to design constraints included?			
	Are all of the requirements related to attributes included?			

		Yes	No	Not Applicable
	Are all of the requirements related to external interfaces included?			
	Are all of the requirements related to databases included?			
	Are all of the requirements related to software included?			
	Are all of the requirements related to communications included?			
	Are all of the requirements related to hardware included?			
	Are all of the requirements related to inputs included?			
	Are all of the requirements related to outputs included?			
	Are all of the requirements related to reporting included?			
	Are all of the requirements related to security included?			
	Are all of the requirements related to maintainability included?			
	Are all of the requirements related to installation included?			
	Are all of the requirements related to criticality included?			
	Are all of the requirements related to the permanency limitations included?			
	Are possible changes to the requirements specified?			
	Is the likelihood of change specified for each requirement?			
Consistency				
	Are there any requirements describing the same object that conflict with other requirements with respect to terminology?			
	Are there any requirements describing the same object that conflict with respect to characteristics?			

		Yes	No	Not Applicable
	Are there any requirements that describe two or more actions that conflict logically?			
	Are there any requirements that describe two or more actions that conflict temporally?			
Clarity				
	Are the requirements described in non-technical understandable language?			
	Are there any requirements which could have more than one interpretation?			
	Is each characteristic of the final product described with a unique terminology?			
	Is there a glossary in which the specific meaning(s) of each term is (are) defined?			
	Could the requirements be understood and implemented by an independent group?			
Traceability				
	Are all requirements traceable back to a specific user need?			
	Are all requirements traceable back to a specific source document or person?			
	Are all requirements traceable forward to a specific design document?			
	Are all requirements traceable forward to a specific software module?			
Verifiability				
	Are any requirements included which are impossible to implement?			
	For each requirement, is there a process that can be executed by either a human or a machine to verify the requirement?			
	Are there any requirements which will be expressed in verifiable terms at a later time?			
Modifiability				
	Is the requirements document clearly and logically organized?			
	Does the organization adhere to an accepted standard?			
	Is there any redundancy in the requirements?			

		Yes	No	Not Applicable
Content				
General				
	Is each requirement relevant to the problem and its solution?			
	Are any of the defined requirements really design details?			
	Are any of the defined requirements really verification details?			
	Are any of the defined requirements really projecting management details?			
	Is there an introduction section?			
	Is there a general description section?			
	Is there a scope section?			
	Is there a definitions, acronyms and abbreviations section?			
	Is there a specific requirements section?			
	Is there a product perspective section?			
	Is there a product functions section?			
	Is there a user characteristics section?			
	Is there a general constraints section?			
	Is there an assumptions and dependencies section?			
	Is there a specific requirements section?			
	Are all of the necessary appendixes present?			
	Are all of the necessary figures present?			

		Yes	No	Not Applicable
	Are all of the necessary tables present?			
	Are all of the necessary diagrams present?			
Specific				
Inputs				
	Are all input sources specified?			
	Is all input accuracy requirements specified?			
	Are all input range values specified?			
	Are all input frequencies specified?			
	Are all input formats specified?			
Outputs				
	Are all output destinations specified?			
	Are all output accuracy requirements specified?			
	Are all output range values specified?			
	Are all output frequencies specified?			
	Are all output formats specified?			
Reports				
	Are all report formats specified?			
	Are all calculations/formulas used in reports specified?			
	Are all report data filter requirements specified?			
	Are all report sorting requirements specified?			
	Are a report totaling requirements specified?			
	Are all report formatting requirements specified?			
Functions				
	Are all software functions specified			
	Are all inputs specified for each function?			

		Yes	No	Not Applicable
	Are all aspects of the processing specified for each function?			
	Are all outputs specified for each function?			
	Are all performance requirements specified for each function?			
	Are all design constrains specified for each function?			
	Are all attributes specified for each function?			
	All security requirements specified for each function?			
	Are all maintainability requirements specified for each function?			
	Are all data base requirements specified for each function?			
	Are all operational requirements specified for each function?			
	Are all installation requirements specified for each function?			
External Interfaces				
	Are all user interfaces specified?			
	Are all batch interfaces specified?			
	Are all hardware interfaces specified?			
	Are all software interfaces specified?			
	Are all communications interfaces specified?			
	Are all interface design constraints specified?			
	Are all interface security requirements specified?			
	Are all interface maintainability requirements specified?			
	Are all human-computer interactions specified for user interfaces?			

		Yes	No	Not Applicable
Internal Interfaces				
	Have all internal interfaces been identified?			
	Have all internal interfaces characteristics been specified?			
Timing				
	Are all expected processing times specified?			
	Are all data transfer rates specified?			
	Are all system through put rates specified?			
Reliability				
	Are the consequences of software failure specified for each requirement?			
	Is the information to protect from failure specified?			
	Is a strategy for error detection specified?			
	Is a strategy for correction specified?			
Trade-offs				
	Are acceptable trade-offs specified for competing attributes?			
Hardware				
	Is the minimum memory specified?			
	Is the minimum storage specified?			
	Is the maximum memory specified?			
	Is the maximum storage specified?			
Software				
	Are the required software environments/OS's specified?			
	Are all of the required software utilities specified?			
	Are all purchased software products that are to be used with the system specified?			
Communications				
	Is the target network specified?			

		Yes	No	Not Applicable
	Are the required network protocols specified?			
	Is the required network capacity specified?			
	Is the required/estimated network throughput rate specified?			
	Is the estimated number of network connections specified?			
	Are minimum network performance requirements specified?			
	Are the maximum network performance requirements specified?			
	Are the optimal network performance requirements specified?			

SUMMARY

- Effective requirements management builds the foundation of any software. Thus, it is important to follow a systematic approach in this phase to avoid issues with the software at the later stages.
- Feasibility study is conducted at the beginning to ensure that all the expectations from the stakeholders are analysed and a consensus is reached on how much of that can be created with the current time and cost constraints in the project.
- Requirement elicitation techniques are used to make sure all the needs from the systems are captured. The different and conflicting viewpoints of the different stakeholders and user groups of the system need to be merged and agreed upon before proceeding to the next step.
- Modeling techniques are used to analyse the requirements and synthesize a solution which becomes the input in the design phase. System analyst will critically analyse the information flow and content, functional behaviour, data flow behaviour and external system interfacing requirements to create a model with which both the customers and the engineers are comfortable.
- Specifying the requirement in correct, complete, clear, verifiable and prioritized fashion is critical to ensure the outcome of the requirement's engineering phase is useful for the subsequent stages of software development life cycle. Review and inspection methodologies are used to ensure the quality of the SRS document.
- Throughout the project life cycle, tracking the requirements for proper implementation and any change is crucial. A requirement traceability matrix (RTM) provides a standard way of tracking the requirements throughout the project life cycle. Along with that a sound change management process and change tracker is recommended to track the changes to the initial requirements and avoid the requirements creep.

EXERCISES

PART A (Objective-type Questions)

1. Which of the following is not a type of requirement?
   A. Functional requirements
   B. Non-functional requirements
   C. Interface-specification requirements
   D. Customer-priortized requirements
2. Which of the following is the definition of Requirements Management?
   A. It is the discipline of planning, monitoring, analysing, communicating and controlling requirements. It is a continuous process throughout a project. It involves communication among project team members and stakeholders and adjustments to requirements changes throughout the course of the project.
   B. It deals with how the existing requirements can be stored and tracked and how the changes to these requirements can be handled during the requirements phase as well as throughout the life cycle of the project.
   C. The set of requirements which defines what the system will do or accomplish.
   D. The quality attributes and the design and architecture constraints that the system must have.
3. Which of the following is the definition of Requirements Management?
   A. It is the discipline that explores the externally imposed conditions on a proposed computer system and tries to identify the capabilities that will meet those imposed conditions and recording the same in the form of documentation called the requirement document of the computer system.
   B. It deals with how the existing requirements can be stored and tracked and how the changes to these requirements and also introduction of new requirements can be handled during the requirements phase as well as throughout the life cycle of the project.
   C. The set of requirements which defines what the system will do or accomplish.
   D. The quality attributes and the design and architecture constraints that the system must have.
4. Which of the following is the definition of Non-functional Requirements?
   A. It is the discipline that explores the externally imposed conditions on a proposed computer system and tries to identify the capabilities that will meet those imposed conditions and recording the same in the form of documentation called the requirement document of the computer system.
   B. It deals with how the existing requirements can be stored and tracked and how the changes to these requirements and also introduction of new requirements can be handled during the requirements phase as well as throughout the life cycle of the project.
   C. The set of requirements which defines what the system will do or accomplish.
   D. The quality attributes and the design and architecture constraints that the system must have.
5. A stakeholder may be a person or an organization?
   A. True
   B. False
6. Which of the following is not an example of Functional Requirements?
   A. Business Logic
   B. Data Manipulation logic
   C. Processing Logic
   D. Security logic

7. Which of the following is not an example of Non-functional Requirements?
   A. Business Logic
   B. Performance Logic
   C. Scalability Logic
   D. Testability Logic

8. Which of the following are Non-functional Requirements related to organization?
   A. Performance requirements
   B. Standard requirements
   C. Scalability requirements
   D. Testability requirements

9. Which of the following are External Non-functional Requirements?
   A. Performance requirements
   B. Standards requirements
   C. Legal requirements
   D. Testability requirements

10. Which of the following is not a step of Requirement Identification?
   A. Feasibility study
   B. Eliciting requirements
   C. Requirement analysis
   D. Requirement stability

11. Which of the following is not a type of feasibility study?
   A. Operational feasibility
   B. Technical feasibility
   C. Customer feasibility
   D. Economic feasibility

12. Which types of feasibility checks the usability of the proposed software?
   A. Operational feasibility
   B. Technical feasibility
   C. Customer feasibility
   D. Economic feasibility

13. Which type of feasibility checks whether the level of technology required for development of the system is available with the software firm?
   A. Operational feasibility
   B. Technical feasibility
   C. Customer feasibility
   D. Economic feasibility

14. Which type of feasibility checks if there is scope for enough return by investing in this software system?
   A. Operational feasibility
   B. Technical feasibility
   C. Customer feasibility
   D. Economic feasibility

15. Which of the following is not a type of Requirement Elicitation techniques?
   A. Brainstorming
   B. Direct observation
   C. Technical feasibility
   D. Apprenticing

16. Which of the following is not a problem during Requirement Elicitation?
   A. Communication gap
   B. Conflictive requirements
   C. Volatile requirements
   D. Unambiguous requirements

17. After successful completion of Requirement Elicitation and Analysis, the next step is
   A. Requirement specification
   B. Feasibility study
   C. Eliciting requirements
   D. Requirement re-analysis

18. Which of the following phase ensures the customer needs are captured completely, clearly and consistently?
   A. Requirement specification
   B. Feasibility study
   C. Eliciting requirements
   D. Requirement validation

19. Which of the following are the steps involved in requirement identification in order?
   A. Feasibility study, Eliciting requirements, Requirement analysis, Requirement specification, Requirement validation
   B. Eliciting requirements, Feasibility study, Requirement analysis, Requirement specification, Requirement validation

C. Feasibility study, Eliciting requirements, Requirement analysis, Requirement validation, Requirement specification
D. Eliciting requirements, Requirement analysis, Feasibility study, Requirement specification, Requirement validation

PART B (Write the answers in one or two lines)—5 Marks

1. Define 'requirements'.
2. What are the types of requirements?
3. Define requirement management.
4. Define stakeholders.
5. Define prototyping.
6. What are functional requirements?
7. Give examples of functional requirements.
8. What is a non-functional requirement?
9. Give some non-functional requirements related to product.
10. Give some non-functional requirements related to organization.
11. Give some examples for external non-functional requirements.
12. Write notes on product oriented vs process oriented approach of NFRs?
13. Write notes on qualitative vs quantitative approach of NFRs?
14. Write notes on interface specification.
15. What are all the steps involved in requirement identification?
16. Define feasibility study.
17. What are all the contents and characteristics of a feasibility study?
18. List down the types of feasibility study?
19. Write notes on operational feasibility.
20. Write notes on technical feasibility.
21. Write notes on economic feasibility.
22. Write notes on requirement elicitation.
23. List down various requirement elicitation techniques you are aware of.
24. List down few problems faced while eliciting requirements.
25. Write notes on requirement analysis.
26. What is requirement traceability?
27. What is requirement specification?
28. What is requirement validation?
29. What is the use of throwaway prototype?

PART C (Descriptive-type Answers)—10 Marks

1. What are the major tasks occur in requirements identification? Discuss in detail.
2. Discuss feasibility study in detail.
3. Discuss the importance of requirements in detail giving an example.
4. Discuss various types of requirements.
5. Discuss the possible problems while eliciting requirements.
6. List down any three requirement elicitation techniques in detail.
7. Discuss various types of focus group techniques in detail.
8. Discuss 'prototype concepts' in details. How it is used for requirement engineering and management?
9. Discuss in detail, the characteristics of a good SRS.
10. Explain the validating requirements and the possible steps.

Section III

Software Project Planning

8

Software Estimation Tools, Techniques and Models

8.1 Introduction

Various types of estimation techniques are available for software engineers and project managers which help them to do the software estimation precisely and accurately. Some of the estimation techniques are expert judgements, top-down estimation, bottom-up estimation, analogous estimation and parametric estimation. Various types of models are available for the estimations which can be used directly while estimating the cost of softwares. In particular, cost estimation models are of bigger help for the estimators and those are being used predominantly. Metrics are of no use if they are not analysed properly and due to this we need to understand various tools which are helpful in the analysis of estimation.

8.2 Definition of Estimation

'To form an approximate notion of the amount, number, magnitude or position of anything, without actual enumeration or measurement.'

—Oxford English Dictionary

To complete any activity in a planned manner, estimation is considered to be very important. For example, if you need to arrive for an interview in a particular time, at first you will estimate how long it will take on travelling so that you can plan of your starting time accordingly. But, as you can understand, this will be the case of estimate by guess. In a multi-million dollar software project, cost estimation is to be executed in a systematic way. Here, the estimation should be more accurate and thus needs to follow some scientific methodologies.

8.3 Importance of Accurate Estimation

The following results occur due to inaccurate estimation:

1. Inaccurate estimate may result in inefficient usage of resources.
2. Inaccurate estimate may result incorrect decision.

3. Inaccurate estimate may result in cost overrun, schedule overrun.
4. Inaccurate estimate may result in customer dissatisfaction.
5. Inaccurate estimate may result in loss of faith and in turn loss of business from the customer.

Discussion Point

Discuss the importance of accurate estimation with examples for the above points.

8.4 Efforts and Duration

In estimation process, we should be very clear with the difference between the efforts and duration. Effort is the exact amount of work required for completing a particular task. Duration is defined as the time elapsed between start and end of the particular task.

Example: For writing a particular piece of code, two resources will be required working for 10 hours each. So, the overall estimation is 20 hours which will take three days duration to complete the task.

Types of Effort

Discrete Effort (DE): The concept of 'discrete effort' applies directly to the specific work efforts that can be directly traced and identified as having a direct tie for ultimate completion of the project-related work and which is also directly measurable.

Apportioned Effort (AE): The concept of 'apportioned effort' applies not directly to the specific work efforts, but related to some other tasks that are apportioned over here. For example, project management efforts for finishing a task.

Level of Effort (LOE): In project management, level of effort (LOE) is a support-type project activity that must be done to support other work activities or the entire project effort.

8.5 Estimation Process

It is the process (Figure 8.1) of calculating, forecasting and approximating the cost, effort and time of completing the project deliverables. The customer expectation along with various constraints and assumptions are also taken into consideration during the estimation process.

The task of balancing the stakeholder expectations and operating within the boundary of the project (constraints, assumptions) at the same time is crucial for the estimation process. Constraints limit various options available. For example, the customer wants to finish the project on a particular date is a constraint and the estimation is based upon it. The number of resources in a project is a constraint in the project, because we need to finish the project only with the available resources. Assumptions are certain statements or actions or events which are considered to be true or false in deriving the estimate. An estimate is always a qualified

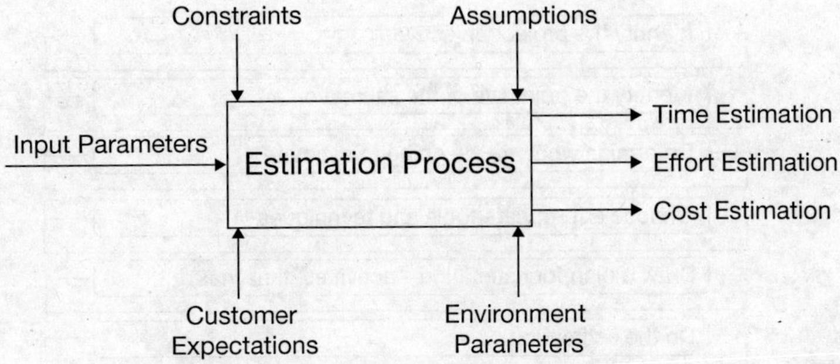

Figure 8.1 Estimation Process

guess based on assumptions. All estimation has its associated assumptions with it, and it needs to be specified, so that the basis of estimate is known to all the stakeholders of the project and can be validated. We make lot of assumptions about the experience and skill-set of the resources during the estimation process. We assume all the resources are uniformly skilled and the customer will give the sign-off on time. If the assumption goes wrong, it creates adverse effect on the estimation. The estimation is right only when the assumption is right.

Customer expectations are also to be considered while estimating the project. Customer expectations also keep on changing. Customer expectations are related with time, schedule, effort and quality parameters of the project. Environment parameters include various environment-related factors which can affect the project. It includes, status of the project, risks involved in the estimation, the project cost involved in the estimation, time involved in the estimation, difficulty of the estimation process, and expertize availability for the estimation, etc.

8.5.1 Basic Steps in Software Estimation Process

Basic steps in software estimation process are shown in Figure 8.2. These steps are described here.

Identify the Project Objectives

The estimation process should be in line with the objective of the project. If the estimation is not in line, we may be measuring and estimating something which is of no use to the project. In particular, the objectives which are related to the context and requirements for the project are crucial to identifying during the estimation.

Identify the Objectives of the Estimation

It states, what we are going to achieve by estimation. The identification of estimation objectives is based on project objectives, business objective and technical team feedback mechanism. During the measurement process, the whole team should be focused on the right estimation objectives.

Determine Parameters and Tools

What we are going to measure is the important parameter in the estimation process. Are we going to measure the height, weight, cost, duration? The identification of parameter helps to choose the appropriate tools for the estimation. For example, the tools and techniques of estimating the cost are different from the schedule.

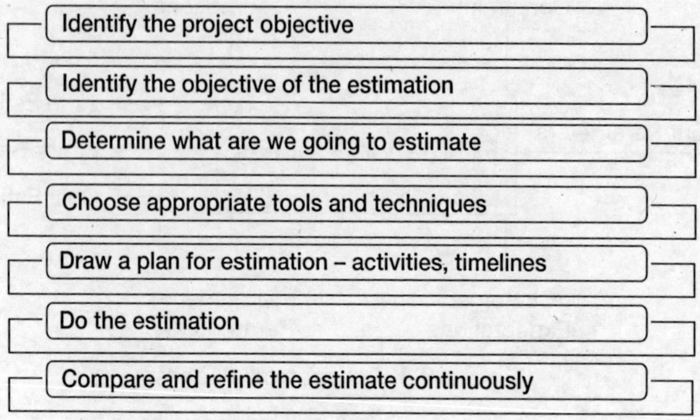

Figure 8.2 Estimation Process Steps

Draw Out a Plan for the Estimation

Planning helps to ensure all the available information is obtained before starting the estimation. Draw out a schedule indicating the various activities of the estimation process along with appropriate time line of the estimation. This helps to monitor and control the estimation process. Resources involved in the estimation process are also listed and mapped against the tasks for better tracking. There is no right plan or wrong plan, whatever that works is fine.

Doing the Estimation

Estimation is a process of doing the calculation to derive the values as per the plan. We are also here to find a value or number that is close enough to the right value (number) and in other words estimations are always approximation.

Refine the Estimation

Continuous refinement of the values and the estimation process makes the success of cost estimation. The value (estimation) is continuously refined if more information about the risks, resources and contexts are known in clear at later point of time. Even if the estimation process is refined based on the continuous feedback and experience. Some uncontrollable events or situations may impose a re-estimation of the cost and schedule.

8.6 Basic Estimation Principles

Following are the basic estimation principles that can be followed with any estimation:

1. Use more than one technique to derive the estimate.
2. Use more than one method of estimation.
3. It is better to obtain at least two estimates using each method.
4. Involve the people who will be doing the actual work.
5. Get the commitment from the team who will be doing the work.
6. Get the feedback from the project sponsor.
7. Ensure the estimation are reviewed independently.

8. Add contingencies based on the risk levels.
9. Ensure the assumptions are clearly documented.
10. Refine the estimate as more information is known.

Discussion Point

Discuss the importance of basic estimation principles. Give examples for each point.

8.7 Estimation Techniques

Estimations techniques are of great help for the estimators and can be used across various situations. We need to find out the appropriate technique according to the environment factors. Various known estimation techniques are: expert judgements, top-down estimation, bottom-up estimation, analogous estimation and parametric estimation. Let's see some of those techniques here which are discussed below. We will learn the cost estimation related techniques in Chapter 11.

8.7.1 Expert Judgement

One or more experts who are good in the particular field of domain/technology/process use their experience to predict the estimation (cost, schedule, etc.). The discussion continues until the consensus is reached. The estimation is accurate if the expert has direct experience on the system and the metrics under study. Finding experts are difficult.

Advantages:

1. It is useful in the absence of quantified data.
2. It can factor in impacts of new technology in the market.
3. It can factor in the experience of the past project which is impossible to quantify and measure otherwise.
4. It can factor in realistic assumptions and constraints based on the past project data.

Disadvantages:

1. Estimate is only as good as expert's opinion.
2. It is hard to express the opinion of the expert.
3. It is hard to justify the accuracy of the output.
4. Different experts differ in their opinion.
5. It is hard to document the factors used by the experts.

8.7.2 Brainstorming

In brainstorming session, the facilitator should guide the entire session and encourage active participation to all those involved. We need to involve participants from various departments across the organization and who have different backgrounds so that they can bring fresh ideas (estimations) that can inspire. It is important that the purpose of the meeting should be explained clearly well in advance to the participants, and it is helpful if they are prepared when they arrive at the meeting. Brainstorming usually effective with groups of 8–12 people and that should be performed in a relaxed environment.

Advantages:

1. It considers the opinion of the entire team.
2. Quick and easy technique.
3. Fresh ideas and large set of ideas possible.

Disadvantages:

1. If the facilitator is not strong enough the technique fails.
2. Positive bias and negative bias surfaces.
3. Opinions of the members are not always useful.
4. Effective only with groups of 8–12 people.

8.7.3 Delphi Technique

The Delphi method relies on a panel of independent experts and is a way to reach consensus among experts on the estimation. After each round, the facilitator provides an anonymous summary of the experts' forecasts of estimates (figures) from the previous round as well as the reasons they provided for their judgments without telling which expert contributed that. Experts are encouraged to revise their earlier estimations and resubmit the answers based on the summary results from previous round. During this process, the group will converge towards the estimation and finally the process is stopped after a pre-defined stop criterion like number of rounds, stability of results. The mean or median scores of the final rounds determine the final result.

Points to Remember

Delphi method is an expert technique and anonymous. The experts may not know the details of other experts involved in the process.

Advantages:

1. Independent experts does the estimation.
2. There is no biasing as anonymous technique followed.
3. Experts are given opportunity to correct and revise their figures based on other people's figures and justification.
4. Final outcome is more accurate.
5. Final outcome accepted by all.

Disadvantages:

1. Time consuming (as it goes for more discussion rounds).
2. The result is as good as the experts chosen for the purpose.
3. Identifying experts takes time.

4. Determining the number of experts to be involved is critical for the success.
5. Facilitator needs to be strong and not biased.
6. Facilitator needs to spend lot of time collating the details.

8.7.4 Parkinson Law

Parkinson law states that work expands to fill the time available. If we have three resources, and the software to be delivered in 10 months, then the efforts required to do the software = 3 × 10 = 30 person month.

Advantages:

1. Easy and quick estimation.
2. All the resources are being utilized in the estimation.

Disadvantages:

1. It is applicable only for smaller companies.
2. The estimation may not be accurate as it does not consider project parameters.
3. This technique considers all the resources of same experience and skill level.

8.8 Tools for Analysing Metrics and Estimations

Metrics are of no use if they are not analysed properly. Ishikawa's 7 'old' tools can be used for this purpose which is listed below:

- Checklist
- Pareto diagram
- Histogram
- Scatter diagram
- Run chart
- Control chart
- Cause-and-effect diagram

8.8.1 Checklists

A checklist is an instruction sheet for an estimator or inspector to use for verification purpose. The checklists are generic in nature and we can use more tailored checklists (if necessary) to meet the needs of a particular project, program or activity. When we prepare a checklist, it indirectly tells that we are planning to do certain defined activities. Checklist will be used to verify whether we did all the activities as per the customized checklist. Checklist can be used to analyze the metrics.

8.8.2 Pareto Diagram

Pareto developed the concept of 80–20 rule, i.e., 80% of the problems are due to 20% of the causes. Pareto chart is a histogram ordered by frequency of occurrence and is used by the

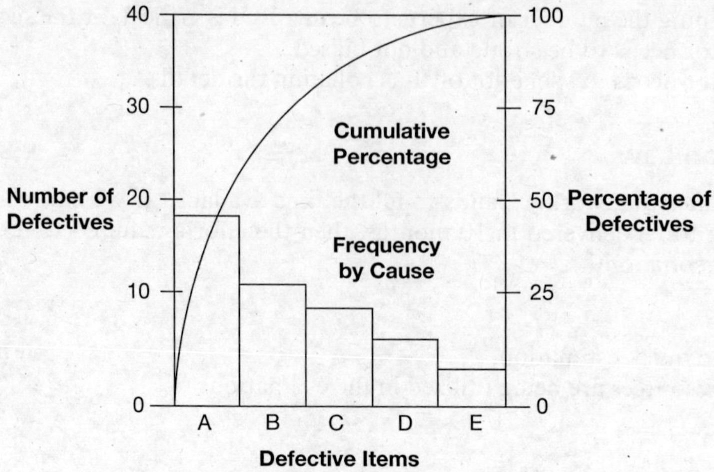

Figure 8.3 Pareto Diagram

project team to find out the causes creating the greatest number of defects. The problems in a process are arranged in the order of importance using factors, such as cost, time delay or some other parameters.

Steps for the Pareto Diagram

1. Determine the classification of defect you will use in the graph (Example: number of defects).
2. Decide on a time period to be covered on the graph.
3. Total the frequency of occurrence for each category for the period and each total will be shown by the length of the bar.

In the above Pareto diagram (Figure 8.3), 'Cause A' alone is responsible for about 50% of the problem with more than 15 defects. If we take steps to remove the defective item A, most of our problems will get solved.

8.8.3 Histogram

It is a graphical representation (Figure 8.4) of the frequency distribution of the variable under consideration and the values of the variables are grouped into intervals which are shown in the horizontal axis and the frequency of occurrence of values in various intervals are shown in the vertical axis.

If any unusual events affected the process during the time period of the histogram, our analysis of the histogram shape probably cannot be generalized to all time periods. First, we need to analyse the meaning of histogram's shape.

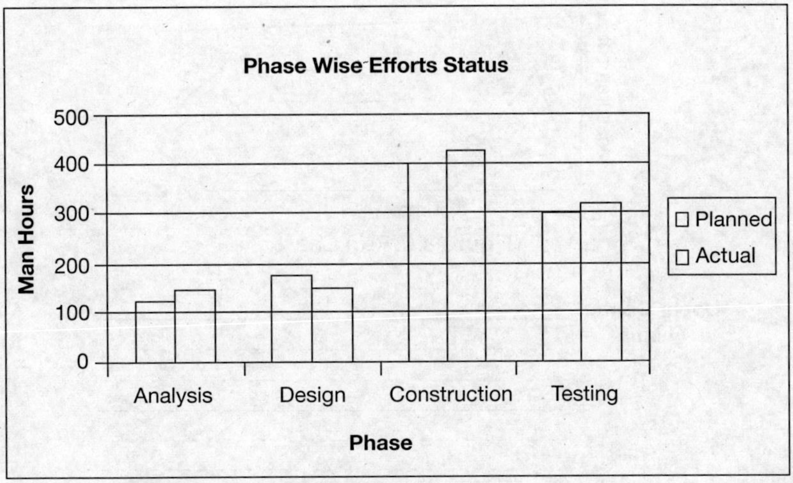

Figure 8.4 Histogram

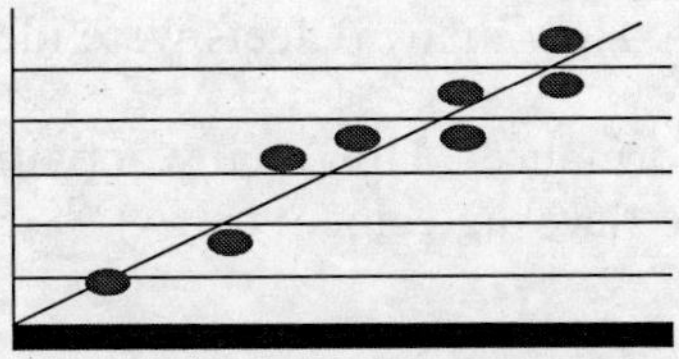

Figure 8.5 Scatter Plot

8.8.4 Scatter Diagram

A scatter diagram has the following components and characteristics:
A scatter diagram (scatter plot in Figure 8.5) used to analyse the relationship between two variables.
Y-axis has the variable to be predicted.
X-axis has the variable to make the prediction.
Correlation is the indicative measure of the relationship between two sets of numbers or variables (here, the variables are plotted at X and Y axis).
Correlated variables form a line or curve kind of structure while plotted in a graph.

8.8.5 Run Chart

A run chart (Figure 8.6) is also called a run-sequence plot. It is a graph that displays observed data in a time sequence. Trend analysis is performed on a run chart to forecast future outcomes based on the historical data.

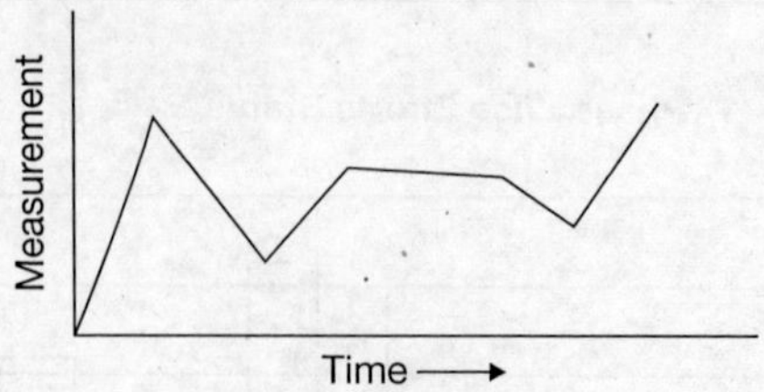

Figure 8.6 Run Chart

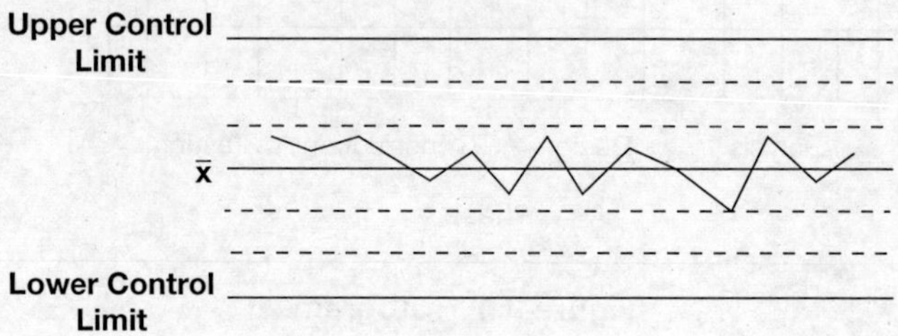

Figure 8.7 Control Chart

1. Technical performance—How many defects were identified and how many defects were closed out of it?
2. Cost and schedule performance—How many activities per period were completed within the defined service level agreement (SLA)?

8.8.6 Control Charts

It (Figure 8.7) is used to assess whether the process is 'in control' and is used to determine whether the observed variations in a process are due to normal process variations or due to any other problems. Control chart helps to do corrections in the process before producing bad output.

Points to Remember

Run of seven continuous ponits toward upper or lower control limit in a particular direction may indicate that the process is out of control. This is called 'Rule of Seven'. Variations may be caused by differences in machines, workers overtime, for which causes are well-known and no need for further investigations and this is called 'Assignable Causes'.

There are two types of control charts, namely, variable control charts and attribute control charts.

Variable control charts deals with items that can be measured like height, cost, schedule, etc. X Bar Chart, R Chart, MA Chart are examples of variable control charts.

Attribute control charts are used to test the attributes of a product in order to find out whether product is going out of control. p-chart, c-chart, u-chart are examples of attribute control charts.

1. Choose the control chart fitting into your data.
2. Determine the appropriate time period required for collecting the data and plotting the data collected.
3. Collect the actual data construct your chart and analyze the data.
4. Look for 'out-of-control signals' on the control chart just drawn and investigate the cause. Document the entire process.

Center line in Control chart represents mean
UCL = 3 × Standard Deviation above mean
LCL = 3 × Standard Deviation below mean

Tolerances: The result is acceptable if it falls within the range specified by the tolerance.
Control limits: The process is said to be in control if the result falls within the control limits.

Out of Control
Process is out of control when one of the following conditions is met:

- At least one point outside the control limits
- Seven points in a row above the average value (even within limit)
- Lot of points in a row near the control limits (this indicates a problem)

8.8.7 Cause and Effect Diagrams

Kaoru Ishikawa developed this diagram. It is known as the Fishbone Diagram or Ishikawa Diagram (Figure 8.8). This diagram is useful in determining the root-cause problems. We can use this to analyse the problem related with metrics. It helps us to analyse all the possible causes associated with the problem under a study.

A possible root–cause can be uncovered by using the Why–Why diagram (Figure 8.9). How–How diagram is shown in Figure 8.10.

The causes in a cause and effect diagram are frequently arranged into five major categories such as manpower, methods, materials, measurement and machinery. More classification can be added as per the situation which suits our need.

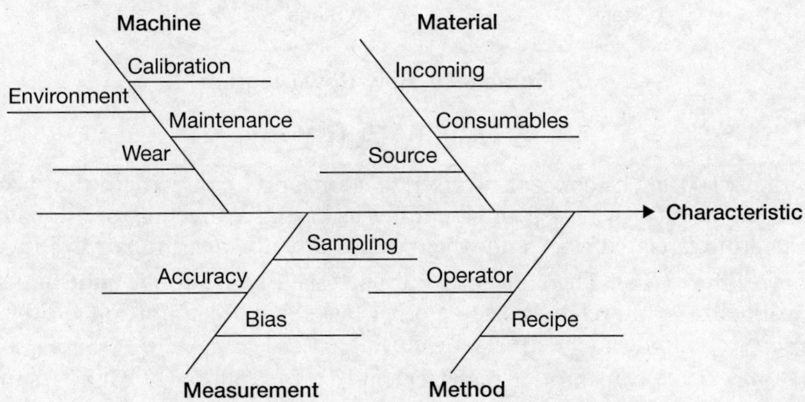

Figure 8.8 Cause and Effect Diagram

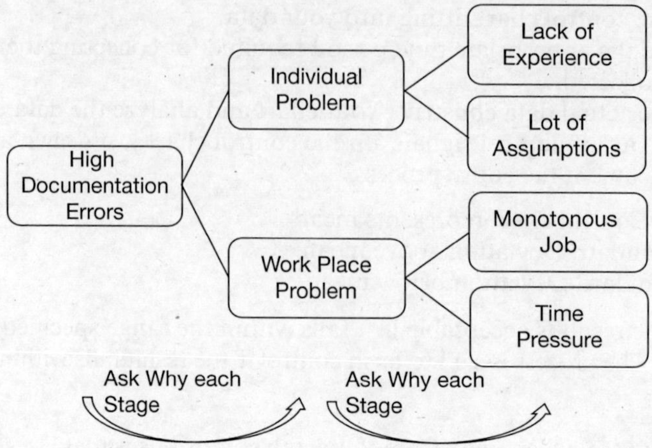

Figure 8.9 Why–Why Diagram

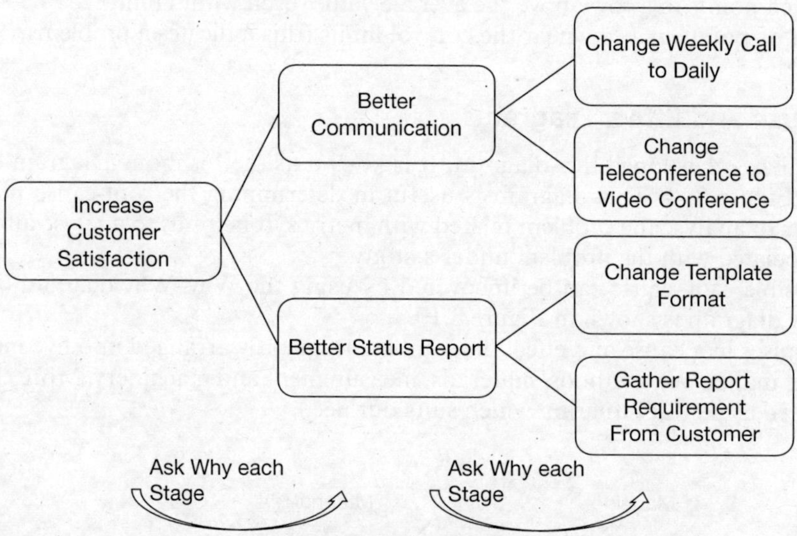

Figure 8.10 How-How Diagram

SUMMARY

- **Discrete Effort (DE):** The concept of discrete effort applies directly to the specific work efforts that can be directly traced and identified as having a direct tie for ultimate completion of the project-related work and which is also directly measurable.
- **Apportioned Effort (AE):** The concept of apportioned effort applies not directly to the specific work efforts, but related to some other tasks that are apportioned over here. For example, project management efforts for finishing a task.
- **Level of Effort (LOE):** In project management, level of effort (LOE) is a support-type project activity that must be done to support other work activities or the entire project effort.

Basic Estimation Principles

1. Use more than one technique to derive the estimate.
2. Use more than one method of estimation.
3. It is better to obtain at least two estimates using each method.
4. Involve the people who will be doing the actual work.
5. Get the commitment from the team who will be doing the work.

Expert Judgement: One or more experts who are good in the particular field of domain/technology/process. Use their experience to predict the estimation (cost, schedule, etc.).

Brainstorming: In a brainstorming session, the facilitator guide the entire session and encourage active participation to all those involved. We need to involve participants from various departments across the organization and who have different backgrounds, so that they can bring fresh ideas (estimations) that may inspire.

The Delphi Method: It is a way to reach consensus among experts on the estimation.

Metrics are no use if they are not analysed properly. Ishikawa's 7'old' tools can be used for this purpose.

- Checklist
- Pareto diagram
- Histogram
- Scatter diagram
- Run chart
- Control chart
- Cause-and-effect diagram

Checklist: A checklist is an instruction sheet for an estimator or inspector to use it for verification purpose.

Pareto Diagram (Pareto Chart): Pareto developed the concept of 80–20 rule, *i.e.*, 80% of the problems are due to 20% of the causes.

Histogram: It is a graphical representation of the frequency distribution of the variable under consideration and the values of the variables are grouped into intervals which are shown in the horizontal axis and the frequency of occurrence of values in various intervals are shown in the vertical axis.

A Scatter Diagram (Scatter Graph): It is used to analyze the relationship between two variables.

A Run Chart: It is also called as a run-sequence plot which is a graph that displays observed data in a time sequence. Trend analysis is performed on a run chart to forecast future outcomes based on the historical data.

Control Charts: It is used to assess whether the process is 'in control' and is used to determine whether the observed variations in a process are due to normal process variations or due to the process getting out of control.

Cause and Effect Diagram: It is also known as the fishbone diagram or Ishikawa diagram and developed by Kaoru Ishikawa. It is useful in determining the root cause problems. We can use this to analyse the problem related with metrics.

EXERCISES

PART A (Objective-type Questions)

1. Exact amount of work required for completing a particular task is called
   A. Effort
   B. Duration
   C. Time
   D. Completion time

2. The time elapsed between start and end of the particular task is called
   A. Effort
   B. Duration
   C. Time
   D. Completion time

3. For writing a particular piece of code, if two resources worked for 10 hours and it took 3 days to complete the tasks. What are the overall estimation and the duration of the tasks?
   A. 20 hours, 3 days
   B. 3 days, 20 hours
   C. 6 hours, 30 days
   D. 2 hours, 30 hours

4. The specific efforts that can be directly traced and identified as having direct tie for ultimate completion of project related work is called
   A. Discrete Effort
   B. Apportioned Effort
   C. Level of Effort
   D. Direct Effort

5. The effort that applies not directly to the specific work efforts, but related to some other tasks is
   A. Discrete Effort
   B. Apportioned Effort
   C. Level of Effort
   D. Direct Effort

6. The effort which is a support-type project activity that must be done to support other work activities or the entire project effort is known as
   A. Discrete Effort
   B. Apportioned Effort
   C. Level of Effort
   D. Direct Effort

7. Which of the following is not an estimation technique?
   A. Expert judgements
   B. Top down estimation
   C. Analogous estimation
   D. Horizontal estimation

8. One or more experts, who are good in the particular field of domain/technology/process, use their experience to predict the estimation (cost, schedule, etc.). It is called
   A. Expert judgements
   B. Top-down estimation
   C. Analogous estimation
   D. Brainstorming technique

9. The type of estimation technique everybody participates to get more ideas is called
   A. Expert judgements
   B. Top-down estimation
   C. Analogous estimation
   D. Brainstorming technique

10. A panel of independent experts are used in the technique and also being used anonymously is known as
    A. Bottom-up estimation
    B. Top-down estimation
    C. Delphi technique
    D. Brainstorming technique

11. Work expands to fill the time available is called Parkinson law
    A. True
    B. False

12. Values of repeated measurements is called
    A. Accuracy
    B. Precision
    C. Metrics
    D. Comparative estimate

13. The measure value is very close to true value means
    A. Accuracy
    B. Precision
    C. Metrics
    D. Comparative estimate

14. Which of the following is not a tool of Ishikawa 7 'old' tools?
    A. Checklist
    B. Histogram
    C. Pareto chart
    D. Flow chart

15. An instruction sheet for an inspector to use for verification purpose is called
    A. Check list
    B. Pareto chart
    C. Histogram
    D. Run chart

16. 80–20 rule based chart is called
    A. Checklist
    B. Pareto chart
    C. Histogram chart
    D. Run chart

17. The graphical representation of the frequency distribution of the variable under consideration and the values of the variables is called
    A. Checklist
    B. Pareto chart
    C. Histogram chart
    D. Run chart

18. The graph that displays observed data in a time sequence is called
    A. Control chart
    B. Pareto chart
    C. Histogram chart
    D. Run chart

19. Two types of control charts are
    A. Variable control charts and attribute control charts
    B. Data control charts and information control charts
    C. Process control charts and product control charts
    D. Cause control charts and problem control charts

20. Which of the following is not a condition of a process said to be out of control in a control chart?
    A. At least one point outside the control limits.
    B. Points moving frequently moving up and down but within the limits.
    C. Seven points in a row above the average value (even within limit).
    D. Lots of points in a row near the control limits (this indicates a problem).

21. Just by adding more resources we cannot finish the project early, addition of more resources may increase overall output in the beginning, but will eventually decrease individual productivity.
    A. True
    B. False

PART B (Write the answers in one or two lines)

1. List down any three importance of accurate estimation in a software project.
2. Define efforts and duration.
3. Give example for the difference between efforts and duration in a software project.
4. Define Discrete Effort (DE).
5. Define Apportioned Effort (AE).
6. Define Level of Effort (LOE).
7. What are estimation techniques?
8. List down various software estimation techniques you are aware of.

9. What is expert judgment technique?
10. What is brainstorming technique?
11. Write notes on Delphi technique.
12. Discuss various tools for analysing metrics and estimations.
13. Write notes on checklist.
14. Write notes on Pareto diagram (Pareto chart).
15. What is histogram?
16. Write notes on run chart.
17. What is control chart?
18. Write notes on two types of control charts?
19. What is the condition of a process to be out of control in control charts?
20. Write notes on cause and effect diagrams.

9

Software Project Management Plan

9.1 Introduction

A Software Project Management Plan (SPMP) is a comprehensive document. It captures the entire project dynamics in one place. This is an overarching document which is used right from the initiation to planning, monitoring and controlling upto the closure of a project. So, it is evident that it is a live document. It is elaborated and updated throughout the project life cycle. All the stakeholders of the project get visibility about what, how and when of the project from the SPMP.

9.2 What is Project Planning?

There is a popular saying 'you can control something only if you can plan it'. It is only possible to control a project efficiently if the planning is done diligently. Project planning encompasses the strategic part of understanding the planning principles and philosophies and the tactical part by following the steps, tools and techniques to create the project plan. Project scenarios are often dynamic in nature making it essential that the project plans also evolve with time. For example, if a project plan is created with an assumption that rightly skilled resources would be available before the beginning of the development phase, but during actual project execution if it is found that such skilled resources are not available, then the project plan is bound to change in handling the new situation.

Cost, time, scope and quality are four prime factors tracked in a project. A project plan has the final objective of controlling these four components involved in projects. Project plan acts as the road map for the entire project. The team may follow it throughout the project life cycle. What level of importance would be given to the project planning activities often depends on the organization's culture. An organization that wants to get into project activities very quickly must not encourage investing much time in planning work, whereas a process-oriented organization, aiming to reduce the uncertainties and gain control over a project, will invest heavily for robust planning.

For software projects, the project plan encompassing all the aspects of the project is documented in the form of Software Project Management Plan (SPMP). This is the key document of the project and has reference to many sub-documents describing plans for different aspects of the project.

9.3 SPMP Structure

There are two main sections in an SPMP. The first section contains the scope, tasks and costs involved in the project which helps all the stakeholders to understand 'when', 'what' and 'how' activities will be performed in the project. The second section contains the process and operational management systems like details about the quality management, configuration, changes, risks, communication and several other factors which make a project successful. These are discussed below along with the description of each subsection and suggestions on how these sections should be addressed during planning process for developing the project management plan. The elements of SPMP are discussed as given below:

Project Overview

1. **Introduction/overview:** This section provides introduction to the project as well as the project management plan. Some background information about the project like who the customer is, how the project was initiated, how the project is funded along with some other information which may be important for the reader of the SPMP like stringent quality norms, safety feature requirements, government policies which are applicable for the project, etc., can also be part of this section.
2. **Mission and Objectives:** The mission statements state the reason for taking up the project. The objective section elaborates the goals that the project should accomplish. It is important to identify and document the key objectives as those will construct the critical success factors for the projects. There are different types of objectives that are specified by different stakeholders ranging from customer organizations to delivery organizations as:

    - Technical objectives
    - Safety objectives
    - Cost objectives
    - Schedule/timeline objectives
    - Reporting objectives
    - Manpower objectives and other related goals

    Clearly, stated objectives help to create a well-defined scope, Work Break down Structure (WBS) and reliable project plan.
3. **Work Scope:** This section ensures that all the in-scope activities and out-of-scope activities are properly understood and agreed between all the parties. This helps in creating the WBS efficiently. Often the work scope and the WBS are developed in parallel. There may be implicit and explicit requirements that need to be delivered to the customer. Other than the design and development of the product or system, there

may also be system integration requirement, data migration requirement, training, deployment and maintenance requirement for the proposed system. The following items comprise a work scope:

- *Project Deliverables or End Products:* Here, list of products, services, documents that should be delivered to the customer over the life cycle of the project are captured clearly.
- *Requirements:* Requirements can be of different categories, like technical requirements, management requirements, data requirements, special instructions, etc. This set of requirement acts as specifications for the projects which need to be followed.

In most of the projects, the technical requirements are captured in a separate document called the Functional Requirement Specification (FRS) document. The Requirement Management chapter of this book discusses the details of activities performed in requirement stage.

The other requirements which are not technical in nature, but still are important for the customer have to be captured in the SPMP as well. For example, there may be a requirement that the project is executed from a Restricted Access Development Centre because of the sensitive data it handles. Then this facility requirement should be captured in SPMP and adhered to it in the project.

Other types of requirements which can be part of this document are operational instructions, training needs, testing requirements and any special support required by the customer. In case some portions of the requirement are developed through sub-contracting, then this may have a reference to the original customer.

- *Excluded Scope:* When there are multiple vendors involved in one project then it is very important for each vendor to spell out what is in-scope and what is out-of-scope for it. For example, if the design, coding, and unit testing is handled by one vendor and then system testing is to be carried out by a different vendor, then it is crucial that both the vendors clearly document where their respective responsibilities start and finish so that any controversy during the project execution can be avoided. For sole vendors also, in case the customer need to handle certain tasks, like hardware procurement or getting government licenses, etc., for making the project successful then those become out of scope for the vendor and should be mentioned clearly in the SPMP.

Project Organization

The project's organizational structures, their boundaries and interfaces as well as role and responsibilities of the participating groups are identified and documented here for various elements of the project.

1. **Organizational Structure:** The internal management structure of the project to depict the lines of authority, lines of reporting and lines of communications within the project are depicted in this section. Organizational structures are often represented graphically using hierarchical organization charts and matrix diagrams. Figure 9.1 shows a sample of organization structure.
2. **Organizational Boundaries and Interfaces:** On the basis of how many teams are involved in the project and with how many external agencies or organizations the teams need to work, the number of organizational boundaries and the complexity

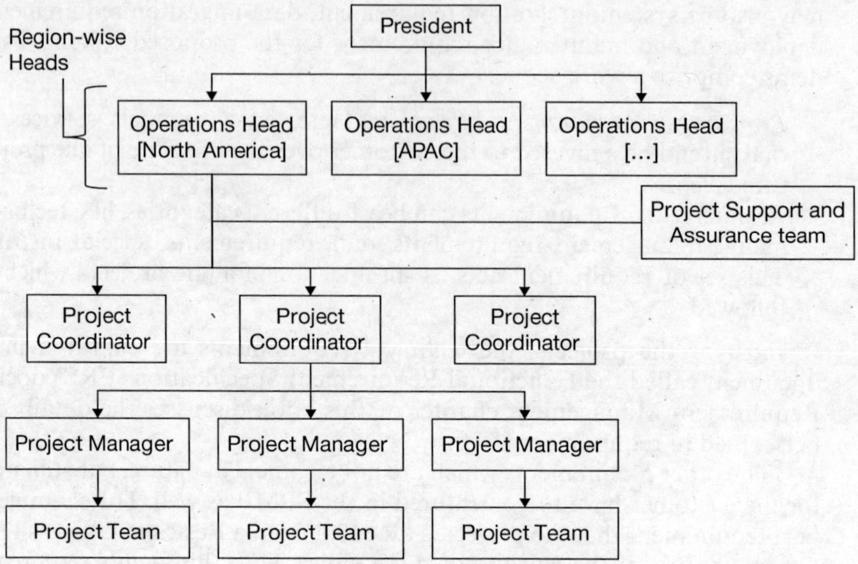

Figure 9.1 Organization Chart

of interfaces increase. It is important to define the boundaries with the other teams, external agencies and consultants early in the project to promote clear communication. Similarly, it is important to define the administrative and managerial boundaries with the internal support services, like quality assurance, human resources, etc., at the early stage of the project.

3. **Roles and Responsibilities:** This section briefly describes the roles and responsibilities of the individuals who are part of the project organization. The RACI matrix is an efficient way of representing the roles and responsibilities in a project. It identifies the persons 'Responsible', 'Accountable', 'Consulted' and 'Informed' in the project throughout its life cycle. Figure 9.2 shows a sample of the RACI matrix.

Management Process

1. **Planning Basis:** Assumptions, constraints, approaches and the other factors that are considered during planning are documented in this section. It is very important to capture the planning basis so that all the stakeholders understand the rationale behind the plan and also these points can be referred and tracked during the project life cycle to monitor any change in scenario and need for re-planning. The items that are addressed in this section are:
   - *Constraints:* All the known constraints at the time of developing the plan should be captured here and, then communicated to all stakeholders. The constraints can be technical or technological constraints, skill availability constraints, date constraints, location constraints or even policy constraints.

   Example of technical constraint is a new technology used in the project that needs initial set-up and training time for the associates. Similarly, there may be acute date constraints from the customer, like the product needs to be launched before the Christmas which drives the whole plan.

Activity/Decision	Director	Sponsor	Project Manager	Team	Client
Provide the necessary hardware and software licenses for the project work	I	I	C	I	R, A
Requirement sign-off	I		A	I	R
Co-ordinate with multiple vendors to freeze the interface definitions	I	R	C	I	A
Interface design creation			A	R	C, I
Shift the project milestones to add functionalities	R	I	A	I	C

R =**Responsible** to do or complete. Can be shared responsibilit.
A = **Accountable.** Ultimately answerable for the results and holds the 'sign off' right.
C = **Consulted.** People who are consulted before a final decision is taken.
I = **Informed.** Individuals who need to know about a decision or action taken.

Figure 9.2 RACI Matrix

In many cases, the government policies, like visa restriction in certain countries or requirement of employing local resources are big constraints for projects. Such factors can affect the project cost and timeline which should be accounted for in the SPMP.

- *Approaches/Strategies:* The approaches and the strategies are considered while developing the project plan as those are playing significant roles throughout the project life cycle. For example, if it is decided that the project needs to fast-tracked by performing the system testing and user acceptance testing with considerable overlap, then the resource and timeline planning changes significantly than the normal back to back scenario. The other strategies like getting a portion of the project developed through a contractor instead of developing it in-house have significant impact on planning and thus to be mentioned in the SPMP.
- *Assumptions:* There must be uncertainties and open clarifications at the beginning of a project. For planning purpose, it is important to assume certain factors and prepare a plan. It is essential that the planning assumptions are available with the project manager as these needs to be validated throughout the lifecycle of the project. The project scenarios might change at any point of time requiring the assumptions to be changed which, in turn, will cause project plan revision.

2. **Resource Plan:** Resources in the project can include the staffs, hardware, software and other infrastructure requirements. This section captures when and what resources are required in the project along with the required quantity and quality. The staffs can be from inside the organization or from other vendors or contractors.
3. **Procurement and Logistics Plan:** On the basis of cost benefit analysis, an organization may decide to get some part of the project handled by a vendor or external agency. This requires the creation and execution of a procurement and logistics plan.

Technical Process

The technical details of the project like methods, tools and techniques, architecture to be used, etc., are captured in this section. Some of the related details, like the plan for software documentation and plans for project support functions, such as quality assurance, configuration management and verification and validation will also be identified in this section.

1. **Methods, Tools, and Techniques:** Projects undergo different stages, like design, build, test, integration, documentation, delivery, modification and maintenance. The important parameters guiding these stages like computing system, development methodology, team structure, programming language, and other notations, tools, techniques, and methods to be used are specified here. Also, the technical standards, policies, procedures and guidelines governing development are either directly included here or those documents are referenced in this section.
2. **Architecture Plan:** The underlying architecture of a project known as the architecture plan is a crucial document and a reference to that plan is mentioned in this section. Because of the highly technical nature and big structure of the architecture plan, a reference is included here instead of writing the full content.
3. **Documentation and Configuration Management Plan:** Documentation is an important part of the project work other than the technical work. A documentation plan can specify what documentation is required to be delivered when it should be delivered and the mode of delivery. An important aspect associated with the documentation requirement is the configuration management and version control requirement in the project. Often, a confirmation manager role is created in the project which controls the versioning, multiple editing, storage and media as well as delivery of documentation.
4. **Project Support Functions:** Support functions are the peripheral systems of a software project that are not part of the direct technical delivery, but helps in making the project a success. These plans are often big enough to become an independent document of their own and referenced in the SPMP document. Some of these support functions are:
   - Configuration management
   - Software quality assurance
   - Verification and validation plans
   - Production support and operational support functions

Work Packages, Schedules and Budget

This is a crucial section of the SPMP as this will specify the work packages, their dependencies, project resource requirements, the budget, the resource requirements and, finally, establish a project schedule.

1. **Work Packages:** This subsection defines the work packages and WBS for the activities and tasks that need to be completed as per project agreement. Work breakdown structure is a powerful representation of all the project work in a hierarchical structure and each lower level in the hierarchy represents more granular details of the project's work. The lowest level called 'work packages' are uniquely identified work items and helps in subsequent stages of estimation, budgeting and planning.

2. **Dependencies:** Ordering of the work packages is driven by the interdependencies among them and also by the dependencies on external events. Techniques like dependency lists, activity networks, and the critical path method are used to depict dependencies among work packages and their ordering.
3. **Resource Requirements:** The resources required (normally the staff) to complete the work packages and the time and duration of their involvement are specified here. Based on the resource calendar, the timeline of the work packages are drawn.
4. **Budget and Resource Allocation:** Based on the resource cost, the overall budget for completing the project is drawn. All the above inputs are crucial for creating the project schedule.
5. **Schedule:** Project schedule is the depiction of project's works on a time scale along with their dependencies, resources, precedence relations and required milestone dates. Schedules may be expressed either in absolute calendar time or as increments to key project milestones.

In the next chapter, the detailed steps for creating the project schedule are discussed.

Project Success Criteria

Multiple elements comprise the criteria which need to be met for the success of the project. Some of these are project milestones and checkpoints, key deliverables, acceptance criteria and management approval process, for project and product deliverables.

1. **Project Milestones:** Project milestones are important and identifiable points in time that specifies the completion of set of task. For example, the completion of design or completion of testing can be treated as important milestones in a project. It is important to adhere to the milestones for the success of the project. So, this section of the SPMP is crucial as all the stakeholders should be aware of the milestones and work together to achieve those.
2. **Approval Process:** This subsection describes the management process for obtaining approval of project deliverables. The approval requirement may be from internal authorization departments or it may also include any approvals needed from anyone outside the agency or group. The process and criteria for 'go/no-go' decision points are also captured here.
3. **Acceptance Criteria:** These are the customer specified criteria or the check points, based on that the customer may accept or reject the work product. A clearly specified list of acceptance criteria helps in avoiding conflict at the later stages of the project. It is important that the acceptance criteria are specific, measurable and quantitative rather than broad based and qualitative.
4. **Critical Success Factors:** It is more than just on time and on budget delivery of the work product that contributes to the success of a project. There may be several objectives which describe critical success factors as identified by the client as the project quality goals. For example, successful on site-offshore collaboration, regular status reporting, error free code, etc., can be mentioned by the client as the important factors which can dictate success and failure of the project.

Data Conversion/Data Migration Plan

Many projects have data conversion and data migration activity as the scope of the project. This subsection describes how the data from the old or legacy system is collected and converted and then finally migrated to production after the application is deployed into production.

Test Strategy

Testing is the crucial part of any project. This ensures that the developed application is doing what it is designed to do. There are several types of testing based on the scope, technique and timeline as Unit Testing, Functional Testing, System Testing, User Acceptance Testing, Regression Testing, and Performance/Scalability Testing. Test strategy captures the expectation from each of these testing processes, the methodologies to be followed, the tools to be used, the important timelines and the resulting documentation which should be generated out of the testing activities. This section should also include Data Verification.

A test strategy may contain details of each of the stages in testing. These are:

1. Unit Testing
2. Functional Testing
3. System Testing
4. User Acceptance Testing
5. Regression Testing
6. Performance/Scalability Testing
7. Data Verification

Deployment Plan

After developing and testing the required software, it is important that it is installed in the production environment successfully. Proper planning is required to ensure that the new system is installed without affecting the customer's business, especially if the new system intends to replace an already existing system. This section describes how the product will be deployed into production.

System Transition/Rollout Plan

The knowledge transfer required for software components, hardware components and transition of knowledge from development to maintenance team is crucial for effectively supporting the product. Along with that, the rollout plan can involve the plan on how to distribute the software to multiple regions and departments and any language translation, training, etc., for achieving this.

Maintenance and Support Plans

Once the product is deployed and rolled out, the maintenance and support team takes over the operations and upgrade part of it. The maintenance and support plan may include activities, like the daily scheduled jobs, clean ups, upgrades, application and database tuning.

Related Plans

As we discussed earlier in this chapter, SPMP is the overarching document comprising of all the plans relevant for a project. Other than the sections we discussed here, there are other plans that are part of the SPMP. As these plans are large enough to qualify for a separate document, the reference to these documents are only maintained in the SPMP most of the times. These plans are:

1. **Communication Management Plan:** This is a crucial plan that outlines the details of communication required in the project. Communication is the key for success in any project. The communication needs for different stakeholders in the project are different and it is important that all the communication needs are met for success of the project. The frequency (daily, weekly, and monthly), mode (mails, phones, and video conference), approach (formal, informal), etc., provide clarity of the communication requirements that the project team should adhere to throughout the span of the project.
2. **Quality and Productivity Management Plan:** It describes the acceptable level of quality parameters of the project and how the project management team will implement the performing organization's quality policies and quality plan. For example, based on the organizational quality policy, the project needs to identify whether they will be following ISO standards or CMMI or Six Sigma. It also includes the approaches for implementing quality control, quality assurance, and quality improvement processes. The roles and responsibilities of the people involved in the quality process along with various tools and techniques that will be used in the quality journey of the project are clearly identified and documented in this plan. This is described in details in Chapter 13.
3. **Training Plan:** There are two types of training that may be part of this document. First part is the training of end users of the product which is often critical for project success. The training needs as specified by the customer needs to be properly planned and executed by the project team. Sometimes, the training requirements can involve many complexities. For example, there may be requirements of performing the training in multiple languages which needs to be planned very carefully. Second type of training plan is based on the skillset requirement and skillset available from the team members. This is called 'skill gap analysis'. Based on the gaps identified, the employee training programs to be planned accordingly in the project.
4. **Risk Management Plan:** This document is prepared to plan, mitigate and monitor the risks in the project, efficiently. Risks are the incidents which can affect the project outcome either positively or negatively. Risk management plan describes how the risks will be identified, their impact and probability of occurrence can be measured and how the mitigation can be achieved. In Chapter 12, we have discussed the components of risk management plan in details.
5. **Change Management Plan:** Changes are inevitable in a project due to several factors like changing in market conditions, change in user requirement, change in timeline, technological advancement, etc. So, it is important that the team is ready with a plan of handling changes as it happens in a project. A change management plan captures the steps that need to be followed from the imitation of a change till the approval process which is called Change Control Mechanism.
6. **Security Plan:** The security requirements are a crucial commitment of any project as it is often backed by the legal contracts and statutory requirements. For example, a financial organization may need that the project to be executed from a secured development center as data protection which is of prime importance.

9.4 Pitfalls in Software Project Planning

There are some common mistakes that project managers commit while creating project plans. It is important to be aware of those common mistakes as those can lead to project failure.

1. **Inadequate Planning:** Planning is often looked down upon as waste of time. Many organizations' culture looks for quick action and result as they feel that it is not worth investing time in planning. Similar mindset is found among new and inexperienced project managers. They get pressurized by the organizations and stakeholders to demonstrate faster result. But, often they succumb to this loophole. The danger is if a project improperly planned, then substantial amount of time, at the later stage, is lost in `fire-fighting'. This happens because unknown risks and unwanted outcomes plague the later stage of the project. Certainly, this stage consumes more effort than in the planning stage.
2. **Lack of Details:** Breaking the project work in sufficient details is crucial for efficient estimation, monitoring and communication. All the project stakeholders should have clear understanding of all the works involved in the project. For achieving this, it is important that the project's scope is broken down into smaller pieces. Accurate estimation of cost and duration is also possible only if the work items are granular enough. Also, at the later stage of the project it is important that the progress is tracked closely which is only possible if the deliverables are broken into smaller chunks of work. For example, if the System Testing activity spans for eight weeks, it will be important to make sure that at the end of each week we can measure whether we are on track in terms of the progress. This is only possible if we break down the testing work in smaller activities like, test case writing, data preparation, test execution, bug fixing, etc.
3. **More Details:** This is just the opposite of the problem stated above. If the project works are broken down in too much details then it may become a management and administration overhead to keep track of all tasks. Moreover, there may be projects which are of small duration or simple ones and may not need so much detailing to be done for planning. So, taking an informed decision of how much granularity is required for planning is a crucial aspect of project planning.
4. **Planning Alone:** The people who will be working in the project should be involved greatly during the planning activity. This ensures that the collected wisdom of experts in different areas is shared during the planning activity making the plan much more realistic than the project manager preparing it alone. Another benefit of involving key stakeholders is that it is easier to get buy in from them during the execution phase as they had created the plan themselves. Planning alone by the project manager is often seen as a cause of failure because of limited exposure to all aspects of project and less buy in from the stakeholders at later stage.
5. **Outdated Plan:** As we discussed earlier in this chapter, a project plan is a live document because of the dynamic nature of the project. Unless the project plan is kept updated with all the changes happening in the project scenario, the project manager will lose track of what needs to be done in the project and deviations and rework in the project will be inevitable after sometime. So, it is of utmost importance that the project plan is updated regularly and shared with all stakeholders.

6. **Ignoring Risks During Project Planning:** One big mistake which many project managers make during the planning phase, is forgetting to take into account the risks and uncertainties. So, the plans they create become the 'best case situation' plan which seldom reflect the real life scenario. There will always be some risk or uncertainties coming to reality during the project and, thus, not planning for those will be disastrous to the project. It is often observed that increase in cost and duration, as a result of accommodating the mitigation of risks, is perceived by organizations as project manager's inability to control the project. It is completely a wrong interpretation of planning for risks.

In summary, too much planning and too less planning both are detrimental for a project. On the basis of project parameters, like size, complexity, importance, organization's expectation, risk and uncertainty involved and stakeholder's profile, a balance needs to be struck.

SUMMARY

- Project planning encompasses the strategic parts of understanding the planning principles and philosophies and the tactical part of following the steps, tools and techniques to create the project plan.
- For software projects the project plan encompassing all the aspects of the project is documented in the form of Software Project Management Plan (SPMP). This is the key document of the project and has reference to many sub-documents describing plans for different aspects of the project.
- A project plan is a live document because of the dynamic nature of the project. Unless the project plan is kept updated with all the changes happening in the project scenario, the project manager will lose track of what needs to be done in the project and deviations and rework in the project will be inevitable after sometime.
- Cost, time, scope and quality are four prime factors tracked in a project. A project plan has the final objective of controlling these four components of the project.
- Project plan acts as the roadmap for the entire project which the team can follow throughout the project life cycle.

EXERCISES

PART A (Objective-type)

1. Project risk management is defined as
   A. The process of defining how to conduct risk management activities for a project.
   B. The process of prioritizing risks for further analysis or action by assessing and combining their probability of occurrence and impact.
   C. The process of developing options and actions to enhance opportunities and to reduce threats to protect objectives.
   D. The process of conducting risk management planning, identification, analysis, response planning and monitoring and controlling a project.

2. Those areas which a project manager considers to be true, real, or certain are called
   A. Constraints
   B. Risks
   C. Assumptions
   D. Project performance
3. A set of interrelated activities and actions performed to achieve pre-specified products, results or services is referred as
   A. A process
   B. Project management
   C. Operation management
   D. Service management
4. Which of the following is a formal document to manage and control project execution?
   A. Statement of work
   B. Risk register
   C. Project charter
   D. Project plan
5. The person who should be in control during the whole lifecycle of the project is called
   A. Sponsor
   B. Project manager
   C. Team member
   D. Stakeholder
6. The sub-section of the SPMP which describes how the support and maintenance activities will be planned in the project is called
   A. Training plan
   B. Deployment plan
   C. Support and maintenance plan
   D. Risk plan
7. In a RACI chart, R stands for:
   A. Responsible
   B. Resource
   C. Requirement
   D. Requested
8. Which is not a common pitfall faced during project planning?
   A. Inadequate planning
   B. Planning alone
   C. Take help of experts as needed
   D. Too much details

PART B (Write the answers in one or two lines)

1. Define project management plan.
2. Name the broad sections in an SPMP.
3. What is the purpose of change management plan?
4. Discuss management process section of an SPMP.
5. Highlight the common pitfalls while creating an SPMP.
6. Describe any two pitfalls that project manager should be aware of while creating an SPMP.
7. Name five related plans referenced in an SPMP.

10

Schedule Management

10.1 Introduction

The backbone of project management is the ability to accurately plan the project activities, resources and costs along with control over the schedule and costs. These are essential in meeting the specified time and cost goals. Schedule management includes the processes required to manage timely completion of a project. In this chapter, we will learn how the overall scope of a project is broken into well-planned tasks trackable till completion.

10.2 Project Schedule

Project schedule is the list of milestones, activities and deliverables put on the timeline and resource information for a particular project. From the schedule, overall project start and end date as well as activity level start and end dates are found. Also, it helps to know which resources would be working on which activities at which point of time. If there are dependencies between the activities, then that should also reflect in the project schedule. Based on the project schedule, various types of analyses become possible. Some examples are: (1) Finding out the critical path for effective risk analysis; (2) Analysis of the delay and possible fast-tracking of projects; and analysis of resource utilization and so on. In the subsequent sections, we will learn how an effective project schedule can be developed.

10.3 Steps to Develop a Project Schedule

The scope of a project should be documented at the beginning of the planning phase. From the planning phase, project manager and the project team needs to identify all the activities or tasks to be performed to get the necessary work done for delivering the scope to the customer. The following six broad steps are followed for creating and maintaining a proper project schedule.

1. Define activities and create Work Breakdown Structure (WBS): The process of defining the work (activities) that must be performed to meet the project objectives.
2. Sequence activities: The process of identifying and documenting the interaction and logical relationships between activities.
3. Estimate activity resources: The process of determining resources (e.g., equipment, materials, manpower, etc.) that are required, quantities of each resource that is planned to be used, and the availability of each resource to perform the project activities.
4. Estimate activity duration: The process of using information on project scope and resources, and developing durations for input to schedules.
5. Develop schedule: The process of determining the start, intermediate milestones, and end dates of project activities.
6. Control schedule: The process of monitoring the status of the project to update project progress and to manage changes to the accepted schedule.

Figure 10.1 explains the steps for developing a project schedule

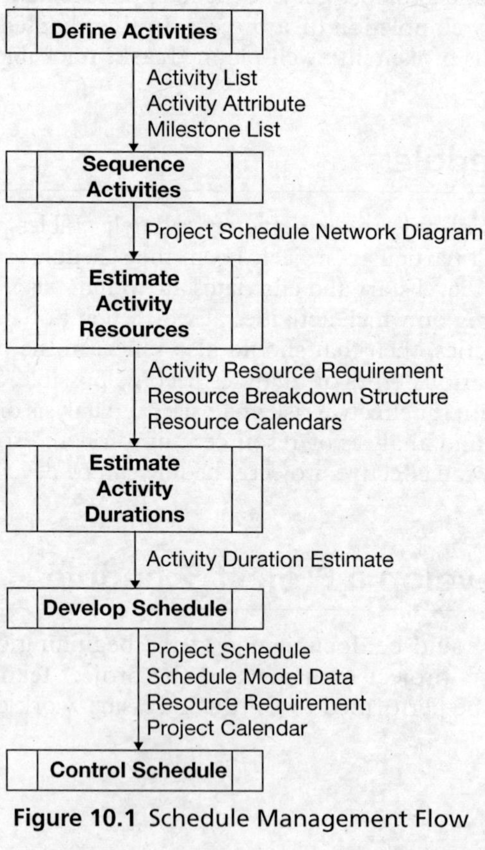

Figure 10.1 Schedule Management Flow

10.3.1 Create Work Breakdown Structure and Define Activities

Every project has definite start and end dates, therefore, a project schedule becomes the basic building block for definition of the entire project. For finding out the start and end date of an entire project, it is necessary to define the start and end dates of all the tasks or activities involved in projects. So, the first step in the Define Activities process is breaking down the project deliverables into smaller and manageable chunks of work called 'Work Breakdown Structure (WBS)'. The lowest tier of a project's WBS is called 'work package'.

Work Breakdown Structure

Work breakdown structure is a deliverable-oriented hierarchical decomposition of the work that needs to be completed by the project team to achieve the project deliverable. Each descending level of the hierarchy represents increasing level of details about the project work. So, a WBS contains all the project work as per the approved scope statement.

The steps involved in creating a WBS are as follows:

- Identify deliverables from the scope statement and related work.
- Structuring and organizing the higher level WBS.
- Decompose upper WBS levels into detailed components at the lower level.
- Assigning identification codes to the WBS components.
- Verify that the degree of decomposition of the work is in accordance to the project needs.

Figure 10.2 shows a sample WBS where the project is broken into phases and then deliverables of each phase are identified. After this, each deliverable is broken into smaller chunks of work called 'work packages'. Work packages have sufficient amount of details and granularity that they

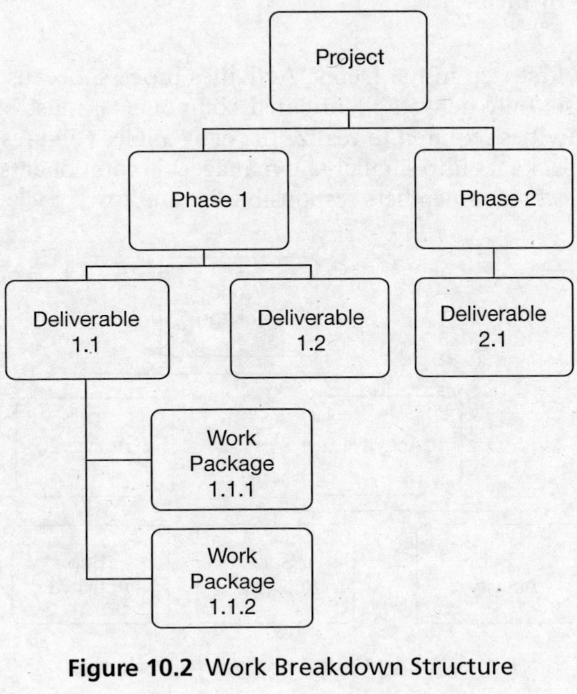

Figure 10.2 Work Breakdown Structure

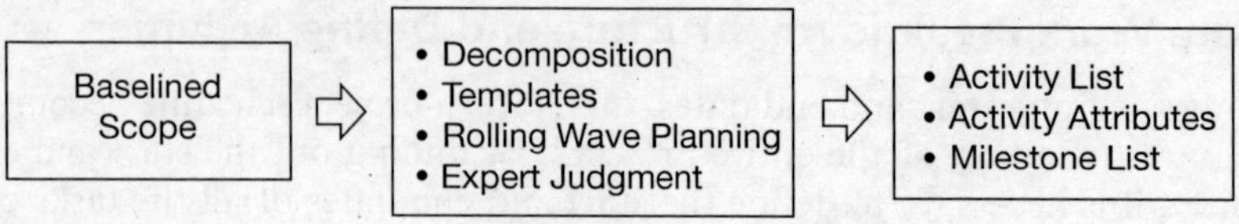

Figure 10.3 Define Activities

can be estimated, planned and tracked in the project life cycle. The list of work packages are documented in the form of a WBS Dictionary comprising details like work package identification number, description of work and responsible organization, resource requirement, cost estimate, acceptance criteria, etc.

Refer to Figure 10.3 for the steps involved in the Define Activities. Decomposition of work packages leads to activities. Activities provide a basis for estimating, scheduling, executing, monitoring, and controlling project work. Project assumptions and constraints, identified and documented in the project's scope statement, also serve as inputs to the process of defining activities. Required quality levels—both stated and implied—serve as project constraints and have a substantial effect on activity definition. Rigorous quality standards would obviously entail more about project activities. At the end of Define Activities process, we generate an activity list which is a list of all activities to be performed as part of a project.

Environmental factors and organizational assets are also used as inputs to the Define Activities process. Organization assets generate the activities related to policies and procedures of a project; it also helps to define activities using historical information and lessons learnt. Environmental factors, such as infrastructure and project management software help to define the activities of the project.

Decomposition:
Decomposition is the first step in the Define Activities process, because the work packages of the WBS which lists only deliverable-oriented components, must be broken down into the actual tasks or activities required to realize the deliverables (Figures 10.4 and 10.5). The sub-division of work packages into smaller and manageable components of activities is often performed by the project team members responsible for that work package. The correct level

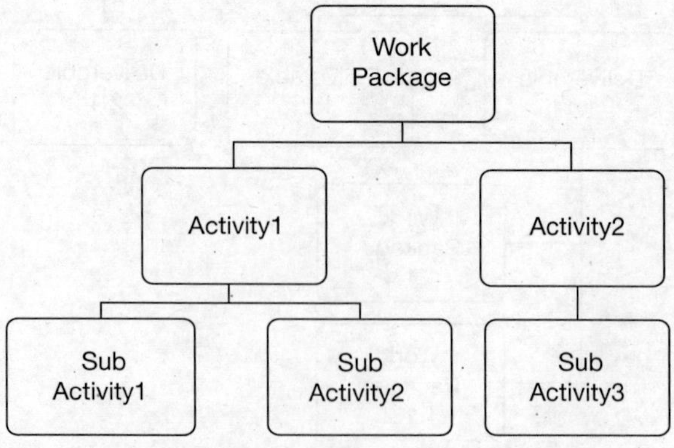

Figure 10.4 Work Packages to Activities

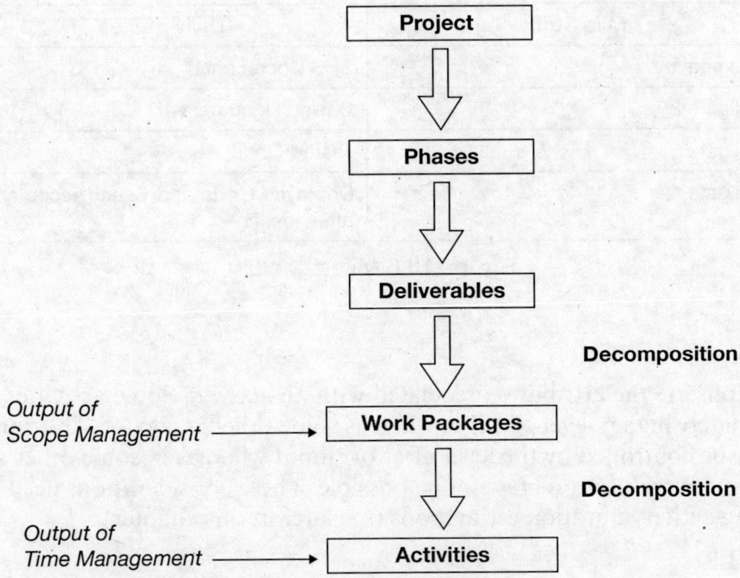

Figure 10.5 Decomposition

of decomposition helps for accurate schedule estimation and timely completion of a project. Correct level of decomposition means decomposing a project to such a level that all efforts related to planning, executing, monitoring and controlling can be readily addressed and managed. Excessive decomposition leads to more work without addition of much value and also leads to inefficient use of resources with decrease in work efficiency.

Templates

Templates from other projects can be used to create activity lists and also to define activity attributes. Templates can be used to define typical milestones as well. Historical data is very useful not only to stop reinventing the wheel, but also to reduce the efforts involved in defining an activity. In a typical project, the Project Management Office provides the templates that can be used in the project. However, it is the project manager's responsibility to customize this template for its purpose.

At the end of the activity identification step, we get an activity list, where attributes and the milestone list are used for sequencing the activities according to project needs.

1. Activity List

At the end of the decomposition process, the activity list of the project gets generated. An activity list is a comprehensive list of all scheduled activities required for a project. It includes the activity identifier and scope of work description for each activity in sufficient detail. An activity identifier is a unique number that identifies a particular activity. It helps in distinguishing an activity from the others that are similar in nature or name. These activity identifiers are unique across the entire project schedule network diagram.

2. Activity Attributes

Activity attributes represent the inherent properties of a particular activity. A WBS identifier, an activity identifier, a predecessor activity, a successor activity, leads, lags, constraints

Mile Stone	Deliverables
Tollgate 1	SRS Document
Tollgate 2	Design Document
Tollgate 3	Tested Code
Tollgate 4	Deployed Code and Client Acceptance after Testing

Figure 10.6 Milestone List

and assumptions are the attributes associated with an activity. Some activities may require a disproportionately higher level of effort whereas some others may not. The duration of some activities may be controlled by the level of effort input whereas in some other activities, such types of control over duration may not be possible. These considerations need to be factored in determining activity duration estimations (see later in this chapter).

3. Milestone Lists

Generally, a milestone list is coupled with a milestone chart and it is used to provide a series of indicators regarding project progress till now and achievements or goals yet to be reached. In Figure 10.6, Tollgate 1 indicates that it will deliver Software Requirement Specification (SRS) document at the end of its phase. Assuming that a project consists of only these four milestones of equal efforts and duration, it can be said that 50% of the project is completed as after crossing Tollgate 2.

10.3.2 Sequencing the Activities

After defining all activities entailed by the project and generating the activity list, the project team needs to arrange these activities in a logical sequence from start to end. In other words, to identify all subsequent processes that require as inputs, the outputs of preceding processes need to be identified. The project team is required to identify the logical relationships, and preferred relationships between all activities. The project team accomplishes this task by identifying project dependencies. Therefore, the sequence activities process is for identifying and documenting such relationships among all project activities. Figure 10.7 shows the steps involved in sequencing the activities.

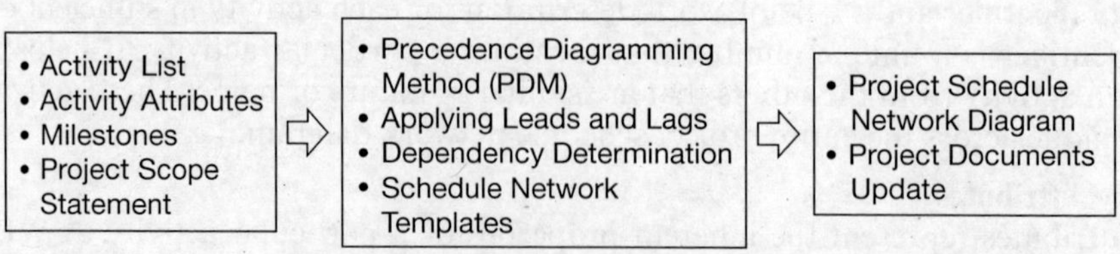

Figure 10.7 Sequence Activities

A project is a series of activities performed in a logical order. The ordering of the activities largely depends on the inter-dependencies between the activities. In the table (below), the different types of dependencies that can be present in a project are described.

Different Types of Activity Dependencies

Dependency Types	Nature	Organizational Control	Example
Mandatory dependencies	Dependencies that are inherent in the nature of the work involved; also called 'hard dependencies.'	Generally, it is difficult to alter this dependency.	In a building project, construction of walls of a house must necessarily precede construction of ceiling.
Discretionary dependencies	Usually defined by the project management team or organization.	It is, generally, within organizational control, but may limit later scheduling options and, hence, must be set with caution; flexible.	Best practices of an organization.
External dependencies	It involves a relationship between project activities and non-project activities.	Organization may not hold much control over these discrepancies compared to the above two.	Organizational dependency on a country's economy, environmental factors, external interfaces.

Precedence Diagramming Method

Precedence Diagramming Method (PDM) is a widely used representation of activity sequencing and, is available in most of the project management scheduling software. Also, PDM employs a diagram that arranges all activities of a project with the relationships and dependencies among them as shown below. The PDM uses the notation of circle or boxes representing the activities called 'nodes'. The arrows that connect these nodes represent the dependency or activity. This technique is also called 'Activity-On-Node (AON)'. Here is an example of PDM:

Activity	Prior Activity
A	None
B	A

Activity A Activity B

Also, PDM is a technique used in the Critical Path Method (CPM), for constructing a Project Schedule Network Diagram (PSND) (see later in this chapter). PDM is not a diagram showing project schedule; rather, it is a technique used before the project schedule is defined. As mentioned earlier, PDM typically uses boxes to indicate project activities and arrows to connect them. A PDM usually has an activity number to identify each activity, a short description of the activity, and indications for early start, early finish, late start, late finish, and

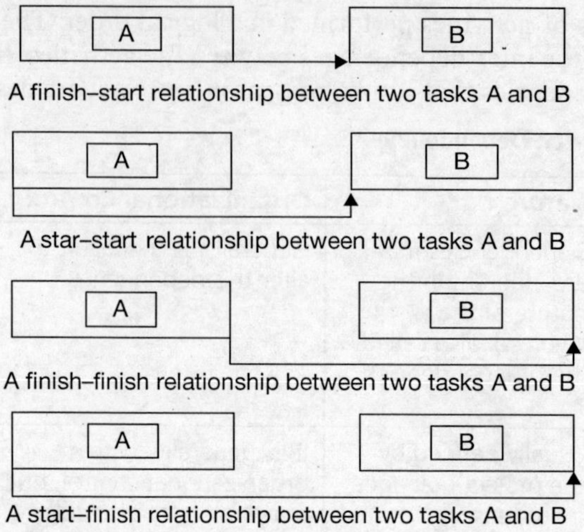

Figure 10.8 Types of Relationship Between Tasks

duration of the activities. An activity might have one, two or more predecessors and one, two or more successors.

Relationships between activities shown in a PDM can be of four types. These four types may be referred as the logical relationships in a PDM.

Logical Relationships

A total of four logical relationships or dependencies are possible between any two activities, because an activity can have start or finish relationship with another (Figure 10.8).

Finish–Start Relationship: Here, the initiation of a successor activity depends on the completion of a predecessor activity. Many project activities bear this relationship with others. For example, the User Acceptance Test (UAT) cannot be started until final deployment into the testing environment is completed. Deployment needs to be completed for UAT to start.

Start–Start Relationship: Here, the initiation of a successor activity depends on the initiation of a predecessor activity (Figure 10.9). Therefore, a subsequent task may start even before a preceding task has been completed; only the latter should have started and—as would be the case—partially completed. In other words, two tasks related by a start–start relationship may be performed in tandem. For example, code review can be started only after writing the codes starts.

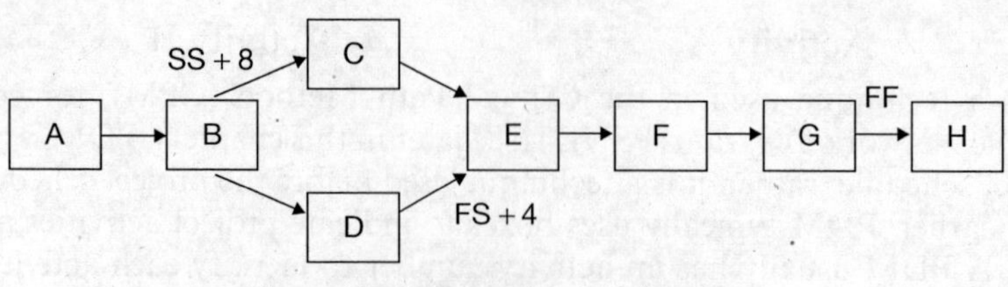

Figure 10.9 Precedence Diagram

Finish–Finish Relationship: Here, the completion of a successor activity depends on the completion of a predecessor activity. For example, a project manager cannot close a project until customer's sign-off has been completed.

Start–Finish Relationship: Here, the completion of a successor activity requires the start of a predecessor activity. Such a relationship is unusual, but is often found in activities involved in just-in-time management processes. When people work in shifts, the beginning of one shift indicates the end of another shift. The project manager of such a project may use this type of relationship.

Leads and Lags

Applying leads and lags is the next step in the activity sequencing process. Leads and lags refer to buffers introduced between tasks for better control of activities.

A lag directs a delay in a successor activity. If a delay of x days is required between the finish of a task and the start of another, then a finish–start dependency may be established with a specification lag time of x days. For example, a technical-writing team can begin editing the draft of a document 10 days after it begins writing. The two tasks, writing and editing—bear a start–start relationship with a 10-day lag.

Lead accelerates the start of the successor activity prior to the completion of the predecessor. For example, the coding team may not wait for the whole design to complete before starting the design in case there is time constraint in the project. In this case, the finish to start relationship between design and coding is established with a lead of x days, which means that coding starts x days prior to the scheduled completion of design. Lead creates parallel activities.

Points to Remember

A lead time tends to accelerate a successor activity. A lag time directs a delay in a successor activity.

Project Schedule Network Diagram

The PSND is a schematic display of project's activities and dependencies, showing the flow of project work, which is then used to develop the project schedule. A sub-network is simply a section of the overall PSND. The PSNDs are created within the Sequence Activities process and it becomes an input to the develop schedule process. PSNDs are generally Activities On the Node (AON) and use all four types of dependencies between activities (i.e., finish–start, finish–finish, start–start, and start–finish) as mentioned above. Following are the advantages of generating PSNDs:

- PSNDs show interdependencies of all activities (a decomposition of WBS).
- They depict project work-flow clearly showing activities that need to be performed in the required sequence.
- They compress the schedule in planning and throughout the life of a project.
- If used for schedule control and reporting, they show project progress.
- They help in justifying the project manager's estimate for the duration of a project.

Figure 10.9 shows an example of a precedence diagram that uses different type of dependencies.

10.3.3 Estimating the Activity Resources

This is the process for determining:

1. The resources (including human resource, equipment and materials) that are required.
2. The quantities of each resource that will be used.
3. The point in time (in the future) when each identified resource will be available to perform assigned project activities.

Figure 10.10 shows the steps involved in this.

Resource Calendars

An important input required for determining the resource requirement and resource availability for a project is the resource calendar. In the context of project management, calendars are of two types: project calendars and resource calendars. Project calendars are related to all the resources involved in a project whereas resource calendars refer to particular resources or groups of resources and their availability. Resource calendars are used to ensure that work is scheduled only when resources are available for work. The working time settings in the resource calendar need to match those in the project calendar. Moreover, there source calendar can be customized to show individual schedule information, such as vacations and leaves of absence. If work time settings of resources involve part-time or the night shift, a separate base calendar for each shift may be set up and applied. Also, project managers can use resource calendars to accommodate exceptions in the work timing of individual resources.

There are different estimation techniques used for estimating the activity resources. These are:

1. Bottom-up Estimating

The bottom-up estimating technique is just the opposite of the top-down estimating. The technique is used to estimate every activity or work item individually and sum that estimate to determine a final estimate. Although, bottom-up estimations are accurate, these are time consuming and are used only when definitive, detailed estimates are required.

2. Published Estimating Data

Production rate and unit cost of the resources can be obtained from published data based on historical information gathered from different companies. This data is useful for determining the resources of an activity. It can be used as the base data to arrive at accurate estimation of resources.

3. Activity Resource Requirements

The activity resource requirement technique is used to identify the type and quantity of resources required for each activity in a work package. These requirements then can be aggregated to determine the estimated resources for each work package. The level of detail varies by application area.

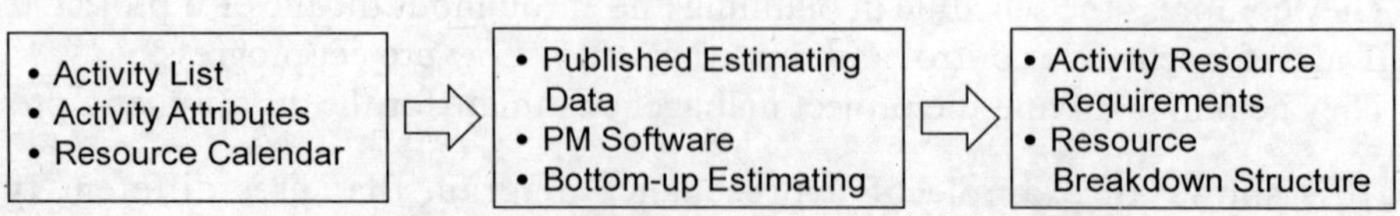

Figure 10.10 Estimate Activity Resources

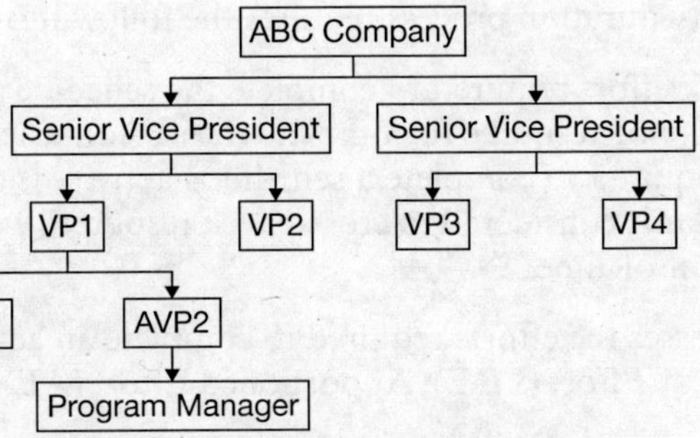

Figure 10.11 Resource Breakdown Structure

At the end of the activity resource estimation stage, a project manager identifies the RBS which depicts the resource requirement to complete the project activities.

Resource Breakdown Structure

A Resource Breakdown Structure (RBS) is a hierarchal structure of human resources, organized by function. For example, the top level of an RBS could be the business unit to which a resource belongs; the second-to-lowest level would be a team manager to whom the resource reports and the final level is the resource itself. In the following table, the resource at Level 3, i.e., the assistant vice president of operations could be provided access to all resources through Level 4 to Level 7 (Figure 10.11).

Level	*Resource*
Level 1	[Organization Name]
Level 2	Senior Vice President
Level 3	Assistant Vice President
Level 4	Project Manager
Level 5	Team Manager
Level 6	Resource A
Level 7	Resource B

10.3.4 Estimating the Activity Duration

This process analyses information on project scope and resources and then develops activity durations from input to schedules. Activity duration refers to the number of work periods needed to complete the activities listed in the activity list. The accuracy of estimates can be improved by considering the amount of risk in the original estimate. More the realistic risks are identified, more estimates become accurate and realistic (Figure 10.12).

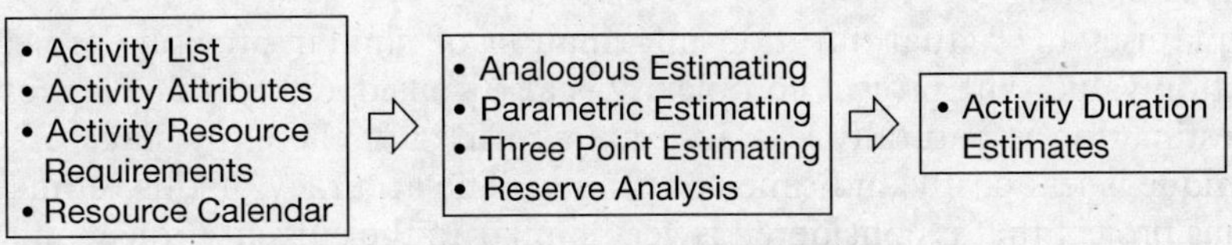

Figure 10.12 Estimate Activity Duration

The estimate activity duration process requires the following:

- Amount of work effort required to complete the schedule activity is estimated.
- Assumed quantity of resource to complete the schedule activity is estimated.
- Work periods required to complete a scheduled activity is calculated.
- Resource calendar is considered to cross-check resources with required skills are available at right point of time.

A related concept addresses the efforts required to complete an activity. There are three types of effort, namely, Level of Effort (LOE), Apportioned Effort (AE), and Discrete Effort (DE).

Level of Effort

Level of Effort (LOE) refers to work of a supportive nature that does not directly add to execution of activities and does not require a definite product outcome. However, it is mandatory, as support for other work activities or the entire project effort, and consists of short amounts of work that must be repeated periodically.

Examples of such an activity are project budget accounting or oiling of machinery in manufacturing.

Apportioned Effort

Apportioned Effort (AE) is the effort that is directly related to some other measured effort and is related and proportional to the measured effort in other work packages. For example, we may consider (apportioned) efforts of the quality assurance division depending on performance of the project team as a whole.

Discrete Effort

These kinds of efforts can be directly traced against each deliverables. It is easily measurable. This is just opposite to AE.

Estimating activity duration accurately is very important for the success of a project. Inaccurate estimation leads to cost and schedule overruns. Moreover, activity duration should allow for leakage time or hidden time and intervening breaks. For example, if an activity takes 1½ days to complete and starts on a Friday morning, Saturday and Sunday being holidays, the activity duration should be calculated considering the two intervening holidays. The activity should be scheduled as complete only on the following Monday afternoon and the elapsed time being 3½ days. In activity duration calculation, the duration of a work package is equal to the amount of time required to do the work, divided by the number of people working. It is given as:

$$\text{Duration} = \text{Work/Unit}$$

Discussed below are the techniques followed during estimation of activity duration.

1. Analogous Estimating

This technique uses the actual duration information of similar previous projects to get a gross estimation value. The project complexity is also considered to achieve more accuracy. Analogous estimation is naturally less accurate and used at the early stage of the project. This is technique is less costly and time consuming. The accuracy of this estimate increases if the previous project that is considered is very similar to the current project and the experts involved in this estimation are very knowledgeable.

2. Parametric Estimating

This estimation technique uses the statistical relationship between historical data and other variables in the project to estimate the duration, cost, budget, etc. By multiplying the quantity of work by the labour hour per unit of work, the duration estimation can be calculated. For example, if one person can complete 20 test cases per day, then to write 200 test cases 10 days will be required.

Parametric estimation can be accurate if the model is sophisticated and the underlying data is accurate.

3. Regression Analysis and Learning Curve Method

When accurate information on an activity is not available, project managers use regression analysis and learning curve methods, for duration estimation. In regression analysis, two variables are plotted on a graph and their relationship is derived using mathematical modeling. The regression equation deals with the following variables:

$Y = f(X, \beta)$

Where,

β is a constant, a scalar or a vector of length k.

X is the independent variable.

Y is the dependent variable.

The Learning Curve Method assumes that a resource consumes progressively less time in carrying out a task, that is, all other work factors being the same, a resource always consumes less time compared to the duration consumed previously to complete a similar activity.

4. Heuristics

Heuristics refers to the 'rule of thumb' estimate, based on knowledge of duration actually consumed after working on large number of similar activities.

5. Three Point Estimation

The Three Point Estimation technique, better known as PERT (program, evaluation, and review technique) improves the accuracy of the estimate manifold by considering the risks in the project. This technique assumes that there is very small probability that a project will be completed on a given date estimated at the beginning of the project. The project manager makes three types of estimations, namely, best, worse, and most likely, for completing an activity. The Expected duration is the weighted average of best case, most likely and worst case estimates.

Expected value = $(P + 4M + O)/6$

$SD = (P - O)/6$

Where

O is the best-case estimate, considering the resource availability, their productivity, dependency of activities, and the interruptions.

M is the most likely estimate made with realistic expectations about the above parameters.

P is the worst-case estimate considering the pessimistic situation for the above parameters.

SD is standard deviation.

This estimate is more accurate as the three points clarify the range of uncertainty of the duration of estimation.

6. Graphical Evaluation and Review Technique

The Graphical Evaluation and Review Technique (GERT) is a combination of network logic and activity duration estimates. Usually, it allows looping. Consider an activity 'A' which is executed five times, continuously. We cannot represent it using the normal diagramming technique. We need to use GERT to represent it. Any graphical method can be used to represent the looping.

7. Reserve Analysis

Reserve analysis addresses buffer in the calculation of duration estimation. Contingency reserve or buffer is generally factored in as a percentage of the overall activity duration estimation. The buffer, often set at 10% of the estimated overall activity duration, is used to manage unknown future project risks.

If we are ready to take more risks in the activity, then reserve can be zero. In order to reduce risks, we add more reserve. However, it is better for the reserve to be always at an optimum level (neither too high nor too low). There can be some minor setbacks for the activity duration since it depends on various factors, such as:

- Resource attrition
- Resource at activity taking leave
- External factors like strike, etc.

We may accommodate the above factors by doing reserve analysis.

The Role of a Project Manager in Estimation

Many of the estimates discussed so far are created not by the project managers, but by the team members or resources are assigned to actually carry out the activities. A project manager, however, provides team members with sufficient information to accurately estimate the duration of activities, after communicating to them the criticality of the accuracy of their estimates. The project manager also performs a sanity check of the estimates received, in addition to formulating a contingency management plan. As in all other processes, the project manager documents the assumptions made during estimating for later review.

At the end of this process, the duration of the project activities are arrived at which gives an indication how big or small the project duration is. It may also include some indication of the range within which the duration can vary in cases of uncertainties in the project.

10.3.5 Developing the Schedule

As we have now identified all the tasks in the project, their dependencies and resource requirements and as we have also estimated the duration that each activity will be taking, now our task is to put all these information together and create the project schedule. So, the next task is to determine the start and end dates of the project activities. Once we put the activities with their start and end dates, connect the activities through their dependencies, put the resource calendar and also analyse the possible options to shorten the schedule, we finally get the project start and end dates. Figure 10.13 shows the steps involved in this process.

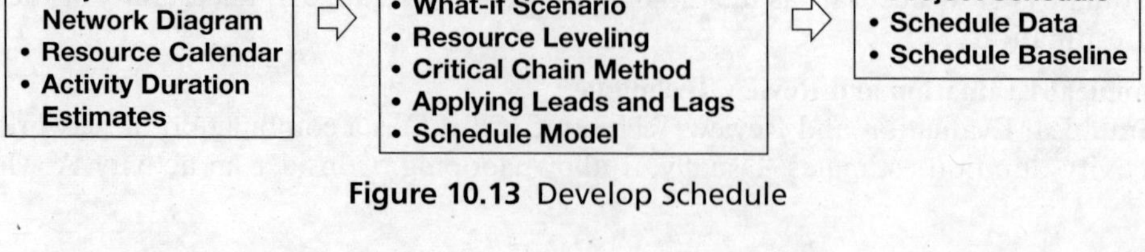

Figure 10.13 Develop Schedule

All the artefacts that we created till the last step are considered while creating the schedule like, activity list, activity attributes, PSDN, resource calendar and activity duration estimates.

Definition of Float/Slack

The concept of float and slack is important for understanding how the project activities are scheduled with sufficient flexibility..

Total Float/Slack: This is the time for which completion of an activity can be delayed without delaying the project end date or an intermediary milestone.

Free Float/Slack: This is the time for which completion of an activity can be delayed without delaying the early start date of its successor activities.

Project Float/Slack: This is the time for which completion of a project work can be delayed without delaying the externally imposed project completion date (imposed by the customer).

Schedule Creation Techniques

Some of the well-known techniques for schedule development are as follows:

1. Schedule Network Analysis

Schedule network analysis is a technique that generates the project schedule using the PSND. It employs various techniques, such as Critical Path Method (CPM), schedule compression techniques, what-if analysis, critical chain analysis, etc. as elaborated here. It also uses resource levelling techniques to compress the schedule by identifying path convergence and path divergence.

2. Critical Path Method (CPM)

In this technique, the theoretical early start and end dates, and late start and end dates for all activities are calculated without considering any resource constraint through forward and backward pass. CPM is a method of using network analysis techniques to identify those tasks that are on the critical path, that is, where any delay in the completion of these tasks will lengthen the project timescale, unless action is taken. Critical path is the longest path which is the minimum duration of a completion of a project. There can be more than one critical path and those increases the risks in the project because all these paths need to be monitored closely to avoid any possible delay. A critical path can change during the project life cycle as the duration, dependency and resource requirement, etc., of the tasks may change over time. These are discussed here:

- The network diagram does not change when the end date changes. The project manager should investigate the options, such as fast-tracking and crashing the schedule to meet the new date and then change the network diagram following the approved changes.
- When a project has a negative float, the project manager should consider compressing the schedule. For all activities in critical path, the float will be zero. Figure 10.14 shows calculation of critical path for a process.
- In the diagram (Figure 10.4) the project has 8 nodes and the activities that need to be performed to move from one node to the next are shown as the arrows (Refer to PSDN for more explanations). The estimated duration of each task is mentioned above the arrow. There are parallel activities that are taking place in this project, but the minimum duration of the project is the length of the critical path as calculated here.

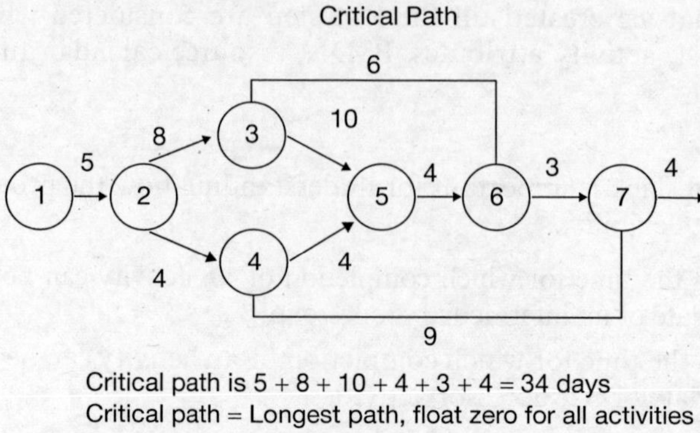

Figure 10.14 Critical Path Calculations

Path Convergence

The merging of different network paths into the same node in a project schedule network diagram is called 'path convergence'. It is usually characterized by a schedule activity with more than one predecessor activity. The merging of different network diagrams into a single node is also called 'path convergence'.

Path Divergence

This is the opposite of path convergence. Branching of different paths from a single path or node is called 'path divergence'. For example, when we are handling a software project, design for different modules can be progressed in parallel after requirement analysis is done.

Figure 10.15 shows an example on path convergence and path divergence.

3. What-If Scenario Analysis

What-If Scenario Analysis (WISA) is a powerful tool that can analyse various 'What-If' scenarios to determine the schedule of a project.

The schedule of a project depends on various parameters including, but not limited to:

1. Resource utilization
2. Cost factors

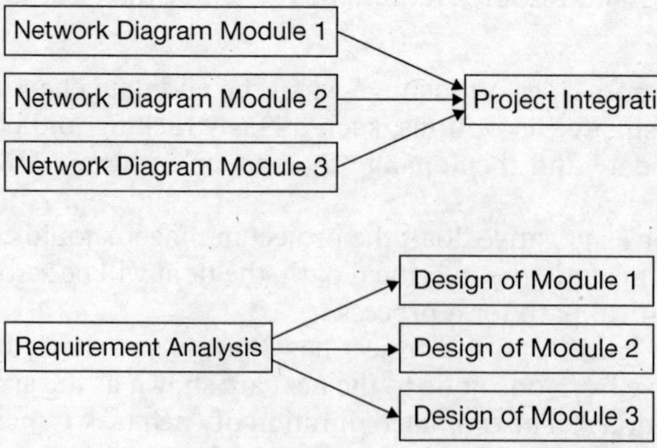

Figure 10.15 Path Convergence and Path Divergence

3. Dependencies of activities
4. Risk parameters
5. Unknown external factors like, strike, storming, etc.

The WISA estimates the effect that each potential event may have on the project schedule. This allows the project team to plan for contingency and mitigation plans in case any adverse scenarios may take place during the project execution. There are several simulation techniques which help in calculating the effect of different combination of scenarios on the project schedule. Monte Carlo simulation is such a powerful simulation technique.

4. Schedule Optimization

Schedule optimization is mandated when execution of a project as per schedule has been affected because of internal or external factors, upon which a project manager is required to optimize schedule. Here is a list of the tools which a project manager commonly uses to optimize a project schedule.

Crashing

Here, total project duration is decreased with minimal compromises on original objectives. We, usually add extra resources to decrease the project duration. Consequently, the cost of the project increases due to the crashing technique.

Fast Tracking

Here, instead of processing in sequence as per the project schedule, the activities are processed parallelly. The risks associated with projects increase by doing things in parallel. Activities in critical path that are to be done in parallel are first identified to reduce the overall project duration. In this technique, either the duration of critical activities is shortened or working hours increased.

5. Resource Levelling

Resource levelling is the reapportioning of available resources to avoid over-allocation or under-allocation and to ensure that activities are performed with maximum efficiency.

Here, peak overloads are reduced by redistributing allocations to activities with float (discussed later in this section). This optimization technique can increase the activity duration.

Figures 10.16 and 10.17 illustrates this tool. Application of resource levelling can result in the same tasks (say Tasks A, B, and C) being completed in five days with only six resources,

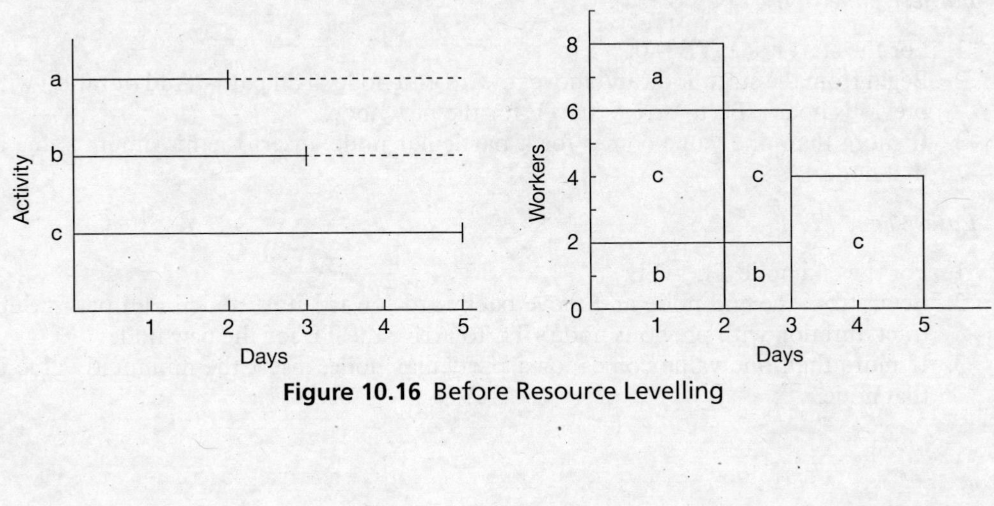

Figure 10.16 Before Resource Levelling

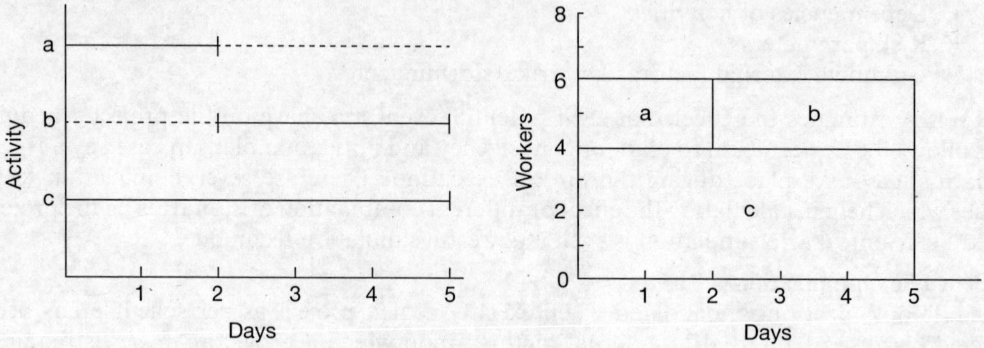

Figure 10.17 After Resource Levelling

whereas without resource levelling tool applied, the tasks may have used eight resources to complete the tasks. The resource leveling tools are as follows:

- *Rule of Thumb*: Allocate scarce resources to critical path activities first.
- *Increased Project Duration*: Often results in a project duration that is longer than the preliminary schedule.
- *Reallocation*: Resource reallocation and adjustments are used to bring the schedule back or as close as possible to the originally intended duration.
- *Reverse Resource Allocation*: Resource is scheduled in reverse from the project end date.
- *Critical Chain*: A technique that modifies the project schedule to account for, and accommodate limited resources.

6. Critical Chain Method

This technique modifies the project schedule to account for limited resources, mixes deterministic and probabilistic approaches, and puts more emphasis on the resources. When resources are always available in unlimited quantities, then a project's critical chain is identical to its critical path. This technique involves adding duration buffers which are not actual activities. In this technique, the following steps used to calculate earliest and latest times:

Earliest Time (TE):

1. For the start node, TE = 0.
2. Begin from the start node and move toward end node in all paths. Add duration with previous node's TE to arrive the TE for the new node.
3. If more than one value comes for a particular node, insert the maximum value in that node.

Latest Time (TL):

1. For the end node TL = TE.
2. Begin from the end node and move backward toward start node in all paths. Subtract duration with previous node's TL to arrive the TL for the new node.
3. If more than one value comes for a particular node, insert the minimum value in that node.

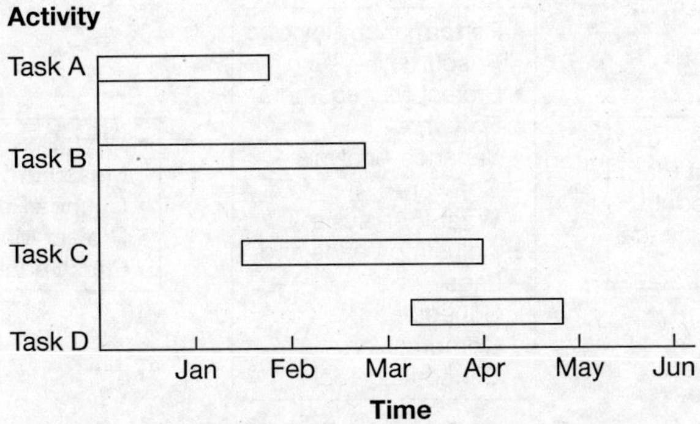

Figure 10.18 Gantt Chart

The schedule created using these tools and techniques which acts as the basis of all the plannings in the project. There are several representations possible for a project schedule, but the most common one is the Gantt chart.

Gantt Chart

The most common representation of the project schedule is through a Gantt chart. The types of Gantt charts mostly used are:

Bar Chart: It displays activity start and end dates as well as expected duration.

Milestone Chart: It displays scheduled start or completion of the major deliverables.

Combination Chart: It displays events and activities as a function of time.

Figure 10.18 represents a bar type Gantt chart.

10.3.6 Controlling the Schedule

During the life cycle of a project, one of the key activities that the project manager needs to perform is to monitor, track and update the project schedule called 'controlling the schedule'. The main steps under this process are:

- Measuring the current status of the project schedule.
- Influencing the factors that cause schedule changes, ensuring that these are agreed upon.
- Determining the reason for the deviation, if any.
- Managing the changes when they occur.

The schedule control process is used to monitor the status of project execution, to update on project progress, and to manage changes in the schedule for its baseline, if required. Following are the important metric and tools concerning schedule control (See Figure 10.19).

Project Schedule: The approved project schedule is called 'schedule baseline'. It provides the basis for measuring and reporting schedule performance.

Work Performance Information: This information updates the project manager on schedule performance, such as which planned dates have been met and which have not.

Performance Reviews (Earned Value): This process involves in the assessment of schedule variations to determine whether they require corrective actions.

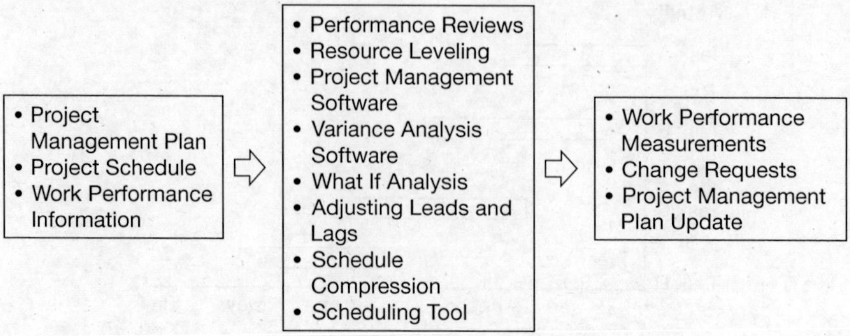

Figure 10.19 Control Schedule

Progress Reporting: The progress reporting and current schedule status include information, such as actual start and end dates as well as the remaining durations for incomplete schedule activities.

PM Software: This schedule-control tool is used for tracking planned dates against actual dates and forecasting.

Variance Analysis: This tool compares the target dates with the actual forecasted start and end dates to analyse variance.

Work Performance Measurements: This tool is used to calculate Schedule Variance (SV) and Schedule Performance Index (SPI) values for WBS components, in particular, the work packages and control accounts, and also document and communicate the same to the stakeholders.

Points to Remember

The following steps are adhered for effective project schedule management:

- Estimation based on a WBS will improve accuracy.
- Activity duration should be estimated by the resource actually performing the activity.
- Use of historical information improves accuracy of estimates.
- A schedule baseline should be maintained and not changed except for approved project changes.
- Estimates are more accurate if smaller-sized work components are estimated. Bottom-up estimation is the most accurate type of estimation.
- Corrective and preventive actions should be recommended when schedule problems occur.
- Continuous monitoring of schedules helps in anticipating deviations.
- Plans should be revised during completion of the work.

10.4 Project Scheduling Tools

Most of the common project management tools provide the facility to create and manage project schedules. The basic capabilities of the scheduling tools are, facility to sequence project activities, mark the activity dependencies and assign dates and resources to them.

More sophisticated scheduling tools provide advanced facilities like resource levelling, critical path analysis and tracking. Scheduling tools may provide support for:

- Defining dependency relationship (single or multiple) types between activities.
- Resource assignment and resource leveling.
- Critical path analysis.
- Estimating activity duration and probability-based simulation.
- Activity cost accounting.

It is expected that the scheduling software should provide information related to the activities, duration, resource availability and planning costs, monitoring and tracking the projects. Scheduling software is expected to provide the following information to different stakeholders:

- Overview of how long the tasks will take to complete.
- Early warning of any risks of schedule failure in the project.
- Information on workload or holiday plans.
- Tracking of actual and planned performance.
- Utilization of available resources.
- Cost of projects.
- Status tracking of projects.

Microsoft Project, ZOHO Projects, FastTrack Schedule 9, Primavera P6 and @task are some of the popular project schedule management tools.

SUMMARY

Time management of a project produces the schedule baseline. From WBS, in particular from the workpackages, individual activities to be scheduled and activity durations for the schedule are determined.The activities are sequenced in a logical order called a network diagram using the PDM method. 'Fast-tracking' and 'crashing' are two techniques for optimizing schedules. Buffering is a technique for adjusting the schedules for accommodating future risks. All activities on critical paths are called 'critical activities'. Slack or float is the time for which a task can be delayed without delaying successor activities.

- **Activity:** Work performed during the course of a project (Normally it has duration, cost, and resource requirements).
- **Critical Path:** Longest path, float less than or equal to specified value, mostly zero. This series of activities determines the earliest completion of the project and, is usually defined as those activities with float less than or equal to a specified value (usually zero).
- **Float:** The overall amount of time that an activity may be delayed from its early start without delaying the project finish date (It is also called 'slack, total float and path float').
- **Lag:** Modification of a logical relationship which directs a delay in the successor task and they are basically inserted waiting times in between tasks.
- **Lead:** A modification of a logical relationship where the successor task can be started earlier than planned. For example, in a Finish to Start relationship with a six day lead, the successor can start six days prior to the completion of the predecessor.
- **Milestone:** A significant event in the project, usually completion of a major deliverable, which determines the signal to go ahead to the next phase or project.

- **Precedence Diagram Method (PDM):** It is the network diagramming technique where activities are represented by nodes. Activities are linked by precedence relationships to show the logical sequence in which the activities are to be performed.
- **Resource Leveling:** Form of network analysis in which start and finish dates are driven by resource management concerns. Resource leveling refers to keeping the resources same across the duration of the project, thereby, avoid resource overloading.

EXERCISES

PART A (Objective-type Questions)

1. Fast-tracking is also known as
A. Overtime
B. Resource leveling
C. Crashing
D. Concurrent engineering

2. Which of the following relationship represents concurrency between two activities?
A. Start-to-start
B. Finish-to-start
C. Start-to-finish
D. Finish-to-finish

3. Fast-tracking usually adds more
A. Cost
B. Risk
C. Time
D. Scope

4. This kind of dependency is difficult to change
A. Mandatory dependencies
B. Discretionary dependencies
C. External dependencies
D. Nothing is difficult to change

5. This kind of dependency is inherent in the nature of the work
A. Mandatory dependencies
B. Discretionary dependencies
C. External dependencies
D. Team dependencies

6. Between any two activities how many logical relationships are possible?
A. 2
B. 4
C. 3
D. 6

7. Which structure is a hierarchal structure of human resources, organized by function?
A. RBS
B. WBS
C. OBS
D. EBS

8. Lag allows the following type of relationship
A. Finish–Start
B. Start–Start
C. Finish–Finish
D. Start–Finish

PART B (Write the answer in one or two lines)

1. What is milestone list?

2. Define lead and lag. Give an example.

3. What is resource breakdown structure? Give example.

4. What is GERT?

5. What are path convergence and path divergence?

6. What are fast-tracking and crashing?

7. Discuss various project time management processes in detail.

8. Discuss three different types of project dependencies in detail with examples.

9. Discuss four different types of relationships possible between any two activities with examples for each.

10. Discuss crashing, fast-tracking, resource leveling with examples.

11

Cost Management

11.1 Introduction

If we are not following a cost management process, then it would be difficult to get control over the profitability of the projects. Poor cost management will also affect funding of the future projects.

Cost, in general, is a resource sacrificed or foregone to achieve a specific objective in a project. Software project costs are those costs that are directly related to the development of software projects. Project cost is usually measured in terms of monetary units and also in Dollars. Cost estimation for a project not just an one time activity. It is done throughout the life-cycle of the projects. Some examples of project costs are the costs of equipment, cost of software, cost of hardware elements, cost of materials, and cost of human resources required to complete various activities of a project. Project costs are to be effectively predicted, managed, and controlled for the betterment of the projects. On the projects with narrow scopes, cost estimating and cost budgeting process can be combined together as a single process. Overall project cost can be fixed only when the scopes of the project is clearly defined. Project cost management refers to the set of process involved in planning, estimating, budgeting, and controlling cost to ensure that the project is completed within the approved budget and schedule.

11.2 Various Categories of Costs

The various categories of costs associated with software project management can be described as follows:

Variables Costs: The costs that change with the project life-cycle as well as effect the number of units produced. For example, costs of material and wages. Marginal cost is a type of variable cost.

Fixed Costs: Fixed costs are those costs which remain indifferent irrespective of the type of the software that a farm produces.

This cost does not change with the number of software sold in the market. For example, rentals, machine costs, etc. are fixed costs. A software development farm must pay its rent and utility bills irrespective of the sales volume of the software it develops.

Note: It is important to understand that fixed costs are 'fixed' only for a specific period of time. When that specific time is over, all fixed costs become variable costs. Rental cost also changes every year.

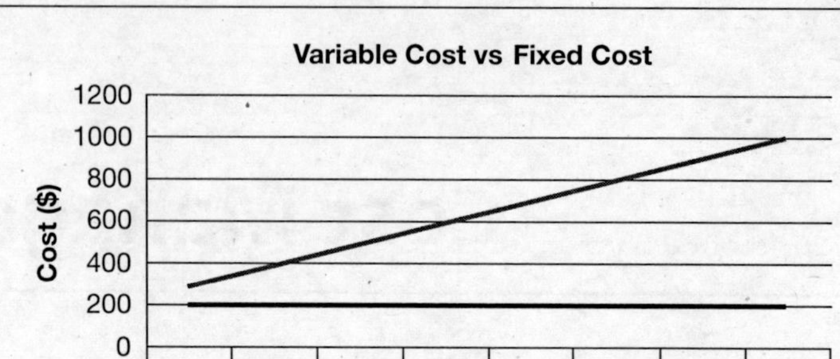

	1	2	3	4	5	6	7	8
— Variable Cost	100	200	300	400	500	600	700	800
— Fixed Cost	200	200	200	200	200	200	200	200

Figure 11.1 Variable Cost vs Fixed Cost

From the above graph, it may be noted that the fixed cost curve is a straight, flat line as it does not change with the units of the software produced. The variable cost curve is constantly moving upwards with an increasing slope as the units of software produced are increased.

Direct Costs: These are costs directly connected and accountable to the work executed on a project and also associated to an objective. The costs of this nature directly affect a project. For an instance, if a particular software is bought and it is exclusively used in developing a project, then this software project cost is treated as a direct cost'. Project travel costs, project-related software sourcing costs are some examples of direct costs.

Indirect Costs: Indirect costs are incurred for the benefit of more than one project. These types of costs affect the company as a whole, not just a single project. The cost of a software director recruited in a company is one fine example. Since he is expected to work across the projects, the costs associated to him can be considered as indirect costs. Cost of software procured to be used across the projects in an organization can be considered as indirect cost. Audit fees and legal expenses are also the examples of indirect costs. The costs related to the training department, cost of furniture and fixtures, administrative costs, support staffs' remuneration in an organization are also the examples of indirect costs. This is because these costs are shared across all the projects developed in an organization.

Opportunity Cost: It is the cost of being not able to do something's because we did something else or lost opportunity. Cost of not pursuing a course of action is called an opportunity cost. Assuming that, you have only 30 resources in your company and being completely utilized in a particular project and your customers is aware of all those resources by their individual names. Now, one more customer is giving you a bigger opportunity of sanctioning a bigger project than the current project, but you are not able to accept the bigger project as all your resources are already engaged in the previous projects. Opportunity cost of the first project is the revenue lost in the second project or the cost of not choosing the second project. Let's look into another example, If there are two projects to choose from project A with net present value of $2 million and project B with a net present value of $0.7 million. Here, the opportunity cost of selecting project A is $0.7 million.

Sunk Cost: The cost already incurred (it is a waste) for a project is called 'sunk cost'. An example of sunk cost is software advertising expenses. Once a company pays out for such an expenditure, no alternative lies reverse it.

A project cost was originally estimated at \$2 million. It is now half-way done, and \$3 million has already been spent. Now, the committee has to decide whether to continue the project or not. Should they consider the fact that \$3 million has already been spent? Expended costs (*i.e.*, sunk costs) are to be ignored when making the decision, whether to continue investing in a project or not.

11.3 Precision vs Accuracy of Cost Estimates

'Precision' means the values of repeated measurements, and 'Accuracy' means the measured value is very close to the true or actual value. Precise measurements need not be accurate.

Example: A project manager forecasts the cost variance at the end of a project will be between 40–60%, based on the most recent data. The actual cost variance at the end of the project turns out to be 53%. In this case, the forecast was accurate, but not very precise. Another Project Manager forecasts cost variance at the end of the project as 51.47%. It turns out to be 62%. This forecast was very precise, but completely inaccurate. A very accurate measurement is not necessarily signifies a precise one. The project management team requires to determine the level of accuracy and precision.

11.4 Accuracy of Cost Estimation

The estimated figures in cost estimation should always be in range. For example, cost of a project can be estimated in the range of \$1 million to \$2 million.

There are three standard ranges used for cost estimation. These are discussed as follows:

Rough Order of Magnitude (ROM): It is made during the project initiation stage. It is an approximate estimate made without detailed data. It is the most difficult estimate as the project information is very less here. This is also called ballpark figure with a typical range of ±50%.

Budgetary Estimate: Budgetary estimate is made during the project planning stage. It is used to obtain approval of a project. Also, it is used to establish and calculate the funds required for execution of a project (development). A budget estimate is more accurate than an order of magnitude estimate. The budget estimate is most often based on analogous estimation which is considering budget lessons learned from a similar project and applying them to the current project. Typical range: –10% to +25%.

Definitive Estimate: Further refinement of an estimate happens as the project progresses and more information about the project is obtained. It is prepared from well-defined specifications, data, drawings, etc. A definitive estimate uses the bottom-up technique, and is the most accurate of all the estimate types. However, it mostly consumes considerable resources and time because of many calculations and data collections are involved. Typical range: ±10% or –5% to +10%.

In earlier stages of the project, estimates are usually wide ranged. As more information about the project becomes available, estimate range is narrowed down over the life-cycle of the project.

Four Common Estimating Styles of Cost

Subjective Estimate: The cost is estimated purely based on personal experience. No logics or formulas are used in this type of cost estimation. It is completely based on intuition. Expert judgement is the best example of the subjective estimation style. The subjective estimation can be improved by using the paired comparison method.

Statistical Estimate: This style is called 'statistical estimation style'. It is completely based on a comprehensive historical data. If the historic data is wrong, then the estimation yields wrong results. Even if the historic data is right, proper interpretation of the data is required for better estimation.

Comparative Estimate: This style is called 'comparative estimation'. It is based on similar types of projects. If the similar projects has no data or wrong data, then it affects the result.

Empirical Estimate: This style is called 'empirical estimation' It is based on the real data of the current project. But proper empirical estimation can be done only at the end of the project. This is because the correct information will be known only at the end. Hence, empirical data cannot be used at the beginning of the project.

11.5 Pricing Factors

There is no simple relationship between the development cost. The price is charged to the customer. Broader organizational, economic, political, and business considerations influence the price charged. Table 11.1 explains some of the possible factors that determine pricing.

Table 11.1 Pricing Factors

Factor	Description
Requirement complexity	Organization runs through the requirements and, if the complexity is low and the requirements are clear, then usually lower price is quoted.
Risks involved (uncertainly)	Organization runs through the requirements and, if there are high risks involved in the project, then higher price to adjust the risks is quoted.
Contractual Terms	If the customer is letting the code developed to be used with other customers, then less price may be charged.
Financial position of the organization	An organization in financial crisis may quote lower price to win a contracts.
Market position	Organizations willing to enter new markets quote lesser price to capture business.

Problems in Estimating Accurate Costs

- Developing an estimate for a large project is a complex task.
- Lots of training and standards are required.
- People usually go by under or overestimation biases.

Basic Estimation Principles

- Use more than one techniques to derive the estimate.
- Use more than one method of estimation.

- It is better to obtain at least two estimates using each method.
- Involve the people who will be doing the actual work.
- Receive a commitment from the team will be handling the project.

11.6 Plan Cost Management Process

Plan cost management is a process that establishes the policies, procedures, and documentation for planning, managing, executing, and controlling project costs. The key benefit of this process is that it ensures the cost management processes and their associated tools and techniques are documented properly. Main output of plan cost management process is the cost management plan.

Analytical Technique of Plant Cost Management

Developing the cost management plan may involve choosing strategic options to fund the project, such as self-funding, funding with equity or funding with debt. The cost management plan may also detail ways to finance project resources, such as purchasing, renting or leasing. These decisions, like other financial decisions affecting the project, may affect project risks. Organizational policies and procedures may influence which financial techniques are employed in these decisions. The techniques may include (but, are not limited to): payback period, return on investment, internal rate of return, discounted cash flow, and net present value.

Cost Management Plan

Cost management plan is a component of project management plan. It describes how the project costs would be planned, structured, monitored, and controlled. The cost management processes and their associated tools and techniques are documented in the cost management plan. It may be formal or informal, highly detailed or broadly framed based on the needs of a project.

A cost management plan can implement the following:

- *Level of Accuracy*: Activity cost estimates will adhere to a rounding of the data to a prescribed precision (*e.g.*, \$100.05, \$100.054, \$100.055) based on the scope of the activities and magnitude of the project, and may include an amount for contingencies.
- *Units of Measure*: Each unit used in measurements (such as staff hours, staff days, weeks, or lump sum) is defined for each of the resources.
- *Organizational Procedures Links*: The Work Breakdown Structure (WBS) provides the framework for the cost management plan, allowing for consistency with the estimates, budgets, and control of costs. The WBS component used for the project cost accounting is called 'Control Account (CA)'. Each control account is assigned a unique code or account number(s) that links directly to the performing organization's accounting system.
- *Control Thresholds*: Variance thresholds for monitoring cost performance may be specified to indicate an agreed-upon amount of variation to be allowed before some action needs to be taken. Thresholds are typically expressed as percentage deviations from the baseline plan.

- *Rules of Performance Measurement*: Earned Value Management (EVM) rules of performance measurement are set. For example, the cost management plan may
  - Establish the earned value measurement techniques (*e.g.*, weighted milestones, fixed-formula, percent complete, etc.) to be employed.
  - Specify tracking methodologies and the earned value management computation equations for calculating projected Estimate at Completion (EAC) forecasts to provide a validity check on the bottom-up EAC.

For more specific information regarding earned value management, refer to the practice standard for earned value management.

- *Reporting Formats*: The formats and frequency for the various cost reports are defined.
- *Process Descriptions*: Descriptions of each of the other cost management processes are documented.
- *Additional Details*: Additional details about cost activities like these, but not limited to: description of strategic funding choices, procedure for recording a cost, and roles and responsibilities of those persons who perform cost activities.

11.7 Estimate Cost Process

Cost estimation is done throughout the life-cycle of the projects. It is based on the project's WBS and project schedule to improve accuracy. Cost estimating includes identifying and considering cost alternatives for managing risks.

Importance of accurate estimation:

1. Inaccurate estimate may result in inefficient usage of resources.
2. Inaccurate estimate may result incorrect decision.
3. Inaccurate estimate may result in cost overrun and schedule overrun.
4. Inaccurate estimate may result in customer dissatisfaction.
5. Inaccurate estimate may result in loss of faith and in turn loss of business from the customer.

Whenever cost-related issues or problems occur, corrective and preventive actions are implemented. If the cost estimates is too high and need to be optimized, then the project manager may consider using reusable components, cut scope, outsourcing options, subcontracting part of the project or use cheaper resources, and at the same time closely monitoring the impact of changes on the project.

The inputs for estimating the cost are discussed as below:

Individual Activities of the Project as Input

This helps in understanding what we are estimating and, also helps to understand what is out of scope, if there are any constraints, etc.

Cost Management Plan as Input

This is a simple document which answers the following questions:

- How to plan cost for a project?
- How to estimate the cost of a project?

- How to effectively manage cost to the baseline?
- How to control cost and manage variances?

It also includes the following elements:

- Units of measures–currency, effort hours, staff days.
- Levels of precision.
- Level of accuracy–for estimates.
- Organizational procedural links—WBS component used for cost accountings are called 'control accounts' and are linked to organizational accounting systems.
- Control thresholds—agreed upon variance limits.
- Rules for performance measurement–earned value measurement.
- Reporting formats to be used:
  - Process description, that is, processes for establishing cost baseline, processes for cost change control.
- Additional details, like:
  - Strategic funding choices.
  - Procedure for handling fluctuations in currency exchange rate.
  - Procedure for project cost recording.

Project Schedule as Input

It contains details of activities, resource assigned, details about when any activity will occur and this will help us to estimate the cost accurately and, also the timing of the cost requirement. This will help us to create a time-phased expenditure plan to control project costs. Cost will also affect the schedule. For example, if something costs more than expected, then you may change the schedule to be able to do that at later point of time or look for options to reduce the cost.

11.8 Tools and Techniques of Cost Estimation

Analogous Estimation Technique

Analogous estimating is used to estimate total project costs when detailed information is limited or no data are available about the project. This process uses the actual cost of previously completed similar projects to predict the cost. Hence, the estimates are based on historical information. Analogous estimating is also a form of expert judgment, as current project requirements are estimated without access to real-time data. It uses a top–down approach, and time required for estimation is less compared to that in bottom–up estimation. It is generally less costly than other estimating techniques, but it is also generally less accurate as we use only the data of similar kind of projects.

Analogous estimation is most reliable, when:

1. The previous projects are similar in fact and not just in appearance.
2. The individuals or groups preparing estimates have the needed expertize to do the estimation.

Advantages:

1. Easy to implement.
2. Cost involved for the estimation is less.
3. Similar projects taken into consideration.
4. Individual tasks need not be identified.

Disadvantages:

1. Project components and activities not considered.
2. Difficult to estimate for projects with uncertainty.
3. Depends entirely on the comparative project.
4. Not possible if data not available for similar projects.
5. Not possible to apply for new kind of projects.

Parametric Estimation Technique

Parametric estimation uses mathematical model with project characteristics (parameters) to predict the cost. Parametric estimation follows analogous estimation for better cost estimation. For an example, one similar module in previous projects cost already $650 per module and this new project has 10 similar modules and, hence, it will cost me $6500.

Parametric estimation is accurate, when:

1. Parameters used for prediction are accurate.
2. Parameters are really quantifiable to be used in a mathematical model.
3. Availability of accurate mathematical model for cost prediction.
4. Model used is scalable depending on the situation.

Two varieties of parametric estimate are:

- *Regression Analysis (Scatter Diagram)*: Tracks two variables to see if they are related to each other. It establishes a mathematical formula to use in future parametric estimating.
- *Learning Curve*: This is a model and is based on the principle that the cost per unit decreases as more work gets completed. Installing floor tiles in the 30th room will take less time due to improved productivity and learning from other floorings.

Advantages:

1. More accurate than analogous estimation.
2. Individual work items and risks of the projects are considered.
3. Micro and macro parameters of the projects are considered.
4. Tries to connect various parameters of the project.

Disadvantage:

Not possible if data not available for the project under consideration.

Bottom–up Estimation Technique

It is the technique of estimating the cost of individual work items in work break-down structure and then sums up the costs to arrive total project cost. It will produce accurate results comparatively as we do calculation for all individual work items (tasks). Bottom-up estimation is performed with the help of team members for high accuracy. It is also driven by the size of the individual work items.

Advantages:

1. More detailed as all individual work items being considered.
2. More accurate than the top–down approach.
3. More details about individual work items comes up during the process.

Disadvantages:

1. More time consuming.
2. System level activities not considered.
3. Cost of doing detailed estimation is very high.
4. Not possible to do at the beginning of a project.
5. Accuracy is driven by the accuracy of the individual estimations.

Top-down Estimation Technique

It is also called 'macro model', because the estimation happens at macro (higher) levels. In this technique, the individual work items are not considered for the estimation. The estimation is based on the external factors and it is partitioned into individual work items (low level components).

Advantages:

1. Requires only minimal detail.
2. System level (higher level) activities considered.
3. It is fast and easy.

Disadvantages:

1. Low level components and activities not considered.
2. Usually not detail.
3. No justification or logic for estimation (it is just distribution technique of available numeric).

Vendor Bid Analysis Technique

Vendor bid analysis as the name implies, it gathers information from vendors to help establish cost estimates. We can accomplish this by requesting bids or quotes or working with some trusted sources of estimates. You will analyse the bids and decide on one contractor for the work. When multiple vendors are involved for each deliverables, then the price of individual deliverables are calculated to derive a cost that supports the final and total project cost.

Advantages:

1. It is the cheapest method for the customer—free of cost.
2. Varieties of estimation techniques can be applied here.
3. Customer can understand the estimation process of vendors.

Disadvantages:

1. It solely depends on the vendors and they may bias the estimation.
2. It is applicable and effective only when multiple vendors are there.
3. Vendors may skew the estimation depending on the demand and the market conditions.

Reserve Analysis Technique

Reserve analysis also considers buffer time to estimate the cost of an activity. Some money needs to be kept aside for cost overruns to accommodate for the risks (future) that remain in the project after the risk management planning processes are completed. The objective of building a reserve component into the estimated cost is to ensure that project objectives are met without cost overruns. Proper reserve analysis will also increase the chance of project success and proper estimation of costs. Adding reserve is not adding padding. It's about calculating additional funds that may be required as justified by risk management planning processes related data points. There are two types of reserves: contingency reserve (Known-Unknowns), management reserve (Unknown-Unknowns).

Contingency reserve deals with known risks, so we need to consider the cost associated dealing with this. This reserve lies at the discretion of project manager, to deal with anticipated, but not certain events emerging out risks associated with the project. Contingency reserve is proportion to the risks exposure of the project.

Management reserve helps to tackle unknown risks and so the impact is also unknown. Fixed amounts, say (10% or 20%) is added with the overall cost to tackle this kind of risks.

Cost of Quality Technique

Quality level determines the cost associated with the quality activities.

The cost of quality is the total cost to produce the product or service of the project according to the quality standards.

Cost of quality related activities are also to be estimated and included in cost budgeting. It is about how much money it takes to complete the project right. It includes costs like reviews, audits, inspections, quality control, etc. If we want to set higher quality levels then obviously the cost of the activities will be more and for lesser quality levels the cost estimation will be lower. The cost of work added to the project to accommodate plan quality, assure quality and control quality should be added to the project cost estimate.

There are three costs associated with the cost of quality, namely:

1. Prevention costs
2. Appraisal costs
3. Failure costs

Prevention means keeping defects out of the hands of the customers. Prevention costs are the costs associated with satisfying customer requirements by producing a product without defects.

Appraisal costs are costs expended to examine the product or process that ensure the requirements are being met. Appraisal costs might include costs associated with things like inspections and testing.

Failure costs are what it costs when things do not go according to the plan. Failure costs are also known as cost of poor quality. There are two types of failure costs, namely, internal failure costs and external failure costs.

Three point Estimation Technique

Accuracy of single-point estimates can be improved by considering the uncertainties and risks associated with the project. Three-point estimates has three estimates that are used to come up with a final estimate. Three point estimation techniques are originated from Program Evaluation and Review Technique (PERT). Optimistic estimate is the fastest estimate and smallest estimate in which the resource assumes that risks are less and always the best results happen. Pessimistic estimate is the slowest estimate in which the resource assumes all the possible risks occurs in the project. Most likely estimate is in between optimistic estimate and pessimistic estimate. Three point estimations Consider Optimistic (CO), Pessimistic (CP) and most likely (CM) cost estimate scenarios to define an approximate range for estimation. Most of the times, we tend to ignore the optimistic and pessimistic estimations which may lead to wrong estimations and, hence, we need to include those while estimating the cost. We need to completely rely on the experienced team members to give these estimates. Expected cost estimation, standard deviation and variances are calculated from these three estimates.

Expected activity cost estimate (CE) = (CO + 4·CM + CP)/6

Activity standard deviation = (CP – CO)/6

Activity variance = [(CP – CO)/6] squared = Standard deviation squared

Pricing to Win Technique

Here, the estimations happen not for the system or any of its parameters, but for the prediction of customer expectation price. Particularly, this happens in cost estimation. We win the deal if we are able to estimate it correctly. This technique (approach) seems to be unethical.

Advantages:

1. It meets customer's expectations.
2. It gets blessings of the customers.
3. Probability of winning a deal is higher by using this estimation.

Disadvantages:

1. It does not consider the characteristics of a project.
2. This may yield worst impact on all the parameters of a project.
3. Project profitability may be impacted, because of this technique (when the price is too low).
4. This technique seems to be unethical. (How we will know the customer's price in ethical way?).

Output of Cost Estimation

Activity Cost Estimate: It is the quantitative assessment of the probable costs required to complete each individual activities in a project. Cost is calculated for all the types of costs like direct costs, indirect costs, etc. This includes the supporting detail, such as:

- Description of estimated scope of work.
- Documentation of any assumptions made.
- Range of possible results.

Basis of Cost Estimation

A Basis of Estimate (BoE) is the documentation of how a time or cost estimates was produced for each lowest level (work package) of the work breakdown structure. It contains the logics and techniques behind the estimation of costs with details which includes the assumptions, constraints considered for the estimation. Minimally, it should include the method used for estimating, assumptions taken, who made the estimate, specific cost figures used (*i.e.*, internal hour rates or external consultants fees, etc.).

Exercise 11.1: Choose the Tool/Technique to Use in the Below Scenario		
You received a new project in a new domain and you called Raja who already worked in that domain and asked his input to estimate the total cost for your project.	Analogous estimation	Parametric Estimation
You estimate the cost for all the activities and rolls up to estimate for the whole project cost estimation.	Top-down approach	Bottom-up approach
You have historical information about similar kind of projects and adjusting the same as per the attributes of the existing project to arrive at the cost estimation.	Analogous estimation	Parametric estimation
You have the estimation for the overall project as a whole, and you are distributing it to the individual activities.	Top-down approach	Bottom-up approach

11.9 Software Cost Estimation Models

Cost estimation models are mathematical algorithms which help the software engineer and the project manager to estimate the cost in a more accurate and sophisticated way. Nowadays, computerized software which is built as per the models help for the estimation along with spreadsheets-based models. Input parameters of the model include the attributes of the product and project under study. Outputs of the models are usually the resource requirements of efforts, cost and time.

Let's look into three famous cost estimation models, namely:

1. SLIM model
2. COCOMO model
3. SEER–SEM model

In almost all the models, cost is estimated as a mathematical function of product, project and process attributes whose values are estimated by project managers. They are called 'algorithmic (parametric) models'.

$$\text{Effort} = A' * \text{Size}^{B'} \times M$$

Where

A is a constant and is organization-dependent.
B is a complexity fator based on size
M is a multiplier representing attributes of product, process, and people

Most models are basically similar in nature, but with different values for A, B, and M. Accuracy of these kind of models can be improved by calibrating (modifying) the model to a specific environment.

11.9.1 Putnam's Software Life Cycle Model

It was created by Lawrence Putnam Sr. in late 1970 based on the analysis of the life cycle and is based on Rayleigh distribution which describes the time and effort required to finish a software project of specified size. It is intended mainly for large projects and has only few parameters as input.

$$\text{Effort} = \left[\frac{\text{Size}}{\text{Productivity} \times \text{Time}^{4/3}}\right]^3 \times \text{B}$$

Where,

'Effort' is the total effort of the project denoted in person-years.
'Size' is the product size (usually ESLOC–Effective Source Line of Code).
'B' is a scaling function and is based on size.
'Productivity' is the product productivity (It is the ability of the organization to create software of a given size at a particular defect rate).
'Time' is the total schedule (duration) of the project in years.

Plotting effort as a function of time, we can yield the Time–Effort curve.

The points along the curve, indicate the estimated total effort to complete the project at a particular time. One of the distinguishing features of the Putnam's model is that the total effort decreases as the time to complete the project is extended.

The three tools derived, based on SLIM model, are namely:

1. SLIM-Estimate
2. SLIM-Control
3. SLIM-Metrics

Advantages:

1. Simple and repeatable estimations.
2. Only few parameters.
3. Easy to refine and customize formulas.

Disadvantages:

1. Unable to deal with exceptional conditions.
2. Experience not quantified.

11.9.2 COCOMO Model

COCOMO model is the famous model of cost estimation and other models are Putnam's Software Life-cycle Model (SLIM), Parametric Review of Information for Costing and Evaluation–Software (PRICE-S), and Software Evaluation and Estimation of Resources–Software Estimating Model (SEER–SEM).

COCOMO stands for Constructive Cost Model. It is a mathematical empirical model. It was developed at TRW Automotive Holdings Corp. An American defense contractor, Boehm, based on a cost database from 63 different historical software projects, in 1981, developed this model. It is well-documented and associated with any specific software vendor.

The COCOMO model exists in three different flavours, namely, basic model, intermediate model, and advanced model.

A. ***Basic Model***: It gives single 'ballpark' estimate based on the product attributes.
B. ***Intermediate Model***: This model modifies the basic estimate (which was based only on the product) attributes using project and process attributes.
C. ***Advanced Model***: This model estimates the project phases and its parts, separately.

A. *Basic COCOMO Model*

It gives single 'ballpark' estimate based on product attributes which can be derived from the equation as given here:

$$PM = C \times KDSI^{S} \times M$$

Where,

PM is the effort measured in person-months.

C is a complexity factor (2.4/3.0/3.6).

KDSI (Kilo Delivered Source Instructions) is a product metric.

Exponent S is close to 1 (1.05/1.12/1.20).

M is a multiplier based on process, product and development attributes (~1).

Project Complexity	Efforts Required	Development Time
Simple	$2.4(KDSI)^{1.05}$	$2.5(Efforts)^{0.38}$
Medium	$3.0(KDSI)^{1.12}$	$2.5(Efforts)^{0.35}$
Embedded	$3.6(KDSI)^{1.20}$	$2.5(Efforts)^{0.32}$

People required = Efforts required/Development time

Simple projects are said to be executed in organic mode. Moderate projects are said to be executed in semi-detached mode, and highly complex projects are said to be executed in embedded mode.

B. *Intermediate COCOMO Model*

The following attributes for the intermediate COCOMO models are taken into consideration:

Product attributes (3 sub-attributes)
Hardware attributes (4 sub-attributes)
Personnel attribute (5 sub-attributes)
Project attributes (3 sub-attributes)

In total, 15 attributes were considered in intermediate the COCOMO model (Table 11.2).

Table 11.2 Intermediate COCOMO Model Attributes

Product Attributes	Hardware Attributes	Personnel Attributes	Project Attributes
1. Reliability	1. Runtime performance	1. Analyst capability	1. Use of software tools
2. Size	2. Memory constrains	2. Engineering capability	2. Application of software engineering methods
3. Complexity	3. Volatility of the virtual machine	3. Applications experience	3. Required development schedule
	4. Required turnaround time	4. Virtual machine experience	
		5. Programming language experience	

The Effort Adjustment Factor (EAF) which varies for the attributes and have typical values ranges from 0.9 (minimum) to 1.4 (maximum) (Table 11.3).

Table 11.3 EAF with Cost Drivers

Cost Drivers	Ratings (EAF)					
	Very Low	Low	Nominal	High	Very High	Extra High
Product Attributes						
Required software reliability	0.75	0.88	1	1.15	1.4	
Size of application database		0.94	1	1.08	1.16	
Complexity of the product	0.7	0.85	1	1.15	1.3	1.65
Hardware Attributes						
Runtime performance constraints			1	1.11	1.3	1.66
Memory constraints			1	1.06	1.21	1.56
Volatility of the virtual machine		0.87	1	1.15	1.3	
Required turnabout time		0.87	1	1.07	1.15	
Personnel Attributes						
Analyst capability	1.46	1.19	1	0.86	0.71	
Application experience	1.29	1.13	1	0.91	0.82	
Software engineer capability	1.42	1.17	1	0.86	0.7	
Virtual machine experience	1.21	1.1	1	0.9		
Programming language experience	1.14	1.07	1	0.95		
Project Attributes						
Application of engineering methods	1.24	1.1	1	0.91	0.82	
Use of software tools	1.24	1.1	1	0.91	0.83	
Required development schedule	1.23	1.08	1	1.04	1.1	

Table 11.4 helps calculating the efforts required using the intermediate model.

Table 11.4 Complexity vs Efforts Required

Project Complexity	Efforts Required
Simple	EAF * $3.2(KLOC)^{1.05}$
Medium	EAF * $3.0(KLOC)^{1.12}$
Embedded	EAF * $3.8(KLOC)^{1.20}$

C. *Advanced (Detailed) COCOMO Model*

The detailed model considers all the parameters of intermediate model. It estimates the project phases (Figure 11.2) and its parts, separately. The effort is calculated as a function of program size.

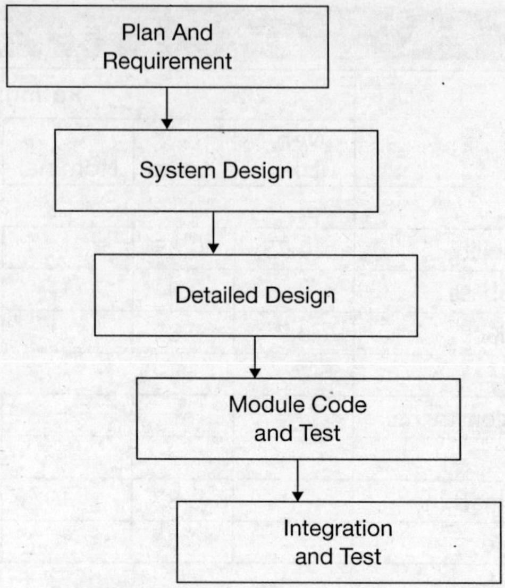

Figure 11.2 Detailed COCOMO Steps

COCOMO II

COCOMO II is the successor of COCOMO 81. It is better suited for estimating modern software development projects. It was released in 1995. COCOMO II addresses the issues on non-sequential and rapid development process models along with reuse-driven and object-oriented approaches.

COCOMO II has three sub-models, namely:

- Early prototyping level
- Early design
- Post-architecture

In the early prototyping model, the estimates are based on the object points. In the early design model, the estimates are based on the function points.

In the post-architecture model, the estimates are based on the source line of code (SLOC).

11.9.3 SEER–SEM Model

- SEER-SEM stands for Software Evaluation and Estimation of Resources–Software Estimating model.
- This model is based on the original Jensen model [Jensen, 1983].
- The Jensen model derives from COCOMO and other models in its mathematical formulation.
- SEER-SEM estimates can be used as part of a composite modeling system for hardware/software systems.
- The scope of the model covers all phases of the project life-cycle, from early specification through design, development, delivery and maintenance.

- Development models covered in this model include object-oriented, reuse, COTS, spiral, waterfall, prototype and incremental development.
- Languages covered in this models are third and fourth generation languages (C++, FORTRAN, COBOL, Ada, etc.) as well as application generators.
- It builds estimates on knowledge, based on the existing projects.
- The SEER-SEM cost model allows probability levels of estimates, constraints on staffing, effort or schedule.
- Estimate outputs of this model include effort of the project, cost, schedule, staffing, and defects.

11.10 Determine Budget Process

Determine budget follows estimate cost process. It is the process of allocating the overall cost estimate of the project into individual activities or work packages in order to establish a cost baseline for measuring project performance of individual activities and, in turn, for the overall project. A cost baseline should not be changed without a proper approval process for change, and these changes are usually approved in the integrated changed control process. We usually add some extra dollar which is not really needed for that purpose and needed for some other purpose. It is called 'padding' and it is not an ethical project management practice. For example receiving cost approval for training and utilizing it for procuring software and vice versa.

Tools and Techniques of Determine Budget

Cost Aggregation Technique: It is a quite straightforward technique. Up to this point, costs have only been estimated at an activity level, but it is important to aggregate, or sum up such costs to the work package level and, then to the overall project level. There may be other levels within the project where costs need to be aggregated, and these may include accounting node points within the work breakdown structure, internal or external accounting departments, and of course at the total project level.

Reserve Analysis Technique: It can reserve both the contingency reserve and management reserve of the project. Contingency reserves are allowances for unplanned, but potentially required changes that can result from realized risk. Management reserve is a separately planned quantity used to allow for future situations which are impossible to predict and they are intended to reduce the risk of missing cost or schedule objectives. Reserve analysis may be calculated on percentage basis, or may only be applied to activities or work packages with higher risks.

There are two schools of thought here, one is that cost reserve to be a simple constant percentage of the overall cost, other one is that cost reserve to be completely based on the risk taking ability and the probability of the risk occurance.

The latter technique would be used to provide the reserve analysis. When it is performed, reserve analysis should be in proportion to the amount of risk associated with a project.

Funding Limit Reconciliation Technique: Expenditure of funds should be reconciled with any funding limits on the commitment of funds for the project. Large variations in the periodic expenditure of funds are usually undesirable for organizational operations. The expenditure of funds is reconciled with the funding limits set by the customer or performing organization on the disbursement of funds for that particular project. Reconciliation will necessitate adjustments of the scheduling to smooth or regulate those expenditures, which is accomplished by placing deadlines and schedule milestones for work packages. This is 'real world', and it is, therefore, important to adjust the project cost baseline to harmonize with such constraints and limitations.

Output of Determine Budget Process

Cost Baseline: The freezing of costs estimation which will be used to measure and monitor the cost performance of the project.

Project Funding Requirements

Funding usually occurs in incremental amounts. It is not a continuous process. The total funds required are those included in the cost baseline plus the management contingency reserve as defined for a project. It is derived and directly based on the cost baseline. It can be established to exceed, usually by a fixed margin, to allow for either early progress or cost overruns which is inevitable.

11.10.1 S-Curve

A simple technique for tracking project costs is to develop a periodical cumulative budget spend plan, and then track actual costs against that plan. The rate of expenditure at the beginning of the project is usually slow. Maximum cost will occur during the execution phase (middle) of a project when the spending rate is higher. As the project comes to an end, the end-stage rates are low and, hence, the slope of the curve is shallow, resulting in 'S' shape. The slope of the graph (Figure 11.3) indicates the project expenditure rate, sometimes called 'burn rate.' By plotting actual costs against the budget planned, one can identify the differences between actual spending and the estimated plan.

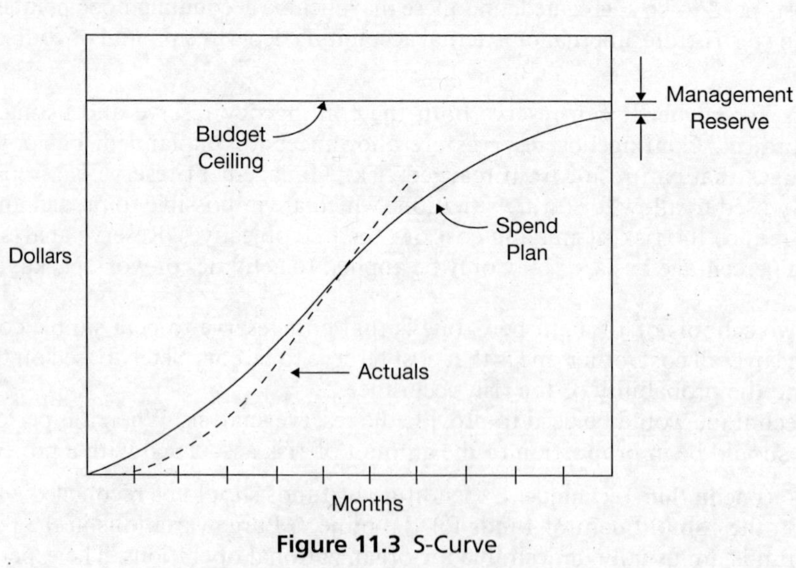

Figure 11.3 S-Curve

Exercise 11.2: Tool Being Used to Build a Budget		
Petrol price suddenly increased by 10% and your project requires extensive travels. So, you reserved $500 aside to deal with the petrol price hike.	Reserve analysis	Cost aggregation
Anand assists Balaji to add up all the estimations to control accounts for ascertaining how much the current costs may stand than the previous account.	Cost aggregation	Funding limit reconciliation
Once the budget is prepared, you are reviewing again to confirm that we can afford everything on time.	Cost aggregation	Funding limit reconciliation

11.11 Control Cost Process

Cost control is easily possible through the proper usage of the earned value reporting system, which makes it possible to measure performance to schedule as well as performance to budget in the same system by using simple formulas.

In this process, the status of the project is monitored to update the project budget and the changes to cost baseline are managed. The actual cost is tracked against the budget. The major task of control cost is monitoring and controlling the expenditure of project fund against the actual work accomplished. Control costs include:

- Influence the factors that create changes to the cost baseline.
- Manage the actual changes when and as they occur.
- Detect variances from the plan.
- Ensure all appropriate changes are recorded.
- Prevent inappropriate or unauthorized changes.
- Inform the appropriate stakeholders about the changes.
- Analyse positive and negative variances.
- Find, how variances affect other control processes.

Inputs of the Control Cost Process

Work Performance Data as Input: Raw observations and measurements identified during activities being performed, to control the cost of the project.

Examples:

1. Percentage of work completed.
2. Actual cost incurred.

Project Management Plan as Input: The project management plan, especially the cost management plan which defines the process of the entire cost control mechanism and acts as input to control the cost process.

Cost Baseline and Project Funding Requirement as Input: Baseline is compared with the work performance information to calculate the variance and appropriate action is taken based on the degree of variance.

Tools and Techniques of Control Cost

Forecasting Techniques

Learning Curve: As time moves on, total costs will increases but the cost per unit drops, because repetition increases efficiency of the work involved in producing the output.

$$Y_x = Kx^{\log_2 b}$$

Where,

K = number of direct work hours to produce the first unit.

Y_x = number of direct work hours to produce the xth unit.

x = number of unit produced.

b = learning percentage.

Law of Diminishing Returns: Just by adding more resources we cannot finish a project early. Addition of more resources may increase the overall output at the beginning, but eventually will decrease individual productivity. Adding three times more manpower to the same task may not complete it three times faster.

Earned Value Technique

The earned value method measures project performance against plans to identify past variances. It may also be used to identify future variances and determine final cost at project completion. The term 'earned value' refers to the actual work completed and the allotted budgeted cost for that portion of work.

For example, if 20% of work on a project with a budget cost of $10,000 (for 20% of work) has been found completed on a given date, the earned value for the performing organization on the date is $10,000 which is the budget cost (not actual cost) of completing 20% of the work. Project managers apply the earned value method to have better control over project execution. Earned value is calculated by comparing the planned amount of work with that actually accomplished, to determine if cost incurred and adherence to schedules and quality standards are set as per baseline projections. The earned value method is favored across the globe and widely used by project managers in project performance measurement. It integrates cost, scope (work) and schedule performance into a single report and helps the project managers to control the entire project.

EV Terms

Data Element	Term	Definition
Scheduled Work	Planned Value (PV)	Budgeted Cost of Work Scheduled (BCWS)
Work Accomplished	Earned Value (EV)	Budgeted Cost of Work Performed (BCWP)
Actual Cost of Work Accomplished	Actual Costs (AC)	Actual Cost of Work Performed (ACWP)
Authorized Work	Budget at Completion	—
Forecasted Cost	Estimate at Completion	—
Work Variance	Schedule Variance	—
Cost Variance	Cost Variance	—
Completion Variance	Variance at Completion	—

Planned Value: It is defined as budgeted cost of work scheduled (BCWS).

Earned Value: It is defined as budgeted cost of work performed (BCWP).

For example, consider a project with a total project budget of \$10,000. Let the total project timeline be 10 months.

Let us assume that we shall be finishing 10% of the work every month. Total project budget (\$10,000) is uniformly distributed (each 10%) across the months to calculate the planned value.

Now, at the end of first month, the planned value is \$1000 where 10% of the work is expected to be completed.

At the end of second month, the planned value is \$2000 where 20% of the work is expected to be completed, and so on.

At the end of tenth month, the planned value is \$10,000 where 100% of the work is expected to be completed.

Now, actually we are at the end of the third month.

When we calculate the actual cost incurred, the amount is \$4000 (AC). There is no formula for actual cost as actual cost is the actual spent from the pocket at that time.

When we calculate the actual percentage of work completed, it is only 20%. So, Earned value = \$2000. We completed work which is worth of \$2000 at the end of third month.

However, we are supposed to complete 30% (as planned). So, Planned Value = \$3000. We planned to completed work which is worth of \$3000 at the end of the third month.

The difference between Earned Value and Planned Value is Schedule Variance,

$$SV = EV - PV$$

The difference between Earned Value and Actual Cost is Cost Variance

$$CV = EV - AC$$

The ratio of earned value to Planned Value (PV) is schedule performance index

$$SPI = EV/PV$$

The ratio of earned value to actual cost is the cost performance index

$$CPI = EV/AC$$

Estimate to Complete (ETC): It is the expected cost needed to complete the project from the point of calculation to the end of the project.

Estimate at Completion (EAC): It is the expected total cost of the project from the beginning to the end of the project (when the defined scope of work has been completed).

There are five different formulas to calculate EAC. These are as follows:

1. An easy way of calculation of EAC is take the Budget-at-Completion, and divide that by the Cost Performance Index, *i.e.*, EAC = BAC/CPI.
2. EAC can also be computed as BAC/(CPI · SPI), which would reflect the compound impact of schedule and cost issues on the project.
3. If you have grounds for believing that all the past problems and issues will get corrected. Then, EAC = actual cumulative cost + ETC.
4. EAC = AC + (BAC – EV)
   (When AC = EV, then EAC = BAC or EAC= BAC/CPI more accurately)
5. EAC = AC + (BAC – EV)/CPI

Formulas 1 and 2 are used when sufficient grounds exist to believe that all past problems and issues will not get corrected and that the same problems will continue. For example, if BAC of the project is \$10,000 and CPI is 0.7 at a particular point of time, we assume that CPI will be 0.7 even at the end of the project. So, EAC = 10,000/0.7 = \$14,285.

Formula 3 is used when sufficient grounds exist to believe that all past problems and issues will get corrected. In this case ETC is freshly calculated and we use the formula:

$$EAC = ACC + ETC,$$

where, ACC is accumulated actual cost.

Formula 4 is an extension of formula 3, EAC = AC + (BAC – EV). This formula assumes that irrespective of the actual costs, the amount allocated for future completion of the remaining work will be budgeted.

If EV = \$2000, AC = \$3000, BAC = \$10,000, then EAC = 3000 + (10,000 – 2000) = 3000 + 8000 = \$11,000.

Formula 5 is an extension of Formula 4 and takes past performance into consideration and, hence, CPI is used.

Variance at Completion (VAC): It is the difference between Budget at Complete (BAC) and estimate at completion (EAC).

$$VAC = BAC - EAC$$

To Complete Performance Index (TCPI)

TCPI = Work Remaining/Cost Remaining

Work remaining is calculated using the formula, BAC – EV. As you know, EV is the actual work completed and BAC is the planned one at the end of the project.

Cost remaining is calculated using the formula, EAC – AC. As you know, AC is the actual cost incurred and EAC is the estimated cost at the end of the project.

Therefore, TCPI = (BAC – EV)/(EAC – AC)

Example 1

PV	EV	AC		
\$1	\$1	\$1	On schedule	On cost
\$2	\$2	\$1	On schedule	Under cost
\$1	\$1	\$2	On schedule	Over cost
\$1	\$2	\$2	Ahead of schedule	On cost
\$1	\$2	\$3	Ahead of schedule	Over cost
\$1	\$2	\$1	Ahead of schedule	Under cost
\$3	\$2	\$1	Behind schedule	Under cost
\$2	\$1	\$3	Behind schedule	Over cost
\$2	\$1	\$1	Behind schedule	On cost

Example 2

BAC = \$40K
EV = \$20K
PV = \$28K
AC = \$26K

- % of Work Scheduled — PV/BAC = \$28K/\$40K = 70%
- % of Budget Spent — AC/BAC = \$26K/\$40K = 65%

- % of Work Accomplished EV/BAC = \$20K/\$40K = 50%
- Cost Variance EV – AC = \$20K – \$26K = –\$6K
- Schedule Variance EV – PV = \$20K – \$28K = –\$8K

If	AC > EV	AC = EV	AC < EV
Then	CV < 0	CV = 0	CV > 0
	CPI < 1	CPI = 1	CPI > 1
The Project is	Overbudget	On Budget	Under Budget

If	PV > EV	PV = EV	PV < EV
Then	SV < 0	SV = 0	SV > 0
	SPI < 1	SPI = 1	SPI > 1
The Project is	Behind Schedule	On Schedule	Ahead of Schedule

Exercise 11.3 EV Calculation Exercise
If EV = \$94000 and SPI = 0.87, what is the planned value?
If PV = \$257000 and BAC = \$330000, what is the scheduled percent complete?

Other Concepts in Costing

Depreciation is the decrease in value of an asset over a period of time for accounting tax and the value calculation after a period of time. Following are some concepts in costing:

- Straightline method (Asset depreciates the same amount every year)
- Double declining balance (In the first year there is a higher deduction in the value of the asset—twice the amount of straightline. Each year after that the deduction is 40% less than the previous year.)
- Sum of year digit method (Lets say, the life of an object is six years. The total of one to six is 21(6 + 5 + 4 + 3 + 2 + 1). In the first year, we deduce 6/21 from the cost, in the second year, we deduce 5/21, and so on.)

Output of Control Cost Process

Budget forecasts: Calculated EAC value represents the budget forecasts and is communicated to all the stakeholders.

Measuring progress of individual tasks: Assuming the duration of a Task is 10 days. The work is planned to start January 1st and gets over by 10th January. The following table may be used to calculate the progress of the task in question.

Measuring Rule for Progress of Individual Tasks			
Rule	Task Begins	Tasks Completed	Percent Progressed
50/50	Y	N	50%
50/50	Y	Y	100%
20/80	Y	N	20%
20/80	Y	Y	100%
0/100	Y	N	0%
0/100	Y	Y	100%

Work Performance Information

Work performance data collected is analysed in context to infer information based on the relationship between the various measured parameters. This is called 'Work Performance Information (WPI)'.

Examples:

1. Schedule Variance (SV)
2. Cost Variance (CV)
3. Estimate at Complete (EAC)
4. Estimate to Complete (ETC)

Discussion Points

- How is historical information useful for the cost management process?
- What are all the difficulties faced by you for calculating the cost of a particular tasks?

SUMMARY

If we are not following cost management process, then it would be difficult to get control over the profitability of the project. Poor cost management will also affect funding of the future projects. The work breakdown structure is the basis of the cost estimate and drawing correct WBS is the first success factor for better cost management. Cost estimation is done throughout the life-cycle of projects. Cost control is easily possible through proper usage of the earned value reporting system which makes it possible to measure performance to schedule and performance to budget in the same system by using simple formulas. Project expenditures are less at the beginning and at the end. The expenditure is more at the middle phase of the project.

Bottom-up Estimation: In this technique, the cost of individual work items are estimated, and then it is summarized rolling-up to get the overall project total. It is more accurate than the top-down approach.

Top-down Estimation: It is also called macro model as the estimation happens at macro (higher) levels. In this technique, the individual work items are not considered for the estimation.

Analogous Estimation: Here, the estimations happen by comparing the project to a similar kind of project (application/domain). Analogous means comparison.

Parametric Estimation: It is an accurate estimation technique out of all the available techniques and uses some formula (statistical relationships) connecting various variables (parameters) of the project for deriving the estimation.

Pricing to Win: Here, the estimations happen not for the system or any of its parameters, but for the prediction of customer expectation price.

Vendor bid Analysis: It analyses the estimated cost of a project. This is done based on the received bids from the qualified vendors, for a specific project (This technique is used by the customers).

Three Point Estimation: Project managers know this technique through PERT (Program, Evaluation, and Review Technique). This technique believes that there is very small probability that a project will be completed on a given date estimated at the beginning of the project.

Estimating Styles:
Subjective Estimate: Based on personal experience.
Statistical Estimate: Based on comprehensive historical data.
Comparative Estimate: Based on similar projects.
Empirical Estimate: Based on real data of the project.

COCOMO Model: COCOMO stands for Constructive Cost Model. It is a mathematical empirical model. It was developed at TRW. An American defense contractor, Boehm, based on a cost database from 63 different historical software projects, in 1981, developed this model. It exists in three different flavours, namely, basic model, intermediate model, and advanced model.

1. Basic: It gives single 'ball-park' estimate based on the product attributes.
2. Intermediate: It modifies the basic estimate (which was based only on the product) attributes using project and process attributes.
3. Advanced: It estimates project phases and its parts, separately.

Learning Curve: As time moves on, the total costs will increase, but the cost per unit will drop, because repetition increases with the efficiency of the work involved in producing the output.

Actual Cost (AC): Actual cost is the total cost incurred in accomplishing the work during a given time period. It is also being referred as ACWP (Actual Cost of Work Performed).

Budgeted Cost of Work Performed (BCWP): This is called 'earned value' and this is the cumulative sum of the approved cost estimates for activities completed during a given period (usually project-to-date).

Budgeted Cost of Work Scheduled (BCWS): The sum of the approved cost estimates for activities scheduled to be performed during a given period as per the plan.

Chart of Accounts: Numbering system used to monitor project costs by category (*e.g.*, wage cost, material cost) and the project chart of accounts is based on the corporate chart of accounts of the main performing organization.

Code of Accounts: Numbering system used to uniquely identify each element of the WBS. Mostly, it is a numeric system for easy identification of the levels.

Contingency Reserve: Time to manage future situations (known-unknowns) intended to reduce the impact of missing cost or scheduled objectives and is included in the project's cost and schedule baselines.

Cost Budgeting: Allocating the cost estimates to each individual project components for better control of the overall project.

Cost Estimating: Cost estimation of the resources needed to complete the defined project activities.

Cost Performance Index (CPI): The ratio of budgeted costs to actual costs (BCWP/ACWP) and CPI is often used to predict the magnitude of a possible cost overrun.

Cost of Quality: Cost to keep the quality to a particular level defined which includes review cost.

Cost Variance (CV): Difference between the estimated cost of an activity and the actual cost of that activity.

Earned Value: It is the method of measuring project performance by comparing the amount of work planned with that of actual accomplishment.

Estimate at Completion (EAC): The expected total cost of an activity, a group of activities, or of the project at the end, EAC = Actual-to-date + ETC.

Estimate to Complete (ETC): The expected cost needed to complete an activity, a group of activities, or the project and this is also known as forecast final cost.

Fixed Costs: Costs that do not change that are based on the number of units and also non-recurring.

Management Reserve: To manage future situations which are impossible to predict ('Unknown-unknowns'). It is used to reduce the risk of missing cost or schedule objectives and use of this requires a change to the project's cost baseline.

Parametric Estimating: An estimating technique that is based on statistical relationship between historical data and other variables to calculate an estimate.

Payback Period: The number of time periods at which cumulative revenues exceed cumulative costs and, therefore, the project has turned a profit.

Planned Value (PV): Planned value is the budgeted cost for the work scheduled to complete an activity and is also referred as BCWS (Budgeted Cost of Work Scheduled).

Schedule Performance Index (SPI): It is the ratio of work performed to work scheduled.

Schedule Variance (SV): It is the difference between scheduled completion of an activity and the actual completion of that activity.

Answers to Exercise Questions

Exercise 11.1 Choose the Tools to be Use(d) in the Following Scenario		
You got a new project in new domain and you called Raja who already worked in that domain and asked his input to estimate the total cost for your project	Analogous Estimation	Parametric Estimation
You estimate the cost for each and every activity and rolls up to estimate for the whole project cost estimation	Top–down Approach	Bottom-up Approach
You have historical information about similar kind of projects and adjusting the same as per the attributes of the existing project to arrive the cost estimation	Analogous Estimation	Parametric Estimation
You have the estimation for the overall project as a whole and you are distributing it to the individual activities	Top–down Approach	Bottom-up Approach

Exercise 11.2		
Petrol price got suddenly increased 10% and your project has lot of travels and so you reserve $500 aside to deal with the petrol hike.	Reserve Analysis	Cost Aggregation
Anand helps Balaji to add up all the estimations to control accounts to find out how much it will costs more than the previous account	Cost Aggregation	Funding Limit Reconciliation
Once the budget is done, you are looking over again to make sure we can afford everything on Time.	Cost Aggregation	Funding Limit Reconciliation

Exercise 11.3 EV Calculation
SPI = EV/PV. So, PV = EV/SPI = 94,000/0.87 = $10,8046
PV = BAC * Schedule % Completion Scheduled % Completion = PV/BAC = 257000/330000 = 77%

EXERCISES

PART A (Objective-type Questions)

1. Earned value is
A. planned work value
B. revenue from customer
C. value given to customer
D. completed work value

2. Mahesh is the project manager of ABC project, and he needs to estimate cost for his project which one of the following will be best input for him?
A. Historical information
B. WBS
C. Bottom up estimation
D. Expert judgment

3. You are the project manager of ABC Project and your manager clearly instructed you to do the estimation as accurately as possible. Which of the following method you will use?
A. Top–down approach
B. Parametric model
C. Bottom–up approach
D. Analogous estimation

4. You are the project manager of ABC project and your manager clearly instructed you to do the estimation as quickly as possible. Which of the following method you will use?
A. Top–down approach
B. Parametric model
C. Bottom–up approach
D. Analogous estimation

5. You are the project manager of ABC project and you tried to approximate the monetary resources needed to complete project activities. Which one of the following is in order of less accurate to most accurate?
A. Order of magnitude, Budget, Definitive
B. Definitive, Budget, Order of magnitude
C. Budget, Order of magnitude, Definitive
D. Budget, Definitive, Order of Magnitude

6. You are the project manager of ABC project and you tried to approximate the monetary resources needed to complete project activities, this is an example of
A. Estimate cost
B. Determine budget
C. Control cost
D. Plan cost

7. You are the project manager of ABC project and you are aggregating the estimated costs of individual activities or work packages to establish an authorized cost baseline, this is an example of
   A. Estimate cost
   B. Determine budget
   C. Control cost
   D. Plan cost management
8. What is the present value of a project which is worth $100,000 after a year and annual interest rate is 5%?
   A. $95,238
   B. $105,000
   C. $95,000
   D. $100,000
9. Cost that doesn't change with the number of units produced is called as:
   A. Variable cost
   B. Indirect cost
   C. Fixed cost
   D. Unit cost
10. Mahesh is the project manager of XYZ project and it is very small project where the scope is very limited. He can combine the following process
    A. Cost estimating and cost budgeting
    B. Cost estimating and cost controlling
    C. Cost budgeting and cost controlling
    D. Cost planning and cost estimating
11. Mahesh who is the senior project manager is telling that cost management plan can be informal. Is it possible and do you agree with this?
    A. True
    B. False
12. Select the best statement regarding cost estimate.
    A. Cost estimate is very accurate in the beginning of the project
    B. Accuracy of cost estimate will increase as the project progresses
    C. The accuracy of cost estimation is same at all levels of the project
    D. Accuracy of cost estimate will decrease as the project progresses
13. Cost estimating is an iterative process from phase to phase.
    A. True
    B. False
14. Mahesh, the project manager of ABC project had only limited amount of information about the project in the beginning stage and which type of estimation technique he would have used in the above situation?
    A. Parametric estimation
    B. Top–down approach
    C. Bottom–up approach
    D. Analogous estimation
15. Mahesh, the senior project manager of ABC project hates using analogous estimation technique. What do you think might be the reason for the same?
    A. It is costly
    B. It is taking more time for estimation
    C. It is generally less accurate
    D. It is not at all accurate
16. Mahesh, the senior project manager of ABC project loves using parametric estimation technique. Because
    A. It is less costly
    B. It is taking less time for estimation
    C. It can produce higher level of accuracy
    D. It is risk free estimation technique
17. Two lines in S curve is made up of
    A. Income vs expenditures
    B. Cost baseline vs expenditures
    C. Cost vs time
    D. Cost estimate vs cost budget
18. X axis of S curve is
    A. Expenditure
    B. Cost baseline
    C. Time
    D. Scope
19. Earned value management integrates the following components
    A. Cost, Scope, Quality
    B. Quality, Scope, Time
    C. Risk, Cost, Time
    D. Cost, Scope, Time

20. When the project is completed which of the following case will be true?
 A. EVM schedule variance will ultimately equal zero
 B. EVM schedule variance will be positive value
 C. EVM schedule variance will be negative value
 D. EVM schedule variance can be positive or negative depending on the project performance

21. SPI value less than one indicate which of the following?
 A. More work was completed than planned
 B. Less work was completed than planned
 C. It indicates nothing
 D. CPI also less than one

22. Analysis which examines project performance over time to determine if performance is improving or deteriorating is called
 A. Trend analysis
 B. Variance analysis
 C. System analysis
 D. EV analysis

23. The cost of investing in a particular project and, therefore, forgoing the potential benefits of other projects is known as
 A. Direct cost
 B. Indirect cost
 C. Opportunity cost
 D. Variable cost

24. Which of the following would closely estimate the actual cost of a project?
 A. Order-of-magnitude
 B. Budget
 C. Definitive
 D. Initial

25. In the EV system, cost variance is computed as
 A. EV−PV
 B. EV−AC
 C. AC−EV
 D. AC−PV
 E. PV−EV

26. Your company got possibilities of choosing only one of the two projects ABC, XYZ. ABC is worth $40,000 and XYZ is worth $60,000. Your company decided to choose the ABC project as it uses less number of resources than XYZ. What is the opportunity cost of choosing ABC project?
 A. $40,000
 B. $60,000
 C. $20,000
 D. $0

27. Which tasks is more over budget?
 A. Task 1
 B. Task 2
 C. Task 3
 D. Task 4

28. Which task is ahead of schedule?
 A. Task 1
 B. Task 2
 C. Task 3
 D. Task 4

29. Which tasks is ahead of schedule and within budget?
 A. Task 1
 B. Task 2
 C. Task 3
 D. Task 4

30. Mahesh is the project manager of ABC project whose budget-at-completion (BAC) is $50,000. The duration of the project is 10 months where Mahesh planned to spent uniformly across all months. The project is at the end of 5th month but completed only 40% of the work. What is the earned value of this project at that point of time?
 A. $25,000
 B. $20,000
 C. $5000
 D. $50,000

31. Which of the following is the disadvantage of SLIM Model?
   A. Simple and repeatable estimations
   B. Experience not quantified
   C. Only few Parameters
   D. Easy to refine and customize formulas
32. Which of the following is not a flavour of COCOMO model?
   A. Basic model
   B. Intermediate model
   C. Advanced model
   D. Complex model
33. COCOMO model stands for
   A. Cost of component model
   B. Code cost model
   C. Constructive cost model
   D. Constructive code based model

PART B (Write the answers in one or two lines)

1. List down various software estimation techniques you are aware of.
2. Write notes on bottom–up estimation technique
3. Write notes on top–down estimation technique.
4. Write notes on analogous estimation technique.
5. Write notes on parametric estimation.
6. Write notes on vendor bid analysis technique of estimation.
7. What are three point estimation techniques? What is the formula used in three point estimation technique?
8. What are all the different estimating styles you are aware of?
9. What is subjective estimation style?
10. What is statistical estimation style?
11. What is comparative estimation style?
12. What is empirical estimation style?
13. Define precision and accuracy.
14. Write notes on cost of a project.
15. What is Variable cost and fixed cost?
16. What is direct cost and indirect cost?
17. What is opportunity cost?
18. Write notes on cost estimation process.
19. Differentiate between cost estimating and pricing.
20. What are all the problems in estimating accurate costs?
21. What are all the types of cost estimates?
22. Write notes on cost estimation models.
23. Give examples for cost estimation models?
24. List down any three advantages of SLIM model.
25. List down the disadvantages of SLIM model.
26. What is COCOMO model?
27. What are all the flavours of COCOMO model?
28. Write notes on Detailed COCOMO model.
29. What is COCOMO II model?
30. Write notes on cost aggregation.
31. What is reserve analysis?
32. What is funding limit reconciliation?
33. Write notes on learning curve.
34. Write notes on law of diminishing returns.
35. Write notes on earned value management (EVM).
36. What is EAC in EV technique?
37. What is VAC in EV technique?
38. What is to Complete Performance Index (TCPI) in EV technique?

Section IV

Software Project Execution, Monitoring and Control

12

Risk Management

12.1 Introduction

There is an element of risk in every activity or enterprise, but effective risk management techniques can mitigate the harmful effects of risks coming to fruition. The American Express Bank, for example, undoubtedly succeeded in managing risk effectively and professionally, because their centers in New York were back in operation just one day after the 9/11 attacks. Project managers, too, are required to plan for and manage risks, because cost overruns, loss of stakeholder confidence, or even outright project failure can result if any or all threats associated with project risks do materialize.

12.2 Reactive vs Proactive Risk Strategies

In reactive risk strategy, nothing is done until something goes wrong in a project. As there is no prior planning on how to handle the occurred risk, the project team will have to move to a fire-fighting mode and, finally, to a crisis management mode after the occurrence of the risks. On the other hand, the proactive risk strategies believe in advanced planning for probable risks and effective handling of it in case the risk occurs. Figure 12.1 shows the difference in approach for reactive and proactive risk strategies.

An important responsibility of a project manager and the project management team is to identify all project risks, analyse and rank them as per importance, and set processes and systems in place to possibly avert the identified threats. Risks are events or consequences that have been estimated to have a non-zero probability of occurrence during execution of a project. Those are always measured by their impacts on a project. Generally, risks entail losses or benefits, contrary to an opinion those risks always represent only threats to a project's success. Therefore, project risk management techniques aim to increase the probability and impact of positive events and decrease the probability and impact of negative events on a project.

A high level pictorial representation of the different phases of risk management is shown in Figure 12.2.

Reactive vs Proactive Risk Strategy	
Reactive Approach	**Proactive Approach**
• The approach is: 'Don't worry, I will think of something'. • Nothing is done until something goes wrong. • Team need to move to a fire-fighting mode to resolve the problem rapidly. • Crisis management is the choice for this management techniques. • Most of the unstructured organizations and inexperienced teams rely on this approach.	• Approach is to avoid risk and create contingency plans for the unavoidable risks. • The risk management process are followed in proactive approach: ▪ Identify possible risks and recognize what may go wrong. ▪ Analyse identified risks to estimate the probability of occurrence and the impact. ▪ Rank the risks by probability and impact. ▪ Develop a mitigation plan and contingency plan to manage risks having high probability and high impact.

Figure 12.1 Reactive and Proactive Risk Management

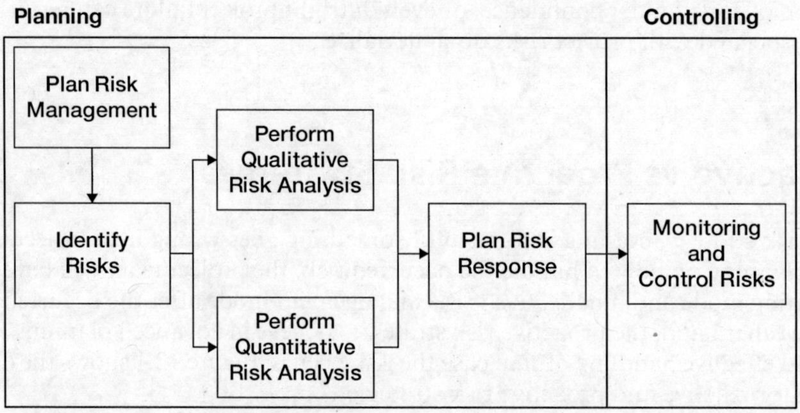

Figure 12.2 Risk Management Process

12.3 Software Risk

The definition of risk is 'A probability or threat of loss or any negative consequence which is caused by external or internal events and that may be avoided through preemptive action.' This means, a risk has the following two types of characteristics:

Uncertainty: In this case, the risk event may happen or may not happen. There is a degree of uncertainty attached to the event.

Loss: If the risk event occurs, there would be certain losses incurred.

12.3.1 Types of Risk

In software projects, there are different types of risks. Those are discussed here.

Project Risk: The project risks impact the project schedule which, in turn, increases the cost of the project. There may be various reasons behind the project risks, which include budget issue, resource issue, requirement issue, customer issue, etc. which can impact a software project.

Technical Risk: The impact of technical risk is mainly on the quality and timeline of the project. There may be potential issues in the design, implementation, interface, maintenance and unknown technology of the software which leads to delay and affect quality in the project.

Business Risk: Every project has some business goals to fulfill. But, if the business alignment of the project or the software to be built is lost, then either it loses the focus of the senior management or the project may be scrapped.

Following are two important concepts related to risk management.

High-risk Area: The intensity of a risk varies over a project's life-cycle. Risk is usually high in the conceptual and developmental phases of a project. It decreases over a project's life-cycle with gradual completion of the project work. Alternatively, the costs at stake is low at the early phases of the life-cycle. It increases as work is accomplished. The area of overlapping is known as the high-risk area. The risk is very high at the beginning, because of uncertainties in the project. The cost at stake is low at the beginning, because we would have just started by investing our money. But, as we move ahead with the project, uncertainties will go down, because the project scope becomes transparent.

But the costs at stake move slowly up as the project progresses. Both these (costs at stake and risk) meet at a point forming an area called 'high-risk area' which needs to be cautiously monitored.

Stakeholder Tolerance: Depending on the criticality of perceived benefits or losses, different stakeholders accept varying degrees of risk in a project. For example, cost variance and scope variance are acceptable up to a certain limit, beyond which it will go out of control. This is called 'stakeholder's tolerance level'.

Let us discuss the plan risk management. It is the first step in the risk management process.

12.4 Plan Risk Management

Careful and explicit risk management planning enhances the probability of success of risk management process. Project scope statement acts as a primary input as the entire project revolves around executing the scope of the project successfully. In addition to this, cost management plan and schedule management plan also act as the inputs for this process, as risk management depends on these plans. The process of how a project manager manages the risk depends on how he manages the schedule and cost of the project (Figure 12.3).

Arranging risk planning meeting is the first step for planning risk management. This meeting should involve the project manager, project team leaders, key stakeholders, and others who may be deemed authorities on providing inputs to risk management. In these meetings, risk management responsibilities are assigned. Cost elements and schedule activities of managing risks are also assigned to the project budget and project schedule, respectively.

Figure 12.3 Plan Risk Management Process

Risk management plans for the similar natured past projects may serve as inputs for preparing the risk management plan for a current project. Templates of similar projects can also be used in assisting to draw up the risk management plan.

Risk categories and a risk breakdown structure are parts of the risk management plan. These are the primary outputs in planning the risk management. Risk categories help in systematic identification of risks and contribute to the effectiveness and quality of the identify risk process. Risk categories are simply list of common areas or sources of risk; typically project management offices have standard lists of risk categories that all projects can use to identify risks easily.

The contents of a typical risk management plan are as follows:

- Methodology to manage risks
- Roles and responsibilities for each action
- Budget
- Frequency of occurrence of meeting
- Risk categories
- Definitions of risk probability and impact
- Probability and impact matrix
- Scoring and interpretation
- Reporting formats

Risk Breakdown Structure

Risk categories in a project can be depicted in a hierarchical format which identifies different levels of project organization which can be potential source of risk arranged according to risk categories and sub-categories. A typical risk breakdown structure (RBDS) (Figure 12.4) lists the categories and sub-categories within which risks for a project may arise.

External Categories: Government regulations, markets, customers, suppliers.
Project Management: Initiation, planning, controlling, resourcing, closing.
Organization: Funding, prioritization.

Risk Mitigation, Monitoring and Management Plan

The purpose of the Risk Mitigation, Monitoring and Management Plan (RMMM) is to effectively identify, monitor and mitigate risk. For delivering a quality product, it is important that organizations should perform risk identification and mitigation activities effectively. It is the responsibility of the whole organization to control risks in projects. Though, the development team is involved in the day to day project activities and will be identifying, monitoring and mitigating the risks continuously, but it is the responsibility of other stakeholders also to be alert on any possible risks occurring. For example, a change in market condition which may affect the viability of a product may be identified by the marketing team and the management is alerted of the possible risks.

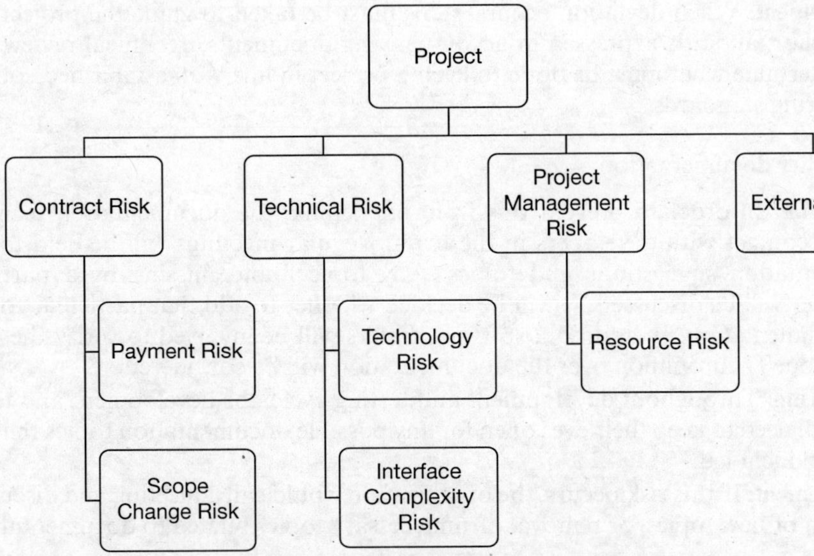

Figure 12.4 Risk Breakdown Structure

There are several factors that the RMMM plan takes into account, like:

1. Project size
2. Requirement stability
3. Business impact
4. Revenue and profitability
5. Timeline and milestones
6. Cost
7. New customer
8. New geography
9. New and unstable technology, etc.

Sometimes, all these factors are put into a form of checklist or questionnaire. The project risks are identified based on the answers captured in the checklist. The RMMM plan not only focuses on identifying risks, but also plans for monitoring, mitigating and managing the risks. Given here are some examples of the RMMM plan:

Risk: Software engineering standards not followed.

- **Mitigation:** While it is possible to deviate from software engineering standards, it is unlikely to occur. All team members have a full understanding of the software process, and how we plan to implement them in the process.
- **Monitoring:** Technical reviews, involving comparison between documentation and the actual project will help to determine if deviation will occur. All relevant documents must be as complete and accurately as possible to ensure that work will conform to expressed software engineering standards.

- **Management:** When deviation occurs, steps must be taken to guide the project back within the standards expressed in accompanying documents. Technical reviews also help determine what must be done to keep a project in line with established software engineering standards.

Risk: Poor quality documentation.

- **Mitigation:** In order to prevent this from happening, the documentation team will keep in contact with developers in the team. Regular meetings will be held to offer documentation suggestions and topics. Any topic found missing by a particular developer will be discussed. It will be decided whether to add that particular topic in the documentation. In addition, software testers will be involved to verify the documentation. Their opinion over the documentation will be considered.
- **Monitoring:** Throughout development and testing cycle, the development and testing team will need to keep their eyes open for any possible documentation topics that have not been included.
- **Management:** If this risk occurs, the organization would call a meeting and discuss the addition of new topics, or removal of unnecessary topics related to documentation.

12.4.1 Identify Risk

The identify risks process (Figure 12.5) involves in the determination of risks that are likely to affect a project and documentation of the characteristics of each risk. Both the positive effects [opportunities or rewards] and negative effects [threats] of risks are documented. The project team, subject matter experts, stakeholders, and other project managers are involved in the risk identification process. This process is iterative, because the identification occurs over the entire life-cycle of the project, that is, from its beginning till the end. Its a continuous process. As because project managers are often called uncertainty managers, it would be fair to call them risk managers as well.

In addition to the formal (already identified) project risks, there are also risks that may evolve over the course of project execution. A risk trigger is a symptom of an indirect manifestation of a risk event; however, risk triggers may prove to be false alarms sometimes their identification does not indicate the certainty of a risk developing. An example of a risk

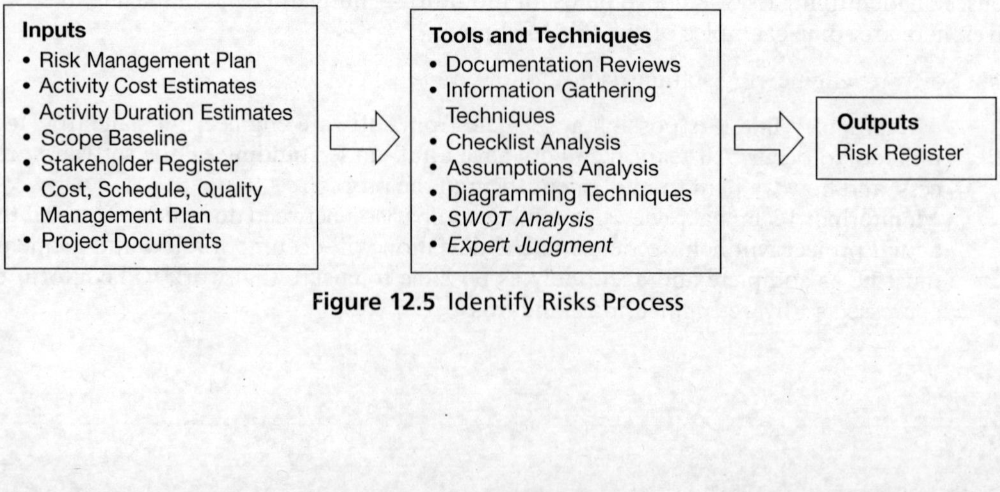

Figure 12.5 Identify Risks Process

trigger is poor team morale. Risk triggers, if identified on time, serves project managers as helpful by warning signs of an emerging risk.

Few ways to identify risks are documentation reviews, brainstorming and information gathering techniques, Delphi technique, checklist analysis, diagramming techniques, assumption analysis, SWOT analysis, and expert judgment.

12.4.1.1 Documentation Review

A structured documentation review comprises review of all project materials, particularly project baseline documents (Figure 12.6). Use of this tool includes review of all project plans, assumptions, lessons learned and risk management plans from previous similar projects, and contractual obligations, if any, for the project. The quality of past risk management plans, agreement, if any, between those plans and requirements and assumptions of those projects, and agreement, if any, between those plans and the actual execution of those projects can be useful sources of indicators of risks in the current project.

Point to Remember

There are many ways to identify risks: documentation reviews, brainstorming and information gathering techniques, Delphi technique, checklist analysis, diagramming techniques, assumption analysis, SWOT analysis, and expert judgment.

12.4.1.2 Information Gathering Techniques

Different information gathering techniques for risk identification are as follows:

1. **Brainstorming:** The main goal of brainstorming, a popular and widely used information-gathering technique in risk identification, is to obtain the material required to generate a comprehensive list of risks as envisioned by all project stakeholders.

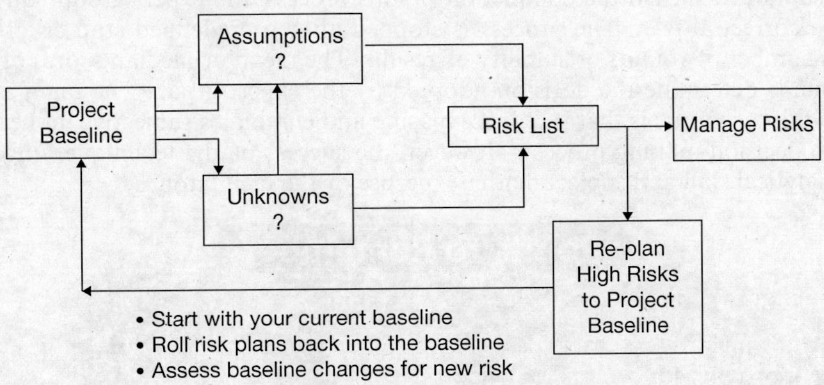

Figure 12.6 Project Baseline

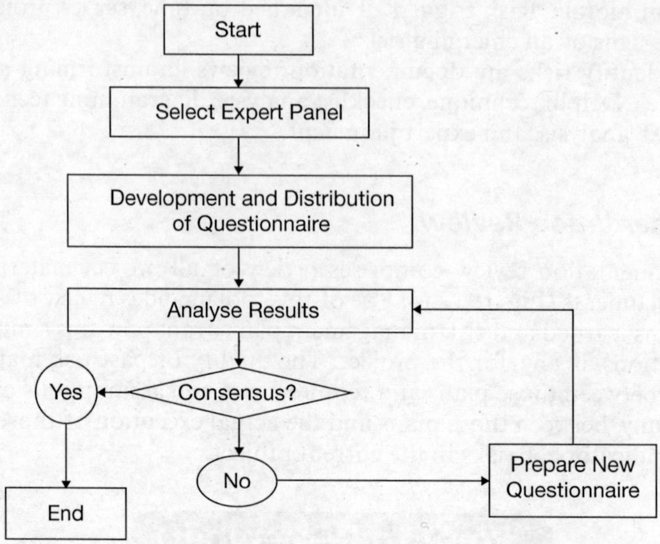

Figure 12.7 Delphi Technique for Risk Identification

An important feature of brainstorming meetings is that they use participants of widely differing functional backgrounds, which enhances the likelihood fresh ideas and innovations being generated.

2. **Delphi Technique:** The Delphi technique (Figure 12.7) is a systematic, interactive forecasting method used for risk identification and it uses a panel of independent experts. It is also used to help the participating experts to reach a consensus. Experts answer questionnaires in two or more rounds. After each round, the session facilitator provides a summary of the forecasts of each expert, one by one, without indicating the identity of the expert.

   The summary also includes the reasons the expert provided for judgments made. After summaries of all experts' views have been, thus, presented, experts are encouraged to revise their forecasts—on the basis of the summaries presented—and resubmit them. On the completion of this process, the expert group converges on the correct answer. The process is stopped after a predefined stop criterion, such as number of rounds or stability of results. The mean or median scores of the final rounds determine the decision adopted by the expert group. The main advantage of this technique is that it reduces biasing and eliminates subjective influences from the decision-making process. However, the success of the technique hinges on the analytical skill and subject matter expertise of the facilitator.

Points to Remember

The main features of the Delphi technique are as follows:

1. Anonymity of the expert participants.
2. Opportunity for experts to review their inputs.
3. Structured information flow.

3. **Interviewing:** In this technique, risks are identified by interviewing the experienced project participants, stakeholders, and subject matter experts.
4. **Root Cause Analysis:** The underlying causes of the problem are identified. Then, a preventive action is planned to prevent any possible problem.

12.4.1.3 Checklist Analysis

Risk identification checklists can be prepared on the basis of historical information available in the similar natured past projects. The lowest level of RBDS can also be used as risk checklist.

12.4.1.4 Diagramming Techniques

There are different diagramming techniques like cause and effect diagrams and system or process flow charts that show how various components of a project are interrelated and this link identification serves as a basis for risk identification. Influence diagrams, pictorial representations of a problem showing causal influences, and time ordering events may also be used as diagramming tools to identify risks.

An influence diagram, also referred to as a decision network, is a graphical and mathematical representation of a decision. It helps to take a decision and the decision is fully based on the influence of various factors associated with the decision. Risks associated with various factors are the sources of risks for the entire decision-making process. For example, assume that you are the project manager of a construction project and you want to plan your vacation based on the weather forecast which is not conducive for the work. Figure 12.8 shows two functional arcs ending in satisfaction, one conditional arc ending in weather forecast, and one informational arc ending in vacation activity. The informational arc ending in vacation activity indicates that the project manager will only know weather forecast, not weather condition, when making a choice. In other words, actual weather will be known after a choice has been made. It also indicates that vacation activity is independent of weather condition, given weather forecast is known from it. Both weather forecasts and actual weather are the sources of risks.

12.4.1.5 SWOT Analysis

SWOT analysis acts as an instrument in strategic planning. Factors internal to an organization can be classified as strengths (S) or weaknesses (W) and those external to the organization classified as opportunities (O) or threats (T). The following list defines the four components of a SWOT analysis (Figure 12.9).

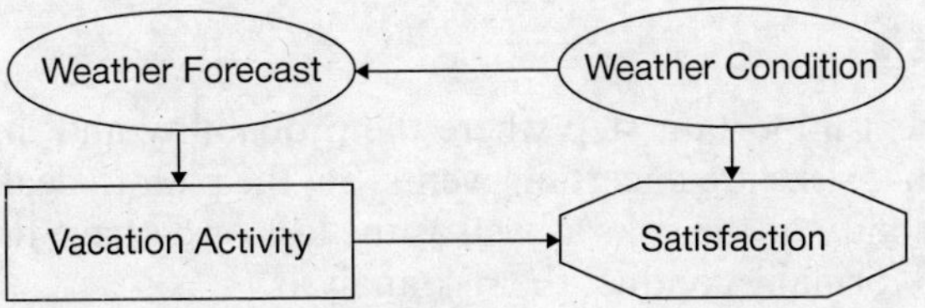

Figure 12.8 Influence Diagram

Figure 12.9 SWOT Analysis

Strengths: Positive tangible and positive intangible attributes internal to an organization that are within the organization's control.

Weakness: Negative attributes that are within an organization's control representing areas of organizational improvement.

Opportunities: Attractive factors external to the organization.

Threats: External risk factors beyond the organization's control; the organization may yet benefit from threats by having contingency plans to effectively address these threats.

Points to Remember

The Dos and Don't of SWOT analysis are as follows:

- Be realistic on all the factors.
- Be specific with the factors and area of comparison.
- Compare factors only with the core mission.
- Keep analysis short and simple.
- Avoid complexity.

The risk register is the primary output of the 'identify risks process'. The register is used updating risk information, because risk identification is an ongoing process. It lists identified risks, potential responses of the risks identified, root causes of identified risks, and updated risk categories.

The risk register is an important project document and it is often referred as a risk tracker sheet.

12.4.2 Risk Analysis

Risk analysis is the next important step where the probability and impact of the risks are identified. We know that risks are uncertain events. So, the plan to deal with the risks should be based on the probability of the risks as well as the loss or damage that the risk may cause. There are two ways to formally conduct the risk analysis.

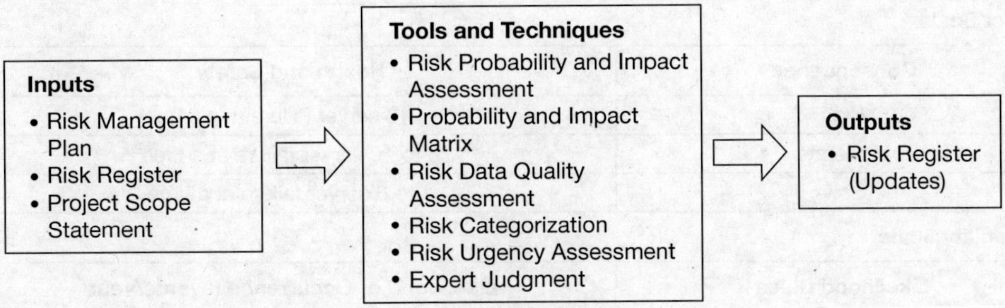

Figure 12.10 Qualitative Risk Analysis

12.4.2.1 Qualitative Risk Analysis Techniques

Qualitative risk analysis process (Figure 12.10) is one of assessment and evaluation of the impacts of and likelihoods of realization related to identified risks. Qualitative risk analysis is a subjective analysis of identified risks. Here, subjective refers to the classification of risks as high-impact, medium-impact, and low-impact risks. Establishing normative standards to classify identified risks, reduces the element of personal bias in the classification process. The perform qualitative risk analysis process is a quick and cost effective means of establishing priorities. However, the outputs of this process are revised during project execution.

Qualitative risk analysis is followed by quantitative risk analysis. First, the risk needs to be qualified as high, medium, or low. Only then can we quantify the risks stating how much high or how much low.

Risk probability is defined as the chance level of risks occurring in a project, whereas risk consequences refer to the impact on projects if identified risks do materialize. Both these important factors are identified and documented in the risk management plan. The levels of risk probability and impact are assessed, measured, and analysed in project team meetings, attended by subject matter experts as well.

12.4.2.1.1 Probability and Impact Matrix A probability and impact matrix is used to assign risk ratings, namely, low, medium, or high (Figure 12.11), to risks on the basis of a combination of: (1) the probability of occurrence of that risk; and (2) its impact of the risk event occurring on project objectives. Risk response action depends on the classification of the risk (Figure 12.12). Risks with high probability and high impact require further analysis, including quantification and timely management. Risks with lower probability and impact may not require action but would typically be monitored.

Ordinal scale is a ranked-order scale, such as very low, medium low, low, moderate, high, and very high. Cardinal scale values are usually linear (0.1/0.3/0.5/0.7/0.9) or non-linear (0.05/0.1/0.2/0.4/0.8). Ordinal scale is an example of Likert scale (*i.e.*, risk effects on a scale of 1 to 5). A rating of 5 would be considered to be high riskier than a rating of 1, but we cannot say that it is five times riskier than the 1. Cardinal scales have an absolute value in them and we can make quantitative comparisons between results.

Impact Scale	
Consequence	**Health and Safety**
High	>10 server failure at a time
Moderate	6 to 10 server failure at a time
Low	1 to 5 server failure at a time
Probability Scale	
Likelihood Class	**Likelihood of Occurrence (events/year)**
Low	<0.01% chance of occurrence
Medium	0.01–10% chance of occurrence
High	>10% chance of occurrence

Figure 12.11 Impact and Probability Scale

PROBABILITY AND IMPACT MATRIX				
Probability	High			**Immediate Attention**
	Medium			
	Low			
		Low	Medium	High
		Impact		

Figure 12.12 Probability and Impact Matrix

12.4.2.1.2 Risk Data Quality Assessment Risk data quality assessment is a technique used to evaluate the degree to which a project data are useful. Needless to say, accurate data are necessary for accurate qualitative risk analysis. The technique (Figure 12.13) involves the following steps:

- Identify the extent of understanding of a risk.
- Check the data available on the risk.
- Check the reliability of data.
- Collection of more reliable data.

12.4.2.1.3 Risk Urgency Assessment Risk urgency assessment is based on the indicators of risk, such as time available to create a risk response, symptoms and warning signs, and the risk ratings (Figure 12.14).

Time-based Action: A positive opportunity may be temporarily available. Only a time-bound risk response action can eliminate the risk and enable in availing of the rewards offered by the opportunity.

Symptoms and Warning Signs of Risk: Such signs may allow only for a short response window, sometimes just a few hours before an intended risk event occurs. Such signs are also referred to as risk triggers.

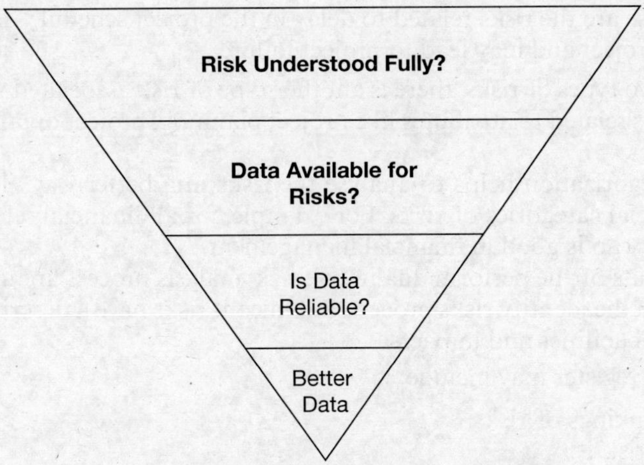

Figure 12.13 Risk Data Quality Assessment

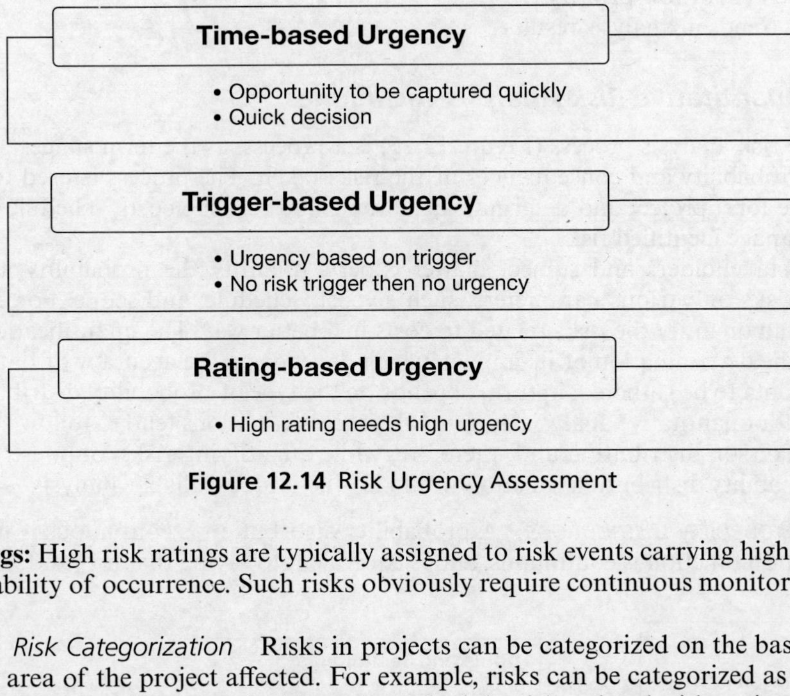

Figure 12.14 Risk Urgency Assessment

Risk Ratings: High risk ratings are typically assigned to risk events carrying high impact and high probability of occurrence. Such risks obviously require continuous monitoring.

12.4.2.1.4 Risk Categorization Risks in projects can be categorized on the basis of source of risks or area of the project affected. For example, risks can be categorized as operational risks, financial risks, risks related with project schedule, risks related with environment, risks related with change, risks related with resources, risks related with timeline, etc. These are described as follows:

Operational Risks: Risks due to operational factors, such as loss due to improper process implementation.
Example: Lack of proper training for resources.

Schedule Risk: These are the risks related to delay in the project schedule. The schedule risks directly affect the project and may lead to project failure.

Apart from these two types of risks, there is another type of risk associated with project management. This risk is related to attributes like project planning, project organization, frequent requirement changes.

The above categorization helps to analyse the risks in a better way. Special treatments can be given to special categories of risks. For example, for all financial related risks, we can assign a risk owner who is good in financial management.

The main outputs of the perform qualitative risk analysis process are updates to the risk register generated in the identify risks process. Significant risks have a description of the basis for the assessed probabilities and impacts.

Updates to the risk register may include:

1. Relative rankings of risks.
2. Causes of risks.
3. Risks requiring response in near term.
4. List of risks for further analysis.
5. Watch list of low priority.
6. Any trends in analysis results.

12.4.2.2 Quantitative Risk Analysis Techniques

Quantitative risk analysis process (Figure 12.15) is a process, as the term suggests, of quantifying the probability and consequences of the risks taken. The process is used to quantify risk exposure for a project and determine achievable and realistic costs, schedules, or scope targets to manage identified risks.

Project stakeholders and subject matter experts quantify the probability and consequences of risks on various parameters, such as cost, schedule, and scope. For example, a cost expert can quantify the risks related to costs in a better way. The quantification of risks is based on the determination of its impact, which depends on the accuracy of data in hand. The type of data to be gathered, in turn, depends on the type of probability distributions that will be used for quantitative analysis. In general, process variations tend to follow a binomial, normal, or Poisson distribution and, therefore, while quantifying risks, only use of the applicable probability distribution function would lead to a more reliable analysis.

12.4.2.2.1 Probability Distributions A probability distribution is continuous if its cumulative distribution function is continuous, and is equivalent to saying that for random variables

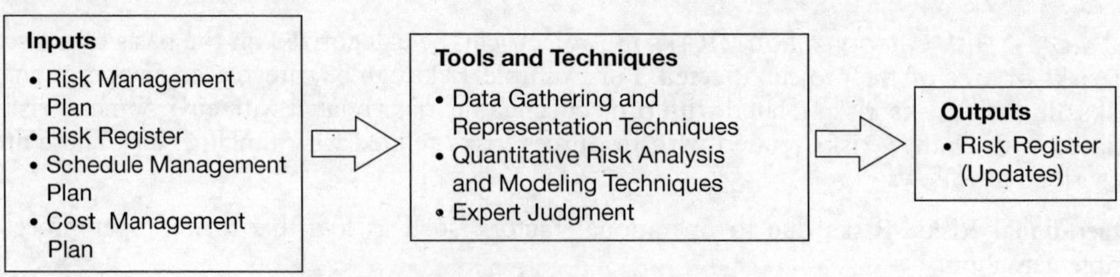

Figure 12.15 Quantitative Risk Analysis

X, P[X = a] = 0 for all real numbers 'a', that is the probability that X attains the value 'a' is zero, for any number a. Here, X is called a continuous random variable. Continuous probability distributions represent uncertainties in values, such as durations of schedule activities and costs of project related components. Process measurements follow discrete probability distributions when they are restricted to being within a predefined list of possible values and the list either has a finite number of members or is at most countable. It can be used to represent uncertain project events, such as the outcome of a test or a possible scenario in a decision tree.

12.4.2.2.2 Decision Tree A decision tree is a tool used in risk analysis and are used to investigate the risks associated with several possible courses of action. In a typical decision tree, a chance node is represented by circle and a decision node represented by a square. In a decision tree analysis, the process of risk analysis starts from the right of the tree diagram and works toward the left, that is, from the future toward the past. Future decisions are made and they are rolled back to become part of the earlier decisions. For example, a future decision can be selection of Project A, selection of Project B, success of Project A after selection, failure of Project A after selection, success of Project B after selection, and failure of Project B after selection.

Uniform distributions are used only if there is no obvious value that is more likely than any other between specified high and low bounds, as in the early concept stage of design.

12.4.2.2.3 Quantitative Risk Analysis and Modeling Techniques For quantifying risks, we need the list of risks identified in the risk register along with the tolerance limits of the stakeholders, approximate cost estimation of the risks, and resources required. Once these lists are available, we can start performing quantitative risk analysis using sensitivity analysis, expected monetary value analysis, and simulation.

1. **Sensitivity Analysis:** Sensitivity analysis is used to determine risks that have potentially the greatest impact on project outcome. This technique is used to examine the extent to which uncertainty associated with each project element affects the overall project objective, while assuming that the uncertainty associated with all other project elements is zero. Sensitivity analysis often involve in the use of Tornado diagrams (Figure 12.16), also called 'Tornado plots' or 'Tornado charts', which are used to examine the relative importance of process variables.

2. **Expected Monetary Value Analysis:** The Expected Monetary Value (EMV) analysis is a technique in which a calculation is made to determine the average of all potential outcomes of an event when the future includes a number of scenarios that may or may not happen. The Expected Monetary Value analysis, referred to as EMV, can be conducted at any point in the life-cycle of a project, but should be done as early as possible to get the better results out of it. Risks with higher EVM need to be addressed as a priority.

   Expected monetary value is given by:

   Expected monetary value = Probability × Cost

   Using this technique, project managers summarize expected values to total project risks. Three probabilities values are used to calculate EMVs (not to be confused with those used in PERT calculations).

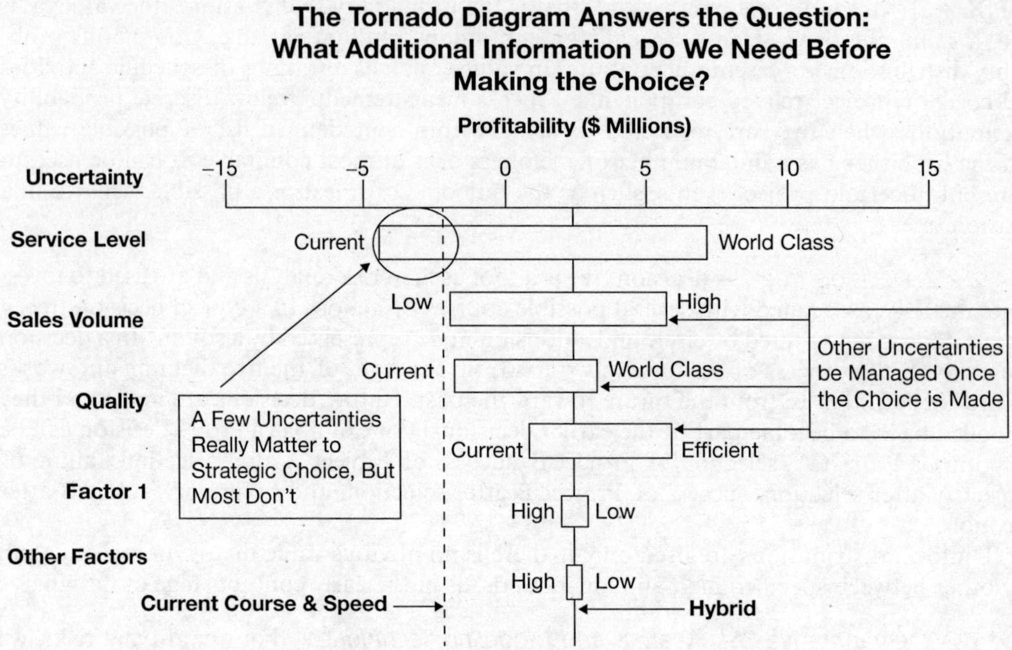

Figure 12.16 Tornado Diagram

The expected value, thus estimated, serves as a guideline for total costs entailed to eliminate identified project risks. For example:

If a project has a 55% chance of a $100,000 profit and a 40% chance of a $300,000 loss, the EMV of the project is calculated as:

EMV = profit of (0.55 × 100,000) + loss of (0.40 × 300,000)
= profit of (55,000) + loss of (120,000)
= loss of $65,000

3. **Modeling and Simulation:** Simulation techniques are widely used to generate models that analyse the behaviour or performance of a system and quantify the effects of identified risks on that system. Project execution is simulated many times to obtain a statistical distribution of calculated results. The Monte Carlo analysis is a good example of simulation techniques. The Monte Carlo analysis represents a class of iterative and computational techniques that produce results to quantify the risks associated with simulated schedules and alternative plans, paths through network diagrams, and strategies for successful project outcome. The analysis result in a probability distribution which may be used as inputs for further analysis.

The following contents of the risk register is updated as part of quantitative risk analysis:

- The probabilistic analysis of the project is updated.
- The probability of achieving time and cost objectives is updated.
- The prioritized list of quantified risks is updated.
- Trends in quantitative risk analysis results are updated.

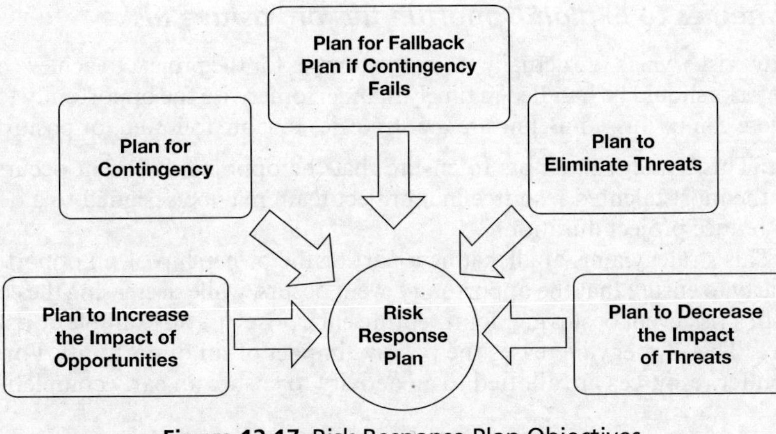

Figure 12.17 Risk Response Plan Objectives

12.4.3 Risk Mitigation Planning

Risk mitigation planning is the process to identify the ways to enhance opportunities and reduce threats to project objectives and determine the action plan to implement those (Figure 12.17). Risk response planning is based on the severity of the identified risk and estimated cost effectiveness in overcoming the challenge. Response plans should be time bound, realistic within the project context, and agreed upon by all parties involved. A risk owner is assigned who takes ownership of the risk. The risk owner has the responsibility of analysing and controlling the project risks. A risk owner is identified based on the skill set and experience level. For example, for all project management related risks, the project manager can be an owner, and for all technical related risks the team leader or architect can be the owner.

Risk responses may include:

- Action plans to eliminate the threats before they happen.
- Action plans to decrease the probability and/or impact of threats.
- Action plans to increase the probability and/or impact of opportunities.
- Contingency plans.
- Fallback plans if contingency measures taken prove to be ineffective.

12.4.3.1 Strategies to Counter Negative Risks or Threats

Negative risks are threats to the project and should be either avoided or the impact is minimized to reduce the damage to the project as much as possible. Below are the strategies that are followed for this:

Avoidance: This strategy attempts to eliminate a specific threat by eliminating its cause. For example, scope creep, which occurs when project scope is not frozen, may be eliminated by freezing project scope at an appropriate point of time.

Transference: This strategy aims at use of contracting, insurance warranties, guarantees, and outsourcing of work, all which transfer risk from the performing organization to a third party.

Mitigation: This strategy attempts to decrease the probability of occurrence of a risk, reduce the risk-event value, or both, thereby reducing the cost of managing that particular risk.

12.4.3.2 Strategies to Exploit Opportunities or Positive Risks

There are positive risks which are actually the opportunities for the project to achieve more than planned. These risks should be handled in timely manner, otherwise the opportunity for reaping benefit from these can be missed. Below are the strategies that are followed for positive risks:

- **Exploit:** This strategy attempts to ensure that the opportunity event occurs. For example, the most talented resource in a project team may be assigned to a demanding task to reduce project duration.
- **Share:** This strategy aims at allocating a part of the ownership of an opportunity to a third party to ensure that the opportunity event occurs, while decreasing the cost associated with a risk event occurring. Joint venture enterprises are an example of risk sharing.
- **Enhance:** This strategy increases the positive impact of an opportunity. For example, more buffer resources are allotted to an activity to ensure an early completion.

12.4.3.3 Strategies for Both Threats and Opportunities

Acceptance is a type of strategy, applicable for both the threats and opportunities. This strategy accepts the risk and develops a contingency plan, when the risk events occur. For example, in a cost plus contract the buyer takes more risks and in a fixed bid project the seller takes more risks. The risks related with the contract are accepted and a contingency plan is developed to tackle it.

Contingency Reserve: This strategy aims at generating a contingency reserve to tackle unknown risks and accepted known risks. The quantum of the contingency reserve which may be in the form of additional time for the project, additional resources, and additional billing to the customer, is based on the expected impact of the risk.

Management Reserve: This strategy generates a separately planned quantity to be used to manage future uncertain scenarios that are impossible to predict—unknown-unknowns. Use of management reserve requires a change to the project's cost and schedule baselines, whereas a contingency reserve is not required to be reflected in cost and schedule baselines.

The main outputs of the plan risk response process are updates to the risk register and include residual risks and contingency plans:

Residual Risks: These are risks that remain after a risk response plan has been determined and put in place. Residual risks are documented and continually monitored.

Contingency Plans: These are plans describing the specific actions that will be taken if identified opportunities or threats occur.

12.4.3.4 Proactive Risk Response Strategies

As discussed earlier, identifying and mitigating the risks well ahead of their occurrence, ensures the effective and well-controlled project execution. The processes that help in proactive risk identification and mitigation are as follows:

Project Risk Response Audits: Risk auditors examine the effectiveness of established risk response plans with respect to risk avoidance, risk transfer, and risk mitigation. Checks are made on whether the organization has adopted appropriate and relevant techniques to assess the severity of the risks and whether a combination of qualitative and quantitative techniques has been used in assessment of the risks. The effectiveness of risks owner is also audited.

Periodic Project Risk Reviews: Established risk response plans are periodically reviewed for their implementation and for their continued relevance and effectiveness. If changes are deemed to be required, risk plans are appropriately updated. Risk reviews also check whether appropriate procedures are being followed.

Technical Performance Measurement: This tool is used to compare technical accomplishments during project execution to the project plan's schedule of technical achievements. Appropriate action is taken wherever deviations are found high.

Additional Risk Response Planning: This technique is used to address risks not identified those are not documented in the risk register that may have emerged over project execution. Additional planning and allocation of resources may also be required if the impact of identified risks proves to be greater than anticipated.

Work-around: These are unplanned responses to unanticipated risk events.

Status Meetings: These are meetings that are convened the deviation from established risk response plans is high. Status meetings are used to review, plan, and if required upgrade existing risk response plans.

Reserve Analysis: Reserve analysis is a technique that is used to identify the quantum of reserve resources that require to be set aside for project contingencies. The magnitude of this quantum depends on the complexity of the project. Reserves may be reallocated if expected threat events do not occur or if expected opportunities do occur. Additional response planning technique is used to address risks not identified, while reserve analysis is used for the identified risks.

12.5 Hazard and Risk

Hazard is a potentially dangerous condition which is caused by an event and results in manpower or economic losses. The probability and impact of the hazard occurring is called 'the risk of hazard'. The hazard analysis steps are similar to the risk assessment steps that we discussed earlier. Figure 12.18 shows the flow of hazard analysis.

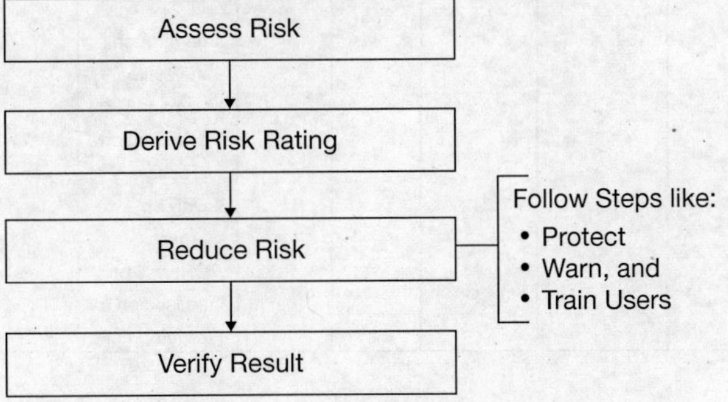

Figure 12.18 Hazard Analysis

SUMMARY

Risks can be effectively managed by practicing the following pre-defined steps. The features of risk management are:

- A project risk is a potential source of deviation from the project plan and can have a negative or positive impact on the project.
- Project risks that represent threats are classified as negative; project risks that represent opportunities are classified positive.
- Risks should be identified in all phases of the project life-cycle; risk identification is an iterative process. Established risk response plans require continual review.
- Work-around is unplanned response to unanticipated risk events.

CASE STUDY

A risk register is the place where the details of the project's risks and their status are maintained. It is to be noted that a risk register is a live document. The information maintained in this document is to be kept updated regularly. It gives visibility to all the stakeholders about the nature and criticality of the risks present in the project along with the plan to mitigate those.

Sample Risk Register

Risk ID	Date Raised	Risk Title	Risk Description	Impact Description	Probability	Impact	Overall Risk Rating	Action Plan	Action Plan Responsibility Owner	Expected Closure Date	Status
1	1-Jan-13	FSD Sign Off	Frequent requirement changes might come after FSD sign-off.	May result in effort and scheduled escalation. Too many changes will threaten go live date.	Medium	Medium	Medium	1. Change management process to be leveraged to treat any change to the signed-off FSD as a CR. 2. All CRs will go through the estimation and prioritization process. 3. Only approved CRs will be passed on for development.	Steve	1-Mar-2013	Open

EXERCISES

PART A (Objective-type questions)

1. Project risk management is defined as
   A. The process of defining how to conduct risk management activities for a project.
   B. The process of prioritizing risks for further analysis or action by assessing and combining their probability of occurrence and impact.
   C. The process of developing options and actions to enhance opportunities and to reduce threats to protect objectives.
   D. The process of conducting risk management planning, identification, analysis, response planning, monitoring and controlling a project.

2. The process of numerically analysing the effect of identified risk on overall project objectives is called
   A. Plan risk responses
   B. Perform quantitative risk analysis
   C. Perform qualitative risk analysis
   D. Plan risk management

3. The process of evaluating the risk process effectiveness throughout the project is called
   A. Plan risk responses
   B. Perform quantitative risk analysis
   C. Perform qualitative risk analysis
   D. Monitor and control risk

4. The process of developing options and actions to enhance opportunities and to reduce threats to project objectives refers to the
   A. Perform quantitative risk analysis
   B. Perform qualitative risk analysis
   C. Plan risk responses
   D. Monitor and control risk

5. Risk experts participate in this technique anonymously.
   A. Brainstorming
   B. Delphi technique
   C. Checklist analysis
   D. Root cause analysis

6. Shutting a project down on account of high risks is which types of risk response plan?
   A. Transfer
   B. Avoid
   C. Accept (Evade)
   D. Mitigate

7. Outsourcing is a part of which risk response plan?
   A. Transfer
   B. Avoid
   C. Accept (Evade)
   D. Mitigate

8. All of the following are examples of positive risks except
   A. Exploit
   B. Share
   C. Accept
   D. Mitigate

9. Monitor and control risks can involve all of the following except
   A. Choosing alternative strategies
   B. Executing a fallback plan
   C. Taking correction action
   D. Analysing the risk

10. How often should identification of risk take place?
    A. Only when the project manager is free
    B. One per phase is enough as the project is big
    C. Throughout the project
    D. One in the planning phase

PART B (Write the answers in one or two lines)

1. Define risk.
2. Name three types of risks.
3. Define high risk area.
4. Write notes on stakeholder tolerance.
5. What is risk management plan? What are all its contents?
6. Write notes on Risk Breakdown Structure.
7. Write notes on Risk Register.
8. What is probability impact matrix?
9. Write notes on Risk Urgency Assessment.
10. Write notes on Risk Data Quality assessment.
11. Write notes on Decision Tree.

13

Quality Management

13.1 Introduction

Quality means different things to different people, according to their positional and influencing roles. A customer may define quality as 'fitness for intended use,' whereas a vendor may define it as 'meeting the requirements.' More formally, the term 'quality' may be used to indicate the degree to which the inherent characteristics of a product or feature meets the stated or implied requirements.

Quality management refers to the processes necessary to ensure that a project will satisfy the needs for which it was undertaken.

Quality management addresses the management of a project and the product of the project. The product of a project relates to the 'what' of the project, whereas the management of a project relates to the 'how' of the project.

13.2 Quality vs Grade

Quality and grade are not one and the same. Quality is 'the degree to which a set of inherent characteristics fulfil the requirements,' whereas grade is a category assigned to products or services that are intended for identical or similar functional applications but possess different technical characteristics.

A software product may be used to explain the difference between the quality and grade of a product. Suppose, a banking-software product has been developed with a view to be used as an extremely user-friendly interface, featuring a large number of on-screen prompts, and that it automates a large number of banking processes, requiring few decisions to be made by its users. Such a product may be called a high grade product.

Alternatively, another banking software product may not attempt to provide such user-friendliness or automation. Users of this software may be required to intervene and make manual decisions often. Such a product can be called a lower-grade product. However, both products can be high quality products they meet the requirements of the stated intended use.

We can conclude that a high-grade product may be a low quality product and a low-grade product a high quality product.

Similarly, gold coins made of 22 carat gold, 20 carat gold, and 18 carat gold, are gold products of stated differing grades. A fitness for intended use comparison of 22 gold and

18 carat gold would not be valid. A fitness-for-intended-use comparison is valid, however, between two 5 g coins of 22 carat gold bought from two vendors, and a proper judgment on the comparative quality of the two coins may be made.

Therefore, a product of low grade is not a problem, but low quality certainly is. In the context of project management, a project management team decides upon and manages the trade-off between the intended levels of quality and grade in a product.

Discussion Point

What are all the quality characteristics you will look into when you are buying a kilogram of brinjal from the market?

Project manager along with the project management team are responsible for managing the trade-off in the levels of quality and grade.

Discussion Point

If there is a trade-off between quality and grade, how will you convince the customer? (Customer usually demands higher quality and higher grade simultaneously.)

13.3 Precision vs Accuracy

Precision refers to the repeatability of measurements made on a process. Accuracy refers to the measured value being close to the true value or target value or target value aimed at by the process; nearness of the process value to the specification value means high accuracy. Precise measurements need not be accurate and vice versa. However, a process that is in control and capable would be characterized by both precision and accuracy. The following example illustrates the difference between precision and accuracy.

For example, a project manager's forecasts of cost variance in five projects, on the basis of the data available at the start of each project were 48%, 57%, 52%, 50%, and 55%. Suppose, the actual cost variance in the five projects turned out to lie between 50% and 55%. In this case, the project manager's forecast may be called accurate, but not precise.

Suppose, another project manager's forecasts of cost variance for five similar projects, each having a cost variance between 50% and 55%, are 59%, 58%, 58%, 59%, and 59%. In this case, the forecast may be called 'precise but not accurate'. Generally, achieving precision is a much more difficult and capital-intensive process compared to one for achieving accuracy.

The project management team bears the responsibility to determine the intended level of accuracy and precision in the various measurements involved in a project.

Discussion Points

How will you determine the level of accuracy and precision for your projects? Will this priority changes over the time with the life-cycle of the project? What is the role of availability of data in calculating precision and accuracy?

13.4 Quality Management and Project Management

Juran defined quality as 'fitness for use,' and Deming developed the 14 Steps to total quality management. Deming also advocated the plan-do-check-act cycle as the basis for quality improvement. Crosby popularized the concept of the cost of poor quality and advocated prevention over inspection and 'zero defects.' Crosby believed that quality is 'conformance to requirements.' JIT stands for Just-in-Time principle, used in inventory concepts. There will not be any excess on-hand inventory but based on the demand the orders will be made. This principle is used to improve efficiency.

Quality management initiatives, such as total quality management complement, project management processes and recognize the importance of the following objectives and processes:

- **Customer Satisfaction:** Understanding, managing and influencing the needs of the customer so that customer expectations are met or always exceeded.
- **Prevention Over Inspection:** The cost of avoiding mistakes is always lower than the cost of correcting them.
- **Management Responsibility:** Even though success requires participation of all members, it is the responsibility of management to provide resources and supports needed.
- **Continuous Improvement:** Plan-Do-Check-Act cycle (Figure 13.1) defined by Shewhart and modified by Deming is a useful tool for continuous improvement and can be used in any process.

Figure 13.1 represents simple steps that can be followed for process improvements like Plan for improvement, Do on small Scale, Check the results, Act by correcting.

Discussion Points

Do you know the quality policy of your organization? What is the importance of quality policy?

Importance of Software Quality

1. It increases customers' confidence level.
2. It helps fixing bugs before it reaches customers.
3. It helps giving predictable delivery.

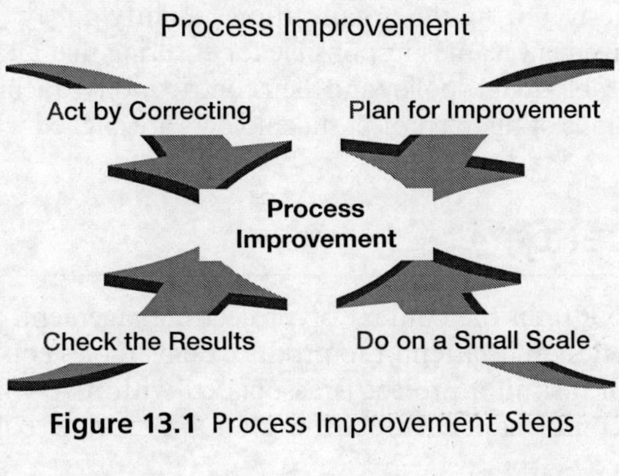

Figure 13.1 Process Improvement Steps

4. It helps identifying the risks of the projects through various audits.
5. It helps executing the project as per the contract by tracking various metrics given in the contract document.
6. It helps systematic production of the software.
7. It ensures a software working in extreme conditions through various stress testing mechanisms.
8. It helps ensuring various components of the project work in integrated mode through integration testing.
9. It helps in defect prevention and defect reduction.

Product vs Process Quality Management

Software product quality is taken care by software testing teams. Process quality is taken care by quality teams or delivery assurance groups.

Product quality only focuses on the end deliverable of the projects. It does not focus on the process aspects of the projects. It concentrates on what is being produced as an outcome and not on how it is being produced. The end result is measured against the standard set by the customer. Software product quality is taken care by software testing team.

Process quality focus on the process. It concentrates on how a product is produced. Process quality is taken care by software quality teams.

The goal of a process quality team is to focus and reduce process variance. Focus on process quality, in turn, generates higher and predictable product quality as a secondary outcome.

Professional project managers concentrate on both process and product quality. In this chapter, we will discuss both these aspects.

13.5 Quality Policy

Quality policy is defined as the 'overall intentions and direction of an organization with regard to quality as formally expressed by the top management.'

- The quality policy of an organization can usually be adopted 'as is' for use in a project.
- If the organization lacks a formal quality policy, or if the project involves multiple performing organizations, the project management team will need to define a quality policy for the project.
- The design and structure of the quality management system of an organization is built upon and derived from the organization's quality policy.
- The project management team is responsible for ensuring that all project stakeholders are aware of the applicable quality policy and their contributions to achieving it. This is to ensure that the contributions of all the project stakeholders are aligned with the quality policy.

13.6 Cost of Quality

The Cost of Quality (COQ), in the context of project management, refers to the total cost incurred by the organization in its attempt to produce deliverables conforming to the requirements in a project. Each task in a project is associated with its own costs, namely, cost of conformance and non-conformance. Establishing an appropriate balance between them is the responsibility of the project team. Categories of costs of quality are prevention costs and appraisal costs. Failure costs are associated with costs of fixing poor quality. In general, costs of quality are discussed under two heads and four subheads: costs of conformance, namely, prevention costs and appraisal costs, and costs of non-conformance, namely, internal failure costs and external failure costs. The following are the examples of these costs.

13.6.1 Costs of Conformance

Costs of conformance refer to accumulated cost related to the work used to confirm the quality aspects in the project. It is the money spent to avoid mistakes, errors and bugs in the product. There are two types of costs of conformance, namely, prevention costs and appraisal costs.

Prevention costs are the costs related to the factors that are used to prevent errors in the products or services, and appraisal costs are the costs related to the factors that are used to appraise the quality standards of the product or service. Activities that are related to prevention costs are quality planning, quality training, statistical process control. Activities that are related to appraisal costs are inspections, reviews/audits, and testing.

13.6.2 Costs of Non-conformance

Costs of non-conformance refer to the accumulation of costs related to the work which are related to fixing and overcoming the defects which already occurred. In this case, money spent to fix bugs, errors and defects in the product.

There are two types of costs of non-conformance, namely, internal failure costs and external failure costs. Internal failure costs are the costs associated with scrap/rework, repair, downtime, defect evaluation, corrective measures. External failure costs are costs associated with rejects, returns, complaints in warranty.

Exercise 13.1: List Down the Actions You will Take as a Project Manager to Maintain Quality in the Project

Exercise 13.1: Possible Answers
Reviewing all the deliverables.
Identify Quality standards that are applicable to the project.
Actions to ensure that quality standards are followed.
Actions to ensure quality process are followed.
Actions to ensure proper quality audit and review happening without fail.

13.7 Procedural Approach to Quality—Plan Quality

It is the process of identifying the quality standards of the project and the product to be developed and determining the manner in which they are to be achieved. The output of the plan quality management process is the quality management plan, which is the basic document for managing the quality of a project.

A quality management team plans addresseing the following aspects:

1. How to manage quality of a project?
2. The process of performing quality assurance activities.
3. The process of controlling quality of a project.
4. Quality standards to follow.
5. Quality measurement protocols to be used in a project.

Quality standard is an agreed-upon quality level to achieve a project result. It is applicable to that project alone. Generic quality standards usually come from within the organization or from government or professional associations. The project manager, however, should have a plan in place, for continually improving the quality standards.

13.7.1 Tools That Helps in Setting Quality Goal

13.7.1.1 Cost-benefit Analysis

The quality level in a project is planned, considering the benefits of meeting quality requirements versus costs incurred in meeting them. The resultant quality level generally proves to the optimum level. Costs and benefits referred here include tangible and intangible elements that are discussed as follows:

1. The cost of losing customers goodwill is more damageable financially than the cost of implementing a process to focus on customer satisfaction. Hence, need to consider both the tangible and intangible costs benefits during the cost-benefit analysis.
2. The cost of reviewing and fixing the errors found may cost the project manager's just one day effort, whereas not implementing the review process will incur him more efforts to fix the same error.

13.7.1.2 Seven Basic Quality Tools

The following tools are referred as the seven basic quality tools:

1. Cause-and-effect diagrams
2. Flow charts
3. Check sheets
4. Pareto diagrams
5. Histogram
6. Control charts
7. Scatter diagrams

We discussed these tools in detail in Chapter 8.

13.7.1.3 Benchmarking

Benchmarking is a technique that compares the standards aimed at one project against those of another project. Another project may from within the same organization or other similar kind of organizations. Based on the comparison, a plan for quality and standards for the current project may be initiated. Benchmarking is commonly used in continuous improvement processes. For example, if a project handled by an organization received an excellence award from a professional body, that project could be used by the organization as a benchmark for all the similar projects it would handle in future. Thus, methodologies and standards that the award-winning project followed could be used for other projects as well. Choosing an appropriate benchmark, however, is very important.

13.7.1.4 Design of Experiment

Every process consists of multiple variable parameters. The impact of one variable on another is identified (formulated) using Design of Experiment (DOE). The DOE, a statistical 'what–if' tool, uses experimentation to statistically determine the process variable that serves as the most critical parameter for process improvement. The DOE technique is generally used in product design and is a good tool to set designs based on quality. Hence, it is included in the plan quality process. The DOE analyst may use one of the several statistical software packages readily available in the market for conducting a DOE. The analyst can view graphical displays, build models, and test assumptions. Because, this is an experimental technique, however, it is as effective as it is expensive.

13.7.1.5 Control Charts

The control chart is also known as the Shewhart chart or process-behaviour chart. It is a tool used to determine whether a process is in statistical control or not. If it is not in statistical control, needless to say, it should be brought into control. Control charts are often used as part of a quality control processes, feedback from which can be used for planning. Therefore, a control chart may also be considered as a planning tool.

13.7.1.6 Brainstorming

It is a group creativity technique that can be used for multiple aspects of project management including collecting quality related requirements. It involves in facilitating a group of individuals to generate as many ideas on a topic as possible. While collecting the quality related requirements using this technique, we should clearly write down the set of rules to be followed. There should not be any arguments on the collected ideas (quality requirements). But the main disadvantage of the brainstorming technique is that it easily gets biased. When an experienced member of the team makes suggestions, the other members of the team tend to agree with him/her rather than come up with their own solutions by thinking creatively or innovatively. The nominal group technique may take brainstorming a step further by including a voting process to rank the ideas that are generated.

13.7.1.7 Affinity Diagram

Figure 13.2 shows an example of the affinity diagram. The affinity diagram helps to group large set of ideas into common themes to understand and plan the ideas. It discovers previously unknown connections between ideas and pieces of information.

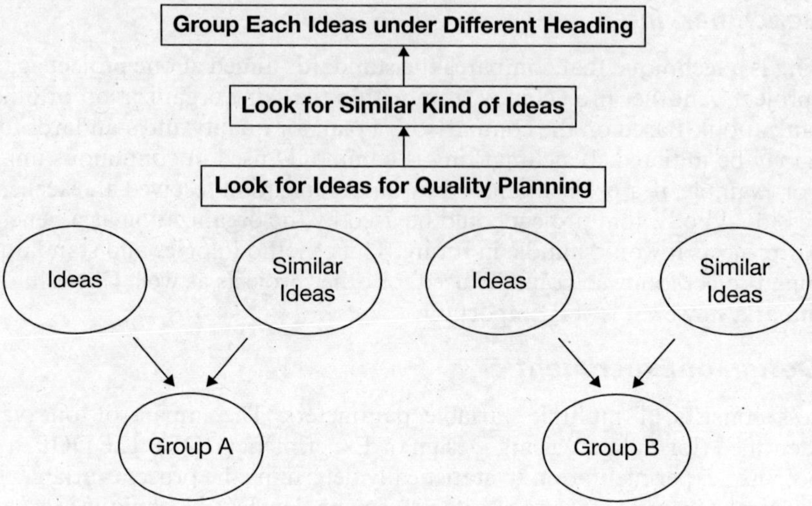

Figure 13.2 Affinity Diagram

The basic steps for constructing an affinity diagram are as follows:

1. Look for ideas.
2. Look for similar ideas.
3. Group these ideas logically.

13.7.1.8 Force Field Analysis

Force Field Analysis (Figure 13.3) is a technique that identifies all forces for and against a quality planning decision. In order to move the quality standards from the current state to a desired state, quality should be planned to overcome the hindering factors and strengthen the

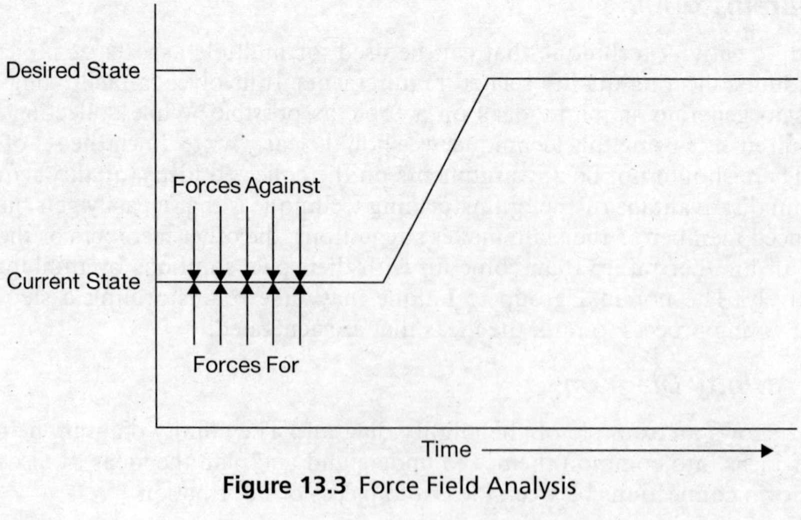

Figure 13.3 Force Field Analysis

forces supporting it. We need to consider both the forces (for, against) before drawing out the quality plan to achieve a desired result.

13.7.2 Outputs of Plan Quality Process

13.7.2.1 Quality Management Plan

The primary output of the plan quality management process is the quality management plan. It describes the acceptable level of quality parameters of the project. It also describes, how a project management team will implement the performing organization's quality policies and quality plan. It also includes the approaches for implementing quality control, quality assurance, and quality improvement processes. It also clearly defines the roles and responsibilities of the people involved in the quality process along with various tools and techniques that will be used in the quality journey of the project. A quality management plan may be formal, informal, highly detailed, or broadly framed depending on the situation. Quality management plan also becomes part of the overall project management plan.

Various Roles Involved in Quality

1. **Quality Manager:** Project manager takes this role most of the time. He defines the quality policy of the project. He also sets the quality plan of the project along with the team. He is responsible for defining quality approach of the project like quality planning approach and quality control approach. He also decides the roles and responsibilities of the other team members of the project with respect to quality. He also initiates the quality management plan and process improvement plan. He is responsible for maintaining relationships and communications within and outside the team on all quality aspects of the projects.
2. **Quality Lead:** A Quality Lead reports to the quality manager of a project. He is responsible for quality aspects of the project along with the quality manager.
3. **Quality Assurance Team:** This team is responsible for auditing of the projects at frequent intervals as per quality management plan as part of quality assurance. Depending on this size of the projects, there can be separate quality assurance managers under whom different quality assurance team members called 'quality representative' of the project works.
4. **Quality Representative:** This team is responsible for actual audit of the project at the ground level. It reports to the quality assurance manager.
5. **Metrics Collection Group:** This group only works on analysis of various metrics that are available at the organization level. It helps setting the benchmark metrics used by the quality assurance department for compliance purpose.
6. **Quality Control Team:** This team works on controlling quality of the projects using various quality control tools like Root Cause Analysis tools, Pareto charts, etc.
7. **Configuration Management Team:** This team is responsible for maintaining various configuration items (code, documents, etc.) of the project so that proper versioning of the configuration items are maintained in the repository. Configuration audit helps inspecting changes from the baseline version and ensuring all changes are approved.

Y	N	?	All stakeholders and stakeholder groups, including other projects identified?
Y	N	?	Has each stakeholder or stakeholder group been classified in terms of their potential impact and influence on the project?
Y	N	?	If 'Yes', is there a plan to manage and communicate with each stakeholder/group to ensure their commitment for the project?

Figure 13.4 Checklist

13.7.2.2 Quality Checklists

A checklist (Figure 13.4) is a set of procedure or process to use for the purpose of quality verification. A checklist indirectly states all defined planning activities. Customized checklists are prepared to meet the needs of a particular project or program.

13.7.2.3 Process Improvement Plan as Output

Set of activities necessary to improve processes are included in the process improvement plan which is part of the overall project management plan. All projects need not have this process improvement plan. It is required only for the projects where improvements in processes are necessary.

13.7.2.4 Performance Metrics

A metric is a verifiable measure stated in quantitative or qualitative terms that translates customer needs into performance measures, for example, defect frequency, failure rate, availability, reliability, and test coverage.

13.8 Perform Quality Assurance Process

Quality assurance refers to the process of auditing and analysing established quality requirements and process results to ensure that appropriate and valid quality standards and operational definitions are in place. Quality assurance refers to the systematic and planned activities implemented to provide confidence to all stakeholders that all processes are established for successful project execution and comply with applicable quality standards. Continuous improvement activities are also part of quality assurance initiatives.

13.8.1 Tools and Techniques of Perform Quality Assurance

13.8.1.1 Quality Audit

Quality audit is the task of systematic examination of the effectiveness of a quality system carried out by a quality auditor or an audit team and is the key engine of a quality system.

The objectives of quality audits are to:

- Identify best practices being implemented.
- Identify gaps and shortcomings of a quality system.
- Share the good practices introduced in similar project.
- Add mistakes to the lessons learned.
- Confirm the implementation, or otherwise, of approved change requests, corrective and preventive actions, and defect repairs.

It is generally a scheduled task. Results of quality audits along with quality control reports form the basis of measuring the functioning of a quality assurance system.

Discussion Points

Discuss the purpose of quality audit. How this is being done in your organization?

Various types of quality audits are as follows:

1. **Project Start-up Audit:** This usually happens at the beginning of the projects to check and set the quality parameters of the project and also helps achieving the quality expectation of the projects so that all the stakeholders are clear.
2. **Process Audit:** This happens only to check the process compliance level of the projects and set action plans to improve it. This audit will not check the delivery output of the projects.
3. **Delivery Audit:** This audit happens whenever there are deliveries (final delivery) to the customers. Audit outcome gives a report with Go/No Go decision based on various parameters set in the quality management plan.
4. **Project Security Audit:** This audit is practiced only to check the security compliance level of the projects. It sets action plans to improve project security. Customers who work in on-site off-shore models and projects involving dealing with customer-specific data requests this kind of audit.
5. **Metrics Audit:** This audit focus only on various metrics parameters of the projects and sets action plans to improve it.
6. **Risk Audit:** This audit focus only on the risks parameters of the projects and ensure risks are being tracked and managed following the risk management plan of the projects.
7. **Project Management Review:** This is conducted usually by senior management to check various parameters of the projects focusing mainly on customer satisfaction index, customer escalations, and profit and loss metrics of the projects.
8. **Configuration Audit:** This helps tracking all the configuration items of the projects. It ensures all the changes from baselines and approved by the authorized people involved the projects.
9. **Closure Audit:** This happens at the end of the projects ensuring project completion and helps to document the lessons learnt and best practices of the project into organization repository. This also baseline various metrics of the project for future analysis.

13.8.1.2 Process Analysis

Process analysis is a part of continuous improvement initiatives. It follows the steps outlined in a process improvement plan to identify the required improvements in the process. Process analysis (Figure 13.5) is used to reduce risk, improve efficiency, and control costs. This analysis also examines the issues in the process, the constraints experienced, and also identify non-value added activities during process execution. It includes causal analysis to analyse a problem or situation, determines the underlying causes that lead to it, and also involves formulation of the preventive actions for similar types of problems.

13.8.1.3 Process Decision Program Chart

A tree diagram is developed for the plan as part of Process Decision Program Chart (PDPC). It depicts objectives, activities and tasks of that plan at various levels.

1. It is used to identify potential problems in an underdeveloped quality plan. Thus, it helps identifying the appropriate counter-measures to resolve those problems.
2. It helps identifying the potential risks and select from a set of possible counter-measures to the risks. Risks associated with every aspects of the plan are identified and the counter-measures to the risks are specified.

The PDPC is used in particular when the quality plan is large and complex. This is also used when the price of failure of quality plan is higher.

13.8.1.4 Inter-relationship Diagram

An inter-relationship diagram is an analysis tool that allows a team to identify the cause-and-effect relationships among critical issues. One cause may lead to another cause. So it is called 'inter-relationship diagram'. This analysis helps a team distinguishing between issues. An inter-relationship diagram is used when a team is struggling to understand the relationships among several issues associated with a process. For example, a simple question such as 'Why did you come late to office today?' may elicit a response that the bus came late. Probing why the bus came late may lead to 'Traffic Jam' as the answer. Further, questioning the reason for traffic jam may point to an 'Improper Signal' which, in turn, may be attributed to a 'technical fault' and so on.

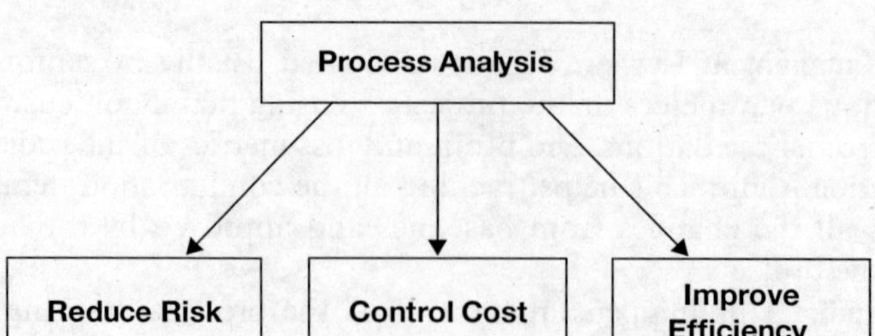

Figure 13.5 Process Analysis

13.9 Quality Control Process

Monitoring quality results to determine if they comply with the already set quality standards and identifying ways to eliminate causes related to problems. Quality control is performed throughout the project life-cycle and is often performed by the quality control department or other similar kinds of departments responsible for quality.

13.9.1 Quality Control Terminologies

Following are some quality control terminologies commonly used:

- Prevention (keeping errors out of the process)
- Inspection (keeping errors out of the hands of the customers)
- Attribute sampling (results either conformed or not conformed)
- Variables sampling (results are rated on continuous scale that measure the degree of conformity)
- Tolerances (specified range of acceptable results)
- Control limits (thresholds which can indicate whether the process is out of control)

A project management team must have the working knowledge of statistical quality control, especially sampling and probability, to help evaluating the quality control outputs.

13.9.2 Quality Control Tools

Ishikawa's 7 'old' tools can be used for this purpose. We discussed all these tools in detail in Chapter 8.

- Checklist
- Pareto diagram
- Histogram
- Scatter diagram
- Run chart
- Control chart
- Cause-and-effect diagram

13.9.3 Standard Control Chart

The simplest and best known indicator is the presence of a point beyond the 3σ control limits. Because we know that in a normal distribution, 99.73% of the population will fall within ±3σ of the mean. We also know that there is only a .27% chance that a point will fall outside those limits. In other words, there is a 99.73% chance that the points outside the limits are the result of non-random causes. It is important to note that if a given phenomenon is unlikely, then it does not mean that it is impossible. For example, a point outside the 3σ limits does not necessarily mean that the process is unstable. It is always a cause for investigation. However, Process Capability (CP) should not be calculated until it has been determined that the evidence of instability is, in fact, a random occurrence. The charts are reviewed for evidence of instability and the 'rules' are intended to provide evidence—not conclusive proof.

13.9.4 Sampling Inspection

An inspection is the examination of the work product to determine whether it conforms to documented standards. The results of an inspection generally performance measurements collection and may be conducted at any level. Inspections may be called reviews, peer reviews, audits or walkthroughs.

13.9.5 Output of Perform Quality Control Process

Validated Deliverable: The main output of a quality control process is the validated deliverables. After validation, only the deliverables are supplied to the customers.
Quality Control Measurements: It is the documented results of quality control activities in the format finalized during the quality planning process.

13.10 Software Testing

One may wonder if testing is really required if the software development was done as per the specification and also if the developers did a good job, then where and what is the necessity for software testing. It is true that these are valid arguments for a perfect world, but reality is far from it. In fact, testing evolved as a separate entity much later in the history of software development. Testing was part and parcel of development up to 1970's and no separate testing teams were involved till then.

We typically build software systems with multiple evolving requirements and stakeholder's expectations. Since software is an evolving product, there is typically nothing called 'complete requirements' or 'requirements freeze'. Requirements keep on coming and it is up to the project team and stakeholders to decide and plan accordingly.

'*Because of human inability to perform and communicate with perfection, software development is accompanied by a quality assurance activity.*'

—Deutsche (1996)

Moreover, software is not something like a physical product like a car or a computer or a manufactured object. It is imperative that software testing must be done using some specific and different methodologies and techniques.

13.10.1 Psychology of Testing

Over the years, as software testing has evolved from being synonymous with debugging to a separate independent competency aimed at improving the overall quality of the products.

The diagram (Figure 13.6) shows how the thought process developed from the testing perspective.

At the very beginning (Rudimentary Level–Phase 0), the aim is to get a bug-free product without any coding errors. Testing is like debugging, so it is not really called 'testing'. A bug free code does not mean that a software product will meet the expected requirements.

The next level (Basic Level–Phase 1) is to show that the software works. This is similar to the development team goal, but testing is clearly different from debugging. We can never say

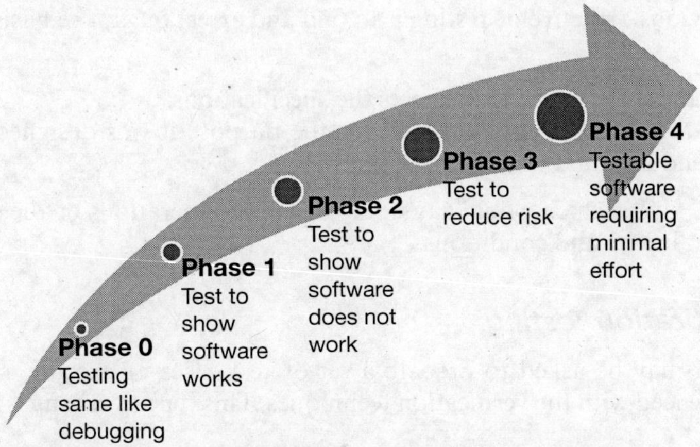

Figure 13.6 Testing Evolution Process

software works under all conditions; we can only test a subset of conditions due to the infinite possibilities. For example, a simple positive integer user input field can take values ranging from zero to infinity. The software may have been passed by over thousand test cases, but all it takes is only one test case to prove that it is not working.

The next level of thinking (Intermediate Level–Phase 2) is to find areas where the software does not work. This is completely opposite to the way of thinking earlier which was along with the developers line of thinking. There is an analogy which Boris Beizer gives here to bring out the difference in thinking like the difference between book keepers and auditors. The job of the book keeper is to present the accounts in the best possible way, but the auditors' job is to prove that in spite of the appearance of balance there has been embezzlement. This type of thinking leads to strong, revealing test cases.

The Advanced level–Phase 3 of thinking evolved based on the level of confidence the tester develops on the software he is testing. Testing cannot be done forever either positive or negative cases, a logical end needs to be met and the product should be released once there is a desired level of confidence in the product. This confidence would come if harsh or difficult test cases are consistently passed by the software.

Finally, the Optimized Level–Phase 4 of thinking is based on a strong expertise in the areas to be tested and identification of what can be tested or not. If the product is testable then the labour for testing is reduced and also testable code will have fewer bugs than code that is hard to test. At this level the testing is optimized and it is most focused and precise. The tester has the expertise to identify the key problem areas and the skill to design test cases to capture them. This comes with the comprehensive knowledge of the multiple testing techniques and their practical applications.

13.10.2 Software Testing Objectives

The first objective of software testing is to prevent bugs from getting into the system. This type of testing is commonly called 'verification testing'. This is the most effective way of minimizing the defects in a software.

The other obvious objective of testing is to find and arrest bugs. The basis of finding the bugs depends on:

1. Whether the software product meets the specifications.
2. Whether the software product is fit for the purpose it was designed. This is more from an end user and usability perspective.

Whether there are faults which would cause failure during operations of the software under various loads, user inputs and conditions.

13.10.2.1 Verification Testing

Typically, a tester may be asked to prepare a set of test cases or execute and may not be familiar or experienced with the verification techniques. This type of testing is a static manual process.

Static testing is done without accessing the actual application, just as the name 'verification testing' suggests, it is done by using review-based techniques (Figure 13.7).

The fundamental theme of verification testing is—Are we building the product right?

The following techniques are useful in verification testing:

Reviews: It is a formal process in which the peers or stakeholders examine a piece of work to ensure correctness. It could be a specification document or a technical design or a piece of code. Its purpose is to uncover errors, ambiguity or lack of expected standards.

Walkthroughs: It is a formal process where the person responsible for a specific unit of work formally presents to a group of reviewers. The work has to be circulated to the reviewer group ahead of the discussion giving ample time for the reviewers to examine, write comments or prepare questions for the walkthrough meeting. The presenter will go through the document line by line during the walkthrough, explaining what has been done and why.

Inspections: It is the most formal type of reviews. Each and every participant has to go through training to participate in the inspections. In the reviews and walkthroughs, the presenter is the original owner of the materials presented, but in inspection the presenter has to learn from the owner along with his interpretations and then present it to other participants who are called 'inspectors'. There could be roles like moderators and recorders also assigned

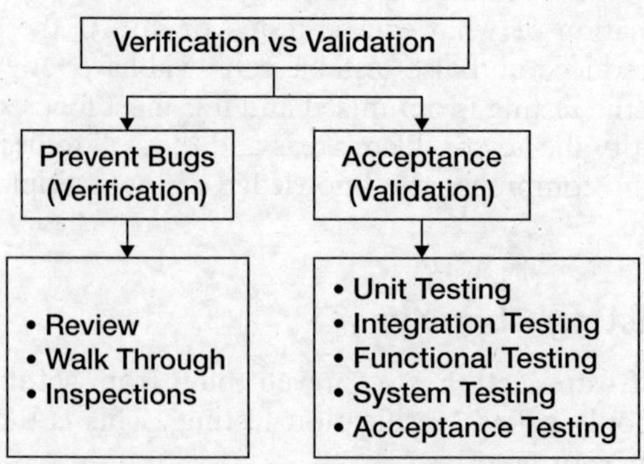

Figure 13.7 Verification and Validation

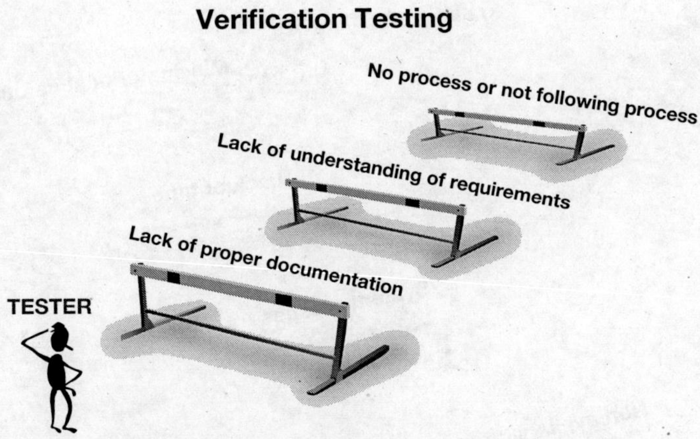

Figure 13.8 Verification—Impacting Issues

to the participants. Inspections have been found to be very effective in uncovering bugs for any software delivery, specifically with respect to the design documents and the code.

Impacting Issues of Verification Testing

Lack of proper documentation, lack of understanding requirements, and people not following process are the impacting issues of verification (Figure 13.8). How we know that we are building a product right if the requirement documents are not available or no clarity on requirements?

13.10.2.2 Validation Testing

The testing activities that are done to evaluate a software in the executable mode can be called 'validation testing'.

The previous verifications activities performed during the requirements, development and coding stages help in minimizing the bugs coming down to the validation phase. Bugs that are discovered during the validation phase are costly to fix than the bugs identified in the verification phase.

This is the reason for early involvement of testers in the software development cycle. A requirement that is corrected in the initial phase is lot cheaper than when it is corrected after becoming a program (coded).

The common tests like unit, system, integration and acceptance tests are performed to ensure that the software works as expected in the executable mode.

Some of the issues that a tester might face during validation (Figure 13.9) are:

Lack of Time: Testing generally takes a hit when development schedules are extended. When this happens, all the planned test cases may not be executed. The number of bugs detected would also be impacted. The tester must ensure that he gets enough time to test a product.

In case a tester does not have enough time, he should prioritize and execute the test cases for critical functionalities then proceed further with other test cases. The risks associated by not being able to execute all the test cases should be communicated to the stakeholders.

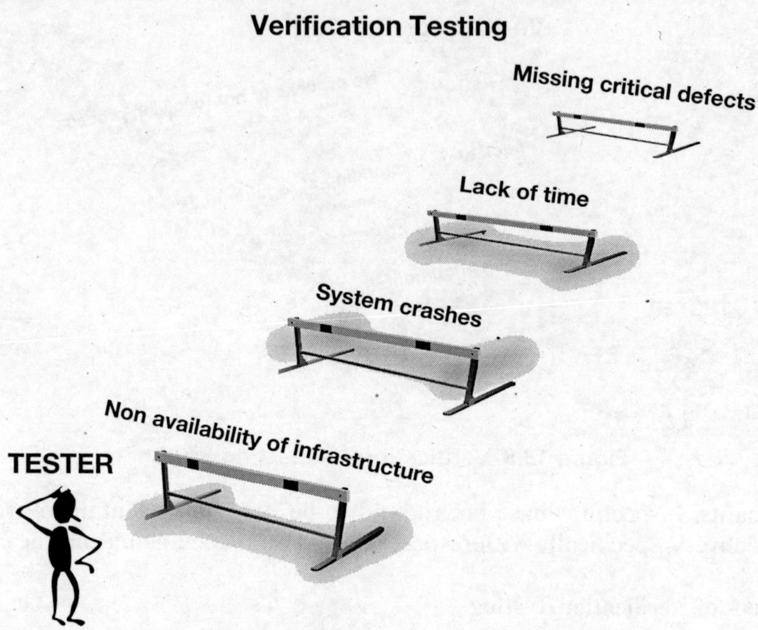

Figure 13.9 Validation Impacting Issues

Software Crashes: A software may not be in a testable stable state. As a result, even some basic test conditions could bring the system down and halt testing completely. These types of delays take away valuable testing team from testers since the application is not available.

Missing Critical Defects: This is related to the two problems commonly faced by testers due to lack of time and time lost due to system crashes. A tester may be too much occupied with these fundamental issues of working. As a result, he may not be able to focus on testing of the critical functionalities.

Validation Testing Basic Phases

Figure 13.10 shows the various phases of development and the corresponding testing phases that could be planned in parallel.

Unit Testing: The smallest testable units of a software which could be individual programs or modules are tested during the unit testing phase. This is usually done by the developer, the tester can verify with the developer if this has been done and study the unit test cases and reports. Generally, the tester is not expected to do unit testing if black-box testing is only in scope. But, if the tester is expected to do white-box testing, then he should perform various white-box testing techniques covered in the following chapter and unit test the code.

Integration Testing: After the individual modules have been tested, the next step is to ensure that the interactions within the software modules. This type of testing is called 'integration testing' and typically bugs could be found at the interfaces and the communication points between the modules.

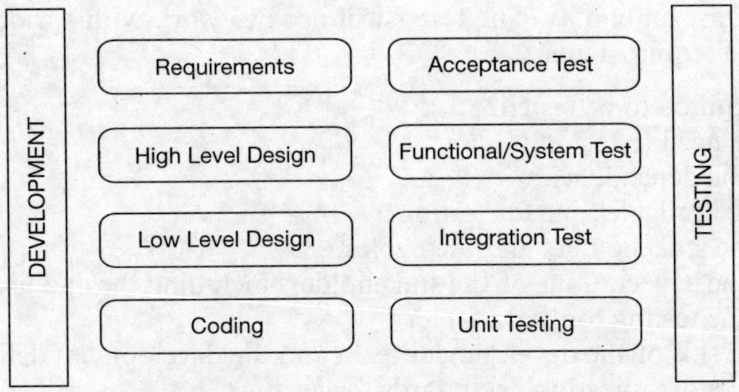

Figure 13.10 Validation Testing Phases

Functional Testing: This is done to verify the end-to-end functionalities of the modules. This ensures whether the business requirements of the application have been satisfied. The tester prepares and executes the test cases based on his understanding of the business, the business requirements and the knowledge gained through the interaction with the business Subject Matter Expert (SME).

Typically, testing of applications would involve functional testing only and then directly into acceptance testing without much of system testing. System testing is more rigorously done for software products.

System Testing: This is a more comprehensive test where all the components of the system— software, hardware, external interfaces are all tested as per the specifications. This is done to ensure the delivery of a complete and fully integrated software product.

Acceptance Testing: This is the final phase of testing where the customer himself will execute a set of test cases to evaluate and accept the product. Here, testing is not that elaborate and if a new product is getting released, the acceptance test cases would have been defined as a part of the requirements phase and executed during this final phase of testing to confirm acceptance of the product.

The final code would be delivered only during the end of the project. But depending on the developmental model, we could get workable units of code in phases in an iterative manner. Based on the delivery schedule, the tester can plan the respective test case preparation and execution.

Even if something works fine, testing needs to be done to confirm that it does what was expected under the given conditions.

When the actual application or part of it is not yet available for testing which would be the case in the initial stages of development, the tester would need to use the techniques of static testing, namely specifications, walkthroughs, pretending like the customer and visualizing the end product of the specifications, desk checking with developers, researching on the usability standards and guidelines, study and review of a similar software that has been developed.

The most important activity for a tester is to understand the requirement specifications. The requirement specifications must typically answer the following questions in no uncertain terms and without any ambiguity. The tester will need to work with various teams to get a better picture of the requirements.

1. What is required to be tested?
2. Why do we need to test it?
3. What are the dependencies?
4. What is the available time for testing?
5. Who are the stakeholders and their roles?
6. What are the expectations of the stakeholders including the end users?
7. What are the testing tools available?
8. What is the size of the development team and the development delivery schedule?
9. What are the organization's standards for testing?
10. What are the details of the development, test and end user environments'?

13.10.3 Types of Software Testing

This is an introductory on the various testing types commonly practiced in the industry. The basic categories of testing namely White- and black-box testing (Figure 13.11) are discussed along with the specific techniques for applying them.

13.10.3.1 Introduction to White-box Testing

Structural or white-box testing is based on knowledge of internal structure and logic of programs, the coverage of specifications is validated in the code.

There are many synonyms for white-box testing as given in the list below:

- Glass-box Testing
- Structural Testing
- Clear-box Testing
- Open Box Testing
- Logical Testing
- Crystal-box Testing
- Basis-path Testing

White-box testing can be quite complex depending on the applications. A small application that performs a few simple operations could be white-box tested quickly say in minutes, while larger programming applications take days, weeks and even longer for completion of test.

White box testing ensures that all independent paths within a module have been exercised at least once. Typically, the software program should have a flow for normal execution and when exceptions are encountered, it should display meaningful error messages and exit gracefully. No unhandled exceptions should be present under any circumstance. The database interactions during the program flow should also be verified like when trying to update a table is not found or a field is not present in the table or if there is no space in the database to create new records.

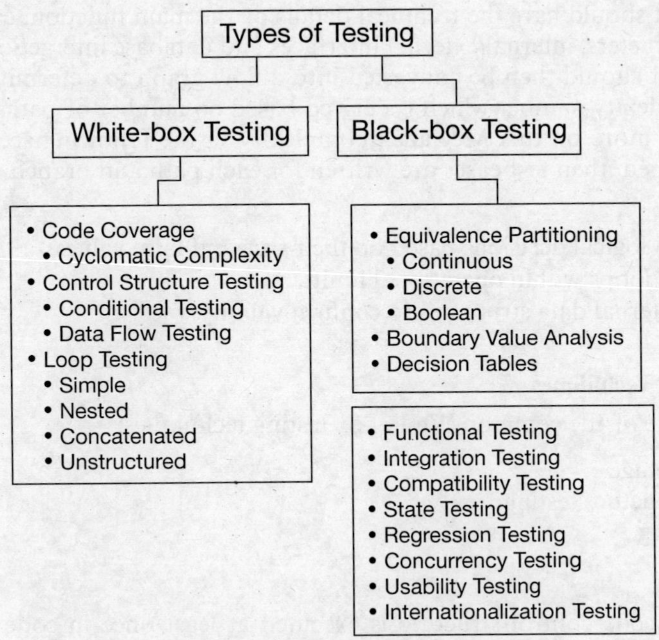

Figure 13.11 Types of Testing

All the logical conditions should be exercised, for example, there may be multiple statements validating 'N' number of conditions as shown below:

IF THEN …

..

ELSE IF…

..

ELSE IF…

..

ELSE

..

END

One area of possible error is that, the program may never pass through the last ELSE statement under normal operations and it is possible that this could have been dropped out of the developers' radar.

13.10.3.1.1 Guidelines for White-box Testing The software application should be first represented as a pseudo-code or flowchart. For our understanding let us assume that the application program or module is converted into a flowchart.

This flowchart should have the technical details of the main function, calling functions, input/output parameters, internal/external interfaces and database interactions.

This flowchart should then be converted into a flow graph to determine the McCabes Cyclomatic Complexity number which is derived based on number of paths and nodes. We will be discussing more on this McCabe's complexity in the following sections. Once the complexity is defined, then test cases are written for each path and branch with the following criteria:

- Exercise all logical decisions based on their true and false values.
- Execute all loops within operational limits.
- Exercise internal data structures to confirm validity.

White-box Testing Techniques

Following are some of the common White-box testing techniques:

- Code Coverage
- Control structure testing
- Loop testing

Code Coverage

Each segment of code control structure is executed at least once in code coverage. Each branch in the software code is taken at least once in each possible direction.

For multiple conditions, you must test not only each direction, but also each possible combination of conditions, which is usually done by using a 'truth table'. Each independent path through the code is taken in a pre-determined order. All possible paths through the code are defined and covered.

Cyclomatic Complexity

It is a quantitative measure of the logical complexity of a program. It defines the number for independent paths on the basis set for a program (Figure 13.12). It provides an upper bound for the number of tests that must be conducted to ensure that all statements have been executed at least once. Independent path is any path through the program that introduces at least one new set of processing statements or a new condition.

McCabe cyclomatic complexity is mathematically defined as

$$M = L - N + 2P$$

Where,

L = the number of links in the graph
N = number of nodes in the graph
P = number of disconnected parts in the graph (like calling program and sub-routine)

McCabe Number = No. of Edges – No. of Nodes + 2 No. of Paths
McCabe Number = 6 – 6 + 2 = 2

This implies only 2 individual paths to be tested.

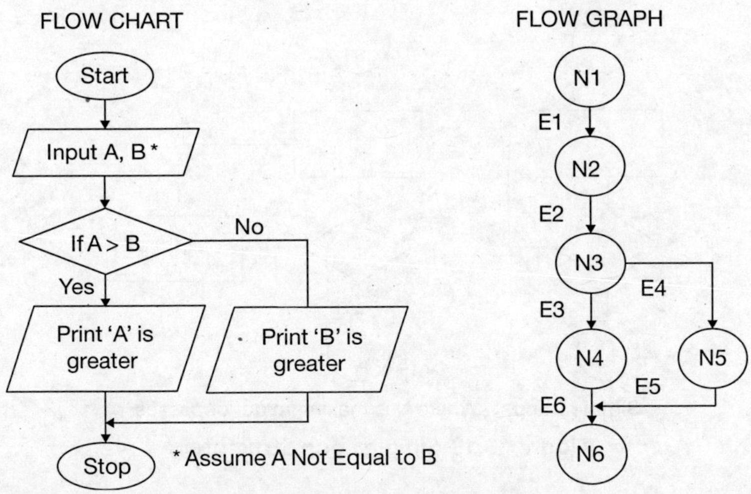

Figure 13.12 Cyclomatic Complexity

Control Structure Testing

Control structure testing involves condition testing and data flow testing:

- *Condition Testing:* It is a test case design method that exercises the logical conditions contained in a program module. The value of a variable would determine the flow of the application which can easily be understood with an example as in the case of Boolean operators like TRUE or FALSE. If TRUE, then the application traverses along a specific path, if FALSE, it will traverse along another path. Similarly, the value of an integer variable like the age can make the application behave in a certain manner. For example, if age is 18 or above certain rules may be triggered and if age is less than 18, certain other conditions may be triggered.
- *Data Flow Testing:* Generally, all applications have variables defined and used according to their specific requirements. When a variable is defined in a program, it is actually allocated a certain portion of the memory so that values could be assigned and reassigned to this memory location during the course of a program execution. Data flow testing is analysing the location and variables assigned or changed or impacted during the execution of a program. The typical errors which could be found by this method are like references may be made to variables which do not exist or the variables may have unexpected values. There are typically two types of data testing, namely, Define/Use where the variables definition and usage is analysed through the course of program execution and program slicing where the programs are sliced to chunks of executable components to observe the impact of changes to a specific variable within these components.

Loop Testing

The validity of loop constructs in a program or code is exclusively focused here. Type of loops are as follows:

- Simple
- Nested
- Concatenated
- Unstructured

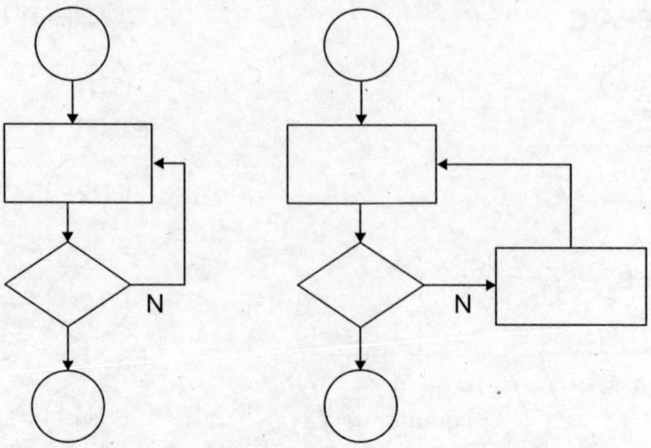

Simple Loops—Where N is maximum no. of passes

Figure 13.13 Simple Loop Structure

Simple Loop: Simple loops (Figure 13.13) are single loops which can be covered by two cases either by looping and non-looping. In loops the bugs are typically found around the minimum iteration and maximum iteration values. The minimum number of iterations is generally zero, but not each time. The minimum conditions to test the simple loop are:

- Skip the loop entirely.
- One pass through the loop.
- Two passes through the loop to check any initialization errors.
- (N – 1), N and (N + 1) passes through the loop.

Nested Loops: Nested loops (Figure 13.14) are two or more loops where at least one of the loops logically begins and ends within another loop. In the following example, Loop 1 begins and ends within Loop 2.

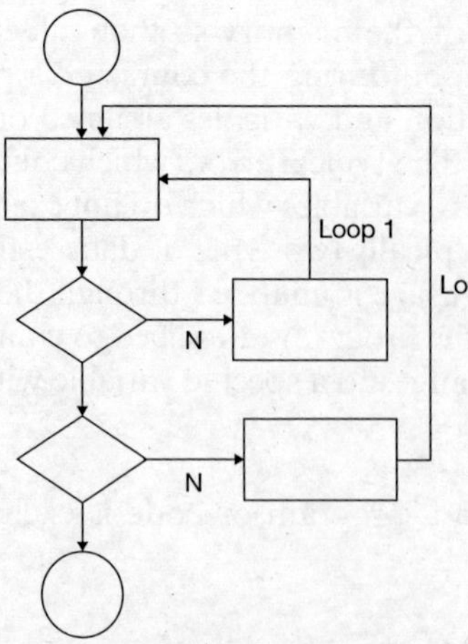

Nested Loops—Where N is maximum no. of passes

Figure 13.14 Nested Loop Structure

The basic test, which we discussed for simple loops, should be completed for each individual loop. The additional tests for nested loop are as follows:

- Start with the innermost loop and set all other loops to minimum value.
- Test the boundaries of the inner loop, Minimum Value –1, Minimum Value +1, Minimum Value, Maximum +1 and Maximum –1. The outer loop should be at minimum value.
- Work outwards keeping inner loops to typical values.
- Repeat the steps with Minimum Value –1, Minimum Value +1, Minimum Value, Maximum +1 and Maximum –1, for all the nested loops simultaneously.

Concatenated Loops: Concatenated loops (Figure 13.15) fall somewhere in between the simple and nested loops from testing perpectives. When we test along a path, if it is possible to enter one loop after exiting from another loop then the two loops are concatenated.

The iteration values in one loop is directly or indirectly dependent on the iteration values of the other loop. If the iteration values are not related then they are not concatenated loops even if the loops are in the same path.

13.10.5.1.2 White-box Testing Tools Given here are some of the tools available for white-box testing:

1. Purify by Rational Software Corporation
   - Run-time error and memory-leak detection
   - C/C++, FORTRAN and Java
   - UNIX, NT, and W2K
2. Insure++ by Parasoft Corporation
   - Run-time error and memory-leak detection
   - Add-on module TCA measures code coverage
   - C/C++
   - UNIX, NT, and W2K

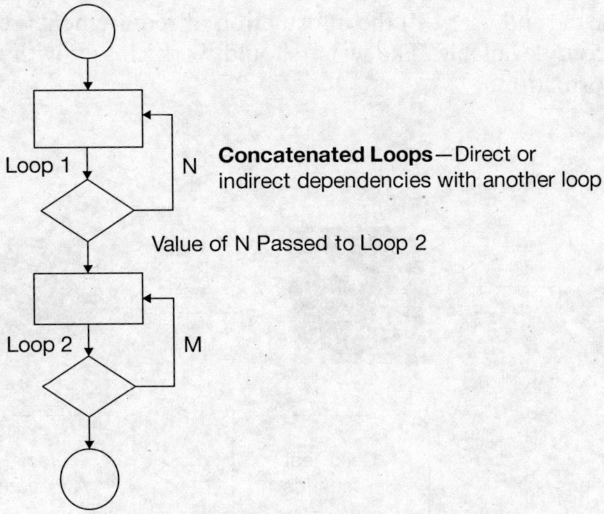

Figure 13.15 Concatenated Loop Structure

3. Quantify by Rational Software Corporation
   - Performance profiling
   - C/C++, Java, and VB
   - UNIX, NT, and W2K
4. Expeditor by One Realm Inc.
   - Source code scanner for I18N errors
   - C/C++, Java, and HTML
   - UNIX, NT, and W2K

13.10.3.2 Black-box Testing

There are many synonyms for black-box testing as given here.

- Specification Testing
  - Conformance Testing
  - Requirements Testing

Black-box testing (Figure 13.16) involves testing the application like an external or end-user by validating the outputs received from the application based on certain inputs given to it. The internal technical mechanisms like the programs and the code infrastructure of the application are not considered in this type of testing. The tester has neither access to the source code nor is expected to be knowledgeable of the programming language and code structure behind the application.

The application is a 'Black Box' to the tester. He is aware of only the functionalities to be tested, the required inputs and the corresponding expected outputs, but nothing about the internal workings. This type of testing requires good knowledge of the business requirements of the application. For example, if it is a mobile application, then the tester needs to have a good understanding of the Internet world and also good analytical skills to see through the requirements to identify problem areas. The tester has to understand the requirements to an extent that he should be able to fill the gap for any missed specifications on both the sides, either the business or the end user. All the information or requirements related to the assignment may not be directly available. The tester should work closely with the stakeholders to get the necessary information.

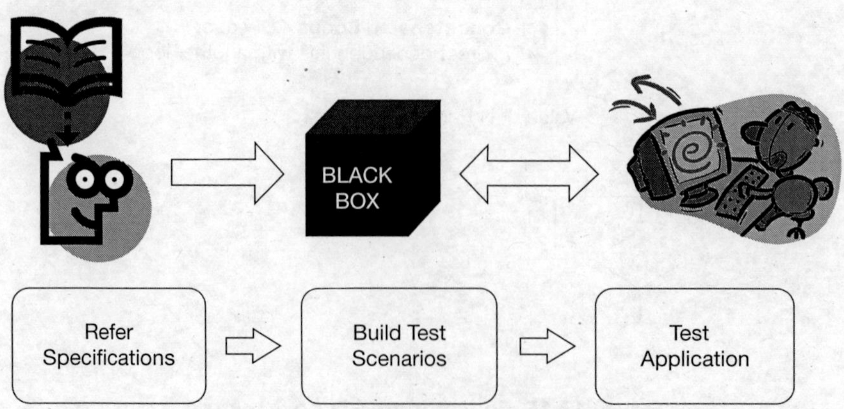

Figure 13.16 Black Box Testing Mechanism

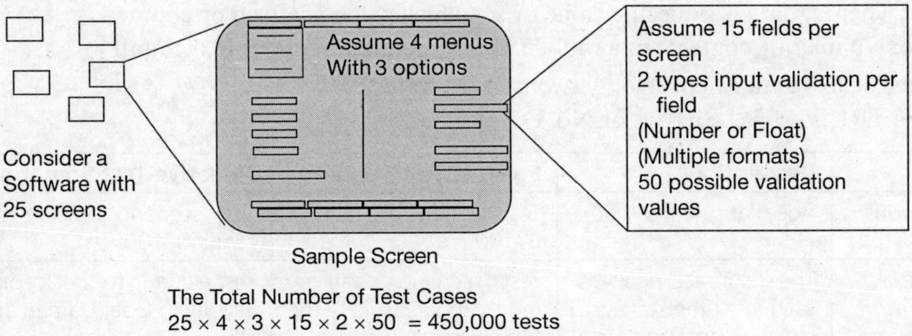

Figure 13.17 Complete Test Case Example

Figure 13.17 shows a sample software application with about 25 screens, each screen having 4 menus, each menu having 3 options and an average of 15 fields per screen. If we calculate the number of test cases, we would need to execute for completely test this application is a mind boggling 4,50,000 test cases. Even if it takes 1 minute to execute a test case, it will take 312.5 days working 24 × 7 to complete testing of the entire set.

The challenge for the testers is mainly of two-fold:

1. Reduce the number of test cases to manageable limits.
2. Ensure that the identified subset of test cases gives sufficient coverage.

The common Black-box testing techniques used in addressing these challenges are:

1. Equivalence Partitioning
2. Boundary Value Analysis
3. Decision Tables

13.10.3.2.1 Equivalence Partitioning One of the key challenges of a tester is reducing the almost infinite set of possible test cases into an effective smaller set of test cases. Equivalence partitioning is a technique used to reduce the number of test cases to a manageable size level while maintaining reasonable test coverage at present. In this testing approach, we partition the input or output space into equivalence classes. An equivalence class is defined in such a way that a member of an equivalence class represents all other members of the class. This provides a way of selecting the most relevant test cases and eliminating the ones that do not have much value. For example, if we need to verify a given input field that accepts integer values of length up to 5, then range of values would extend from 0–10000 in both positive and negative directions which would be highly laborious to test for each and every value. Instead by applying equivalence partitioning, we could have 4 classes here—Positive Integer, Negative Integer, 0 and Fractions (for negative scenario). Just 4 test values representing the 4 equivalence classes would give us the required test coverage.

Types of Equivalence Partitions

Continuous: The test data is a measured value. It can take any value within a given range.

Example: Temperature in a city, the height of persons, etc.

Discrete: The test data is a specific value or set which can be defined or counted.
Example: Number of contacts in a mobile phone, number of states in a country.

Boolean: The test data can have only two possible values.
Example: TRUE or FALSE, Yes or No, On or Off.

Type	Description	Positive Test Scenario	Negative Test Scenario
Continuous	Age of insured (0–100).	Test scenario for range 0–100.	Test scenario outside the range 0–100.
Discrete	The insurance policy is valid in all the states of India except Goa, Diu and Daman.	Test scenario confirming the policy validity for the given set of states in India.	Test scenario to check policy validity in Goa, Daman and Diu.
Boolean	Existing customer.	Test scenario with 'Yes'.	Test scenario with 'No'.

Guidelines for Equivalence Partitions

The complete input domain data should be divided into relevant equivalence data classes as given below.

1. Dividing the data into two or more groups based on one of the following classes:
   - Ranges (Continuous)
   - Number values (Discreet)
   - Sets (Boolean, Continuous, Discreet)
2. Writing test cases for each VALID input.
3. Writing at least one test case for each INVALID input.

13.10.5.2.2 Boundary Value Analysis This technique is a logical next step after identifying the equivalence classes. Here the test cases are defined at the boundaries of equivalence classes rather than at the middle of the input data domain since the probability of finding errors is more at the boundaries.

Create test cases for each boundary value by choosing one point on the boundary, one point just below the boundary, and one point just above the boundary. 'Below' and 'above' are relative terms and depend on the data value's units. This ensures testing the application at the border of its planned operational limits.

Consider the example of a continuous data class like age of the insured person which is defined as between 1–100.

Now two equivalence classes can be identified for testing are:

1. All Ages between 1–100.
2. All Ages below 1 and above 100.

The corresponding boundary values that could be tested for the above classe s are:

1. 0, 1 and 2 – Lower Boundary
2. 99, 100 and 101 – Upper Boundary

The test cases with the above 6 data sets (3 lower and 3 upper boundaries) could be used to test the application. For the values 0 and 101, the application must not accept the values, all the other values 1, 2, 99 and 100 should be acceptable. Most bugs can be identified by creating two equivalence classes as above, one with the data which we expect to work and the other with the data which we do not expect to work.

Guidelines for Boundary Value Analysis

1. If input is a range between values A and B, test cases should be designed with values A and B and just above and just below A and B values.
2. If input specifies a number of values, test cases should be designed to exercise minimum, maximum, and just above and below minimum and maximum values.
3. Apply the same above two for output conditions.
4. Design test cases to exercise data structures at its boundaries.

Input Data Fields Testing Checklist

Generally, applications have user interface through which the user input values which are processed by the application and corresponding outputs are generated. The input fields could be numeric, alphabets, texts or special characters. Each of the input fields could be tested for these inputs.

- Enter a valid value within the boundary limits.
- Enter the value 0.
- Press Enter do not type anything.
- Certain fields may have defaults, if so clear the defaults.
- Enter upper bound (UB) value for no : of characters/digits.
- Enter UB + 1.
- Enter UB – 1.
- Enter Lower Bound (LB) value for number of characters/digits.
- Enter LB + 1.
- Enter LB – 1.
- Enter negative values.
- Type special characters like/ : ;
- Check with wrong data types like number for character.
- Enter upper case letters.
- Enter lower case letters.
- Enter an expression.
- Enter special ASCII values like 255 (End of File).
- Leading space or zeros.
- Reserved words of the programming language.
- Any operating system filename reserved characters like: . , \ , *.
- Check with function keys, ALT, CTL, Shift, other similar combinations.
- Simulate time outs by waiting on the field without entering.
- Move to another application and get back.
- Overwrite the entered values verify mouse and keyboard activities.

13.10.3.2.3 Decision Tables Decision table's documents complex business rules that a system must implement. Here, the focus is on validating business rules, conditions, constraints and corresponding responses and actions of a software component.

Basic Approach:

- Identify and list all possible 'conditions' (inputs) and all possible 'actions' (outputs).
- Define test case to cover each case.

The general format of a decision table is given in Table 13.1.

Table 13.1 Decision Table Format

	Rules			
Conditions	**Rule 1**	**Rule 2**	**...**	**Rule p**
Condition 1				
...				
Condition m				
Actions				
Action 1				
...				
Action n				

Consider an example of an auto insurance company which gives discounts to drivers who are married and/or student. Let's begin with the conditions.

The following decision table has two conditions, each one of which takes on the values Yes or No.

- A decision table with two binary conditions.
- The possible combinations are {Yes, Yes}, {Yes, No}, {No, Yes}, and {No, No}. Each rule represents one of these combinations.

Table 13.2 Decision Tree – Binary Table- Limited Entry Decision Tables

CONDITION	RULE 1	RULE 2	RULE 3	RULE 4
Married	Yes	No	Yes	No
Student	No	Yes	Yes	No
ACTIONS				
Discount %	20	30	40	0

The decision tables which use binary conditions like TRUE/FALSE are known as limited entry decision tables (Table 13.2). The decision tables which use multiple conditions are known as extended entry decision tables.

Guidelines for Creating Decision Tables

- Prepare a list of all the conditions to be tested.
- Calculate the approximate number of rules to be tested which is 2^n where 'n' is the number of conditions. If number of conditions is 2 as in the example the number of rules is $2^2 = 4$.

- Define all the combinations in the table.
- Verify if there are any redundancies in the rules or inconsistencies in the combinations.
- Fill the actions for all the combinations.

The three main functional testing methods (Equivalence Partitions, Boundary Value and Decision tables) complement each other to give a more effective testing outcome which would not be possible with just one or two of the methods. The decision table testing and boundary value analysis have evolved from equivalence class testing. Here, the input and outputs are grouped together into equivalence classes and the logical dependencies of the rules are tested.

Black-box testing tries to find errors in the following categories.

- Incorrect or missing functions
- Interface errors
- Errors in data structures
- Errors in external data base access
- Behavioural or performance errors
- Initialization and termination errors

The following testing types can be categorized under black-box testing:

- Functional Testing
- Integration Testing
- Compatibility Testing
- State Testing
- Regression Testing
- Concurrency Testing
- Usability Testing
- Internationalization Testing

13.10.3.2.4 Functional Testing The objective of functional testing is to make sure that the software application meets the intended requirements. The requirements may be defined in specifications document which is typically the document shared with development team for building the software or in some cases the document may not be available which means the testing team would have to create one. Functional testing can be conducted both manually or by using automated tools.

The testing team understands the application by studying the requirements document. The testing team will have to work with many stakeholders to ensure that they have the required information for creating a test plan and design the test cases. The testing team prepares test cases which will ensure coverage of the functionality of the system. These test cases are reviewed for coverage, correctness and efficiency. The test cases are then executed and the defects are recorded. The defects are reported to the development team for fixing. The testing cycle is normally iterative and continues for an agreed number of iterations or until the defects have reduced to an acceptable level.

Testing Type	Pre-requisites	Expected Deliverables
Functional	• Requirements specifications • Access to application during Test execution • Automation tool if applicable	• Functional test plan • Manual test cases • Automation test cases • Defect report

13.10.3.2.5 Integration Testing Generally, software applications consist of multiple software modules. These modules might be coded by different programmers may or may not be within the same hardware or software platforms. In Integration testing, we focus on checking data communication amongst these modules.

Integration testing is also known as 'String Testing' or 'Thread Testing'. The objective of integration testing is to verify that different working components of the system perform as expected when assembled.

Testing Type	Pre-requisites	Expected Deliverables
Integration	• Technical architecture document detailing the interfaces. • Unit testing completed for the modules.	• Integration test plan • Manual test cases • Defect report

13.10.3.2.6 Compatibility Testing Compatibility helps to determine if a product will function correctly with other hardware/software in the intended environment.

Software testing requires functional validation across a wide variety of hardware platforms, operating systems, databases, browsers, servers and various networks. Failure to perform these tests can introduce costly bugs. Investing in compatibility testing early helps reduce tech support costs at later stage.

Testing Type	Pre-Requisites	Expected Deliverables
Compatibility testing	• Understanding of the multiple platforms where the software will be used • Availability of the required hardware for testing	• Compatibility test plan • Manual test cases • Defect report

13.10.3.2.7 State Testing The present condition of a software application is called 'a state'. The application goes through various states during the course of its usage. The verification of the programs logical flow through the various states is known as state testing. Since the state of an application is constantly changing and the application is expected to be tested with relevant inputs for each specific state. This can be understood more clearly with examples like software games or drawing applications.

Consider an example of a simple SUDOKU application on your mobile (Figure 13.18). The initial state of the application would be something like a set of squares partially filled. The final state of the application would be with all the empty squares filled with relevant values. Each time the user makes an entry, the state of the application changes, certain validations takes place and user is informed if his action is correct. The user is also able to toggle back and forth between the various states starting from the initial state to the final state through the 'N' number of states in between (Figure 13.19).

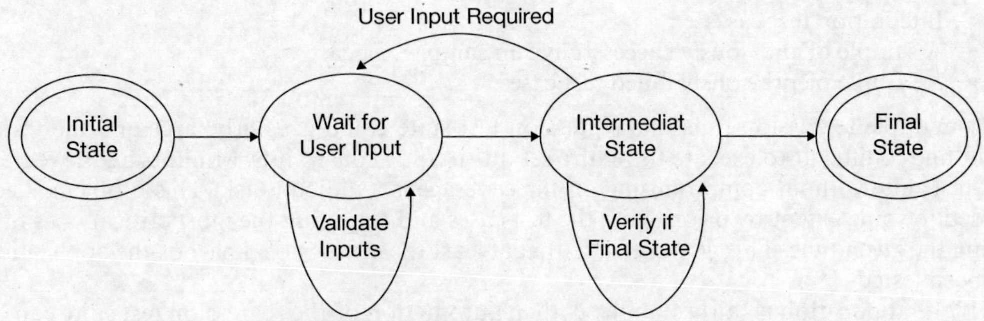

State Diagram for SUDOKU Application

Figure 13.18 State Diagram–SUDOKU

Testing Type	Pre-requisites	Expected Deliverables
State testing	• Understanding of the various application states • Conditions which trigger movement from one state to another	• State test plan • Manual test cases • Defect report

13.10.3.2.8 Regression Testing Regression testing involves reuse of the existing test cases to retest the application after any change has been made. This is done to ensure that the new changes made to the software do not affect any of the existing functionality.

Regression testing is typically done after fixing bugs, new enhancements, modification of code due to change in requirements and performance issue fixes.

Depending on the time constraints or requirements the tester may execute the complete set of test cases or only a partial set of test cases. The test cases to be executed for regression testing and can be identified using the following guidelines:

- Test cases which verify critical business functionalities. The tester needs to identify these test cases and prioritize them.
- Test cases which frequently fail or have a high probability of failing based on past experience.

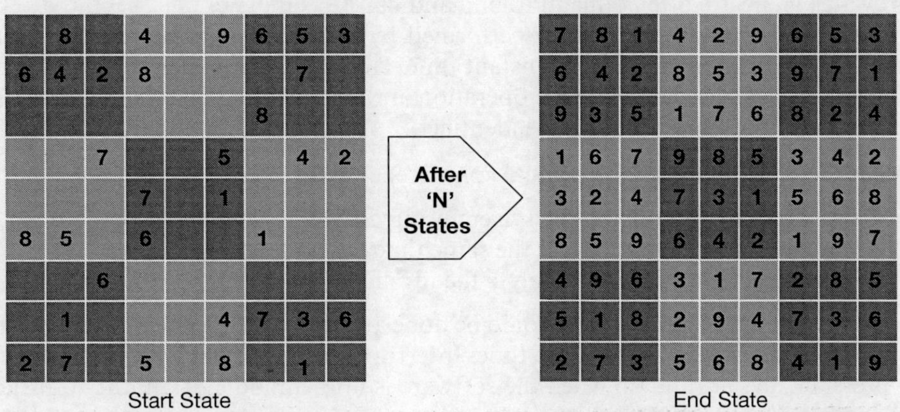

Figure 13.19 State Diagram–SUDOKU–Start and End States

- Integration test cases.
- A sample of previously successfully run sample test cases.
- A sample of previously failed test cases.

After multiple regression runs, the regression test suite could get fairly large and the tester might find it difficult to execute the entire set due to time constraints. Minimizing the regression test suite without compromising on the coverage is a difficult task. This problem is addressed to some extent by prioritizing the test cases and executing the most critical ones first during the given time. This would ensure that at least the most critical part of the application has been tested.

If the application is fairly stabilized, then automation of the regression test suite can be considered. There are tools like Quick Test Pro (QTP), Selenium, and Rational Functional Tester (RFT) which can be used for regression automation. The decision to automate should be based on the frequency of regression and a favourable Return on Investment (ROI) on automation. There may be no point in automation if the regression suite is run just once in a year only for a 2 week period. We can complete this type of testing manually itself unless there are some strong reasons like lack of availability of manual testers for the 2 week period for a very niche and critical application which requires special testing skills not easily available.

Testing Type	Pre-requisites	Expected Deliverables
Regression testing	• Availability of existing set of test cases • Prioritizing of the test cases based on criticality • Detailed understanding of what is changed in the application and why	• Regression test plan • Automation feasibility report • Manual test cases • Defect report

13.10.3.2.9 Concurrency Testing Concurrency testing is performed to identify race conditions in an application which may occur when two or more users perform exactly the same transaction at the same instant of time. This results in the two or more threads competing for the same application resources like database, memory, printer, communication mechanism or other hardware. These are often difficult to find and hard to simulate.

Manual concurrency testing can be performed by making two or more users perform exactly the same operation at the same instant time. However, this does not ensure or guarantee that the users will execute the same operation at the same time. The test may need to be conducted several times for an issue to be identified.

Following are some of the steps for manual concurrency test:

1. Login two or more users on the system using different machines.
2. Execute the same transaction at the same time for both users.
3. Validate the transaction and analyse the result.

Some of the common transactions that could be done are sharing the same printer and trying to print a document exactly at the same time. Interrupting the system with multiple mouse clicks or pressing keys at random when the software is in the middle of another transaction or changing states.

Testing Type	Pre-requisites	Expected Deliverables
Concurrency testing	• Technical architecture of the system with its interfaces • Determine the possible concurrency scenarios • Identify necessary hardware and users	• Concurrency test plan • Automation plan (if applicable) • Defect report

13.10.3.2.10 Usability Testing For any application, the comfort of the end user is a very important requirement. The more the ease with which the users can learn and use the application the better it is. In usability testing the tester looks out for various aspects of usability like efficiency, intuitiveness, aesthetics and ergonomics. Usability testing has to be preferably done early in the life-cycle so that user interface and workflow changes do not cause substantial rework later.

Testers, first, get familiar with the domain and application functionalities. They identify different roles, corresponding workflows and tasks performed by the end users. Each tester performs the identified tasks to evaluate the application for usability by identifying violations of usability standards, inconsistencies and overall look and feel. Then, finally recommendations are made to rectify issues.

Testing Type	Pre-requisites	Expected Deliverables
Usability testing	• End user requirements • Use cases • User interface details • Screen prototypes • Detailed screen flows • User manual	• Usability test plan • Usability test cases • Test results • Recommendations

13.10.3.2.11 Internationalization Testing This is an extension of the usability testing to ensure that the application could be used in multiple countries with different languages and culture.

This includes testing for globalization as well as localization. Testing for globalization which ensures the application can be used across multiple countries and languages. This precedes the testing for localization which is more focused on testing the usage for a specific area or country. In general, the user interface should able to handle the specific linguistic and cultural expectation of the users in different countries. Language experts could be used for checking the user messages and verifying the contextual layout of the application for appropriateness. Identify and verify features of the product which may be useful in some countries and may not be relevant to others. If the features are not required, verify whether these are disabled. Data storage and data retrieval from multilingual application should be tested since the unicode formats for storage and retrieval may be different.

Testing Type	Pre-requisites	Expected Deliverables
Internationalization testing	• User requirements for globalization • User requirements for localization • Design document for internationalization	• Test plan • Test cases • Test results • Recommendations

CASE STUDY

Let us take an example of testing a mobile application which will help in compressing and decompressing files like .zip, .RAR, TAR, .gzip.

This is a very useful application in mobile phones, for reading documents and archiving them.

Given below are some of the activities that would be done to test the application. Please identify the testing type they would be fall in most appropriately (Answers are given in brackets):

1. User able to download the application (Functional).
2. Check the time it took to download the application (Functional).
3. INSTALL the application on the mobile (Functional).
4. Extract all the data from a compressed file (Functional).
5. Verify if the files extracted are functional as expected – audio, video, data (Functional).
6. Apply any restrictions for download depending on country or age (Functional).
7. Check how easy it was to use the application (Usability).
8. Check the impact on the memory usage on your mobile (White Box).
9. Check if there are any vulnerabilities for hacking and security threats (White Box).
10. Check the CPU usage on your mobile for the application in various states (State Testing).
11. Analyse the impact of the application when the mobile receives a call (Concurrency).
12. Analyse the impact of the application on the battery (Functional).
13. Check the functionalities of free and cost downloads (Functional).
14. Check the complete billing flow if the download has a cost (Functional).
15. Check all the above functionalities of the application with different mobile brands (Compatibility).
16. Verify the application across multiple operating like Android, OS-X and Windows (Compatibility).
17. Check if any additional info ID displayed like advertisements, other downloads, etc. (Functional).
18. Check how clean is the UNINSTALL (Functional).
19. Check if the application connects to the internet and transmits any information (White Box).
20. Check impact of any upgrades or patches to the application (Functional).
21. Check the usability of application in various countries (Internationalization).

SUMMARY

The main aim of quality is to ensure 'Conformance to requirements' and 'fitness for use'. Quality is (and must) planned in and not inspected in. Prevention is very important than inspection.

The three areas of quality management are plan quality, perform quality assurance, and perform quality control. Quality planning involves ensuring that the appropriate and relevant project management principles have been applied and another aspect of project quality planning involves planning for the quality of the deliverables involved. The cost of quality is the profit of quality. Quality control involves operational techniques meant to ensure proper quality standards as per the plan are getting followed. Quality assurances are activities that boost the confidence surrounding quality.

Control Charts: A graphic display of the results, over time and against established control limits which is used to determine if the process is in control or in need of adjustment.

Corrective Action: Changes made to bring back the expected future performance of the project in line with the plan.

Cost of Quality: The cost incurred to ensure quality which includes quality planning, quality control, quality assurance, and rework.

Pareto Diagram: A histogram ordered by frequency of occurrence that shows number of results against identified cause.

Performance Reporting: Collecting and disseminating information about project performance for project progress.

Quality Assurance (QA): Process of evaluating overall project performance to provide confidence that the project will satisfy the relevant quality standards and this usually occurs in regular intervals.

Quality Control (QC): Process of monitoring particular project results to determine if they comply with the quality standards and identifying ways to eliminate causes related with the problems.

Quality Plan: A document setting out the specific quality practices, resources and process relevant to a particular product, service, contract or project.

Quality Policy: The overall quality intentions and direction of quality, as formally expressed by top management.

Quality Planning: Identifying quality standards related to projects and determining the process to satisfy them.

Total Quality Management (TQM): A common approach to implementing a quality improvement program within an organization. Deming suggested a process of plan-do-check-act (PDCA) cycle for the same.

Kaizen Theory: Continuous improvements to reduce costs and ensure consistency.

Marginal Analysis: We compare the cost of incremental quality improvements against the increase in revenue and optimal quality is reached when cost of improvement is same as the costs to achieved quality.

Rule of Seven: In control charts, if there are seven points on one direction, then an assignable cause must be found.

Prevention vs Inspection: Cost of preventing defects is much lower than the cost of correcting them later.

- **Application software testing** is testing the common applications which we see every day and mostly used for data processing like Banking System, Insurance, Payroll, Inventory Management System, Hospital Management Systems and also Mobile Applications.

- **Systems software testing** is done on the programs written for running the computer/system itself which facilitate, enhance and control various programs like the operating system, complier and interpreter.
- We had seen the **basic approaches to testing** namely verification and validation. The different phases of testing like unit, integration, system and acceptance testing were also introduced. The evolution of testing and the current expectation from tester were also studied.
- **Verification testing** is done by using review based techniques. The fundamental theme of verification testing is—Are we building the product right?
- The testing activities that are done to evaluate the software in the executable mode can be called as **validation testing.**
- **Test strategy** is a high level plan based on the understanding of multiple factors involved in a software development.
- The two fundamental testing approaches, **White Box and Black box testing** were discussed and the various testing techniques under each of them were studied.
- **Structural or white box testing** is based on knowledge of internal structure and logic of programs, the coverage of specifications is validated in the code.
- **Black box testing** involves in testing the application like an external or end-user by validating the outputs received from the application based on certain inputs given to it.
- When we get testing requirements, it is typically for black box testing unless specifically stated otherwise. The different types of black box testing were studied with the general approach, pre-requisites and the delivery expectations for functional, compatibility, integration, regression, concurrency, state, usability and internationalization testing.

EXERCISES

PART A (Objective-type questions)

1. The definition of quality management is
   A. The process of identifying quality requirements or standards for the project and product, and documenting how the project will demonstrate compliance.
   B. The process of auditing the quality requirements and the results from quality control measurements to ensure appropriate quality standards and operational definitions are used.
   C. The process of monitoring and recording results of executing the quality activities to assess performance and recommend necessary changes.
   D. It includes the processes and activities of the performing organization that determine quality policies, objectives, and responsibilities so that the project will satisfy the needs for which it was undertaken.

2. Which of the following is true?
   A. Project quality management addresses the management of the project only.
   B. Project quality management addresses the management of the product only.

C. Project quality management addresses the management of the project and product of the project.
D. It applies to projects based on the nature of the project.

3. The degree to which a set of inherent characteristics fulfill requirements is called
A. Grade
B. Quality
C. Scope
D. Accuracy

4. Category assigned to products having same functional use, but different technical characteristics is called
A. Grade
B. Quality
C. Scope
D. Accuracy

5. Your manager asked you to develop a product in two different technologies in order to increase the marketability. These two products are called different
A. Grade
B. Quality
C. Scope
D. Accuracy

6. You are discussing with all the stakeholders regarding quality and grade to be decided and fixed for the project. Who is responsible for the trade-off between quality and grade?
A. Project manager and the project management team
B. Project Stakeholder
C. Client
D. Project Sponsor

7. Precise measurements are not necessarily accurate.
A. True
B. False

8. Total cost of all efforts related to quality throughout the product life-cycle is called
A. Cost of conformance
B. Cost of non-conformance
C. Cost of quality
D. Efforts of quality

9. Quality checklist is the output of which of the following process?
A. Plan Quality
B. Perform Quality Assurance
C. Perform Quality Control
D. Measure Quality

10. Process improvement plan is the output of which of the following process?
A. Plan Quality
B. Perform Quality Assurance
C. Perform Quality Control
D. Measure Quality

11. Failure Cost are often classified as
A. Parallel Cost, Vertical Cost
B. Standard Cost, Variable Cost
C. Internal Cost, External Cost
D. Fixed Cost, Variable Cost

12. Your manager is ready to spend extra cost and asked you to take more time to do it right. This is called
A. Appraisal Costs
B. External Failure Costs
C. Internal Failure Costs
D. Prevention Costs

13. Your manager is ready to spend extra cost to do rework on the project before submitting to the customer. This is called
A. Appraisal Costs
B. External Failure Costs
C. Internal Failure Costs
D. Prevention Costs

14. Your manager has requested PMO to do frequent inspection on the project to assess the quality and is an example of
A. Appraisal Costs
B. External Failure Costs
C. Internal Failure Costs
D. Prevention Costs

15. Warranty work is an example of
A. Appraisal Costs
B. External Failure Costs
C. Internal Failure Costs
D. Prevention Costs

16. A quality control manager knows that the standard deviations from two sources are '0.14' and '0.23', respectively. What is the total standard deviation assuming there is no other deviation?
A. 0.23 inch
B. 0.14 inch
C. 0.27 inch
D. 0.47 inch

17. Your manager asked you to conduct a quality audit at the end of every phase in a project. The audit is part of organization's
A. Quality Assurance Process
B. Quality Control Process
C. Quality Planning Process
D. Process Improvement Program

18. Control limits are generally set as
A. $\pm 3\ \sigma$
B. $\pm 1\ \sigma$
C. $\pm 2\ \sigma$
D. $\pm 6\ \sigma$

19. Your manager asked you to set quality metrics based on the competitor is an example of
A. Benchmark
B. Quality Control
C. Quality Assurance
D. Quality Policy

20. Statistical method for identifying which factors may influence specific variables of a product or process under development or in production is called
A. Benchmark
B. Quality Control
C. Quality Assurance
D. Design of Experiment

21. Which document describes how the project management team will implement the performing organization's quality policy?
A. Quality Management Plan
B. Quality Policy Document
C. Quality Assurance Document
D. Quality Control Document

22. A structured tool used to determine whether project activities comply with organizational and project policies, processes and procedures is called as
A. Design of Experiment
B. Checklist
C. Cost of Quality
D. Quality Audit

23. __________ is an analytical technique which helps in identifying which variables have the most influence on the overall outcome.
A. Design of Experiments
B. Benchmarking
C. Quality Audit
D. Quality Checklist

24. What is the primary objective of Verification Testing?
A. Prevent Bugs in the product
B. Identify Bugs in the product
C. Customer Satisfaction
D. Creating Quality Product

25. Which of the following is not a technique of verification testing?
A. Reviews
B. Walkthroughs
C. Inspections
D. Audit

26. It is a formal process in which the peers or stakeholders examine a piece of work to ensure correctness and is known as
A. Reviews
B. Walkthroughs
C. Inspections
D. Audit

27. It is a formal process where the person responsible for a specific unit of work formally presents his work to a group of reviewers and is known as
A. Reviews
B. Walkthroughs
C. Inspections
D. Audit

28. It is a formal process in which the presenter has to learn from the owner along with his interpretations and then present it to other participants and is known as:

A. Reviews
B. Walkthroughs
C. Inspections
D. Audit

29. Bugs that are discovered during the validation phase are costly to fix than the bugs identified in the verification phase.
A. True
B. False

30. The smallest testable part of software which could be individual programs or modules are tested during this type of testing is
A. Unit Testing
B. Integration Testing
C. System Testing
D. Acceptance Testing

31. This type of testing is to ensure that the interactions within the software modules are intact.
A. Unit Testing
B. Integration Testing
C. System Testing
D. Acceptance Testing

32. This type of testing is more comprehensive to test the components like hardware, software, external interfaces.
A. Unit Testing
B. Integration Testing
C. System Testing
D. Acceptance Testing

33. The final phase of testing where the customer himself will execute a set of test cases to evaluate and accept the product is called
A. Unit Testing
B. Integration Testing
C. System Testing
D. Acceptance Testing

34. Which of the following is not the name of White box testing?
A. Glass Box Testing
B. Structural Testing
C. Clear Box Testing
D. Conformance Testing

35. Which of the following is not a type of White Box Testing?
A. Code Coverage Testing
B. Boundary Value Analysis
C. Control Structure Testing
D. Loop Testing

36. Each segment of the code control structure is executed at least once in
A. Code Coverage Testing
B. Boundary Value Analysis
C. Control Structure Testing
D. Loop Testing

37. Number of independent paths in the basis set of a program is called as
A. Equivalence Partitions
B. Boundary Value Analysis
C. Cyclomatic Complexity
D. Flow of the program

38. Which of the following is not a type of Equivalence partition?
A. Continuous
B. Discrete
C. Boolean
D. String

39. The technique which is a logical next step after identifying the equivalence classes is
A. Equivalence Partitions
B. Boundary Value Analysis
C. Cyclomatic Complexity
D. Flow of the Program

40. The type of testing make sure that the software application meets the intended requirements is
A. Functional Testing
B. Compatibility Testing
C. State Testing
D. Regression Testing

41. The type of testing helps to determine if a product will function correctly with other hardware/software in the intended environment is
A. Functional Testing
B. Compatibility Testing
C. State Testing
D. Regression Testing

42. The type of testing helps to determine the current condition of a software application is known as

A. Functional Testing
B. Compatibility Testing
C. State Testing
D. Regression Testing

43. The type of testing involves in reuse of the existing test cases to retest the application after any change has been made
A. Functional Testing
B. Concurrency Testing
C. Usability Testing
D. Regression Testing

44. This type of testing is used to identify race conditions in an application which may occur when two or more users perform exactly the same transaction at the same instant of time.
A. Functional Testing
B. Concurrency Testing
C. Usability Testing
D. Regression Testing

45. The type of testing takes care of the comfort of the end user is called:
A. Functional Testing
B. Concurrency Testing
C. Usability Testing
D. Regression Testing

PART B (Write the answers in one or two lines)

1. Distinguish between precision and accuracy.
2. What is quality policy of an organization?
3. Define Cost of Quality (COQ) of a project.
4. What are all the categories of Cost of Quality (COQ) of a project?
5. Define cost of conformance.
6. Define cost of non-conformance.
7. What are all the types of cost of non-conformance?
8. Write notes on Plan Quality Process.
9. Define Benchmarking.
10. What is DOE?
11. Write notes on Control Charts.
12. Write notes on Brainstorming Technique.
13. What is Force Field analysis?
14. What is Quality Management Plan?
15. Define Check list.
16. Write notes on quality assurance process.
17. Write notes on Quality Control process.
18. Write the objectives of doing Software Testing.
19. Write notes on Verification Testing.
20. What are all the three techniques used for Software Verification?
21. How reviews are useful for verification?
22. How walkthroughs are useful for verification?
23. Write notes on Inspections.
24. What is Validation Testing?
25. What are all the issues of Validation Testing?
26. Write notes on Unit Testing.
27. Write notes on Integration Testing.
28. Write notes on System Testing.
29. Write notes on Acceptance Testing.
30. What is White Box Testing?
31. Write few other names of White box testing?
32. What are all the types of White Box Testing?
33. Write notes on Code Coverage Testing.
34. Write notes on Cyclomatic complexity.
35. What is Black Box Testing?
36. What are all the types of Equivalence Partitions?
37. What is Boundary Value Analysis?
38. What is Functional Testing?
39. What is Compatibility Testing?
40. What is State Testing?
41. What is Regression Testing?
42. What is Concurrency Testing?
43. What is usability testing?
44. What is the difference between Quality and Grade?

14

Software Measurement, Metrics and Estimations

14.1 Introduction

Nothing can be more true than the saying, 'which can't be measured can't be controlled'. Metrics and measurement are crucial parts for executing software projects successfully. The topic of Software Measurement and Metrics has created a lot of interest over the last two decades. In 1960s and 1970s, the main focus of IT was on product evaluation. In 1980s and 1990s, the focus shifted to process evaluation as it was understood that only an efficient process can create an effective product. In the late 1990s, the integration of measurement process with the software life-cycle began, because it was evident that to create an efficient process the measurement of 'how the process is performing' is very important. In this chapter, we will discuss the details of measurement and metrics in the software domain.

14.1 Measurement

Measurement is the process or the result by which numbers or symbols are assigned to attributes of entities in the real world to describe them into clearly defined rules. Some examples are, length, time, temperature. Each of the measurements describes some attributes of the objects in the real world.

Software measurement is a quantified attribute or characteristic of a software product or the software process. The content of software measurement is defined and governed by ISO Standards (ISO 15939–software measurement process).

Example: Number of lines of code and number of classes and interfaces provides us some idea about volume of the code as well as complexity of the developed software.

A unit of measurement (as per standard definition) is a definite magnitude of a physical quantity, defined and adopted by convention or by law, that is used as a standard for measurement of the same physical quantity.

Example: Length of a single brick = 40 centimetre.

In the above Example, length is a physical quantity, and centimetre is a unit of length that represents a definite predetermined length.

'When you can measure what you are speaking about and express it in numbers, you know something about it; but when you cannot measure, when you cannot express it in numbers, your knowledge is of a meager and unsatisfactory kind: it may be the beginning of knowledge, but you have scarcely, in your thoughts, advanced to the stage of science.'

— Lord Kelvin

14.1.1 Why Measurement is Important in Life?

Measurement is not only important for a software, it is also important in our day-to-day life (Figure 14.1). Think about some familiar scenarios that which refers how measurement plays crucial role in our day-to-day life:

1. To take proper medicine (1 spoon, 2 spoon).
2. To cook correctly (Correctly measured ingredients).
3. To fill sufficient fuel in car (How many liters?).
4. To fill sufficient water in overhead tank.
5. To pay correct money at shop/hotels.
6. To decide winning side in sports (High Goal, Score).
7. To measure performance of the students (Higher marks).
8. Performance appraisal at office.
9. To reach at office on time (Time measurement).
10. To fix office temperature (AC cool measurement).
11. Proper use of capacity (Room/Office).
12. Proper use of goods (Inventory measurement).
13. Measuring investments (ROI).
14. Measuring cash outflow/inflow.

All the above instances indicates the importance of measurement in our day-to-day life.

Figure 14.1 Measurements in Life

14.1.2 Why to Measure Software?

'You cannot control what you cannot measure.'—De Marco, 1982

'What is not measurable, make miserable.' —Galileo

Measurement is important in software development, for the following reasons (not limited).

To Understand What We Do: It helps to understand the past by measuring the product and the process already executed and, thereby, helps to compare different process and products. It also helps understand the process and the product on hand.

For Realistic Planning (Future Prediction): To plan and predict the future based on the past measurements.

For Control: To compare the actual parameter values against the planned values and take necessary actions if there is deviation.

To Improve the Process and Product: Measurement provides baseline measures for making improvements in the process and the product.

Benchmarking: Software metrics help to create benchmarks with similar kind of organizations.

Cost Reduction: Cost reduction is possible only after the measurement of the current cost.

To Define Quality Level: We need measurement on software so that we can understand and agree on product quality.

14.1.3 Characteristics of Effective Measurement Program

Proper focus on measurement at the organization level will yield the intended benefit.

To keep the measurement program effective, we should have the following basic characteristics (Figure 14.2):

1. Aligned with the organization business objectives.
2. Tied to decision making at lowest level possible.
3. Balanced metrics at all levels.
4. Focused on measuring processes.
5. Viewed as mission critical.

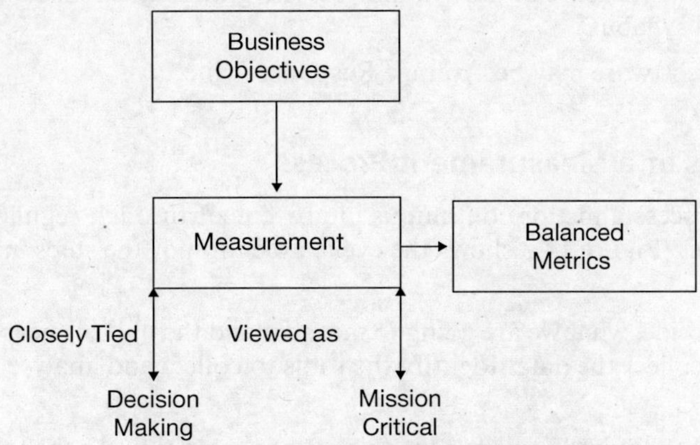

Figure 14.2 Effective Measurement

Discussion Points

1. Discuss characteristics of effective measurement program in detail with known examples (in a student life at college).
2. Discuss characteristics of effective measurement program in detail with known examples (in a student life in the society).

14.1.4 Types of Measure

Direct Measures
It is measured directly in terms of the observed attribute (usually by counting). For example, length of source-code written, time taken for a process execution, number of defects discovered in a particular phase of the project.

Indirect Measures
It is calculated from different direct and indirect measures.

Example 1: Module defect density = Number of defects discovered/Length of source.
Example 2: Temperature (usually derived from the length of a liquid column).

True Performance Measures
Customers use 'true' performance measures. True performance measures are used by customers to measure the performance of the products they use, in their own language as per their own view.

Example 1: A true measure of a book may be 'easy to read'.
Example 2: A true measure of software may be 'fast response'.

True performance measures typically vary from customer to customer. The parameter and the calculation logic also changes form the customer to customer.

Substitute Performance Measures
Producers use 'substitute' performance measures. Substitute measures are quantifiable units.

Example: A substitute measure of a book may be 'less grammatical mistakes, less number of pages, covering full syllabus'.

A true measure of software may be 'Average Response Time'.

14.1.5 Activities of a Measurement Process

A measurement process aims for continuous improvement through regular checking of the current performance. Figure 14.3 shows the cyclic execution of the steps in measurement.

Plan
First, we need to decide, what we are going to measure and the unit of measurement. Identify the mechanism to collect the data. Identify the tools to collect and analyse the metrics.

Collect
Accumulate the data required to derive the formulated metrics using the tool, if any.

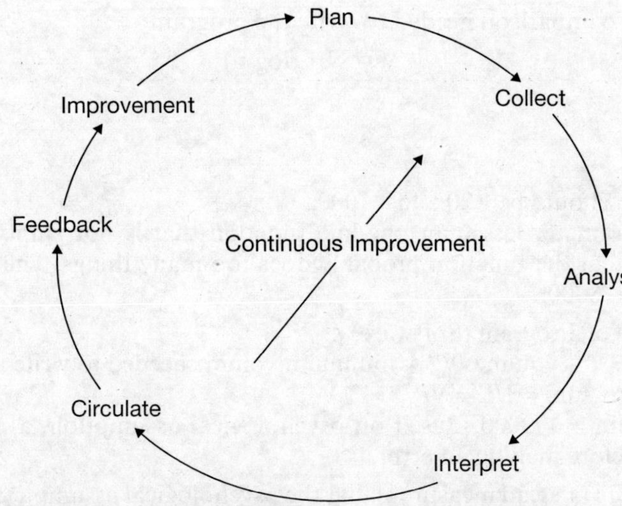

Figure 14.3 Activities of a Measurement Process

Analyse

The computation of metrics and also the application of tools to analyse the metrics happen over here. This step combines various metrics data. It also use the filtration of metrics based on the plan. It is better to automate the data collection and analyse process.

Interpret

Actual interpretation of the metrics used to give meaningful thoughts and also steps or actions to be taken based on the analysed metrics happens over here. Interpretative guidelines and recommendations should be established well ahead of each metrics, so that interpretation takes place methodologically. Target dates should be defined against each action points.

Circulate

Interpretation along with the steps or actions is passed onto the software development team for taking necessary actions as defined.

Feedback

Get feedback from the team to gain insight into the effectiveness of the measurement/metrics along with the effectiveness of the action taken to produce the desired results.

Improvement

Continuous improvement of the measurement process based on the feedback received by incorporating changes in the process and the metrics, if required.

14.1.6 Halstead Measure

Maurice Halstead of Purdue University attempted to tie physical, syntactical objects and psychological measurements together with a set of definitions:

n_1 = total number of unique operators in a program (software)
n_2 = total number of unique operands in a program (software)
N_1 = total number of occurrences of the operators
N_2 = total number of occurrences of the operands

Volume (V) = mental comparison needed to write the program

$$V = N * (\log_2 n)$$

Where,

$N = N_1 + N_2$

$n = n_1 + n_2$

Volume of a function should be >20 and <1000.

Volume of a parameter less than one-line function that is not empty is about 20. A volume >1000, tells that the function probably does too many things. The volume of a file should be >100 and < 8000.

Level (L) = Level of Program (Software)

L = V*/V (where, V = volume; V* = minimum volume needed to write the program)

Difficulty of a program = 1/L = V/V*

Faults of program = V/3000. Based on psychological assumption, a person can make 3000 decisions before making an error.

The problem with Halstead measure is that the psychological assumptions along with the projections of numbers have been subject to dispute.

14.1.7 Cyclomatic Measure

This measure was introduced by McCabe to look at the number of unique paths for testing. Initially, it was based on graph theory, but can also be attained by:

M = Number of binary decisions + 1

There have been numerous studies that looked for correlations between cyclomatic complexity and defect rate. Here, results have been much more positive than the Halstead measure.

14.2 Metrics

Metric is a standard of measurement. A metric indicates the nature or strength of an attribute, usually by means of a number, often in conjunction with a unit. When we state 40 centimetre (in the above example), it actually means 40 times of the definite pre-determined length called '1 centimetre'. Software metric relates individual measures in a meaningful way.

In Figure 14.4, a person is mapped to height. When we state 182 centimetre, it actually mean 182 times the definite predetermined length called '1 centimetre'.

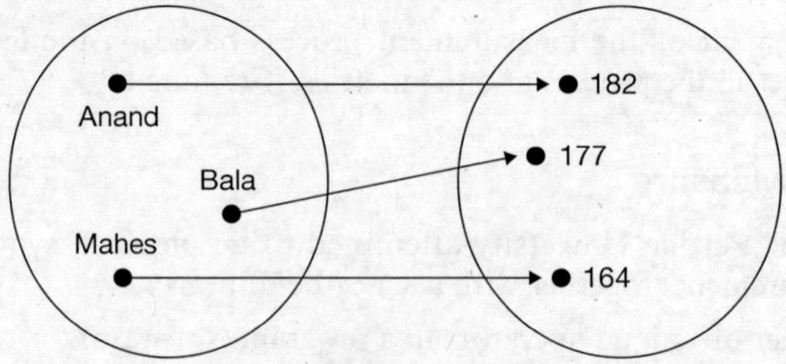

Figure 14.4 Measure Mapping Height Attribute of a Person on a Number Representing Height in Centimetre

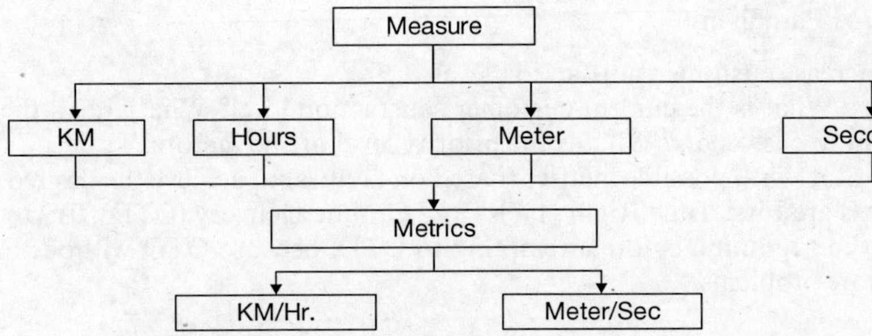

Figure 14.5 Relationship Between Measure and Metrics

Software metric relates individual measures of software(s) in a meaningful (as discussed about metrics in day-to-day life).

Software metrics are quantifiable measures that could be used to measure characteristics of a software system (product) or the software development process, through which a software is developed. Figure 14.5 shows how metrics and measurement are related.

Measurement and metrics are required for effective management. Managers need quantifiable information (metrics) to take appropriate action.

'*A quantitative measure of the degree to which a system, component or process possesses a given attribute*'

—IEEE Standard Glossary

14.2.1 Goal-Question-Metric Paradigm of Metrics

The Goal-Question-Metric (GQM) identifies the meaningful metrics of a product by following three important steps (Figure 14.6). These steps are:

1. Establish the measurement goal that is specific to the process or product under study.
2. Define a set of questions that are appropriate and which are necessary in order to achieve the specified goal identified in Step 1.
3. Identify metrics that help answering the questions identified in Step 2.

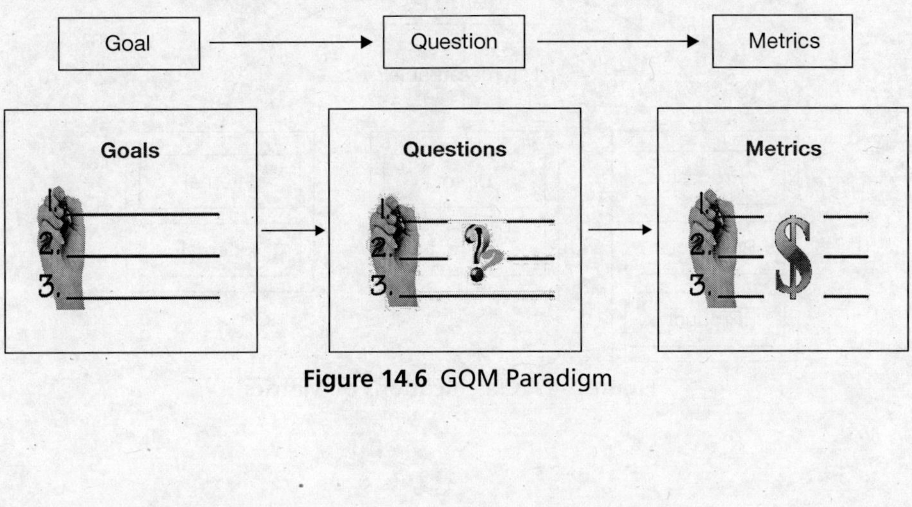

Figure 14.6 GQM Paradigm

Examples for GQM Paradigm

1. *Goals:* Increase customer satisfaction level.
2. *Questions:* What is the current customer satisfaction level? What are all the factors important to customers? What is the priority level of the factors?
3. *Metrics:* Start with possible metrics (based on factors) to achieve the desired level. If the factors are First Time Right (FTR) and Ontime Delivery (OTD). Try to achieve FTR at the beginning before attempting to OTD, because OTD without FTR will create more problems.

14.2.2 Black Box and White Box Metrics

Metrics are also classified as Black Box Metrics and White Box Metrics.

If the inside and outside logic of a metrics (how the metric is calculated) is not known, then it is called 'Black Box Metric'. Example: Function Point (FP) metrics (where the inside logic is not known).

If the inside and outside logic of a metrics (how the metric is calculated) is clearly known, then it is called White Box Metric. Example: Lines of Code (LOC) (where the inside and outside logic is clearly known).

14.2.3 Types of Software Metrics

Matrices are classified into the following categories (Figure 14.7).

Product Metrics: Metrics related to products. (LOC)

Process Metrics: Metrics related to process of development (length of the iteration).

Resources Metrics: Metrics related to the usage of personnel and resources along with their properties (developer productivity).

External Metrics: Measured with respect to environment/context (productivity, usability).

Internal Metrics: Not dependent on the environment/context (LOC).

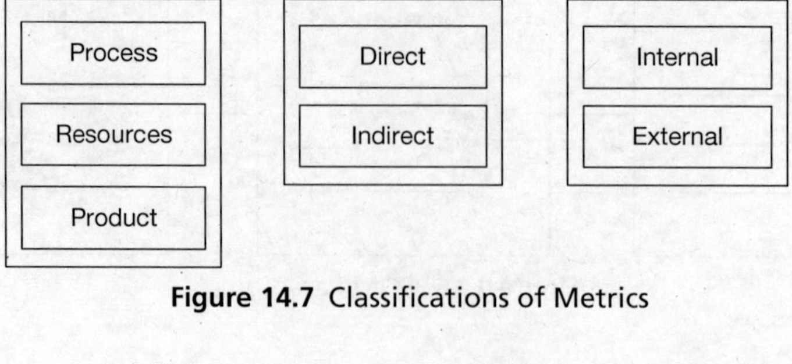

Figure 14.7 Classifications of Metrics

Direct Metrics: Directly Measurable (LOC, FP).

Indirect Metrics: Not measurable directly (code quality, defect density, temperature).

14.2.3.1 Product Metrics

Metrics that are related to the software product developed is called 'product metrics' (Figure 14.8). They quantify the characteristics of the product being developed.

Example: Size of the product (lines of code), complexity of a product, test metrics (product-related) and quality metrics of a product. It focuses on the quality of the deliverables.

McCall's Quality Factors

McCall, Richards, and Walters group the quality factors of a product into three categories which are focused on three aspects of a software product (Product Operation, Product Orientation, and Product Transition), shown in Figure 14.8. The three categories are:

1. **Product Operation:** It focuses on operational characteristics of a product (correctness, reliability, usability, integrity and efficiency)
2. **Product Revision:** It focuses on the revision characteristics of a product when undergoes change (maintainability, flexibility and testability)
3. **Product Transition:** It focuses on the product adaptability to the new environments (portability, reusability, interoperability)

1. Product Operation

Correctness: The extent to which a software (product) meets its specifications (requirement documentation) is called 'correctness'. If correctness is 100%, then it signifies that the product exactly meets the requirement.

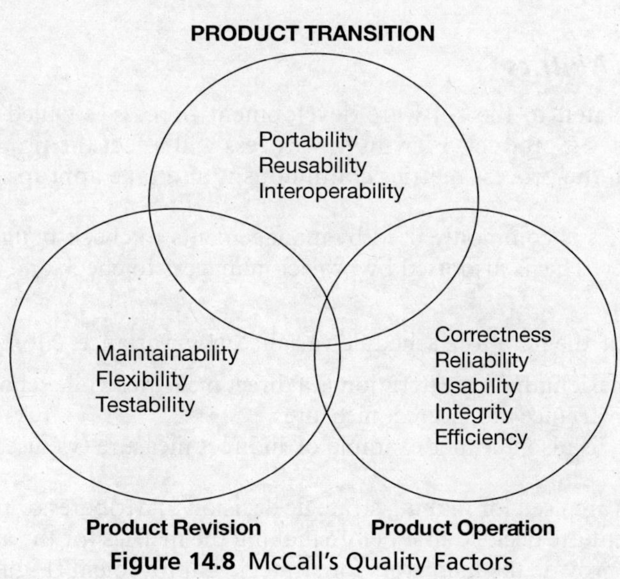

Figure 14.8 McCall's Quality Factors

Reliability: The extent to which a software (product) perform its intended function is called 'reliability'. If the reliability is 100%, then it means it exactly does the intended function.

Usability: Usability is the ease of use and learn-ability of a software (product).

Integrity: Integrity indicates how a software (product) is protected from unauthorized usage (unauthorized user accessing the product, user accessing unauthorized data).

Efficiency: The effort, time, cost required to produce the desired output in a product. It is the ability to produce specific outcome effectively with minimum input.

2. **Product Revision**

   When a product undergoes change, the main focus remains on the revision characteristics of it. These are maintainability, flexibility and testability.

   Maintainability: The effort required to find out correct mistakes in a product.

   Flexibility: The effort required to modify a part of software (product).

   Testability: The effort required to test software (product) to ensure that it works properly and does the intended purpose.

3. **Product Transition**

   This focuses on the product adaptability to new environments and the characteristics that are measured, that is portability, reusability and interoperability.

   Portability: The effort required to transfer a software (product) from one environment (hardware) to another.

   Reusability: The extent to which part of a product or the full product can be used in making a new software (product).

   Interoperability: The extent to which a product can be coupled with another product.

14.2.3.2 Process Metrics

Metrics that are related to the software development process is called 'process metrics'. Set of process creates a product. Flaw in the process will affect the product and, hence, it is required to watch the process metrics continuously, and take appropriate action at right time.

A process metrics is commonly used by managements to check budgets and office procedures for efficiency. This is also used by project managers to check and control projects in efficient manner.

Examples: Length of the iteration, schedule variance, cost variance, effort variance.

In the above example, length of the iteration is a direct measure, while schedule variance, cost variance and effort variance are indirect measures.

Process stability is also another example of indirect measure (we use different formulas to derive it).

Process metrics are used for making strategic decisions. Attributes or properties of a process, for improvement are decided first before making the metrics for the attributes. Then the metrics are used to provide the indicators for strategic improvement (Figure 14.9).

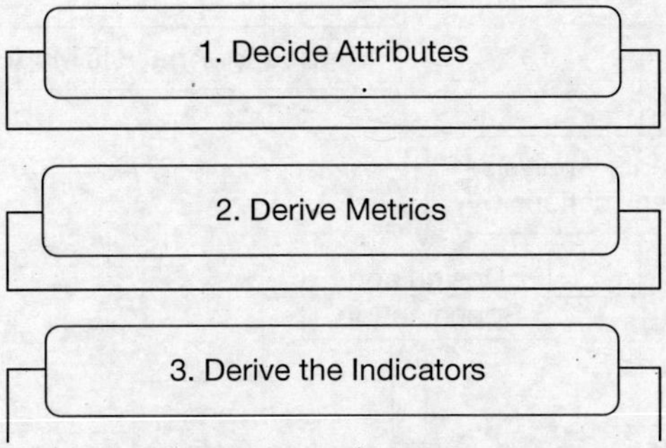

Figure 14.9 Process Metrics Steps

Process effectiveness is measured based on the outcome of the process. These are work products delivered, human effort expended, calendar time expended, conformance to the schedule, time and effort to complete each generic activities.

14.2.3.3 Resource Metrics

Metrics related to the resources (including human resources) are called 'resource metrics'.

Example 1:

- Effort per function point per resource.
- Cost per function point per resource.
- Defects per function point per resource.

The aforementioned examples are the indirect measures. On the other hand, the costs for human resource is a direct measure.

Example 2:

Resource metrics are usually used for:

1. Project management purpose.
2. Financial purpose.
3. HR management purpose.

Project Manager: To complete a work on time, Kumar needs to spend extra two hours per day.
Finance: Putting Kumar into the new project will cost $5 per function point.
HR Management: On an average, Kumar produce 10 defects per day.

14.2.4 Metrics for the Analysis Model

Requirement analysis phase (Figure 14.10) happens after collecting the requirments from the customer and, also, requirement-related metrics are part of this phase of the project. From the requirments, we can state:

1. How many functionalities the system will deliver? —Functionality delivered.
2. What is the size of the system to be developed? —Size of the system to be developed.
3. What is the quality level of the requirement? —Quality of the requirement (level of completeness).

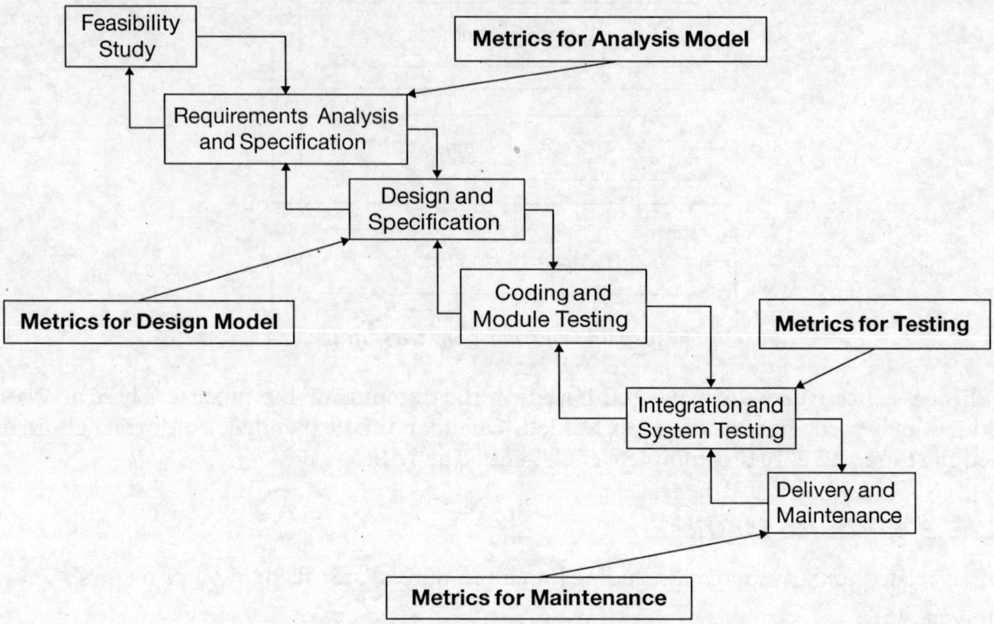

Figure 14.10 Metrics Appliciability at SDLC Stages

14.2.5 Metrics for the Design Model

Design phase (Figure 14.10) happens after the requirement analysis phase. The metrics we use for the design model are:

Architectural Metrics: Provide an indication of the quality of the architectural design.

Component-level metrics: Measure the complexity of software components and other characteristics that have a bearing on quality.

Interface Design Metrics: Focus primarily on usability.

Specialized Object-oriented Design Metrics: Measure characteristics of classes their communication, and collaboration characteristics (Refer to next chapter on object-oriented design metrics).

14.2.6 Metrics for Testing

Testing phase (Figure 14.10) happens after the coding phase. The metrics we use during testing phase are:

- *Defect-related metrics*
  - Focus on defects (*i.e.*, bugs) found, rather than on the tests themselves.
- *Testing effectiveness metrics*
  - Provide a real-time indication of the effectiveness of tests that have been conducted.

- *In-process metrics*
  - Process-related metrics that can be determined as testing is conducted.
- *Statement and branch coverage metrics*
  - Lead to the design of test cases that provide program coverage.

Metrics for Testing (process related)

Examples for testing-related metrics are:

1. Defect removal effectiveness (DRE)
2. Response time for fixing
3. Productivity metrics

1. Defect Removal Effectiveness

The metric can be calculated for the entire development process, for each phase or before code integration as given below:

DRE = Metrics for design model/Metrics for analysis model

The higher the value, the more effective the development process and fewer defects escaping to next phase or the field.

Phase defect removal effectiveness and related metrics are useful for quality management and planning. Measurements that indicate clearly which phase of the process needs improvement and should be focused on. Using the right tools, analysis can be done for the entire project as well as for local areas.

Points to Remember

Every organization set some benchmark for the important metrics. DRE is one of them. The project team tries to make sure that the DRE value is at least minimum the benchmark value or better than it.

2. Response Time for Fixing (Metrics for Testing)

Most organizations have established guidelines on the time limit within which the fixes should be available for the reported defects. Severe problems are usually fixed as soon as possible. The less severe defects more relaxed time. The fix response time metric is usually calculated for all problems as follows:

Mean time of all problems from open to closed. Sometimes, there are less severe problems that customers ignore, so the problem remains open for a long time which are given below:

- Distortion of mean time.
- In these cases, medians should be used instead of mean time values.

Idea: Short time in fix process leads to customer satisfaction and determines how good the process is in this field.

14.2.7 Metrics for Maintenance

Software Maturity Index (SMI): It provides an indication of the stability of a software product based on changes that occur for each release.

SMI = (Total Modules – Changed Modules)/Total Modules

Software maturity index will go down if the changes occur in higher number of modules.

Changed modules includes, number of added module + number of changed module + number of deleted modules.

The product is stable when SMI is nearby 1. The average time to produce a release can be proportional to SMI. When SMI is near zero, it will take more time to deliver the changes.

Figure 14.10 shows what metrics is applicable to which software development life-cycle (SDLC) stage of the software development.

14.2.8 Productivity Metrics

Software productivity is a complex subject concerning many factors (resources, quality, time). Metrics like LOC/hour, FP/person-month, hours/class and average person-days/class (in object metrics), etc. Usually, number of units of output per unit of effort can be used to increase development by focusing on certain not-efficient phases – usually problematic in other sense, too.

Law of Diminishing Returns: Just by adding more resources we cannot finish a project early. Addition of more resources may increase overall output at the beginning, but will eventually decrease individual productivity. Engaging three times more people to the same task may not help the task to be finished three times faster.

14.2.9 Characteristics of a Good Metrics

If we do not follow the correct metrics, then it will be the 'Consistent Reliable LIER' that we need to remember as the characteristics of the metrics.

Consistent – *required*
Reliable – *required*
Linear – *nice, but not necessary*
Independent – *required*
Easy to use – *nice, but not necessary*
Repeatable – *required*

Consistent metric means it is comparable across systems indicating the meaning and the logics of measurement and is consistent across various systems. If it is inconsistent, it is impossible to compare across systems.

Reliability of a metrics is the ability to perform and maintain its functions in routine as well as unexpected circumstances.

Linear performance of metrics is the ability to maintain its linear level. For example, if metric increases two times, then the performance also increases two times.

Independency of a metric indicates that it is not dependent on external pressure or influence of other metrics. For example, pressure to change the meaning of a metric/pressure to change the definition of a metric/pressure to influence the definition of a metric.

Easy to use character of a metric indicates that the metric should always be easy to use. No one will use if it is hard.

Repeatability is the important characteristics of metrics. Same value is measured each time when an experiment is performed.

14.2.10 Measurement and Metrics Indicators

Indicators are the metrics or combination of metrics that provides insight into the software process, project, or product itself which helps taking a decision. Earned value metrics is one such example.

Earned Value Management

It is a method of measuring project performance and any professional project manager/scrum master should know how to calculate this for better control on the project. It is calculated by comparing planned amount of work with the actually accomplished. It is practiced to determine if cost and schedule performance are going as per the plan. We will be discussing more about earned value in the upcoming chapters.

Points to Remember

It is important for the project team to look out for indicators throughout the project life-cycle. These provide insight into the problems and improvement areas.

14.3 Kaner and Bond's Evaluation Framework for Metrics

The researchers Kaner and Bond developed a general framework for evaluating a metric. They laid out 10 points to check for, on the basis of the IEEE software metric criteria. Figure 14.11 provides an explanation of this framework.

1. What is the purpose of the measure? It helps us to understand the stakes in making the measurement so that we know how much to invest for ensuring its validity.
2. What is the scope of the measure? Does it impact one team or developer or multiple parts of a large project? The authors point out that as the scope broadens so does the number of confounding variables to the system.

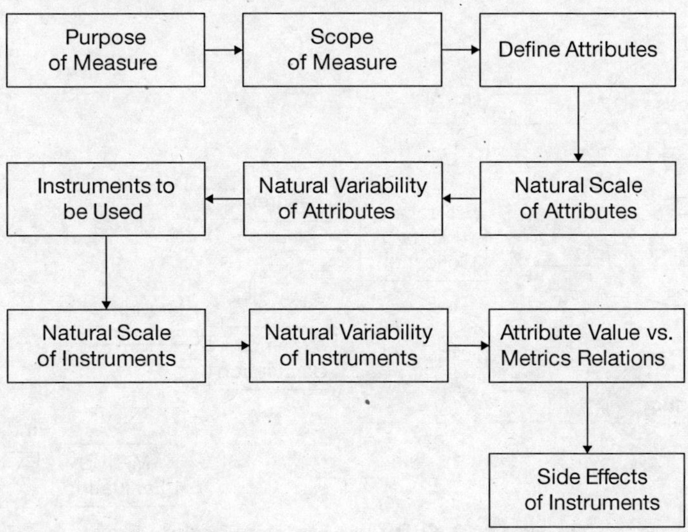

Figure 14.11 Kaner and Bond's Evaluation Framework for Metrics

3. What attribute of the software is being measured?
4. What is the natural scale of the attribute we are trying to measure?
5. What is the natural variability of the attribute? What numbers do you expect to see?
6. What measuring instrument do we use to perform the measurement?
7. What is the natural scale for this metric?
8. What is the natural variability of readings from this instrument? Are small differences to be expected or does even the slightest change mean that a huge improvement has been reached?
9. What is the relationship of the attribute to the metric value? It makes sure that we are measuring the right thing.
10. What are the natural and foreseeable side effects of using this instrument? If a metric is used, will the effects of writing code that makes the metric better be what we want them to be? The authors point out that an improvement in the metric should mean an equal increase in code quality too, or else there may be something the metric isn't showing you.

14.4 Software Metrics Baseline Steps

In order to baseline the metrics, we analyse the data (measures, metrics and indicators) from various similar-natured processes, projects and products. It can be filleted out or modified before baselining the metrics for the current project. The data is to be collected from as many similar projects as possible with consistent measures. After data collection, the metrics are computed and baseline is established (Figure 14.12).

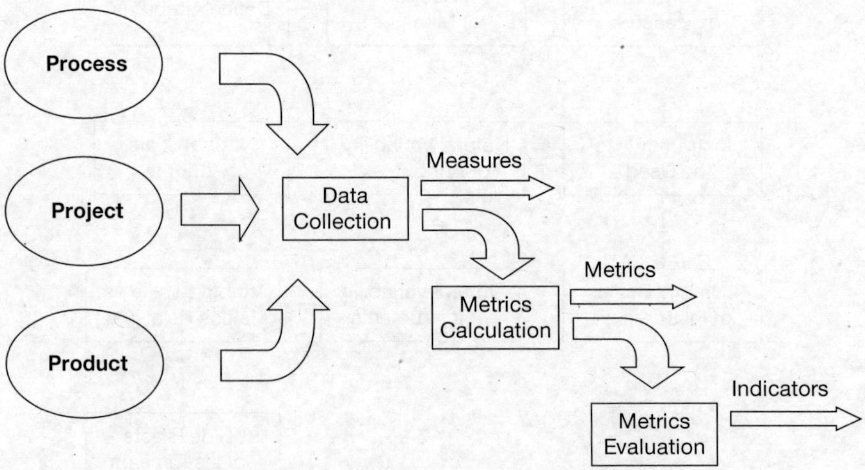

Figure 14.12 Software Metrics Baseline Steps

14.5 Other Concepts

14.5.1 S-Curve

A simple technique for tracking project costs is to develop a periodical cumulative budget spend plan and, then, track actual costs against the plan. The slope of the graph indicates the project expenditure rate, sometimes called the 'burn rate.' (Cost Burn up Graph)

By plotting actual costs against the budget planned, you can see differences between actual spending and the plan (Figure 14.13).

14.5.2 Learning Curve

Learning curve theory indicates that because of learning, people will start doing the work efficiently and, thereby, overall cost will reduce. As time moves on, total costs will increase; but the cost per unit will drop, because repetition increases efficiency of the work involved in producing the output.

$$Y_x = K_x^{\log_2 b}$$

Where,

K = the number of direct work hours to produce the first unit.
Y_x = the number of direct work hours to produce the x-th unit.
x = the number of units produced.
b = the learning percentage.

The above is also applicable for Agile Projects, and so the customer expects the team to improve the productivity thereby delivering more velocity as the iteration cycle progresses.

Discussion Points

Discuss how learning curve affects the estimations?

Discuss the various metrics associated with a college student?

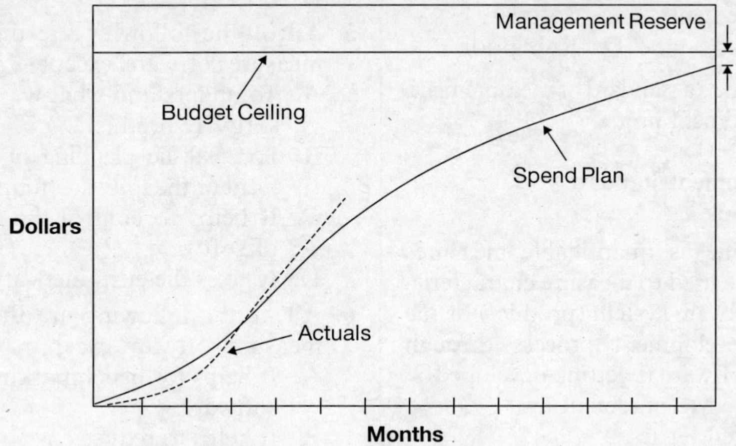

Figure 14.13 S-curve

SUMMARY

This chapter gives an introduction to various terms related to measurement, metrics, and estimations. Once the estimation and planning part is complete for a project, the metrics come handy for tracking execution and progress of the project. In this chapter, we discussed the concepts of measurement, metrics, types of software metrics, Halstead metrics, Kaner and Bond's evaluation framework for metrics, and Cyclomatic measure.

- Measurement is the process or the result by which numbers or symbols are assigned to attributes of entities in the real world to describe them following clearly defined rules. Some examples are, length, time, and temperature. Measurement is not only important for a software, it is important in our day-to-day life also. Maurice Halstead of Purdue University attempted to tie physical, syntactical objects and psychological measurements together with a set of definitions. Cyclomatic measure was introduced by McCabe to look at the number of unique paths for testing.
- Metric is a standard of measurement. A metric indicates the nature and strength of an attribute, usually by means of a number, often in conjunction with a unit. GQM Paradigm of metrics stands for Goal, Question and Metric).
- We also discussed various types of software metrics in this chapter. If we do not follow the correct metrics, then it will be the 'Consistent Reliable LIER'. This is what we need to remember as the characteristics of the metrics.
- Kaner and Bond's evaluation framework for metrics discussed in detail.

EXERCISES

PART A (Objective-type Questions)

1. This is defined as the process or the result by which numbers or symbols are assigned to attributes of entities in the real world in such a way as to describe them to clearly defined rule is
   A. Measurement C. Software
   B. Metrics D. Rule Book
2. This is defined as a standard of measurement.
   A. Measurement unit
   B. Metrics
   C. Measurement standard
   D. Rule Book
3. This is define as quantifiable measures that could be used to measure characteristics of a software system (product) or the software development process through which the software is getting developed.
   A. Software Measurement unit
   B. Software Metrics
   C. Software Measurement standard
   D. Rule Book
4. This is a quantified attribute of a characteristic of a software product or the software process.
   A. Software Measurement
   B. Software Metrics
   C. Software Measurement standard
   D. Rule Book
5. All of the following are the reasons to measure software, except
   A. To understand what we do inside the software product.
   B. For realistic planning of the development of the software (future prediction).
   C. It helps to control the development of software.
   D. It gives the customer satisfaction
6. All of the following are the reasons to measure software, except
   A. It helps for benchmarking with other software.
   B. It helps to reduce cost.
   C. It helps to define quality level.
   D. It gives the customer satisfaction.

7. Following are the characteristics of effective measurement program, except
   A. It is to be aligned with the organization business objectives.
   B. Tied to decision making at lowest level possible.
   C. Balanced metrics at all levels available.
   D. It should be easy and simple to measure.
8. Following are the types of measure, except
   A. Personal Measure
   B. True Performance Measures
   C. Substitute Performance Measures
   D. Indirect Measures
9. Module Defect Density = Number of defects discovered/Length of source is an example of which type of measure?
   A. Direct Measure
   B. True Performance Measures
   C. Substitute Performance Measures
   D. Indirect Measures
10. Who uses true performance measures?
    A. Software Engineers
    B. Producers
    C. Customers
    D. Testers
11. A measure of 'Fast Response' of software is an example of
    A. Direct Measure
    B. True Performance Measures
    C. Substitute Performance Measures
    D. Indirect Measures
12. Who uses substitute performance measures?
    A. Software Engineers
    B. Producers
    C. Customers
    D. Testers
13. If the inside and outside logic of a metrics (how the metric is calculated) is not known, then it is called
    A. Black Box Metrics
    B. White Box Metrics
    C. Brown Box Metrics
    D. Gray Box Metrics
14. If the inside and outside logic of a metrics (how the metric is calculated) is clearly known, then it is called
    A. Black Box Metrics
    B. White Box Metrics
    C. Brown Box Metrics
    D. Gray Box Metrics
15. Which measure was introduced by McCabe to look at the number of unique paths for testing?
    A. Cyclone Measure
    B. Cyclomatic Measure
    C. McCabe Measure
    D. McCabe Unique Path Measure
16. All of the following are examples of product revision metrics, except
    A. Maintainability C. Flexibility
    B. Portability D. Testability
17. The effort required to modify a part of software is called
    A. Maintainability C. Flexibility
    B. Portability D. Testability
18. The effort required to determine and correct mistakes in a product is called
    A. Maintainability C. Flexibility
    B. Portability D. Testability
19. All of the following are examples of product transition metrics, except
    A. Maintainability
    B. Portability
    C. Reusability
    D. Interoperability
20. The effort required to transfer the software product from one environment to another is referred as
    A. Maintainability
    B. Portability
    C. Reusability
    D. Interoperability
21. The extent to which a product can be coupled with another product is referred as
    A. Maintainability C. Reusability
    B. Portability D. Interoperability
22. Which of the following activities of a measurement process are in order?
    A. Plan, Collect, Analyse, Interpret, Circulate, Feedback, Improvement
    B. Collect, Plan, Analyse, Interpret, Circulate, Feedback, Improvement

C. Plan, Collect, Analyse, Circulate, Interpret, Feedback, Improvement
D. Plan, Collect, Analyse, Interpret, Circulate, Improvement, Feedback

23. Which of the following measure attempted to tie physical, syntactical objects and psychological measurements together with a set of definitions?
A. Halstead Measure
B. Cyclomatic Measure
C. McCabe Measure
D. McCabe Unique Path measure

24. In GQM Paradigm, Q stands for
A. Quantitative C. Quality
B. Qualitative D. Question

25. In GQM Paradigm, M stands for?
A. Metrics
C. Maintainability
B. Measures
D. Mute

26. In GQM Paradigm, G stands for
A. Goat C. Goal
B. Get D. Government

27. McCall's Quality factors concentrate on the following aspects of a product, except
A. Product Operation
B. Product Orientation
C. Product Transition
D. Product Support

28. All of the following are examples of operational aspects of a product, except
A. Correctness C. Portability
B. Reliability D. Usability

29. All of the following are examples of revisional characteristics of a product, except
A. Correctness
B. Testability
C. Maintainability
D. Flexibility

30. All of the following are examples of adaptability characteristics of a product, except
A. Portability
C. Maintainability
B. Reusability
D. Interoperability

31. The extent to which software product perform its intended function is called
A. Integrity C. Maintainability
B. Reusability D. Reliability

32. Which of the following indicates how software product is protected from unauthorized usage?
A. Integrity C. Maintainability
B. Reusability D. Reliability

PART B (Write the answers in one or two lines)

1. Define the term 'measurement'.

2. Define the term 'software measurement'.

3. Define the term 'unit of measurement'.

4. Why do we measure software?

5. Name the characteristics of effective measurement program?

6. Name the various types of measure.

7. What is direct measures?

8. What is indirect measures?

9. What is true performance measures?

10. What is substitute performance measures?

11. Name the various activities of a measurement process.

12. Define the term 'metrics'.

13. Define software metrics.

14. Draw a simple diagram depicting the relationship between measure and metrics.

15. What is Black Box Metrics?

16. What is White Box Metrics?

17. Define Cyclomatic measure.

18. Write notes on productivity metrics.

19. Write notes on product revision and its metrics.

20. Write notes on product transition and its metrics.

21. What are all the metrics that are applicable to the analysis phase of a project?

15

Lines of Code, Function Point and Object-oriented Metrics

15.1 Introduction

There are different types of metrics and measurement techniques that software project managers often use while executing projects. More complex a project, it becomes more important that correct metrics and measurements are in place to aid the project managers and the project team, for remaining on-course during the entire project duration. The metrics and measures used in the software domain are quite different from that in traditional industries. The ways how the robust size or complexity of a software system is depicted are quite different from how it is done in other industries like civil or manufacturing, etc. In this chapter, we will discuss the various types of measurements and metrics in softwares.

15.1 Lines of Code

Lines of Code (LOC) specifically include all lines containing program headers, declarations, and executable and non-executable codes in a software program. Source Lines of Code (SLOC) is a software metric that is used to measure the size of a software program by just counting the number of lines in the source code of the program. The SLOC is used to predict (approximate) the efforts required to write the code and is also used to estimate the maintainability hours after a code is written.

15.1.1 Types of SLOC Measures

Figure 15.1 depicts the following SLOC types:

1. Physical SLOC (PLOC)
2. Logical SLOC (LLOC)
3. Comment SLOC (CLOC)
4. Reused SLOC (RLOC)

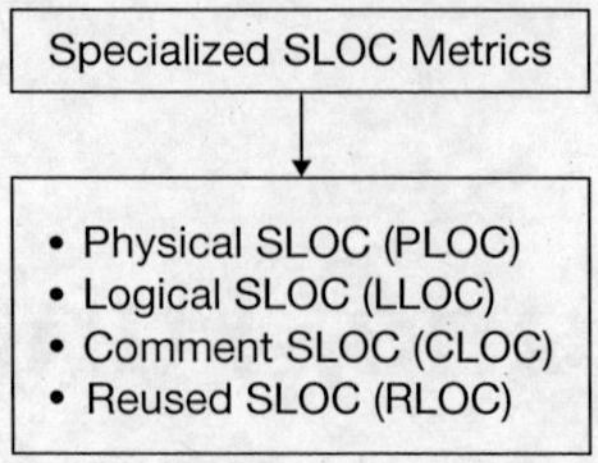

Figure 15.1 Specialized SLOC Metrics

Physical SLOC is a count of lines in the text of the physical source code which includes comment lines, declarations, and blank lines.

Logical SLOC is a count of lines of the only 'executable statements'. Lines of the comments, declarations and blank lines are not counted for this purpose. This definition varies with computer language, because the meaning of the 'executable statements' varies across computer language. The LLOC is widely used concepts for various LOC estimations.

Comment LOC is count of lines consisting of only the comments in the source code. Codes written without any comments are considered as poor code. Good codes are tending to have appropriate comments.

Reusable Line of Code (RLOC) is the count of lines reused in the particular code which will not be counted for calculating the efforts. People encouraged for writing and using the reusable code which saves lot of efforts during the development process.

Points to Remember

Physical SLOC is a count of lines in the text of the physical source code including comment lines, declarations, and blank lines. Logical SLOC is count of lines of the only executable 'statements'. Lines of the comments, declarations and blank lines are not counted for this purpose.

Example

Following are some lines of a C program.

```
/* Beginning of the for Loop */
for (i = 50; i < 0; i – = 1)
{
printf('Hai Students');
}
/* End of the for Loop */
```

Physical SLOC is represented by PLOC
Logical SLOC is represented by LLOC
Comment SLOC is represented by CLOC

How many lines of code are there in the above program?
How many executable lines of code are there in the above program?
How many comments lines of code are there in the above program?

PLOC = 6 (totally there are 6 lines – Line 1 to 6)
LLOC = 2 (totally there are 2 executable lines – Line 2 and 4)
CLOC = 2 (totally there are 2 comments line – Line 1 and 6)

FORTRAN and Assembler are line-oriented languages in which the lines of code concepts are used effectively.

Various widely used LOC measurements along with their meaning are given in Table Table 15.1.

Table 15.1 LOC Measurement and Meanings

Measurement	Meaning
KLOC	1,000 lines of code
KDLOC	1,000 delivered lines of code
KSLOC	1,000 source lines of code
MLOC	1,000,000 lines of code
GLOC	1,000,000,000 lines of code

15.1.2 Advantages of Line of Code Measurements

1. Easy to learn
2. Easy to measure (Scope of automated counting)
3. Easy to report and check
4. Complex formulas are not used
5. Repeatability is possible
6. Measurements are easily automatable

Since it is easy to calculate, easy to measure and easy to report (Figure 15.2), even juniors can use LOC for estimation purpose.

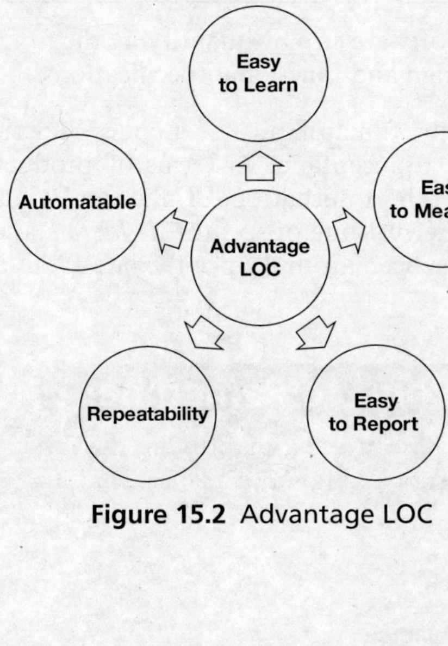

Figure 15.2 Advantage LOC

15.1.3 Drawbacks of the Line of Code Measure

1. There is no standard definition of LOC. There are different versions of measurements.
2. Functionality of the code not taken into consideration for calculation. This is the big drawback of LOC.
3. Skilled coders can develop the same code with less lines (as per LOC, they are considered as less productive, but it is not correct).
4. Developers who produces more lines does not mean that they are productive.
5. Complexity of codes not taken into consideration (complex codes may be written in few lines, but it takes time).
6. LOC is non-comparable across languages (Java program LOC is not comparable with C language LOC).
7. Estimates, based on lines of code, can adversely go wrong, because LOC is not a direct measure of functionality or productivity.
8. If LOC is used for measurements, people may add junk code j to increase LOC which may not add any value to anybody.
9. Low utility as sizing measure.

Constructive Cost Model (COCOMO) is a series of models written by Barry Boehm. This model uses SLOC as an input parameter. We will be discussing this model (COCOMO) in detail later in this chapter.

> *'Measuring software productivity by lines of code is like measuring progress on an airplane by how much it weighs.'*
>
> —Bill Gates

LOC should not be used to measure software productivity.

15.2 Function Point Count

Function Points (FP) measure software size by quantifying the functionality provided to the users based solely on logical design and functional specifications.

Note: LOC does not consider the functionality of a code. Function points are often preferred over SLOC. It has gained acceptance in terms of productivity (for example, FP/year) and quality (defects/FP). The International Function Point Users Group (IFPUG) counting practices committee (www.ifpug.org) is the *de facto* standard for counting methods. Function point analysis has been around since the late 1970s and is still used by many organizations.

Point to Remember

Function points measure software size by quantifying the functionality provided to the user based solely on logical design and functional specifications.

15.2.1 Function Point Analysis

Function Point Analysis (FPA) is a method of quantifying size and complexity of a software system in terms of the functions that the system delivers to the users. Function point analysis is independent of the computer language, development methodology, technology or capability of the project team used for developing an application.

15.2.2 Function Point History

1. It was developed by Allan Albrecht in the late 1970s while working at IBM.
2. The function point counting manual was produced by IBM's GUIDE organization in the early 1980s.
3. The International Function Point Users Group (IFPUG) was founded in the late 1980s and produced its own counting practices manual.
4. In 1994, IFPUG produced Release 4.0 of its counting practices manual.
5. The Function Point Counting Practices Manual 4.1 was released in 1999.

15.2.3 Objectives of Function Point Counting

Following are the objectives of function point counting.

1. It measures functionality that the user requests and receives (which is the not part of LOC).
2. It is simple enough to minimize the overhead of the measurement process.
3. It is a consistent measure among various projects and organizations.

15.2.4 The Function Point Estimation Process Steps

In FP, only logical files are internal, because it is internal to the system. Input is called 'external input', since the input is coming external to the system. Output is called 'external output'. Inquiries are called 'external queries'. Interface files are called 'external interface file' (Figure 15.3).

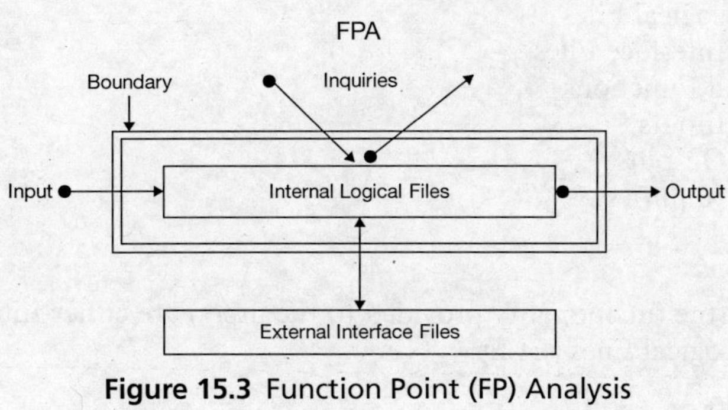

Figure 15.3 Function Point (FP) Analysis

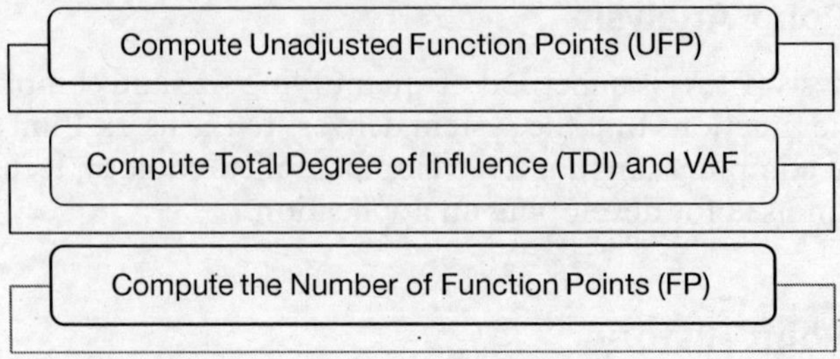

Figure 15.4 Function Point (FP) Process Steps

Internal logical files and external interface files are called 'data functions'. Others (External inputs, External outputs, External Inquiries) are called 'transactional functions'. These are as follows:

- Data Functions
  - Internal Logical Files
  - External Interface Files
- Transactional Functions
  - External Inputs
  - External Outputs
  - External Inquiries

Process Steps

Step 1: Compute Unadjusted Function Points (UFP).
Step 2: Compute Total Degree of Influence (TDI) and Value Adjustment Factor (VAF).
Step 3: Compute the number of Function Points (FP).

15.2.4.1 Step 1: Compute Unadjusted Function Point Count

The UFP reflects the specific countable functionality provided to the users through projects or applications. The UFP calculation is broken into two categories with five sub-categories:

- Data Functions
  - Internal Logical Files
  - External Interface Files
- Transactional Functions
  - External Inputs
  - External Outputs
  - External Inquiries

Count Data Functions

Data functions are (the functionality provided to the users) are either Internal Logical Files (ILF) or External Logical Files (ELF).

An ILF is a user-identifiable group of logically related data or control information maintained within the boundary of the application.

An EIF is a user identifiable group of logically related data or control information referenced by the application, but maintained within the boundary of another application. It resides entirely outside the application. It is maintained by another application. It is an ILF for another application.

Assign each identified ILF and EIF a functional complexity based on the number of Data Element Types (DETs) and Record Element Types (RETs) associated with the ILF or EIF.

DET is a unique user recognizable field from a business perspective which participates in a transaction or is stored on a logical data file. RET is a user recognizable subgroup of data elements within an ILF or EIF.

Count Transactional Functions

Transactional functions represent the functionality provided to the user to process data. Transactional functions are external inputs, external outputs, or external inquiries.

An External Input (EI) is an elementary process that processes data or control information that comes from outside the application's boundary.

Examples of external input:

1. Data input screen
2. Another application
3. Business data does update ILF
4. Control data does not update ILF

An External Output (EO) is an elementary process that sends data or control information outside the application's boundary.

Examples of external output:

1. Creates reports.
2. Creates output files sent to other applications.
3. Created from ILF and ELF.

An External Inquiry (EQ) is an elementary process that sends data or control information outside the application boundary. It is an elementary process with both input and output components that result in data retrieval from one or more ILF and ELF.

1. EQ is sent outside the application boundary.
2. It is an input process and does not update ILF.
3. Output side does not contain derived data.

Assign each identified EI, EO and EQ a functional complexity based on the number of File Types Referenced (FTRs) and Data Element Types (DETs).

Example

In a particular development program, we have five data functions (2 Internal Logical Files, and 1 External Interface Files), 13 Transaction Functions (3 External Input, 4 External output, 6 External Queries).

Table 15.2 represents complexity split up.

Table 15.2 Components vs. Complexity

Components vs Complexity	Number of Components		
	Simple	**Average**	**Complex**
External Input (EI)	2	0	1
External Output (EO)	0	2	2
External Query (EQ)	2	1	3
Internal Logical Files (ILF)	2	0	2
External interface Files (EIF)	0	0	1

Table 15.3 represents the above table along with the weighting factor of complexity calculating UFP (unadjusted function point).

Table 15.3 Complexity Weighing Factor

Software System Components	Complexity Level									Total UFP
	Simple			Average			Complex			
	Count	Weight Factor	Points	Count	Weight Factor	Points	Count	Weight Factor	Points	
	A	B	C = A × B	D	E	F = D × E	G	H	I = G × H	
External Input (EI)	2	3	6	—	4	—	1	6	6	12
External Output (EO)	—	4	—	2	5	10	2	7	14	24
External Query (EQ)	2	3	6	1	4	4	3	6	18	28
Internal Logical files (ILF)	2	7	14	—	10	—	2	15	30	44
External interface Files (EIF)	—	5	—	—	7	—	1	10	10	10
Total UFP										118

15.2.4.2 Step 2: Compute Total Degree of Influence and Value Adjustment Factor

Value Adjustment Factor (VAF) indicates the general functionality provided to the users of the application. The VAF comprises 14 General System Characteristics (GSCs) that assess general functionality of the application. Each characteristic has associated with descriptions that helps determining the degree of influence of the characteristics. The degrees of influence range on a scale from 0–5 (from no influence to strong influence).

Evaluate each of the 14 general system characteristics on a scale from 0–5 (Table 15.4) to determine the Degree of Influence (DI). Add the degrees of influence for all the 14 general system characteristics to produce the Total Degree of Influence (TDI).

Put the TDI in the following equation to derive the value adjustment factor.

$$VAF = (TDI \cdot 0.01) + 0.65$$

Table 15.4 Value Adjustment Factor and Degree of Influence

		0 – No Influence 5 – Strong Influence
S. No.	**Value Adjustment Factors**	**Degree of Influence**
1	Data communication	0 1 2 3 4 5
2	Distributed data processing	0 1 2 3 4 5
3	Performance	0 1 2 3 4 5
4	Heavily used configurations	0 1 2 3 4 5
5	Transaction rate	0 1 2 3 4 5
6	Online data entry	0 1 2 3 4 5
7	End user efficiency	0 1 2 3 4 5
8	Online update	0 1 2 3 4 5
9	Complex processing	0 1 2 3 4 5
10	Reusability	0 1 2 3 4 5
11	Installation ease	0 1 2 3 4 5
12	Operational ease	0 1 2 3 4 5
13	Multiples sites	0 1 2 3 4 5
14	Facilitate change	0 1 2 3 4 5

In the previous example, the following value adjustment factor is calculated if there are two degrees of influence for each of the 14 GSC descriptions $(2 \cdot 14)$:

That is,

$$VAF = (28 \cdot 0.01) + 0.65$$
$$VAF = 0.93$$

15.2.4.3 Step 3: Compute the Function Point

Function point count is calculated by using a specific formula. For a development project, enhancement project or application (system baseline) function point count is:

$$FP = (UFP + CFP) \times (0.65 + 0.01 \times TDI)$$
$$FP = (UFP + CFP) \times VAF$$

Here, CFP is the unadjusted function points added by the conversion unadjusted function point count.

The development project function point calculation consists of three components of functionality:

1. Application functionality included in the user requirements for the project.
2. Conversion functionality included in the user requirements for the project.
3. Application value adjustment factor.

Development project function point formula is:

$$DFP = (UFP + CFP) \times VAF$$

where,

DFP is the development project function point count.

UFP is the unadjusted function point count for the functions that will be available after installation.

CFP is the unadjusted function points added by the conversion unadjusted function point count.

VAF is the value adjustment factor.

15.2.5 Applications of Function Points

Function points are used to measure productivity (*e.g.*, number of function points achieved per work hour expended), to measure quality (*e.g.*, rate of change, completeness), financial measurements (*e.g.*, cost per function point), maintenance measurements (*e.g.*, maintainability).

15.2.5.1 Function Point for Productivity

Hours per Function Point

It measures the number of hours required to develop a function point. It is given by:

Total no. of project hrs/No. of function point delivered.

Information Technology Productivity

It is the overall productivity of the IT department. It is given by:

Total function points/Total IT work effort.

Delivered Functionality and Development Functionality

It indicates how much functionality was actually delivered to the end users in relation to the rate of productivity of the developed functionality. It is given by:

Total cost/Total functionality delivered

or,

Total development effort hours/Total functionality developed in-house.

15.2.5.2 Function Point for Quality Measurement

Functional Requirement Size: It measures the total number of functions requested by end users expressed in terms of function points. The calculation derives the function points required by a requesting user organization.

Completeness: It measure the functionality delivered versus the functionality originally requested.

Rate of Change: It measure calendar time to deliver the required software solution to end users. It is given by:

Number of function point/Elapsed calendar time

Defect Removal Efficiency: Formula for Defect Removal Efficiency:

Total number of defects found prior to delivery/Total number of defects.

Defect Density: It measures the number of defects identified across one or more phases of the development project life-cycle and compare that value to the total size of application. Formula for defect density:

Total number of defects/Total number of function points

Test Case Coverage: It measures number of test cases that are necessary to adequately support thorough testing of a development project.

Formula for test case coverage = Number of test cases/Total number of function points.

Volume of Documentation: It measure or estimate the number of pages produced or anticipated in support of the development effort.

Formula for volume of documentation = Number of pages/Total number of function points.

15.2.5.3 Function Point for Financial Measurement

Cost per Function Point: It identifies the cost for each function point developed. Formula for cost per function point:

Total cost/Total function points.

Repair Cost Ratio: It is used to track the costs to repair applications that are operational. It is commonly used as a monitoring metric for a newly installed application. Formula for repair cost ratio:

Total hrs to repair × Cost per hr/Release function point

15.2.5.4 Function Point for Maintenance Measurement

Maintainability: It measures the cost required to maintain an application. Formula for maintainability:

Maintenance cost/Application function points

Reliability: It measure the number of failures an application experience relative to its function size. Formula for reliability:

Number of production failures/Total application function point

Assignment Scope: It measures the number of FTE resources required to support an application. Formula for assignment scope:

Total application function points/Number of full time resources required to support the application

Rate of Growth: It measures the growth of an application's functionality over the specific period of time. Formula for rate of growth:

Current number of function points/Original number of function point

Backfire Value: It is the number of lines of code factored by a language complexity multiplier to derive the number of function points.

Stability Ratio: It is used to monitor how effectively an application or enhancement has met expectations of the users (based on the number of changes that were required during the first 60–90 days of production). Formula for stability ratio:

Number of changes/Number of application function points.

Discussion Points

1. How can we use maintenance measurement in a project?
2. How can we use function point for financial measurement?

Point to Remember

Function points are used to measure productivity (Example: Number of function points achieved per work hour expended) to measure quality (Example: Rate of change, completeness), financial measurement (Example: Cost per function point), maintenance measurement (Example: maintainability).

Exercise 15.1

PIMS is a basic project invoice management system. It is planned to serve a business employing 5,000 people.

The system is planned to have interfaces to the company's other software packages, such as Attendance System, which tracks attendance of all the people engaged in the project; Project System, which tracks all the projects executed by the organization. A Report-Master is planned to produce several reports and online queries.

Table 15.5 Components vs Complexity

	Number of Components		
Components vs Complexity	**Simple**	**Average**	**Complex**
External Input (EI)	2	0	1
External Output (EO)	1	2	2
External Query (EQ)	2	1	2
Internal Logical Files (ILF)	2	1	0
External Interface Files (EIF)	0	1	1

Calculate function point of the system using the same complexity factors as defined above for the components. Considering the value adjusted factor as 1.3.

15.2.6 Benefits of FPA

1. Improves return on IT investments.
2. Improves the estimation process.
3. Communication of workload happens clearly.
4. Improves understanding of business functions.
5. Improves traceability of requirements through implementation.
6. Improves allocation of resources and reduces overtime.

15.2.7 Drawbacks of FPA

1. The calculation of function counts tends to take a black-box view of the system.
2. Accurate counting requires certified function point specialists.
3. The user-defined function types may not be wholly appropriate for current technology.
4. The classification of the user function types into simple, average, and complex appears to be oversimplified.
5. The choice of weights was determined by debate and trial.
6. The restriction to 14 processing complexity factors is not going to be satisfactory for all time. What if a new complexity factor to be factored in?
7. The calculation logic is more subjective and may vary from person to person.
8. There are about 20 variations of function point logics available in the market.

15.3 Extended Function Point Metrics

There are lot of metrics (Figure 15.5) which are called 'extended function point metrics'. These are the modified versions of function points (Example: Use case points, Object points, Feature points, Story points).

15.3.1 Use Case Points

Use Case Points (UCPs) allow the estimation of an application's size and effort from its use cases. UCPs are based on the number of factors, scenarios, and various technical and environmental factors in the use case diagram.The UCPs Estimation Method was introduced by Gustav Karner and can be implemented using a spreadsheet.

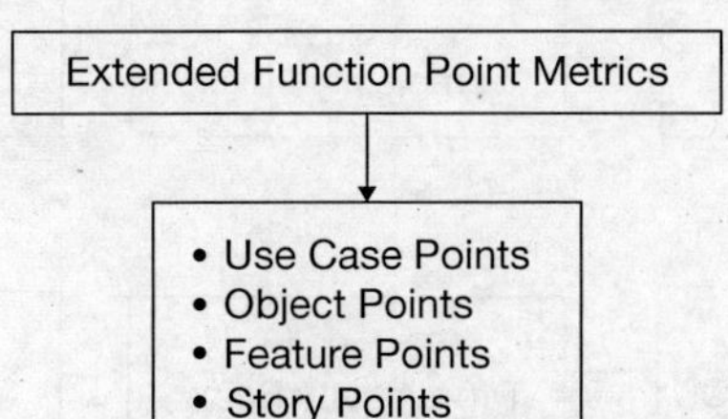

Figure 15.5 Extended Function Point Metrics Types

Usually, the UCP equation is based on four variables. These are:

- Technical Complexity Factor (TCF)
- Environment Complexity Factor (ECF)
- Unadjusted Use Case Points (UUCP)
- Productivity Factor (PF)

The UCP equation is given by:

$$UCP = TCP \times ECF \times UUCP \times PF$$

The use case point's method has produced estimates close to actual effort in several projects. This indicates that the use case point's method may support expert knowledge when a use case model for the project is available. Some tailoring to the company may be useful to obtain maximum benefits from the method.

15.3.2 Object Points

Object points (alternatively named, application points) are an alternative function-related measure to function points when 4GLs or similar languages are used for development.

The number of object points in a program is a weighted estimate of:

- The number of separate screens that are displayed.
- The number of reports that are produced by the system.
- The number of program modules that must be developed to supplement the database code.

Object-point Estimation Procedure

Figure 15.6 depicts the object-point estimations procedures as noted here.

1. Assess **object-counts** in the system: number of screens reports, and 3GL.
2. Assess complexity level for each object (use table): simple, medium and difficult.
3. Calculate new object point 'NOP' the **object-point count** of the system: add all weights for all object instances.
4. Estimate the percentage of reuse and compute the adjusted NOP 'New Object Points' to be developed.
5. Determine the productivity rate PROD (use metrics table).
6. Compute the adjusted effort PM (Person month) = adjusted NOP/PROD.

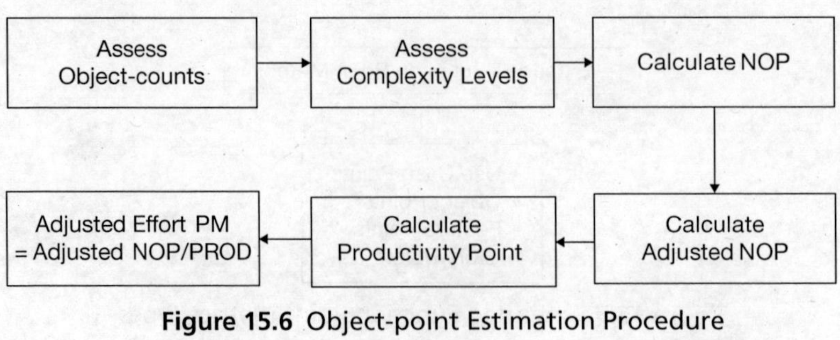

Figure 15.6 Object-point Estimation Procedure

Object points are easier to estimate from a specification than function points as they are simply concerned with screens, reports and programming language modules. They can, therefore, be estimated at a fairly early point in the development process. At that stage, it is very difficult to estimate the number of lines of code in a system.

Example

Assessment of a software system shows that (Table 15.6) 20% of the objects could be supplied from previously developed components. Lets compute the estimated effort 'Person-months' needed to develop the system.

Table 15.6 Complexity Table

	Complexity		
	Simple	**Medium**	**Difficult**
Screen	2	0	1
Report	1	2	2
Language	2	1	2

Object Counts

Table 15.7 NOP – Object Count

	NOP			
	Simple	**Medium**	**Difficult**	**Total**
Screen	2 × 1 = 2	0 × 2 = 0	1 × 3 = 3	5
Report	1 × 3 = 3	2 × 5 = 10	2 × 8 = 16	29
Language	2 × 5 = 10	1 × 8 = 8	2 × 10 = 20	38
			Total	72

NOP is calculated (Table 15.7) by the sum of the individual complexity factors of each of the screen, report and language.

$$\begin{aligned}\text{Adjusted NOP} &= \text{NOP} \times (1 - \%\ \text{reuse}/100)\\ &= 72 \times (1 - 20/100)\\ &= 72 \times (0.8)\\ &= 58\end{aligned}$$

For high productivity (metric table): PROD = 25 OP/P-M

Estimated effort person-month = Adjusted NOP/PROD = 58/25= 2.32 person months.

15.3.3 Feature Point Estimation

The feature point measure accommodates applications in which the algorithmic complexity is high. For more complex systems, the feature point count is 20–35% higher than the count determined using function points alone. Algorithm is extra measurement added in feature point estimation comparing to function point estimation. An algorithm is defined as a bounded computational problem that is included within a specific computer program. The feature point metric was so named, because telecommunications software engineers used the term 'feature' for major functions being developed for switching systems. (The author, Capers Jones, had worked on telecommunications systems)

Only single weight value is used for each measurement as shown in Table 15.8.

Table 15.8 Feature Point Estimation – Component vs Factor

Feature Point Estimation	
Component	**Feature Point Factor**
User Input	4
User Output	5
User Inqueries	4
Files	7
External Interfaces	7
Algorithms	3

Overall feature point is calculated using the feature point factor along with the adjustment factor (as per FP).

15.3.4 Story Point Sizing

A story point is actually a measure of complexity and this is used in relative estimation techniques of agile projects to size its story. Story is in the form of a card called 'story cardin' which the requirement is written in the form of a story. Story point is not a direct measure of the estimates (similar to function point) and is a relative measurement.

If we have two user stories with story point 1 and 4, it means that the second story is four times complex than the first user story. User story with story point 3 is three times complex than user story with point 1.

But we need to first baseline a story which all in the team can relate to for sizing other stories.

Example: A team has 3 user stories to estimate.

1. A login screen to be developed.
2. A screen for entering customer data is required.
3. A mailing module will send periodic mails to the customers.

All the team members are very clear about what they need to do in the customer data entry screen (Second story). So they took it as the baseline and assigned it the story point of 6 [any arbitrary number]. When they started estimating the login screen (First story), they found that the login screen validations and functionalities are simpler than the customer data entry screen (Second story) and, thus, they assigned it a number 2 (relative to the customer data entry screen story point). This means, the team agrees that the customer data screen (Second story) is 3 times more complex than the login screen (First story). similarly, all the user stories are estimated relative to the baselined story point.

So, we measure complexity using story point, but in order to calculate the effort, we need to consider the person who will implement the story along with the complexity factors. Remember, for every team, story size could mean different things depending on what baseline they chose. If two teams are given exactly the same set of stories, one can say their total story point estimate is 41 and the other can say 14. It depends on what numbers they chose. That means, story point of one project is not comparable with story point of another project.

15.3.4.1 Story Points Measurement

Agile estimation uses non-linear scale for story points. As we have discussed, story points are a relative number of complexities. Some people use the numbers 1 to 10. Some people use the number 10 to 100. We need not only assign numbers to story points. Some innovative people assign T-shirt sizes to story points, say S, M, L, XL, XXL, XXL, etc. Some people uses Fibonacci series numbers to story points (0, 1, 1, 2, 3, 5, 8, 13, 21, etc). Some people use variety of animal names for user stories (cat, dog, lion, and elephant) to indicate dog is bigger than cat, lion is bigger than dog and elephant is the biggest.

15.3.4.2 Planning Poker

Planning poker provides an excellent way of estimation. It is the most widely used estimation technique of agile projects. It is simple, makes fun and results in reliable estimates. Table 15.9 indicates the story point estimated by different estimators at Round 1 and Round 2.

Table 15.9 Planning Poker Steps

Shrikrishna	Manas	Estimator
Assess object-counts	Calculate Productivity Point	2
Assess complexity levels	Adjusted effort PM = adjusted NOP / PROD	1
Calculate NOP	Anand	4
Calculate adjusted NOP	Balaji	10

Rules for Planning Poker: Every team members (estimators) given with a card (which has numbers). Client reads the story which needs to be sized with explanations required, if any. All the team members (estimators) choose a card, but do not show it to others. Then the client asks the estimators to show the card and everybody shows their cards at a time. Customer goes through the story points chosen by different estimators for the same story. Any disagreement in story points are resolved in the following ways.

- Reaching consensus with discussion
- Go with majority
- Go with high estimates
- Go with average after few rounds
- Three point estimates

A veteran team of expert estimators performing this task will reach to consensus very quickly.

From Table 15.9, if we want to go with majority, then we can select 5. If we want to go with high estimates (safety side) we can select 6. Sometime, we can go with averaging all the estimates.

We can also choose three point estimations (PERT estimation) for resolving disagreements.

Choose the highest estimation (pessimistic), choose the lowest estimation (optimistic), calculate average of the remaining (most likely). Use PERT formula to calculate the estimation.

$$\text{PERT Estimation} = (\text{Optimistic} + 4 \times \text{Most likely} + \text{Pessimistic})/6$$

15.3.4.3 Velocity

Velocity is the sum of story points delivered by a team per cycle of the iteration (sprint). Sprint is usually time boxed. So we can say, velocity is the story points delivered for a period of time, it indirectly the amount of work delivered by the team over a period of time. Period of time is usually 1–4 weeks which is of normal sprint duration. Figure 15.7 depicts the relationship between velocity and various sprints.

Velocity actually changes with every iteration and the team needs to recalculate its velocity at the end of each iteration in order to have a realistic estimation.

By comparing the velocity over a set of iterations (Figure 15.7) we can find out whether the team is getting faster or slower and the customer expects the velocity to get improved over a period of time. Velocity is directly affected by the number of resources working on Sprint.

Customers always expect the velocity to increase over a period of time, but sudden increase in velocity is also a concern as it may be related to the problems in the estimation (high estimation).

Sprint	Velocity
Sprint 1	20
Sprint 2	30
Sprint 3	28
Sprint 4	32
Sprint 5	33
Sprint 6	35

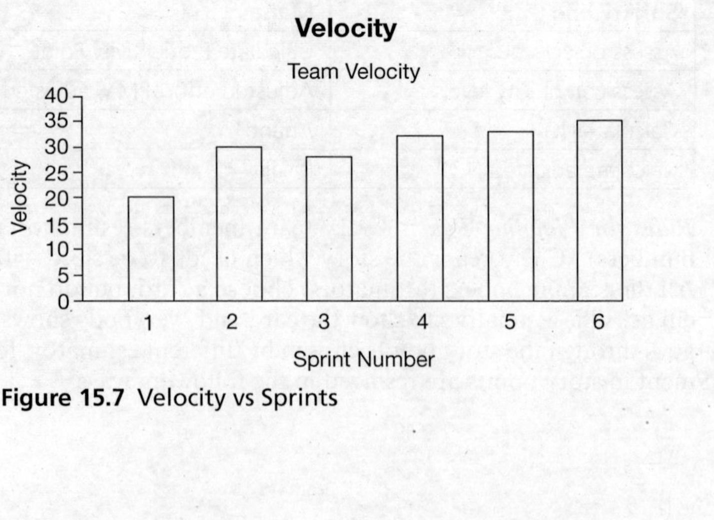

Figure 15.7 Velocity vs Sprints

Velocity of two teams are not comparable as the estimation logic differs between teams (Story point 1 in one team may be different in another team). Velocity is also proportional to the team composition; experienced team member does more work thereby more story points whereas inexperienced team member takes more time. Velocity is expected to increases with team's tenure, because the team gets mature and expected to execute more story points. Velocity is not a measure of productivity. We should not include bugs and rejected stories while calculating velocity. By knowing and understanding the team's velocity helps to make commitments upfront and also with confidence. It also helps to select the story points that fit into the iteration. Customers also need to help the team by doing proper prioritization of the story points.

15.4 Object-oriented Metrics

As the object-oriented (OO) paradigm began to spread throughout the software community during C++ and Java usages, people felt the need for the estimation techniques based on objects and its characteristics rather than following traditional techniques.

Some of the specialized OO metrics constructs (factors) include:

1. Number of classes in the overall program.
2. Weighted methods per class.
3. Number of children per class.
4. Depth of inheritance tree.
5. Types of inheritance used in the overall program.
6. Coupling between objects in the program.
7. Types of methods used within the class.
8. Number of variables used in the program.
9. Number of similar variables used in the program.
10. Duplication of class structures.
11. Operating complexity.
12. Attributes complexity.
13. Reuse metrics like reusable class, reusable objects, etc.

15.4.1 Specialized OO Metrics

Some of the specialized OO metrics (Figure 15.8) include:

1. Chen Metrics
2. Morris Metrics
3. MOOSE (Metrics for Object-oriented System Environments) or (Metrics for Object-oriented Software Engineering). It is also called 'Chidamber and Kemerer—USA' Metrics. It is also called 'CK Metrics'.
4. MOOD (Metrics for Object-oriented Design). It is also called 'Abrieu–Portugal' metrics/ AP Metrics.
5. EMOOSE

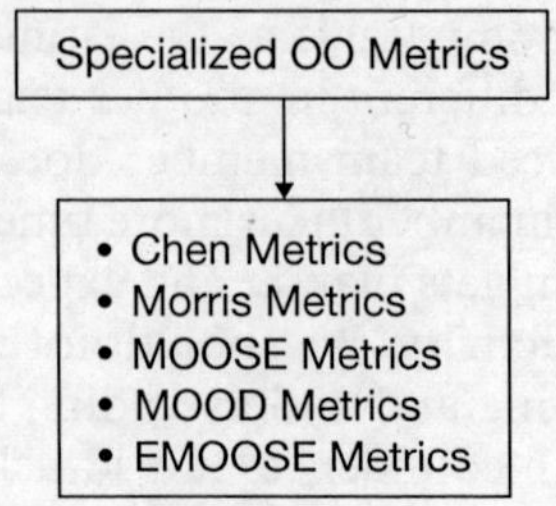

Figure 15.8 Specialized OO Metrics Types

15.4.1.1 Chen Metrics

It uses (Table 15.10) the coupling, cohesion and complexity metrics of objects.

Coupling: Degree of dependence among components. High coupling makes modifying parts of the system difficult, *e.g.*, modifying a component affects all the components to which the component is connected.

Cohesion: The degree to which all elements of a component are directed towards a single task and all elements directed towards that task are contained in a single component.

Table 15.10 Chen Metrics

Chen Metrics		
Coupling	**Cohesion**	**Complexity**
Class Coupling	Cohension	Attribute Complexity
Opearing Coupling		Operating Complexity

It uses Class Coupling Metrics (CCM), Operating Coupling Metrics (OCM). It uses Cohesion Metrics (CM). It uses Attribute Complexity Metrics (ACM), Operating Complexity Metrics (OXM). Reuse Metrics is a Boolean metrics with value of 0 or 1 indicating whether reusable objects available or not available.

15.4.1.2 Morris Metrics

Morris defined the complexity of the object-oriented system in the form of the depth of the tree using sub-nodes. More sub-nodes indicate the system more complex.

15.4.1.3 MOOSE Metrics/CK Metric Suite

Metrics for Object-oriented System Environments (MOOSE) consists of 6 metrics (Table 15.11).

1. Weighted Methods per Class (WMC)
2. Response for Class (RFC)
3. Number of Children for Class (NOC)

Table 15.11 Moose Metrics/CK Metrics

Moose Metrics/CK Metrics		
Class	**Coupling**	**Cohension**
Weighted methods per Class	Coupling between Objects	Lack of Cohension in Methods
Response for Class		
Number of children for Class		
Depth of Inheritance Tree		

4. Depth of Inheritance Tree (DIT)
5. Coupling Between Objects (CBO)
6. Lack of Cohesion in Methods (LCOM)

WMC: This measure the complexity of the methods in a class. Here, complexity is determined based on the time required to complete (write) the method and the technical difficulties involved in writing the method. A relative value is used to figure out the complexity of the methods so that all the methods inside the class are comparable. High value of WMC indicates the class is more complex.

RFC: This measure the set of methods executed in response to the class execution and the number of messages received by the class in response to the class execution by the object of the class. High value of RFC indicates the class is more complex and the testing efforts also increased.

NOC: This measure the number of subclasses (Number of Children) for a class (Figure 15.9) and also deals with method inheritance. Inheritance is a form of reuse and greater this number indicates greater potential for reuse. Higher number of NOC indicates that reuse also increases which causes increase of testing efforts.

DIT: It measures the length of the maximum path from root to the end node of the tree (Figure 15.9). It represents the complexity. Higher value of the depth indicates that more classes and methods are inherited and is an indication of complexity. Large DIT values indicate that many methods may be reused.

CBO: This measures the number of classes to which the specific class is coupled (linked to). Higher value indicates it as less attractive for reusing and also more sensitive to change,

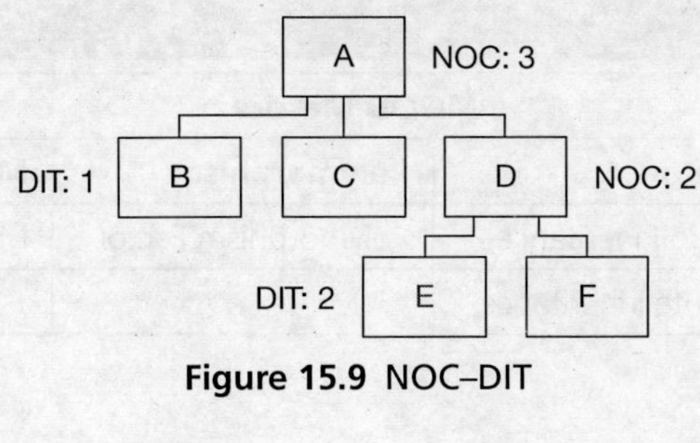

Figure 15.9 NOC–DIT

because changing one class will affect the other coupled classes. When CBO increases, the reusability of the class decreases and it also complicates the modifications. We need to keep CBO value of class as low as possible.

LCOM: It measures the number of disjoint method pairs minus the number of similar method pairs used. If LCOM increases the coupling between methods increases and, therefore, the complexity also increases.

15.4.1.4 MOOD Metrics

Metrics for Object-oriented Design (MOOD) refers a structural model of the Object-oriented paradigm (Table 15.12) using Object-oriented techniques, like encapsulation, inheritance, polymorphism and message passing. It uses two main features of a class, namely, methods and attributes. Methods are the functions which are used to modify the status of the objects; attributes are the status and characteristics of the objects.

The metrics can be classified into different categories and sub-categories as follows:

Encapsulation Metrics: Method Hiding Factor (MHF), Attribute Hiding Factor (AHF).

Inheritance Metrics: Method Inheritance Factor (MIF), Attribute Inheritance Factor (AIF).

Polymorphism Metrics: Polymorphism Factor (PF).

Message Passing Metrics: Coupling Factor (CF).

MHF: It is defined as the ratio of the sum of the invisibilities of all methods defined in all classes to the total number of methods defined in the system under consideration.

AHF: It is defined as the ratio of the sum of the invisibilities of all attributes defined in all classes to the total number of attributes defined in the system under consideration.

MIF: It is defined as the ratio of the sum of the inherited methods in all classes of the system under consideration to the total number of available methods for all classes.

AIF: It is defined as the ratio of the sum of the inherited attributes in all classes of the system under consideration to the total number of available attributes for all classes.

PF: It is defined as the ratio of the actual number of possible different polymorphic situation for class to the maximum number of possible distinct polymorphic situations for class.

CF: It is defined as the ratio of the maximum possible number of couplings in the system to the actual number of couplings not imputable to inheritance.

Table 15.12 MOOD Metrics

MOOD Metrics			
Encapsulation	**Inheritance**	**Polymorphism**	**Massage Passing**
Method Hiding	Method Inheritance	Polymorphism Factor	Message Coupling Factor
Attribute Hiding	Attribute Inheritance		

Table 15.13 E-Moose Metrics

E-Moose Metrics		
Class	**Coupling**	**Cohension**
Weighted methods for Class	Coupling between Objects	Lack of Cohension in Methods
Response for Class	Message Pass Coupling	
Number of Children for Class	Data Abstraction Coupling	Size 1 and size 2
Depth of Inheritance Tree		
Number of methods in Class		

15.4.1.5 EMOOSE Metrics

In Extended Metrics for Object-oriented Software Engineering (EMOOSE) metrics, message and data coupling as well as data abstraction are considered which is not part of the original MOOSE metrics. In addition to the six metrics defined in MOOSE, the following five metrics are also used in the extended model bringing the total count of metrics to eleven (Table 15.13).

Message Pass Coupling (MPC): It means that the number of message that can be sent by the class operations.

Data Abstraction Coupling (DAC): It is used to count the number of classes which an aggregated to current class and also defined the data abstraction coupling.

Number of Methods (NOM): It is used to count the number of operations that are local to the class, *i.e.*, only those class operation which can give the number of methods to measure it.

Size 1: It is used to find the number of lines of code.

Size 2: It is used to count the number of local attributes and the number of operations defined in the class.

15.4.2 Advantages of Object-oriented Metrics

The main strengths of OO metrics are:

1. The OO metrics uses various object-oriented terms which are understandable easily by the object-oriented community.
2. The OO metrics distinguishes easy project vs. complex projects.
3. The OO metrics are easily comparable across projects.
4. The OO metrics are easily related with the structure of the program which is not possible with other metrics.

15.4.3 Disadvantages of Object-oriented Metrics

The main drawbacks of OO metrics are:

1. The OO metrics not applicable for testing or maintenance. It is applicable only for development project.
2. The OO metrics not supported by various estimating tools available in the market.
3. The OO metrics are unrelated to all other known software metrics. Converting OO metrics to FP or LOC is difficult.
4. The OO metrics do not deal with full life-cycle issues.

15.5 DeMarco's System BANG

DeMarco suggested another measure of system size similar to function point and is called 'system BANG'. This term was dervied from 'big bang' approach.

System specification document is divided into number of functional primitives which are described as a trivial piece that is too small to justify further positioning. Values of functional primitives are further adjusted based on Halstead's volume-vocabulary relationship. Each functional primitive is given an empirical complexity correction factor depending on the class of primitive function. DeMarco defined 16 classes of primitives. Each weighted functional primitive is multiplied by its complexity correction factor and the resulting functional primitive values are summed to give total system BANG called 'Function Bang'. DeMarco also suggests the users to define our own classes and complexity factor.

System BANG Based on Data Objects: If the system possesses significant database, then BANG of the system can be calculated from the objects in the database (Figure 15.10). Each object is corrected based on the relationships at the bounded and then corrected objects are summed up to calculate Data Bang. For systems containing both data strong and function strong, two sets of BANG metrics can be used. The two predictors (Function Bang and Data Bang) should not be combined together.

System Bang is very easy to use when it is automated, otherwise it is very subjective in nature.

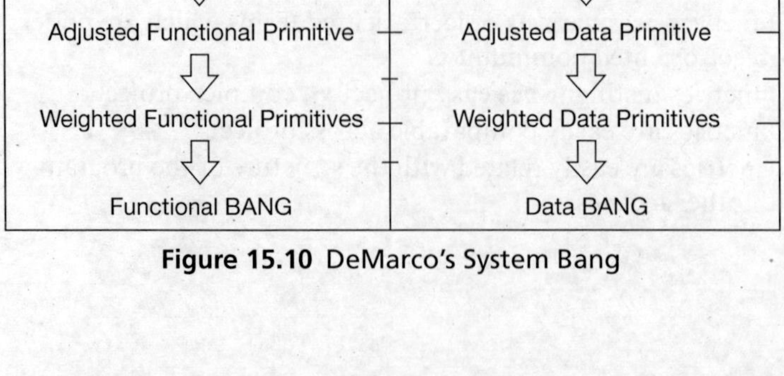

Figure 15.10 DeMarco's System Bang

Discussion Points

1. Compare and contrast LOC with FP estimation.
2. Compare UCP and object point.

SUMMARY

This chapter explains the concepts of Lines of Code (LOC) and Function Point Estimation (FP Estimation). Lines of Code specifically include all lines containing program headers, declarations, and executable and non-executable codes in a software program. Since it is easy to calculate, measure, report—even juniors can use LOC for estimation purpose. The 'Functionality of the Code' not taken into consideration for calculation of LOC. Function point analysis is a method of quantifying the size and complexity of a software system in terms of the functions that the system delivers to the user. FPA (Function Point Analysis) is independent of the computer language, development methodology, technology or capability of the project team used to develop the application. An object point (alternatively named, application points) is an alternative function-related measure to function points when 4GLs or similar languages are used for development. A story point is actually a measure of complexity and this is used in relative estimation techniques of agile projects to size its story. Velocity is the sum of story points delivered by a team per cycle of the iteration or sprint. This chapter is also discussed the following specialized object-oriented (OO) metrics in detail, like Chen Metrics, Morris Metrics, MOOSE Metrics, MOOD Metrics, and EMOOSE Metrics. This chapter also discuss the DeMarco's System Bang.

Answers to Exercise Questions

Exercise 15.1

PIMS is a basic Project Invoice Management System that is planned to serve a business employing 5000 people.

Component Analysis:

Number of Components			
Components Vs Complexity	**Simple**	**Average**	**Complex**
External Iuput (EI)	2	0	1
External Output (EO)	1	2	2
External Query (EQ)	2	1	2
Internal Logical Files (ILF)	2	1	0
External Interface Files (EIF)	0	1	1

Calculate function point of the system using the same complexity factor defined before for the components considering the value adjusted factor as 1.3.

Function Point Calculation:

Software System Components	Complexity Level									Total UFP
	Simple			Average			Complex			
	Count	Weight Factor	Points	Count	Weight Factor	Points	Count	Weight Factor	Points	
	A	B	C = A × B	D	E	F = D × E	G	H	I = G × H	
External Input (EI)	2	3	6	–	4	–	1	6	6	**12**
External Output (EO)	1	4	4	2	5	10	2	7	14	**28**
External Query (EQ)	2	3	6	1	4	4	2	6	12	**22**
Internal Logical Files (ILF)	2	7	14	1	10	10	–	15	–	**24**
External Interface Files (EIF)	–	5	–	1	7	7	1	10	10	**17**
Total UFP										**103**

FP = 103 × 1.3 = 133.9

EXERCISES

PART A (Objective-type questions)

1. Lines of Code specifically include all lines containing program headers, declarations, and executable and non-executable codes in a software program.

A. True

B. False

2. SLOC stands for

A. Structured Lines of Code
B. Source Lines of Code
C. Size Lines of Code
D. Stable Lines of Code

3. All of the following are types of SLOC, except

A. Physical SLOC
B. Logical SLOC
C. Comment SLOC
D. Used SLOC

4. Count of lines in the text of the physical source code including comment lines, declarations and blank lines is called
A. Physical SLOC
B. Logical SLOC
C. Comment SLOC
D. Re-used SLOC

5. Count of lines of the only 'executable statements' is called
A. Physical SLOC
B. Logical SLOC
C. Comment SLOC
D. Re-used SLOC

6. Count of lines consisting of only the Comments in the Source Code is called
A. Code SLOC
B. Count SLOC
C. Comment SLOC
D. Name SLOC

7. All of the following are the advantages of the Line of Code Measure, except
A. Skilled coders can develop the same code with less line
B. Complex formulas not used
C. Repeatability is possible
D. Measurement easily automatable

8. LOC does not consider the functionality of the code.
A. True
B. False

9. Which of the following measures software size by quantifying the functionality provided to the user based solely on logical design and functional specifications?
A. LOC
B. Function Point
C. Object Point
D. Story Point

10. FPA (Function Point Analysis) is independent of the computer language, development methodology, technology or capability of the project team used to develop the application.
A. True
B. False

11. Which of the following is not an objective of Function Point Counting?
A. Measure functionality that the user requests and receives.
B. Simple enough to minimize the overhead of the measurement process.
C. A consistent measure among various projects and organizations.
D. Compute Total Degree of Influence (TDI) for the project.

12. Data functions is a combination of
A. Internal Logical Files and External Interface Files
B. External Inputs and External Outputs
C. Internal Logical Files and External Logical Files
D. External Inquiries and Internal Inquiries

13. A user identifiable group of logically related data or control information maintained within the boundary of the application is called
A. External Logical File
B. Internal Logical File
C. Boundary Data
D. Boundary Control Information

14. User identifiable group of logically related data or control information referenced by the application, but maintained within the boundary of another application is called
A. External Logical File
B. EInternal Logical File
C. Boundary Data
D. Boundary Control Information

15. Unique user recognizable field from a business perspective which participates in a transaction or is stored on a logical data file is called

A. RET
B. DEA
C. DET
D. LDF

16. User recognizable subgroup of data elements within an ILF or EIF is called
A. RET
B. DEA
C. DET
D. LDF

17. External inputs, external outputs, or external inquiries are called
A. Data Functions
B. Transactional Functions
C. External Functions
D. Control Functions

18. Which of the following is not an example of External Input?
A. Data Input Screen
B. Another Application
C. Reports Creation
D. Business Data

19. Elementary process that sends data or control information outside the application's boundary is called as External Output.
A. True
B. False

20. An Elementary process that sends data or control information outside the application boundary is called
A. External Inquiry
B. External Files
C. Internal Inquiry
D. External Control

21. Which of the following is not true?
A. EQ is sent outside the application boundary.
B. EQ is an input process that does not update ILF.
C. Output side does not contain derived data.
D. EQ is a data or control information that comes from outside the application's boundary.

22. How many value adjustment factors are available in function point analysis?
A. 4
B. 12
C. 14
D. 24

23. Correct Formula for Value Adjustment Factor is
A. VAF = (TDI · 0.02) + 0.65
B. VAF = (TDI · 0.10) + 0.65
C. VAF = (TDI · 0.01) + 0.45
D. VAF = (TDI · 0.01) + 0.65

24. Which of the following is not part of development function point component?
A. Application Functionality
B. Conversion Functionality
C. Application Value Adjustment Factor
D. Conversional Functionality Adjustment Factor

25. Which of the following is the formula for Development Function Point?
A. DFP = (UFP + CFP) × VAF
B. DFP = (UFP × VAF) + CFP
C. DFP = (UFP/VAF) + CFP
D. DFP = (UFP – CFP) × VAF

26. Which of the following is not the use of function points?
A. It is used to measure productivity
B. Maintenance measurement
C. Financial measurement
D. Operational measurement

27. Which of the following measures the total number of functions requested by end user expressed in terms of function points?
A. Function Point
B. Functional Requirement Size
C. Reliability
D. Maintainability

28. What is the formula for maintainability in terms of Function Points?
A. Maintainability = Maintenance cost/Application function points
B. Maintainability = Application function Points/Maintenance cost

C. Maintainability = Maintenance cost × Application function points
D. Maintainability = Maintenance cost + Application function points

29. What is the formula for Reliability in terms of Function Points?
A. Reliability = Number of Production failures × Total application function points
B. Reliability = Number of production failures/Total application function points
C. Reliability = Number of production failures + Total application function points
D. Reliability = Total application function points × Number of production success

30. Which of the following measures the number of FTE resources required to support an application?
A. Assignment Scope
B. Rate of Growth
C. Backfire Value
D. Support Scope

31. Which one in the following list, measures the growth of application's functionality over a specific period of time?
A. Functional Scope
B. Rate of Growth
C. Backfire Value
D. Support Scope

32. What is the formula for rate of growth with respect to function points?
A. Current number of function points/ original number of function point
B. Original number of function points/ current number of function point
C. Current number of function points – original number of function point
D. Current number of function points + original number of function point

33. Which is the number of lines of code factored by a language complexity multiplier to derive the number of function points?
A. Functional Scope
B. Rate of Growth
C. Backfire Value
D. Stability Ratio

34. It is used to monitor how effectively an application or enhancement has met the expectations of the user (based on the number of changes that were required during the first 60–90 days of production).
A. Functional Scope
B. Rate of Growth
C. Backfire Value
D. Stability Ratio

35. Formula for stability Ratio:
A. Number of application function points/Number of changes
B. Number of changes/Number of application function points
C. Current number of function points/ Original number of function point
D. Number of production failures/ Total application function points

36. Which of the following is not a benefit of function point analysis?
A. Improves the understanding of business functions.
B. Improves traceability of requirements through implementation.
C. Improves the allocation of resources and reduces overtime.
D. The calculation of function counts tends to take a black box view of the system.

37. Which of the following is not an example of extended function points?
A. Line of Points
B. Use Case Points
C. Object Points
D. Feature Points

38. Which of the following allow the estimation of an application's size and effort from its use cases?

A. Line of Points
B. Use Case Points
C. Object Points
D. Feature Points

39. What is the formula for UCP?
A. UCP = TCP × ECF × UUCP × PF
B. UCP = TCP + ECF + UUCP + PF
C. UCP = (TCP / ECF) × UUCP × PF
D. UCP = UUCP × PF

40. Which of the following measures and accommodates applications in which the algorithmic complexity is high?
A. Line of Points
B. Use Case Points
C. Object Points
D. Feature Points

41. Which of the following is actually a measure of complexity and this is used in relative estimation techniques of agile projects?
A. Line of Points
B. Use Case Points
C. Story Points
D. Feature Points

42. Sum of story points delivered by a team per cycle of the iteration (sprint) is called
A. Total Story Points
B. Velocity
C. Delivery Points
D. Sprint Points

43. Velocity actually changes with every iteration and the team needs to recalculate its velocity at the end of each iteration.
A. True
B. False

44. All of the following are examples of specialized OO metrics, except
A. MOOSE Metrics
B. EMOOSE Metrics
C. Morris Metrics
D. EMORRIS Metrics

45. Class coupling metrics are used in
A. Chen Metrics
B. Morris Metrics
C. MOOD Metrics
D. MOOSE Metrics

46. Degree of dependence among components is called
A. Coupling
B. Cohesion
C. Degree of dependence
D. Intra-component dependency

47. High value of WMC indicates the class is more complex.
A. True
B. False

48. High value of RFC indicates the class is more complex and the testing efforts also increases?
A. True
B. False

49. Higher number of NOC indicates that reuse also increases. It also indicates that testing efforts will increase?
A. True
B. False

50. Which of the following measures the length of the maximum path from root to the end of node of the tree?
A. CBO
B. NOC
C. DIT
D. RFC

51. Which of the following increase in this Morris Metrics indicates the decrease in reusability?
A. CBO
B. NOC
C. DIT
D. LCOM

52. Increase in this Morris Metrics indicates the increase in coupling and complexity.
A. CBO
B. NOC
C. DIT
D. LCOM

53. Structural model of the object-oriented paradigm is called

A. MOOD
B. MOOSE
C. MORRIS
D. CHEN

54. Total number of EMOOSE metrics are
A. 21
B. 11
C. 12
D. 5

PART B (Write the answers in one or two lines)

1. Write notes on Lines of Code.

2. What are all the types of SLOC measures?

3. What is Physical SLOC?

4. What is Logical SLOC?

5. What is Comment SLOC?

6. What is RLOC?

7. Write any three advantages of the Line of Code Measure.

8. List down any three drawbacks of the Line of Code Measure.

9. Write notes on Function Point Count.

10. What is Function Point Analysis?

11. What are all the objectives of Function Point Counting?

12. List down three stages of FP calculation steps.

13. List the various elements used in Function Point (FP) Analysis.

14. What is data functions and Transactional Function in FP?

15. Write notes on Data Functions.

16. Write notes on DET and RET related with function points.

17. Write notes on Transactional Functions of FP.

18. What is External Input (EI) related to function point?

19. What is External Output (EO) related to Function point Analysis?

20. What is External Inquiry (EQ) related to function point?

21. What is Value Adjustment Factor (VAF) in function point analysis?

22. What is Function Point Count? Give an example for its calculation.

23. Write notes on development project function point calculation.

24. What are the uses of function points?

25. Write notes on delivered functionality and development functionality.

26. What is functional requirement size?

27. How function point is used in Financial Measurement of projects?

28. What is maintainability and reliability with respect to function points?

29. What is assignment scope with respect to function points?

30. Write notes on 'rate of growth' with respect to function points.

31. What is Backfire value and Stability Ratio with respect to function points?

32. Write any three benefits of function point analysis?

33. Write any three drawback of Function Point Analysis?

34. Write notes on Extended Function Point Metrics.

35. What is Use Case Points?

36. What are all the variables involved in Use Case Point (UCP) equation?

37. What is Object Points?

38. What is Feature Point Estimation?

39. What is Story Point Sizing?

40. Define velocity.

41. Write notes on Velocity vs Sprints.

42. What is Object-oriented Metrics?

43. List down various types of Specialized OO Metrics.
44. Write notes on Chen Metrics.
45. What is coupling and Cohesion?
46. Write names of six Morris Metrics.
47. Write notes on WMC Morris Metrics.
48. Write notes on RFC Morris Metrics.
49. Write notes on NOC Morris Metrics.
50. Write notes on DIT Morris Metrics.
51. Writes notes on CBO Morris Metrics.
52. Write notes on LCOM Morris Metrics.
53. Write notes on MOOD Metrics.
54. What are all the MOOD Metrics related to Encapsulation?
55. What is MHF of Mood Metrics?
56. What is AHF of Mood Metrics?
57. What is MIF of Mood Metrics?
58. What is AIF of Mood Metrics?
59. What is PF of Mood Metrics?
60. What is CF of Mood Metrics?
61. What is EMOOSE Metrics?
62. What are all the advantages of Object-oriented Metrics?
63. What are all the disadvantages of Object-oriented Metrics?

16

Software Configuration Management

16.1 Introduction

Configuration Management (CM) is the discipline of controlling the evolution of complex systems and, thus, managing the costs incurred in making changes to the system. Software Configuration Management (SCM) is its specialization for computer programs and associated documents.

SCM encompasses the initiation, evaluation and control of changes to a software product during its evolution, deployment and maintenance. According to ISO 9001 guideline, the definition of SCM is configuration management provides a mechanism for identifying, controlling and tracking the versions of each software item. In many cases, earlier versions still in use must also be maintained and controlled. SCM is also called 'Software Control Management'.

ISO 9001 also specifies the high level capabilities of a SCM system.

It should:

1. Identify uniquely the identity of each software item.
2. Identify the versions of each software item which together constitute a specific version of a complete product.
3. Identify the build status of software products in development or delivered and installed.
4. Control simultaneous updating of a given software item by more than one person.
5. Provide coordination for updating of multiple products in one or more locations as required.
6. Identify and track all actions and changes resulting from a change request, from initiation to release.

16.2 Basic Concepts of Configuration Management

The important terms that one should understand before exploring CM:

- Configuration Item
- Change Request
- Versions and configurations
- Promotion
- Release
- Repository
- Workspace

A piece of software or work product which is subject to change is a **Configuration Item.**

A **Version** identifies the state of a particular configuration item or a configuration at a well-defined point in time.

A **Promotion** is a version of a configuration item/CM aggregate that has been available to other developers in a project.

A **Release** is a version that has been available to the user or the client.

A **Repository** stores the various releases of a CM item/aggregate. It is a library of promotions.

16.3 Software Configuration Management Process

The four key aspects that must be defined for each software project to ensure that a good SCM process is implemented are as follows:

- Configuration Identification
- Configuration Control
- Configuration Status Accounting
- Configuration Authentication

16.4 Configuration Identification

Any software is usually made up of several programs. Each program, its related documentation and data can be called 'Configurable Item (CI)'. The number of CIs in any software project and the grouping of artifacts that make up a CI is a decision made by the project. The end product is made up of a bunch of CIs.

The status of the CIs at a given point of time is called 'a baseline' which serves as a reference point in the software development life cycle. Each new baseline is the sum total of an older baseline plus a series of approved changes made on the CI. The IEEE definition of baseline is as follows:

> A specification or product that has been formally reviewed and agreed to by responsible management that thereafter serves as the basis for further development, and can be changed only through formal change control procedures.

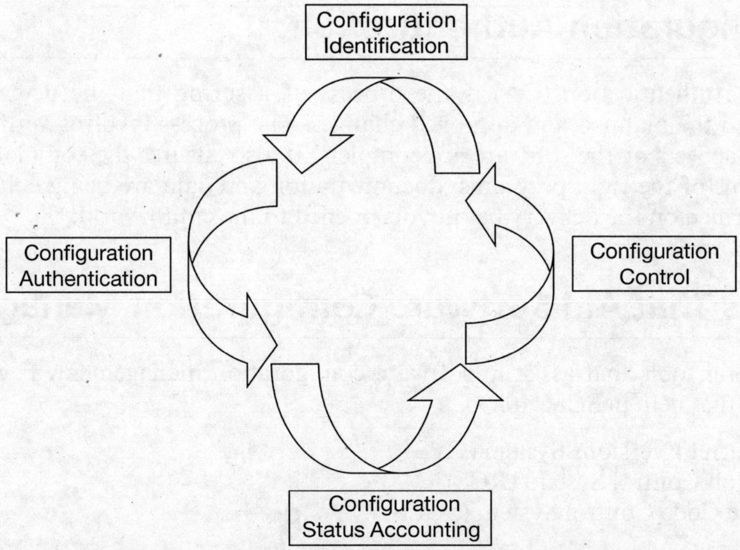

Figure 16.1 Configuration Management Concepts

A baseline is considered to have the following attributes:

1. **Functionally Complete**: A baseline will have a defined functionality. The features and functions of this particular baseline will be documented and available for reference. Thus, the capabilities of the software at a particular baseline are well known.
2. **Known Quality**: The quality of a baseline will be well-defined, that is, all known bugs will be documented and the software would have undergone a complete round of testing before being defined as baseline.
3. **Immutable and Completely Re-creatable**: A baseline, once defined, cannot be changed. The list of the CIs and their versions are set in stone. Also, all the CIs will be under version control so the baseline can be recreated at any point in time.

16.5 Configuration Control

The process of deciding and coordinating the approved changes for the proposed CIs and also implementing the changes on the appropriate baseline is called 'Configuration Control (CC)'.

It should be kept in mind that CC only addresses the process after changes are approved. The act of evaluating and approving changes to software comes under the purview of an entirely different process called change control.

16.6 Configuration Status Accounting

Configuration Status Accounting (CSA) is the bookkeeping process of each release. This procedure involves tracking of what is in each version of software and the changes that lead to this version.

CSA keeps a record of all the changes made to the previous baseline to reach the new baseline.

16.7 Configuration Authentication

Configuration Authentication (CA) is the process of assuring that the new baseline has incorporated all the planned and approved changes. The process involves verifying that all the functional aspects of the software are complete. It also ensures the completeness of the delivery in terms of the right programs; documentation and data are being delivered. CA is an audit performed on the delivery before it is opened to the entire world.

16.8 Tools That Aid Software Configuration Management

There are several tools that assist in software configuration management. Few of the free software tools that help in SCM are:

1. Concurrent Versions System (CVS)
2. Revision Control System (RCS)
3. Source Code Control System (SCCS)

Concurrent Versions System (CVS)

CVS is a version control system. Using it, we can record the history of the source files. For example, sometimes defects are introduced when software is modified and you might not be able to detect the defect until a long time after you make the modification. With CVS, you can easily retrieve old versions to see exactly which change caused the defect. This can sometimes be a big help.

Revision Control System (RCS)

To change a configuration item, a developer has to lock that item first, preventing other developers from changing the item at the same time.

The developer specifies a label for each configuration item. Using this label the developers can check out consistent set of versions [Herbert, 1999].

Source Code Control System (SCCS)

The SCCS is a complete system of commands that allows specified users to control and track changes made to SCCS file. These files allow several versions of the same file to exist simultaneously, which can be helpful when developing a project requiring many versions of large files.

Commercial Tools:

1. Rational Clear Case
2. PVCS
3. Microsoft Visual SourceSafe

16.9 SCM and SEI Capability Maturity Model

The Capability Maturity Model (CMM) defined by the Software Engineering Institute (SEI) describes the principles and practices to achieve a certain level of software process maturity.

The model is intended to help software organizations improve the maturity of their processes in terms of an evolutionary path from ad-hoc and chaotic to a disciplined one. The CMM is designed towards organizations in improving their software processes for building better one faster and at a lower cost.

The SEI defines five levels of maturity of a software development described here.

Associated with each level from level two onwards are key areas which an organization is required to focus on to move to the next level. Such focus areas are called 'Key Process Areas (KPA)' in CMM parlance.

16.10 Configuration Management Activities

The Configuration Manager, in a software project, takes the responsibility of identifying, managing and controlling the configuration items. The activities performed by the configuration manager are:

- Configuration Item/CM Aggregate Identification
- Promotion Management
- Release Management
- Branch Management
- Change Management
- Variant Management

Configuration Item Identification: This activity involves creating a model of the system as a collection of evolving components.

Promotion Management: This activity ensures creation of versions of development components for other developers.

Release Management: During this activity, the versions for the clients and users are created.

Change management: This activity ensures proper handling, approving and tracking of change requests.

Branch Management: This activity becomes important when there is a need to manage concurrent development.

Variant Management: This activity is essential if there is a need for multiple versions which are intended to co-exist and rightly managing them.

16.11 Software Configuration Management Plan

A SCMP documents the way the configuration management will be implemented and followed in an organization. Before the teams can actually follow the CM steps, it is important that they prepare the plan highlighting areas like items to be put under CM, the tool to be used for it, the persons who will be handling the different roles of CM, the audits to be performed, etc. This plan should be developed early in the lifecycle of a project to control the changes from the beginning. A SCMP should contain the key sections as described later.

16.11.1 Purpose

This is a generic section which explains the purpose of CM and why it is important. The purpose of SCM is to establish and control the integrity of work products using:

- Configuration Identification
- Configuration Control
- Configuration Status Accounting
- Configuration Audit

These steps are briefly explained in this section of the plan.

16.11.2 Objectives

What we are planning to convey though this plan is described in this section. An example of the content of this section:

'This SCM Plan defines the configuration management policies and procedures to be followed for this project. In this plan we will first address activities that are platform independent. As the project advances through the life cycle stages, this plan will be expanded to reflect platform specific activities'.

16.11.3 Software Configuration Management Resources

This section identifies the different roles of individuals as well as groups that will participate in the SCM process. It also describes the relationships between individuals and groups. The key points documented in this sub-section are: SCM related Roles and Responsibilities of Project Manager, Configuration Management Manager (CMM), Configuration Control Board (CCB) etc., are mentioned here. Let us look into few sample roles and responsibilities of these resources.

Project Manager (PM)

- Frame the overall project schedule for SCM-related activities along with CMM.
- Ensure team members have received enough training and knowledge about SCM concepts and techniques and applied to project activities.
- Make sure that the SCM standards and procedures set by the CMM, the CCB, and any other affected groups as outlined in this plan are followed by the team.

Configuration Manager (CM)

This is the most important role in terms of SCM. This person is responsible to create and/or update the SCM Plan with assistance from the Project Manager as well as communicating the contents of the plan to the project team.

- Identify the Configuration Items (CIs).
- Create and maintain the SCM Plan, standards, and procedures.
- Communicate the new as well as updated SCM Plan, standards, and procedures to all stakeholders.
- Make sure that all project team members are aware of the SCM process through training on their roles.

- Create SCM products (baselines, application environments) and get those authorized by the CCB.
- Process and track change requests.
- Ensure that configuration item change requests and problem reports for all CIs follow the steps like initiation, recording, review, approval, and tracking according to the SCM Plan.
- Make sure the functional and physical configuration audits are performed.

Configuration Control Board (CCB)

- Monitor the changes/updates to project requirements.
- Approve the identified list of CIs and the baseline of the same.
- Review and approve changes to the baselines.
- Review, discuss, prioritize and approve the change requests.

16.11.4 Software Configuration Management Tasks

This section contains detailed steps for completing the CM tasks.

- **Identification of Configuration Items and Baseline:** The project team along with the CMM should identify the items that they need to monitor and update under the CM framework. These items are properly labelled. A baseline version is created which acts as the foundation of the CM system. At this step, the CIs are grouped, categorized and labelled in a logical fashion so that it is easy to refer to any of the items at a later point of time. This is also called 'CI Register'. Table 16.1 shows a sample CI register.

Table 16.1 CI Register

Configuration Items	Item Code	Responsible for Placing Ttem Under Control	When Item is Put Under Control
Project Plan	PPM-0003	Project Manager	Initiation & Planning Stage End
Requirements Specification	RES-0402	Business Owner	Requirements Stage End
Requirements Traceability Matrix	RES-0403	Project Manager/DTMB Analyst	Requirements Stage End
Test Plan	TST-0601	Business Owner/Test Manager	System Design Stage End
Test Type Approach (1…n)	TST-0603	Business Owner/Test Manager	System Design Stage End
Design Document	DES-0204	Project Manager/DTMB Analyst	System Design Stage End
Test Case Document	TST-0606	Project Manager/DTMB Analyst	Coding End
Etc…			

- **Version Control (Control changes before and after release to customer):** Each work product under CM may undergo changes due to many reasons like multiple people working on the same item; the user initiated changes, the review comments to be incorporated, etc. so, it is important that the CM system engages a version control system to maintain and track the different versions of the work products which allows to refer to any previous version incase needed. The hierarchical approach and proper labelling done in the previous step ensures success of this step.
- **Change Control:** The tasks involved in this step are like checking out the existing work product from the system, making changes to it, synchronizing the versions, branching off the versions. In case multiple people are working on the same item, merging multiple versions, approving the changes and then checking in the changed version into the repository so that the change control process takes help of the version control task.
- **Configuration Auditing:** Periodic audit or authentication ensures that changes are made properly and processes are followed. Configuration audits focus on identifying the robustness of the CM process and whether for each item the CM processes are followed properly. The attributes of the CI's should reflect the correct status and the changes to pass the audit process.
- **Reporting:** This is also a periodic task where each stakeholder is apprised of the updates and changes to the configuration database, problems found, steps taken to arrest future problems and other configuration audit findings.

16.11.5 Configuration Management Schedule

In this section, the sequence and coordination of CM activities with the project milestones are established.

16.11.6 Change Requests and Approvals

SCM Plan documents the procedures for initiating change requests, enforcing the flow of the change process, prioritizing the changes, capturing CCB decisions, and reporting the process information. Some of the tools used for controlling change request work flow are:

- Remedy Flow and Procedures
- Rational Software
- Serena Team Track
- Microsoft Excel
- Microsoft Word

16.11.7 Change Control Process

Controlling the changes to the configuration items is one of the main tasks of a CM system. This section highlights how the CCB should control changes that impact schedule, function, and the configuration of the system as a whole.

16.11.8 Management of Release Documentation

Releasing the correct version of the document and software to the stakeholders is key to the success of any project. The CM system ensures that when the CIs are released to external stakeholders a consistent process is followed. The following documents are normally required for the release to production:

- Installation Plan (including a rollback plan)
- Release Notes
- Updated User Documentation
- Training Materials

16.11.9 Configuration Control Tools and Techniques

This section focuses on the tools and techniques that will be employed for implementing the SCM processes. The purpose of these tools may be to manage access to the repositories, to process change requests and to report status of CIs.

The basic set of tools includes:

- Database Management Systems.
- Report Generators.
- Tools for maintaining separate dynamic and controlled repositories.
- File system with the capability to manage the check in and check out of units, for controlling compilations, and capturing the resulting products.

Some examples of specific tools are:

- Infrastructure Configuration Management Build Application
- Remedy
- Issue Tracker
- Oracle Repository
- Serena Version Manager

16.11.10 Configuration Management Update

After all the processes for CM are established in the above sections, this section mentions how the SCMP will be kept updated during the project life cycle.

SUMMARY

CM is very crucial for evolving software systems. Change in many large software systems is inevitable. Careful planning is required considering the components that are likely to be changed, any other subsystems that may have to be changed for the modification of the given system, analysis of cost, etc. CM makes sure that these changes do not cause undesired impact on the other subsystems.

- **Basic configuration management activities are:**
  - Configuration Identification
  - Configuration Control
  - Configuration Status Accounting
  - Configuration Authentication
- **Few common version management tools are:**
  - Concurrent Versions System (CVS)
  - Revision Control System (RCS)
  - Source Code Control System (SCCS)
- **Software configuration management plan includes:**
  - Purpose
  - Objectives
  - Software Configuration Management Resources
  - Software Configuration Management Tasks
  - Change Requests and Approvals
  - Change Control Process
  - Management of Release Documentation
  - Configuration Control Tools and Techniques

EXERCISES

PART A (Objective-type Questions)

1. SCM stands for
   A. Software Configuration Management
   B. Software Control Management
   C. Software Change Management
   D. Software Code Management

2. A piece of software work product which is subject to change is called
   A. Change Item
   B. Change Request
   C. Work Item
   D. Configuration Item

3. The process of deciding, coordinating the approved changes for the proposed CIs and implementing the changes on the appropriate baseline are called
   A. Change Control
   B. Change Request
   C. Work Item
   D. Configuration Control

PART B (Short Questions)

1. What are the SCM tools you are aware of?

2. What are the traditional SCM processes steps?

3. What is configuration control?

17

Managing People and Organizing Teams

17.1 Introduction

Managing the project team is crucial for the success of any project delivery. Project managers will be required to motivate the project team in times of temporary reverses, help resolve conflicts that may arise among stakeholders, or address team retention, labour relations, and performance appraisals over the life-cycle of a project. Team communication management refers to the process of timely and appropriate development, collection, dissemination, storage, and disposition of project related information. Generally, more than 90% of a project manager's time spend for communication.

17.2 Managing the Project Team

Project managers are expected to be effective leaders, communicators, negotiators, problem solvers, and capable of influencing stakeholders to their behaviours and activities that would result in overall project success. Project human resource management, thus comprises a set of processes required to make effective use of the people involved in a project. These peoples are recognized as sponsors, customers, project team members, and subcontractors.

The following points elaborate the important factors that a project manager need to address as part of team management:

- Selection of techniques those are appropriate for personal and organizational relationships.
- Choice of techniques that are appropriate to the current needs of the project. For example, project human resource requirements may change over the course of project execution, the number of project stakeholders may change as the project moves from one phase to another, and their impacts may vary over time.
- Awareness of the administrative human resource requirements of the performing organization to ensure compliance. Project manager ensures team awareness.
- Actions undertaken to influence project team members toward professional and ethical behaviour.

17.3 Organizational Theories

Organizational theories explain how groups and individuals behave in differing organizational arrangements. Those were derived from organizational structures and procedures that took shape during the industrial revolution in England and Europe. Organizational theories provide information regarding the way people function and how organizations behave. Project managers apply these theories to identify strengths and weaknesses of their teams, and to reduce time and costs of projects. Organizational theories represent one of the bases for generating an effective human resource plan. Three such theories are presented here.

17.3.1 McGregor's Theory of X and Y

This theory postulates that there are two types of employees. Theory X employees, who avoid work, do not take responsibility, and generally dislike work, are to be watched, cannot be trusted, and need to be micromanaged. Theory Y employees, who are motivated, take responsibilities, they like work, to be provided challenging assignments, and encouraged to work independently.

17.3.2 Z Theory

As per the Z theory, workers need to be involved in the decision-making process; it will make them more responsible and accountable for their decisions.

17.3.3 Maslow's Hierarchy of Needs

This well-known organizational theory postulates that there exists a hierarchy of human needs. People seek higher-level needs only when their lower-level needs have been satisfied. The hierarchy of these needs, from the highest to lowest, is as follows:

- Self-actualization needs—seek knowledge and maximize potential.
- Esteem needs—respect for others, self-respect, freedom and recognition.
- Social needs—community and social anxieties.
- Safety needs—job security, financial security.
- Physiological needs—basic needs like water, shelter and food.

Points to Remember

The popular organizational theories are McGregor's Theory of X and Y, Maslow's hierarchy of needs and Z theory which are useful in understanding the employee behaviour and effective team management.

17.4 Team Communication

Project managers generate a communication management plan, prepare reports based on it, ask and discuss with stakeholders about their needs, identify what communication processes they need, and frequently revisit communication needs of stakeholders at team meetings to avoid communication related problems.

On a high level, the processes involved in the effective communication management are:

1. **Plan Communication:** This process determines the information needs of the project stakeholders and establishes a communications system.
2. **Manage Communication:** Manage communication is a process of implementing the communication management plan and responding to unexpected requests for information.
3. **Control Communication:** This is a process of collecting and presenting performance information to stakeholders on how resources are being used to achieve the project objectives and take appropriate actions to control it.

Project managers are always at the centre of communications and the primary key to success in their role is to understand the various ways to interact with different stakeholders and also with others inside and outside of an organization. There are different dimensions of communications, such as internal vs external, formal vs informal, vertical vs horizontal, official vs unofficial, written vs oral, and verbal vs non-verbal. Choosing a particular dimension depends on the situation and context in which the communication evolves and also the purpose of the communication. About 55% of communications are nonverbal communications. Figure 17.1 for various dimensions of communications along with the purpose of each dimension.

Internal vs External

- Internal means with the project team
- External means with customers, other projects and media

Formal vs Informal

- Formal includes memos, reports, briefings
- Email and ad-hoc communications are informal

Vertical vs Horizontal

- Vertical means communication with peers at same level

Official vs Unofficial

- News letter and annual reports are official communications
- Off the record communication are unofficial communication

Written vs Oral

- Any documents in writing be classified as written communication

Verbal vs Non-verbal

- Non-verbal communication includes voice fluctuation and body language
- About 55% of communication are non-verbal communication

Figure 17.1 Dimensions of Communication

17.5 Forms of Communication

The term 'forms of communication' refers to the physical medium through which communication is made. In organizational contexts, such media may of formal or informal, oral or written. The choice of the form of communication to be used to make a communication varies over situations, priorities, and organizational cultures. Table 17.1 summarizes the different forms of communication that may exist in an organization.

Table 17.1 Forms of Communication in Organizations

Forms of Communication	Characteristic	Examples
Written formal	Precise; transmitted through the medium of correspondence.	Project charter, scope statement, project plan, WBS, project status, contract related communication.
Written informal		E-mails, notes, memos, letters
Oral formal	High degree of flexibility; use the medium of personal contact, group meetings or telephone.	Presentations, speeches
Oral informal		Conversations with team members Project meetings. Leisure room or war room conversations.
Non-verbal communication	About 55% of total communication.	Facial expressions, hand movements, tone of voice while speaking.

17.6 Process of Communication

The actual process of communication involves the following three components:

- Sending the communication
- Receiving the communication
- Eliciting feedback on the communications made

A fourth component could be understanding of the possible organizational barriers to effective communication. Organizations address these barriers to communication by establishing formal procedures for communication and, thereby, facilitate the aforementioned three components.

Sending Messages: There are four elements involved in sending a message: (1) formulate the message of communication; (2) consider possible barriers to the communication that is going to be made; (3) encode the message, and (4) clearly communicate (send) the message.

The knowledge of formulating a message to be communicated is an art. First, the sender needs to be clear in what he communicates, why he communicates; the message should not give dubious meaning; it should be clear and accurate. The format of the message also varies depending on the type of message (formal vs informal), choosing appropriate formats is also important for communication. The sender should consider the different barriers to communication, such as:

1. Lack of clear communication channels—Using email, where the server is not working properly.
2. Garrulous and voluble communication—We should not communicate to others rapidly without determining the understanding level of other persons.
3. Physical distance—People sitting in different physical working areas separated from each other.
4. Jargons used in technical communication—Using technical jargons are to be avoided when communication with different groups. For example, RAM means both Random Access Memory and Responsibility Assignment Matrix.
5. Distracting environmental factors—Background noise in working environments is a good example.

Figure 17.2 shows the various components of communication skill a project manager needs to possess for effectively building and managing the team.

17.6.1 Encoding the Message

Converting the message which is feasible enough to communicate directly is referred as encoding. For example, our voice message should be converted to digital signal before transmitting it through media.

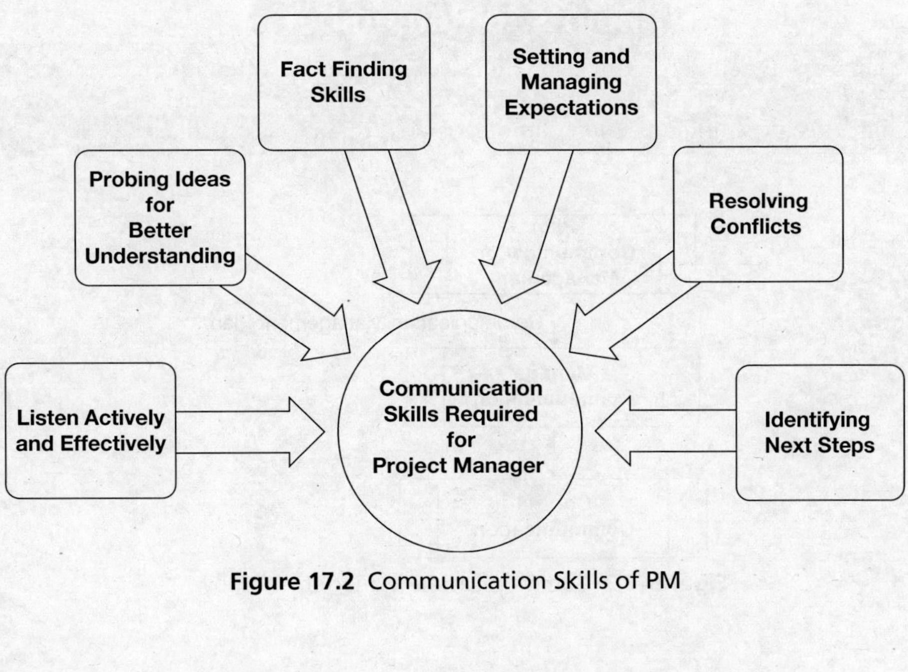

Figure 17.2 Communication Skills of PM

Receiving Messages: Recipients receive the message, but the latter is generally affected by external barriers and the recipient's own internal barriers, if any. Possible internal barriers are the recipient's experience level, understanding of the message, and attitude towards the subject matter of the communication made by the sender. Recipients decode the message contained in the communication that is received by means of mental images. Human mind always links the message with the information that we already know in order to understand the message clearly. For example, 'sky blue' colour is more understandable instead of saying light blue color.

Feedback: After a communication has been made, the senders generally confirm on the receipt of the message contained in the communication. This process of eliciting feedback may entail the sender asking the receiver questions such as 'Do you understand what I say?'

17.7 Handling Communication in Software Project

Effective communication is said to have been made when information has been provided in the right format, at the right point in time, and with the right impact on both the sender and receiver.

Here, 'right impact' means the purpose of passing the message should be achieved. For example, if you send a message stating a proposed delay in a project along with the reasons for the delay, then the client on getting the message, should accept the delay and the reasons you describe. That is effective communication. Efficient information, on the other hand, refers only to the process of providing the required information when needed. Figure 17.3 shows the various communication-related processes.

Number of communication channels = $N \times (N - 1)/2$

Here, N refers to the number of team members. Therefore, if there are 6 resources in a project team, there would be 15 communication channels between them.

Points to Remember

As the number of members in the team increases, the number of communication channels increase as well. This brings a lot of complexities in the team management and, thus, for big teams, effective communication planning is the primary task of the leads.

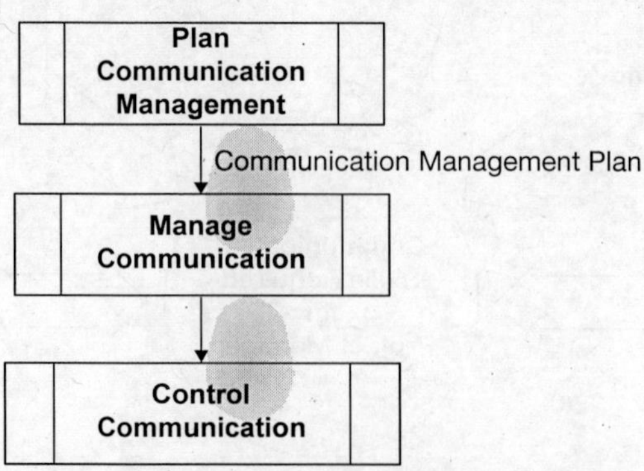

Figure 17.3 Communication Management Flow

17.7.1 Communication Technologies

Communication technologies are used to transfer information back and forth among project elements. Communications can take place in many ways, like face to face, via fax, via e-mail, over phone, through net meetings, video conferences, etc. The choice of which technology to use is based on the following factors:

- Urgency of the need of information
- Availability of the technologies identified
- Expected project staffing of the project
- Duration of the project using the technology
- Project environment where communication technologies are applied

17.7.2 Communication Methods

There exist three types of communication methods: push communication, pull communication, and interactive communication.

1. **Push Communication:** Here, a communication is sent (pushed) to the receiver without confirmation or certification as whether it has reached the intended recipient (*e.g.*, letters, e-mails, faxes).
2. **Pull Communication:** Here, recipients access the communication (pull) at their discretion. Pull communication methods are employed when large volumes of information need to be transferred (*e.g.*, intranet).
3. **Interactive Communication:** Here, both the push method and pull methods are used (phone, video conferencing).

Effective distribution of information includes a number of techniques such as choosing appropriate sender-receiver models, correct choice of communication media, writing style of the message, presentation methods, facilitation, etc.

Sender-receiver Models: An appropriate sender-receiver model is based on aspects such as whether it is a one-to-one communication or one-to-many communication, a push communication (e-mail) or pulls communication (records retrieval), etc.

Choice of Media: Choosing the right media to convey the information will make the process effective. For example, some types of information can be passed on through e-mail, while others may be best disclosed face-to-face.

- **Writing style of messages:** Key elements that make an e-mail (or any other message effective) include choosing an appropriate and meaningful 'subject line', use of proper salutation in the message, correct sentence structure, and appropriate use of active and passive voice.
- **Meeting management techniques:** Agenda, conflicts
- **Presentation styles:** Body language
- **Facilitation techniques:** Building consensus

Although, several techniques exist for managing communication, team meetings continue to be the most preferred. The following guidelines are used conducting effective team meetings:

- Set and enforce strict time lines for meetings.
- Meet team members regularly, but not frequently. It may distract them from their work.

- Involve team members to generate agenda for the meeting.
- Ensure that only the points on the agenda would be discussed.
- Distribute the agenda before hand to the members.
- Revisit the minutes of previous meetings and address pending action items, if any.
- Let the team members know what is expected out of them in advance.
- Invite only those team members to the meetings who are important.
- Set and enforce ground rules for discussions in the meetings.
- Properly document and communicate the minutes of all the meetings.

Table 17.2 Information Gathering and Retrieval Systems

Technique	Examples
Information gathering and retrieval systems	Manual filing systems, electronic-text databases, project management software, systems that allow to access for technical documentation such as engineering drawings.
Information distribution methods	Project meetings, hard-copy document distribution, shared access to networked electronic databases, faxes, e-mails, voice mails, and video conferencing sessions.

17.8 The Five Phases of Team Building

Five team building phases are defined in the PMBOK®—Project Management Body of Knowledge is forming, storming, norming, performing, and adjourning.

1. **Forming:** Team members are introduced to each other in the forming phase. This phase is characterized by politeness and formality in the relationships between team members.
2. **Storming:** The team starts to move from 'as is' to 'to be'. Some team members may be in conflict with others in a clash for control or in a clash of individual identities or cultures. Hence, the term storming. During the storming phase, team members tend to disagree with each other. The team's leadership or the management, however, exerts effort to overcome their differences, ensuring they are resolved.
3. **Norming:** Following the 'storm,' team members reach a consensus on the 'to be' process and learn to work together. However, when issues or concerns surface the team may return to the storming phase. Also, when a new member joins the team, the phases of norming and storming would be reenacted for the entire team. It is in this phase that unique, team-specific norms assume shape and get entrenched with all team members; hence the term norming.
4. **Performing:** Once the important team members have resolved their differences and established strong work relationships, the team is said to be ready for high performance. While in the performing phase, the team seldom falls back into the storming phase. In this phase, a team is characterized by high levels of initiative.
5. **Adjourning:** Here, the team shares its improved processes with other teams. Many relationships formed within a team continue long after dispersement of the team following project completion.

17.9 Conflict Management

Conflict in organizations is inevitable and is actually the difference of opinion between people. Evading conflict could lead to be more negative consequences or destructive than dealing with the conflict itself. Innovative ideas emerge when there is difference of opinion. The starting point for any healthy discussion is difference of opinion and hence, conflict is inevitable.

Project managers address conflicts early and usually engage the conflicting parties in private, using a direct, collaborative approach. They consider conflict as a team issue and during the process of conflict resolution, focus: (1) on the present and not the past, and (2) on the issue involved in the conflict and not the individuals involved. The commonly used conflict resolution techniques are as follows:

Problem Solving: This technique confronts the problem head on, using research and objective analysis as its tools. It is widely considered as the preferred approach and aims at a healthy win–win solution to the problem.

Compromise: This technique searches for a solution that conflicting parties find moderately satisfying and entails both parties giving up a part of their demands. This approach generally leads to lose–lose solution and is primarily used to avoid build-up of conflict levels.

Forcing: In this approach, the conflicting party with less power is simply asked to accept the other more powerful side's demands, leading to a win–lose solution. Because this approach seriously damages relationships, it is only adopted by project managers rarely when the gravity of the crisis calls for it.

Smoothing: Project managers use this approach to emphasize areas of agreement, and aim to ignore areas of disagreement, between conflicting parties. Obviously, this approach leads only to a temporary solution.

Collaborating: This technique incorporates multiple view points and insights from differing perspectives, leading to consensus and commitment. This approach may lead to a win–win solution.

Withdrawing: Project managers use this approach when they believe that it is better than conflicting parties avoid each other. This technique generally does not solve a problem, but may introduce a 'cooling' period.

SUMMARY

- Organizational theories explain how groups and individuals behave in differing organizational arrangements and are derived from organizational structures and procedures that took shape during the Industrial Revolution in England and Europe.
- **Maslow's Hierarchy of Needs:** This well-known organizational theory postulates that there exists a hierarchy of human needs. People seek higher-level needs only when their lower level needs have been satisfied. The hierarchy of these needs, from the highest to lowest, is as follows:

- Self-actualization needs—seek knowledge, maximize potential
- Esteem needs—respect for others, self-respect, freedom, recognition
- Social needs—community and social anxieties
- Safety needs—job security, financial security
- Physiological needs—basic needs like water, shelter, and food

- Five team-building phases are defined in the PMBOK are forming, storming, norming, performing, and adjourning.
- Conflict in organizations is inevitable and is actually the difference of opinion between people.
- Memos, e-mails are examples of non-formal communication while reports and metrics are example of formal communication. Approximately, 70–90% of project manager's time goes only for communicating. A project manager spends ~50% of his time in meetings.
- Formula for calculating number of communication channel is $N \times (N - 1)/2$, where N is the number of people involved.
- Team communication management refers to the process of timely and appropriate development, collection, dissemination, storage, and disposition of project related information. Generally, more than 90% of a project manager's time expend for communication.
- On a high level, the processes involved in the effective communication management are
  - *Plan Communications:* This process determines the information needs of the project stakeholders and establishes a communications system.
  - *Manage Communications:* Manage communications is a process of implementing the communication management plan and responding to unexpected requests for information.
  - *Control Communications:* This is a process of collecting and presenting performance information to stakeholders on how resources are being used to achieve project objectives and take appropriate actions to control it.
- There are different dimensions of communications such as internal vs external, formal vs informal, vertical vs horizontal, official vs unofficial, written vs oral, verbal vs nonverbal. Choosing a particular dimension depends on the situation or context in which the communication evolves and also the purpose of the communication.
- The actual process of communication involves following three components:
  - Sending the communication
  - Receiving the communication
  - Eliciting feedback on the communications made
- Communication technologies are used to transfer information back and forth among project elements. Communications can take place in many ways: face to face, via fax, via e-mail, over phone, or by net meetings, video conferences, etc.

EXERCISES

PART A (Objective-type Questions)

1. Which of the following is not an example of organizational theory?
   A. Maslow's hierarchy of needs
   B. Theory of X and Y
   C. Theory Z
   D. Damien's principle

2. What percentage of time project managers spend after communication?
   A. 62%
   B. 70%
   C. 82%
   D. 90%

3. Project status report is which form of communication?
   A. Formal written communication
   B. Informal written communication
   C. Informal verbal communication
   D. Informal verbal communication

4. Effective communication means information is provided in right _____ at right _____ and with the right_____
   A. Format, Time, Impact
   B. Meaning, Quality, Analysis
   C. Format, Time, Language
   D. Meaning, time, Impact

5. A project team have 11 stakeholders. How may communication channels it has?
   A. 11
   B. 10
   C. 55
   D. 66

6. Which of the following is not an example of judgmental method?
   A. Composite forecasts
   B. Delphi method
   C. Scenario building
   D. ARMA

PART B (Write the answers in one or two lines)

1. What are all the factors that project managers requires to address as part of team management?

2. Write notes on Organization Theories (OT).

3. Write notes on McGregor's Theory of X and Y.

4. What is Z Theory?

5. Write notes on Maslow's Hierarchy of Needs.

6. What are all the process involved in communication management?

7. What are all the components of communication?

8. What is encoding of a message?

9. Write notes on communication technologies.

10. What are all the factors that affects communication technologies?

11. Write notes on Push and Pull communication methods.

12. Explain 'forming' and 'storming' phases of team building.

13. Write notes on norming phases of team building.

14. Write notes on conflict management.

15. Explain how forcing can be used as a technique of conflict management.

16. Explain how withdrawing can be used as a technique of conflict management.

18

Software Project Reviews

18.1 Introduction

Organization is a complex equilibrium of interactions between its organizational structure, systems, performance measures, culture and the associated people. It is a big structure with each component exercising its influence on others and, thereby, molding or modifying them. Hence, even the best designed organizations need periodic tuning and recalibration of its components to refocus and rededicate itself to its objectives. An organization strives to offer new and innovative solutions in order to remain competitive. Its delivery processes also need to be dynamic and adaptive to the changing market scenarios. Besides this, organization has been witnessing quite aggressive growth. A flip side of this is, of course, the people are continuously challenged and, hence, tend to make compromises to meet delivery schedules. Some of these compromises may give short-term dividends, but have long-term impacts on quality of products, delivery processes, etc. Hence, they have an impact on the organization's reputation. Software project reviews help overcoming these difficulties.

A software review is 'A process in which a software product or process is examined by managers, users, customers, users' representatives, or stakeholders, for comments or approvals.'

18.2 Objectives of Reviews

Project reviews help to recalibrating and fine-tuning the delivery processes to make them aligned with the organizational realities. The following reviews are helpful in a delivery process:

- Identify gaps in the process and product.
- Validation of the work done.
- Tuning of the existing processes and product.
- Ensure quality assurance.
- Ensure customer satisfaction.
- It is also form of knowledge transfer.
- It also helps for team building.

Identification of gaps in the process and product is possible by reviewing various documents and artifacts of the projects starting from process documents, customer requirements, design document, developed code, test case document, test design document, project management plan, and deployment document.

A review process for the documents needs to be defined clearly along with a project review checklist that can be used to review those documents to ensure review covers all the items.

18.3 Types of Reviews

Stakeholder-based Classification

There are two types of reviews, namely, formal review and informal review depending on the participative stakeholders of the review. Formal reviews includes following formal process involving subject matter experts for doing the review. Subject matter experts may be internal to the project or external. Informal reviews also may follow a structure, but in informal manner. Two more types of review for stakeholder-based classifications are peer review vs internal review. Internal review involves review with internal people. It focuses on team rather than work. It helps finding early recovery of bugs and problems. Peer review is an alternate to internal review. Peer team members do the review. Peer review focus on work rather than project team.

Level-based Classification

There are two types of reviews namely technical review and general project management review depending on the levels to be reviewed. Technical review involves technical people and deal only with technical issues and problems of the project whereas general project management review deals with project management aspects of the project like scope review, cost review, time review, risks review, and communication review, etc.

Orientation-based Classification

There are two types of reviews, namely, output-oriented review and process-oriented review. Output-oriented review concentrates on reviewing the outcome rather than the process of creation. It helps identifying issues in final outputs. It primarily focuses on short-term issues of the output. Process-oriented review identifies issues in the overall process. It primarily focuses on long-term issues of the process.

Project Life-cycle-based Classification

Reviews can be classified based on project life-cycle stages. Start-up review happens at the beginning of projects ensuring all are rightly set for starting the project. Phase-end review happens at the end of the phases ensuring that phases are completed as per the expectations of that phase. Process review happens in between the phases ensuring process are being followed properly. Delivery audit happens before delivery of the products ensuring work completion and the outcome can be delivered to the customers. Project closure audit happens at the end of the projects ensuring the project completion procedures are taken care.

18.4 Timing of Reviews

There are numerous junctures in project management life-cycle at which a review of artifacts or process can be carried out. The number of reviews and timing of reviews are dependent on various parameters like size of a project, complexity of a project, importance of a project, schedule of a project. Timing needs to be chosen in such a way that all relevant information about the review is available with the reviewers before starting a review process. If relevant information is not available, then review outcome will not be very effective. A delayed review also will not add any value as the commitment might be given to the customer already. Choosing optimum time for review is essential.

18.5 Stakeholders of Review Process

One of the crucial aspects to ensuring an effective review is the selection of the participants of review. Key participants in the review process include the Chairperson of the review, team, subject matter experts, and customer of the project.

Chairperson

Project manager usually plays this role as complete review of the project is his responsibility. Chairperson is one who initiates the review process by connecting various stakeholders, identifying timing of review, preparing alternate plan and ensure check-lists are available for review, conducting review meeting, follow-up with the outcome and implementation of the review. Project manager can also appoint somebody as the chairperson of the review depending on the situation. For example, project manager can appoint a lead designer as a chairperson when design document is being reviewed. Project manager can appoint a technical leader as a chairperson when the coding is being reviewed. Depending on the size and complexity of the project, co-chairperson can also be employed for effective review process.

Team

Team is an important stakeholder of any review who can explain the context to the reviews and clarifying doubts if any. While reviewing the design of a project, design team will represent the review, while reviewing the coding of the project, coding team will represent the review. It may not be possible to include entire team for review, but key team members need to be identified in order to take better advantage of the review.

Subject Matter Experts

The SME needs to be selected based on the artifacts under review. For a technical review, SME can be a technical expertise whereas for a project management review, a project management expert needs to play this role. Subject matter experts can be better from outside the project team who are not involved in the life-cycle of the project. One of the subject matter experts is called 'lead reviewer' who would lead the entire review.

Customer

Representatives from customer organization can also take care in the review process, for effective outcome of the review. This will ensure duplication of review at the customer's side.

18.6 Characteristics of Reviews

Review is a well-established way of improving the quality of project life-cycle and its outcomes.

Reviews are Independent

Subject matter experts can be better from outside the project team, who are not involved in the life cycle of the project and who are independent of the project outcome. Independent reviews are always out of bias. Independent reviews are mostly straightforward and honest in nature. Independent reviews can be trusted easily.

Reviews are Timely

Timely review of projects and artifacts are very important. If reviews started earlier than planned, then the reviewer may not have sufficient information to do the reviews properly. If reviews started late, then the review outcome may not be fully utilized and the team may not have sufficient time to fix the review outcomes.

Reviews are Transparent

Reviews needs to be as transparent as possible. It should not hide anything from the team. This will ensure trust and at the same time will help the team to fix the review outcome easily. Transparent review also minimizes bias. Transparent review also ensures that reviews are realistic in nature.

Reviews are Multidisciplinary

Multidisciplinary review ensures the reviews covers all the aspects of the agenda completely. Multidisciplinary also ensures views of various stakeholders to be considered for review and needs to satisfy various stakeholders. Multidisciplinary includes taking care of understanding and reviewing various linkages between elements of documents or software under review. Multidisciplinary reviews ensure that reviews taken place considering holistic view of the system.

Reviews are Objective

Review outcomes needs to be objective rather than subjective. Objective also ensures complete quantitative outcome without any doubts or clarifications. Review outcome should not be stated in doubtful manner and needs to be clear and crisp.

Reviews are Accessible

Review outcomes needs to be accessible for all the stakeholders involved, enabling them to fix the issues raised. There is no meaning for review outcome, if it is not accessible by the stakeholders.

18.7 Initiating Review

Initiation phase of the review forms the foundation of starting the planning phase of the review. It sets the goals of the review and determines the length of the review along with the formalities involved in the overall review process. Notifications given to the expert team to start the planning phase. Initiation phase usually gets executed by chairperson of the review.

18.8 Planning Review

Initiation phase of the review sets the goals of the review and planning phase and takes it as input when planning the next step of the review. This phase determines the timeline of the review in detail along with cost and other constraints. This step also decides the structure of the review and participants of the review in each phase. Performance baseline is also agreed by all stakeholders for review. This step also builds the questionnaire and checklists required to start the review.

18.9 Data Collection Phase

All the required data to start the review is being collected in this phase. If the reviewers are required to go through any other data which are essential to conduct the review, it is being facilitated here.

The reviewers individually prepare for group examination of the work under review by examining the data and artifacts carefully for anomalies. This individual preparation will vary depending on the types of reviews.

18.10 Structure of Review Meeting

Length of a review meeting can be hours to days to weeks depending on the complexity or scope of the project, review resources availability. It is not necessarily to review all the aspects of a phase in a single sitting of review; it can be planned in iterations also. The purpose of review is to improve the product or developing superior product and not finding fault with the person or product.

Agenda for Review

An well-prepared agenda ensures 50% completion of review and as per the plan helps in the smooth execution of review. Agenda lists down who is responsible for review, duration of review, distribution of review for various items, place of review, mode of review like telephone, and in person video conference.

Welcome and Introduction

Usually, 5% of the overall time spent in this process. Introduction is given by the chairperson of the review. Review stakeholders are also introduced to each other stating their experience, organization and area of expertise.

Review Purpose and Review Process

Usually, 5% of the overall time spent over here detailing out the purpose and process of review. The chairperson explains this to all the stakeholders. He will seek constructive inputs from all the review stakeholders.

Background of Review

Usually, 10% of the overall time spent over here. Actual review starts from this section. Review background is clearly explained to all stakeholders listing down the circumstance of review. This section clearly links previous review outcome with the current review.

Discussion of Project and Product

Usually, 60–65% of the overall time spent over this process. Presentation and discussion of each item under review are discussed here. Complete traceability of the items under review, process of creation of items under review is discussed. It discusses assumptions considered while creating the items under review along with clarifications of uncertainty.

Wrap-up

Usually, 10% of the overall time is spent in this process. Outcome of the review is discussed over here. Identification of issues and recommendations are discussed as an outcome of the review. Action items are summarized. Post review activities are also discussed. Chairperson also thanks the reviewers and other participants.

Example: If total review duration = 100 minutes, then we can split the timeline of a review meeting as follows:

Welcome and introduction time = 10 minutes
Review purpose = 5 minutes
Background Review = 10 minutes
Project discussion = 65 minutes
Project wrap-up = 10 minutes

18.11 Post Review Follow-up and Review Report

Post-review Follow-up

Once the reviews are complete, somebody needs to follow-up the action items of the review to ensure it is completely addressed. Chairperson of the review, usually the project manager, needs to take this role. All items identified as an outcome of review, need to be addressed in timely manner for effective outcome and benefits.

Review Report

The structure of a review report depends on the type of review. The items under review are usually agreed by all stakeholders well before beginning the review. A review report needs to be issued within a week time of the review with recommended action items. A follow-up status report on review needs to be issued within a month with status of action items and detailed resolution of items. Following are the contents of a review report:

- Introduction: Review scope, Review Objectives
- Current Project Status: Project ecosystem
- Recommendations: Action items, timelines, budget of action items
- Current Status of Action Items: Open/closed/on hold/rejected/WIP
- Limitations and Assumptions of the Review: If any

18.12 Software Estimation Review Process

Accurate estimations of time, cost, scope and risks are the pillars for effective project planning and execution. Project estimation is a crucial element of project. It needs to be reviewed in order to have right estimation technique and right estimation outcomes. A structured estimation process should produce quality estimate, consistency in estimation, improving accuracy, and saving time.

Pre-requisite for Review

Estimate is developed by the project team. This process involves the following six steps:

1. Notify the Estimation Review Team and take an appointment.
2. Provide the estimate developed by the project team to the Estimation Review Team.
3. Provide required knowledge transition to the Estimation Review Team to facilitate review process.
4. Estimation Review Team reviews the estimation and provides review comments (if applicable).
5. Project team incorporates the review comments (if applicable) received from Estimation Review Team and jointly finalize upon the revised estimation.
6. Project team submits the revised estimation to the customer.

Notes

1. The estimation review process may continue for two weeks.
2. Steps 4 and 5 might be iterative.
3. On completion of review process, Estimation Review Document should be prepared by the project team.

18.13 Software Design Review Process

A design review is a milestone of the design phase of the project. Design is reviewed against its requirements for identifying and closing issues before committing or delivering design documents to the customer. Design review can be made compulsory depending on the product being developed. Cost of rework increases through the development life-cycle. Design review is a classic example of quality efforts. Design can be evaluated based on the already defined set of criteria, such as non-functional requirements, functional requirements, usability, etc. Design review can be formal or informal depending on the situations.

Pre-requisite

Design document developed by the project team. This process involves the following 5 steps:

1. Notify the Design Review Team and take an appointment.
2. Provide the design document developed by the project team to the Design Review Team.

3. Design Review Team reviews the design documents and provides review comments.
4. Project team incorporates the review comments received from Design Review Team and produces the modified final design documents.
5. Project team submits the final design documents to the customer for sign-off.

Notes

1. The design review process may last for two weeks.
2. Steps 3 and 4 might be iterative.
3. On completion of review process, Design Review Documents should be prepared by the project team.

18.14 Software Coding Review Process

Pre-requisites

Developed code and design documents agreed upon by project team and Design Review Team.

This process involves the following four steps:

1. Notify the Code Review Team and take an appointment.
2. Provide the design documents agreed upon by the Project Team and Design Review Team with the Code Review Team.
3. Code Review Team reviews codes based on the information provided in the design documents and provides its review comments.
4. Project team modifies the codes based on the review comments received from the Code Review Team.

Notes:

1. Code Review Team ensures coding is complete as per design.
2. Code Review Team also uses standard checklists for consistency.
3. The code review process may span two weeks.
4. Steps 3 and 4 might be iterative.
5. On completion of review process, Code Review Document should be prepared by the Project Team.

18.15 Project Review Checklist

Project review checklists help the reviewer to execute review in better way. Checklists also ensures all the aspects of the reviews are covered objectively. A checklist can just be 'Yes/No' type or it can be score-driven (1/2/3/4/5), but clear-cut definition is important to maintain consistency.

Sample Project Planning Review Checklist

Given here a detailed checklist to assist reviewing the health of Project Planning.

Relevance (at this time)	Practice (at this time)
(How relevant is this attribute to this project or review?)	(An indication of this attribute's strength or weakness)
1 — Little/none; 3 — Moderate; 5 — Critical	1 — Not addressed; 3 — Adequate; 5 — Well-covered

Item	Attribute	Relevance	Practice	Remarks
1	**Project Planning Review**			
1.1	Formal Project Management Plan available? And all the key elements are available?			
1.2	Have all the stakeholders been identified? Stakeholder register available?			
1.3	Is a Stakeholder Management Plan in place?			
1.4	Responsible Accountable Consultative Involved (RACI) Chart clearly defined for all the stakeholders?			
1.5	Objectives of projects communicated to all stakeholders of the project?			
1.6	Communication Management Plan of the project available?			
1.7	Have project management standards and procedures been established and documented?			
1.8	Governance committee in place?			
1.9	Are there procedures in place to effectively manage interdependencies with other projects/systems?			

Sample User Requirement Review Checklist

Item	Yes / No / NA
1. Does the User Requirements Documentation (URD) provide a good idea about the objectives of the project?	Yes
2. Has the scope of the project been clearly defined?	Yes

3. Have all external interfaces been defined (in case the system is not a stand-alone one)?	Yes
4. Has the target environment been clearly defined?	Yes
5. Has the development environment been clearly defined (in case it is different from the target environment)?	NA
6. Functional attributes (Performance, Interface, Operational, Acceptance, Documentation and Verification) defined clearly?	Yes
7. Is it clear what kind of users will be using the system? Is there enough information about the kind of user interface that is required?	Yes
8. In identifying general constraints, have all possible constraints been considered?	Yes
9. Have all the assumptions, dependencies and risks been identified?	NA
10. Are the externalizing parameters identified and listed?	Yes
11. Have the statutory and regulatory requirements related to the product been identified, if any?	Yes
12. Have the security requirements been identified?	Yes
13. Is the Use Case IDs provided are clear and consistent?	NA
14. Is the confidentiality status (Project/department/organization) in the footer of the URD updated?	Yes

18.16 Review Feedback Form

A review feedback form helps collecting feedback from the stakeholders. It helps improving the overall review process. It will be used to increase the service level and make next reviews more effective for various participants. Review feedback form helps receiving feedbacks from the following questions:

- Rating scale of overall performance of review?
- Expectation set clearly before starting the review?
- This review 'added value' to the project?
- All findings were adequately discussed at the end of the review?
- The review recommendations were constructive, relevant and actionable?
- Reviewer is knowledgeable?
- Reviewer exhibited professionalism and courtesy?

18.16.1 Sample Review Feedback Form

Project Review

Purpose

This form was designed to help us collect feedback from you as a participant of the review. Your opinion is important to us and will be used for increasing our service level and make our next review more effective for the participants. We thank you in advance for the time and effort you are investing in filling out this form.

Identification Details

Your Name ______________________

ID ______________________

Location & Date ______________________

Project Name ______________________

Reviewer Name ______________________

Rating Scale for Performance

1	Extremely poor	6	Satisfactory
2	Very poor	7	Good
3	Poor	8	Very good
4	Below average	9	Great
5	Average	10	Excellent

Assessment (Please Tick the Appropriate Rating)

1.	Expectation is clearly before beginning the review?	1	2	3	4	5	6	7	8	9	10
2.	This review is an 'added value' to the project?	1	2	3	4	5	6	7	8	9	10
3.	All the findings were adequately discussed at the end of the review?	1	2	3	4	5	6	7	8	9	10
4.	The review recommendations were constructive, relevant and actionable?	1	2	3	4	5	6	7	8	9	10
5.	The reviewer is knowledgeable?	1	2	3	4	5	6	7	8	9	10
6.	Reviewer exhibited professionalism and courtesy?	1	2	3	4	5	6	7	8	9	10

18.17 NAH Syndrome

NAH stands for Not Applicable. Team members may feel that review outcome may not be applicable in their environment or team situation. They may feel that review outcome may not provide any benefit to the team. It may even say review recommendations are not valid and this is called 'NAH syndrome' of review outcomes. Overcoming NAH syndrome is within the control of the Project Manager of the project. He needs to have continuous conversation with the team to ensure that they understand the importance of review. In order to overcome this syndrome, project managers need to use evidence from within the own organization to convince the team members rather than using the evidence or data from other organization. In order to prove the effectiveness of the review and overcoming NAH syndrome of the organization, review process can first be used in some set of sample projects. As the data and evidences are within the organization, other team may easily accept it.

18.18 Value of Reviews

The following points show the value of reviews.

- Software reviews identify software issues earlier and avoid rework in the software at later point of time.
- Review helps the team to identify the issues themselves before it reaches the customer.
- Cost of identifying and fixing the defects earlier through review is much lesser than the cost of fixing it at testing phase of the project.
- Review is another form of knowledge transfer.
- Review helps for team building (Team knows how to work with each other).

SUMMARY

Project Reviews helps recalibrates and fine-tune the delivery processes to make them aligned with the organizational realities..

Objectives of Review:

- Identify gaps in the process and products.
- Validation of the work accomplished.
- Tuning of the existing processes and products.
- Ensure quality
- Ensure customer satisfaction.
- It is also a form of knowledge transfer.
- It also helps in team building.

Stakeholder-based Classification: There are two types of reviews. These are Formal Review and Informal Review. It depends on the participative stakeholders of the review.

Level-based Classification: There are two types of reviews. These are Technical Review and General Project Management review. These depends on the levels to be reviewed.

Orientation-based Review: There are two types of reviews namely output oriented review and process oriented review.

Project life-cycle-based Classification: Reviews can be classified based on project life-cycle stages.

Characteristics of Reviews:

- Reviews are Independent
- Reviews are Timely
- Reviews are Transparent
- Reviews are Multidisciplinary
- Reviews are Objective
- Reviews are Accessible

Structure of Review Meeting: If total review duration = 100 minutes, then we can split time line like below, for various activities of review meeting:

- Welcome and introduction time = 10 minutes
- Review purpose = 5 minutes
- Back ground review = 10 minutes
- Discussion of project = 65 minutes
- Wrap-up = 10 minutes

Following are the contents of a review report:

- Introduction: Review Scope, Review objectives
- Current Project Status: Project ecosystem
- Recommendations: Action items, Time lines, Budget of action items
- Current Status of Action Items: Open/closed/on-hold/rejected/WIP
- Limitations and Assumptions of the Review: If any

Project Review Checklist: A project review checklist helps the reviewer to execute review in a better way. It also ensure all the aspects of the reviews are covered objectively. Checklist can just be 'Yes/No' type or it can be score driven (1/2/3/4/5), but clear-cut definition is important to maintain consistency.

NAH Syndrome

NAH stands for **N**ot **A**pplicable **H**ere. Team members may feel that review outcome may not be applicable in their environment or team situation. They may feel that review outcome may not provide any benefit to the team and may even say review recommendations are not valid and this is called 'NAH Syndrome of Review Outcomes'.

Value of Reviews

- Software reviews identify software issues earlier and avoid rework in the software at some later point of time.
- A review helps the team to identify the issues by themselves before it reaches to the customers.
- Cost of identifying and fixing the defects earlier through review is much lesser than the cost of fixing it at testing phase of the project.
- Review is another form of knowledge transfer.
- Review helps for team building (Team knows how to work with each other).

EXERCISES

PART A (Objective-type Questions)

1. Which of the following is not an objective of the review process?
   A. Ensure quality assurance
   B. Identify gaps in the process
   C. Ensure customer satisfaction
   D. Find people's faults
2. Which of the following is not a type of review classification?
   A. Customer-based classification
   B. Stakeholder-based classification
   C. Level-based classification
   D. Orientation-based classification
3. Which of the following is not a characteristic of the review process?
   A. Transparent
   B. Objective
   C. Timely
   D. Negotiable
4. NAH Syndrome stands for
   A. National Highway Syndrome
   B. Not Applicable Here Syndrome
   C. Not Active Here Syndrome
   D. Not Accurate Here Syndrome

PART B (Write the answers in one or two lines)

1. List down any three objectives of software reviews.
2. Write notes on stakeholder-based classification of reviews.
3. Write notes on level-based classification of reviews.
4. Write notes on orientation-based classification of reviews.
5. Write notes on timing of reviews.
6. Write notes on Chairperson of the review process.
7. Write notes on Subject Matter Experts of the review process.
8. Explain any two characteristics of review.
9. Write notes on NAH syndrome of review.
10. List down any three values of reviews.

19

Project Tracking and Reporting

19.1 Introduction

A project execution process is performed to complete the project works as defined in the project management plan. This is because project execution remains ridden with uncertainties and changes in objectives. Setting up a standard process is required over the course of work execution. Such changes require formal approval and documentation. Hence, entailing a formal process for documentation and recording of the work results and changes. Effective tracking of the project activities as well as monitoring and controlling progress are critical for success of any project. Along with this, it is important that the stakeholders are regularly appraised with the progress and issues during the project life-cycle known as reporting. In this chapter, we will discuss the various processes involved in project execution, monitoring and reporting.

19.2 Project Execution

Project execution is a process that coordinates the works of the team members who have been allocated to a project for performing the tasks needed to complete the project.

At a higher level, the job of project execution can be thought a collection of activities such as:

1. Create the project deliverables.
2. Recruit staffs; train and manage them.
3. Issue change requests and adapt the approved changes.
4. Manage risks and implement the risk response activities.
5. Collect and document the lessons learnt.

As the project scenarios are dynamic in nature, changes are inevitable in a project. Thus, project execution also requires implementation of the approved changes covering:

1. **Corrective Action:** Documented direction for executing the project work to bring back the expected future performance of the project work in-line with the project management plan.
2. **Preventive Action:** A documented direction to perform an activity that can reduce the probability of negative consequences associated with project risks.

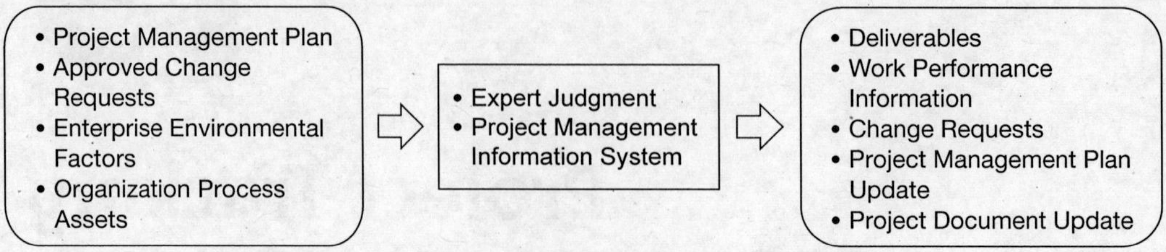

Figure 19.1 Project Execution Flow Chart

3. **Defect Repair:** The identification of defects that is formally documented in a project component with a recommendation to either repair the defect or completely replace certain components.

The project manager and the project team perform activities to accomplish project objectives and in order to do that, a project manager obtains and manages resources including people, materials, equipments and facilities. He/she manages risks of the project and implements risk response activities. He/she is responsible for maintaining project communication channels and reports with respect to costs, schedule, etc. (Figure 19.1) for overall flow of project execution.

19.2.1 Project Management Information Systems

Project Management Information Systems (PMISs) are important parts of enterprise environmental factors prevalent in an organization. These systems typically provide a user access to the in-house automated tools, the information collection and distribution systems or the web interfaces to online automated systems used during the tracking and controlling project execution efforts. For example, a configuration management tool is a subsystem of overall PMISs and is used mainly for monitoring and controlling emerging project scopes against the baseline scope. Its purpose is to control changes throughout the project. It focuses on the physical characteristics of the project and not on the overall project scope and defines the steps required to control changes to them.

Configuration management activities are crucial for keeping projects on track and it involves:

1. *Configuration Identification:* Selection and identification of a configuration item provides the basis on which product configuration is defined and verified. It is based on that products and documents are labeled. Accountability is maintained though this activity.
2. *Configuration Status Accounting:* Information is recorded and reported as to when the appropriate data about the configuration item is to be provided.
3. *Configuration Verification and Auditing:* It ensures the configuration items are correct, corresponding changes are recorded, assessed, approved, tracked, and correctly implemented.

A configuration management system along with change control processes accomplishes three main objectives:

1. Establishes a method to consistently identify and request changes to established baselines and to assess the value and effectiveness of those changes.
2. Provide opportunities to continuously validate and improve the project by considering the impact of each change.
3. It provides the mechanism for the project management team to consistently communicate all approved and rejected changes to the stakeholders in a formal way.

19.2.2 Deliverables

When a project is being executed, we finally expect deliverables out of it. The deliverables produced at the project execution phase needs to be validated (validated deliverable) and the customer has to accept it (accepted deliverable). Deliverable is defined as the unique and verifiable products or results that must be produced to complete the project (or sub-project).

19.2.3 Work Performance Information

Work Performance Information (WPI) can be related to various performance results routinely collected as part of the project management plan and fed into the performance reporting process which includes, but is not limited to the following:

- Schedule progress
- Deliverable status
- Schedule activities started
- Costs authorized and incurred
- Resource utilization detail

Project Management Plan Updates: At any point of time we need to keep the plan and execution in sync. This is an important activity expected to be performed by every professional project manager. During project execution, there may be a need for change in the plan and so we may update a few subsidiary management plans, such as Scope Management Plan, Cost Management Plan, etc. and their baselines depending on the need.

Project Document Updates: Documents for which updates may be provided includes Requirement documents, Issue documents, Risk register, and the Stakeholder register.

19.3 Monitoring and Controlling Project Work

Monitor and controlling process is the process of tracking, reviewing, regulating and controlling the progress to meet the performance objectives as per the Project Management Plan. Monitoring is an aspect of project management performed throughout the project (Figure 19.2). This process includes the following objectives:

1. Controlling changes and recommending preventive actions.
2. Monitoring the ongoing project activities.

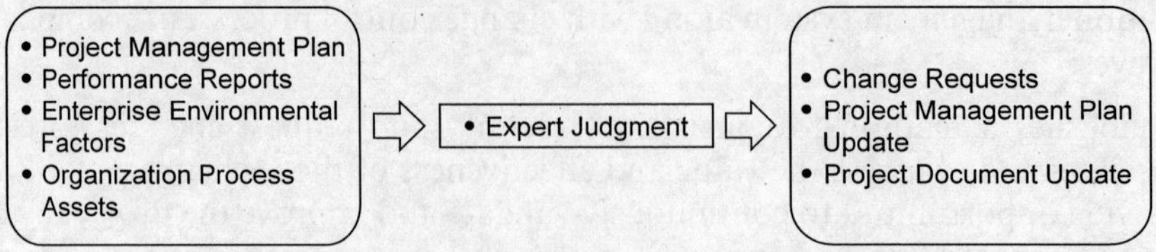

Figure 19.2 Monitor and Control Project Work

3. Influencing the factors that could circumvent integrated change control so that only the approved change requests are implemented.
4. Collect, analyse, and distribute performance information.
5. Compare the actual performance information against the plan.
6. Assess the trends.
7. Change the plan or change the execution if required.
8. Identify new risks and monitor the existing risks.

Monitoring the project effort and the work done provides an opportunity for the project team to get an insight into the health of the project and to identify the areas that may require additional attention. For example, an increasing trend in number of bugs reported in the test environment may call for strengthening the code review activity. For a multi-phase or release-based project, this insights are very helpful as the project team can plan the necessary corrective actions to be implemented in the subsequent stages based on the problems indemnified in the current stage. Monitoring also gives the team an opportunity for mid-term course correction (Figure 19.3). The gap between where we are (current state) and where we want to be (target state) reveals the corrections required to align the project with the intended outcome.

19.3.1 Perform Integrated Change Control

Change control is an important control process, because owing to the uncertainties inherent in project execution, changes are bound to surface and effectively managing and documenting change is critical for project success. Integrated change control is a process whereby changes

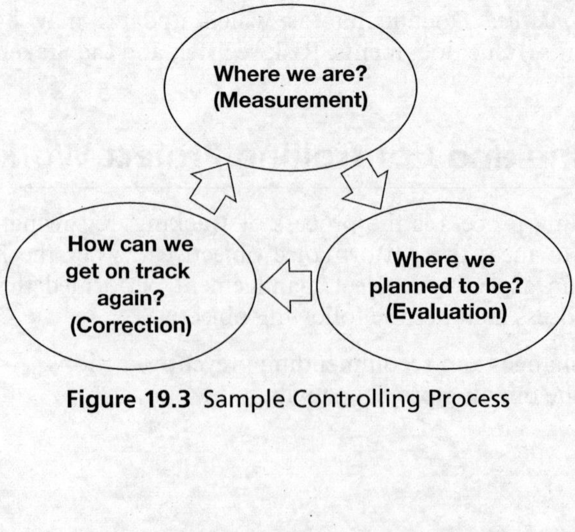

Figure 19.3 Sample Controlling Process

approved and documented are readily shared and applied across several similar projects being managed at a given point in time. The process of reviewing all change requests, approving changes, and controlling changes to deliverables and organizational process assets includes recommendations for changes, corrective action, preventive action, and defect repairs. These recommendations are evaluated and either approved or rejected by the project manager. The approved change requests are implemented (executed) as project work.

The project manager has authority to approve some change requests in emergency situations as per the procedures defined in preceding text.

Overall change control is concerned with: (1) influencing the factors that create change; (2) determining that a change has occurred; and (3) managing the actual changes when they occur.

Integrated change control is the process which ensures that all the project deliverables including the project management plans are maintained and configured carefully. Changes are monitored carefully, and are either approved or rejected. Integrated change control also ensures that approved changes are incorporated and rejected changes are not incorporated into the product. Scope, cost, and time are together called 'triple constraints, and are to be monitored closely in integrated change control' (Figure 19.4).

Activities performed during change control are as follows:

1. Identifying that a change has occurred.
2. Checking whether only the approved changes are being implemented.
3. Reviewing and approving the requested changes as per guidelines.
4. Managing the approved changes as and when they occur.
5. Maintaining integrity of the baseline scopes using various mechanisms such as review and inspections.
6. Controlling and updating scope, budget, schedule, and quality.
7. Documenting the impact of requested changes on project parameters and deliverables.

Integrated change control process not only just approves or rejects the change requests, but also approves the necessary preventive and corrective actions necessary to ensure that the change is beneficial to the project.

1. Approved change requests (planned and executed)
2. Rejected change requests
3. Project management plan (updates)
4. Project scope statement (updates)

Figure 19.4 Integrated Change Control

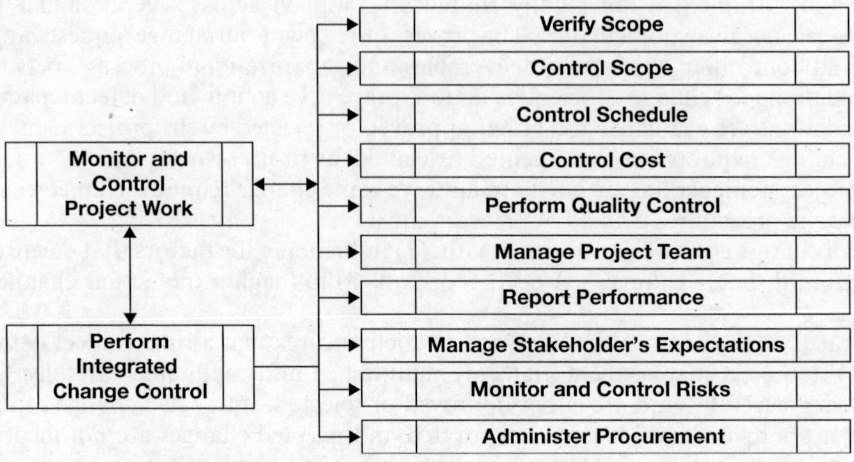

Figure 19.5 Monitoring and Controlling Process

Figure 19.5 shows the different project management activities performed for monitoring and controlling projects are described here:

Verify Scope: The deliverables are validated according to the acceptance criteria formalized with the stakeholders. This step may give rise to change requests which are the requirements over and above the initial agreed upon requirements set.

Control Scope: Throughout the project life-cycle, the changes to the project scope needs to be monitored and controlled closely to make sure that only the works agreed upon with the customer are delivered. Requirement Traceability Matrix (RTM) is a useful artifact for maintaining the list of items in project scope and making sure that all the works are delivered. Scope control mechanisms were discussed in the Requirements Management chapter.

Control Schedule: Monitoring the progress of the project and comparing that with the project schedule helps in managing any change in the schedule baseline. As we discussed earlier, time is one of the important constraint in any project and thus any deviation in project timeline or milestones need to be reported to all the stakeholders as soon as it is known. The techniques of controlling schedule were discussed in the Schedule Management chapter.

Control Costs: The second important constraint of a project is cost. Every project starts with a fixed budget and the sponsors requires to take decisions and initiate actions in case the cost of the project varies from the initial estimate. So, budget forecasts and the change requests need to be closely tracked for monitoring and controlling costs. We discussed the cost control mechanisms in the Cost Management chapter.

Perform Quality Control: Every project has certain quality goals based on the type and criticality of the product or service it is delivering. At the initial stages of project planning, the quality metrics and work performance measurement criteria are defined for the project. At the execution stage, quality is monitored and the necessary corrective actions taken to bring the quality of intermediate deliverables at the controlled limits so that the final deliverables meet the overall quality goal. We discussed more about quality control in the Quality Management chapter.

Monitor and Control Risks: As we have already discussed in the Risk Management chapter, monitoring and controlling the project risks are critical for success of any project. Monitoring is important to identify new risks as well as occurrence of any predicted risk and, then, controlling the impact of the risk so that the project outcomes are not affected negatively.

19.4 Project Performance Reports

The project performance report deals with collection and distribution of performance information which includes status reports, forecasts and progress measurements. Project plan, schedule, budget forecasts and work performance measurements are important inputs for reporting the project's progress properly.

19.4.1 Types of Performance Reports

Project performance is measured against the performance measurement baselines defined in the project management plan. The different types of performance reports are:

- *Status Report:* It presents the current status of a project.
- *Forecasting Report:* It presents an estimate of the future project status.
- *Trend Report:* It presents an analysis of the project results over time to check whether performance has improved or deteriorated.
- *Variance Report:* It presents a comparison of actual results the baseline targets.

Performance reports generally provide information on scope, schedule, cost, quality, and possible risks and lessons learned. They represent a basis for corrective actions and mid-course corrections, if any.

Common Formats for Performance Reports: There are different formats of performance reports like bar charts, S-curves, histogram, tables, variance analysis report, earned value analysis.

Bar Charts: A bar chart is a chart with rectangular bars and its length proportional to the values they represent on the X-axis. These bars can also be plotted horizontally with the values represented on the Y-axis.

S-curves Report: Other name of S-curve is Sigmoid curve and measures performance of the project over time. It displays planned value vs actual value and also planned value vs Earned Value. Shape is looking like 'S' because of the slow progress in the beginning and end of the project.

Histogram Report: Histogram is used to analyse transactional data. Histogram uses the form of aggregation or frequency distribution. More than one variable can be included in Histogram.

Variance Analysis Report: This report identifies and quantifies the differences in project parameters in time. For example, how the revenue, expenditure, effort variation, schedule variation, project quality, etc., are varying with time is demonstarted with this report.

Earned Value analysis: It is a popular method for measuring project performance. It integrates cost, schedule and scopes and can be used to forecast future performance and project completion dates.

A project manager with effective team-communication skills would:

- Be an effective communicator of project information.
- Avoid communication blockers wherever possible.
- Use a single office, if possible, for all project team members.
- Make meetings effective by preparing agendas and follow-ups.

The following methods are widely used in the forecasting methods which help to prepare performance reports.

Time Series Methods: These techniques are used to make forecasts on the basis of past patterns in the available data. Time is set as an independent variable to forecast demand. Measurements are taken at successive points or over successive periods (Examples: every hour, day, week, month, year, or at any other regular or irregular intervals).

Judgmental Methods: These methods incorporate intuitive judgments based on opinions and subjective estimates. Forecast by analogy, composite forecasts, Delphi method, and scenario building (analysing possible future events based on different possible outcomes) are examples of judgmental method.

Causal Econometric Methods: Such techniques use the assumption that the underlying factors that influence the forecast variables may be identified with confidence. For example, use of many trainees in a project as the key resources would lead to more escalations in the project. If causes are understood, projections of the influencing variables can be predicted. Auto Regressive Moving Average (ARMA), regression analysis, and non-linear regression are examples of causal econometric methods.

Point to Remember

Forecasting methods include time-series methods, causal econometric methods, and judgmental methods.

19.4.2 Performance Communication Channels

These channels are used to exchange information about project progress and performance. They are also used to analyse the project performance and progress. In this case, the project manager generally uses 'push communication' technique.

Reporting Systems: Standard tools to capture, store, and distribute the needed information to stakeholders are helpful to a project manager for reporting the performance and progress of the project.

Expert Judgment: The expertise gained from similar projects worked on earlier is used to manage and control communication process of communication management. The Dos and Don'ts are implemented based on the expertise gained from previous projects.

Meetings: In order to control communications and also to make the control realistic and accepted by the entire team, it is better to conduct team meetings. This meeting should also be attended by other stakeholders such as project sponsors and others who have a stake in the project. The project manager can also conduct this meeting with selected team members to control the communication. The project manager has to ensure through the selected few that communication is happening as per the communication management plan.

SUMMARY

- Project execution is a process that coordinates the works of the team members who have been allocated to a project for performing the tasks which are needed to complete the project.
- Approved changes cover:
  - Corrective Action: Documented direction for executing the project work to bring back the expected future performance of the project work in line with the project management plan.
  - Preventive Action: A documented direction to perform an activity that can reduce the probability of negative consequences associated with project risks.
  - Defect Repair: The formally documented identification of defect in a project component with a recommendation to either repair the defect or completely replace the component.
- Work Performance Information (WPI) can be related to various performance results routinely collected as part of the project management plan and fed into the performance reporting process.
- Monitor and controlling processes is the process of tracking, reviewing, regulating and controlling the progress to meet the performance objectives as per the project management plan.
- Integrated change control is a process where changes are approved and documented. These are readily shared and applied across several similar projects managed at a given point in time.
- There are different types of performance reports:
  - Status Report: It presents the current status of a project.
  - Forecasting Report: It presents an estimate of the future project status.
  - Trend Report: It presents an analysis of project results over time to check whether performance has improved or deteriorated.
  - Variance Report: It presents a comparison between actual results and baseline targets.

EXERCISES

PART A (Objective-type Questions)

1. Forecast by analogy is an example of the judgmental method. Which of the following is not an example of judgmental method?

A. Composite forecasts
B. Delphi method
C. Scenario building
D. ARMA

2. All of the following are input of report performance process, except

A. Budget forecasts
B. Work performance information
C. Work performance measurements
D. Variance analysis

3. In the change control process, which of the following would be the top priority of a project manager?

A. Making necessary changes per plan
B. Analysing the impact of changes
C. Informing the stakeholders about the impact of changes
D. Preventing unnecessary changes

4. A change to documented plans to reflect modified or additional ideas or content regarding deliverables is an instance of

A. Corrective action
B. Preventive action
C. Defect repair
D. Updates

5. A documented action plan to ensure that the future performance of a project task is brought in-line to comply with the project management plan is an instance of
A. Corrective action
B. Preventive action
C. Defect repair
D. Accepted deliverable

6. All of the following are examples of Work Performance Information (WPI) except
A. Deliverable status
B. Schedule progress
C. Costs incurred
D. PMIS

7. Suppose, when your project is in the execution stage, a change in legal requirements entails a change in the scope of your project. What would be your first response?
A. Create a documented change request.
B. Proceed as per the existing plan.
C. Consult with the project sponsor and the stakeholders.
D. Hold project execution until the issue is resolved.

8. Which of the following is not an example of causal/econometric method?
A. ARMA
B. Regression analysis
C. Non-linear regression
D. Forecast by analogy

PART B (Write short answers)

1. Explain what Approved Changes cover.
2. Describe PMIs.
3. What is WPI?
4. Briefly describe Integrated Change Control process.
5. What are all the various types of performance report?
6. Explain in detail Trend Report and Variance Report.

Section V

Project Closure and Maintenance

20

Software Project Closure

20.1 Introduction

Projects are temporary in nature. Every project must have a specific start date and end date. Projects are initiated for a specific outcome and when it is delivered, it comes to an end. This 'end' is a process in itself and is formally referred as project closure. Closing processes discuss the steps necessary for completing project, phase, contract and describes different techniques to enact those steps. Closure procedure of the project begins after the client has accepted all the project deliverables. One key benefit of project closure is to ensure that the project have met expectations and another is to collect and document lessons learned and best practices, so the project team can incorporate successes and avoid problems their future work.

20.2 Why Closure?

In a software project management, closure is required for the following reasons:

- To ensure the project requirements are met as per customer satisfaction: This is the idealistic way to close a project successfully. A project can be closed, once all the objectives of the projects are met.
- To transit complete software product to their long-term operational status (support and maintenance). Once the project is complete it moves to operational mode of support and maintenance.
- To transit the project team to operational positions.
- To release the project team to other projects.
- To measure and recognize the work and commitment of various project stakeholders.
- To check the complement against contractual obligations as per the contract.
- To create repository of project documents for organizational process assets.
- To measure degree of success and failure against some pre-built parameters called 'acceptance criteria'.
- To create best practices and lessons learnt while executing a software project.
- To close all financial reports.
- To improve estimates for future projects.

20.3 Acceptance Criteria

Acceptance criteria defines the form and functions of the project deliverables, establishing end-user expectations and requirements, and forming the basis by which project deliverables are accepted or rejected. Acceptance criteria can be defined as one form of 'contract' under which the project will perform its expectations. Acceptance criteria may not be changed as the work progresses forms the basis of project's success measurement.

20.4 Major Activities in Close Project

The close project process facilitates in the documentation of any changes made throughout the project life-cycle. The process also helps in documentation of the corrective actions that had been taken over the course of project execution. This documentation of corrective action is made retrospectively; it has the benefit of hindsight and helps the organization in taking effective and preventive measures by establishing robust systems, to avoid reinventing the wheel or redundancies. The following activities are performed during when a project is closed:

1. Actions and activities necessary to satisfy completion or exit criteria for the phase or project.
2. Actions and activities necessary to transfer the project's products, services and results to the next phase or to production and operation.
3. Activities necessary to collect project or phase records, audit project success or failure, gather lessons learned, and archive project information for future use by the organization.

20.5 Administrative Closure and Contract Closure

There are two types of closures, namely, administrative closure and contract closure. Administrative closure is performed after contract closure.

Contract Closure Procedures (from Procurement): Contractual closure deals with project elements that were external to the organization. This is an element of procurement management.

- Close all contracts.
- Confirm if all work is completed correctly and satisfactorily as per the contract.
- Formal acceptance of deliverables as per the previously defined requirements.
- Update and archive contract records for future reference/check/audit.
- Final documentation that the contract is complete.
- Final payment.

Administrative Closure: Administrative closure involves bring to completion all internal and administrative aspects of the project concerning team members, management, other stakeholders, financials and equipment.

- Integrated activities needed to collect project records. Record the current status of the project in a document.
- Analyse a project's success or failure. Document the lessons learnt (shortcomings) and best practices (success) of the project.
- Archive project information for future use by the organization. Prepare final project reports for the benefits of all stakeholders.
- Release all the resources. Close all project accounts.
- Prepare a summary of the above information, including any open issues, and distribute it among the appropriate stakeholders.

20.6 Project Closure Process

The closing process (Figure 20.1) finalizes all activities across all process groups. It gathers complete project information and stores the same for future reference. Stakeholders approve formal closure of the project. Documentation of the best practices, lessons learnt and archival of the project artifacts happens in this process group. It also gives clear signal to the resource manager to re-assign the resources to other projects. It is essential to complete the closing process at the conclusion of a project even if the project is prematurely terminated. Prematurely terminated projects include aborted projects, cancelled projects, projects in exception, etc. Additionally, the project manager will be concerned about the disposition of this project team and their immediate future. A project closure plan lists all the activities required to close a project, to ensure that a project closure process took place smoothly and efficiently.

Inputs for Project Closure Process

- Project Management Plan (For referring the closure procedure): A project management plan becomes the agreement between the project manager and project sponsor, defining what constitutes project completion.
- Contract Documentation: It includes the contract itself as well as changes to the contract and other documentation (such as the technical approach, product description, acceptance criteria).

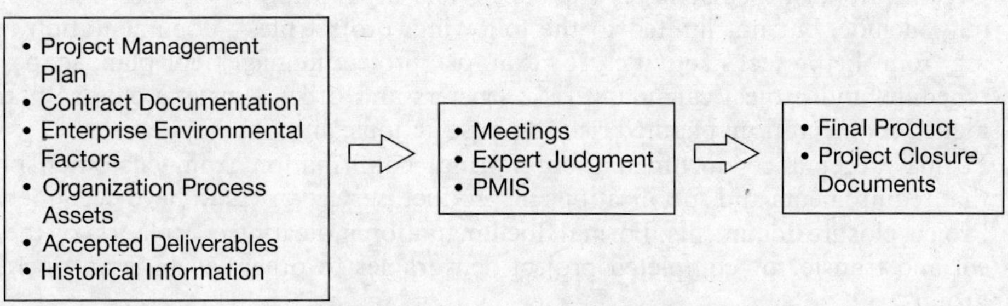

Figure 20.1 Project Closure Process

- Enterprise Environmental Factors: Example: Government regulations.
- Organizational Process Assets: Example: Formal sign-off forms. The organizational process assets may include, but not limited to the following. Project or phase closure guidelines or requirements (*e.g.*, administrative procedures, project audits, project evaluations and transition criteria).
- Work Performance Information: Example: All invoices from procurement.
- Acceptable Deliverables: A project can be closed only after the deliverables are accepted by the customer. Accepted deliverables may include approved product specifications, delivery receipts and the work performance documents. Partial or interim deliverables may also be included for the phased or cancelled projects.
- Historical information and lessons learned knowledge base (*e.g.*, project records and documents, all project closure information and documentation, information about both the results of past project selection decisions and past project performance information, and information from risk management activities).

Tools and Techniques of Close Project Process

- Closure Analysis Meetings: These types of meetings takes place face-to-face, virtual, formal, or informal manner. This may include the project team members and the relevant stakeholders. The closure analysis meetings include, but are not limited to the lessons learnt, closed, user groups, and review meetings.
- Project Management Information System (PMIS): This helps to know the project status and metrics.
- Expert Judgment: Expert judgment is applied when performing administrative closure activities. These experts ensure the project or phase closure is performed to the appropriate standards.
- Examples of analytical techniques used in project closeout are regression analysis. trend analysis.

Outputs of Close Project Process

- Final Product, Service or Result: This output refers to the transition of the final product, service, or result that the project was authorized to produce (or in the case of phase closure, the intermediate product service, or result of that phase).
- Formal acceptance/handover of the final product, service or result.
- Receipt of formal statement that contract terms have been met.
- Organizational Process Assets (updates): The organizational process assets update may include, but not limited to the following: project files—documentation resulting from the project's activities, for example, project management plan; scope, cost, schedule, and project calendars; risk registers and other registers; change management documentation; planned risk response actions; and risk impact.
- Formal acceptance documentation: Formal confirmation from customer/sponsor that requirements and specifications of product, service or result have been met.
- Project closure documents: Formal documentation indicating completion of the project and transfer of completed project deliverables to others such as an operations group.

- Historical information: Historical information and lessons-learnt information are transferred to the lessons-learnt knowledge base for use in future projects. Historical information and lessons-learned information are transferred to the lessons-learned knowledge base for use in future projects or phases. This can include information on issues and risks as well as techniques that worked well that can be applied to future projects.
- Project closure documents: Project or phase closure documents, consisting of formal documentation that indicates completion of the project or phase and the transfer of the completed project or phase deliverables to others, such as an operations group or to the next phase. During project closure, the project manager reviews prior phase documentation, customer acceptance documentation from the 'validate scope' process, and the contract (if applicable), to ensure that all project requirements are completed prior to finalizing the closure of the project. If the project was terminated prior to completion, the formal documentation indicates why the project was terminated and formalizes the procedures for the transfer of the finished and unfinished deliverables of the cancelled project to others.

20.7 Project Termination

It is essential to complete the closing process at the conclusion of a project even if the project is prematurely terminated. Prematurely terminated projects include aborted projects, cancelled projects, projects in exception, etc. Additionally, the project manager will be concerned both about the disposition of this project team and their immediate future. When a decision is taken to prematurely abandon a project, there is a compelling urgency to stop all further funding also transferring the workforce for other productive deployment. As a matter of fact, project termination activities must form part of the original project plan and not hurriedly be undertaken as an afterthought.

20.7.1 Reasons for Project Termination

Some of the reasons for the project termination are:

1. Interim audit indicates that the project will not achieve the desired objectives.
2. Because of organizational changes at the customer side.
3. Senior team members of the project leaving the vendor organization and no replacement, available.
4. Funding issues at the customer's side.
5. When the output of the project is not cost effective.
6. Technology advances warrants changes in the engineering aspects.
7. Better alternate utilization of funds and personal available.

20.7.2 Different Ways to Terminate Project

There are four different fundamental ways to terminate a project: extinction, addition, integration, and starvation.

Termination by Extinction

These are projects brought to an end (often before completion it stops), because they are unsuccessful, fail to meet customer's objectives, are superseded by technical advances that make the project obsolete or because cost escalations destroy economic viability of the project or product. A project can said to be terminated when works are slowed down or ceased to the point that further progress is no longer feasible and will further damage the project.

1. The project may end, because it has successfully achieved its goals and now moves out of the organization.
2. The project may also be stopped, because it is unsuccessful due to various reasons. For example, interim audit indicates that the project will not achieve the desired objectives.
3. A special case of termination by extinction is 'termination by murder' and project death is sure. For example: (1) Due to organizational changes at the customer side a project may lose its priority and gets closed, (2) Senior team member of the project leaving out the vendor organization and there is no replacement available.

Termination by Addition

Project is terminated because it is getting 'added' to another organization or to another division of the same organization or to its parent organization. The project is terminated because it is 'Completed' and 'Success'. Project may be added 'to continue as it is' or 'to merge with already existing project'. Termination by addition happens when a project ends successfully and then migrates into the parent organization as a new business unit or product line. A project may be added 'to continue as it is' to parent organization or new division as it is successful and for further development. A project may be added 'to merge with already existing project' of the parent organization or new division. Project resources migrate from project division to product division because of this termination.

Termination by Integration

This happens due to mergers and acquisitions in which the project becomes standardized. One division or company gets integrated with another division or company. This method of terminating projects is the most common way of dealing with successful projects. The project associated with one company is moved to the parent company. For example, if company X buys company Y, then all the projects of company Y will be integrated with company X projects. Company Y projects will become zero and company X projects will increase in all parameters. Termination by integration needs to consider the people who worked in pervious project, accounting and finance of previous projects, engineering aspects of previous projects, software used by previous projects, new marketing strategy to be planned out.

Termination by Starvation

This type of project termination is a 'slow starvation due to budget constraints'. Project is not getting cancelled by management, but it automatically happens due to budget reduction. In reality, this is not a termination.

20.7.3 Termination Process

The termination process has two distinct parts. First is the 'decision', whether or not to terminate (Terminate, Don't Terminate). Second is 'implementation', *i.e.*, to terminate the project or execute termination process.

Decision Aiding Models

Decision-aiding models for the termination decision fall into two generic categories:

1. Criteria-based Model: Criteria-based model tests the project against the set of predefined criteria of successful or unsuccessful projects. Criteria for termination projects can be of low profitability, market potential of the product, schedule delays, change in competitive strategy. Criteria are derived from goals.
2. Goal-based Model: Goal-based model tests the project against set of goals set in the beginning of the same project. Goal should be SMART which means, Specific, Measurable, Achievable, Realistic, Time-bound.

Implementation Process

Special termination managers are involved in the process of shutting down a project. It follows the closure procedures defined above.

20.8 Project Closure Analysis

A project closure analysis document lists the closure activities and any outstanding matters and recommends how they should be addressed. The project closure report is usually developed, once the project is completed and all the project outputs have been delivered to the business owner(s) or it has been decided to close the project for some other reasons. This may be the result of a recommendation from a review of the project where the findings are negative or may be the result of changed priorities within the agency, division or business unit.

20.8.1 Objectives of Closure Analysis

- Determine what went right and wrong.
- Determine what worked and what did not work.
- Outline outstanding issues, risks, operational matters and recommendations.
- How to make it better next time.
- Collecting relevant information which helps for future projects.
- Collecting project metrics for future analysis.
- Collecting lessons learnt which helps future projects.

20.9 Final Closure Report

Closure report is produced as an outcome of closure analysis. The project final report documents the knowledge and experience gained from the project along with various artifacts of the project. The Project Closure Report is the document produced by the project team and is used by senior management to 'tidy up' any loose ends and formally close the project. Final closure reports need to be written without ambiguity. Final closure report is being shared by project managers to all stakeholders which addresses project delivery performance, project administrative performance, project structure, life-cycle followed along with timelines. Other reports of the projects, feedbacks from the customers, best practices and the lessons learnt, project management techniques followed, lists of various audits and reviews conducted with its evaluations and action reports, master project plan. The fundamental purpose of the final reports is to improve the future projects to be executed and, hence, comments are necessary at all places which will help future project managers to execute its projects successfully.

20.9.1 Elements of a Project Closure Report

Finance and Administration Records

After each deliverable, all the sets of records which include administrative and financial aspects are documented clearly. This will be helpful while facing legal actions if any in the future. This will also be helpful for future estimation (cost and financial related). This will be archived along with other project records.

Resource Performance Reporting

Performance of the resources while they worked in the project to be documented, this also includes the resources not directly reporting to the project manager. This will help for future performance appraisal, promotions, salary hike, etc.

Project Metrics Performance

Project performance metrics such as project size, project efforts and project defects are to be documented. This will help for future analysis of metrics and also improves future estimation of projects.

Project Size Metrics

How project was classified (categorized) in terms of size, such as simple, medium, complex. How data was used to measure the size? What estimation technique was used (such as LOC, function point, etc.)? Project Efforts Metrics: In this category, we document, what is the method of estimation? What is the planned effort? What is the actual effort? What is the deviation? What is the reason for deviation? What is the analysis of variation? What is the rework effort? What is cost of rework? What is the effort spent on Reviews?

Project Defect Metrics

Here is a list of project defect metrics:

- How many defects identified stage wise?
- How many defect classification models used?

- What is all the severity of the defects identified?
- Program module wise defect classification, what is the defect injection rate?

Staff Release Procedure

We need to release the remaining staff as a part of closure procedure. Plan of releasing the resources to be communicated to those staff members, so that they can plan their future. This early communication can happen through a formal meeting conducted by project managers.

Risk Management Process

In this part, the procedure of identifying risks and mitigation steps which includes in the plan is given here. The effectiveness of those processes is also documented. Top risks of the projects are also analysed to manage this kind of risks in the future projects.

Quality Management Process

- What is a quality management process?
- What are all the quality issues faced?
- What is the effectiveness of a quality management process?
- What are the quality metrics measures and its effectiveness?
- How quality control measures provides assurance of quality?

Communication Management Process

- What is the communication management process?
- What is the effectiveness of communication management process?
- What changes were made in communication management process?

Issue Management Process

- What is the issue management process?
- What are all the issues faced?
- What is the effectiveness of issue management process?

Customer Expectation Management Process

- What is the customer expectation management process?
- What is the effectiveness of customer expectation management process?
- Did these expectations vary during the project execution?

Casual Analysis

- List of casual analysis done on the project using Pareto Chart and Root-cause Analysis procedure.
- What are all the action items and outcome of those analysis?
- How those analysis helped the project?
- What is the effectiveness of those analysis?

Lessons Learnt

The following are the sources for identifying the lessons learnt:

- Change request documents
- Changes in project management plan
- Changes in project documents
- Project reviews and it outcomes
- Project performance records
- Feedback from the customers
- One more project review at the closure
- Interviewing project stakeholders

Project Closure Recommendation

What are all the recommendations based project closure analysis?

SUMMARY

Projects are temporary in nature. Every project will have a specific start date and end date. Projects are initiated for a specific outcome and when it is delivered, it comes to an end. This 'end' is a process in itself and is formally referred to as project closure.

Acceptance criteria define the form and functions of project deliverables, establishing end-user expectations and requirements, and forming the basis by which project deliverables are accepted or rejected.

There are two types of closure, namely, administrative closure and contract closure. Administrative closure is performed after contract close out while contractual closure deals with project elements that were external to the organization.

Administrative Closure: Administrative closure involves bring to completion all internal and administrative aspects of the project concerning team members, management, other stakeholders, financials, and equipment.

The closing process finalizes all the activities across all the process groups. It gathers complete project information and stores the same for future reference. Stakeholders approve formal closure of the projects. Documentation of the best practices, lessons learnt and archival of the project artifacts happens in this process group.

Termination by Extinction: These are projects brought to an end (often, before completion it stops), because they are unsuccessful, fail to meet customer objectives, are superseded by technical advances that make the project obsolete, or due to cost escalations which destroy economic viability of the project or product.

Termination by Addition: Project is terminated, because it is getting 'added' to another organization or to another division of the same organization or to its parent organization. Project is terminated, because it is 'completed' and 'success'. Project may be added 'to continue as it is' or 'to merge with already existing projects'.

Termination by Integration: This happens due to mergers and acquisitions and the project become standardized. One division or a company gets integrated with another division or company. This method of terminating projects is the most common way of dealing with successful projects. The project associated with one company is moved to the parent company.

Termination by Starvation: This type of project termination is a 'slow starvation due to budget constraints'. Project is not getting cancelled by management, but it automatically cancelled due to budget reduction. In reality, this is not a termination.

Termination Process: The termination process has two distinct parts. First is the 'decision', whether or not to terminate (Terminate, Don't Terminate). Second is the 'implementation', decision is to terminate the project or execute termination process.

Closure report is produced as an outcome of closure analysis. The project final Report documents the knowledge and experience gained from the project along with various artifacts of the project. The project closure report is the document produced by the project team and used by senior management to 'tidy up' any loose ends and formally close the project. Final closure reports need to be written without any ambiguity.

EXERCISES

PART A (Objective-type Questions)

1. This is a form of 'contract' under which the project will perform its expectations.
   A. Acceptance criteria
   B. Expectation document
   C. Performance document
   D. Contract document

2. There are two types of closure of project
   A. Administrative closure and legal closure
   B. Project closure and resource closure
   C. Project closure and product closure
   D. Administrative closure and contract closure

3. All of the following are inputs to closure process, except
   A. Project management plan
   B. Contract documentation
   C. Closure analysis meeting
   D. Historical information

4. Projects are terminated, because they are unsuccessful, fail to meet customer objectives, are superseded by technical advances that make the project obsolete, or because cost escalations destroy economic viability of the project or product. This is an example of
   A. Termination by extinction
   B. Termination by addition
   C. Termination by integration
   D. Termination by starvation

PART B (Write the answers in one or two lines)

1. What is acceptance criteria?

2. What are all the high level activities performed during the close project process?

3. What is the difference between contract closure and administrative closure?

4. Write notes on project closure process.
5. What are the tools and techniques of closure process?
6. What is project termination?
7. What are all the reasons for project termination?
8. What is termination by extinction?
9. What is termination by addition?
10. What is termination by integration?
11. What is termination by starvation?
12. What is project closure analysis?
13. What are all the objectives of closure analysis?

21

Software Maintenance, Support, and Implementation

21.1 Introduction

Software maintenance is the core aspect of software engineering. A system is deployed to the production environment after their development. The process of modifying the production system after the delivery, in order to correct the faults, improving performance and adapting the changing environment is called 'software maintenance'.

Software evolution and maintenance was first addressed by Lehman in 1969. The key findings of his research (Lehman 97) called 'Lehman law' which states that maintenance decisions depends on what happens to systems (and softwares) over time. According to him, "the software systems continuously evolve over a period of time with more complexity".

Let's see the difference between the development and maintenance (Table 21.1) which will help us understanding the maintenance-related activities in detail.

21.2 Development vs Maintenance

Table 21.1 Difference Between Development and Maintenance

Development	Maintenance
Application is not in the production environment.	Application is already in the production environment.
End users are not using the system.	End user started using the system.
It is not driven by the end users. It is driven by the project team.	It is completely driven by the end users.
Opportunity for innovation is wider.	Opportunity for innovation is less.
Time frame to fix bugs is well framed.	Time frames to fix bugs are not well-framed. It varies depending on the nature of the bugs.
Team has freedom to decide what is necessary for the situation.	Team may not have such freedom and constraint by the production system and end user preference.

(Continued)

Table 21.1 *(Continued)*

Defects have no immediate effect on the production system.	Defects may disrupt production system if not addressed properly.
Developing a new system from the scratch is something unique.	Maintenance activities are mostly repetitive in nature.

21.3 Maintenance Activities

There are four types of maintenance activities, namely:

1. Adaptive maintenance
2. Corrective maintenance
3. Perfective maintenance
4. Preventive maintenance

Let us discuss all these four activities.

21.3.1 Adaptive Maintenance

Adjusting the system adaptively based on the environment changes is called 'adaptive maintenance'. The system has no faults (errors) on its own, but needs adaptation (changing) as per the environment changes. For example, healthcare related systems needs to be updated during protocol changes by the Health Insurance Portability and Accountability Act (HIPAA). Adjusting the system parameters as per the new hardware changes/OS changes is also an example of adaptive maintenance. Mostly in adaptive maintenance, there will not be a change in functionality. Adaptive maintenance cost can be minimized by isolating system dependency features. Figure 21.1 shows how a website is upgraded once after the newer version of the Internet Explorer browser was released. A maintenance program undertaken to make the website compatible with the new version of the software is an example of adaptive maintenance.

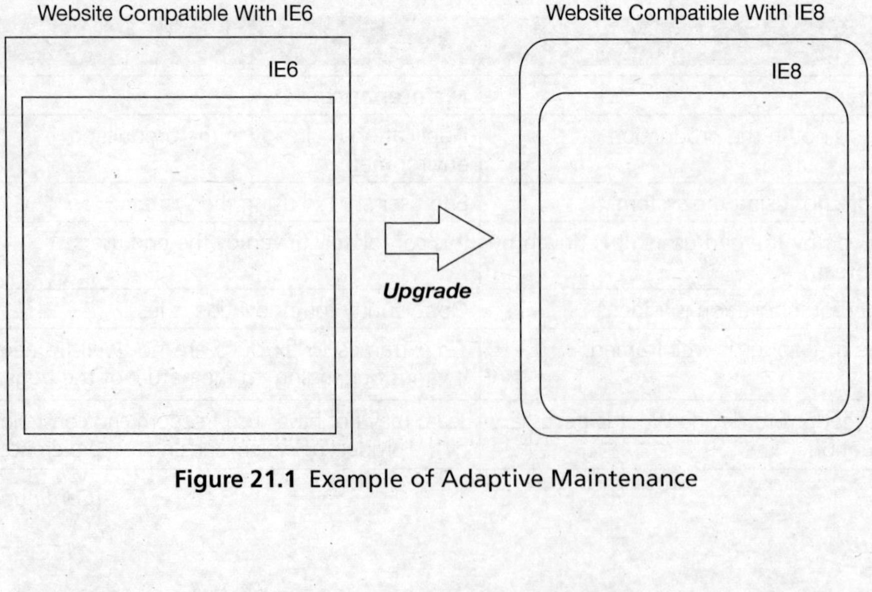

Figure 21.1 Example of Adaptive Maintenance

21.3.2 Corrective Maintenance

It is the process of identifying, isolating and repairing the faults (errors) that are discovered in the system so that the system can be restored and remains operational. Corrective maintenance includes repair or replacement of equipment. This activity may be the result of a regular inspection which identifies the failure (errors) in time and leads to corrective maintenance. Corrective maintenance takes place after the fault occurs.

Types of corrective maintenance:

1. Immediate corrective maintenance (actual work starts immediately after failure and is critical in nature).
2. Deferred corrective maintenance (in which work is delayed in conformance to the stakeholders).

Faults (errors) can be user-based, coding-(software) based or hardware-based. The following life-cycle is being followed for corrective maintenance:

1. Notify helpdesk
2. Diagnose the error
3. Fix the error
4. Test the error
5. Plan the release (installation)
6. Release
7. Post-release activities

21.3.3 Perfective Maintenance

It is the system upgrade kind of work which makes the system working more efficiently. About 50% of the maintenance is perfective maintenance. Upgrading hardware, upgrading software, upgrading bandwidths are examples of perfective maintenance. This type of maintenance happens due to adapting changes and the user's requirements.

Examples:

1. Providing shortcut commands for the system.
2. Performance tuning, to increase the speed of the server.
3. Applications consolidations, for easy management.
4. Automatic help to users to choose data.

The older version of the keyboards did not have multimedia keys (Figure 21.2). But with the popularization of multimedia applications, it became necessary to provide the users some shortcut keys for accessing multimedia functionalities directly from the keyboard. This is an example of the predictive maintenance from the keyboard manufacturing companies.

As per a survey (Figure 21.3) adaptive and perfective maintenance alone contributes up to 75% of the maintenance works.

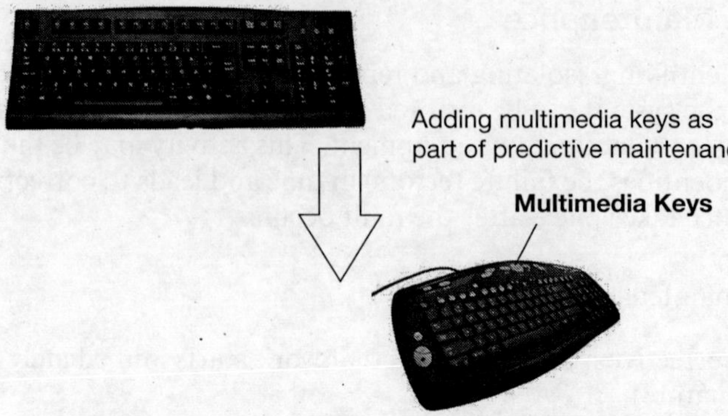

Figure 21.2 Example of Perfective Maintenance

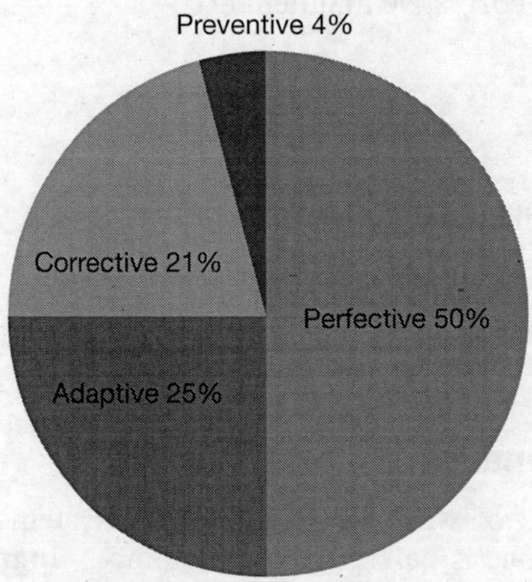

Figure 21.3 Maintenance Type Ratio Chart

21.3.4 Preventive Maintenance

Activities that are aimed at increasing the maintainability are called 'preventive maintenance'. Such activities avoid system outages and errors. In automobile, car's engine oil is changed after a car travels every 5000 kms. This is practiced to prevent errors and is an example of preventive maintenance. Documenting the existing system is the best example for preventive maintenance. Identifying system component that may fail depending on the trend is an example of preventive maintenance. Continuously monitoring the size of a database as the system grows to prevent sizing-related errors are examples of preventive maintenance.

Figure 21.3 shows a maintenance type ratio chart. It clearly indicates that perfective maintenance is more than any type and it contributes 50%. Only 4% of maintenance types are preventive maintenance.

21.4 Maintenance Process and Change Request Management

Maintenance process (Figure 21.4) depends on the software being maintained. It varies considerably depending on the types of softwares. But still we can list the common maintenance activities executed in software maintenance. Let us take a look at the information.

Change request are the part and parcel of all the software maintenance process. Change request are usually raised by the end users requesting for a change in the system that are being used by them. Sometimes the change requests are raised by the management.

Once the change request is received, it should be analysed (impact analysis). The purpose of the analysis is to find out whether the change is necessary. We need to avoid unnecessary changes at this stage itself. Once it is decided that we are going to implement the changes we need to find out the impact of that particular change request on any other part of the system. Change in one component may impact over other components and we need to carefully analyse those dependent components and its impact.

Change implementation will happen after the doing thorough impact analysis in consistent with the release plan. Change implementation strategy should be in sync with the release plan strategy. Delay in the implementation part of the change will affect the release plan.

System release will happen once the change is implemented and thoroughly tested.

In practice, some change request are implemented urgently and directly into the production environment due to business emergencies (or change in production environment) which needs to be avoided as it caters to lot of risks to the environment and the product.

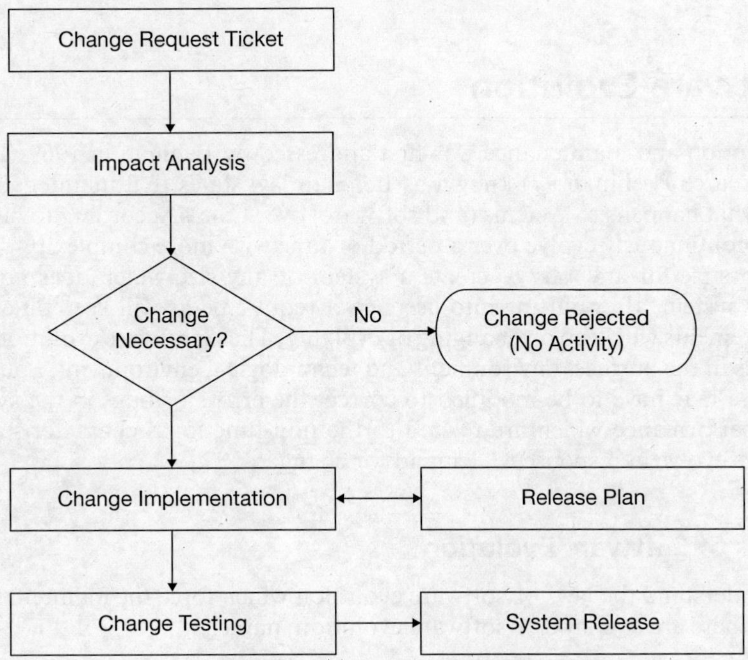

Figure 21.4 Maintenance Process

21.5 Maintenance Cost

Maintenance cost is usually higher than the overall development cost of the software. Sometimes it is 100 times of the development cost. Aging software requires higher support costs as compared to the latest technology-based software. This happens, because sourcing specialized technical resources for upgrading the old technology-based software is highly difficult. Moreover, the maintenance activities often corrupt the old software structures and increase the software maintenance cost. The following factors determine software maintenance cost:

1. Complexity of the System: When the complexity of the system to be maintained increases, the maintenance cost also increases.
2. Volume of Work Involved: Sometimes the complexity may be less, but the volume of work involved in the maintenance activities may be higher. Hence, the cost of maintenance also comes higher.
3. Ageing of the Software: As the software age increases, the structure is degraded, hence it becomes tough to maintain and, thereby, increases the overall maintenance cost of those systems.
4. Soft Skills: Maintenance cost also involves various types of skills required to maintain softwares. It not only depends on the quantity of the skills required, but also on the experience level of the people required to support the system.
5. Contractual Responsibility: Maintenance cost also depends on the contractual responsibilities of the vendor. If there is no incentive, the vendor may not be interested for quick changes in the system.

21.6 Software Evolution

Software evolution and maintenance was first addressed by Lehman in 1969. The key findings of his research (Lehman 97) known as Lehman law states that maintenance decisions depends on 'what happens to systems (and software) over time'. According to him, "the software systems continuously evolve over a period of time with more complexity".

It is impossible for anybody to create a system of any size which does not need to be changed. Any system, after putting into use, newer requirements will keep on emerging; the existing requirements will keep on changing or evolving. These software evolutions are mainly due to changes in the business environment and technological environment. Sometimes, part of the software may have to be modified to correct the errors or bugs in the system and to improve the performance which are related to the non-functional characteristics. Software systems always evolve in response to demand for change.

21.6.1 Laws of Software Evolution

We need to understand the laws of software evolution which force the maintenance to occur. For example, there are two laws of software evolution, namely:

1. Law of increasing complexity
2. Law of continuing change

Law of increasing complexity: As the system evolves over a period of time the complexity of the system also increases. This will also increase the overall maintenance cost.

Law of continuing change: A system that is being used goes for continual change, until it is judged more cost effective to restructure the entire system or replace it by a completely new version.

21.7 Reverse Engineering

The reverse engineering (Figure 21.5) concept is helpful for maintaining the software.

This engineering process helps building the system based on the system requirements and the system design. Reverse engineering is analysing the software system to identify and understand the overall system components, design and the requirement flow of the system. It helps to understand the relationships between various components.

The reverse engineering concept helps reconstructing the lost blueprint of the system. It is a design recovery process.

In many legacy systems, the system documents a design documents, etc. are not present. Only the software source code as the reliable information to understand the overall system is available. Reverse engineering helps reconstructing the requirements, design, test case and user documentation in consistent with the source code of the system.

Design recovery after reengineering result at higher level of abstraction and redocumentation result is at the same level of abstraction.

In the reverse engineering process, all the information about the system is generated (automatic generation and manual generation) and stored in a database before producing the documents. Reverse engineering is a three-step process, namely:

1. Generation of information
2. Storage of information
3. Creation of documents

Reverse engineering is often the initial activity in a reengineering project. Let us see what is reengineering in the subsequent sections.

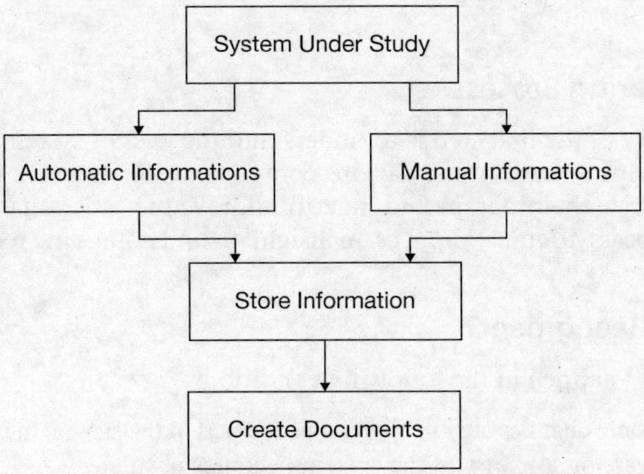

Figure 21.5 Reverse Engineering Process

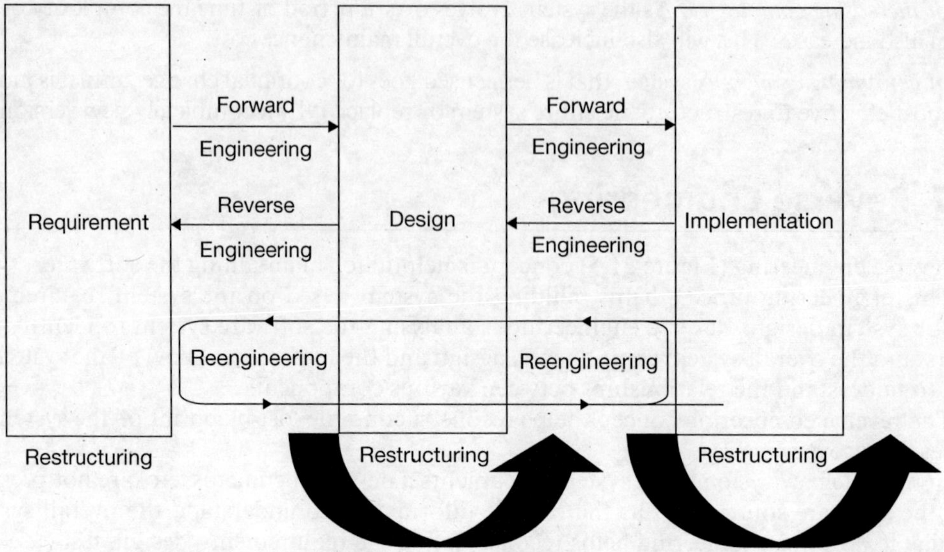

Figure 21.6 Forward, Reverse, Re-engineering, Restructuring

21.8 Reengineering

Reengineering (Figure 21.6) involves putting efforts to make the system easier to maintain. In this process, the source code is getting changed for easy maintenance and functionality of the system and also gets changed during the process. Code cleaning happens over here along with the enhancement of the system.

Reengineering may also lead to rewriting the software in entirely new programming language.

Reengineering may lead to redocumentation of the system. Reengineering reduces the risks of the overall maintenance of the system. The cost of reengineering is usually lesser than the cost of developing the new software.

21.8.1 Reengineering Process

In reengineering process, the first step is to understand the overall system. Implement reverse engineering which helps to understand various components. Restructure the system in a logical manner. Modularize the program and data to improve the functionality and to complete the reengineering process. Figure 21.7 gives an insight on understanding reengineering process.

21.8.2 When to Reengineer?

Reengineering should happen in the following conditions:

1. When the system changes are mostly confined to part of the system then reengineer that part.
2. When hardware or software of the system becomes obsolete.
3. When tools to support restructuring are available.

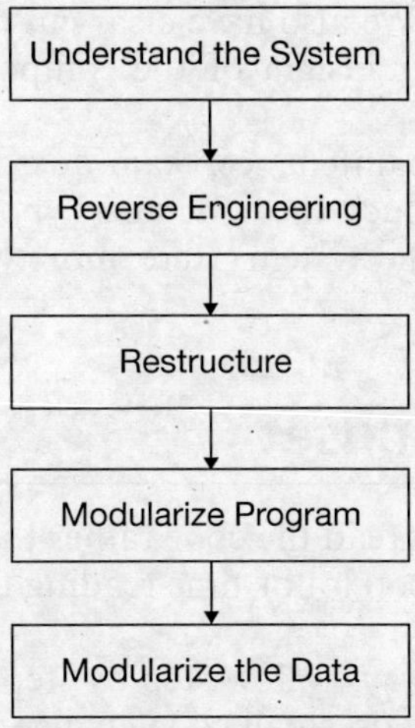

Figure 21.7 Reengineering Process

21.8.3 Advantages of Reengineering

The advantages of the reengineering process are as follows:

1. It Reduces Risks: There may be high risks while developing new software. Risks may be related to staffing problems, design problems, specifications problems. In reengineering process, the first step is to understand the overall system, thereby helps in mitigating the risks properly.
2. It Reduces Costs: The cost of reengineering is usually lesser than the cost of developing new software.

21.9 Restructuring

Restructuring is similar to reengineering. Here, the transformation of a system from one representation to another happens at the same level of abstraction. Functionality of the system does not change here except code cleaning. Revamping of the screens of the software can happen here. Migration from one version of the software to another version of the software is the best example of restructuring.

21.10 Maintenance Strategies

Maintenance strategies are of the following two types:

1. Systematic strategy
2. As-needed Strategy

In the systematic strategy everything happens in a systematic and planned manner. The maintenance team understand the overall system under maintenance. A systematic top-down study of the system happens here. We also have clear-cut documentation for the entire flow of the system. The team has better insight of the components and its causal relationship between them.

In the as-needed strategy of maintenance, team does not maintain any documentation of the system. The team directly touch the code and hypothesis is formulated based on the local information available about the system. Here, more we need a technical team than the systematic strategy.

21.11 Maintenance Mindset

Maintenance programmers directly read the code rather than studying the documentation.

Maintenance programmers spend lot of time reading the code than the time taken to fix or change the code.

Maintenance programmers always follow step by step approach rather than a big bang approach for fixing problems. They do small code change and test it completely before proceeding to the next code change.

Maintenance programmers always follow stereotypical action that means they just concentrate whether the code works or not rather than studying the set of code copied from other source.

Maintenance programmers do not change the code unless, otherwise, they are 100% sure on it.

21.12 Service Perspective to Software Maintenance

There are many differences (Table 21.2) between a product and service. Software maintenance can be attributed to service part also. Before getting into the service perspective of software maintenance, let us see the difference between the product and service.

Table 21.2 Difference between Product and Service

Product	Service
1. Product is tangible	1. Services are intangible
2. Product is perishable	2. Services are not perishable
3. Produced and consumed at later point of time	3. Produced and consumed at the same time
4. Product articulation is easy	4. Service articulation is difficult
5. Centralization and mass production is possible	5. Centralization and mass production is difficult

Sometimes, maintenance is seen as providing service to end-users as opposed to delivering a product. We need to judge the maintenance quality that is different from the development. Service capacity, service efficiency and service responsiveness are considered important factors in maintenance.

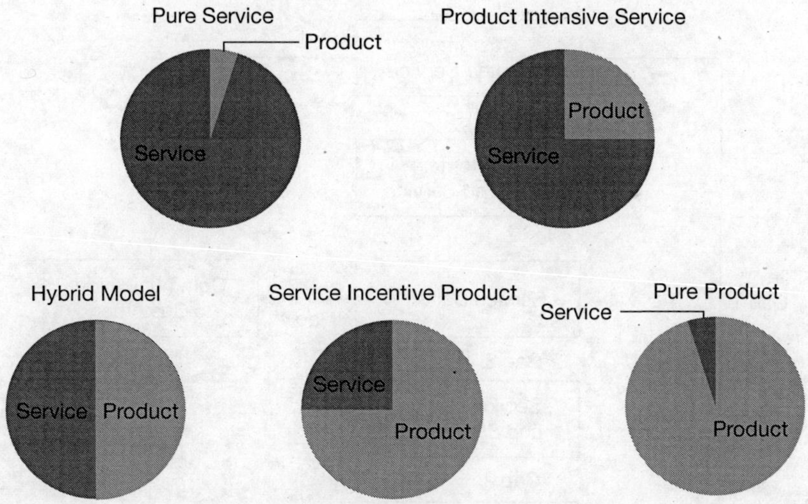

Figure 21.8 Pure Service to Pure Product

Information Technology Infrastructure Library (ITIL) is being followed as default practices in software maintenance. The ITIL is a set of practices for Information Technology Service Management (ITSM) that focuses on aligning IT services with business needs of the organization.

Also, ITIL describes processes, procedures, tasks and checklists for establishing integration with the organization's vision, strategy, value and overall maintaining a minimum level of competency.

Maintenance always has some percentage of service associated with it. The percentage will vary from situation to situation (Figure 21.8) as given below:

- A hybrid model of maintenance has exactly 50% product and 50% service.
- In service intensive product, the service percentage is more than 25%.
- In productive intensive service, the product percentage is more than 25%.

21.13 Gap Model Service

Gap model (Figure 21.9) is used to illustrate the difference between expected service and the service delivery. The Gap model service is categorized into five different types as follows:

1. Gap 1 is the difference between the expected service perceived by the service provider and the expected service by the customer. This focuses the service provider to focus on something which is not relevant to the customer. In order to bridge the gap, the service provider needs to clearly document and translate the customer service expectations into a service agreement.
2. Gap 2 is the difference between the written service specification and the expected service perceived by the service provider. Customer expects immediate response or work around when a production server goes down, but service provider will start doing the analysis as per the service specification agreed.

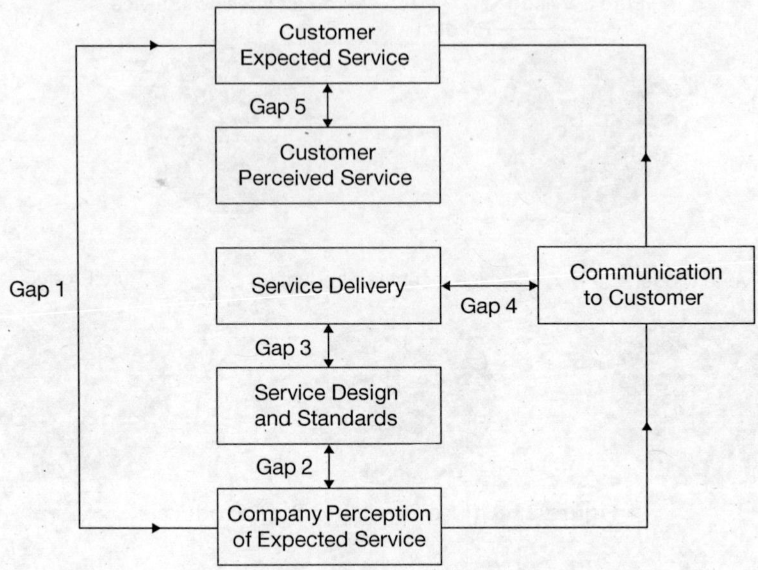

Figure 21.9 Gap Model Service

3. Gap 3 is the difference between the written specification and the actual service delivery. This may be due to human resource efficiency, balancing demand and supply, customer not doing his role, customers not following rules written.
4. Gap 4 is the difference between the actual delivery and communication about the service. Ineffective horizontal communication is the best example for this Gap. Here, the service provider will simply send an e-mail to the customer stating all the problems solved and services restored, but the customer will still be facing the problem. This is mainly due to the communication gap. It can be addressed through a common bug-tracking tool.
5. Gap 5 is the difference between the customer perceived service and the actual expectation of the customer. Most of the projects fail due to this reason.

21.14 Software Maintenance Tools

There are lot of software tools available in the market that can be used by the software maintenance team for different purpose.

Tools to Maintain Version History and Document Repository: Tools like Visual SourceSafe (VSS) and CVS (Open Source Tool) are used to maintain the versions of various documents and software. This software has features like check in and checkout which ensures only one person is changing the code which ensures consistency.

Tools for Bug Tracking: Tools like Bug Zilla and Mantis are used to track and report errors. These tools also helps doing easy root-cause analysis and aging of various bugs reported. Service-level tracking and reporting is easy with these tools.

Tools to Manage Issues: Tools like Trac is used for issue tracking. It also has features like Wiki, and integration to sub-version. This also helps to do easy milestone tracking.

Static Behaviour Analysis Tools: There are tools available to do static behaviour analysis of various softwares which can be used to do the forward and backward engineering. This helps understanding the coding without actually executing the code. Static code analyser tool varies with programming languages as the structure of the program changes. It also helps understanding the security vulnerable if any in the code.

Dynamic Behaviour Analysis Tools: There are tools available to understand the various flows within the system by executing the code. Dynamic code analyzer executes all the possible flow within the system and, thereby, helps the programmer to understand the system easily.

21.15 Issues in Software Maintenance

The following issues are found in software maintenance.

1. Alignment with end user's priorities during maintenance.
2. Staffing people who has the system experience.
3. Estimating the cost of maintenance.
4. Measuring the maintenance (maintain ability).
5. Testing the system.
6. Understanding the system.
7. Unstructured code.
8. Insufficient documentation.

In the above list, the first three items are management issues and the last five items are technical issues. These issues are discussed here.

During the maintenance process, each and every end-user may expect the team to solve its own problems on priority basis. When the number of problems or issues is more, alignment with the end-users priorities becomes difficult. End-user's priorities, mostly based on business priorities, and not based on technical feasibilities and possibilities.

Staffing suitable people who has the system experience under maintenance is always a difficult task. Understanding the system which is already there in the production is difficult and retaining the experienced resources is still difficult.

Estimating the cost of maintenance is difficult not only at the customer side, but also at the performing organization's side (vendor side). The basic parameters based on which we usually estimate the maintenance cost keep on changing. The ballpark estimate says that cost of maintenance is 50% of the full life-cycle cost of development. This does not consider the complexity of the system and, hence, may not hold good for all the systems.

Defining measurable metrics for maintenance is always difficult, in particular, for a new system. The main objective in maintenance is to fix the defects as soon as possible and also with excellent quality of services delivering best customer satisfaction. Usually, when defects are quickly fixed, it may lead to quality-related issues which may also lead to customer dissatisfaction and, hence, defining measurable metrics is difficult.

Defects need to be fixed as well as tested quickly. Testing only the modified code may not be a problem, but testing the inter-dependencies of the code change is difficult as time constraint is a big factor in maintenance.

Completely understanding a system, then addressing the defects is difficult, because most of the systems have unstructured code and inefficient documentations. In most cases, a system is divided into some modules. A set of specific people are deployed to those modules. Coordinating changes across modules and understanding the same is a difficult job.

Other issues in software maintenance are quality of the original application under maintenance, quality of the documentation for the existing system, lack of time for updating the documentation, poor maintenance management and lack of model for maintenance, different programming styles of people, people not showing interest in the maintenance as not much of learning after a certain point of time.

21.16 Difference between Software Maintenance and Support

Maintenance comes in the form of change request (which is also being raised in the form of ticket). Maintenance part is directly linked to changes in application.

As already discussed, the four types of maintenance activities are:

1. Adaptive Maintenance
2. Corrective Maintenance
3. Perfective Maintenance
4. Preventive Maintenance

Adaptive Maintenance: The system has no faults (errors) on its own, but adapting (changing) as per the environmental changes.

Corrective Maintenance: It is the process of identifying, isolating and repairing the faults (errors) that are discovered in the system so that the system can be restored and operational.

Perfective Maintenance: It is the system upgrade kind of work which makes the system to work more efficiently.

Preventive Maintenance: These kinds of activities avoid system outages and avoid errors.

Support usually follows ITIL Framework (Incident management, problem management, SLA Management, etc). Support part is directly linked to serving (supporting) the customer to do their jobs. There are three levels of support, namely, Level 1, 2 and 3.

Level 1 support will act as interface point to the customer (end-user's). It is called 'service desk'. Service desk need not have any technical capability to solve customer problems, but will understand their pain points and record it. Service desk people talk in the language of the customer. Few tickets will get closed at this level itself (if the pain area is known and the solution or the reason is known to the service desk). If the ticket is not solved at this level, it will get passed to Level 2, but still service desk will track the ticket until closure.

Level 2 support will do quick fix (minor enhancements or changes) with the application directly at the production environment. If not able to solve at this level, it is forwarded to Level 3.

Level 3 focuses on corrective modifications and changes and will plan for the releases.

21.17 Common Metrics in Software Maintenance and Support

Client Satisfaction Index (CSI): It is also called 'customer Satisfaction Index'. What the customer feels about the quality of the service in the main index. Customer satisfaction index helps to channelize the overall maintenance efforts towards the customer critical activities. It also helps us to understand our service rating against other service providers. Usually CSI is obtained from the customer in the form of a survey, at least once in a quarter. Various components (parameters) of CSI are: 1. Product related feedback (rating) 2. Service related feedback (rating) 3. Sales related feedback (rating) 4. Quality related feedback (rating) and 5. Feedback against other providers etc. Depending on the environment, these parameters can be customized. These parameters are measured in the scale of 1 to 5.

Acknowledgement Service Level Agreement (SLA) Percentage for Closed Tickets: The formula for calculating Acknowledgement SLA Percentage for closed tickets is, Number of tickets acknowledged within target time/Total tickets closed × 100. This is usually calculated for tickets of a particular period (usually 1 month duration).

Example 1

ABC project closed 400 tickets last month and out of this 380 tickets were acknowledged within target acknowledgement limit. Find out Acknowledgement SLA Percentage for closed Tickets.

Acknowledgement SLA Percentage = Number of tickets acknowledged with in target time/ Total tickets closed × 100.

Acknowledgement SLA Percentage = (380/400) × 100 = 95%

Example 2

Green way project's Ticket Acknowledgement distribution is given below. SLA for acknowledgement of any ticket is less than or equal to 20 minutes. Calculate Acknowledgement SLA Percentage for closed tickets.

Sl. No.	Acknowledgement Time	Total Tickets
1	1 to 5 minutes	15
2	6 to 10 minutes	150
3	11 to 20 minutes	180
4	21 to 55 minutes	55

Acknowledgement SLA Percentage = Number of tickets acknowledged with in target time/ Total tickets closed × 100

Acknowledgement SLA Percentage = ((15 + 150 + 180)/400) × 100 = (345/400) × 100 = 86.25%

Acknowledgement SLA Percentage for Open Tickets: The formula for calculating Acknowledgement SLA Percentage for open tickets is Number of tickets acknowledged with in target time for open tickets/Total tickets open × 100. This is usually calculated for tickets of a particular period (usually 1 month duration).

Example 1

Number of open tickets in ABC project is 134 out of which 120 tickets were acknowledged within the set acknowledgement limit. Calculate Acknowledgement SLA Percentage for open tickets.

Acknowledgement SLA Percentage for open tickets is, Number of tickets acknowledged within target time for open tickets/Total tickets open × 100.

Acknowledgement SLA Percentage = (120/134) × 100 = 89.55%

Example 2

Green way project's Ticket Acknowledgement distribution is shown below. SLA for acknowledgement of any ticket is less than or equal to 20 minutes. Calculate Acknowledgement SLA Percentage for Open Tickets.

Sl. No.	Acknowledgement Time	Total Tickets	Closed Tickets
1	1–5 minutes	15	10
2	6–10 minutes	150	125
3	11–20 minutes	180	180
4	21–55 minutes	55	45

First we need to calculate number of open tickets in each stage.

Sl. No.	Acknowledgement Time	Open Tickets
1	1–5 minutes	5
2	6–10 minutes	25
3	11–20 minutes	0
4	21–55 minutes	10

Total number of open tickets = 40

Total number of open tickets within Acknowledgement limit = 30
Acknowledgement SLA Percentage for open tickets is The Number of tickets acknowledged with in target time for open tickets/Total tickets open × 100.
Acknowledgement SLA Percentage for Open Defects = (30/40) × 100 = 75%

Resolution SLA Percentage for Closed Tickets: The formula for calculating Resolution SLA Percentage for Closed Tickets is Number of tickets resolved within Target time/Total tickets closed × 100. This is usually calculated for tickets of a particular period (usually 1 month duration).

Example 1

The following represents SLA Agreement for ABC Project.

	Service Level Agreement				
	Category	**Overall**	**Response**	**Resolution**	**Availibility**
Service Level Class	Platinum	Sev1	25 mins	3 hrs	99.50%
		Sev2	25 mins	5 hrs	
		Sev3	45 mins	10 hrs	
		Sev4	1 hr 45 mins	80 hrs	
	Gold	Sev1	25 mins	3 hrs	97.00%
		Sev2	40 mins	5 hrs	
		Sev3	1.2 mins	10 hrs	
		Sev4	1 hrs 45 mins	80 hrs	
	Silver	Sev1	35 mins	5 hrs	96.00%
		Sev2	1.2 hrs	6 hrs	
		Sev3	2.2 hrs	25 hrs	
		Sev4	3.2 hrs	90 hrs	
	Bronze	Sev1	1.2 hrs	5 hrs	95.00%
		Sev2	2.2 hrs	6 hrs	
		Sev3	2.2 hrs	25 hrs	
		Sev4	4 hrs	90 hrs	

The following table indicates the resolution trend for a particular period for Platinum Sev1 Category of tickets. Calculate Resolution SLA Percentage for Closed Tickets for Platinum Sev 1 Category.

Sl. No.	Resolution Time (in minutes) (Sev1 Platinum)	Total Tickets Closed for the Period
1	1–30	15
2	31–60	120
3	61–180	160
4	181–300	55

Resolution SLA Percentage for Closed Tickets is Number of tickets resolved within Target time/Total tickets closed × 100.

Resolution SLA Percentage for closed tickets = (15 + 120 + 160)/(15 + 120 + 160 + 45) = (295/350) × 100 = 84.2%.

Ticket Backlog Percentage: The formula for calculating ticket backlog percentage for a particular period is [(Number of tickets carry forwarded from pervious periods + Number of new tickets received in the reporting period – Number of tickets closed during the reporting period)/(Number of tickets carry forwarded from pervious periods + Number of new tickets received in the reporting period)] × 100.

Backlog Management Index (BMI): (Number of tickets closed during the period/Number of tickets arrived during the period) × 100.

Percentage of Improvement in Mean Time to Resolve (MTTR): Formula for calculating Percentage of improvement in Mean Time to Resolve is ((Baseline MTTR – Current MTTR)/ Baseline MTTR) for the reporting period ×100. Baseline MTTR is the average MTTR for previous periods (usually over 6 month's period).

Ticket Productivity: Formula for calculating ticket productivity is (Actual effort of closed tickets/Number of closed tickets) for the reporting period.

Load Factor of Maintenance Team: Actual effort spent on maintenance activities/Overall available effort of the team.

Cost of Poor Quality (COPQ): Formula for calculating COPQ is given as (Effort expended on rework/Actual effort) for the reporting period × 100.

Cost of Quality (COQ): Formula for calculating COQ is given as (Effort spent on Appraisal Cost + Effort spent on Prevention Cost + Effort spent on Failure Cost)/(Effort spent on Prevention Cost + Effort spent on Appraisal Cost + Effort spent on Failure Cost + Effort spent on Production Cost) ×100.

Defect Density by Effort: Formula for calculating Defect Density by Effort is ((Number of pre-shipment Defects + Number of post-shipment Defects + Number of post-production Defects)/(Overall Actual Effort)) for the reporting period.

Defect Removal Efficiency Percentage: Formula for calculating Defect Removal Efficiency Percentage is Pre-shipment Defects/(Pre-shipment Defects + Post shipment Defects + Post production Defects) × 100.

Example

The Table, below, represents the distribution of defects. Calculate Defect Removal Efficiency Percentage.

Sl. No.	Defect Type	Number of Defects
1	Pre-shipment Defects	10
2	Post-shipment Defects	11
3	Post-production Defects	6
4	Total	27

Defect Removal Efficiency Percentage = Pre-shipment Defects/(Pre-shipment + Post-shipment Defects + Post-production Defects) × 100 = (10/27) × 100 = 37%

21.18 System Implementation

Systems implementation is the construction of the new system and the delivery of that system into production. It consists of two phases, namely:

1. Construction of the new system.
2. Delivery of that system into production environment.

Construction of the new system consists of various implemented elements. Delivery of that system into production environment happens by combining various elements into a system in the production environment as a whole.

Phase 1: Construction of the New System

Construction of the new system starts by gathering requirements. Software engineers, then apply design principles on the requirements and, then, fabricate that into a code, in order to create each system elements. Each system elements can be verified against the standard descriptions of the requirements. If verification and validation reveal discrepancies against the requirements, then the system elements are fixed through modifications, repair before proceeding further.

Phase 2: Delivery of the System into Production

Phase 2 is called System Integration Phase. It combines various system elements developed in Phase 1 into the production environment as a whole. Phase 2 of the implementation also involves deploying, packaging, and storage which depends on the technologies and where (Hardware) or when (Timing of the implementation) the integration happens.

System Manual Preparation: Preparing system manuals (How the system operations), maintenance and operation documents, installation documents is also part of the implementation process. These documents will be utilized either in the deployment of the system or in the continuous maintenance of the system.

Artifacts involved in system implementation are:

- An implemented system document
- Implementation tools document
- Implementation procedures document
- An implementation strategy document
- Verification reports documents
- Issues of the implementation
- Change request documents

Activities in the System Implementation Process

The following major activities and tasks are performed during this process.

Defining the Implementation Strategy: This can be a single-time activity or repeated iterative activity depending on the types of system getting implemented. During multiple releases, this implementation strategy is getting fine-tuned for iterations. Implementation strategy decides what tools, equipment, and process to be used during the implementation along with the acceptance criteria for the implementation along with tolerance limit. The implementation strategy also consists of arrangements for packaging, storing, and deploying the implemented system element. Implementation strategy also talks about forming a controlling committee who are the owners of the tasks, commissioning a communication model involving various stakeholders so that the communication is smooth, forming a governance model ensuring the system implementation is on time, clarifying doubts, resolving conflicts.

Realize the Individual System Elements: This activity involves realizing the individual system elements and integrating the same to form the system as a whole. The realization happens as per the implementation strategy defined before. It follows the governance model set which takes care of environmental guidelines, legislation procedure, and security of the system. This step also takes care of process combining hardware and software. This step also analyse training capability, initial operations and maintenance.

Provide Evidence of Compliance: This step gives the evidence that the implemented individual system elements meet the user requirements through continuous verification and validation of the integrated system.

Deploying Implemented Element: How the system as a whole will get deployed into production environment that can be used by the end-users.

We can classify the roles of users in the overall system implementation into four types, namely:

- Organizational role
- Competency role
- Education and training role
- System coach role

Organizational role involves deciding and finalizing the time of roll out (system implementation), deciding on tasks to be carried out before the implementation date, forming a controlling committee who are the owners of the tasks, commissioning a communication model involving various stakeholders so that the communication remains smooth, forming a governance model ensuring the system implementation is on time, clarifying doubts, resolving conflicts. Forming right information model along with communication to ensure smooth flow of information for various stakeholders, getting their buy-in and involvement for the system implementation.

Competency role is connected with competence and skills possessed by the key users. This role needs to utilize end users competency, knowledge, skills in order to ensure smooth implementation of the system. This role needs to know organization strategies, plans, process to carry out system implementation in multiple stages. This role needs to ensure that the key users actively participate in explaining as-is system to IT implementation team along with to-be system expectations also. In order to explain to-be system, they also need to have knowledge of Information Technology. These key users are also getting involved in checking the final system and give sign-off approval.

Educational and training role supports the IT implementation team for carrying out training to all the end users of the system once it is implemented (after go live). Competency role members can take this role easily, but this role requires different types of skills. They need to prepare complete training materials about the system in such a way that all the end users understand it clearly. This role needs to have training skills, presentation skills in addition to the knowledge about the system and should possesses the ability to present the individual merits of the implemented system. This role also conveys the functionalities of the system to senior management who are not directly involved in the implementation process.

System Coach Role is taken by one of the key users of the system who are well-versed with the newly implemented system. They are actually users with thorough system knowledge who also understands company environment and line of business. They act as the change agents. They transfer their knowledge to rest of the employees in the organization.

21.19 User Acceptance Testing

This is the final phase of testing. In this process, customers execute a set of test cases to evaluate and accept the final product. Acceptance test cases would have been defined as a part the requirements phase and executed during this final phase of testing to confirm acceptance of the final product. The final code would be delivered only at the end of the project. But depending on the developmental model, we could get workable units of code in phases in an iterative manner. Based on the delivery schedule, the tester may plan the respective test case preparation and execution. The most important activity for a tester is to understand the requirement specifications. The requirement specifications must typically answer the following questions in no uncertain terms and without any ambiguity. The tester will need to work with various teams to get a better picture of the requirements as given below:

1. What is required to be tested?
2. Why do we need to test it?
3. What are the dependencies?
4. What is the available time for testing?
5. Who are the stakeholders and their roles?
6. What are the expectations of the stakeholders including the end-users?
7. What are the testing tools available?
8. What is the size of the development team and the development delivery schedule?
9. What are the organization's standards for testing?
10. What are the details of the development, test, and end user environments?

SUMMARY

Software maintenance is the core aspect of software engineering. After the system development, the system gets deployed into the production environment. The process of modifying the production system after the delivery, in order to correct the faults, improving performance and adapting to the changing environment is called 'software maintenance'.

There are four types of maintenance activities, namely: Adaptive Maintenance, Corrective Maintenance, Perfective Maintenance and Preventive Maintenance.

1. **Adaptive Maintenance:** Adjusting the system adaptively based on the environment changes is called 'adaptive maintenance'. The system has no faults (errors) on its own, but adapting (changing) as per environmental changes.
2. **Corrective Maintenance:** It is the process of Identifying, Isolating and repairing the faults (errors) that are discovered in the system so that the system can be restored and operational. Corrective maintenance includes repair or replacement of equipment.
3. **Perfective Maintenance:** It is the system upgrade kind of work which makes the system to work more efficiently. About 50% of the maintenance is perfective maintenance. Upgrading hardware, software, band-widths are examples of perfective maintenance.

4. **Preventive Maintenance:** Activities that are aimed at increasing the maintainability is called 'preventive maintenance'. Preventive maintenance activities avoid system outages and avoid errors.

Maintenance Process: Maintenance process depends on the software being maintained and it varies considerably across softwares. But still we can list down the common maintenance activities that are executed across all the software maintenance works.

Maintenance Cost: Maintenance cost is usually higher than the overall development cost of the software and sometimes it is 100 times higher than the development cost. Old-aging softwares involves expensive support costs than the modern technology-based software. This happens, because sourcing specialized technical resources is difficult for the old technology-based softwares. Furthermore, the maintenance activities also tend to corrupt the software structure further by increasing the software maintenance cost.

Laws of Software Evolution: We need to understand the laws of software evolution which force maintenance to take place. For example, let us see two laws of software evolution, namely: (1) Law of increasing complexity; (2) Law of continuing change.

- Reverse engineering is analysing a software system to identify and understand the overall system components, design and the requirement flow of the system. It helps to understand the relationships between various components.
- Reengineering involves putting efforts to make a system easier to maintain. In this process, the source code changed for easy maintenance and functionality of the system also changed during the process. Code cleaning happens over here along with the enhancement of the system.
- Restructuring is similar to re-engineering. Here, the transformation of a system from one representation to another happens at the same level of abstraction. Functionality of the system does not change except code cleaning.
- Maintenance Strategies: There are two types of maintenance strategies: (1) Systematic strategy; (2) As needed strategy.
- There are several difference between a product and service; software maintenance can be attributed to service part also.

EXERCISES

PART A (Objective-type questions)

1. All of the following are types of maintenance activities, except
   A. Adaptive Maintenance
   B. Corrective Maintenance
   C. Perfective Maintenance
   D. Proactive Maintenance

2. Opportunity for innovation is less in maintenance projects.
   A. True B. False

3. Maintenance activities are not repetitive in nature.
   A. False
   B. True

4. Adjusting the system based on environment changes is called
   A. Adaptive Maintenance
   B. Corrective Maintenance
   C. Perfective Maintenance
   D. Preventive Maintenance

5. Which type of maintenance is the process of identifying, isolating and repairing the faults (errors) that are discovered in the system so that the system can be restored and operational?
A. Adaptive maintenance
B. Corrective maintenance
C. Perfective maintenance
D. Preventive maintenance

6. Which type of maintenance happens after a fault?
A. Adaptive maintenance
B. Corrective maintenance
C. Perfective maintenance
D. Preventive maintenance

7. Two types of corrective maintenance are: immediate corrective maintenance and deferred corrective maintenance.
A. True
B. False

8. Which of the following is not a phase of corrective maintenance?
A. Notify Helpdesk
B. Diagnose the Error
C. Fix the Error
D. Automatic help to users to choose data

9. It is the system upgrade kind of work which makes the system to work more efficiently.
A. Adaptive maintenance
B. Corrective maintenance
C. Perfective maintenance
D. Preventive maintenance

10. All of the following are examples of perfective maintenance, except
A. Documenting the existing system
B. Performance tuning—to increase the speed of the server
C. Applications consolidations—for Easy management
D. Automatic help to users to choose data

11. Activities that are aimed at increasing the maintainability are called
A. Adaptive maintenance
B. Corrective maintenance
C. Perfective maintenance
D. Preventive maintenance

12. Documenting the existing system is the best example of
A. Adaptive maintenance
B. Corrective maintenance
C. Perfective maintenance
D. Preventive maintenance

13. Complexity of a system is directly proportional to the maintenance cost of the system.
A. True
B. False

14. Volume of a system is directly proportional to the maintenance cost of the system.
A. True
B. False

15. Aging of a system is not related to the maintenance cost of the system.
A. True
B. False

16. Contractual responsibility of a system is not related to the maintenance cost of the system.
A. True
B. False

17. It is impossible for anybody to create a system of any size which does not need to be changed.
A. True
B. False

18. Two laws of Software Evolution are Law of decreasing complexity and Law of continuing change.
A. True
B. False

19. As the system evolves over a period of time, the complexity of the system decreases.
A. True
B. False

20. Analysing a software system to identify and understand the overall system components, design and the requirement flow of the system is known as
A. Reverse Engineering
B. Reengineering
C. Structuring
D. Restructuring

21. Which of the following is not a step of reverse engineering process
A. Generation of Information
B. Storage of information
C. Creation of documents
D. Creation of information

22. In which of the following process the source code is changed for easy maintenance and functionality of the system also gets changed during the process?
A. Reverse Engineering
B. Reengineering
C. Structuring
D. Restructuring

23. All of the following are about reengineering, except
A. It may lead to re-writing the software
B. It may lead to re documentation of the system.
C. It reduces the risks of the overall maintenance of the system.
D. The cost of reengineering is higher than the cost of developing the new software.

24. First step in reengineering is to understand the overall system.
A. True
B. False

25. Which of the following is false about re-engineering?
A. It reduces the cost
B. It increases the risk
C. It may lead to re-writing the software
D. It may lead to re-documentation of the system.

26. Restructuring is similar to
A. Reverse engineering
B. Reengineering
C. Structuring
D. Restructuring

27. Migration from one version of the software to another version is the best example of
A. Reverse Engineering
B. Reengineering
C. Structuring
D. Restructuring

28. Here, the transformation of a system from one representation to another happens at the same level of abstraction.
A. Reverse Engineering
B. Reengineering
C. Structuring
D. Restructuring

29. Which of the following is the difference between the expected service perceived by the service provider and the expected service by the customer?
A. Gap 1
B. Gap 2
C. Gap 3
D. Gap 4

30. Which of the following is the difference between the written service specification and the expected service perceived by the service provider?
A. Gap 1
B. Gap 2
C. Gap 3
D. Gap 4

31. Which of the following is the difference between the written specification and the actual service delivery?
    A. Gap 1
    B. Gap 2
    C. Gap 3
    D. Gap 4

32. Which of the following is the difference between the actual delivery and communication about service?
    A. Gap 1
    B. Gap 2
    C. Gap 3
    D. Gap 4

33. Ineffective horizontal communication is the best example of
    A. Gap 1
    B. Gap 2
    C. Gap 3
    D. Gap 4

34. Which of the following is the difference between the customer perceived service and the actual expectation of the customer?
    A. Gap 2
    B. Gap 3
    C. Gap 4
    D. Gap 5

PART B (Write the answers in one or two lines)

1. Opportunity for innovation is less in maintenance projects. Explain and write notes on this.
2. Maintenance activities are mostly repetitive in nature. Explain and write notes on this.
3. List down four types of maintenance activities.
4. Write notes on adaptive maintenance.
5. Write notes on corrective maintenance.
6. What are all the types of corrective maintenance?
7. List down the lifecycle activities of corrective maintenance.
8. What is perfective maintenance?
9. Give examples for perfective maintenance.
10. What is preventive maintenance?
11. Give examples for preventive maintenance?
12. Write notes on maintenance cost of a software?
13. How the complexity of a system is related to maintenance cost of the system?
14. How the volume of a system is related to the maintenance cost of the system?
15. How the aging of a system is related to the maintenance cost of the system?
16. How the soft skills are related to the maintenance cost of the system?
17. How the contractual responsibility is related to the maintenance cost of the system?
18. Write notes on software evolution.
19. What are all the laws of software evolution?
20. Write notes on the law of increasing complexity of software evolution?
21. Write notes on the law of continuing change of software evolution?
22. Write notes on reverse engineering of a system?
23. What are all the steps of reverse engineering process of a system?
24. Write notes on the reengineering process of a system?

25. What are all the steps involved in reengineering of a system?
26. When to reengineer a system?
27. List down any two advantages of reengineering?
28. What is restructuring?
29. What are the two types of maintenance strategies?
30. Write notes on systematic strategy of maintenance?
31. Write notes on the as-needed strategy of maintenance?
32. Write notes Gap 1 Service Model of maintenance?
33. Write notes Gap 2 Service Model of maintenance?
34. Write notes Gap 3 Service Model of maintenance?
35. Write notes Gap 4 Service Model of maintenance?
36. Write notes Gap 5 Service Model of maintenance?
37. List down any fours issues of software maintenance.

Section VI

Emerging Trends in Project Management

22

Managing Global Projects

22.1 Introduction

With the increasing trend of deploying onsite-offshore teams, most of the projects span across multiple geographies now-a-days. Along with that, the big organizations are becoming truly global through expansion, acquisition and merger by spanning their projects and products across the globe. So, project managers need to handle a team spread across multiple geographies. They need to deal with different cultures, time zones and levels of communication. In this chapter, we will discuss about the framework that is fully responsible in handling truly global projects.

22.2 Why Global Projects Exist?

The following reasons are responsible for the existence of global projects:

1. **Efficient Resourcing:** One of the main drivers for selecting global teams to deliver projects is making the projects financially more viable. The popular terminology, 'onsite-offshore' model reflects the project-team structure where the customer facing teams are outsourced either to the customer location or very close to customer location by making sure that there is no gap in communication between the customer and the supplier. But, this team is kept at a minimal number and the actual delivery team is based out of one or more economic locations. The team or resources spread across different locations calls for measures to integrate the output of the teams and to make seamless communication among the teams.
2. **Compliance:** The labour laws of many countries have mandated that local resources should be used for staffing the projects. For this reason, the organizations are compelled to build teams in customer's location as well as manage the project in multiple locations.
3. **Performance:** Availability of skilled resources in case of some niche skill requirement for the project may also lead to executing the projects from multiple locations. As all the project team members should work towards a single goal, it is important that the niche skilled resources must work collaboratively with other team members to deliver the project works.
4. **Global Roll-out:** With the recent trend of multi-national companies that are implementing software products and which can cater to the needs of all their branches

spread across multiple countries, the implementation of global roll-out of projects becomes necessary. In this case, a core solution is developed in a central location and then it is taken up by the local teams in multiple geographies which is then customized according to the local needs and rolled out to the corresponding locations.

22.3 Challenges in Managing Global Projects

Following are the challenges in managing global projects:

1. **Geography, Time-zone and Jurisdiction Difference:** Managing the logistics across multiple geographies due to different time zones and difference in jurisdiction becomes very complex. For example, the organization structure may vary in regions due to the jurisdictions and local laws. Similarly, local holidays, hours of operation, national laws differ across countries and this means that for global projects multiple sets of these parameters need to be managed. The time-zone difference may cause in the increased number of teleconferences and challenges in accommodating everyone in team meetings or discussion. This, in turn, may cause delays in finalizing decisions.
2. **Communication Barriers:** There are several factors due to which communication among teams spread across different locations can be impeded. Time-zone difference is one of the critical factors. Along with this, the cultural or language barrier may also pose threat to effective communication.
3. **Cultural Differences:** Awareness about cultural alignment of the globally distributed team is critical. Cultural differences may give rise to conflicts due to the expectation mismatch regarding what is right and what is wrong, such as organizational hierarchy, value conflicts and may get worse with the language barriers.
4. **Stakeholder Management:** Stakeholders are the persons whose interests are positively or negatively impacted by the outcome of the project. With cultural and geographical differences this gets more complicated than the collocated project teams. The primary challenge is to make all the stakeholders align to the justification of the project. Due to the differences in values, culture and jurisdictions, the outcome expectation of stakeholders from different locations may be very different from each other. It is important to communicate the purpose and align everyone towards the same goal at the beginning of the project with a planned kick-off. Face-to-face kick-off with all the critical stakeholders is highly recommended for success of the global projects.
5. **Solution Design:** To implement the requirements, laid down by the customer, in the approach of a project is often termed as the solution. A solution has different components like architecture, processes and the core or mandatory rules. A comprehensive business and technical architecture is essential for designing a truly global solution. Similarly, clear processes need to be laid down for all the locations to make sure that the core processes are followed consistently across all locations. There may be core and mandatory rules which need to be followed throughout the project for its success. For example, the need of a secured workplace for financial data, irrespective of the location of project execution. Such requirements need to be communicated to

all global locations in same manner. Other project requirements that need to be fulfilled along with providing the deliverables like supporting business as usual or documentation are also critical success factors which need to be communicated across all locations.

6. **Financial Control:** Some of the challenges faced in managing financial control across geographies are difference in fiscal years, tax rules and benefits realization, etc. All the locations should have clarity on the budgetary target, benefit target and financial governance mechanism.
7. **Multi-vendor Coordination:** Large multinational contracts normally involve with multiple vendors across the geographies and coordinating their work is important to implement the final solution. Lack of clarity on the roles and responsibility of the vendors is noted as the biggest challenge in a multi-vendor scenario. There may be a challenge of difference in capability of the resources in different regions within the same vendor.

22.4 Various Factors Considered for Managing Global Projects

Controlling global projects need changes in the project delivery framework. Some important considerations that play a significant role in the success of global projects are discussed below:

1. **Onsite-offshore Time-overlap:** In a distributed team setup (Figure 22.1), it is very important that the onsite and offshore teams are in sync for the activities they perform. It is very essential to make sure that, there is sufficient overlap between the onsite and offshore working hours. To achieve it, the offshore team may work in shifted working hours.

   Typical offshore day activities shown in Figure 22.1.

   This model has certain benefits, like it allows adequate overlap between the remote teams. It also provides a time window every morning (US time)—to resolve queries and interact directly with requirement team, users and customer point of contacts. This also can help in joint development as the code is handed over to the other location at the end of the day from each location to their counterpart.
2. **Communication:** For a distributed team, communication is the biggest challenge which needs to be planned effectively for success.

   The various modes of communication, such as e-mail, telephone and face-to-face conversation can be placed on a 'richness' scale, which looks something like Figure 22.2.

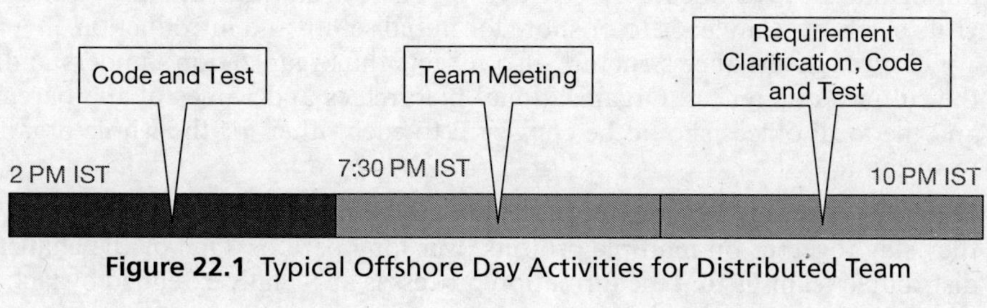

Figure 22.1 Typical Offshore Day Activities for Distributed Team

'Richer' Communication

↑

Face-to-face conversation with a physical whiteboard
High-resolution, large-screen videoconference with a virtual whiteboard
High-resolution, large-screen videoconference
Low-resolution, small-screen videoconference
Telephone call using high quality phone hardware and a clear connection
Telephone call using poor quality phone hardware and VOIP (= noisy connection)
Instant messaging and real-time text chat
Wikis and electronic discussion boards
Email

↓

'Poorer' Communication

Figure 22.2 Communication Effectiveness

The project managers need to help everyone in the distributed team to shift away from e-mail as the primary means of communication. This starts with making live communication as effortless as possible. The group needs to agree that wherever possible, conversations should take place live rather than via e-mail. If the conversation needs to be documented, either party required to send a brief e-mail summary after the call. It is important for the members from both onsite and offshore team to clearly communicate for which it is acceptable to phone with quick and urgent questions without any 'pre-scheduling'; otherwise, many teams will assume that it is not appropriate to call, and will thereby use e-mail by default. The use of Wiki, IM, conference call and communication log are the preferred mode of communication in a distributed environment.

An effective communication plan helps in bridging the gap in communication among the stakeholders situated in multiple locations. It should clearly capture the different needs, source, form and frequency of communication.

3. **Cultural Alignment:** Teamwork is the key enabler of any project. It is very important at the beginning of the project to bridge the cultural difference of the onsite (client) team and the offshore team, so that the mutual trust is built between the teams. One of the most critical steps for the success of a global project is that the distributed teams should come together in person at the beginning and spend quality time sharing key project information and building a relationship with each other. This call for significant investments by HR to impart cross-cultural trainings and planning visits by client team leads to offshore for initial set up and introduction.

   Project governance structure also reflects the organization's understandings of the cultural differences. Organizational hierarchies and values of the parent office and the local offices should be congenial to each other for the whole organization to sustain.

4. **Build the Team Over Time:** Good teams take long time to form, but work best if they stay together on multiple projects over long periods. One of the challenges of distributed teams is that the formation process is artificially extended by lack of face

to face communications. New team members take longer time to ramping up on the team's practices as well as on the customer problem domain. It also takes longer for team members to get to know each other on the personal level that is required for a really effective work. Therefore, reorganizing distributed teams is even more disruptive than with a collocated team.

Special attention must be given to new team members who are working remotely after joining a project. Consider assigning them a buddy or mentor to help them catch up optimum speed. Distributed teams may produce additional artifacts like Wiki pages to document designs and processes solely meant for the purpose of helping new team members pick up speed.

A set of core members who will be on a project for several releases will also be helpful in building a team. By adding other team members who are there for shorter periods will then be less disruptive as they can learn from the team's core members. The makeup of the core team may also slowly change as the time gradually changes. Avoid teams that are working from the scratch level for each project as no continuity is guaranteed from them between projects.

5. **Usage of Tools:** For a colocated team, the process of getting to know the scopes, requirements and progress is easy as physical documents, dashboards, team interactions are readily available. Obviously, this is not possible for a remote team. Remote teams need tools to do this, and those tools must be very flexible. Sometimes, in global teams one set of code is worked upon by multiple teams. So, it is important to check that every piece of code is thoroughly unit-tested and the final code is regression tested after all the incremental developments are done. Few important areas where usage of tool helps in a global project environment are as follows:

   Project Management System: In Project Management System (PMS), project management tools like MS-Project, NetSuite, OpenProject, etc. are used which provide a high level as well as granular view of the health of a project and enable an end-to-end collaboration through workflows between management, development and testing teams for the successful delivery of a project that becomes critical for handling global projects.

   Automated and Complete Unit Testing: Code coming out of the developer's workshop should have undergone complete unit testing amounting to 100% of achievable code coverage. It is important to put an automated unit test framework, so that multiple code changes can be executed with minimal additional effort. Whenever a new code unit is tested, the previously released units should be tested as a sort of regression.

   Automate Regression Testing: One of the most important testing in distributed development environment is regression testing. It will be almost impossible to ensure full coverage and quality outcome without the help of automation because of the repetitive nature of regression testing. So, the plan to invest in the automation tool and including the efforts of keeping the automation suite up-to-date in the budget become necessary for global projects.

6. **Continuous Integration:** The development process becomes difficult to manage when the team members across geographies work on the same functionalities and modification by one team member may break the functionality of any other team member.

In this situation, it is essential to consider frequent incremental integration instead of big-bang integration. Some of the key points related to continuous integration are:

- It eliminates high-risk integration issues which may lie hidden till the end in a big-bang integration scenario.
- Quick turnaround time for integration defects, where development or testing is not held up for long periods.
- Only 100% unit tested code qualifies for continuous integration. Any integration issues should not be arised due to code defects that are missed during unit testing.
- The frequency of integration varies which depends upon the maturity of team, complexity of requirements, and percentage of User Interface (UI) component in application, etc.
- Validation: Each of the cone integrations shall be smoke-tested, and milestones shall be system tested.

7. **Managing Multiple Vendors:** The importance of maintaining a global plan often called as the program management plan is crucial for coordinating the multi-vendor scenarios. Also, there should be some representative in each location for monitoring the progress, so that the plan will be tracked till completion. The processes or rules to be followed by each vendor need to be clearly articulated at the beginning of the project or may be even in the contract document.

   So, here is the summary of points to be considered for managing global projects successfully (Figure 22.3).

   - **Do** work to maximize the available communication bandwidth available to the team. Provide communications tools like conference phone, webcams, and hands-free headsets, for the team and help them to adapt their existing practices to distribution.

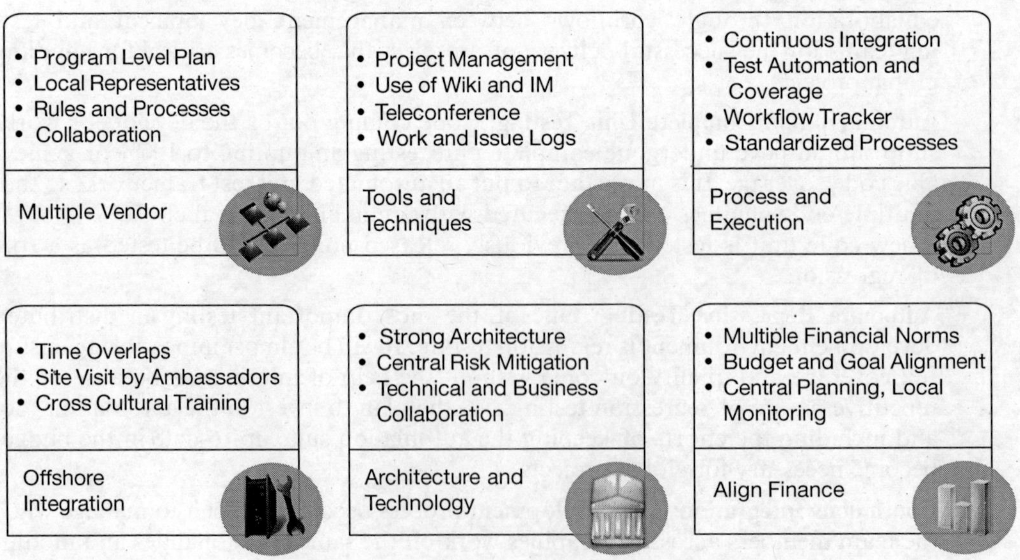

Figure 22.3 Global Team Considerations

- **Do not** continually reorganize the teams for every new project. Building teams takes time, building distributed teams takes even longer. Maximize the investments in team building by minimizing churn on teams.
- **Do** plan to travel, especially at the project's pivotal points. Bring everyone together for the first couple of iterations, periodically during the project, and right before final release.
- **Do** provide tools to augment or replace those that only work within a team room—like a work item tracking system to replace with the sticky notes on whiteboards.
- **Do not** let remote team members be forgotten in the team meetings. Pair them up with a buddy and try putting everyone on the same footing by having at least all members call into conference calls occasionally.
- **Do** evolve the team's practices as they identify better ways to deal with the challenges of geographic dispersion. Frequent feedback sessions are the key for convincing a team to consider, how to improve.
- **Do** plan for multi-vendor situations differently. Setting the expectations and the work rules right at the beginning helps.

SUMMARY

The challenges in handling global projects include:

- Geography
- Time-zone and jurisdiction difference
- Communication barriers
- Cultural differences
- Stakeholder management
- Solution design
- Financial control
- Multi-vendor coordination

The best practices that help in handling global projects are:

- Onsite-offshore time-overlap
- Communication
- Cultural alignment
- Build the team over time
- Usage of tools
- Continuous integration
- Managing multiple vendors

EXERCISES

PART A (Write the answers in one or two lines)

1. Briefly describe why we take up global projects.
2. Describe top three challenges in handling global projects.
3. Describe how we bridge the communication gap in distributed teams.
4. Describe how usage of tools help in managing global projects.
5. Mention few Dos and Don'ts for handling global projects.

23

Agile Software Project Management

23.1 Introduction

Agile is a topic of growing importance in the software industry. It helps organizations becoming more flexible to change and to deliver workable software in a shorter turnaround and, thus, benefiting customers and the executing organizations. Whether Agile is a superior methodology in comparison to the traditional Waterfall model had been a subject of debate since its inception. Understanding the difference in the philosophy of the traditional project execution model vs Agile is important before exploring the Agile methodologies and the related management strategies. In this chapter, we will learn the basic principles of Agile and the management philosophies applied in Agile software projects.

23.2 Why Agile?

After executing software development projects in traditional methodologies for a long time, the limitations of this methodology which the Agile Framework tried to address can be learnt. Here are the limitations of the traditional project execution methodologies:

1. Modern projects are constrained by lot of uncertainties more on what is expected or what is anticipated in the beginning of the project.
2. Even though, organizations have processes to handle difficult situations, but people are yet to be empowered to execute those.
3. It is difficult to change the plan once it is baselined. Customer needs to follow a change control system. Customers require to pay even for genuine changes.
4. End-users see the end product only at the end of the projects.
5. There is a huge gap between the expectations of the customers and the end-users of the product. As a result, most of the IT projects face problem in the User Acceptance Testing (UAT) phase.
6. Projects are often isolated from the changing business scenario. Most of the times, it is very difficult to inserted the changes by the customer once initiated, how genuine case it may be.

7. Most of the projects are scrapped due to change in technologies and business conditions during execution of the projects.
8. Based on the scope of a project, traditional project management tries to define the timeline and cost. With progress of time the scope changes, but no alteration in the timeline makes the project team frustrated.
9. Often, customers end up paying more than what was estimated at the beginning of a project.
10. As team is not empowered to take decisions, the execution part is entirely different from the planning part (mostly owned by project manager). Most of the time, execution does not happen as per the initial plan.
11. A customer only sees the interim deliverables during various phases of a project, which may not reflect the actual final product.

How Agile methodologies overcame the limitations of traditional project execution?

1. Agile project involves the end user throughout the life-cycle of a project to avoid conflicts at later stage.
2. Agile project produces incremental products at the end of every phase of the project (The concept of phase is changed).
3. Agile project delivers important features first.
4. Customers are given flexibility to add, modify or delete the requirement until the team actually starts working on it. Customers are also given options to prioritize their requirements.
5. Agile project engages all the stakeholders (Usually in traditional project management, we involve and engage only the team).
6. Agile project gets the commitment from the Team (In traditional project management, we only allocate the tasks to the team without their commitment).
7. Agile project does planning at multiple levels of the projects (In traditional project management, we do only high level planning and once it is fixed we start executing it. We do not have plans at the execution levels).
8. Agile project encourages proactive risk identification.
9. Agile project allows open and transparent project management.
10. Agile project continuously improves product, process, people (In traditional project management, we concentrate more on process).

23.3 What is Agile?

Agility: Agility is the ability to both create and respond for the change in a turbulent business environment and depends on common sense. A teams common sense is the primary driving factor of Agile.

Agile: As per Scott Ambler: 'Agile is an iterative and incremental (evolutionary) approach to software development which is performed in a highly collaborative manner with 'just enough' ceremony that produces high quality softwares which meets the changing needs of its stakeholders'. Iterative means 'Re Do or Repeat'. Incremental means 'add on to'.

Agile is a philosophy that uses organizational models based on people, collaboration and shared values (*Source:* PMI Agile Specification). From these definitions of Agile, we can clearly infer that Agile is both iterative and incremental way of developing software which delivers continuous value to the customer. Agile inherits the advantages of both iterative and incremental software development methodologies. Incremental and iterative development gives us the opportunities not only to improve the development process, but also to adjust the requirements to the continuous changing world. At the end of each iterative cycle, we get incremental working product rather than interim deliverable. The traditional project tries to give more interim deliverables (documents) before releasing the final product. But Agile project tries to give incremental product itself at every stage of the project rather than giving an interim deliverable in the form of documents.

Agile project actually considers every project as business rather than seeing it as an individual project. Agile project tries to understand business problem at every stage of the execution whereas traditional project considers this at the beginning of the project only and tries to freeze the plan and tries to execute that plan in a single stretch. Agile projects are being executed closer to the business and interacts with business often and involves the end users in every iterations, thereby it actually feels and understand business pain. Agile project does not kill business people with plan. Agile project management actually tries to do inward orientation as well as outside orientation simultaneously, whereas the traditional project management does only inward orientation and it does not do outward orientation.

23.4 Various Characteristics of Agile Projects

Adaptability in Agile Projects

In traditional projects (all at once development), the adaptability is there only in the beginning of the project and it goes down drastically once we start the project. There is no adaptability in the traditional projects once we start executing the project. In Agile project, since it follows an iterative development approach, the adaptability is maintained throughout the life-cycle of the project and is depicted in Figure 23.1. Agile is adaptable to each and every iteration.

Visibility in Agile Projects

In traditional projects (all at once development), the visibility of the product is high only at the end of the project as the product is given to the customer only at the final phase of the project. There is no visibility in the traditional projects until the end of the execution of the project. In agile project, since it follows an iterative development approach, the visibility is maintained throughout the life-cycle of the project (Figure 23.2). Visibility is maintained throughout the project and the customer knows what he expects and what is happening.

Value in Agile Projects

In traditional projects (all at once development), the value is delivered to the customers and end-users only at the end, so the value map increases only at the end. But, in Agile project,

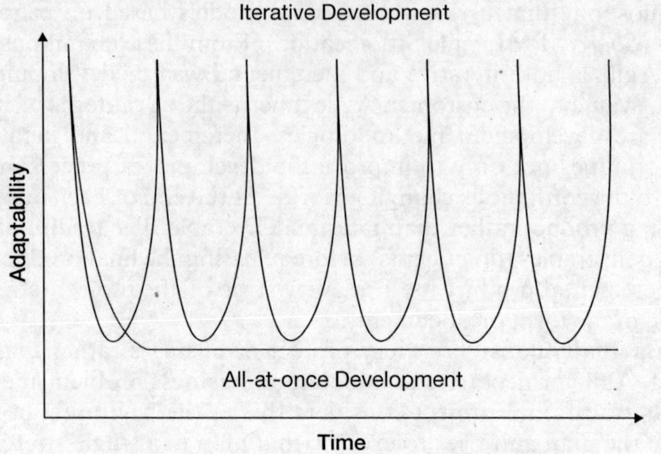

Figure 23.1 Adaptability in Agile Projects

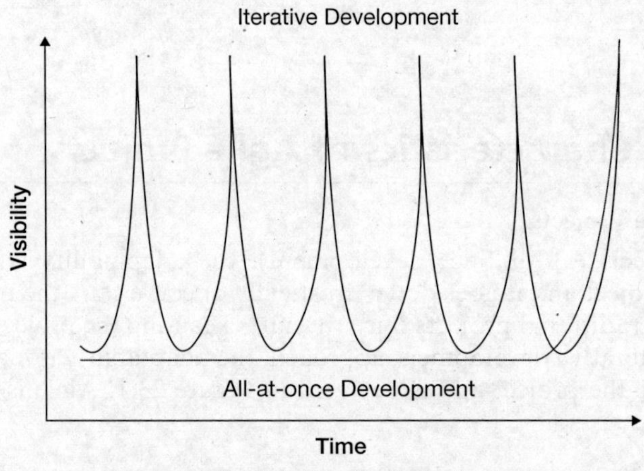

Figure 23.2 Visibility in Agile Projects

due to its incremental nature, the value is delivered incrementally in steps (Figure 23.3). Customers get the value earlier in the Agile projects than in traditional projects.

Risks in Agile Projects

In traditional projects (all at once development), the risk levels get lowered only at the end after delivery of the final product to the customer. In Agile project, the risks are decreased in each iteration as the high-risk items are executed in the first few iterations (Figure 23.4). Fail early is the principle of Agile.

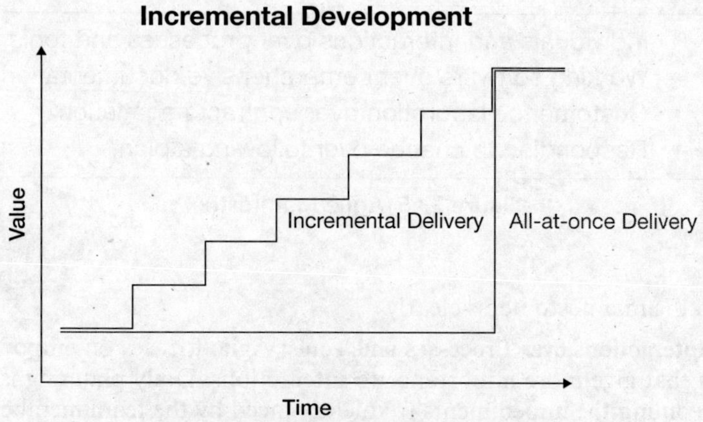

Figure 23.3 Value in Agile Projects

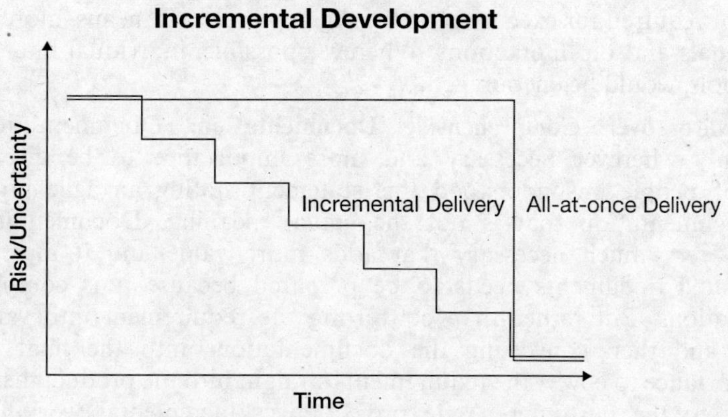

Figure 23.4 Risks in Agile Projects

23.5 Agile Manifesto

Different people called their methodology as Agile, but there were no generic definition and guidelines. In order to derive an understanding and listing down the common aspects across all the agile methodologies, seventeen prominent figures those are regarded as catalysts of Agile methodologies and who are representatives from Extreme Programming, SCRUM, DSDM, Adaptive Software Development, Crystal, Feature-driven Development, Pragmatic Programming, and others sympathetic to the need for an alternative to documentation driven, heavy weight software development processes convened in a place in 2001 at the Snowbird Ski Resort in Utah, and they coined the terms 'Agile Software Development' and 'Agile methods' and they also created the Agile manifesto. Agile manifesto talks about four values and twelve principles applicable for Agile projects.

A public declaration of the Agile philosophy and principles created in February 2001. (*Source:* http://agilemanifesto.org/principles.html)

There are four values of Agile as per Agile (Figure 23.5).

- Individuals and Interactions over processes and tools
- Working software over comprehensive documentation
- Customer collaboration over contract negotiation
- Responding to change over following a plan

Figure 23.5 Agile Manifesto

Let's understand the manifesto items clearly.

Individuals and Interactions over Processes and Tools: Agile focuses on empowered and self-organized teams that give more importance to interactions. Daily planning is based on this value helps overcoming the impediments frequently faced by the team members. Regular interactions also help a team remain committed and focused on the assignments it is handling. This helps the team members co-operating each other. But, this does not mean that process and tools are not required for execution of the Agile projects. It means, more importance is given to individuals and on interactions. Wherever possible, individual interactions, rather than usage of tools, would be encouraged.

Working Software over Comprehensive Documentation: Documentation needs to be prepared only wherever necessary and more importance to be given to working software. Lot of people misunderstood this statement stating an agile project does not require any documentation that is not the actual meaning. Documentations like end user manual is very much necessary that adds more value and it must be prepared. Compliance related documents needs to be prepared because it is compliant with the rules and regulations. But rather than converting the requirement into various types of documentation and then converting the documentations into the final product, agile stresses the importance to covert the requirements straight into the product thereby delivering the value early to the customer. Agile project gives incremental working software as deliverable rather than documentations like what we do with traditional project management. Measurement of the project progress not measured based on the milestone deliverables but based on the features delivered into the system incrementally.

Customer Collaboration over Contract Negotiation: In traditional projects, we decide everything (scope, price, and time) upfront and put it in a contract before starting a project. There are many disadvantages because of this. The whole team stretches their working hours and they work day and night to meet the deadline, because of which the quality of the product may go down. Since the scope is fixed, even for a minor change, the vendor is asking for a change request and the customer gets frustrated. Customer collaboration process makes the customer as part of the development process. The customer understands the trouble of the team members and they help to overcome the difficulties they face. Customer collaboration also happens in sharing the profit with the customer and, thereby, both the parties are benefited..

Responding to Change over Following a Plan: Agile project plan is prepared just in time. In the plan-driven development the requirements get agreed upon upfront, but the plan can be accurate only at the end of the project. Agile manifesto does not say that plan is not required or not important, but preference is given only to responding the change. Agile follows a rolling wave approach, thereby responding to change.

23.5.1 Twelve Principles Behind Agile Manifesto

Fundamental truths and shared values that drive the Agile methodologies are called 'Agile principles'. These managing change, uncertainties, increase efficiency, reduce cost, increase value to the stakeholders, and improve project progress predictability. The twelve principles as follows derived based on the four values of the Agile Manifesto.

1. Our highest priority is to satisfy customer through early and continuous delivery of valuable software.
2. Welcome changing requirements, even late in development. Agile processes harness changes for the customer's competitive advantage.
3. Deliver working software frequently, from a couple of weeks to a couple of months, with a preference to the shorter timescale.
4. Business people and developers must work together throughout the project in daily basis.
5. Build projects around motivated individuals. Give them the environment and support they need, and trust them to get the job done.
6. The most efficient and effective method of conveying information to and within a development team is face-to-face conversation.
7. Working software is the primary measure of progress.
8. Agile processes promote sustainable development.
9. Continuous attention to technical excellence and good design enhances agility.
10. Simplicity, the art of maximizing the amount of work not done, is essential.
11. The best architectures, requirements, and designs emerge from self-organizing teams.
12. At regular intervals, the team reflects on how to become more effective, then tunes and adjusts its behaviour accordingly.

23.5.2 Benefits of Using Agile Methodologies

What kind of organization structure best fits for Agile project execution?

Agile fits best with projectized structure where the team will have more authority than other structures. Team is characterized by nimble results, adaption to change, more scope for innovation, but Agile also fits well with matrix kind of organization structure which gets the benefit of both the functional and projectized structure. In matrix kind of structure, Agile works well only when the Functional Manager and Project Manager understand each other well and tries to complement each other. If they try to compete with each other it will be a difficult situation for executing Agile projects. The team will be more empowered when the collaboration happens. When multiple organizations involved in the same project, then agile may not be suitable, but the same project is being integrated (managed) by the customer, then Agile may be possible, basically the style of project management needs to be fine-tuned depending on the situation.

As per Dr Dobbs, Agile Community Survey (Figure 23.6), 82% of the people agreed that using Agile methodologies improves productivity. Only 18% felt there is no improvement or decrease in productivity while using Agile methodologies. 87% of the people felt that quality is improved while using Agile methodologies. 78% of the people felt that Agile project execution increases business stakeholder's satisfaction levels. 72% of the people felt that cost of system development goes down while using Agile methodologies.

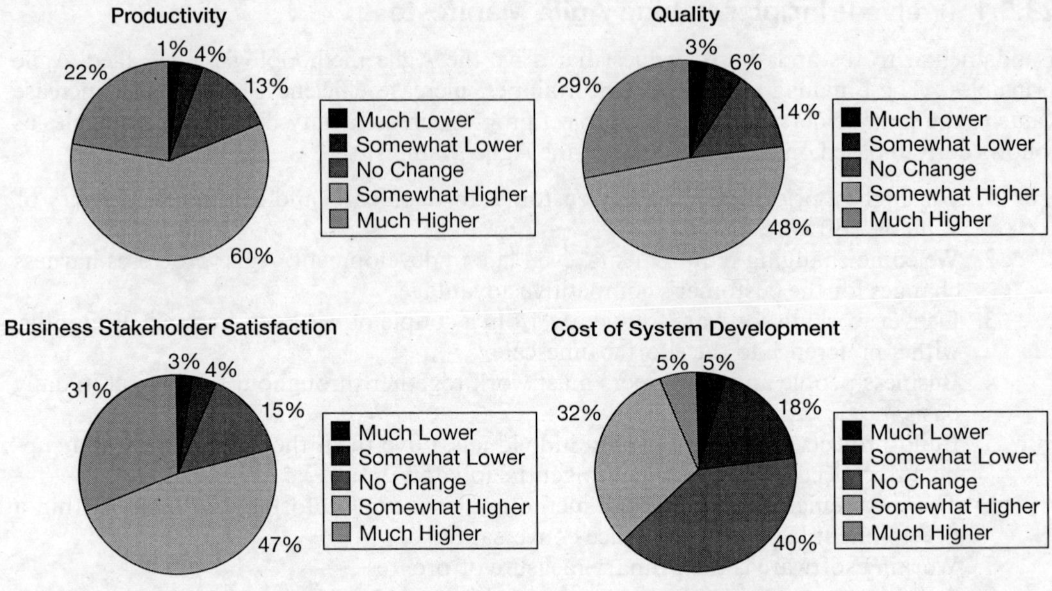

Source: Dr Dobbs Agile Community Survey.

Figure 23.6 Benefits of Agile Methodologies

As per Agile Consortium Survey 2007 (Figure 23.7), Agile project development is 61% cheaper than traditional project execution. Agile project is 24% faster than traditional project execution methodology. 83% improvement in defects while using agile methodologies.

All of these data indicates that agile project execution not only delivers value to the customers and end users, but also to the executing organizations.

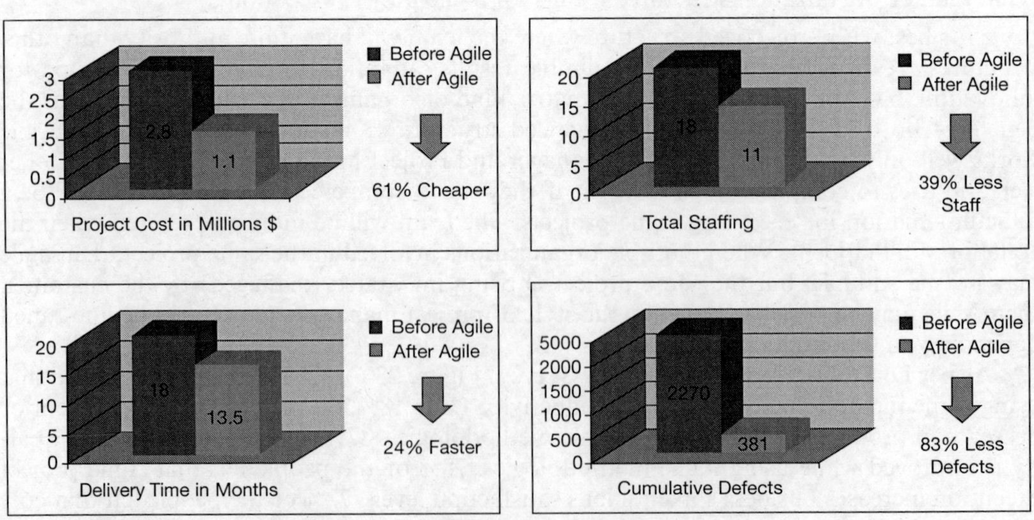

Source: Cutter Consortium Survey 2007.

Figure 23.7 Benefits of Agile Projects

23.6 Agile Project Management Stages

A simplified life-cycle for Agile project management is shown in Figure 23.8. In agile projects, the customer requirements are called 'backlogs'. Product requirements are called 'product backlog' that are created as an outcome of the product vision phase of a project.

Product Visioning: This planning helps to get the commitment from all the stakeholders involved in creating the product by determining money involved in each level of the iterative cycle. Product vision document has the components, namely, vision of the product owner, overall efforts involved in creating the product, target customers, key differentiator of the product. Rolling wave planning and progressive elaboration are the techniques used in creating this plan which will be described in detail in the subsequent chapters.

Release Planning: It happens in repeated flow creating release plan which also determines the number of iterations inside each releases. Release period depends on the following factors:

Deadline from competitors, supporting the contract, to meet predetermined schedule, supporting a financial deadline, when there is enough value, to test the product. Release is actually a set of iterative cycles and, so, a release consists of multiple related iterative cycles. Sometimes separate iterative cycle will be executed by separate teams. This is particularly applicable when multiple teams are involved. A typical release happens in 2–4 months. Release plan is also being defined by the product owner. The delivery team and the product owner need to agree on the number of iterative cycles (sprints) in each release. Release planning usually happens throughout one day. The purpose of release planning is actually to establish a sense of how big a release might be. Release plan actually determines the time plan (time box) for each release and, in turn, for each iterative cycle by determining the current team capacity. During release planning, the set of selected user stories are split into much smaller user stories that focus on narrower features.

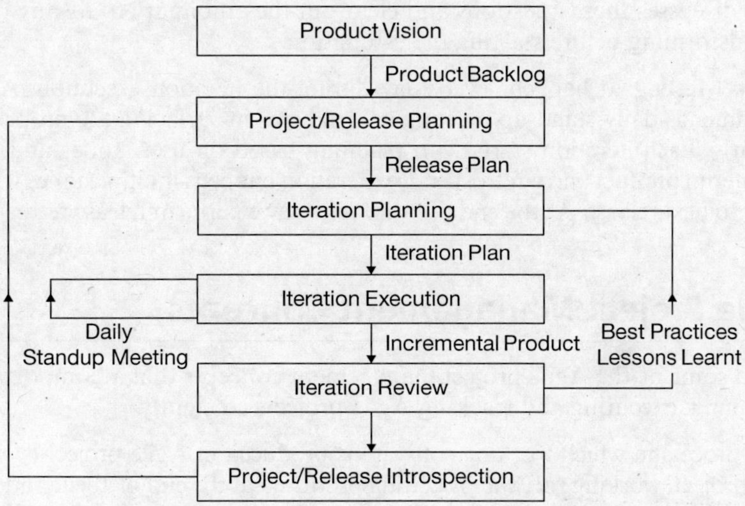

Figure 23.8 Agile Project Management Flow

Types of Release Plan: Usually, there are two basic types of release plans that are widely used are, scope-boxed release plans and time-boxed release plans. In a scope-boxed plan, the work what the team will do is defined in advance, but the release date (time) is uncertain. In a time-boxed plan, the time and release date is defined in advance, but the specific work what people will do is uncertain and is being elaborated with time. Time-boxed plans are mostly preferred way of release planning. This will constrain the amount of work and people will automatically start doing the prioritization which is the fundamental concepts of agile.

At the beginning of each iteration, iteration planning happens followed by iteration execution, iteration demo and iteration retrospection. In an Agile project, the team works in iterations to deliver the final end product.

Iteration Plan: It consists of iteration backlog, assumptions, risks, actions, dependencies, and communication. Team will determine what features can be accommodated in the current iterative cycle (Sprint). It also orders (priorities) the features of the current immediate iterative cycle. Features are decomposed into tasks (minute level). Now, the team can determine the capacity of the team and the tasks on hand in the current iterative cycle (sprint) and both should be mapped.

The team is responsible to come up with the exhaustive list of tasks. The team brainstorms the tasks that they need in order to finish all the iteration's stories. Some tasks will be specific to a single story; others may be useful for multiple stories. Take the opportunity to brainstorm the high level design or the ideas on how to develop the software during this session without going too much into details. This sometimes brings out the perspectives that a single developer or tester would have missed during the actual software development. Take advantage of your on-site customer's presence to ask about the detailed requirements for each story. What is the customer's expectation when the story is done? This will make the acceptance test criteria for your iteration and is the most important piece for getting the customer sign-off. After you've finished brainstorming tasks, list those out on a sequential manner and spread them out on the table and look at the whole picture. The team should discuss 'Are these tasks enough to finish all of the stories and are there any duplicates or overlaps?' If anybody is uncertain about how the plan works with the way the software is currently designed then discusses these questions and clear out the ambiguity to fix any problems and finish the brainstorming before starting the estimation.

Daily Stand-up Meeting: It happens every day during the iteration execution. Agile principle strongly recommends daily stand-up meeting as this helps in surfacing the problems early and attacking it early. Each iteration starts with planning based on user stories and closes with a demo of the interim product and a retrospective. Iteration happens multiple times within a release before moving to next release. At the end of every release we perform release retrospection.

23.7 Agile Project Management Concepts

Let's look into some of the Agile project management concepts that are important to understand for planning, executing and tracking Agile projects efficiently.

Iteration: The process in which working software is produced in Agile project is called as iteration. In Agile project, working software is getting produced at the end of the iteration. The result of an iteration which is usually working software is being used as the starting point of the next subsequent iteration. Iteration demo to the customer happens at the end of the iteration and followed by iteration retrospection which helps improvising the next iteration cycle execution. Iteration is usually a time-boxed event.

Adaptive Planning: Adaptive planning expects to define only a high-level plan for the far-end features, but a detailed plan for the next immediate iteration. This is always a more comfortable and realistic situation to live in, right? This is also referred to as rolling wave planning as the process of planning for a project is happening in waves as the project becomes clearer and complexities unfold. Only key milestones are highlighted in the initial stages for reference.

Time Boxing: It is a fixed time frame within which the team tries to achieve the planned tasks for the iteration and stops the iteration as soon as the timeline is over. Iterations follow a consistent, unchanging schedule in which each activity is executed and these events are called 'time-boxed events' as given below:

- Demonstrate finished iteration outcome (up to an hour)
- Hold retrospective on previous iteration (one hour)
- Plan iteration (half an hour to four hours)

This helps the team keep focused on the main activities and avoid spending time on the low-priority tasks.

Minimally Marketable Future: Minimally Marketable Future (MMF) is the basic minimum feature of the product so that people can start using it rather than waiting for all the futures. There will be a release after MMFs gets created. It actually enables incremental delivery of the product. Multiple MMF makes the whole product. Minimally marketable future has value to the end-user on its own.

Agile Triangle: In traditional projects, the scope is fixed; time and cost are the deriving factors of scope. In Agile projects, time and costs and fixed through time boxing but scope is not fixed for the entire project in a single stretch. It is being developed using just in time plan for the iteration. So, Agile triangle is the inverse triangle of traditional project where time and cost are represented at the top and scope is derived from those which are at the lower side.

Customer Involvement: Agile manifesto recommends active customer participation and involvement rather than time and effort expended on negotiating contracts. Agile software development stresses in evolving requirements accomplished by direct user involvement in the development process, rapid iterations in small and frequent releases (Gaurav Kumar, Pradeep Kumar Bhatia, 2012). Customer involvement in the software development process is very critical to the success of the project. The Agile method states that customer should be part of the development process from analysis and design to implementation and maintenance (Juyun Cho, 2008).

Refactoring: Restructuring the code without changing the functionality is called 'refactoring'. It helps to strengthen the code by enabling for further addition of functionalities. It helps to simplify the code. In Agile projects, the same piece of code is getting refactored multiple times to enable future requirement to be fitted in.

Servant Leader: Servant-leadership represents a model of leadership in Agile projects in which the leader assumes a service orientated role as servant, serving the team. Servant leader will find the need of the team and helps the team to solve the problem. Servant leader will not give any instructions or commands to the team rather help them by servicing and empowering the team.

Spike: Spike can be defined as a small learning period or technical investigation for solving a problem. Spike explores potential solutions for a difficult technical or design problem which can be used to provide a more accurate estimate. If the team does not know whether a particular design approach will work out or not, it is recommended to do spikes to find out which design approach will work out for the team. Spike solutions use controlled experiments to provide information.

Technical Debt: Technical debt is the total amount of less-than-perfect design and implementation decisions in the Agile project. It is a known technical problem in the code. As the technical debt decreases, velocity (number of story points completed per iteration) will start rise again. A good rule of thumb in Agile project is to spend 10% of the iteration on technical debt.

Pair Programming: Two people sit opposite to each other to code the program while the first person is actually coding the program, and another one is checking the possible errors that might occur as reviewer of the code. They also exchange the seats and, thereby, the roles (coders, reviewers). Pair programming doubles the brainpower available during coding, and gives one person in each pair the opportunity to think about strategies and long-term issues.

23.8 Requirements Management in Agile—Epics, Features, User Stories

In Agile projects, the requirements are maintained in the forms of epics, features and user stories. Epics are collections of features, typically 1–3 months in duration. Features are smaller than epics, typically executed in 2–4 weeks in duration. User stories are the smallest increment of value (created from feature) typically executed less than a week. A user story describes what the user does with the software and how the software responds. A user story is a functional requirement that resembles a use case and test case. In agile terminology product features are otherwise called 'user stories'. User stories are much smaller than the usage requirement artifacts such as use cases or usage scenarios; user stories will be captured in the dialogue format and anybody can understand it easily. Three parts (3Cs) of user stories are Card, Conversation and Confirmation. In Agile, stories are written in the form of a card (postal card size). In Agile, stories are written in the form of conversation and it has a format: As a [Role] I want to do [feature] so that I can do [Reason/Benefit]. It is actually the format of [Who] [What] [Why].

Example

As an end user, I want to purchase the model question papers online so that I can avoid delay in purchase. [Why] part is optional, but it is better to describe that. Confirmation is the acceptance criteria of a user story. The customer captures these criteria in acceptance tests, designed to exercise the system in enough ways to demonstrate that the feature really works.

Types of User Stories

User stories are of three types, namely, business user story, technical user story and bug user story. A technical story is a non-functional requirement that describes the functionality supporting the user-facing features in user Stories. Technical stories are usually written by team members and are added to the product backlog. The product owner must be familiar with these stories and understand the dependencies between these and user stories in order to rank all stories for implementation.

Backlogs

In Agile projects, the requirements are maintained in the name of backlogs. It is actually a 'To-do List' of the project. Backlogs contain epics, features, user stories, bugs and errors. Iterative cycle backlog (sprint backlog) is a to-do list of that particular iterative cycle (sprint). Iterative cycle backlog is being created by the team based on the high priority list of release backlog. A release consists of multiple iterative cycles (sprints).

23.9 Communication Management in Agile Projects

Daily Stand-up Meeting (Daily Scrum Meeting)

Agile team works as per the principle of TEAM (Together Everybody Achieve More). Each Agile team member tries to help other team members to finish their tasks. Team commitment is more important in Agile projects. Nobody allocates tasks to the team members and team decides what tasks needs to be executed on a particular day in a ceremony called 'daily stand-up meeting'. They are short (15 minutes maximum), but structured meetings that aim at uncovering any impediments (backlogs) in executing the assigned tasks. Every team member gathers in a regular place and everyone updates the team about what tasks they have executed yesterday, what tasks they are going to execute today and what all the impediments while executing the tasks. No discussions or debates take place in this meeting. It is not a status report meeting as in the Agile projects team does not report status to anybody. But, they simply move the `task-board' to reflect the current status of the assignments which will act as information radiators for others.

Information Radiators

Agile has a practice called `informative workspace'. It is similar to war room of a traditional project team where the team displays the product backlogs, release backlogs, iteration backlogs usually in the form of story cards or task cards on the wall. Other graphs and charts prepared by the team are also fixed on the wall. These are sometimes called `information radiators' or `visible big charts'. There is no hard and fast rule for the information radiators. The team displays the items they feel is useful to them and for execution of the projects.

Burn Charts

The Burn charts help tracking Agile projects. It helps showcasing the amount of work completed, amount of work remaining, and project completion dates. Team members are actually motivated seeing the amount of pending work sharply reducing. There are three types of Burn charts, these are:

- Burn-down chart
- Burn-up chart
- Combined chart

Burn charts are used for sprints as well as for releases. A burn-down chart is also called 'estimate to complete chart'. Since moves downward so it is called Burn-down chart. It actually draws the story points (measure of story) yet to be completed. As we move on, we do some story points and so pending story points starts to come down and, hence, the chart points goes down. A sprint burn-down chart or 'sprint burn-down graph' compares actual and expected progress. It shows whether the team is ahead or behind expectations. Expected progress line is a line drawn between total story points to be completed and zero. Burn-down chart is drawn either with the story points or time estimate. It is up to the team to decide which chart to choose for the project. The comfortable one for the team can is selected. A team can draw the Burn-down graph for sprint, release, and for multiple releases also. Time scale is longer for release and multiple release charts.

Burn-down chart shows only how much work is pending at the end of each iteration. It does not show whether there is any change in the total story points. It does not show how much work actually accomplished in each iteration. A Burn-up chart is helpful in showcasing how much work completed in real sense.

A combined chart is a combination of the burn-down and burn-up charts. Both the charts are shown in a single graph.

Retrospection

Agile is not a prescriptive methodology, but it is a framework that is adapted according to the nature of a project, team, and specific circumstances. The iteration retrospective is an important mechanism that allows a team to continuously evolve and improve through the life of a project. Key elements of the retrospective meeting are:

- Process improvements are made at the end of every iteration which ensures that the project team is always in self-improving mode.
- The retrospective is a collaborative process between all the members of the team.
- All team members identify what went well and what can be improved.
- The actions and lessons learnt are prioritized based on the team's directions.
- Team works out solution to most prominent problems that helps building the team ownership and self-management.
- Helps the team formation and bonding as the areas of conflict can be identified and dealt with.

Osmotic Communication

Osmotic communication means information flows into the background hearing of members of the team, so that they pick up relevant information as though by osmosis. In osmotic communication, the information flow happens at the same time with all the stakeholders. Members pick the relevant information, answer the relevant questions whose answers they know, ask questions if any to clarify doubts. This is normally accomplished by seating them in the same room. Usually, when one person asks a question, others in the room can either tune in or tune out, contributing to the discussion or continuing with their works. The cost associated with osmotic communication is low, but it is very effective in Agile project communication. The feedback rate is also very high while using osmotic communication in the Agile projects. It usually happens within the war room. An Agile project team is always a self-organized and self-disciplined team. Hence, this kind of communication is highly effective.

Example

A team member, Lisa, is writing an e-mail notification module and asking her peer how to integrate the solution with Microsoft outlook. They are working in a collocated facility in an Agile project. David, another team member sitting in the same war room, had worked on a similar thing in his previous project. When he overhears their conversation, he walked in and provided the guidance which immediately resolved the problem Lisa was facing. Here, a lot of back and forth communication channel is saved because of the osmotic communication channel available to the team. But do not assume that the osmotic communication is possible only if the team is collocated; with effective use of SharePoint, Wiki and other collaboration tools this can easily be achieved for the distributed team as well.

23.10 Different Agile Methodologies

Frameworks and process which are based on Agile Manifesto are called 'Agile methodologies'. Agile is a principle which is followed in different project execution methodologies based on the type of engagement and project dynamic (Figure 23.9). Here, we will discuss the most popular Agile methodologies and the situations where each of these is most relevant.

Examples of Agile methodologies:

1. Scrum Methodology
2. Extreme Programming (XP)
3. Dynamic System Development Method (DSDM)
4. Agile Unified Process (AUP)
5. Feature-driven Development (FDD)
6. Lean Software Development
7. Crystal Methods

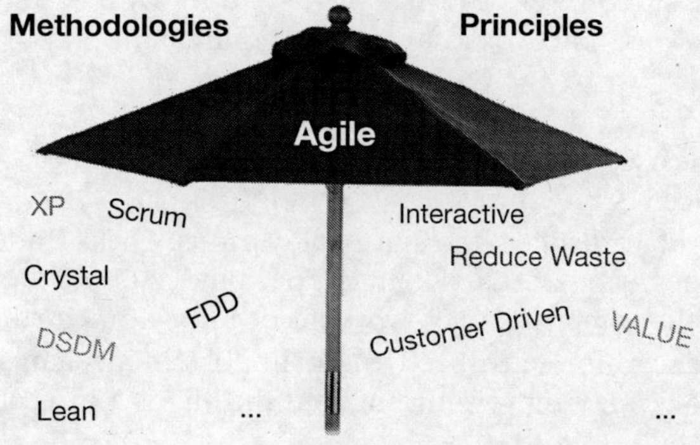

Figure 23.9 Agile Project Methodologies vs Principles

SUMMARY

- Time Boxing: It is a fixed time frame within which the team tries to achieve the planned tasks for the iteration. It stops the iteration as soon as the timeline is over.
- Osmotic communication means information flows into the background hearing of members of the team, so that they pick up relevant information as though by osmosis. In osmotic communication, the information flow happens at the same time to all the stakeholders and people pick the relevant information, answer the relevant question whose answers they know, ask questions, if any, to clarify the doubts.
- Minimally Marketable Future (MMF): MMF is the basis minimum feature of the product so that people can start using it rather than waiting for all the futures. There will be a release after minimal marketable futures gets created. It actually enables incremental delivery of the product. Multiple MMF makes the whole product. MMF has value to the end-users on its own.
- In Agile projects, the requirements are maintained in the forms of epics, features and user stories. Epics are collections of features, typically 1–3 months of duration. Features are smaller than epics, typically executed in 2–4 weeks of duration. User stories are the smallest increment of value (created from feature) typically executed in less than a week.
- Unlike traditional project delivery models where the detailed plan is baselined before the work started in the project, the approach that Agile projects take is more like evolving the plan over time. Also, the project monitoring and tracking approach is quite different from the traditional model as more focus is given in making the progress information available to the stakeholders and making the team self-organized so that they can correct the problems. In this chapter, we discussed the concepts of adaptive planning, progressive elaboration, User story, Agile planning, Time boxing, Agile contracting, Agile project tracking using the information radiators like burn-up chart, burn-down chart, Kanban board, the importance of retrospective and how innovation games can improve the quality of retrospectives.
- Adaptive Planning/Rolling, Wave Planning/Progressive Elaboration: A multi-step, intermittent process of planning which is based on the philosophy that the plan can be detailed out only as more details are revealed with time and with the changing scenario in the project.
- User Story: A user story describes what the user does with the software and how the software responds. A user story is a functional requirement that resembles an 'use case' and a 'test case'.
- Burn Charts: The pictorial representation of the remaining work for an iteration or release which can be used to predict whether all the tasks can be completed for iteration with the current pace.
- Task/Kanban Board: It displays the status of various works under different stages at certain point of time. A look at the Kanban board indicates how much a team has progressed and where they are, how much work needs to be done further.
- Retrospectives: The iteration retrospective is an important mechanism that allows a team to continuously evolve and improve throughout the life of a project.

EXERCISE

PART A (Objective-type Questions)

1. Agile Manifesto talks about—values and—principles applicable for Agile projects.
A. 4, 12
B. 12, 4
C. 4, 5
D. 6, 12

2. Daily stand-up meeting happens in
A. Any period as per the team wish
B. Less than 15 minutes
C. More than 15 minutes
D. More than 1 hour

3. Choose the correct Agile philosophy as per the Agile manifesto.
A. Individuals and interactions over processes and tools.
B. Working software over following a plan.
C. Responding to change over comprehensive documentation.
D. Stop all project work until the issues if any is resolved.

4. Agile is based on
A. Only iterative model
B. Only incremental model
C. Iterative and incremental model
D. Neither iterative nor incremental model

5. Which of the following is the best approach for determining the iteration (time box) length in agile projects?
A. Iterations (time boxes) should always be 4 weeks.
B. The team calculates iteration (time box) length by dividing the total number of story points by the average velocity of the team.
C. Ideal iterations (time boxes) is two weeks.
D. The team will consider the size and complexity of the project into and should agree on the length of the iteration (time box) through discussion.

6. Which of the statements best represents the Agile's approach towards planning?
A. Everything is ad-hoc; there is no scope for planning in agile.
B. Planning should be done in detail at the beginning of the project and then not to be revisited.
C. Planning is an iterative job and should involve the whole team.
D. Planning is done by the project manager and the team members follow the plan.

7. Why the presence of customer representative is made mandatory in Agile projects?
A. The customer representative is the main judge for business value.
B. The project leader should build rapport with the customer representative.
C. The customer representative can dictate the project plan.
D. Customer representative acts as project manager controlling the project.

8. Which of the following statement is true about an Agile approach?
A. Get something as quickly as possible without thinking about quality.
B. Get something simple up and running as quickly as possible.
C. Get business-values delivered as quickly as possible, consistent with the right level of quality.
D. Even half-done items can be delivered and approved.

9. While creating the release plan for a project, the team is exploring the basic minimum features of the product so that people can start using it rather than waiting for something else. What is this set of features called?
   A. Minimally marketable feature
   B. Product backlog
   C. Sprint backlog
   D. Basic feature list

10. In terms of size, what is the ordering of the following items from biggest to smallest?
    A. Epic, theme, story
    B. Theme, story, epic
    C. Story, theme, epic
    D. These are not related at all.

PART B (Write the answers in one or two lines)

1. List down any three Agile methodologies you are aware of.
2. What is adaptive planning?
3. What are the points discussed in a daily stand-up meeting?
4. Mention the four values as defined in the Agile manifesto.
5. What are the main elements of a user story?
6. Write notes on time-boxing element of Agile.
7. Write notes on pair programming concept.
8. Write notes on refactoring in agile projects.
9. Write notes on servant leadership.

Index